HIGHWAY LAWS OF VIRGINIA

2007 SUPPLEMENT

Issued by The Department of Transportation

Reprinted from the Code of Virginia of 1950
and the 2007 Cumulative Supplement

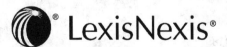

QUESTIONS ABOUT THIS PUBLICATION?

For CUSTOMER SERVICE ASSISTANCE concerning replacement pages, shipments, billing, reprint permission, or other matters,

please call Customer Service Department at 800-833-9844
email *customer.support@lexisnexis.com*
or visit our interactive customer service website at *www.lexisnexis.com/printcdsc*

For EDITORIAL **content questions** concerning this publication,

please call 800-446-3410 ext. 7447
or email: *LLP.CLP@lexisnexis.com*

For **information on other LEXISNEXIS MATTHEW BENDER publications**,

please call us at 800-223-1940
or visit our online bookstore at *www.lexisnexis.com/bookstore*

ISBN: 0-8205-6676-4

Matthew Bender & Company, Inc.
Editorial Offices
P.O. Box 7587
Charlottesville, VA 22906-7587
800-446-3410
www.lexisnexis.com

Product Number 3548118

(Pub. 35511)

Foreword

This 2007 Supplement to the *Highway Laws of Virginia* contains both updated and new material pertaining to highways and related subjects contained in the 2006 edition. Changes in transportation statutes, as well as related subjects, have occurred since the *Highway Laws of Virginia* was last published, and this Supplement should be used in conjunction with the 2006 edition.

The purpose of this volume is to present certain pertinent information, primarily for the utilization and benefit of those personnel within the Virginia Department of Transportation whose tasks and duties require such an immediately available reference. It is also intended to be a convenience to members of this Office and various special counsel employed by the Department.

It is important to note, however, that the utilization of this publication is limited inasmuch as it presents only a small selected portion of the Code of Virginia (1950), as amended. Furthermore, the law must be interpreted in a manner that considers the interrelationship of the Common Law and all sections of the Code that are pertinent to the problem; accordingly, the layman is cautioned not to utilize this reference to the exclusion of advice from counsel.

David S. Ekern, P.E.
Commonwealth Transportation Commissioner

August, 2007

Table of Contents

———

	Page
FOREWORD	iii
SECTIONS AFFECTED BY 2007 LEGISLATION	ix

———

STATUTES:

Title 2.2. Administration of Government.
SUBTITLE I. Organization of State Government.
    Part A. Office of the Governor.
    Chap. 2. Governor's Secretaries, §§ 2.2-228, 2.2-229 1
    Part B.
    Chap. 5. Department of Law, § 2.2-514 2
    Part C. State Agencies Related to the General Operation of Government.
    Chap. 8. Department of Accounts, §§ 2.2-814, 2.2-815 3
    Chap. 11. Department of General Services, §§ 2.2-1111, 2.2-1149, 2.2-1150, 2.2-1155, 2.2-1156 3
    Chap. 15. Department of Planning and Budget, §§ 2.2-1505, 2.2-1514 6
    Chap. 20.1. Virginia Information Technologies Agency, § 2.2-2009 7
    Part E. State Officers and Employees.
    Chap. 30. State Grievance Procedure, § 2.2-3000 9
    Chap. 31. State and Local Government Conflict of Interests Act, §§ 2.2-3100, 2.2-3103, 2.2-3112 9
SUBTITLE II. Administration of State Government.
    Part A. General Provisions.
    Chap. 33. State Holidays and Other Special Days, § 2.2-3300 10
    Part B. Transaction of Public Business.
    Chap. 37. Virginia Freedom of Information Act, §§ 2.2-3700, 2.2-3701, 2.2-3703, 2.2-3704, 2.2-3705.1, 2.2-3705.6, 2.2-3705.7, 2.2-3706, 2.2-3707, 2.2-3707.1, 2.2-3708, 2.2-3708.1, 2.2-3711, 2.2-3712, 2.2-3713 10
    Chap. 38. Government Data Collection and Dissemination Practices Act, §§ 2.2-3806, 2.2-3808.1, 2.2-3808.2 27
    Chap. 40. Administrative Process Act, §§ 2.2-4000, 2.2-4001, 2.2-4002, 2.2-4003, 2.2-4006, 2.2-4007, 2.2-4007.01, 2.2-4007.02, 2.2-4007.03, 2.2-4007.04, 2.2-4007.05, 2.2-4007.06, 2.2-4007.07, 2.2-4007.1, 2.2-4009, 2.2-4011, 2.2-4012, 2.2-4012.1, 2.2-4013, 2.2-4014, 2.2-4015, 2.2-4019, 2.2-4020, 2.2-4027, 2.2-4029, 2.2-4030, 2.2-4031 29
    Chap. 43. Virginia Public Procurement Act, §§ 2.2-4300, 2.2-4301, 2.2-4310, 2.2-4317, 2.2-4327, 2.2-4335, 2.2-4341, 2.2-4343, 2.2-4354, 2.2-4360, 2.2-4363, 2.2-4364, 2.2-4369 42

Title 8.01. Civil Remedies and Procedure.
    Chap. 3. Actions, §§ 8.01-187, 8.01-192, 8.01-193, 8.01-195.3, 8.01-195.6, 8.01-195.7 48

Title 10.1. Conservation.
SUBTITLE II. Activities Administered by Other Entities.
    Chap. 11.1. Department of Environmental Quality, §§ 10.1-1186.01, 10.1-1186.5, 10.1-1188, 10.1-1190 50
SUBTITLE III. Activities Administered by the Department of Historic Resources.
    Chap. 22. Historic Resources, § 10.1-2202.1 55

Page

Title 11. Contracts.
    Chap. 1. General Provisions, § 11-4.5 55

Title 15.2. Counties, Cities and Towns.
SUBTITLE II. Powers of Local Government.
    Chap. 9. General Powers of Local Governments, § 15.2-968.1 56
    Chap. 12. General Powers and Procedures of Counties, § 15.2-1209.1 58
    Chap. 18. Buildings, Monuments and Lands Generally, § 15.2-1800 58
    Chap. 19. Condemnation, § 15.2-1904 59
    Chap. 20. Streets and Alleys, §§ 15.2-2000, 15.2-2001, 15.2-2007.1 59
    Chap. 22. Planning, Subdivision of Land and Zoning, §§ 15.2-2200, 15.2-2202,
              15.2-2204, 15.2-2209, 15.2-2220, 15.2-2222.1, 15.2-2223, 15.2-2223.1,
              15.2-2224, 15.2-2232, 15.2-2241, 15.2-2241.1, 15.2-2242, 15.2-2244,
              15.2-2244.1, 15.2-2245, 15.2-2255, 15.2-2259, 15.2-2260, 15.2-2263,
              15.2-2266, 15.2-2269, 15.2-2280, 15.2-2283.1, 15.2-2285, 15.2-2286,
              15.2-2288.3, 15.2-2291, 15.2-2298, 15.2-2299, 15.2-2303.1, 15.2-2303.2,
              15.2-2305, 15.2-2306, 15.2-2307, 15.2-2308, 15.2-2309, 15.2-2314,
              15.2-2316.1, 15.2-2316.2, 15.2-2317, 15.2-2318, 15.2-2319, 15.2-2320,
              15.2-2321, 15.2-2322, 15.2-2323, 15.2-2324, 15.2-2325, 15.2-2326,
              15.2-2327, 15.2-2328, 15.2-2329 60
SUBTITLE IV. Other Governmental Entities.
    Chap. 48.2. Northern Virginia Transportation Authority, §§ 15.2-4830, 15.2-4838.1,
              15.2-4839, 15.2-4840 92

Title 17.1. Courts of Record.
    Chap. 2. Clerks, Clerks' Offices and Records, §§ 17.1-275, 17.1-292, 17.1-293 94

Title 18.2. Crimes and Offenses Generally.
    Chap. 7. Crimes Involving Health and Safety, §§ 18.2-323.02, 18.2-323.1 98

Title 19.2. Criminal Procedure.
    Chap. 23. Central Criminal Records Exchange, § 19.2-389 98

Title 22.1. Education.
    Chap. 9. School Property, § 22.1-129 102

Title 25.1. Eminent Domain.
    Chap. 1. General Provisions, §§ 25.1-100, 25.1-108 102
    Chap. 2. Condemnation Procedures, §§ 25.1-203, 25.1-204, 25.1-205.1, 25.1-219,
              25.1-220, 25.1-229, 25.1-245 103
    Chap. 4. Relocation Assistance and Real Property Acquisition Policies, § 25.1-417.1 105

Title 28.2. Fisheries and Habitat of the Tidal Waters.
SUBTITLE III. Habitat.
    Chap. 13. Wetlands, § 28.2-1300 106

Title 33.1. Highways, Bridges and Ferries.
    Chap. 1. Commonwealth Transportation Board and Highways Generally, §§ 33.1-3,
              33.1-12, 33.1-13, 33.1-13.01, 33.1-13.02, 33.1-19.1, 33.1-23.02, 33.1-23.03,
              33.1-23.03:002, 33.1-23.03:2, 33.1-23.03:8, 33.1-23.03:9, 33.1-23.03:10,
              33.1-23.05, 33.1-23.1, 33.1-23.2, 33.1-23.3, 33.1-23.4, 33.1-23.4:01,
              33.1-23.5:1, 33.1-41.1, 33.1-44, 33.1-46.2, 33.1-70.3, 33.1-84.1, 33.1-90,
              33.1-94, 33.1-125, 33.1-198, 33.1-198.1, 33.1-199, 33.1-221.1:8,
              33.1-223.2:12, 33.1-223.2:17 106
    Chap. 2. Local Authority Over Highways, § 33.1-225 126
    Chap. 3. Ferries, Bridges and Turnpikes, §§ 33.1-268, 33.1-269, 33.1-277 127
    Chap. 7. Outdoor Advertising in Sight of Public Highways, § 33.1-370 132
    Chap. 9. Adjustment of Claims Resulting From Contracts Executed After June 30,
              1976, for Construction of State Highways, § 33.1-386 132

Page

Chap. 10.1. Department of Rail and Public Transportation, § 33.1-391.5 133
Chap. 10.2. Hampton Roads Transportation Authority, §§ 33.1-391.6, 33.1-391.7, 33.1-391.8, 33.1-391.9, 33.1-391.10, 33.1-391.11, 33.1-391.12, 33.1-391.13, 33.1-391.14, 33.1-391.15 134

Title 34. Homestead and Other Exemptions.
Chap. 4. Wages Exempt, §§ 34-29, 34-34 137

Title 46.2. Motor Vehicles.
SUBTITLE I. General Provisions; Department of Motor Vehicles.
Chap. 1. General Provisions, § 46.2-100 138
Chap. 2. Department of Motor Vehicles, § 46.2-206.1 144
SUBTITLE II. Titling, Registration and Licensure.
Chap. 6. Titling and Registration of Motor Vehicles, §§ 46.2-625, 46.2-629, 46.2-665, 46.2-667, 46.2-685, 46.2-694, 46.2-694.1, 46.2-697, 46.2-702.1, 46.2-739, 46.2-752 145
SUBTITLE III. Operation.
Chap. 8. Regulation of Traffic, §§ 46.2-804, 46.2-805, 46.2-808, 46.2-819.1, 46.2-819.3, 46.2-819.4, 46.2-870, 46.2-871, 46.2-873, 46.2-874.1, 46.2-891, 46.2-894, 46.2-905, 46.2-908.1, 46.2-915, 46.2-932 154
Chap. 10. Motor Vehicle and Equipment Safety, §§ 46.2-1110, 46.2-1130.1, 46.2-1135, 46.2-1143, 46.2-1144.1, 46.2-1149.3, 46.2-1149.5 163
Chap. 12. Abandoned, Immobilized, Unattended and Trespassing Vehicles; Parking, §§ 46.2-1216, 46.2-1219.2, 46.2-1222.2 168
Chap. 13. Powers of Local Governments, §§ 46.2-1304, 46.2-1307, 46.2-1307.1 169

Title 53.1. Prisons and Other Methods of Correction.
Chap. 2. State Correctional Facilities, § 53.1-21 170

Title 54.1. Professions and Occupations.
SUBTITLE II. Professions and Occupations Regulated by the Department of Professional and Occupational Regulation and Boards Within the Department.
Chap. 4. Architects, Engineers, Surveyors, Landscape Architects and Interior Designers, § 54.1-402.2 170

Title 56. Public Service Companies.
Chap. 1. General Provisions, § 56-15 171
Chap. 22. Public-Private Transportation Act of 1995, §§ 56-556, 56-573.1:1 171

Title 58.1. Taxation.
SUBTITLE I. Taxes Administered by the Department of Taxation.
Chap. 8. State Recordation Tax, § 58.1-815.4 172
Chap. 17. Miscellaneous Taxes, §§ 58.1-1724.2, 58.1-1724.3, 58.1-1724.4, 58.1-1724.5, 58.1-1724.6, 58.1-1724.7 173
SUBTITLE II. Taxes Administered by Other Agencies.
Chap. 22. Virginia Fuels Tax Act, §§ 58.1-2217, 58.1-2249, 58.1-2289 173
Chap. 24. Virginia Motor Vehicle Sales and Use Tax, §§ 58.1-2402.1, 58.1-2403, 58.1-2425 176
SUBTITLE III. Local Taxes.
Chap. 37. License Taxes, § 58.1-3713 178

INDEX:
Statutes 181

Sections Affected by 2007 Legislation

Code of Va. Section	Action	Chapter No.	Bill No.	Sec. No.
2.2-229	Amended	80	SB 1199	1
2.2-229	Amended	219	HB 2850	1
2.2-514	Amended	217	HB 2835	1
2.2-1111	Amended	630	HB 2137	1
2.2-1150	Amended	624	HB 1997	1
2.2-1514	Amended	896	HB 3202	1
2.2-2009	Amended	769	SB 0845	1
2.2-2009	Amended	775	SB 1029	1
2.2-3112	Amended	613	SB 1400	1
2.2-3701	Amended	945	SB 1001	1
2.2-3703	Amended	438	HB 1790	1
2.2-3703	Amended	548	SB 0824	1
2.2-3703	Amended	626	HB 2062	1
2.2-3704	Amended	439	HB 1791	1
2.2-3705.6	Amended	374	SB 1002	1
2.2-3705.6	Amended	693	HB 3171	1
2.2-3705.7	Amended	406	HB 2259	1
2.2-3705.7	Amended	652	HB 2418	1
2.2-3705.7	Amended	660	HB 2558	1
2.2-3705.7	Amended	737	SB 1295	1
2.2-3705.7	Amended	739	SB 1369	1
2.2-3706	Amended	133	HB 2858	1
2.2-3707	Amended	300	HB 2758	1
2.2-3707.1	Amended	300	HB 2758	1
2.2-3708	Amended	512	HB 2669	1
2.2-3708	Amended	945	SB 1001	1
2.2-3708.1	Enacted	945	SB 1001	1
2.2-3711	Amended	133	HB 2858	1
2.2-3711	Amended	374	SB 1002	1
2.2-3711	Amended	566	SB 1111	1
2.2-3711	Amended	739	SB 1369	1
2.2-3713	Amended	560	SB 1003	1
2.2-3806	Amended	232	HB 2527	1
2.2-3808.1	Amended	548	SB 0824	1
2.2-3808.1	Amended	626	HB 2062	1
2.2-3808.2	Repealed	548	SB 0824	5
2.2-3808.2	Repealed	626	HB 2062	5
2.2-4001	Amended	873	HB 2537	1
2.2-4001	Amended	916	SB 1139	1
2.2-4002	Amended	41	HB 2082	1
2.2-4002	Amended	870	HB 2450	1
2.2-4002	Amended	932	SB 1413	1
2.2-4003	Amended	873	HB 2537	1
2.2-4003	Amended	916	SB 1139	1
2.2-4006	Amended	873	HB 2537	1
2.2-4006	Amended	916	SB 1139	1
2.2-4007	Amended	873	HB 2537	1
2.2-4007	Amended	916	SB 1139	1
2.2-4007.01	Enacted	873	HB 2537	1
2.2-4007.01	Enacted	916	SB 1139	1
2.2-4007.02	Enacted	873	HB 2537	1
2.2-4007.02	Enacted	916	SB 1139	1
2.2-4007.03	Enacted	873	HB 2537	1
2.2-4007.03	Enacted	916	SB 1139	1
2.2-4007.04	Enacted	873	HB 2537	1
2.2-4007.04	Enacted	916	SB 1139	1
2.2-4007.04	Amended	316	HB 1942	1
2.2-4007.04	Amended	561	SB 1012	1
2.2-4007.05	Enacted	873	HB 2537	1

Code of Va. Section	Action	Chapter No.	Bill No.	Sec. No.
2.2-4007.05	Enacted	916	SB 1139	1
2.2-4007.06	Enacted	873	HB 2537	1
2.2-4007.06	Enacted	916	SB 1139	1
2.2-4007.07	Enacted	873	HB 2537	1
2.2-4007.07	Enacted	916	SB 1139	1
2.2-4007.1	Amended	873	HB 2537	1
2.2-4007.1	Amended	916	SB 1139	1
2.2-4009	Amended	873	HB 2537	1
2.2-4009	Amended	916	SB 1139	1
2.2-4011	Amended	873	HB 2537	1
2.2-4011	Amended	916	SB 1139	1
2.2-4012	Amended	873	HB 2537	1
2.2-4012	Amended	916	SB 1139	1
2.2-4012.1	Amended	873	HB 2537	1
2.2-4012.1	Amended	916	SB 1139	1
2.2-4013	Amended	873	HB 2537	1
2.2-4013	Amended	916	SB 1139	1
2.2-4014	Amended	873	HB 2537	1
2.2-4014	Amended	916	SB 1139	1
2.2-4015	Amended	873	HB 2537	1
2.2-4015	Amended	916	SB 1139	1
2.2-4027	Amended	873	HB 2537	1
2.2-4027	Amended	916	SB 1139	1
2.2-4031	Amended	300	HB 2758	1
2.2-4031	Amended	873	HB 2537	1
2.2-4031	Amended	916	SB 1139	1
2.2-4310	Amended	787	SB 1145	1
2.2-4317	Amended	154	SB 1089	1
2.2-4327	Amended	681	HB 3002	1
2.2-4343	Amended	434	HB 1740	1
2.2-4343	Amended	697	HB 2391	1
8.01-187	Amended	450	HB 1800	1
8.01-187	Amended	720	SB 1068	1
8.01-195.3	Amended	250	HB 1723	1
8.01-195.6	Amended	368	SB 0913	1
10.1-1186.01	Enacted	851	HB 1710	1
10.1-1186.01	Enacted	900	SB 0771	1
10.1-1188	Amended	896	HB 3202	1
15.2-968.1	Enacted	836	HB 1778	1
15.2-968.1	Enacted	903	SB 0829	1
15.2-1209.1	Amended	203	HB 2547	1
15.2-1800	Amended	882	HB 2954	1
15.2-1800	Amended	901	SB 0781	1
15.2-1800	Amended	926	SB 1296	1
15.2-2007.1	Amended	813	HB 2928	1
15.2-2202	Amended	761	HB 3031	1
15.2-2204	Amended	761	HB 3031	1
15.2-2204	Amended	813	HB 2928	1
15.2-2220	Amended	813	HB 2928	1
15.2-2222.1	Amended	792	SB 1200	1
15.2-2223	Amended	761	HB 3031	1
15.2-2223.1	Enacted	896	HB 3202	1
15.2-2224	Amended	761	HB 3031	1
15.2-2232	Amended	801	SB 1351	1
15.2-2241.1	Enacted	420	HB 3011	1
15.2-2242	Amended	813	HB 2928	1
15.2-2244.1	Amended	856	HB 1968	1
15.2-2259	Amended	202	HB 2544	1
15.2-2260	Amended	202	HB 2544	1
15.2-2263	Amended	813	HB 2928	1
15.2-2266	Amended	279	HB 2265	1
15.2-2269	Amended	202	HB 2544	1
15.2-2283.1	Enacted	878	HB 2776	1
15.2-2286	Amended	821	SB 1412	1

Code of Va. Section	Action	Chapter No.	Bill No.	Sec. No.
15.2-2286	Amended	937	HB 2261	1
15.2-2288.3	Amended	611	SB 1205	1
15.2-2288.3	Amended	657	HB 2493	1
15.2-2291	Amended	813	HB 2928	1
15.2-2298	Amended	324	HB 2500	1
15.2-2303.1	Amended	813	HB 2928	1
15.2-2303.2	Amended	321	HB 2380	1
15.2-2305	Amended	695	HB 2010	1
15.2-2305	Amended	713	SB 0955	1
15.2-2308	Amended	813	HB 2928	1
15.2-2316.1	Amended	363	SB 0869	1
15.2-2316.1	Amended	410	HB 2503	1
15.2-2316.2	Amended	363	SB 0869	1
15.2-2316.2	Amended	410	HB 2503	1
15.2-2317	Amended	896	HB 3202	1
15.2-2318	Amended	896	HB 3202	1
15.2-2319	Amended	896	HB 3202	1
15.2-2320	Amended	896	HB 3202	1
15.2-2321	Amended	896	HB 3202	1
15.2-2322	Amended	896	HB 3202	1
15.2-2323	Amended	896	HB 3202	1
15.2-2324	Amended	896	HB 3202	1
15.2-2325	Amended	896	HB 3202	1
15.2-2326	Amended	896	HB 3202	1
15.2-2327	Amended	896	HB 3202	1
15.2-2328	Enacted	896	HB 3202	1
15.2-2829	Enacted	896	HB 3202	1
15.2-4838.1	Enacted	896	HB 3202	1
15.2-4839	Amended	896	HB 3202	1
15.2-4840	Amended	896	HB 3202	1
17.1-275	Amended	548	SB 0824	1
17.1-275	Amended	626	HB 2062	1
17.1-275	Amended	646	HB 2339	1
17.1-292	Enacted	548	SB 0824	1
17.1-292	Enacted	626	HB 2062	1
17.1-293	Enacted	548	SB 0824	1
17.1-293	Enacted	626	HB 2062	1
18.2-323.02	Enacted	436	HB 1777	1
19.2-389	Amended	12	SB 1195	1
19.2-389	Amended	361	SB 0800	1
19.2-389	Amended	495	HB 2517	1
19.2-389	Amended	572	SB 1207	1
22.1-129	Amended	813	HB 2928	1
25.1-108	Amended	882	HB 2954	1
25.1-108	Amended	901	SB 0781	1
25.1-108	Amended	926	SB 1296	1
25.1-229	Amended	450	HB 1800	1
25.1-229	Amended	720	SB 1068	1
25.1-245	Amended	895	HB 3199	1
25.1-417.1	Enacted	895	HB 3199	1
33.1-3	Amended	896	HB 3202	1
33.1-12	Amended	337	HB 2854	1
33.1-13	Amended	863	HB 2228	1
33.1-13	Amended	896	HB 3202	1
33.1-13	Amended	928	SB 1312	1
33.1-13.02	Enacted	335	HB 2838	1
33.1-13.02	Enacted	355	SB 1128	1
33.1-19.1	Amended	896	HB 3202	1
33.1-23.03	Amended	896	HB 3202	1
33.1-23.03:8	Amended	896	HB 3202	1
33.1-23.03:10	Enacted	477	HB 2314	1
33.1-23.1	Amended	305	HB 2785	1
33.1-23.2	Amended	146	SB 0887	1
33.1-23.2	Amended	178	HB 1685	1

Code of Va. Section	Action	Chapter No.	Bill No.	Sec. No.
33.1-23.4	Amended	153	SB 1059	1
33.1-23.4:01	Enacted	896	HB 3202	1
33.1-41.1	Amended	813	HB 2928	1
33.1-44	Amended	813	HB 2928	1
33.1-46.2	Amended	317	HB 2132	1
33.1-70.3	Enacted	382	SB 1181	1
33.1-94	Amended	755	HB 2538	1
33.1-198	Amended	863	HB 2228	1
33.1-198	Amended	928	SB 1312	1
33.1-198.1	Enacted	863	HB 2228	1
33.1-198.1	Enacted	928	SB 1312	1
33.1-199	Amended	863	HB 2228	1
33.1-199	Amended	928	SB 1312	1
33.1-223.2:12	Amended	896	HB 3202	1
33.1-223.2:17	Enacted	304	HB 2781	1
33.1-225	Amended	813	HB 2928	1
33.1-268	Amended	896	HB 3202	1
33.1-269	Amended	896	HB 3202	1
33.1-277	Amended	896	HB 3202	1
33.1-386	Amended	162	SB 1194	1
33.1-391.5	Amended	435	HB 1746	1
33.1-391.6	Enacted	896	HB 3202	1
33.1-391.7	Enacted	896	HB 3202	1
33.1-391.8	Enacted	896	HB 3202	1
33.1-391.9	Enacted	896	HB 3202	1
33.1-391.10	Enacted	896	HB 3202	1
33.1-391.11	Enacted	896	HB 3202	1
33.1-391.12	Enacted	896	HB 3202	1
33.1-391.13	Enacted	896	HB 3202	1
33.1-391.14	Enacted	896	HB 3202	1
33.1-391.15	Enacted	896	HB 3202	1
34-34	Amended	302	HB 2766	1
46.2-100	Amended	209	HB 2674	1
46.2-100	Amended	325	HB 2501	1
46.2-100	Amended	366	SB 0898	1
46.2-100	Amended	393	SB 1383	1
46.2-206.1	Enacted	896	HB 3202	1
46.2-625	Amended	325	HB 2501	1
46.2-625	Amended	393	SB 1383	1
46.2-629	Amended	225	HB 3071	1
46.2-694	Amended	896	HB 3202	1
46.2-694.1	Amended	896	HB 3202	1
46.2-697	Amended	896	HB 3202	1
46.2-702.1	Enacted	896	HB 3202	1
46.2-739	Amended	715	SB 0993	1
46.2-752	Amended	213	HB 2793	1
46.2-752	Amended	230	HB 3143	1
46.2-752	Amended	813	HB 2928	1
46.2-752	Amended	865	HB 2362	1
46.2-804	Amended	501	HB 2534	1
46.2-808	Amended	209	HB 2674	1
46.2-808	Amended	366	SB 0898	1
46.2-819.1	Amended	78	SB 1100	1
46.2-819.1	Amended	200	HB 2462	1
46.2-819.3	Amended	78	SB 1100	1
46.2-819.3	Amended	200	HB 2462	1
46.2-819.4	Enacted	848	HB 1653	1
46.2-870	Amended	222	HB 3024	1
46.2-870	Amended	544	SB 0783	1
46.2-871	Amended	98	HB 1729	1
46.2-873	Amended	813	HB 2928	1
46.2-874.1	Amended	813	HB 2928	1
46.2-891	Amended	189	HB 2163	1
46.2-891	Amended	918	SB 1144	1

Code of Va. Section	Action	Chapter No.	Bill No.	Sec. No.
46.2-905	Amended	209	HB 2674	1
46.2-905	Amended	366	SB 0898	1
46.2-908.1	Amended	209	HB 2674	1
46.2-908.1	Amended	366	SB 0898	1
46.2-915	Amended	111	HB 2113	1
46.2-932	Amended	209	HB 2674	1
46.2-932	Amended	366	SB 0898	1
46.2-932	Amended	813	HB 2928	1
46.2-1130.1	Enacted	177	HB 1679	1
46.2-1130.1	Enacted	540	SB 0742	1
46.2-1135	Amended	896	HB 3202	1
46.2-1143	Amended	523	HB 2917	1
46.2-1144.1	Enacted	738	SB 1321	1
46.2-1149.3	Amended	738	SB 1321	1
46.2-1149.5	Enacted	429	HB 1645	1
46.2-1216	Amended	813	HB 2928	1
46.2-1219.2	Enacted	263	HB 1986	1
46.2-1222.2	Enacted	487	HB 2387	1
46.2-1304	Amended	813	HB 2928	1
46.2-1307	Amended	74	SB 1360	1
46.2-1307	Amended	187	HB 2025	1
46.2-1307	Amended	310	HB 3046	1
46.2-1307.1	Amended	187	HB 2025	1
54.1-402.2	Enacted	618	HB 1801	1
56-15	Amended	813	HB 2928	1
56-573.1:1	Amended	374	SB 1002	1
58.1-815.4	Enacted	896	HB 3202	1
58.1-1724.2	Enacted	896	HB 3202	1
58.1-1724.3	Enacted	896	HB 3202	1
58.1-1724.4	Enacted	896	HB 3202	1
58.1-1724.5	Enacted	896	HB 3202	1
58.1-1724.6	Enacted	896	HB 3202	1
58.1-1724.7	Enacted	896	HB 3202	1
58.1-2217	Amended	896	HB 3202	1
58.1-2249	Amended	896	HB 3202	1
58.1-2289	Amended	896	HB 3202	1
58.1-2402.1	Enacted	896	HB 3202	1
58.1-2403	Amended	896	HB 3202	1
58.1-2425	Amended	896	HB 3202	1
58.1-3713	Amended	57	HB 1628	1
58.1-3713	Amended	586	SB 0734	1

Highway Laws of Virginia

2007 Supplement

Title 2.2.
Administration of Government.

SUBTITLE I.
ORGANIZATION OF STATE GOVERNMENT.

PART A.
Office of the Governor.

CHAPTER 2.
GOVERNOR'S SECRETARIES.

Article 10.

Secretary of Transportation.

Sec.
2.2-229. Office of Intermodal Planning and Investment of the Secretary of Transportation.

ARTICLE 10.

Secretary of Transportation.

§ 2.2-228. Position established; agencies for which responsible.

Editor's note. — Acts 2006, Sp. Sess. I, c. 3, as amended by Acts 2007, c. 847, effective for the biennium ending June 30, 2008, in Item 427 A, provides: "A. The transportation policy goals enumerated in this Act shall be implemented by the Secretary of Transportation, including the Secretary acting as Chairman of the Commonwealth Transportation Board.

"1. The maintenance of existing transportation assets to ensure the safety of the public shall be the first priority in budgeting, allocation, and spending. The highway share of the Transportation Trust Fund shall be used for highway maintenance and operation purposes prior to its availability for new development, acquisition, and construction.

"2. The efficient and cost-effective movement of people and goods will consider the needs in, and connectivity of, all modes of transportation, including bicycling, walking, public transportation, highways, freight and passenger rail, ports, and airports. The planning, development, construction, and operations of Virginia's transportation facilities will reflect this goal.

"3. Stewardship of the environment will be a priority in the allocation of resources and the planning and evaluation of projects and activities by transportation agencies.

"4. To the greatest extent possible, the appropriation of transportation revenues shall reflect planned spending of such revenues by agency and by program. The maximization of all federal transportation funds available to the Commonwealth shall be paramount in the budgetary, spending, and allocation processes. The Secretary is hereby authorized to take all actions necessary to ensure that federal transportation funds are allocated and utilized for the maximum benefit of the Commonwealth, whether such funds are authorized under P.L. 109-59 of the 109th Congress, or any successor or related federal transportation legislation."

§ 2.2-229. Office of Intermodal Planning and Investment of the Secretary of Transportation.
— There is hereby established the Office of Intermodal Planning and Investment of the Secretary of Transportation, consisting of a director, appointed by the Secretary of Transportation, and such additional transportation professionals as the Secretary of Transportation shall determine. The goals of the Office are to provide solutions that link existing systems; reduce congestion; improve safety, mobility, and accessibility; and provide for greater travel options. It shall be the duty of the director of the office to advise the Secretary and the Commonwealth Transportation Board on intermodal issues, generally.

The purpose of the Office shall be:

1. To coordinate and oversee major multimodal corridor studies as directed by the Secretary;

2. To assist the Commonwealth Transportation Board in the Development of the Statewide Transportation Plan pursuant to § 33.1-23.03;

3. To advocate multimodal planning solutions as part of the six-year improvement program;

4. To work with and coordinate action of the Virginia Department of Transportation, the Virginia Department of Rail and Public Transportation, the Virginia Port Authority, and the Virginia Department of Aviation to promote intermodal and multimodal solutions in each agency's strategic and long-range plans;

5. To work with and review plans of regional transportation agencies and authorities to promote intermodal and multimodal solutions;

6. To assess implementation of intermodal planning, including periodic comparisons between and among statewide and regional multimodal plans;

7. To work with and coordinate actions of the agencies of the transportation Secretariat to assess

freight movements and promote intermodal and multimodal solutions to address freight needs;

8. To assess and coordinate transportation safety needs related to passenger and freight movements by all transportation modes;

9. To coordinate the adequate accommodation of pedestrian, bicycle, and other forms of nonmotorized transportation in the six-year improvement program and other state and regional transportation plans;

10. To develop transportation performance measures and prepare an annual performance report on state and regional efforts;

11. To inventory and assess intermodal facilities of statewide importance, prioritize new facilities, and recommend facilities for consideration in the six-year improvement program; and

12. To identify and facilitate public and private partnerships to achieve the goals of state and regional plans. (2002, c. 361; 2006, c. 942; 2007, cc. 80, 219.)

The 2007 amendments. — The 2007 amendments by cc. 80 and 219 are identical, and in the first paragraph, substituted "Office of Intermodal Planning and Investment" for "Intermodal Office"; transferred the former last paragraph to the second sentence in the first paragraph; added subdivisions 1, 2, 7 through 9 and 12; and redesignated former subdivisions 1 through 6 as present subdivisions 3 through 6, 10 and 11.

PART B.

CHAPTER 5.

DEPARTMENT OF LAW.

Article 1.

General Provisions.

Sec.
2.2-514. Compromise and settlement of disputes.

Michie's Jurisprudence. — For related discussion, see 2A M.J. Attorney General, §§ 1, 2.

ARTICLE 1.

General Provisions.

§ 2.2-514. Compromise and settlement of disputes. — A. Except as provided in this section or subsection B of § 23-38.33:1, the Attorney General

may compromise and settle disputes, claims and controversies involving all interests of the Commonwealth including, but not limited to the Virginia Tort Claims Act (§ 8.01-195.1 et seq.), and may discharge any such claims, but only after the proposed compromise, settlement or discharge, together with the reasons therefor, have been submitted in writing to the Governor and approved by him. Where any dispute, claim or controversy involves the interests of any department, institution, division, commission, board, authority or bureau of the Commonwealth, the Attorney General may compromise and settle or discharge the same provided the action is approved both by the Governor, as provided in this section, and by the head, or his designee, of the department, institution, division, board, authority or bureau that is interested. However, when any dispute, claim or controversy arises under the Virginia Tort Claims Act (§ 8.01-195.1 et seq.) or otherwise involves the interests of any department, institution, division, commission, board, authority or bureau of the Commonwealth, and the settlement amount does not exceed $250,000, the Attorney General or an assistant Attorney General assigned to such department, institution, division, commission, board, authority or bureau, or such other designee of the Attorney General, may compromise and settle or discharge the same provided the action is approved by the head, or his designee, of the department, institution, division, board or bureau whose interests are in issue. When the dispute, claim or controversy involves a case in which the Commonwealth has a claim for sums due it as the result of hospital, medical or dental care furnished by or on behalf of the Commonwealth, the Attorney General or such assistant Attorney General may compromise and settle and discharge the same when the settlement amount does not exceed $250,000.

B. No settlement under subsection A shall be made subject to a confidentiality agreement that prohibits the Commonwealth, a state agency, officer or employee from disclosing the amount of such settlement except where such confidentiality agreement is imposed by a court of competent jurisdiction or otherwise is required by law.

C. No settlement under subsection A shall be made subject to a confidentiality agreement if such settlement requires that a matter or issue shall be the subject of (i) regulatory action pursuant to Article 2 (§ 2.2-4006 et seq.) of Chapter 40 of this title, or (ii) legislation proposed to be introduced in the General Assembly. (Code 1950, § 2-92; 1956, c. 387; 1966, c. 677, § 2.1-127; 1973, c. 219; 1979, c. 266; 1986, c. 180; 1989, c. 75; 1995, cc. 359, 384; 2001, cc. 118, 844; 2004, c. 729; 2007, c. 217.)

The 2007 amendments. — The 2007 amendment by c. 217 substituted "and the settlement amount does not exceed $250,000" for "and the amount in dispute does not exceed $50,000" in the third and fourth sentences of subsection A.

PART C.

State Agencies Related to the General Operation of Government.

CHAPTER 8.

DEPARTMENT OF ACCOUNTS.

ARTICLE 2.

Claims Against Commonwealth.

§ 2.2-814. To whom claims presented; Comptroller to furnish forms.

Law Review. — For article reviewing recent developments and changes in legislation, case law, and Virginia Supreme Court Rules affecting civil litigation, "Civil Practice and Procedure," see 40 U. Rich. L. Rev. 95 (2005).

CASE NOTES

Claim presentation. — Professor's breach of contract claim against a state university and its provost for failure to reappoint him as department chair was barred by the Eleventh Amendment and the university, as a branch of the state, did not waive its sovereign immunity to such suit because the professor failed to comply with the procedures set forth in § 2.2-814 for pursuit of a pecuniary claim against the Commonwealth. Amaram v. Va. State Univ., 476 F. Supp. 2d 535, 2007 U.S. Dist. LEXIS 15389 (E.D. Va. 2007).

CIRCUIT COURT OPINIONS

Claim presentation.
University's plea in bar was overruled as the developers complied with the basic statutory requirements for filing a pecuniary claim against the Commonwealth of Virginia; while a demand failed to make a demand for damages, an affiant averred that the developers discussed their damages claims with the university's president, who disallowed the claims. The developers' motion to amend their complaint to add the Virginia Comptroller as a necessary party was granted. Geographic Network Affiliates-International, Inc. v. Enter. for Empowerment Found., 69 Va. Cir. 428, 2006 Va. Cir. LEXIS 94 (Norfolk 2006).

§ 2.2-815. Claims to be examined and forwarded to Comptroller; what Comptroller may allow.

CIRCUIT COURT OPINIONS

Basic statutory requirements for filing pecuniary claim against Commonwealth met. — University's plea in bar was overruled as the developers complied with the basic statutory requirements for filing a pecuniary claim against the Commonwealth of Virginia; while a demand failed to make a demand for damages, an affiant averred that the developers discussed their damages claims with the university's president, who disallowed the claims. The developers' motion to amend their complaint to add the Virginia Comptroller as a necessary party was granted. Geographic Network Affiliates-International, Inc. v. Enter. for Empowerment Found., 69 Va. Cir. 428, 2006 Va. Cir. LEXIS 94 (Norfolk 2006).

CHAPTER 11.

DEPARTMENT OF GENERAL SERVICES.

Article 3.

Division Of Purchases And Supply.

Sec.
2.2-1111. Purchases to be made in accordance with the Virginia Public Procurement Act (§ 2.2-4300 et seq.) and regulations of Division; exempt purchases.

Article 4.

Division Of Engineering And Buildings.

2.2-1150. Conveyance and transfers of real property by state agencies; approval of Governor and Attorney General; notice to members of General Assembly.

ARTICLE 3.

Division Of Purchases And Supply.

§ 2.2-1111. Purchases to be made in accordance with the Virginia Public Procurement Act (§ 2.2-4300 et seq.) and regulations of Division; exempt purchases. — A. All purchases made by any department, division, officer or agency of the Commonwealth shall be made in accordance with the Virginia Public Procurement Act (§ 2.2-4300 et seq.) and such regulations as the Division may prescribe.

B. The regulations adopted by the Division shall:

1. Include a purchasing plan that shall be on file at the Division and shall be available to the public upon request;

2. Require that before any public body procures any computer system, equipment or software, it shall consider whether the proposed system, equipment or software is capable of producing products that facilitate the rights of the public to access official records under the Freedom of Information Act (§ 2.2-3700 et seq.) or other applicable law;

3. Require state public bodies to procure only shielded outdoor light fixtures and provide for waivers of this requirement when the Division determines that a bona fide operational, temporary, safety or specific aesthetic need is indicated or that such fixtures are not cost effective over the life cycle of the fixtures. For the purposes of this subdivision, "shielded outdoor light fixture" means an outdoor light fixture that is (i) fully shielded so that no light rays are emitted by the installed fixture above the horizontal plane or (ii) constructed so that no more than two percent of the total luminaire lumens in the zone of 90 to 180 degrees vertical angle is permitted, if the related output of the luminaire is greater than 3200 lumens. In adopting regulations under this subdivision, the Division shall consider national standards for outdoor lighting as adopted by the Illuminating Engineering Society of North America (IESNA).

For any project initiated on or after July 1, 2003, the Virginia Department of Transportation shall design all lighting systems in accordance with current IESNA standards and recommended practices. The lighting system shall utilize fixtures that minimize glare, light trespass, and skyglow, all as defined by the IESNA, while still providing a comfortable, visually effective, safe, and secure outdoor environment in a cost-effective manner over the life cycle of the lighting system.

4. Establish the conditions under which a public body may use, as a basis for the procurement of goods and nonprofessional services, a particular vendor's contract-pricing that has been negotiated and accepted by the U.S. General Services Administration;

5. Establish procurement preferences for products containing recycled oil (including reprocessed and rerefined oil products) and recycled antifreeze no later than December 31, 2002;

6. Establish conditions under which a public body shall demonstrate a good faith effort to ensure that state contracts or subcontracts for goods or services that involve the manual packaging of bulk supplies or the manual assemblage of goods where individual items weigh less than 50 pounds be offered to nonprofit sheltered workshops or other nonprofit organizations that offer transitional or supported employment services serving the handicapped; and

7. Require that on or before October 1, 2009, and every two years thereafter, the Director of the Department of General Services shall solicit from each state agency and public institution of higher education a list of procurements falling under the Department's authority that were competed with the private sector that appear on the Commonwealth Competition Council's commercial activities list and were, until that time, being performed by each state agency and public institution of higher education during the previous two years, and the outcome of that competition. The Director shall make the lists available to the public on the Department of General Services' website.

C. The Division may make, alter, amend or repeal regulations relating to the purchase of materials, supplies, equipment, nonprofessional services, and printing, and may specifically exempt purchases below a stated amount or particular agencies or specified materials, equipment, nonprofessional services, supplies and printing. (Code 1950, § 2-251; 1958, c. 124; 1966, c. 677, § 2.1-275; 1977, c. 672, § 2.1-442; 1979, c. 508; 1980, c. 357; 1982, c. 647; 1996, c. 435; 1997, c. 907; 2001, cc. 569, 844; 2002, c. 504; 2003, c. 294; 2005, c. 817; 2007, c. 630.)

Cross references. — As to the use of cooperative procurement agreements under the Virginia Public Procurement Act, see § 2.2-4304.

Editor's note. — Acts 2001, c. 569 amended § 2.1-442, from which this section is derived. Pursuant to § 30-152, Acts 2001, c. 569 has been given effect in this section as set out above. The 2001 amendment by c. 569, in subsection B, deleted "and" at the end of subdivision 2, inserted "and" at the end of subdivision 3, and added subdivision 4.

The 2005 amendments. — The 2005 amendment by c. 817 inserted subdivision B 6 and made a related change.

The 2007 amendments. — The 2007 amendment by c. 630 added subdivision A 6 [now A 7] and made related changes.

Law Review. — For article, "Environmental Law," see 35 U. Rich. L. Rev. 601 (2001).

ARTICLE 4.

Division Of Engineering And Buildings.

§ 2.2-1149. Department to review proposed acquisitions of real property; approval by the Governor; exceptions.

Editor's note. — Acts 2006, Sp. Sess. I, c. 3, as amended by Acts 2007, c. 847, effective for the biennium ending June 30, 2008, in Item 203 K 4, provides: "Notwithstanding Section 2.2-1149 of the Code of Virginia, Virginia Commonwealth University is authorized to approve operating, income and capital leases in Qatar under policies and procedures developed by the University."

Acts 2006, Sp. Sess. I, c. 3, as amended by Acts 2007, c. 847, effective for the biennium ending June 30, 2008, in § 4-2.01 a., provides: "a. SOLICITATION AND ACCEPTANCE OF DONATIONS, GIFTS, GRANTS, AND CONTRACTS:

"1. No state agency shall solicit or accept any donation, gift, grant, or contract without the written approval of the Governor except under written guidelines issued by the Governor which provide for the solicitation and acceptance of nongeneral funds.

"2. The Governor may issue policies in writing for procedures which allow state agencies to solicit and accept nonmonetary donations, gifts, grants, or contracts except that donations, gifts and grants of real property shall be subject to § 4-4.00 of this act and § 2.2-1149, Code of Virginia. This provision shall apply to donations, gifts and grants of real property to endowment funds of institutions of higher education, when such endowment funds are held by the institution in its own name and not by a separately incorporated foundation or corporation.

"3.a) The preceding subdivisions shall not apply to property and equipment acquired and used by a state agency or institution through a lease purchase agreement and subsequently donated to the agency or institution during or at the expiration of the lease purchase agreement, provided that the lessor is the Virginia College Building Authority.

"b) The use of endowment funds for property, plant or equipment for state-owned facilities is subject to §§ 4-2.03 Indirect Costs, 4-4.01 Capital Projects-General and 4-5.03 Services and Clients of this act."

§ 2.2-1150. Conveyance and transfers of real property by state agencies; approval of Governor and Attorney General; notice to members of General Assembly. — A. When it is deemed to be in the public interest.

1. Property owned by the Commonwealth may be sold, leased, or other interests therein conveyed to political subdivisions, public authorities, or the federal government, for such consideration as is deemed proper; and

2. Property owned by the Commonwealth and held in the possession of a department, agency or institution of the Commonwealth may be transferred to the possession of another department, agency or institution of the Commonwealth by the execution of an agreement between the heads of such departments, agencies or institutions.

B. No transaction authorized by this section shall be made without the prior written recommendation of the Department to the Governor, the written approval of the Governor of the transaction itself, and the approval of the Attorney General as to the form of the instruments prior to execution.

Prior to entering into any negotiations for the conveyance or transfer of any portion of Camp Pendleton or any military property that has been or may be conveyed to the Commonwealth pursuant to a recommendation by the Defense Base Closure Realignment Commission, the Department shall give written notice to all members of the General Assembly within the planning district in which such property is located. If, within 30 days of receipt of the Department's notice, 25 percent of such members of the General Assembly give notice to the Department that they object to such conveyance or that they require additional information, the Department shall conduct a meeting, with written notice thereof to all members of the General Assembly within that planning district, at which the Department and such members shall discuss the proposed transaction. Members of the General Assembly objecting to the proposed transaction after the meeting shall convey their objections in detail to the Governor, who shall consider the objections. Certification of compliance with the foregoing requirements by the Governor in a deed or other instrument conveying or transferring any portion of Camp Pendleton or any such military property, absent knowledge by the purchaser or transferee to the contrary, shall serve as prima facie evidence of compliance with this subsection.

C. Notwithstanding the provisions of subsection B, a public institution of higher education may convey an easement pertaining to any property such institution owns or controls provided that the institution meets the conditions prescribed in subsection B of § 23-38.88 and § 23-38.112 (regardless of whether or not the institution has been granted any authority under Subchapter 3 (§ 23-38.91 et seq.) of Chapter 4.10 of Title 23). (1984, c. 641, §§ 2.1-504.3, 2.1-504.4; 1986, c. 536; 1989, c. 710; 1996, c. 442; 2001, c. 844; 2005, cc. 933, 945; 2007, c. 624.)

The 2007 amendments. — The 2007 amendment by c. 624 added the second paragraph of subsection B.

§ 2.2-1155. Temporary transfer of use of property between state agencies and institutions; lease to private entities.

Editor's note. — Acts 2006, Sp. Sess. I, c. 3, as amended by Acts 2007, c. 847, effective for the biennium ending June 30, 2008, in Item C-52 2., provides: "Authority is also granted to enter into, as needed, capital leases for any components of an agreement authorized by paragraph 1 of this Item that may qualify as capital lease agreements. GMU shall identify any components of such agreement that qualify as capital leases, as defined by Generally Accepted Accounting Principles (GAAP), and report such leases to the Department of Accounts, the Department of the Treasury and the Department of Planning and Budget. Any such agreement is exempt from § 4-3.03 b.2. of this act. If any such agreement contemplates the lease of property in the possession or control of GMU, this Item shall constitute the approval required by subsection B of § 2.2-1155 of the Code of Virginia for the term of such lease to be in excess of 50 years, up to and including the useful life of the improvements to such property, provided that the Governor also approves such a term."

Acts 2006, Sp. Sess. I, c. 3, as amended by Acts 2007, c. 847, effective for the biennium ending June 30, 2008, in § 4-4.01 u., provides: "Facility Lease Agreements Involving Institutions of Higher Education: In the case of any lease agreement involving state-owned property controlled by an institution of higher education, where the lease has been entered into consistent with the provisions of § 2.2-1155, Code of Virginia, the Governor may amend, adjust or waive any project review and reporting procedures of Executive agencies as may reasonably be required to promote the property improvement goals for which the lease agreement was developed."

§ 2.2-1156. Sale or lease of surplus property.

Editor's note. — Acts 2006, Sp. Sess. I, c. 3, as amended by Acts 2007, c. 847, effective for the biennium ending June 30, 2008, in Item 311 C, provides: "Notwithstanding § 4-5.12 of this act and paragraph C of § 2.2-1156, Code of Virginia, the Department of Mental Health, Mental Retardation and Substance Abuse Services is hereby authorized to deposit the entire proceeds of the sales of surplus land at state-owned mental health and mental retardation facilities into a revolving trust fund. The trust fund may initially be used for expenses associated with restructuring such facilities. Remaining proceeds after such expenses shall be dedicated to continuing services for current patients as facility services are restructured. The trust fund will receive any savings resulting from facility restructuring. Thereafter, the fund will be used to enhance services to individuals with mental illness, mental retardation and substance abuse problems."

Acts 2006, Sp. Sess. I, c. 3, as amended by Acts 2007, c. 847, effective for the biennium ending June 30, 2008, in Item 370 F, provides: "The Department of Historic Resources is authorized to accept a devise of certain real property under the will of Elizabeth Rust Williams known as Clermont Farm located on Route 7 east of the town of Berryville in Clarke County. If, after due consideration of options, the department determines that the property should be sold or leased to a different public or private entity, and notwithstanding the provisions of § 2.2-1156, Code of Virginia, the department is further authorized to sell or lease such property, provided such sale or lease is not in conflict with the terms of the will. The proceeds of any such sale or lease shall be deposited to the Historic Resources Fund established under § 10.1-2202.1, Code of Virginia."

Acts 2006, Sp. Sess. I, c. 3, as amended by Acts 2007, c. 847, effective for the biennium ending June 30, 2008, in Item 387 D, provides: "All residential staff housing properties owned by the Commonwealth and in the possession of the Department of Corrections are authorized to be sold as surplus property pursuant to § 2.2-1156, Code of Virginia. Notwithstanding the provisions of § 2.2-1156 D, Code of Virginia, all net proceeds from the sale of such property after provision is made for any bonds outstanding on such property, as appropriate, shall be deposited into the general fund. Prior to the sale of these properties the Department of General Services shall obtain an appraisal of the fair market value of such properties. Current employees of the Department of Corrections who are currently residing in such residential staff housing shall be granted the first right of refusal to purchase these residences at fair market value."

Acts 2006, Sp. Sess. I, c. 3, as amended by Acts 2007, c. 847, effective for the biennium ending June 30, 2008, in § 3-1.01 BB, provides: "The Department of Alcoholic Beverage Control shall sell the building in which the Alexandria Regional office is currently located. Notwithstanding the provisions of § 2.2-1156, Code of Virginia, all the proceeds from the sale of such property, estimated to be $15,000,000, shall be deposited into the general fund no later than June 30, 2008."

Acts 2006, Sp. Sess. I, c. 3, as amended by Acts 2007, c. 847, effective for the biennium ending June 30, 2008, in § 4-4.01 t., provides: "The Governor may authorize the conveyance of any interest in property or improvements thereon held by the Commonwealth to the educational or real estate foundation of any institution of higher education where he finds that such property was acquired with local or private funds or by gift or grant to or for the use of the institution, and not with funds appropriated to the institution by the General Assembly. Any approved conveyance shall be exempt from § 2.2-1156, Code of Virginia, and any other statute concerning conveyance, transfer or sale of state property. If the foundation conveys any interest in the property or any improvements thereon, such conveyance shall likewise be exempt from compliance with any statute concerning disposition of state property. Any income or proceeds from the conveyance of any interest in the property shall be deemed to be local or private funds and may be used by the foundation for any foundation purpose."

Acts 2006, Sp. Sess. I, c. 3, as amended by Acts 2007, c. 847, effective for the biennium ending June 30, 2008, in § 4-5.09, provides: "a. Notwithstanding the provisions of § 2.2-1156, Code of Virginia, the departments, divisions, institutions, or agencies of the Commonwealth, or the Governor, shall sell or lease surplus real property only under the following circumstances:

"1. Any emergency declared in accordance with §§ 44-146.18:2 or 44-146.28, Code of Virginia, or

"2. Not less than thirty days after the Governor notifies, in writing, the Chairmen of the House Appropriations and Senate Finance Committees regarding the planned conveyance, including a statement of the proceeds to be derived from such conveyance and the individual or entity taking title to such property.

"3. Surplus property valued at less than $5,000,000 that is possessed and controlled by a public institution of higher education, pursuant to §§ 2.2-1149 and 2.2-1153, Code of Virginia.

"b. In any circumstance provided for in subsection a of this section, the cognizant board or governing body of the agency or institution holding title or otherwise controlling the state-owned property shall approve, in writing, the proposed conveyance of the property."

CHAPTER 15.

DEPARTMENT OF PLANNING AND BUDGET.

Sec.
2.2-1514.   (Contingent expiration date — see Editor's notes) Designation of general fund for nonrecurring expenditures.

§ 2.2-1505. Estimates by nonstate agencies of amounts needed.

Editor's note. — Acts 2006, Sp. Sess. I, c. 3, as amended by Acts 2007, c. 847, effective for the biennium ending June 30, 2008, in Item 249, provides: "A. This appropriation represents the Commonwealth of Virginia's contribution to the Jefferson Science Associates, LLC, for the support of the Thomas Jefferson National Accelerator Facility (Jefferson Lab) located at Newport News, Virginia. This contribution includes funds to support faculty positions and industry-led research that will promote economic development opportunities in the Commonwealth.

"B. This nonstate agency is exempt from the match requirement of § 2.2-1505, Code of Virginia and § 4-5.05 of this act."

Acts 2006, Sp. Sess. I, c. 3, as amended by Acts 2007, c. 847, effective for the biennium ending June 30, 2008, in Item 481 E, provides: "The distribution of a grant originally appropriated to Merchants Hope Church within Chapter 951 of the Acts of Assembly of 2005 shall not be contingent upon the organization providing any source of matching funds as is normally required by §§ 2.2-1505 and 10.1-2213, Code of Virginia, or § 4-5.05 of this act."

§ 2.2-1514. (Contingent expiration date — see Editor's notes) Designation of general fund

for nonrecurring expenditures. — A. As used in this section:

"The Budget Bill" means the "The Budget Bill" submitted pursuant to § 2.2-1509, including any amendments to a general appropriation act pursuant to such section.

"Nonrecurring expenditures" means the acquisition or construction of capital outlay projects as defined in § 2.2-1503.2, the acquisition or construction of capital improvements, the acquisition of land, the acquisition of equipment, or other expenditures of a one-time nature as specified in the general appropriation act. Such term shall not include any expenditures relating to transportation, including but not limited to transportation maintenance.

B. At the end of each fiscal year, the Comptroller shall designate within his annual report pursuant to § 2.2-813 as follows: one-third of the remaining amount of the general fund balance that is not otherwise reserved or designated shall be designated by the Comptroller for nonrecurring expenditures, and two-thirds shall be designated for deposit into the Transportation Trust Fund. No such designation shall be made unless the full amounts required for other reserves or designations including, but not limited to, (i) the Revenue Stabilization Fund deposit pursuant to § 2.2-1829, (ii) the Virginia Water Quality Improvement Fund deposit pursuant to § 10.1-2128, (iii) capital outlay reappropriations pursuant to the general appropriation act, (iv) (a) operating expense reappropriations pursuant to the general appropriation act, and (b) reappropriations of unexpended appropriations to certain public institutions of higher education pursuant to § 2.2-5005, (v) pro rata rebate payments to certain public institutions of higher education pursuant to § 2.2-5005, (vi) the unappropriated balance anticipated in the general appropriation act for the end of such fiscal year, and (vii) interest payments on deposits of certain public institutions of higher education pursuant to § 2.2-5005 are set aside. The Comptroller shall set aside amounts required for clauses (iv) (b), (v), and (vii) beginning with the initial fiscal year as determined under § 2.2-5005 and for all fiscal years thereafter.

C. The Governor shall include in "The Budget Bill" pursuant to § 2.2-1509 recommended appropriations from the general fund or recommended amendments to general fund appropriations in the general appropriation act in effect at that time an amount for nonrecurring expenditures and an amount for deposit into the Transportation Trust Fund equal to the amounts designated by the Comptroller for such purposes pursuant to the provisions of subsection B. Such deposit to the Transportation Trust Fund shall not preclude the appropriation of additional amounts from the general fund for transportation purposes. (2002, cc. 839, 888; 2005, cc. 933, 945; 2007, c. 896.)

The section above is effective until December 31 of any year revenues designated to the Highway Maintenance and Operating

Fund or the Transportation Trust Fund are used for non-transportation related purposes. For this section as effective December 31 of any year revenues designated for the Highway Maintenance and Operating Fund or the Transportation Trust Fund are used for non-transportation related purposes according to Acts 2007, c. 896 see the section as set out in the 2006 Edition.

Editor's note. — Acts 2007, c. 896, cl. 3, provides: "That the revenues generated by the provisions of this act shall not be used to calculate or reduce the share of local, federal, and state revenues otherwise available to participating jurisdictions. Further, such revenues and moneys shall not be included in any computation of, or formula for, a locality's ability to pay for public education, upon which appropriations of state revenues to local governments for public education are determined."

Acts 2007, c. 896, cl. 21, provides: "That the revenue generated by this act shall be used solely for transportation purposes."

Acts 2007, c. 896, cl. 22, provides: "That the provisions of this act which generate additional revenue for the Transportation Trust Fund, established under § 33.1-23.03:1 of the Code of Virginia, or the Highway Maintenance and Operating Fund shall expire on December 31 of any year in which the General Assembly appropriates any of the revenues designated under general law to the Highway Maintenance and Operating Fund or the Transportation Trust Fund for any non-transportation related purpose."

Acts 2007, c. 896, cl. 23 contains a severability clause.

The 2007 amendments. — The 2007 amendment by c. 896 inserted the second sentence in the definition of "Nonrecurring expenditures"; in subsection B, substituted the language beginning "as follows: one-third of the remaining" at the end of the first sentence for "an amount for nonrecurring expenditures, which shall equal the remaining amount of the general fund balance that is not otherwise reserved or designated"; and in subsection C, inserted "and an amount for deposit into the Transportation Trust Fund" following "nonrecurring expenditures," substituted "amounts" for "amount" and "purposes" for "purpose," and deleted "of this section" following "subsection B" in the first sentence and added the second sentence. For contingent expiration, see Acts 2007, c. 896, cl. 22.

CHAPTER 20.1.

Virginia Information Technologies Agency.

Article 1.

General Provisions.

Sec.
2.2-2009. (Effective until July 1, 2008) Additional duties of the CIO relating to security of government information.
2.2-2009. (Effective July 1, 2008) Additional duties of the CIO relating to security of government information.

Article 1.

General Provisions.

§ 2.2-2009. (Effective until July 1, 2008) Additional duties of the CIO relating to security of government information. — A. To provide for the security of state government electronic information from unauthorized uses, intrusions or other security threats, the CIO shall direct the development of policies, procedures and standards for assessing security risks, determining the appropriate security measures and performing security audits of government electronic information. Such policies, procedures, and standards will apply to the Com-

monwealth's executive, legislative, and judicial branches, and independent agencies and institutions of higher education. The CIO shall work with representatives of the Chief Justice of the Supreme Court and Joint Rules Committee of the General Assembly to identify their needs.

B. The CIO shall also develop policies, procedures, and standards that shall address the scope of security audits and the frequency of such security audits. In developing and updating such policies, procedures, and standards, the CIO shall designate a government entity to oversee, plan and coordinate the conduct of periodic security audits of all executive branch and independent agencies and institutions of higher education. The CIO will coordinate these audits with the Auditor of Public Accounts and the Joint Legislative Audit and Review Commission. The Chief Justice of the Supreme Court and the Joint Rules Committee of the General Assembly shall determine the most appropriate methods to review the protection of electronic information within their branches.

C. The CIO shall report to the Governor and General Assembly by December 2008 and annually thereafter, those executive branch and independent agencies and institutions of higher education that have not implemented acceptable policies, procedures, and standards to control unauthorized uses, intrusions, or other security threats. For any executive branch and independent agency or institution of higher education whose security audit results and plans for corrective action are unacceptable, the CIO shall report such results to the (i) Information Technology Investment Board, (ii) affected cabinet secretary, (iii) Governor, and (iv) Auditor of Public Accounts. Upon review of the security audit results in question, the Information Technology Investment Board may take action to suspend the public bodies information technology projects pursuant to subdivision 3 of § 2.2-2458, limit additional information technology investments pending acceptable corrective actions, and recommend to the Governor any other appropriate actions.

D. All public bodies subject to such audits as required by this section shall fully cooperate with the entity designated to perform such audits and bear any associated costs. Public bodies that are not required to but elect to use the entity designated to perform such audits shall also bear any associated costs.

E. The provisions of this section shall not infringe upon responsibilities assigned to the Comptroller, the Auditor of Public Accounts, or the Joint Legislative Audit and Review Commission by other provisions of the Code of Virginia.

F. The CIO shall promptly receive reports from directors of departments in the executive branch of state government made in accordance with § 2.2-603 and shall take such actions as are necessary, convenient or desirable to ensure the security of the Commonwealth's electronic information. (2000, c. 961, §§ 2.1-563.42 — 2.1-563.44; 2001, c. 844, §§ 2.2-136 — 2.2-138; 2002, c. 247, § 2.2-226.1; 2003, cc. 981, 1021; 2004, c. 638; 2007, c. 775.)

The 2007 amendments. — The 2007 amendment by c. 775 rewrote subsections A and B; inserted subsection C and redesignated the remaining subsections accordingly; in subsection D, added "and bear any associated costs" to the end of the first sentence, and added the second sentence; and substituted "electronic information" for "databases and data communications" in subsection F.

§ 2.2-2009. (Effective July 1, 2008) Additional duties of the CIO relating to security of government information. — A. To provide for the security of state government electronic information from unauthorized uses, intrusions or other security threats, the CIO shall direct the development of policies, procedures and standards for assessing security risks, determining the appropriate security measures and performing security audits of government electronic information. Such policies, procedures, and standards will apply to the Commonwealth's executive, legislative, and judicial branches, and independent agencies and institutions of higher education. The CIO shall work with representatives of the Chief Justice of the Supreme Court and Joint Rules Committee of the General Assembly to identify their needs.

B. The CIO shall also develop policies, procedures, and standards that shall address the scope of security audits and the frequency of such security audits. In developing and updating such policies, procedures, and standards, the CIO shall designate a government entity to oversee, plan and coordinate the conduct of periodic security audits of all executive branch and independent agencies and institutions of higher education. The CIO will coordinate these audits with the Auditor of Public Accounts and the Joint Legislative Audit and Review Commission. The Chief Justice of the Supreme Court and the Joint Rules Committee of the General Assembly shall determine the most appropriate methods to review the protection of electronic information within their branches.

C. The CIO shall report to the Governor and General Assembly by December 2008 and annually thereafter, those executive branch and independent agencies and institutions of higher education that have not implemented acceptable policies, procedures, and standards to control unauthorized uses, intrusions, or other security threats. For any executive branch and independent agency or institution of higher education whose security audit results and plans for corrective action are unacceptable, the CIO shall report such results to the (i) Information Technology Investment Board, (ii) affected cabinet secretary, (iii) Governor, and (iv) Auditor of Public Accounts. Upon review of the security audit results

in question, the Information Technology Investment Board may take action to suspend the public bodies information technology projects pursuant to subdivision 3 of § 2.2-2458, limit additional information technology investments pending acceptable corrective actions, and recommend to the Governor any other appropriate actions.

D. All public bodies subject to such audits as required by this section shall fully cooperate with the entity designated to perform such audits and bear any associated costs. Public bodies that are not required to but elect to use the entity designated to perform such audits shall also bear any associated costs.

E. The provisions of this section shall not infringe upon responsibilities assigned to the Comptroller, the Auditor of Public Accounts, or the Joint Legislative Audit and Review Commission by other provisions of the Code of Virginia.

F. To ensure the security and privacy of citizens of the Commonwealth in their interactions with state government, the CIO shall direct the development of policies, procedures, and standards for the protection of confidential data maintained by state agencies against unauthorized access and use. Such policies, procedures, and standards shall include, but not be limited to:

1. Requirements that any state employee or other authorized user of a state technology asset provide passwords or other means of authentication to (i) use a technology asset and (ii) access a state-owned or operated computer network or database; and

2. Requirements that a digital rights management system or other means of authenticating and controlling an individual's ability to access electronic records be utilized to limit access to and use of electronic records that contain confidential data to authorized individuals.

G. The CIO shall promptly receive reports from directors of departments in the executive branch of state government made in accordance with § 2.2-603 and shall take such actions as are necessary, convenient or desirable to ensure the security of the Commonwealth's electronic information and confidential data. (2000, c. 961, §§ 2.1-563.42 — 2.1-563.44; 2001, c. 844, §§ 2.2-136 — 2.2-138; 2002, c. 247, § 2.2-226.1; 2003, cc. 981, 1021; 2004, c. 638; 2007, cc. 769, 775.)

Editor's note. — Acts 2007, c. 769, cl. 2, provides: "That the provisions of this act shall become effective on July 1, 2008."

The 2007 amendments. — The 2007 amendment by c. 769, effective July 1, 2008, inserted subsection E [now subsection F] and redesignated the remaining subsections accordingly; and added "and confidential data" to the end of subsection F [now subsection G] and made related changes.

The 2007 amendment by c. 775 rewrote subsections A and B; inserted subsection C and redesignated the remaining subsections accordingly; in subsection D, added "and bear any associated costs" to the end of the first sentence, and added the second sentence; and substituted "electronic information" for "databases and data communications" in subsection F.

PART E.
State Officers and Employees.

CHAPTER 30.
STATE GRIEVANCE PROCEDURE.

§ 2.2-3000. Policy of the Commonwealth; responsibilities of state agencies under this chapter.

CASE NOTES

State grievance process subject to *Rooker-Feldman* doctrine. — In an action by a former state employee against his former state employer and former supervisors, a magistrate correctly found that the court lacked subject matter jurisdiction over the employee's complaint based on the *Rooker-Feldman* doctrine because, although 28 U.S.C.S. § 1257 did not explicitly mention decisions by lower state courts or administrative agencies, the state grievance process under § 2.2-3000 et seq., which the employee had invoked, was an adjudicatory process subject to the *Rooker-Feldman* doctrine. Horner v. Dep't of Mental Health, — F. Supp. 2d —, 2003 U.S. Dist. LEXIS 26935 (W.D. Va. May 1, 2003).

CHAPTER 31.
STATE AND LOCAL GOVERNMENT CONFLICT OF INTERESTS ACT.

Article 4.
Prohibited Conduct Relating to Transactions.

Sec.
2.2-3112. Prohibited conduct concerning personal interest in a transaction; exceptions.

ARTICLE 1.
General Provisions.

§ 2.2-3100. Policy; application; construction.

CASE NOTES

Applicability. — Since a majority of council members did not vote on the retailer's applications for rezoning and special use permits, the town council's vote, by less than a majority of council members, meant that a quorum had not voted on the applications, and, thus, the three council members vote to approve the applications was invalid; too, it did not matter that some of the missing council members had absented themselves pursuant to the State and Local Government Conflict of Interests Act (COIA), § 2.2-3100 et seq., since COIA did not apply the laws involving "Meetings of Governing Bodies" since those laws had nothing to do with conflicts of interests. Jakabcin v. Town of Front Royal, 271 Va. 660, 628 S.E.2d 319, 2006 Va. LEXIS 49 (2006).

ARTICLE 2.
Generally Prohibited and Unlawful Conduct.

§ 2.2-3103. Prohibited conduct.

OPINIONS OF THE ATTORNEY GENERAL

Health regulatory board members. — It is not a violation of the State and Local Government Conflict of Interests Act or the Virginia Public Procurement Act for a member of a health regulatory board to vote to authorize the board to contract with or join an organization in the business of adminstering licensure examinations, where the Department of Health Professions reimburses the board member for per diem and expenses as allowable under state law and travel regulations. See opinion of Attorney General to Mr. Robert A. Nebiker, Director, Department of Health Professions, 05-029 (6/21/05).

It would be a violation of the State and Local Government Conflict of Interests Act or the Virginia Public Procurement Act for a board member to vote to approve a contract or to join an organization where, at the time of the vote, there is an existing arrangement concerning prospective employment of such board member after departure from the board or the board member accepts the payment of monies in excess of allowable per diem payments and travel reimbursement allowances. See opinion of Attorney General to Mr. Robert A. Nebiker, Director, Department of Health Professions, 05-029 (6/21/05).

ARTICLE 4.
Prohibited Conduct Relating to Transactions.

§ 2.2-3112. Prohibited conduct concerning personal interest in a transaction; exceptions.
— A. Each officer and employee of any state or local governmental or advisory agency who has a personal interest in a transaction:

1. Shall disqualify himself from participating in the transaction if (i) the transaction has application solely to property or a business or governmental agency in which he has a personal interest or a business that has a parent-subsidiary or affiliated business entity relationship with the business in which he has a personal interest or (ii) he is unable to participate pursuant to subdivision 2, 3 or 4. Any disqualification under the provisions of this subdivision shall be recorded in the public records of the officer's or employee's governmental or advisory agency. The officer or employee shall disclose his personal interest as required by § 2.2-3114 E or 2.2-3115 E and shall not vote or in any manner act on behalf of his agency in the transaction. The officer or employee shall be prohibited from (i) attending any portion of a closed meeting authorized by the Virginia Freedom of Information Act (§ 2.2-3700 et seq.) when the matter in which he has a personal interest is discussed and (ii) discussing the matter in which he has a personal interest with other governmental officers or employees at any time;

2. May participate in the transaction if he is a member of a business, profession, occupation, or group of three or more persons the members of which are affected by the transaction, and he complies with the declaration requirements of § 2.2-3114 F or 2.2-3115 G;

3. May participate in the transaction when a party to the transaction is a client of his firm if he does not personally represent or provide services to such client and he complies with the declaration requirements of § 2.2-3114 G or 2.2-3115 H; or

4. May participate in the transaction if it affects the public generally, even though his personal inter-

est, as a member of the public, may also be affected by that transaction.

B. Disqualification under the provisions of this section shall not prevent any employee having a personal interest in a transaction in which his agency is involved from representing himself or a member of his immediate family in such transaction provided he does not receive compensation for such representation and provided he complies with the disqualification and relevant disclosure requirements of this chapter.

C. Notwithstanding any other provision of law, if disqualifications of officers or employees in accordance with this section leave less than the number required by law to act, the remaining member or members shall constitute a quorum for the conduct of business and have authority to act for the agency by majority vote, unless a unanimous vote of all members is required by law, in which case authority to act shall require a unanimous vote of remaining members. Notwithstanding any provisions of this chapter to the contrary, members of a local governing body whose sole interest in any proposed sale, contract of sale, exchange, lease or conveyance is by virtue of their employment by a business involved in a proposed sale, contract of sale, exchange, lease or conveyance, and where such member's or members' vote is essential to a constitutional majority required pursuant to Article VII, Section 9 of the Constitution of Virginia and § 15.2-2100, such member or members of the local governing body may vote and participate in the deliberations of the governing body concerning whether to approve, enter into or execute such sale, contract of sale, exchange, lease or conveyance. Official action taken under circumstances that violate this section may be rescinded by the agency on such terms as the interests of the agency and innocent third parties require.

D. The provisions of subsection A shall not prevent an officer or employee from participating in a transaction merely because such officer or employee is a party in a legal proceeding of a civil nature concerning such transaction.

E. The provisions of subsection A shall not prevent an employee from participating in a transaction regarding textbooks or other educational material for students at state institutions of higher education, when those textbooks or materials have been authored or otherwise created by the employee. (1987, Sp. Sess., c. 1, § 2.1-639.11; 2001, c. 844; 2003, c. 694; 2007, c. 613.)

The 2007 amendments. — The 2007 amendment by c. 613 inserted "Notwithstanding any other provision of law" and "constitute a quorum for the conduct of business and" in the first sentence of subsection C.

CASE NOTES

Applicability. — Since a majority of council members did not vote on the retailer's applications for rezoning and special use permits, the town council's vote, by less than a majority of council members, meant that a quorum had not voted on the applications, and, thus, the three council members vote to approve the applications was invalid; too, it did not matter that some of the missing council members had absented themselves pursuant to the State and Local Government Conflict of Interests Act (COIA), § 2.2-3100 et seq., since COIA did not apply the laws involving "Meetings of Governing Bodies" since those laws had nothing to do with conflicts of interests. Jakabcin v. Town of Front Royal, 271 Va. 660, 628 S.E.2d 319, 2006 Va. LEXIS 49 (2006).

SUBTITLE II.

ADMINISTRATION OF STATE GOVERNMENT.

PART A.

General Provisions.

CHAPTER 33.

STATE HOLIDAYS AND OTHER SPECIAL DAYS.

§ 2.2-3300. Legal holidays.

Editor's note. — Acts 2007, c. 124, cl. 1, provides: "That the Department of Education shall make available to local school divisions information regarding the commemoration of Veterans Day in the public schools. Such information shall include, but need not be limited to (i) history of the holiday, (ii) discussion topics, (iii) activities, and (iv) appropriate instructional materials."

Acts 2007, c. 132, cl. 1, provides: "That the Department of Education shall make available to local school divisions information regarding the commemoration of George Washington's birthday on or around February 22 in the public schools. Such information shall include, but need not be limited to, (i) discussion topics, (ii) activities, and (iii) appropriate instructional materials about George Washington."

PART B.

Transaction of Public Business.

CHAPTER 37.

VIRGINIA FREEDOM OF INFORMATION ACT.

Sec.
2.2-3701. Definitions.
2.2-3703. Public bodies and records to which chapter inapplicable; voter registration and election records; access by persons incarcerated in a state, local, or federal correctional facility.
2.2-3704. Public records to be open to inspection; procedure for requesting records and responding to request; charges.
2.2-3705.6. Exclusions to application of chapter; proprietary records and trade secrets.

Sec.
2.2-3705.7. Exclusions to application of chapter; records of specific public bodies and certain other limited exemptions.
2.2-3706.   Disclosure of criminal records; limitations.
2.2-3707.   Meetings to be public; notice of meetings; recordings; minutes.
2.2-3707.1. Posting of minutes for state boards and commissions.
2.2-3708.   Electronic communication meetings; applicability; physical quorum required; notice; report.
2.2-3708.1. Participation in meetings in event of emergency; certain disabilities; distance from meeting location for certain public bodies.
2.2-3711.   Closed meetings authorized for certain limited purposes.
2.2-3713.   Proceedings for enforcement of chapter.

§ 2.2-3700. Short title; policy.

CASE NOTES

Applied in White Dog Publ., Inc. v. Culpeper County Bd. of Supervisors, 272 Va. 377, 634 S.E.2d 334, 2006 Va. LEXIS 81 (2006).

§ 2.2-3701. Definitions. — As used in this chapter, unless the context requires a different meaning:

"Closed meeting" means a meeting from which the public is excluded.

"Electronic communication" means any audio or combined audio and visual communication method.

"Emergency" means an unforeseen circumstance rendering the notice required by this chapter impossible or impracticable and which circumstance requires immediate action.

"Meeting" or *"meetings"* means the meetings including work sessions, when sitting physically, or through telephonic or video equipment pursuant to § 2.2-3708, as a body or entity, or as an informal assemblage of (i) as many as three members or (ii) a quorum, if less than three, of the constituent membership, wherever held, with or without minutes being taken, whether or not votes are cast, of any public body. The gathering of employees of a public body shall not be deemed a "meeting" subject to the provisions of this chapter.

"Open meeting" or *"public meeting"* means a meeting at which the public may be present.

"Public body" means any legislative body, authority, board, bureau, commission, district or agency of the Commonwealth or of any political subdivision of the Commonwealth, including cities, towns and counties, municipal councils, governing bodies of counties, school boards and planning commissions; boards of visitors of public institutions of higher education; and other organizations, corporations or agencies in the Commonwealth supported wholly or principally by public funds. It shall include (i) the Virginia Birth-Related Neurological Injury Compensation Program and its board of directors established pursuant to Chapter 50 (§ 38.2-5000 et seq.) of Title 38.2 and (ii) any committee, subcommittee, or other entity however designated, of the public body created to perform delegated functions of the public body or to advise the public body. It shall not exclude any such committee, subcommittee or entity because it has private sector or citizen members. Corporations organized by the Virginia Retirement System are "public bodies" for purposes of this chapter.

For the purposes of the provisions of this chapter applicable to access to public records, constitutional officers shall be considered public bodies and, except as otherwise expressly provided by law, shall have the same obligations to disclose public records as other custodians of public records.

"Public records" means all writings and recordings that consist of letters, words or numbers, or their equivalent, set down by handwriting, typewriting, printing, photostatting, photography, magnetic impulse, optical or magneto-optical form, mechanical or electronic recording or other form of data compilation, however stored, and regardless of physical form or characteristics, prepared or owned by, or in the possession of a public body or its officers, employees or agents in the transaction of public business.

"Regional public body" means a unit of government organized as provided by law within defined boundaries, as determined by the General Assembly, whose members are appointed by the participating local governing bodies, and such unit includes two or more counties or cities.

"Scholastic records" means those records containing information directly related to a student and maintained by a public body that is an educational agency or institution or by a person acting for such agency or institution. (1968, c. 479, § 2.1-341; 1970, c. 456; 1974, c. 332; 1975, c. 307; 1977, c. 677; 1978, cc. 573, 826; 1979, cc. 369, 687; 1980, c. 754; 1984, c. 252; 1989, c. 358; 1990, c. 538; 1993, cc. 270, 720; 1994, cc. 845, 931; 1996, c. 609; 1997, c. 641; 1999, cc. 703, 726; 2001, c. 844; 2002, c. 393; 2003, c. 897; 2007, c. 945.)

The 2007 amendments. — The 2007 amendment by c. 945 added the definitions of "Electronic communication" and "Regional public body."

§ 2.2-3703. Public bodies and records to which chapter inapplicable; voter registration and election records; access by persons incarcerated in a state, local, or federal correctional facility. — A. The provisions of this chapter shall not apply to:

1. The Virginia Parole Board, except that (i) information from the Virginia Parole Board providing the number of inmates considered by such Board for discretionary parole, the number of inmates granted or denied parole, and the number of parolees returned to the custody of the Department of Corrections solely as a result of a determination by such Board of a violation of parole shall be open to inspection and available for release, on a monthly basis, as provided by § 2.2-3704 and (ii) all records concerning the finances of the Virginia Parole Board

shall be public records and subject to the provisions of this chapter. The information required by clause (i) shall be furnished by offense, sex, race, age of the inmate, and the locality in which the conviction was obtained, upon the request of the party seeking the information;

2. Petit juries and grand juries;

3. Family assessment and planning teams established pursuant to § 2.2-5207;

4. The Virginia State Crime Commission; and

5. The records required by law to be maintained by the clerks of the courts of record, as defined in § 1-212, and courts not of record, as defined in § 16.1-69.5. However, other records maintained by the clerks of such courts shall be public records and subject to the provisions of this chapter.

B. Public access to voter registration and election records shall be governed by the provisions of Title 24.2 and this chapter. The provisions of Title 24.2 shall be controlling in the event of any conflict.

C. No provision of this chapter or Chapter 21 (§ 30-178 et seq.) of Title 30 shall be construed to afford any rights to any person (i) incarcerated in a state, local or federal correctional facility, whether or not such facility is (a) located in the Commonwealth or (b) operated pursuant to the Corrections Private Management Act (§ 53.1-261 et seq.) or (ii) civilly committed pursuant to the Sexually Violent Predators Act (§ 37.2-900 et seq.). However, this subsection shall not be construed to prevent such persons from exercising their constitutionally protected rights, including, but not limited to, their right to call for evidence in their favor in a criminal prosecution. (1999, cc. 703, 726, § 2.1-341.2; 2001, c. 844; 2003, cc. 989, 1018; 2004, cc. 398, 690; 2007, cc. 438, 548, 626.)

The 2007 amendments. — The 2007 amendment by c. 438 rewrote subsection C, by redesignating former clauses (i) and (ii) as (a) and (b), inserting a new clause (i) designator, inserting clause (ii), and making minor stylistic changes.

The 2007 amendments by cc. 548 and 626 are identical, and added subdivision A 5 and made related changes.

CASE NOTES

Constitutionality.

Prisoner exclusion provision of the Virginia Freedom of Information Act, subsection C of § 2.2-3703, was not facially unconstitutional as there were numerous rational reasons for it, such as preventing frivolous requests that would unduly burden state resources, and it was not unconstitutional as applied to an inmate, who sought records regarding his medical condition to determine if he had a viable claim against various state department of correction officials, because even if the inmate's request was not frivolous, he was not thereby denied equal protection, and the exclusion did not deny the inmate's access to the courts as it did not obstruct his ability to file suit challenging his medical treatment. Giarratano v. Johnson, 456 F. Supp. 2d 747, 2006 U.S. Dist. LEXIS 74882 (W.D. Va. 2006).

§ 2.2-3704. Public records to be open to inspection; procedure for requesting records and responding to request; charges. — A. Except as otherwise specifically provided by law, all public records shall be open to inspection and copying by any citizens of the Commonwealth during the regular office hours of the custodian of such records. Access to such records shall not be denied to citizens of the Commonwealth, representatives of newspapers and magazines with circulation in the Commonwealth, and representatives of radio and television stations broadcasting in or into the Commonwealth. The custodian may require the requester to provide his name and legal address. The custodian of such records shall take all necessary precautions for their preservation and safekeeping.

B. A request for public records shall identify the requested records with reasonable specificity. The request need not make reference to this chapter in order to invoke the provisions of this chapter or to impose the time limits for response by a public body. Any public body that is subject to this chapter and that is the custodian of the requested records shall promptly, but in all cases within five working days of receiving a request, provide the requested records to the requester or make one of the following responses in writing:

1. The requested records are being entirely withheld because their release is prohibited by law or the custodian has exercised his discretion to withhold the records in accordance with this chapter. Such response shall identify with reasonable particularity the volume and subject matter of withheld records, and cite, as to each category of withheld records, the specific Code section that authorizes the withholding of the records.

2. The requested records are being provided in part and are being withheld in part because the release of part of the records is prohibited by law or the custodian has exercised his discretion to withhold a portion of the records in accordance with this chapter. Such response shall identify with reasonable particularity the subject matter of withheld portions, and cite, as to each category of withheld records, the specific Code section that authorizes the withholding of the records. When a portion of a requested record is withheld, the public body may delete or excise only that portion of the record to which an exemption applies and shall release the remainder of the record.

3. The requested records could not be found or do not exist. However, if the public body that received the request knows that another public body has the requested records, the response shall include contact information for the other public body.

4. It is not practically possible to provide the requested records or to determine whether they are available within the five-work-day period. Such response shall specify the conditions that make a response impossible. If the response is made within five working days, the public body shall have an additional seven work days in which to provide one of the four preceding responses.

C. Any public body may petition the appropriate court for additional time to respond to a request for records when the request is for an extraordinary volume of records or requires an extraordinarily lengthy search, and a response by the public body within the time required by this chapter will prevent the public body from meeting its operational responsibilities. Before proceeding with the petition, however, the public body shall make reasonable efforts to reach an agreement with the requester concerning the production of the records requested.

D. Subject to the provisions of subsections G and J, no public body shall be required to create a new record if the record does not already exist. However, a public body may abstract or summarize information under such terms and conditions as agreed between the requester and the public body.

E. Failure to respond to a request for records shall be deemed a denial of the request and shall constitute a violation of this chapter.

F. A public body may make reasonable charges not to exceed its actual cost incurred in accessing, duplicating, supplying, or searching for the requested records. No public body shall impose any extraneous, intermediary or surplus fees or expenses to recoup the general costs associated with creating or maintaining records or transacting the general business of the public body. Any duplicating fee charged by a public body shall not exceed the actual cost of duplication. The public body may also make a reasonable charge for the cost incurred in supplying records produced from a geographic information system at the request of anyone other than the owner of the land that is the subject of the request. However, such charges shall not exceed the actual cost to the public body in supplying such records, except that the public body may charge, on a pro rata per acre basis, for the cost of creating topographical maps developed by the public body, for such maps or portions thereof, which encompass a contiguous area greater than 50 acres. All charges for the supplying of requested records shall be estimated in advance at the request of the citizen.

G. Public records maintained by a public body in an electronic data processing system, computer database, or any other structured collection of data shall be made available to a requester at a reasonable cost, not to exceed the actual cost in accordance with subsection F. When electronic or other databases are combined or contain exempt and nonexempt records, the public body may provide access to the exempt records if not otherwise prohibited by law, but shall provide access to the nonexempt records as provided by this chapter.

Public bodies shall produce nonexempt records maintained in an electronic database in any tangible medium identified by the requester, including, where the public body has the capability, the option of posting the records on a website or delivering the records through an electronic mail address provided by the requester, if that medium is used by the public body in the regular course of business. No public body shall be required to produce records from an electronic database in a format not regularly used by the public body. However, the public body shall make reasonable efforts to provide records in any format under such terms and conditions as agreed between the requester and public body, including the payment of reasonable costs. The excision of exempt fields of information from a database or the conversion of data from one available format to another shall not be deemed the creation, preparation or compilation of a new public record.

H. In any case where a public body determines in advance that charges for producing the requested records are likely to exceed $200, the public body may, before continuing to process the request, require the requester to agree to payment of a deposit not to exceed the amount of the advance determination. The deposit shall be credited toward the final cost of supplying the requested records. The period within which the public body shall respond under this section shall be tolled for the amount of time that elapses between notice of the advance determination and the response of the requester.

I. Before processing a request for records, a public body may require the requester to pay any amounts owed to the public body for previous requests for records that remain unpaid 30 days or more after billing.

J. Every public body of state government shall compile, and annually update, an index of computer databases that contains at a minimum those databases created by them on or after July 1, 1997. "Computer database" means a structured collection of data or records residing in a computer. Such index shall be a public record and shall include, at a minimum, the following information with respect to each database listed therein: a list of data fields, a description of the format or record layout, the date last updated, a list of any data fields to which public access is restricted, a description of each format in which the database can be copied or reproduced using the public body's computer facilities, and a schedule of fees for the production of copies in each available form. The form, context, language, and guidelines for the indices and the databases to be indexed shall be developed by the Virginia Information Technologies Agency in consultation with the Librarian of Virginia and the State Archivist. The public body shall not be required to disclose its software security, including passwords. (1968, c. 479, § 2.1-342; 1973, c. 461; 1974, c. 332; 1975, cc. 307, 312; 1976, cc. 640, 709; 1977, c. 677; 1978, c. 810; 1979, cc. 682, 684, 686, 689; 1980, cc. 678, 754; 1981, cc. 456, 464, 466, 589; 1982, cc. 225, 449, 452, 560, 635; 1983, cc. 372, 462, 607; 1984, cc. 85, 395, 433, 513, 532; 1985, cc. 81, 155, 502, 618; 1986, cc. 273, 291, 383, 469, 592; 1987, cc. 401, 491, 581; 1988, cc. 39, 151, 395, 411, 891, 902; 1989, cc. 56, 358, 478; 1990, cc. 217, 538, 721, 819, 968; 1991, cc. 213, 561; 1992, cc. 40, 150, 167, 200, 203, 207, 593, 612; 1993, cc. 205, 270, 296, 537, 552, 638, 750, 883; 1994, cc.

485, 532, 606, 839, 853, 918; 1995, cc. 299, 362, 499, 562, 638, 722, 812, 837; 1996, cc. 168, 469, 589, 599, 783, 786, 794, 855, 862, 902, 905, 1001, 1046; 1997, cc. 198, 295, 439, 567, 636, 641, 777, 782, 785, 838, 861; 1998, cc. 427, 891; 1999, cc. 438, 703, 726; 2001, c. 844; 2002, cc. 715, 830; 2003, cc. 275, 981, 1021; 2007, c. 439.)

The 2007 amendments. — The 2007 amendment by c. 439 inserted "provide the requested records to the requestor or" in the introductory paragraph of subsection B; deleted subdivision B 1, which read: "The requested records will be provided to the requestor"; redesignated former subdivisions B 2 and B 3 as present subdivisions B 1 and B 2; in present subdivision B 1, substituted "are being" for "will be" near the beginning, deleted clause (i), which read: "be in writing," deleted the clause designations (ii) and (iii); in present subdivision B 2, substituted "are being" for "will be" and inserted "are being" near the beginning, deleted clause (i), which read: "be in writing," and deleted the clause designations (ii) and (iii); added present subdivision B 3; in subdivision B 4, deleted "be in writing and" following "Such response shall" near the beginning of the second sentence and substituted "four" for "three" in the last sentence; and inserted "or requires an extraordinarily lengthy search" in the first sentence in subsection C.

§ 2.2-3705.1. Exclusions to application of chapter; exclusions of general application to public bodies.

CASE NOTES

Documents to be made part of record on appeal. — Trial court erred in refusing to require a university to produce reports sought under the Freedom of Information Act so they could be made part of the record under Va. Sup. Ct. R. 5:10(a)(3), as the refusal prevented review by the appellate court of a professor's request for reports made by the university to an accrediting agency, and confidential personnel information under § 2.2-3705.1 could have been shielded by a protective order. Bland v. Va. State Univ., 272 Va. 198, 630 S.E.2d 525, 2006 Va. LEXIS 55 (2006).

§ 2.2-3705.6. Exclusions to application of chapter; proprietary records and trade secrets.
— The following records are excluded from the provisions of this chapter but may be disclosed by the custodian in his discretion, except where such disclosure is prohibited by law:

1. Proprietary information gathered by or for the Virginia Port Authority as provided in § 62.1-132.4 or 62.1-134.1.

2. Financial statements not publicly available filed with applications for industrial development financings in accordance with Chapter 49 (§ 15.2-4900 et seq.) of Title 15.2.

3. Confidential proprietary records, voluntarily provided by private business pursuant to a promise of confidentiality from the Department of Business Assistance, the Virginia Economic Development Partnership, the Virginia Tourism Authority, the Tobacco Indemnification and Community Revitalization Commission, a nonprofit, nonstock corporation created pursuant to § 2.2-2240.1, or local or regional industrial or economic development authorities or organizations, used by the Department, the Partnership, the Authority, or such entities for busi-

ness, trade and tourism development; and memoranda, working papers or other records related to businesses that are considering locating or expanding in Virginia, prepared by such entities, where competition or bargaining is involved and where, if such records are made public, the financial interest of the governmental unit would be adversely affected.

4. Information that was filed as confidential under the Toxic Substances Information Act (§ 32.1-239 et seq.), as such Act existed prior to July 1, 1992.

5. Fisheries data that would permit identification of any person or vessel, except when required by court order as specified in § 28.2-204.

6. Confidential financial statements, balance sheets, trade secrets, and revenue and cost projections provided to the Department of Rail and Public Transportation, provided such information is exempt under the federal Freedom of Information Act or the federal Interstate Commerce Act or other laws administered by the Surface Transportation Board or the Federal Railroad Administration with respect to data provided in confidence to the Surface Transportation Board and the Federal Railroad Administration.

7. Confidential proprietary records related to inventory and sales, voluntarily provided by private energy suppliers to the Department of Mines, Minerals and Energy, used by that Department for energy contingency planning purposes or for developing consolidated statistical information on energy supplies.

8. Confidential proprietary information furnished to the Board of Medical Assistance Services or the Medicaid Prior Authorization Advisory Committee pursuant to Article 4 (§ 32.1-331.12 et seq.) of Chapter 10 of Title 32.1.

9. Proprietary, commercial or financial information, balance sheets, trade secrets, and revenue and cost projections provided by a private transportation business to the Virginia Department of Transportation and the Department of Rail and Public Transportation for the purpose of conducting transportation studies needed to obtain grants or other financial assistance under the Transportation Equity Act for the 21st Century (P.L. 105-178) for transportation projects, provided such information is exempt under the federal Freedom of Information Act or the federal Interstate Commerce Act or other laws administered by the Surface Transportation Board or the Federal Railroad Administration with respect to data provided in confidence to the Surface Transportation Board and the Federal Railroad Administration. However, the exemption provided by this subdivision shall not apply to any wholly owned subsidiary of a public body.

10. Confidential information designated as provided in subsection D of § 2.2-4342 as trade secrets or proprietary information by any person who has submitted to a public body an application for

prequalification to bid on public construction projects in accordance with subsection B of § 2.2-4317.

11. a. Memoranda, staff evaluations, or other records prepared by the responsible public entity, its staff, outside advisors, or consultants exclusively for the evaluation and negotiation of proposals filed under the Public-Private Transportation Act of 1995 (§ 56-556 et seq.) or the Public Private Education Facilities and Infrastructure Act of 2002 (§ 56-575.1 et seq.), where (i) if such records were made public prior to or after the execution of an interim or a comprehensive agreement, § 56-573.1:1 or 56-575.17 notwithstanding, the financial interest or bargaining position of the public entity would be adversely affected, and (ii) the basis for the determination required in clause (i) is documented in writing by the responsible public entity; and

b. Records provided by a private entity to a responsible public entity, affected jurisdiction, or affected local jurisdiction pursuant to the provisions of the Public-Private Transportation Act of 1995 or the Public-Private Education Facilities and Infrastructure Act of 2002, to the extent that such records contain (i) trade secrets of the private entity as defined in the Uniform Trade Secrets Act (§ 59.1-336 et seq.); (ii) financial records of the private entity, including balance sheets and financial statements, that are not generally available to the public through regulatory disclosure or otherwise; or (iii) other information submitted by the private entity, where, if the records were made public prior to the execution of an interim agreement or a comprehensive agreement, the financial interest or bargaining position of the public or private entity would be adversely affected. In order for the records specified in clauses (i), (ii) and (iii) to be excluded from the provisions of this chapter, the private entity shall make a written request to the responsible public entity:

1. Invoking such exclusion upon submission of the data or other materials for which protection from disclosure is sought;

2. Identifying with specificity the data or other materials for which protection is sought; and

3. Stating the reasons why protection is necessary.

The responsible public entity shall determine whether the requested exclusion from disclosure is necessary to protect the trade secrets or financial records of the private entity. To protect other records submitted by the private entity from disclosure, the responsible public entity shall determine whether public disclosure prior to the execution of an interim agreement or a comprehensive agreement would adversely affect the financial interest or bargaining position of the public or private entity. The responsible public entity shall make a written determination of the nature and scope of the protection to be afforded by the responsible public entity under this subdivision. Once a written determination is made

by the responsible public entity, the records afforded protection under this subdivision shall continue to be protected from disclosure when in the possession of any affected jurisdiction or affected local jurisdiction.

Except as specifically provided in subdivision 11 a, nothing in this subdivision shall be construed to authorize the withholding of (a) procurement records as required by § 56-573.1:1 or 56-575.17; (b) information concerning the terms and conditions of any interim or comprehensive agreement, service contract, lease, partnership, or any agreement of any kind entered into by the responsible public entity and the private entity; (c) information concerning the terms and conditions of any financing arrangement that involves the use of any public funds; or (d) information concerning the performance of any private entity developing or operating a qualifying transportation facility or a qualifying project.

For the purposes of this subdivision, the terms "affected jurisdiction," "affected local jurisdiction," "comprehensive agreement," "interim agreement," "qualifying project," "qualifying transportation facility," "responsible public entity," and "private entity" shall mean the same as those terms are defined in the Public-Private Transportation Act of 1995 or in the Public-Private Education Facilities and Infrastructure Act of 2002.

12. Confidential proprietary information or trade secrets, not publicly available, provided by a private person or entity to the Virginia Resources Authority or to a fund administered in connection with financial assistance rendered or to be rendered by the Virginia Resources Authority where, if such information were made public, the financial interest of the private person or entity would be adversely affected, and, after June 30, 1997, where such information was provided pursuant to a promise of confidentiality.

13. Confidential proprietary records that are provided by a franchisee under Article 1.2 (§ 15.2-2108.19 et seq.) of Chapter 21 of Title 15.2 to its franchising authority pursuant to a promise of confidentiality from the franchising authority that relates to the franchisee's potential provision of new services, adoption of new technologies or implementation of improvements, where such new services, technologies or improvements have not been implemented by the franchisee on a nonexperimental scale in the franchise area, and where, if such records were made public, the competitive advantage or financial interests of the franchisee would be adversely affected. In order for confidential proprietary information to be excluded from the provisions of this chapter, the franchisee shall (i) invoke such exclusion upon submission of the data or other materials for which protection from disclosure is sought, (ii) identify the data or other materials for which protection is sought, and (iii) state the reason why protection is necessary.

14. Documents and other information of a proprietary nature furnished by a supplier of charitable gaming supplies to the Department of Charitable Gaming pursuant to subsection E of § 18.2-340.34.

15. Records and reports related to Virginia apple producer sales provided to the Virginia State Apple Board pursuant to §§ 3.1-622 and 3.1-624.

16. Trade secrets, as defined in the Uniform Trade Secrets Act (§ 59.1-336 et seq.) of Title 59.1, submitted by CMRS providers as defined in § 56-484.12 to the Wireless Carrier E-911 Cost Recovery Subcommittee created pursuant to § 56-484.15, relating to the provision of wireless E-911 service.

17. Records submitted as a grant application, or accompanying a grant application, to the Commonwealth Health Research Board pursuant to Chapter 22 (§ 23-277 et seq.) of Title 23 to the extent such records contain proprietary business or research-related information produced or collected by the applicant in the conduct of or as a result of study or research on medical, rehabilitative, scientific, technical, or scholarly issues, when such information has not been publicly released, published, copyrighted, or patented, if the disclosure of such information would be harmful to the competitive position of the applicant.

18. Confidential proprietary records and trade secrets developed and held by a local public body (i) providing telecommunication services pursuant to § 56-265.4:4 and (ii) providing cable television services pursuant to Article 1.1 (§ 15.2-2108.2 et seq.) of Chapter 21 of Title 15.2, to the extent that disclosure of such records would be harmful to the competitive position of the locality. In order for confidential proprietary information or trade secrets to be excluded from the provisions of this chapter, the locality in writing shall (i) invoke the protections of this subdivision, (ii) identify with specificity the records or portions thereof for which protection is sought, and (iii) state the reasons why protection is necessary.

19. Confidential proprietary records and trade secrets developed by or for a local authority created in accordance with the Virginia Wireless Service Authorities Act (§ 15.2-5431.1 et seq.) to provide qualifying communications services as authorized by Article 5.1 (§ 56-484.7:1 et seq.) of Chapter 15 of Title 56, where disclosure of such information would be harmful to the competitive position of the authority, except that records required to be maintained in accordance with § 15.2-2160 shall be released.

20. Trade secrets as defined in the Uniform Trade Secrets Act (§ 59.1-336 et seq.) or financial records of a business, including balance sheets and financial statements, that are not generally available to the public through regulatory disclosure or otherwise, provided to the Department of Minority Business Enterprise as part of an application for (i) certification as a small, women- or minority-owned business

in accordance with Chapter 14 (§ 2.2-1400 et seq.) of this title or (ii) a claim made by a disadvantaged business or an economically disadvantaged individual against the Capital Access Fund for Disadvantaged Businesses created pursuant to § 2.2-2311. In order for such trade secrets or financial records to be excluded from the provisions of this chapter, the business shall (a) invoke such exclusion upon submission of the data or other materials for which protection from disclosure is sought, (b) identify the data or other materials for which protection is sought, and (c) state the reasons why protection is necessary. (1999, cc. 485, 518, 703, 726, 793, 849, 852, 867, 868, 881, § 2.1-342.01; 2000, cc. 66, 237, 382, 400, 430, 583, 589, 592, 594, 618, 632, 657, 720, 932, 933, 947, 1006, 1064; 2001, cc. 288, 518, 844, § 2.2-3705; 2002, cc. 87, 155, 242, 393, 478, 481, 499, 522, 571, 572, 633, 655, 715, 798, 830; 2003, cc. 274, 307, 327, 332, 358, 704, 801, 884, 891, 893, 897, 968; 2004, cc. 593, 690; 2005, cc. 258, 411; 2006, cc. 73, 76, 467, 831, 921, 936; 2006, Sp. Sess. I, c. 1; 2007, cc. 374, 693.)

The 2006 amendments. — The 2006 amendment by Special Session I, c. 1, effective July 1, 2006, and which expires July 1, 2007, inserted "Memoranda staff evaluations ... the responsible public agency" at the beginning of subdivision 11.

The 2007 amendments. — The 2007 amendment by c. 374, designated the provisions of subdivision 11 as subdivision 11 b; added subdivision 11 a; in subdivision 11 b, deleted "(§ 56-556 et seq.)" following "the Public-Private Transportation Act of 1995" and "(§ 56-575.1 et seq.)" following "Public-Private Education Facilities and Infrastructure Act of 2002"; in the first undesignated paragraph of subdivision 11, substituted "entity" for "body" following "by the responsible public" and deleted "to which such records are provided by the responsible public entity"; and substituted "Except as specifically provided in subdivision 11 a, nothing" for "Nothing" at the beginning of the second undesignated paragraph of subdivision 11.

The 2007 amendment by c. 693 inserted "a nonprofit, nonstock corporation created pursuant to § 2.2-2240.1" in subdivision 3.

§ 2.2-3705.7. Exclusions to application of chapter; records of specific public bodies and certain other limited exemptions. — The following records are excluded from the provisions of this chapter but may be disclosed by the custodian in his discretion, except where such disclosure is prohibited by law:

1. State income, business, and estate tax returns, personal property tax returns, scholastic and confidential records held pursuant to § 58.1-3.

2. Working papers and correspondence of the Office of the Governor; Lieutenant Governor; the Attorney General; the members of the General Assembly or the Division of Legislative Services; the mayor or chief executive officer of any political subdivision of the Commonwealth; or the president or other chief executive officer of any public institution of higher education in Virginia. However, no record, which is otherwise open to inspection under this chapter, shall be deemed exempt by virtue of the fact that it has been attached to or incorporated within any working paper or correspondence.

As used in this subdivision:

"Office of the Governor" means the Governor; his chief of staff, counsel, director of policy, Cabinet Secretaries, and the Director of the Virginia Liaison Office; and those individuals to whom the Governor has delegated his authority pursuant to § 2.2-104.

"Working papers" means those records prepared by or for an above-named public official for his personal or deliberative use.

3. Library records that can be used to identify both (i) any library patron who has borrowed material from a library and (ii) the material such patron borrowed.

4. Contract cost estimates prepared for the confidential use of the Department of Transportation in awarding contracts for construction or the purchase of goods or services, and records and automated systems prepared for the Department's Bid Analysis and Monitoring Program.

5. Lists of registered owners of bonds issued by a political subdivision of the Commonwealth, whether the lists are maintained by the political subdivision itself or by a single fiduciary designated by the political subdivision.

6. Records and writings furnished by a member of the General Assembly to a meeting of a standing committee, special committee or subcommittee of his house established solely for the purpose of reviewing members' annual disclosure statements and supporting materials filed under § 30-110 or of formulating advisory opinions to members on standards of conduct, or both.

7. Customer account information of a public utility affiliated with a political subdivision of the Commonwealth, including the customer's name and service address, but excluding the amount of utility service provided and the amount of money paid for such utility service.

8. Personal information, as defined in § 2.2-3801, (i) filed with the Virginia Housing Development Authority concerning individuals who have applied for or received loans or other housing assistance or who have applied for occupancy of or have occupied housing financed, owned or otherwise assisted by the Virginia Housing Development Authority; (ii) concerning persons participating in or persons on the waiting list for federally funded rent-assistance programs; (iii) filed with any local redevelopment and housing authority created pursuant to § 36-4 concerning persons participating in or persons on the waiting list for housing assistance programs funded by local governments or by any such authority; or (iv) filed with any local redevelopment and housing authority created pursuant to § 36-4 or any other local government agency concerning persons who have applied for occupancy or who have occupied affordable dwelling units established pursuant to § 15.2-2304 or 15.2-2305. However, access to one's own information shall not be denied.

9. Records regarding the siting of hazardous waste facilities, except as provided in § 10.1-1441, if disclosure of them would have a detrimental effect upon the negotiating position of a governing body or on the establishment of the terms, conditions and provisions of the siting agreement.

10. Records containing information on the site specific location of rare, threatened, endangered or otherwise imperiled plant and animal species, natural communities, caves, and significant historic and archaeological sites if, in the opinion of the public body that has the responsibility for such information, disclosure of the information would jeopardize the continued existence or the integrity of the resource. This exemption shall not apply to requests from the owner of the land upon which the resource is located.

11. Records, memoranda, working papers, graphics, video or audio tapes, production models, data and information of a proprietary nature produced by or for or collected by or for the State Lottery Department relating to matters of a specific lottery game design, development, production, operation, ticket price, prize structure, manner of selecting the winning ticket, manner of payment of prizes to holders of winning tickets, frequency of drawings or selections of winning tickets, odds of winning, advertising, or marketing, where such official records have not been publicly released, published, copyrighted or patented. Whether released, published or copyrighted, all game-related information shall be subject to public disclosure under this chapter upon the first day of sales for the specific lottery game to which it pertains.

12. Records of the Virginia Retirement System, acting pursuant to § 51.1-124.30, or of a local retirement system, acting pursuant to § 51.1-803, or of the Rector and Visitors of the University of Virginia, acting pursuant to § 23-76.1, relating to the acquisition, holding or disposition of a security or other ownership interest in an entity, where such security or ownership interest is not traded on a governmentally regulated securities exchange, to the extent that: (i) such records contain confidential analyses prepared for the Rector and Visitors of the University of Virginia, prepared by the retirement system or provided to the retirement system under a promise of confidentiality, of the future value of such ownership interest or the future financial performance of the entity; and (ii) disclosure of such confidential analyses would have an adverse effect on the value of the investment to be acquired, held or disposed of by the retirement system or the Rector and Visitors of the University of Virginia. Nothing in this subdivision shall be construed to prevent the disclosure of records relating to the identity of any investment held, the amount invested, or the present value of such investment.

13. Names and addresses of subscribers to Virginia Wildlife magazine, published by the Department of Game and Inland Fisheries, provided the individual subscriber has requested in writing that the Department not release such information.

14. Financial, medical, rehabilitative and other personal information concerning applicants for or recipients of loan funds submitted to or maintained by the Assistive Technology Loan Fund Authority under Chapter 11 (§ 51.5-53 et seq.) of Title 51.5.

15. Records of the Virginia Commonwealth University Health System Authority pertaining to any of the following: an individual's qualifications for or continued membership on its medical or teaching staffs; proprietary information gathered by or in the possession of the Authority from third parties pursuant to a promise of confidentiality; contract cost estimates prepared for confidential use in awarding contracts for construction or the purchase of goods or services; data, records or information of a proprietary nature produced or collected by or for the Authority or members of its medical or teaching staffs; financial statements not publicly available that may be filed with the Authority from third parties; the identity, accounts or account status of any customer of the Authority; consulting or other reports paid for by the Authority to assist the Authority in connection with its strategic planning and goals; the determination of marketing and operational strategies where disclosure of such strategies would be harmful to the competitive position of the Authority; and data, records or information of a proprietary nature produced or collected by or for employees of the Authority, other than the Authority's financial or administrative records, in the conduct of or as a result of study or research on medical, scientific, technical or scholarly issues, whether sponsored by the Authority alone or in conjunction with a governmental body or a private concern, when such data, records or information have not been publicly released, published, copyrighted or patented.

16. Records of the Department of Environmental Quality, the State Water Control Board, State Air Pollution Control Board or the Virginia Waste Management Board relating to (i) active federal environmental enforcement actions that are considered confidential under federal law and (ii) enforcement strategies, including proposed sanctions for enforcement actions. Upon request, such records shall be disclosed after a proposed sanction resulting from the investigation has been proposed to the director of the agency. This subdivision shall not be construed to prohibit the disclosure of records related to inspection reports, notices of violation, and documents detailing the nature of any environmental contamination that may have occurred or similar documents.

17. As it pertains to any person, records related to the operation of toll facilities that identify an individual, vehicle, or travel itinerary including, but not limited to, vehicle identification data, vehicle enforcement system information; video or photographic images; Social Security or other identification numbers appearing on driver's licenses; credit card or bank account data; home addresses; phone numbers; or records of the date or time of toll facility use.

18. Records of the State Lottery Department pertaining to (i) the social security number, tax identification number, state sales tax number, home address and telephone number, personal and lottery banking account and transit numbers of a retailer, and financial information regarding the nonlottery operations of specific retail locations; and (ii) individual lottery winners, except that a winner's name, hometown, and amount won shall be disclosed.

19. Records of the Board for Branch Pilots relating to the chemical or drug testing of a person regulated by the Board, where such person has tested negative or has not been the subject of a disciplinary action by the Board for a positive test result.

20. Records, investigative notes, correspondence, and information pertaining to the planning, scheduling and performance of examinations of holder records pursuant to the Uniform Disposition of Unclaimed Property Act (§ 55-210.1 et seq.) prepared by or for the State Treasurer, his agents, employees or persons employed to perform an audit or examination of holder records.

21. Records of the Virginia Department of Emergency Management or a local governing body relating to citizen emergency response teams established pursuant to an ordinance of a local governing body, to the extent that such records reveal the name, address, including e-mail address, telephone or pager numbers, or operating schedule of an individual participant in the program.

22. Records of state or local park and recreation departments and local and regional park authorities to the extent such records contain information identifying a person under the age of 18 years, where the parent or legal guardian of such person has requested in writing that such information not be disclosed. However, nothing in this subdivision shall operate to prohibit the disclosure of information defined as directory information under regulations implementing the Family Educational Rights and Privacy Act, 20 U.S.C. § 1232g, unless the public body has undertaken the parental notification and opt-out requirements provided by such regulations. Access shall not be denied to the parent, including a noncustodial parent, or guardian of such person, unless the parent's parental rights have been terminated or a court of competent jurisdiction has restricted or denied such access. For records of such persons who are emancipated, the right of access may be asserted by the subject thereof.

23. Records submitted for inclusion in the Statewide Alert Network administered by the Department of Emergency Management, to the extent that they reveal names, physical addresses, email addresses, computer or internet protocol information, telephone numbers, pager numbers, other wireless or portable communications device information, or operating schedules of individuals or agencies,

where the release of such information would compromise the security of the Statewide Alert Network or individuals participating in the Statewide Alert Network.

24. Records of the Judicial Inquiry and Review Commission made confidential by § 17.1-913.

25. Records of the Virginia Retirement System acting pursuant to § 51.1-124.30 or of a local retirement system acting pursuant to § 51.1-803 (hereinafter collectively referred to as "the retirement system") relating to:

a. Internal deliberations of or decisions by the retirement system on the pursuit of particular investment strategies, or the selection or termination of investment managers, prior to the execution of such investment strategies or the selection or termination of such managers, to the extent that disclosure of such records would have an adverse impact on the financial interest of the retirement system; and

b. Trade secrets, as defined in the Uniform Trade Secrets Act (§ 59.1-336 et seq.), provided by a private entity to the retirement system, to the extent disclosure of such records would have an adverse impact on the financial interest of the retirement system.

For the records specified in subdivision b to be excluded from the provisions of this chapter, the entity shall make a written request to the retirement system:

(1) Invoking such exclusion prior to or upon submission of the data or other materials for which protection from disclosure is sought;

(2) Identifying with specificity the data or other materials for which protection is sought; and

(3) Stating the reasons why protection is necessary.

The retirement system shall determine whether the requested exclusion from disclosure meets the requirements set forth in subdivision b.

Nothing in this subdivision shall be construed to authorize the withholding of the identity or amount of any investment held or the present value and performance of all asset classes and subclasses.

26. Records of the Department of Corrections made confidential by § 53.1-233.

27. **(Expires July 1, 2008)** Information relating to the breed of the vaccinated animal, and any personal identifying information relating to the animal owner that is not made a part of the animal license application, contained in rabies vaccination certificates provided to local treasurers as required by § 3.1-796.87:1. (1999, cc. 485, 518, 703, 726, 793, 849, 852, 867, 868, 881, § 2.1-342.01; 2000, cc. 66, 237, 382, 400, 430, 583, 589, 592, 594, 618, 632, 657, 720, 932, 933, 947, 1006, 1064; 2001, cc. 288, 518, 844, § 2.2-3705; 2002, cc. 87, 155, 242, 393, 478, 481, 499, 522, 571, 572, 633, 655, 715, 798, 830; 2003, cc. 274, 307, 327, 332, 358, 704, 801, 884, 891, 893, 897, 968; 2004, cc. 426, 690, 832; 2005, cc. 165, 508; 2007, cc. 406, 652, 660, 737, 739.)

Editor's note. — Acts 2007, c. 660, which added subdivision 27, in cl. 2 provides: "That the provisions of this act shall expire on July 1, 2008."

The 2007 amendments. — The 2007 amendment by c. 406 inserted "and local and regional park authorities" in subdivision 22.

The 2007 amendments by cc. 652 and 737 are identical, and added subsection 25 (now 26).

The 2007 amendment by c. 660 added subdivision 25 (now 27). See Editor's note for expiration date.

The 2007 amendment by c. 739, effective March 21, 2007, added subdivision 25.

§ 2.2-3706. Disclosure of criminal records; limitations. — A. As used in this section:

"Criminal incident information" means a general description of the criminal activity reported, the date and general location the alleged crime was committed, the identity of the investigating officer, and a general description of any injuries suffered or property damaged or stolen.

B. Law-enforcement agencies shall make available upon request criminal incident information relating to felony offenses. However, where the release of criminal incident information is likely to jeopardize an ongoing investigation or prosecution, or the safety of an individual; cause a suspect to flee or evade detection; or result in the destruction of evidence, such information may be withheld until the above-referenced damage is no longer likely to occur from release of the information. Nothing in this subsection shall be construed to prohibit the release of those portions of such information that are not likely to cause the above-referenced damage.

C. Information in the custody of law-enforcement agencies relative to the identity of any individual, other than a juvenile, who is arrested and charged, and the status of the charge or arrest shall be released.

D. The identity of any victim, witness or undercover officer, or investigative techniques or procedures need not but may be disclosed unless disclosure is prohibited or restricted under § 19.2-11.2.

E. The identity of any individual providing information about a crime or criminal activity under a promise of anonymity shall not be disclosed.

F. The following records are excluded from the provisions of this chapter, but may be disclosed by the custodian, in his discretion, except where such disclosure is prohibited by law:

1. Complaints, memoranda, correspondence, case files or reports, witness statements, and evidence relating to a criminal investigation or prosecution, other than criminal incident information as defined in subsection A;

2. Adult arrestee photographs when necessary to avoid jeopardizing an investigation in felony cases until such time as the release of the photograph will no longer jeopardize the investigation;

3. Reports submitted in confidence to (i) state and local law-enforcement agencies, (ii) investigators authorized pursuant to § 53.1-16 or § 66-3.1, and (iii) campus police departments of public institutions of higher education established pursuant to Chapter 17 (§ 23-232 et seq.) of Title 23;

4. Portions of records of local government crime commissions that would identify individuals providing information about crimes or criminal activities under a promise of anonymity;

5. Records of local law-enforcement agencies relating to neighborhood watch programs that include the names, addresses, and operating schedules of individual participants in the program that are provided to such agencies under a promise of anonymity;

6. All records of persons imprisoned in penal institutions in the Commonwealth provided such records relate to the imprisonment;

7. Records of law-enforcement agencies, to the extent that such records contain specific tactical plans, the disclosure of which would jeopardize the safety or security of law-enforcement personnel or the general public;

8. All records of adult persons under (i) investigation or supervision by a local pretrial services agency in accordance with Article 5 (§ 19.2-152.2 et seq.) of Chapter 9 of Title 19.2; (ii) investigation, probation supervision or monitoring by a local community-based probation services agency in accordance with Article 9 (§ 9.1-173 et seq.) of Chapter 1 of Title 9.1; or (iii) investigation or supervision by state probation and parole services in accordance with Article 2 (§ 53.1-141 et seq.) of Chapter 4 of Title 53.1; and

9. Records of a law-enforcement agency to the extent that they disclose the telephone numbers for cellular telephones, pagers, or comparable portable communication devices provided to its personnel for use in the performance of their official duties.

G. Records kept by law-enforcement agencies as required by § 15.2-1722 shall be subject to the provisions of this chapter except:

1. Those portions of noncriminal incident or other investigative reports or materials containing identifying information of a personal, medical or financial nature provided to a law-enforcement agency where the release of such information would jeopardize the safety or privacy of any person;

2. Those portions of any records containing information related to plans for or resources dedicated to undercover operations; or

3. Records of background investigations of applicants for law-enforcement agency employment or other confidential administrative investigations conducted pursuant to law.

H. Records of the Sex Offender and Crimes Against Minors Registry maintained by the Department of State Police pursuant to Chapter 9 (§ 9.1-900 et seq.) of Title 9.1 are excluded from the provisions of this chapter, including information obtained from state, local and regional officials, except to the extent that information is required to be posted on the Internet pursuant to § 9.1-913.

I. In the event of conflict between this section as it relates to requests made under this section and other provisions of law, this section shall control.

(1999, cc. 703, 726, § 2.1-342.2; 2000, c. 227; 2001, c. 844; 2002, cc. 393, 715, 769, 830; 2004, cc. 685, 735; 2006, cc. 857, 914; 2007, c. 133.)

The 2007 amendments. — The 2007 amendment by c. 133 substituted "services agency" for "program" in clause (ii) of subdivision F 8.

§ 2.2-3707. Meetings to be public; notice of meetings; recordings; minutes. — A. All meetings of public bodies shall be open, except as provided in §§ 2.2-3707.01 and 2.2-3711.

B. No meeting shall be conducted through telephonic, video, electronic or other communication means where the members are not physically assembled to discuss or transact public business, except as provided in § 2.2-3708, 2.2-3709 or as may be specifically provided in Title 54.1 for the summary suspension of professional licenses.

C. Every public body shall give notice of the date, time, and location of its meetings by placing the notice in a prominent public location at which notices are regularly posted and in the office of the clerk of the public body, or in the case of a public body that has no clerk, in the office of the chief administrator. All state public bodies subject to the provisions of this chapter shall also post notice of their meetings on their websites and on the electronic calendar maintained by the Virginia Information Technologies Agency commonly known as the Commonwealth Calendar. Publication of meeting notices by electronic means by other public bodies shall be encouraged. The notice shall be posted at least three working days prior to the meeting. Notices for meetings of state public bodies on which there is at least one member appointed by the Governor shall state whether or not public comment will be received at the meeting and, if so, the approximate point during the meeting when public comment will be received.

D. Notice, reasonable under the circumstance, of special or emergency meetings shall be given contemporaneously with the notice provided members of the public body conducting the meeting.

E. Any person may annually file a written request for notification with a public body. The request shall include the requester's name, address, zip code, daytime telephone number, electronic mail address, if available, and organization, if any. The public body receiving such request shall provide notice of all meetings directly to each such person. Without objection by the person, the public body may provide electronic notice of all meetings in response to such requests.

F. At least one copy of all agenda packets and, unless exempt, all materials furnished to members of a public body for a meeting shall be made available for public inspection at the same time such documents are furnished to the members of the public body.

G. Nothing in this chapter shall be construed to prohibit the gathering or attendance of two or more members of a public body (i) at any place or function where no part of the purpose of such gathering or attendance is the discussion or transaction of any public business, and such gathering or attendance was not called or prearranged with any purpose of discussing or transacting any business of the public body or (ii) at a public forum, candidate appearance, or debate, the purpose of which is to inform the electorate and not to transact public business or to hold discussions relating to the transaction of public business, even though the performance of the members individually or collectively in the conduct of public business may be a topic of discussion or debate at such public meeting. The notice provisions of this chapter shall not apply to informal meetings or gatherings of the members of the General Assembly.

H. Any person may photograph, film, record or otherwise reproduce any portion of a meeting required to be open. The public body conducting the meeting may adopt rules governing the placement and use of equipment necessary for broadcasting, photographing, filming or recording a meeting to prevent interference with the proceedings.

I. Minutes shall be recorded at all open meetings. However, minutes shall not be required to be taken at deliberations of (i) standing and other committees of the General Assembly; (ii) legislative interim study commissions and committees, including the Virginia Code Commission; (iii) study committees or commissions appointed by the Governor; or (iv) study commissions or study committees, or any other committees or subcommittees appointed by the governing bodies or school boards of counties, cities and towns, except where the membership of any such commission, committee or subcommittee includes a majority of the governing body of the county, city or town or school board.

Minutes, including draft minutes, and all other records of open meetings, including audio or audio/visual records shall be deemed public records and subject to the provisions of this chapter.

Minutes shall include, but are not limited to, (i) the date, time, and location of the meeting; (ii) the members of the public body recorded as present and absent; and (iii) a summary of the discussion on matters proposed, deliberated or decided, and a record of any votes taken. In addition, for electronic communication meetings conducted in accordance with § 2.2-3708, minutes of state public bodies shall include (a) the identity of the members of the public body at each remote location identified in the notice who participated in the meeting through electronic communications means, (b) the identity of the members of the public body who were physically assembled at the primary or central meeting location, and (c) the identity of the members of the public body who were not present at the locations identified in clauses (a) and (b), but who monitored such meeting through electronic communications means. (1968, c. 479, § 2.1-343; 1973, c. 461; 1976, c. 467; 1977, c.

677; 1982, c. 333; 1989, c. 358; 1990, c. 538; 1993, c. 720; 1995, c. 562; 1999, cc. 696, 703, 726; 2000, c. 227; 2001, c. 844; 2004, cc. 730, 768; 2005, c. 352; 2007, c. 300.)

The 2007 amendments. — The 2007 amendment by c. 300, in subsection C, substituted "their websites and on the electronic calendar maintained by the Virginia Information Technologies Agency commonly known as the Commonwealth Calendar" for "the Internet" at the end of the second sentence.

§ 2.2-3707.1. Posting of minutes for state boards and commissions. — All boards, commissions, councils, and other public bodies created in the executive branch of state government and subject to the provisions of this chapter shall post minutes of their meetings on such body's website, if any, and on the electronic calendar maintained by the Virginia Information Technologies Agency commonly known as the Commonwealth Calendar. Draft minutes of meetings shall be posted as soon as possible but no later than ten working days after the conclusion of the meeting. Final approved meeting minutes shall be posted within three working days of final approval of the minutes. (2002, cc. 580, 618; 2006, cc. 474, 595; 2007, c. 300.)

The 2007 amendments. — The 2007 amendment by c. 300 substituted "electronic calendar maintained by the Virginia Information Technologies Agency commonly known as the Commonwealth Calendar" for "Virginia Regulatory Town Hall."

§ 2.2-3708. Electronic communication meetings; applicability; physical quorum required; notice; report. — A. Except as expressly provided in § 2.2-3708.1, no local governing body, school board, or any authority, board, bureau, commission, district or agency of local government, any committee thereof, or any entity created by a local governing body, school board, or any local authority, board, or commission shall conduct a meeting wherein the public business is discussed or transacted through telephonic, video, electronic or other communication means where the members are not physically assembled. Nothing in this section shall be construed to prohibit the use of interactive audio or video means to expand public participation.

B. Except as provided in subsection D of § 2.2-3707.01, state public bodies may conduct any meeting wherein the public business is discussed or transacted through electronic communication means, provided (i) a quorum of the public body is physically assembled at one primary or central meeting location, (ii) notice of the meeting has been given in accordance with subsection C, and (iii) the remote locations, from which additional members of the public body participate through electronic communication means, are open to the public. All persons attending the meeting at any of the meeting locations shall be afforded the same opportunity to address the public body as persons attending the primary or central location. Public bodies, however, may meet by electronic communication means without a quorum of the public body physically assembled at one location when (i) the Governor has declared a state of emergency in accordance with § 44-146.17, (ii) the meeting is necessary to take action to address the emergency, and (iii) the public body otherwise complies with the provisions of this section.

If an authorized public body holds an electronic meeting pursuant to this section, it shall also hold at least one meeting annually where members in attendance at the meeting are physically assembled at one location and where no members participate by electronic communication means.

C. Notice of any meetings held pursuant to this section shall be provided at least three working days in advance of the date scheduled for the meeting. The notice shall include the date, time, place, and purpose for the meeting; shall identify the locations for the meeting; and shall include a telephone number that may be used at remote locations to notify the primary or central meeting location of any interruption in the telephonic or video broadcast of the meeting to the remote locations. Any interruption in the telephonic or video broadcast of the meeting shall result in the suspension of action at the meeting until repairs are made and public access restored.

D. Agenda packets and, unless exempt, all materials that will be distributed to members of the public body and that have been made available to the staff of the public body in sufficient time for duplication and forwarding to all locations where public access will be provided shall be made available to the public at the time of the meeting. Minutes of all meetings held by electronic communication means shall be recorded as required by § 2.2-3707. Votes taken during any meeting conducted through electronic communication means shall be recorded by name in roll-call fashion and included in the minutes.

E. Three working days' notice shall not be required for meetings authorized under this section that are continued to address an emergency or to conclude the agenda of the meeting for which proper notice has been given, when the date, time, place, and purpose of the continued meeting are set during the meeting prior to adjournment. Public bodies conducting emergency meetings through electronic communication means shall comply with the provisions of subsection D requiring minutes of the meeting. The nature of the emergency shall be stated in the minutes.

F. Any authorized public body that meets by electronic communication means shall make a written report of the following to the Virginia Freedom of Information Advisory Council and the Joint Commission on Technology and Science by December 15 of each year:

1. The total number of electronic communication meetings held that year;

2. The dates and purposes of the meetings;

3. The number of sites for each meeting;

4. The types of electronic communication means by which the meetings were held;

5. The number of participants, including members of the public, at each meeting location;

6. The identity of the members of the public body recorded as absent and those recorded as present at each meeting location;

7. A summary of any public comment received about the electronic communication meetings; and

8. A written summary of the public body's experience using electronic communication meetings, including its logistical and technical experience. (1984, c. 252, § 2.1-343.1; 1989, c. 358; 1991, c. 473; 1992, c. 153; 1993, c. 270; 1995, c. 278; 1996, c. 289; 1999, cc. 703, 726; 2001, c. 844; 2003, cc. 981, 1021; 2005, c. 352; 2007, cc. 512, 945.)

The 2007 amendments. — The 2007 amendment by c. 512 added the last sentence in the second paragraph (now the first paragraph) of subsection B.

The 2007 amendment by c. 945 rewrote the section.

§ 2.2-3708.1. Participation in meetings in event of emergency; certain disabilities; distance from meeting location for certain public bodies.

— A. A member of a public body may participate in a meeting governed by this chapter through electronic communication means from a remote location that is not open to the public only as follows and subject to the requirements of subsection B:

1. If, on the day of a meeting, a member of the public body holding the meeting notifies the chair of the public body that such member is unable to attend the meeting due to an emergency and identifies with specificity the nature of the emergency, and the public body holding the meeting (a) approves such member's participation by a majority vote of the members present and (b) records in its minutes the specific nature of the emergency and the remote location from which the member participated.

Such participation by the member shall be limited each calendar year to two meetings or 25 percent of the meetings of the public body, whichever is fewer;

2. If a member of a public body notifies the chair of the public body that such member is unable to attend a meeting due to a temporary or permanent disability or other medical condition that prevents the member's physical attendance and the public body records this fact and the remote location from which the member participated in its minutes; or

3. If, on the day of a meeting, a member of a regional public body notifies the chair of the public body that such member's principal residence is more than 60 miles from the meeting location identified in the required notice for such meeting and the public body holding the meeting (a) approves such member's participation by a majority vote of the members

present and (b) records in its minutes the remote location from which the member participated.

B. Participation by a member of a public body as authorized under subsection A shall be only under the following conditions:

1. A quorum of the public body is physically assembled at the primary or central meeting location; and

2. The public body makes arrangements for the voice of the remote participant to be heard by all persons at the primary or central meeting location. (2007, c. 945.)

§ 2.2-3711. Closed meetings authorized for certain limited purposes. — A. Public bodies may hold closed meetings only for the following purposes:

1. Discussion, consideration, or interviews of prospective candidates for employment; assignment, appointment, promotion, performance, demotion, salaries, disciplining, or resignation of specific public officers, appointees, or employees of any public body; and evaluation of performance of departments or schools of public institutions of higher education where such evaluation will necessarily involve discussion of the performance of specific individuals. Any teacher shall be permitted to be present during a closed meeting in which there is a discussion or consideration of a disciplinary matter that involves the teacher and some student and the student involved in the matter is present, provided the teacher makes a written request to be present to the presiding officer of the appropriate board.

2. Discussion or consideration of admission or disciplinary matters or any other matters that would involve the disclosure of information contained in a scholastic record concerning any student of any Virginia public institution of higher education or any state school system. However, any such student, legal counsel and, if the student is a minor, the student's parents or legal guardians shall be permitted to be present during the taking of testimony or presentation of evidence at a closed meeting, if such student, parents, or guardians so request in writing and such request is submitted to the presiding officer of the appropriate board.

3. Discussion or consideration of the acquisition of real property for a public purpose, or of the disposition of publicly held real property, where discussion in an open meeting would adversely affect the bargaining position or negotiating strategy of the public body.

4. The protection of the privacy of individuals in personal matters not related to public business.

5. Discussion concerning a prospective business or industry or the expansion of an existing business or industry where no previous announcement has been made of the business' or industry's interest in locating or expanding its facilities in the community.

6. Discussion or consideration of the investment of public funds where competition or bargaining is involved, where, if made public initially, the finan-

cial interest of the governmental unit would be adversely affected.

7. Consultation with legal counsel and briefings by staff members or consultants pertaining to actual or probable litigation, where such consultation or briefing in open meeting would adversely affect the negotiating or litigating posture of the public body; and consultation with legal counsel employed or retained by a public body regarding specific legal matters requiring the provision of legal advice by such counsel. For the purposes of this subdivision, "probable litigation" means litigation that has been specifically threatened or on which the public body or its legal counsel has a reasonable basis to believe will be commenced by or against a known party. Nothing in this subdivision shall be construed to permit the closure of a meeting merely because an attorney representing the public body is in attendance or is consulted on a matter.

8. In the case of boards of visitors of public institutions of higher education, discussion or consideration of matters relating to gifts, bequests and fund-raising activities, and grants and contracts for services or work to be performed by such institution. However, the terms and conditions of any such gifts, bequests, grants, and contracts made by a foreign government, a foreign legal entity, or a foreign person and accepted by a public institution of higher education in Virginia shall be subject to public disclosure upon written request to the appropriate board of visitors. For the purpose of this subdivision, (i) "foreign government" means any government other than the United States government or the government of a state or a political subdivision thereof; (ii) "foreign legal entity" means any legal entity created under the laws of the United States or of any state thereof if a majority of the ownership of the stock of such legal entity is owned by foreign governments or foreign persons or if a majority of the membership of any such entity is composed of foreign persons or foreign legal entities, or any legal entity created under the laws of a foreign government; and (iii) "foreign person" means any individual who is not a citizen or national of the United States or a trust territory or protectorate thereof.

9. In the case of the boards of trustees of the Virginia Museum of Fine Arts, the Virginia Museum of Natural History, and The Science Museum of Virginia, discussion or consideration of matters relating to specific gifts, bequests, and grants.

10. Discussion or consideration of honorary degrees or special awards.

11. Discussion or consideration of tests, examinations, or other records excluded from this chapter pursuant to subdivision 4 of § 2.2-3705.1.

12. Discussion, consideration, or review by the appropriate House or Senate committees of possible disciplinary action against a member arising out of the possible inadequacy of the disclosure statement filed by the member, provided the member may request in writing that the committee meeting not be conducted in a closed meeting.

13. Discussion of strategy with respect to the negotiation of a hazardous waste siting agreement or to consider the terms, conditions, and provisions of a hazardous waste siting agreement if the governing body in open meeting finds that an open meeting will have an adverse effect upon the negotiating position of the governing body or the establishment of the terms, conditions and provisions of the siting agreement, or both. All discussions with the applicant or its representatives may be conducted in a closed meeting.

14. Discussion by the Governor and any economic advisory board reviewing forecasts of economic activity and estimating general and nongeneral fund revenues.

15. Discussion or consideration of medical and mental records excluded from this chapter pursuant to subdivision 1 of § 2.2-3705.5.

16. Deliberations of the State Lottery Board in a licensing appeal action conducted pursuant to subsection D of § 58.1-4007 regarding the denial or revocation of a license of a lottery sales agent; and discussion, consideration or review of State Lottery Department matters related to proprietary lottery game information and studies or investigations exempted from disclosure under subdivision 6 of § 2.2-3705.3 and subdivision 11 of § 2.2-3705.7.

17. Those portions of meetings by local government crime commissions where the identity of, or information tending to identify, individuals providing information about crimes or criminal activities under a promise of anonymity is discussed or disclosed.

18. Those portions of meetings in which the Board of Corrections discusses or discloses the identity of, or information tending to identify, any prisoner who (i) provides information about crimes or criminal activities, (ii) renders assistance in preventing the escape of another prisoner or in the apprehension of an escaped prisoner, or (iii) voluntarily or at the instance of a prison official renders other extraordinary services, the disclosure of which is likely to jeopardize the prisoner's life or safety.

19. Discussion of plans to protect public safety as it relates to terrorist activity and briefings by staff members, legal counsel, or law-enforcement or emergency service officials concerning actions taken to respond to such activity or a related threat to public safety; or discussion of reports or plans related to the security of any governmental facility, building or structure, or the safety of persons using such facility, building or structure.

20. Discussion by the Board of the Virginia Retirement System, acting pursuant to § 51.1-124.30, or of any local retirement system, acting pursuant to § 51.1-803, or of the Rector and Visitors of the University of Virginia, acting pursuant to § 23-76.1, regarding the acquisition, holding or disposition of a security or other ownership interest in an entity, where such security or ownership interest is not traded on a governmentally regulated securities

exchange, to the extent that such discussion (i) concerns confidential analyses prepared for the Rector and Visitors of the University of Virginia, prepared by the retirement system or provided to the retirement system under a promise of confidentiality, of the future value of such ownership interest or the future financial performance of the entity, and (ii) would have an adverse effect on the value of the investment to be acquired, held or disposed of by the retirement system or the Rector and Visitors of the University of Virginia. Nothing in this subdivision shall be construed to prevent the disclosure of information relating to the identity of any investment held, the amount invested or the present value of such investment.

21. Those portions of meetings in which individual child death cases are discussed by the State Child Fatality Review team established pursuant to § 32.1-283.1, and those portions of meetings in which individual child death cases are discussed by a regional or local child fatality review team established pursuant to § 32.1-283.2, and those portions of meetings in which individual death cases are discussed by family violence fatality review teams established pursuant to § 32.1-283.3.

22. Those portions of meetings of the University of Virginia Board of Visitors or the Eastern Virginia Medical School Board of Visitors, as the case may be, and those portions of meetings of any persons to whom management responsibilities for the University of Virginia Medical Center or Eastern Virginia Medical School, as the case may be, have been delegated, in which there is discussed proprietary, business-related information pertaining to the operations of the University of Virginia Medical Center or Eastern Virginia Medical School, as the case may be, including business development or marketing strategies and activities with existing or future joint venturers, partners, or other parties with whom the University of Virginia Medical Center or Eastern Virginia Medical School, as the case may be, has formed, or forms, any arrangement for the delivery of health care, if disclosure of such information would adversely affect the competitive position of the Medical Center or Eastern Virginia Medical School, as the case may be.

23. In the case of the Virginia Commonwealth University Health System Authority, discussion or consideration of any of the following: the acquisition or disposition of real or personal property where disclosure would adversely affect the bargaining position or negotiating strategy of the Authority; operational plans that could affect the value of such property, real or personal, owned or desirable for ownership by the Authority; matters relating to gifts, bequests and fund-raising activities; grants and contracts for services or work to be performed by the Authority; marketing or operational strategies where disclosure of such strategies would adversely affect the competitive position of the Authority; members of its medical and teaching staffs and

qualifications for appointments thereto; and qualifications or evaluations of other employees.

24. Those portions of the meetings of the Intervention Program Committee within the Department of Health Professions to the extent such discussions identify any practitioner who may be, or who actually is, impaired pursuant to Chapter 25.1 (§ 54.1-2515 et seq.) of Title 54.1.

25. Meetings or portions of meetings of the Board of the Virginia College Savings Plan wherein personal information, as defined in § 2.2-3801, which has been provided to the Board or its employees by or on behalf of individuals who have requested information about, applied for, or entered into prepaid tuition contracts or savings trust account agreements pursuant to Chapter 4.9 (§ 23-38.75 et seq.) of Title 23 is discussed.

26. Discussion or consideration, by the Wireless Carrier E-911 Cost Recovery Subcommittee created pursuant to § 56-484.15, of trade secrets, as defined in the Uniform Trade Secrets Act (§ 59.1-336 et seq.), submitted by CMRS providers as defined in § 56-484.12, related to the provision of wireless E-911 service.

27. Those portions of disciplinary proceedings by any regulatory board within the Department of Professional and Occupational Regulation, Department of Health Professions, or the Board of Accountancy conducted pursuant to § 2.2-4019 or 2.2-4020 during which the board deliberates to reach a decision or meetings of health regulatory boards or conference committees of such boards to consider settlement proposals in pending disciplinary actions or modifications to previously issued board orders as requested by either of the parties.

28. Discussion or consideration of records excluded from this chapter pursuant to subdivision 11 of § 2.2-3705.6 by a responsible public entity or an affected local jurisdiction, as those terms are defined in § 56-557, or any independent review panel appointed to review information and advise the responsible public entity concerning such records.

29. Discussion of the award of a public contract involving the expenditure of public funds, including interviews of bidders or offerors, and discussion of the terms or scope of such contract, where discussion in an open session would adversely affect the bargaining position or negotiating strategy of the public body.

30. Discussion or consideration by the Commonwealth Health Research Board of grant application records excluded from this chapter pursuant to subdivision 17 of § 2.2-3705.6.

31. Discussion or consideration by the Commitment Review Committee of records excluded from this chapter pursuant to subdivision 9 of § 2.2-3705.2 relating to individuals subject to commitment as sexually violent predators under Chapter 9 (§ 37.2-900 et seq.) of Title 37.2.

32. [Expired.]

33. Discussion or consideration of confidential proprietary records and trade secrets excluded from this chapter pursuant to subdivision 18 of § 2.2-3705.6.

34. Discussion or consideration by a local authority created in accordance with the Virginia Wireless Service Authorities Act (§ 15.2-5431.1 et seq.) of confidential proprietary records and trade secrets excluded from this chapter pursuant to subdivision 19 of § 2.2-3705.6.

35. Discussion or consideration by the State Board of Elections or local electoral boards of voting security matters made confidential pursuant to § 24.2-625.1.

36. Discussion or consideration by the Forensic Science Board or the Scientific Advisory Committee created pursuant to Article 2 (§ 9.1-1109 et seq.) of Chapter 11 of Title 9.1 of records excluded from this chapter pursuant to subdivision F 1 of § 2.2-3706.

37. Discussion or consideration by the Brown v. Board of Education Scholarship Program Awards Committee of records or confidential matters excluded from this chapter pursuant to subdivision 3 of § 2.2-3705.4, and meetings of the Committee to deliberate concerning the annual maximum scholarship award, review and consider scholarship applications and requests for scholarship award renewal, and cancel, rescind, or recover scholarship awards.

38. Discussion or consideration by the Virginia Port Authority of records excluded from this chapter pursuant to subdivision 1 of § 2.2-3705.6.

39. Discussion or consideration by the Board of Trustees of the Virginia Retirement System acting pursuant to § 51.1-124.30, or the Investment Advisory Committee appointed pursuant to § 51.1-124.26, or by any local retirement system, acting pursuant to § 51.1-803 of records excluded from this chapter pursuant to subdivision 25 of § 2.2-3705.7.

B. No resolution, ordinance, rule, contract, regulation or motion adopted, passed or agreed to in a closed meeting shall become effective unless the public body, following the meeting, reconvenes in open meeting and takes a vote of the membership on such resolution, ordinance, rule, contract, regulation, or motion that shall have its substance reasonably identified in the open meeting.

C. Public officers improperly selected due to the failure of the public body to comply with the other provisions of this section shall be de facto officers and, as such, their official actions are valid until they obtain notice of the legal defect in their election.

D. Nothing in this section shall be construed to prevent the holding of conferences between two or more public bodies, or their representatives, but these conferences shall be subject to the same procedures for holding closed meetings as are applicable to any other public body.

E. This section shall not be construed to (i) require the disclosure of any contract between the Intervention Program Committee within the Department of Health Professions and an impaired practitioner entered into pursuant to Chapter 25.1 (§ 54.1-2515 et seq.) of Title 54.1 or (ii) require the board of directors of any authority created pursuant to the Industrial Development and Revenue Bond Act (§ 15.2-4900 et seq.), or any public body empowered to issue industrial revenue bonds by general or special law, to identify a business or industry to which subdivision A 5 applies. However, such business or industry shall be identified as a matter of public record at least 30 days prior to the actual date of the board's authorization of the sale or issuance of such bonds. (1968, c. 479, § 2.1-344; 1970, c. 456; 1973, c. 461; 1974, c. 332; 1976, cc. 467, 709; 1979, cc. 369, 684; 1980, cc. 221, 475, 476, 754; 1981, cc. 35, 471; 1982, cc. 497, 516; 1984, cc. 473, 513; 1985, c. 277; 1988, c. 891; 1989, cc. 56, 358, 478; 1990, cc. 435, 538; 1991, c. 708; 1992, c. 444; 1993, cc. 270, 499; 1995, c. 499; 1996, cc. 855, 862, 902, 905, 1046; 1997, cc. 439, 641, 785, 861; 1999, cc. 485, 518, 703, 726, 849, 867, 868; 2000, cc. 382, 400, 720, 1064; 2001, cc. 231, 844; 2002, cc. 87, 393, 455, 478, 499, 655, 715, 830; 2003, cc. 274, 291, 332, 618, 703; 2004, cc. 398, 690, 770; 2005, cc. 258, 411, 568; 2006, cc. 430, 499, 518, 560; 2007, cc. 133, 374, 566, 739.)

The 2007 amendments. — The 2007 amendment by c. 133 deleted former subdivision A 18, which read: "Discussion, consideration, review, and deliberations by local community corrections resources boards regarding the placement in community diversion programs of individuals previously sentenced to state correctional facilities" and redesignated former subdivisions A 19 through A 39 as present subdivisions A 18 through A 38.

The 2007 amendment by c. 374, rewrote subdivision A 29 [now A 28].

The 2007 amendment by c. 566 added the language beginning "or discussion of reports or plans" at the end of subdivision A 20 [now A 19].

The 2007 amendment by c. 739, effective March 21, 2007, added subdivision A 40 [now A 39].

CASE NOTES

Closed meeting to discuss previously awarded public contract improper. — Subdivision A 30 [now A 29] of § 2.2-3711 does not allow a public body to close a meeting in order to discuss the application or enforcement of the scope or terms of a previously awarded public contract. White Dog Publ., Inc. v. Culpeper County Bd. of Supervisors, 272 Va. 377, 634 S.E.2d 334, 2006 Va. LEXIS 81 (2006) (decided prior to 2007 amendments to subdivision A 29 of this section and subdivision 11 of § 2.2-3705.6).

CIRCUIT COURT OPINIONS

Discussion of zoning application improper in executive session — Written demurrer of defendants was overruled because the complaint set forth sufficient allegations that matters not lawfully exempted under the Freedom of Information Act were discussed at a county board of supervisors' executive session. While it is proper for a county board of supervisors to go into executive session for the purpose of consultation with legal counsel on specific legal matters requiring provision of legal advice under subdivision A 7 of § 2.2-3711, this does not authorize a general discussion of the merits of a zoning application or a decision to approve the application while in executive session. Robinson v. Brugiere, — Va. Cir. —, 2006 Va. Cir. LEXIS 191 (Amherst County Sept. 21, 2006).

§ 2.2-3712. Closed meetings procedures; certification of proceedings.

CASE NOTES

Closed meeting to discuss previously awarded public contract improper. — Subdivision A 30 [now A 29] of § 2.2-3711 does not allow a public body to close a meeting in order to discuss the application or enforcement of the scope or terms of a previously awarded public contract. White Dog Publ., Inc. v. Culpeper County Bd. of Supervisors, 272 Va. 377, 634 S.E.2d 334, 2006 Va. LEXIS 81 (2006).

Attorney's fees and costs. — As newspaper publishers "substantially prevailed" in their suit against a county board of supervisors for violating the Virginia Freedom of Information Act, § 2.2-3700 et seq., by holding a closed meeting, they were entitled to an award of attorney's fees and reasonable costs under subsection D of § 2.2-3713. The fact that the board's violation was not willful and knowing was not a "special circumstance" that would make such an award unjust. White Dog Publ., Inc. v. Culpeper County Bd. of Supervisors, 272 Va. 377, 634 S.E.2d 334, 2006 Va. LEXIS 81 (2006).

§ 2.2-3713. Proceedings for enforcement of chapter. — A. Any person, including the attorney for the Commonwealth acting in his official or individual capacity, denied the rights and privileges conferred by this chapter may proceed to enforce such rights and privileges by filing a petition for mandamus or injunction, supported by an affidavit showing good cause. Venue for the petition shall be addressed as follows:

1. In a case involving a local public body, to the general district court or circuit court of the county or city from which the public body has been elected or appointed to serve and in which such rights and privileges were so denied;

2. In a case involving a regional public body, to the general district or circuit court of the county or city where the principal business office of such body is located; and

3. In a case involving a board, bureau, commission, authority, district, institution, or agency of the state government, including a public institution of higher education, or a standing or other committee of the General Assembly, to the general district court or the circuit court of the residence of the aggrieved party or of the City of Richmond.

B. In any action brought before a general district court, a corporate petitioner may appear through its officer, director or managing agent without the assistance of counsel, notwithstanding any provision of law or Rule of the Supreme Court of Virginia to the contrary.

C. The petition for mandamus or injunction shall be heard within seven days of the date when the same is made. However, any petition made outside of the regular terms of the circuit court of a county that is included in a judicial circuit with another county or counties, the hearing on the petition shall be given precedence on the docket of such court over all cases that are not otherwise given precedence by law.

D. The petition shall allege with reasonable specificity the circumstances of the denial of the rights and privileges conferred by this chapter. A single instance of denial of the rights and privileges conferred by this chapter shall be sufficient to invoke the remedies granted herein. If the court finds the denial to be in violation of the provisions of this chapter, the petitioner shall be entitled to recover reasonable costs and attorneys' fees from the public body if the petitioner substantially prevails on the merits of the case, unless special circumstances would make an award unjust. In making this determination, a court may consider, among other things, the reliance of a public body on an opinion of the Attorney General or a decision of a court that substantially supports the public body's position.

E. In any action to enforce the provisions of this chapter, the public body shall bear the burden of proof to establish an exemption by a preponderance of the evidence. Any failure by a public body to follow the procedures established by this chapter shall be presumed to be a violation of this chapter.

F. Failure by any person to request and receive notice of the time and place of meetings as provided in § 2.2-3707 shall not preclude any person from enforcing his rights and privileges conferred by this chapter. (1968, c. 479, § 2.1-346; 1976, c. 709; 1978, c. 826; 1989, c. 358; 1990, c. 217; 1996, c. 578; 1999, cc. 703, 726; 2001, c. 844; 2007, c. 560.)

The 2007 amendments. — The 2007 amendment by c. 560 rewrote subsections A and B; and added subsection F.

CASE NOTES

Mandamus erroneously denied.

Newspaper publishers that sued a county board of supervisors for holding a closed meeting in violation of subsection A of § 2.2-3712 had been entitled to a writ of mandamus, as subdivision A 30 [now A 29] of § 2.2-3711 did not allow the board to close the meeting in order to discuss the application or enforcement of a previously awarded public contract. White Dog Publ., Inc. v. Culpeper County Bd. of Supervisors, 272 Va. 377, 634 S.E.2d 334, 2006 Va. LEXIS 81 (2006).

Attorney's fees and costs erroneously denied. — As newspaper publishers "substantially prevailed" in their suit against a county board of supervisors for violating the Virginia Freedom of Information Act, § 2.2-3700 et seq., they were entitled to an award of attorney's fees and reasonable costs under subsection D of § 2.2-3713. The fact that the board's violation was not willful and knowing was not a "special circumstance" that would make such an award unjust. White Dog Publ., Inc. v. Culpeper County Bd. of Supervisors, 272 Va. 377, 634 S.E.2d 334, 2006 Va. LEXIS 81 (2006).

CHAPTER 38.

GOVERNMENT DATA COLLECTION AND DISSEMINATION PRACTICES ACT.

Sec.
2.2-3806.   Rights of data subjects.
2.2-3808.1. Agencies' disclosure of certain account information prohibited.
2.2-3808.2. [Repealed.]

§ 2.2-3806. Rights of data subjects. — A. Any agency maintaining personal information shall:

1. Inform an individual who is asked to supply personal information about himself whether he is legally required, or may refuse, to supply the information requested, and also of any specific consequences that are known to the agency of providing or not providing the information.

2. Give notice to a data subject of the possible dissemination of part or all of this information to another agency, nongovernmental organization or system not having regular access authority, and indicate the use for which it is intended, and the specific consequences for the individual, which are known to the agency, of providing or not providing the information. However documented permission for dissemination in the hands of the other agency or organization shall satisfy the requirement of this subdivision. The notice may be given on applications or other data collection forms prepared by data subjects.

3. Upon request and proper identification of any data subject, or of his authorized agent, grant the data subject or agent the right to inspect, in a form comprehensible to him:

a. All personal information about that data subject except as provided in subdivision 1 of § 2.2-3705.1, subdivision 1 of § 2.2-3705.4, and subdivision 1 of § 2.2-3705.5.

b. The nature of the sources of the information.

c. The names of recipients, other than those with regular access authority, of personal information about the data subject including the identity of all persons and organizations involved and their relationship to the system when not having regular access authority, except that if the recipient has obtained the information as part of an ongoing criminal investigation such that disclosure of the investigation would jeopardize law-enforcement action, then no disclosure of such access shall be made to the data subject.

4. Comply with the following minimum conditions of disclosure to data subjects:

a. An agency shall make disclosures to data subjects required under this chapter, during normal business hours, in accordance with the procedures set forth in subsections B and C of § 2.2-3704 for responding to requests under the Virginia Freedom of Information Act (§ 2.2-3700 et seq.) or within a time period as may be mutually agreed upon by the agency and the data subject.

b. The disclosures to data subjects required under this chapter shall be made (i) in person, if he appears in person and furnishes proper identification, or (ii) by mail, if he has made a written request, with proper identification. Copies of the documents containing the personal information sought by a data subject shall be furnished to him or his representative at reasonable charges for document search and duplication in accordance with subsection F of § 2.2-3704.

c. The data subject shall be permitted to be accompanied by a person of his choosing, who shall furnish reasonable identification. An agency may require the data subject to furnish a written statement granting the agency permission to discuss the individual's file in such person's presence.

5. If the data subject gives notice that he wishes to challenge, correct, or explain information about him in the information system, the following minimum procedures shall be followed:

a. The agency maintaining the information system shall investigate, and record the current status of that personal information.

b. If, after such investigation, the information is found to be incomplete, inaccurate, not pertinent, not timely, or not necessary to be retained, it shall be promptly corrected or purged.

c. If the investigation does not resolve the dispute, the data subject may file a statement of not more than 200 words setting forth his position.

d. Whenever a statement of dispute is filed, the agency maintaining the information system shall supply any previous recipient with a copy of the statement and, in any subsequent dissemination or use of the information in question, clearly note that it is disputed and supply the statement of the data subject along with the information.

e. The agency maintaining the information system shall clearly and conspicuously disclose to the data subject his rights to make such a request.

f. Following any correction or purging of personal information the agency shall furnish to past recipients notification that the item has been purged or corrected whose receipt shall be acknowledged.

B. Nothing in this chapter shall be construed to require an agency to disseminate any recommendation or letter of reference from or to a third party that is a part of the personnel file of any data subject nor to disseminate any test or examination used, administered or prepared by any public body for purposes of evaluation of (i) any student or any student's performance, (ii) any seeker's qualifications or aptitude for employment, retention, or promotion, or (iii) qualifications for any license or certificate issued by any public body.

As used in this subsection, "test or examination" includes (i) any scoring key for any such test or examination and (ii) any other document that would jeopardize the security of the test or examination. Nothing contained in this subsection shall prohibit the release of test scores or results as provided by law, or to limit access to individual records as provided by law; however, the subject of the employment tests shall be entitled to review and inspect all documents relative to his performance on those employment tests.

When, in the reasonable opinion of the public body, any such test or examination no longer has any potential for future use, and the security of future tests or examinations will not be jeopardized, the test or examination shall be made available to the public. Minimum competency tests administered to public school children shall be made available to the public contemporaneously with statewide release of the scores of those taking such tests, but in no event shall such tests be made available to the public later than six months after the administration of such tests.

C. Neither any provision of this chapter nor any provision of the Freedom of Information Act (§ 2.2-3700 et seq.) shall be construed to deny public access to records of the position, job classification, official salary or rate of pay of, and to records of the allowances or reimbursements for expenses paid to any public officer, official or employee at any level of state, local or regional government in the Commonwealth. The provisions of this subsection shall not apply to records of the official salaries or rates of pay of public employees whose annual rate of pay is $10,000 or less.

D. Nothing in this section or in this chapter shall be construed to require an agency to disseminate information derived from tax returns in violation of §§ 2.2-3705.7 and 58.1-3. (1976, c. 597, § 2.1-382; 1978, c. 810; 1979, cc. 683, 688, 689; 1983, c. 372; 1995, c. 400; 2001, c. 844; 2004, c. 690; 2007, c. 232.)

The 2007 amendments. — The 2007 amendment by c. 232 insertd "in accordance with the procedures ... agreed upon by the agency and the data subject" at the end of subdivision A 4 a, and deleted "standard" preceding "charges" and added "in accordance with subsection F of § 2.2-3704" in the second sentence of subdivision A 4 b.

§ 2.2-3808.1. Agencies' disclosure of certain account information prohibited.

— Notwithstanding Chapter 37 (§ 2.2-3700 et seq.) of this title, it shall be unlawful for any agency to disclose the social security number or other identification numbers appearing on driver's licenses or information on credit cards, debit cards, bank accounts, or other electronic billing and payment systems that was supplied to an agency for the purpose of paying fees, fines, taxes, or other charges collected by such agency. The prohibition shall not apply where disclosure of such information is required (i) to conduct or complete the transaction for which such information was submitted or (ii) by other law or court order. (2001, c. 415, § 2.1-385.1; 2007, cc. 548, 626.)

The 2007 amendments. — The 2007 amendments by cc. 548 and 626 are identical, and deleted "or § 2.2-3802" following "this title" and deleted "or court clerk" following "agency" three times in the first sentence.

§ 2.2-3808.2: Repealed by Acts 2007, cc. 548 and 626, cl. 5.

Cross references. — For current provisions as to posting and availability of certain information on the Internet, see § 17.1-293.

CHAPTER 40.

ADMINISTRATIVE PROCESS ACT.

Article 1.

General Provisions.

Sec.
2.2-4001. Definitions.
2.2-4002. Exemptions from chapter generally.
2.2-4003. Venue.

Article 2.

Regulations.

2.2-4006. Exemptions from requirements of this article.
2.2-4007. Petitions for new or amended regulations; opportunity for public comment.
2.2-4007.01. Notice of intended regulatory action; public hearing.
2.2-4007.02. Public participation guidelines.
2.2-4007.03. Informational proceedings; effect of noncompliance.
2.2-4007.04. Economic impact analysis.
2.2-4007.05. Submission of proposed regulations to the Registrar.
2.2-4007.06. Changes between proposed and final regulations.
2.2-4007.07. State Air Pollution Control Board; variances.
2.2-4007.1. Regulatory flexibility for small businesses; periodic review of regulations.
2.2-4009. Evidentiary hearings on regulations.
2.2-4011. Emergency regulations; publication; exceptions.
2.2-4012. Purpose; adoption; effective date; filing; duties of Registrar of Regulations.
2.2-4012.1. Fast-track rulemaking process.
2.2-4013. Executive review of proposed and final regulations; changes with substantial impact.
2.2-4014. Legislative review of proposed and final regulations.
2.2-4015. Effective date of regulation; exception.

Article 5.

Court Review.

2.2-4027. Issues on review.

Article 6.

Virginia Register of Regulations.

2.2-4031. Publication of Virginia Register of Regulations; exceptions; notice of public hearings of proposed regulations.

ARTICLE 1.

General Provisions.

§ 2.2-4000. Short title; purpose.

Editor's note. — Acts 2006, Sp. Sess. I, c. 3, as amended by Acts 2007, c. 847, effective for the biennium ending June 30, 2008, in Item 271 F, provides: "F.1. The State Treasurer is authorized to charge qualified public depositories holding public deposits, as defined in § 2.2-4401, Code of Virginia, an annual administrative fee of not more that one-half of one basis point of their average public deposit balances over a twelve month period. The State Treasurer shall issue guidelines to effect the implementation of this fee. However, the total fees collected from all qualified depositories shall not exceed $100,000 in any one year.

"2. Any regulations or guidelines necessary to implement or change the amount of the fee may be adopted without complying with the Administrative Process Act (§ 2.2-4000 et seq.) provided that input is solicited from qualified public depositories. Such input requires only that notice and an opportunity to submit written comments be given."

Acts 2006, Sp. Sess. I, c. 3, as amended by Acts 2007, c. 847,

effective for the biennium ending June 30, 2008, in Item 291 F, provides: "The Special Supplemental Nutrition Program for Women, Infants, and Children is exempt from the requirements of the Administrative Process Act (§ 2.2-4000 et seq.)."

§ 2.2-4001. Definitions. — As used in this chapter, unless the context requires a different meaning:

"*Agency*" means any authority, instrumentality, officer, board or other unit of the state government empowered by the basic laws to make regulations or decide cases.

"*Agency action*" means either an agency's regulation or case decision or both, any violation, compliance, or noncompliance with which could be a basis for the imposition of injunctive orders, penal or civil sanctions of any kind, or the grant or denial of relief or of a license, right, or benefit by any agency or court.

"*Basic law*" or "*basic laws*" means provisions of the Constitution and statutes of the Commonwealth authorizing an agency to make regulations or decide cases or containing procedural requirements therefor.

"*Case*" or "*case decision*" means any agency proceeding or determination that, under laws or regulations at the time, a named party as a matter of past or present fact, or of threatened or contemplated private action, either is, is not, or may or may not be (i) in violation of such law or regulation or (ii) in compliance with any existing requirement for obtaining or retaining a license or other right or benefit.

"*Guidance document*" means any document developed by a state agency or staff that provides information or guidance of general applicability to the staff or public to interpret or implement statutes or the agency's rules or regulations, excluding agency minutes or documents that pertain only to the internal management of agencies. Nothing in this definition shall be construed or interpreted to expand the identification or release of any document otherwise protected by law.

"*Hearing*" means agency processes other than those informational or factual inquiries of an informal nature provided in §§ 2.2-4007.01 and 2.2-4019 and includes only (i) opportunity for private parties to submit factual proofs in formal proceedings as provided in § 2.2-4009 in connection with the making of regulations or (ii) a similar right of private parties or requirement of public agencies as provided in § 2.2-4020 in connection with case decisions.

"*Hearing officer*" means an attorney selected from a list maintained by the Executive Secretary of the Supreme Court in accordance with § 2.2-4024.

"*Public assistance and social services programs*" means those programs specified in § 63.2-100.

"*Rule*" or "*regulation*" means any statement of general application, having the force of law, affecting the rights or conduct of any person, adopted by an agency in accordance with the authority conferred on it by applicable basic laws.

"*Subordinate*" means (i) one or more but less than a quorum of the members of a board constituting an agency, (ii) one or more of its staff members or employees, or (iii) any other person or persons designated by the agency to act in its behalf. (1975, c. 503, § 9-6.14:4; 1977, cc. 377, 381; 1979, c. 613; 1984, c. 187; 1985, cc. 67, 602; 1997, c. 11; 2001, c. 844; 2002, c. 747; 2007, cc. 873, 916.)

The 2007 amendments. — The 2007 amendments by cc. 873 and 916 are identical, and substituted "2.2-4007.01" for "2.2-4007" in the definition of "Hearing."

§ 2.2-4002. Exemptions from chapter generally.

— A. Although required to comply with § 2.2-4103 of the Virginia Register Act (§ 2.2-4100 et seq.), the following agencies shall be exempted from the provisions of this chapter, except to the extent that they are specifically made subject to §§ 2.2-4024, 2.2-4030 and 2.2-4031:

1. The General Assembly.

2. Courts, any agency of the Supreme Court, and any agency that by the Constitution is expressly granted any of the powers of a court of record.

3. The Department of Game and Inland Fisheries in promulgating regulations regarding the management of wildlife and for all case decisions rendered pursuant to any provisions of Chapters 2 (§ 29.1-200 et seq.), 3 (§ 29.1-300 et seq.), 4 (§ 29.1-400 et seq.), 5 (§ 29.1-500 et seq.), and 7 (§ 29.1-700 et seq.) of Title 29.1.

4. The Virginia Housing Development Authority.

5. Municipal corporations, counties, and all local, regional or multijurisdictional authorities created under this Code, including those with federal authorities.

6. Educational institutions operated by the Commonwealth, provided that, with respect to § 2.2-4031, such educational institutions shall be exempt from the publication requirements only with respect to regulations that pertain to (i) their academic affairs, (ii) the selection, tenure, promotion and disciplining of faculty and employees, (iii) the selection of students, and (iv) rules of conduct and disciplining of students.

7. The Milk Commission in promulgating regulations regarding (i) producers' licenses and bases, (ii) classification and allocation of milk, computation of sales and shrinkage, and (iii) class prices for producers' milk, time and method of payment, butterfat testing and differential.

8. The Virginia Resources Authority.

9. Agencies expressly exempted by any other provision of this Code.

10. The Department of General Services in promulgating standards for the inspection of buildings for asbestos pursuant to § 2.2-1164.

11. The State Council of Higher Education for Virginia, in developing, issuing, and revising guidelines pursuant to § 23-9.6:2.

12. The Commissioner of Agriculture and Consumer Services in adopting regulations pursuant to subsection B of § 3.1-726 and in adopting regulations pursuant to § 3.1-741.6.

13. The Commissioner of Agriculture and Consumer Services and the Board of Agriculture and Consumer Services in promulgating regulations pursuant to subsections B and C of § 3.1-106.4, subsection B of § 3.1-126.12:1, §§ 3.1-271.1, 3.1-530.1, and 3.1-398, subsections B and C of § 3.1-828.4, and subsection A of § 3.1-884.21:1.

14. The Board of Optometry when specifying therapeutic pharmaceutical agents, treatment guidelines, and diseases and abnormal conditions of the human eye and its adnexa for TPA-certification of optometrists pursuant to Article 5 (§ 54.1-3222 et seq.) of Chapter 32 of Title 54.1.

15. The Virginia War Memorial Foundation.

16. The Virginia Medicaid Prior Authorization Advisory Committee in making recommendations to the Board of Medical Assistance Services regarding prior authorization for prescription drug coverage pursuant to Article 4 (§ 32.1-331.12 et seq.) of Chapter 10 of Title 32.1.

17. The State Board of Education, in developing, issuing, and revising guidelines pursuant to § 22.1-203.2.

18. The Virginia Racing Commission, (i) when acting by and through its duly appointed stewards or in matters related to any specific race meeting or (ii) in promulgating technical rules regulating actual live horse racing at race meetings licensed by the Commission.

19. The Virginia Small Business Financing Authority.

20. The Virginia Economic Development Partnership Authority.

21. The Board of Agriculture and Consumer Services in adopting, amending or repealing regulations pursuant to subsection A (ii) of § 59.1-156.

22. The Insurance Continuing Education Board pursuant to § 38.2-1867.

23. The Board of Health in promulgating the list of diseases that shall be reported to the Department of Health pursuant to § 32.1-35 and in adopting, amending or repealing regulations pursuant to subsection C of § 35.1-14 that incorporate the Food and Drug Administration's Food Code pertaining to restaurants or food service.

24. The nonprofit, nonstock corporation established by the Commissioner of Agriculture and Consumer Services pursuant to § 3.1-14.01.

25. **(Expires December 31, 2010)** The Secretary of Natural Resources in setting a date of closure for the Chesapeake Bay purse seine fishery for Atlantic menhaden for reduction purposes pursuant to § 28.2-1000.2.

B. Agency action relating to the following subjects shall be exempted from the provisions of this chapter:

1. Money or damage claims against the Commonwealth or agencies thereof.

2. The award or denial of state contracts, as well as decisions regarding compliance therewith.

3. The location, design, specifications or construction of public buildings or other facilities.

4. Grants of state or federal funds or property.

5. The chartering of corporations.

6. Customary military, naval or police functions.

7. The selection, tenure, dismissal, direction or control of any officer or employee of an agency of the Commonwealth.

8. The conduct of elections or eligibility to vote.

9. Inmates of prisons or other such facilities or parolees therefrom.

10. The custody of persons in, or sought to be placed in, mental, penal or other state institutions as well as the treatment, supervision, or discharge of such persons.

11. Traffic signs, markers or control devices.

12. Instructions for application or renewal of a license, certificate, or registration required by law.

13. Content of, or rules for the conduct of, any examination required by law.

14. The administration of pools authorized by Chapter 47 (§ 2.2-4700 et seq.) of this title.

15. Any rules for the conduct of specific lottery games, so long as such rules are not inconsistent with duly adopted regulations of the State Lottery Board, and provided that such regulations are published and posted.

16. Orders condemning or closing any shellfish, finfish, or crustacea growing area and the shellfish, finfish or crustacea located thereon pursuant to Article 2 (§ 28.2-803 et seq.) of Chapter 8 of Title 28.2.

17. Any operating procedures for review of child deaths developed by the State Child Fatality Review Team pursuant to § 32.1-283.1.

18. The regulations for the implementation of the Health Practitioners' Intervention Program and the activities of the Intervention Program Committee pursuant to Chapter 25.1 (§ 54.1-2515 et seq.) of Title 54.1.

19. The process of reviewing and ranking grant applications submitted to the Commonwealth Neurotrauma Initiative Advisory Board pursuant to Chapter 3.1 (§ 51.5-12.1 et seq.) of Title 51.5.

20. Loans from the Small Business Environmental Compliance Assistance Fund pursuant to Article 4 (§ 10.1-1197.1 et seq.) of Chapter 11.1 of Title 10.1.

21. The Virginia Breeders Fund created pursuant to § 59.1-372.

22. The types of pari-mutuel wagering pools available for live or simulcast horse racing.

23. The administration of medication or other substances foreign to the natural horse.

C. Minor changes to regulations published in the Virginia Administrative Code under the Virginia Register Act, Chapter 41 (§ 2.2-4100 et seq.) of this title, made by the Virginia Code Commission pursuant to § 30-150, shall be exempt from the provisions of this chapter. (1985, c. 602, § 9-6.14:4.1; 1986, c. 615; 1987, cc. 375, 652; 1988, cc. 364, 424, 498, 723, 765, 820; 1989, cc. 54, 299, 478; 1990, cc. 721, 968; 1991, cc. 80, 294, 344; 1992, cc. 200, 409, 488, 592, 793; 1993, cc. 537, 669, 898; 1994, cc. 237, 577, 649, 740, 743, 801; 1995, cc. 103, 499, 516; 1996, cc. 51, 152, 158, 189, 205, 279, 320, 345, 573, 590, 598, 638, 705, 735, 818, 1012; 1997, cc. 87, 88, 109, 212, 390, 439, 567, 624, 785, 806, 845, 850, 861, 868; 1998, cc. 39, 619, 784; 1999, cc. 412, 421, 433, 603; 2000, cc. 382, 400, 924, 1011; 2001, cc. 465, 523, 688, 820, 844; 2003, cc. 639, 695; 2004, c. 802; 2006, c. 442; 2007, cc. 41, 870, 932.)

Editor's note. — Acts 2007, c. 41, which added subdivision A 25, in cl. 2 provides: "The provisions of this act shall expire on December 31, 2010."

Acts 2007, cc. 870 and 932, cl. 3, provides: "That the Commissioner of Agriculture and Consumer Services shall implement the provisions of this act consistent with an opinion of the Attorney General dated April 18, 2006, within 90 days of the effective date of this act."

The 2007 amendments. — The 2007 amendment by c. 41, which expires December 31, 2010, added subdivision A 24 [now 25]. The 2007 amendments by cc. 870 and 932, effective April 4, 2007, are identical, and added subdivision A 24.

§ 2.2-4003. Venue. — In all proceedings under § 2.2-4019 or 2.2-4020 venue shall be in the city or county where the administrative agency maintains its principal office or as the parties may otherwise agree. In all proceedings under § 2.2-4026, venue shall be as specified in subdivision 1 of § 8.01-261. (1975, c. 503, § 9-6.14:5; 1977, c. 624; 2001, c. 844; 2007, cc. 873, 916.)

The 2007 amendments. — The 2007 amendments by cc. 873 and 916 are identical, and rewrote this section.

ARTICLE 2.

Regulations.

§ 2.2-4006. Exemptions from requirements of this article. — A. The following agency actions otherwise subject to this chapter and § 2.2-4103 of the Virginia Register Act shall be exempted from the operation of this article:

1. Agency orders or regulations fixing rates or prices.

2. Regulations that establish or prescribe agency organization, internal practice or procedures, including delegations of authority.

3. Regulations that consist only of changes in style or form or corrections of technical errors. Each promulgating agency shall review all references to sections of the Code of Virginia within their regulations each time a new supplement or replacement volume to the Code of Virginia is published to ensure the accuracy of each section or section subdivision identification listed.

4. Regulations that are:

a. Necessary to conform to changes in Virginia statutory law or the appropriation act where no agency discretion is involved;

b. Required by order of any state or federal court of competent jurisdiction where no agency discretion is involved; or

c. Necessary to meet the requirements of federal law or regulations, provided such regulations do not differ materially from those required by federal law or regulation, and the Registrar has so determined in writing. Notice of the proposed adoption of these regulations and the Registrar's determination shall be published in the Virginia Register not less than 30 days prior to the effective date of the regulation.

5. Preliminary program permit fees of the Department of Environmental Quality assessed pursuant to subsection C of § 10.1-1322.2.

6. Regulations of the Pesticide Control Board adopted pursuant to subsection B of § 3.1-249.51 or clause (v) or (vi) of subsection C of § 3.1-249.53 after having been considered at two or more Board meetings and one public hearing.

7. Regulations of the regulatory boards served by (i) the Department of Labor and Industry pursuant to Title 40.1 and (ii) the Department of Professional and Occupational Regulation or the Department of Health Professions pursuant to Title 54.1 that are limited to reducing fees charged to regulants and applicants.

8. The development and issuance of procedural policy relating to risk-based mine inspections by the Department of Mines, Minerals and Energy authorized pursuant to §§ 45.1-161.82 and 45.1-161.292:55.

9. General permits issued by the (a) State Air Pollution Control Board pursuant to Chapter 13 (§ 10.1-1300 et seq.) of Title 10.1 or (b) State Water Control Board pursuant to the State Water Control Law (§ 62.1-44.2 et seq.), Chapter 24 (§ 62.1-242 et seq.) of Title 62.1 and Chapter 25 (§ 62.1-254 et seq.) of Title 62.1, (c) Virginia Soil and Water Conservation Board pursuant to the Virginia Stormwater Management Act (§ 10.1-603.1 et seq.) of Title 10.1, and (d) the development and issuance of general wetlands permits by the Marine Resources Commission pursuant to subsection B of § 28.2-1307, if the respective Board or Commission (i) provides a Notice of Intended Regulatory Action in conformance with the provisions of § 2.2-4007.01, (ii) following the passage of 30 days from the publication of the Notice of Intended Regulatory Action forms a technical advisory committee composed of relevant stakeholders, including potentially affected citizens groups, to assist in the development of the general permit, (iii) provides notice and receives oral and written comment as provided in § 2.2-4007.03, and (iv) conducts at least one public hearing on the proposed general permit.

10. The development and issuance by the Board of Education of guidelines on constitutional rights and restrictions relating to the recitation of the pledge of allegiance to the American flag in public schools pursuant to § 22.1-202.

11. Regulations of the Board of the Virginia College Savings Plan adopted pursuant to § 23-38.77.

12. Regulations of the Marine Resources Commission.

13. Regulations adopted by the Board of Housing and Community Development pursuant to (i) Statewide Fire Prevention Code (§ 27-94 et seq.), (ii) the Industrialized Building Safety Law (§ 36-70 et seq.), (iii) the Uniform Statewide Building Code (§ 36-97 et seq.), and (iv) § 36-98.3, provided the Board (a) provides a Notice of Intended Regulatory Action in conformance with the provisions of § 2.2-4007.01, (b) publishes the proposed regulation and provides an opportunity for oral and written comments as provided in § 2.2-4007.03, and (c) conducts at least one public hearing as provided in §§ 2.2-4009 and 36-100 prior to the publishing of the proposed regulations. Notwithstanding the provisions of this subdivision, any regulations promulgated by the Board shall remain subject to the provisions of § 2.2-4007.06 concerning public petitions, and §§ 2.2-4013 and 2.2-4014 concerning review by the Governor and General Assembly.

14. Amendments to the list of drugs susceptible to counterfeiting adopted by the Board of Pharmacy pursuant to subsection B of § 54.1-3307.

B. Whenever regulations are adopted under this section, the agency shall state as part thereof that it will receive, consider and respond to petitions by any interested person at any time with respect to reconsideration or revision. The effective date of regulations adopted under this subsection shall be in accordance with the provisions of § 2.2-4015, except in the case of emergency regulations, which shall become effective as provided in subsection B of § 2.2-4012.

C. A regulation for which an exemption is claimed under this section or § 2.2-4002, or 2.2-4011 and that is placed before a board or commission for consideration shall be provided at least two days in advance of the board or commission meeting to members of the public that request a copy of that regulation. A copy of that regulation shall be made available to the public attending such meeting. (1985, c. 602, § 9-6.14:4.1; 1986, c. 615; 1987, cc. 375, 652; 1988, cc. 364, 424, 498, 723, 765, 820; 1989, cc. 54, 299, 478; 1990, cc. 721, 968; 1991, cc. 80, 294, 344; 1992, cc. 200, 409, 488, 592, 793; 1993, cc. 537, 669, 898; 1994, cc. 237, 577, 649, 740, 743, 801; 1995, cc. 103, 499, 516; 1996, cc. 51, 152, 158, 189, 205, 279, 320, 345, 573, 590, 598, 638, 705, 735, 818, 1012; 1997, cc. 87, 88, 109, 212, 390, 439, 567, 624, 785, 806, 845, 850, 861, 868; 1998, cc. 39, 619, 784; 1999, cc. 412, 421, 433, 603; 2000, cc. 382, 400, 924, 1011; 2001, c. 844; 2003, c. 436; 2005, c. 102; 2006, cc. 632, 719; 2007, cc. 873, 916.)

The 2007 amendments. — The 2007 amendments by cc. 873 and 916 are identical, and substituted "§ 2.2-4007.01" for "subsection B of § 2.2-4007" and "§ 2.2-4007.03" for "subsection F of § 2.2-4007" in subdivisions A 9 and 13; and substituted "§ 2.2-4007.06" for "subsection K of § 2.2-4007" in subdivision A 13.

§ 2.2-4007. Petitions for new or amended regulations; opportunity for public comment.

— A. Any person may petition an agency to request

the agency to develop a new regulation or amend an existing regulation. The petition shall state (i) the substance and purpose of the rulemaking that is requested, including reference to any applicable Virginia Administrative Code sections, and (ii) reference to the legal authority of the agency to take the action requested.

B. Within 14 days of receiving a petition, the agency shall send a notice identifying the petitioner, the nature of the petitioner's request and the agency's plan for disposition of the petition to the Registrar for publication in the Virginia Register of Regulations in accordance with the provisions of subsection B of § 2.2-4031.

C. A 21-day period for acceptance of written public comment on the petition shall be provided after publication in the Virginia Register. The agency shall issue a written decision to grant or deny the petitioner's request within 90 days following the close of the comment period. However, if the rulemaking authority is vested in an entity that has not met within that 90-day period, the entity shall issue a written decision no later than 14 days after it next meets. The written decision issued by the agency shall include a statement of its reasons and shall be submitted to the Registrar for publication in the Virginia Register of Regulations. Agency decisions to initiate or not initiate rulemaking in response to petitions shall not be subject to judicial review. (1984, c. 5, § 9-6.14:7.1; 1985, c. 602; 1989, c. 71; 1991, c. 488; 1993, cc. 898, 944; 1994, c. 938; 1995, cc. 25, 677, 717, 790; 1997, c. 87; 2001, c. 844; 2002, cc. 241, 391, 747; 2003, c. 224; 2005, cc. 619, 682; 2007, cc. 873, 916.)

Editor's note. — Acts 2007, cc. 316 and 561, amended former subsection H, which was deleted by Acts 2007, cc. 873 and 916. At the direction of the Virginia Code Commission, amendments by Acts 2007, cc. 316 and 561, have been given effect in § 2.2-4007.04

The 2007 amendments. — The 2007 amendments by cc. 873 and 916 are identical, and deleted subsections B through M, pertaining to notice of intended regulatory actions, informational proceedings, effect of noncompliance, and economic impact analysis and made related changes.

§ 2.2-4007.01. Notice of intended regulatory action; public hearing. — A. In the case of all regulations, except those regulations exempted by § 2.2-4002, 2.2-4006, 2.2-4011, or 2.2-4012.1, an agency shall provide the Registrar of Regulations with a Notice of Intended Regulatory Action that describes the subject matter and intent of the planned regulation. At least 30 days shall be provided for public comment, to include an on-line public comment forum on the Virginia Regulatory Town Hall, after publication of the Notice of Intended Regulatory Action. An agency shall not file proposed regulations with the Registrar until the public comment period on the Notice of Intended Regulatory Action has closed.

B. Agencies shall state in the Notice of Intended Regulatory Action whether they plan to hold a public hearing on the proposed regulation after it is pub-

lished. Agencies shall hold such public hearings if required by basic law. If the agency states an intent to hold a public hearing on the proposed regulation in the Notice of Intended Regulatory Action, then it shall hold the public hearing. If the agency states in its Notice of Intended Regulatory Action that it does not plan to hold a hearing on the proposed regulation, then no public hearing is required unless, prior to completion of the comment period specified in the Notice of Intended Regulatory Action, (i) the Governor directs the agency to hold a public hearing or (ii) the agency receives requests for a public hearing from at least 25 persons. (2007, cc. 873, 916.)

§ 2.2-4007.02. Public participation guidelines. — A. Public participation guidelines for soliciting the input of interested parties in the formation and development of its regulations shall be developed, adopted, and used by each agency pursuant to the provisions of this chapter. The guidelines shall set out any methods for the identification and notification of interested parties and any specific means of seeking input from interested persons or groups that the agency intends to use in addition to the Notice of Intended Regulatory Action. The guidelines shall set out a general policy for the use of standing or ad hoc advisory panels and consultation with groups and individuals registering interest in working with the agency. Such policy shall address the circumstances in which the agency considers the panels or consultation appropriate and intends to make use of the panels or consultation.

B. In formulating any regulation, including but not limited to those in public assistance and social services programs, the agency pursuant to its public participation guidelines shall afford interested persons an opportunity to submit data, views, and arguments, either orally or in writing, to the agency, to include an on-line public comment forum on the Virginia Regulatory Town Hall, or other specially designated subordinate. However, the agency may begin drafting the proposed regulation prior to or during any opportunities it provides to the public to submit comments. (2007, cc. 873, 916.)

§ 2.2-4007.03. Informational proceedings; effect of noncompliance. — A. In the case of all regulations, except those regulations exempted by § 2.2-4002, 2.2-4006, or 2.2-4011, the proposed regulation and general notice of opportunity for oral or written submittals as to that regulation shall be posted on the Virginia Regulatory Town Hall and published in the Virginia Register of Regulations in accordance with the provisions of subsection B of § 2.2-4031. In addition, the agency may, in its discretion, (i) publish the notice in any newspaper and (ii) publicize the notice through press releases and such other media as will best serve the purpose and subject involved. The Register and any newspaper publication shall be made at least 60 days in advance of the last date prescribed in the notice for such submittals. All notices, written submittals, and transcripts and summaries or notations of oral presentations, as well as any agency action thereon, shall be matters of public record in the custody of the agency.

B. If an agency wishes to change a proposed regulation before adopting it as a final regulation, it may choose to publish a revised proposed regulation, provided the latter is subject to a public comment period of at least 30 additional days and the agency complies in all other respects with this section.

C. In no event shall the failure to comply with the requirements of this section be deemed mere harmless error for the purposes of § 2.2-4027. (2007, cc. 873, 916.)

§ **2.2-4007.04. Economic impact analysis.** — A. Before delivering any proposed regulation under consideration to the Registrar as required in § 2.2-4007.05, the agency shall submit on the Virginia Regulatory Town Hall a copy of that regulation to the Department of Planning and Budget. In addition to determining the public benefit, the Department of Planning and Budget in coordination with the agency shall, within 45 days, prepare an economic impact analysis of the proposed regulation, as follows:

1. The economic impact analysis shall include but need not be limited to the projected number of businesses or other entities to whom the regulation would apply; the identity of any localities and types of businesses or other entities particularly affected by the regulation; the projected number of persons and employment positions to be affected; the impact of the regulation on the use and value of private property, including additional costs related to the development of real estate for commercial or residential purposes; and the projected costs to affected businesses, localities, or entities of implementing or complying with the regulations, including the estimated fiscal impact on such localities and sources of potential funds to implement and comply with such regulation. A copy of the economic impact analysis shall be provided to the Joint Commission on Administrative Rules;

2. If the regulation may have an adverse effect on small businesses, the economic impact analysis shall also include (i) an identification and estimate of the number of small businesses subject to the regulation; (ii) the projected reporting, record-keeping, and other administrative costs required for small businesses to comply with the regulation, including the type of professional skills necessary for preparing required reports and other documents; (iii) a statement of the probable effect of the regulation on affected small businesses; and (iv) a description of any less intrusive or less costly alternative methods of achieving the purpose of the regulation. As used in this subdivision, "small business" has the same meaning as provided in subsection A of § 2.2-4007.1; and

3. In the event the Department cannot complete an economic impact statement within the 45-day period, it shall advise the agency and the Joint Commission on Administrative Rules as to the reasons for the delay. In no event shall the delay exceed 30 days beyond the original 45-day period.

B. Agencies shall provide the Department with such estimated fiscal impacts on localities and sources of potential funds. The Department may request the assistance of any other agency in preparing the analysis. The Department shall deliver a copy of the analysis to the agency drafting the regulation, which shall comment thereon as provided in § 2.2-4007.05, a copy to the Registrar for publication with the proposed regulation, and an electronic copy to each member of the General Assembly. No regulation shall be promulgated for consideration pursuant to § 2.2-4007.05 until the impact analysis has been received by the Registrar. For purposes of this section, the term "locality, business, or entity particularly affected" means any locality, business, or entity that bears any identified disproportionate material impact that would not be experienced by other localities, businesses, or entities. The analysis shall represent the Department's best estimate for the purposes of public review and comment on the proposed regulation. The accuracy of the estimate shall in no way affect the validity of the regulation, nor shall any failure to comply with or otherwise follow the procedures set forth in this subsection create any cause of action or provide standing for any person under Article 5 (§ 2.2-4025 et seq.) or otherwise to challenge the actions of the Department hereunder or the action of the agency in adopting the proposed regulation. (2007, cc. 316, 561, 873, 916.)

Editor's note. — Acts 2007, c. 316, amended former subsection H of § 2.2-4007. The language from subsection H was rewritten as this section as enacted by Acts 2007, cc. 873 and 916. At the direction of the Virginia Code Commission, the amendment by Acts 2007, c. 316, was given effect in this section by deleting "and" preceding "a copy" and inserting "and an electronic copy to each member of the General Assembly" following "regulation" in the third sentence of subsection B.

Acts 2007, c. 561, amended former subsection H of § 2.2-4007. The language from subsection H was rewritten as this section as enacted by Acts 2007, cc. 873 and 916. At the direction of the Virginia Code Commission the amendments by Acts 2007, c. 561, were given effect in this section by inserting "including additional costs related to the development of real estate for commercial or residential purposes" following "private property" in the first sentence and adding the last sentence of subdivision A 1.

§ **2.2-4007.05. Submission of proposed regulations to the Registrar.** — Before promulgating any regulation under consideration, the agency shall deliver a copy of that regulation to the Registrar together with a summary of the regulation and a separate and concise statement of (i) the basis of the regulation, defined as the statutory authority for promulgating the regulation, including an identification of the section number and a brief statement relating the content of the statutory authority to the specific regulation proposed; (ii) the purpose of the regulation, defined as the rationale or justification for the new provisions of the regulation, from the standpoint of the public's health, safety, or welfare; (iii) the substance of the regulation, defined as the identification and explanation of the key provisions of the regulation that make changes to the current status of the law; (iv) the issues of the regulation, defined as the primary advantages and disadvantages for the public, and as applicable for the agency or the state, of implementing the new regulatory provisions; and (v) the agency's response to the economic impact analysis submitted by the Department of Planning and Budget pursuant to § 2.2-4007.04. Any economic impact estimate included in the agency's response shall represent the agency's best estimate for the purposes of public review and comment, but the accuracy of the estimate shall in no way affect the validity of the regulation. Staff as designated by the Code Commission shall review proposed regulation submission packages to ensure that the requirements of this subsection are met prior to publication of the proposed regulation in the Register. The summary; the statement of the basis, purpose, substance, and issues; the economic impact analysis; and the agency's response shall be published in the Virginia Register of Regulations and be available on the Virginia Regulatory Town Hall, together with the notice of opportunity for oral or written submittals on the proposed regulation. (2007, cc. 873, 916.)

§ 2.2-4007.06. Changes between proposed and final regulations. — If one or more changes with substantial impact are made to a proposed regulation from the time that it is published as a proposed regulation to the time it is published as a final regulation, any person may petition the agency within 30 days from the publication of the final regulation to request an opportunity for oral and written submittals on the changes to the regulation. If the agency receives requests from at least 25 persons for an opportunity to submit oral and written comments on the changes to the regulation, the agency shall (i) suspend the regulatory process for 30 days to solicit additional public comment and (ii) file notice of the additional 30-day public comment period with the Registrar of Regulations, unless the agency determines that the changes made are minor or inconsequential in their impact. The comment period, if any, shall begin on the date of publication of the notice in the Register. Agency denial of petitions for a comment period on changes to the regulation shall be subject to judicial review. (2007, cc. 873, 916.)

§ 2.2-4007.07. State Air Pollution Control Board; variances. — The provisions of §§ 2.2-4007 through 2.2-4007.06 shall not apply to the issuance by the State Air Pollution Control Board of variances to its regulations. (2007, cc. 873, 916.)

§ 2.2-4007.1. Regulatory flexibility for small businesses; periodic review of regulations. — A. As used in this section, *"small business"* means a business entity, including its affiliates, that (i) is independently owned and operated and (ii) employs fewer than 500 full-time employees or has gross annual sales of less than $6 million.

B. In addition to the requirements of §§ 2.2-4007 through 2.2-4007.06, prior to the adoption of any proposed regulation, the agency proposing a regulation shall prepare a regulatory flexibility analysis in which the agency shall consider utilizing alternative regulatory methods, consistent with health, safety, environmental, and economic welfare, that will accomplish the objectives of applicable law while minimizing the adverse impact on small businesses. The agency shall consider, at a minimum, each of the following methods of reducing the effects of the proposed regulation on small businesses:

1. The establishment of less stringent compliance or reporting requirements;

2. The establishment of less stringent schedules or deadlines for compliance or reporting requirements;

3. The consolidation or simplification of compliance or reporting requirements;

4. The establishment of performance standards for small businesses to replace design or operational standards required in the proposed regulation; and

5. The exemption of small businesses from all or any part of the requirements contained in the proposed regulation.

C. Prior to the adoption of any proposed regulation that may have an adverse effect on small businesses, each agency shall notify the Joint Commission on Administrative Rules, through the Virginia Regulatory Town Hall, of its intent to adopt the proposed regulation. The Joint Commission on Administrative Rules shall advise and assist agencies in complying with the provisions of this section.

D. In addition to the requirements of § 2.2-4017, on or before July 1, 2009, an agency shall review its existing regulations to determine whether they should be continued without change or be amended or repealed, consistent with the stated objectives of applicable law, to minimize the economic impact of regulations on small businesses. If an agency head determines that completion of the review of existing regulations is not feasible by July 1, 2009, that agency shall publish a statement certifying that determination. An agency may extend the date required by this subsection in increments of one year, not to exceed a total of five years.

E. In addition to other requirements of § 2.2-4017, all final regulations adopted after July 1, 2005, shall be reviewed every five years to ensure that they minimize the economic impact on small businesses in a manner consistent with the stated objectives of applicable law.

F. The regulatory review required by this section shall include consideration of:

1. The continued need for the rule;

2. The nature of complaints or comments received concerning the regulation from the public;

3. The complexity of the regulation;

4. The extent to which the regulation overlaps, duplicates, or conflicts with federal or state law or regulation; and

5. The length of time since the regulation has been evaluated or the degree to which technology, economic conditions, or other factors have changed in the area affected by the regulation. (2005, cc. 619, 682; 2007, cc. 873, 916.)

The 2007 amendments. — The 2007 amendments by cc. 873 and 916 are nearly identical, and inserted "2.2-4007.06" in the introductory language of subsection B and made related changes; and inserted "through the Virginia Regulatory Town Hall" in subsection C.

Subsection C is set out in the form above at the direction of the Virginia Code Commission.

§ 2.2-4009. Evidentiary hearings on regulations.

— Where an agency proposes to consider the exercise of authority to promulgate a regulation, it may conduct or give interested persons an opportunity to participate in a public evidentiary proceeding; and the agency shall always do so where the basic law requires a hearing. Evidentiary hearings may be limited to the trial of factual issues directly related to the legal validity of the proposed regulation in any of the relevant respects outlined in § 2.2-4027 of this chapter.

General notice of the proceedings shall be published as prescribed in § 2.2-4007.01. In addition, where the proposed regulation is to be addressed to named persons, the latter shall also be given the same notice individually by mail or otherwise if acknowledged in writing. The proceedings may be conducted separately from, and in any event the record thereof shall be separate from, any other or additional proceedings the agency may choose or be required to conduct for the reception of general data, views, and argument pursuant to § 2.2-4007.02 or otherwise. Any probative evidence may be received except that the agency shall as a matter of efficiency exclude irrelevant, immaterial, insubstantial, privileged, or repetitive proofs, and may deny rebuttal, or cross-examination. Testimony may be admitted in written form provided those who have prepared it are made available for examination in person.

The agency or one or more of its subordinates specially designated for the purpose shall preside at the taking of evidence and may administer oaths and affirmations. The proceedings shall be recorded verbatim and the record thereof shall be made available to interested persons for transcription at their expense or, if transcribed by or for the agency, for inspection or purchase at cost.

Where subordinates preside at the taking of the evidence, they shall report their recommendations and proposed findings and conclusions that shall be made available upon request to the participants in the taking of evidence as well as other interested persons and serve as a basis for exceptions, briefs, or oral argument to the agency itself. Whether or not subordinates take the evidence, after opportunity for the submittal of briefs on request and such oral argument as may be scheduled, the agency may settle the terms of the regulation and shall promulgate it only upon (i) its findings of fact based upon the record of evidence made pursuant to this section and facts of which judicial notice may be taken, (ii) statements of basis and purpose as well as comment upon data received in any informational proceedings held under § 2.2-4007.01 and (iii) the conclusions required by the terms of the basic law under which the agency is operating. (1975, c. 503, § 9-6.14:8; 1985, c. 602; 2001, c. 844; 2007, cc. 873, 916.)

The 2007 amendments. — The 2007 amendments by cc. 873 and 916 are identical, and substituted "2.2-4007.01" for "2.2-4007" in the second and fourth paragraphs; and substituted "2.2-4007.02" for "2.2-4007" in the second paragraph.

§ 2.2-4011. Emergency regulations; publication; exceptions.

— A. Regulations that an agency finds are necessitated by an emergency situation may be adopted by an agency upon consultation with the Attorney General, which approval shall be granted only after the agency has submitted a request stating in writing the nature of the emergency, and the necessity for such action shall be at the sole discretion of the Governor.

B. Agencies may also adopt emergency regulations in situations in which Virginia statutory law or the appropriation act or federal law or federal regulation requires that a regulation be effective in 280 days or less from its enactment, and the regulation is not exempt under the provisions of subdivision A. 4. of § 2.2-4006. In such cases, the agency shall state in writing the nature of the emergency and of the necessity for such action and may adopt the regulations. Pursuant to § 2.2-4012, such regulations shall become effective upon approval by the Governor and filing with the Registrar of Regulations.

C. All emergency regulations shall be limited to no more than twelve months in duration. During the twelve-month period, an agency may issue additional emergency regulations as needed addressing the subject matter of the initial emergency regulation, but any such additional emergency regulations shall not be effective beyond the twelve-month period from the effective date of the initial emergency regulation. If the agency wishes to continue regulating the subject matter governed by the emergency regulation beyond the twelve-month limitation, a regulation to replace the emergency regulation shall be promulgated in accordance with this article. The Notice of Intended Regulatory Action to promulgate a replacement regulation shall be filed with the Registrar within sixty days of the effective date of the emergency regulation and published as soon as practicable, and the proposed replacement regulation shall be filed with the Registrar within 180 days after the effective date of the emergency regulation and published as soon as practicable.

D. In the event that an agency concludes that despite its best efforts, a replacement regulation cannot be adopted before expiration of the 12-month period described in subsection C, it may seek the prior written approval of the Governor to extend the duration of the emergency regulation for a period of not more than six additional months. Any such request must be submitted to the Governor at least 30 days prior to the scheduled expiration of the emergency regulation and shall include a description of the agency's efforts to adopt a replacement regulation together with the reasons that a replacement regulation cannot be adopted before the expiration of the emergency regulation. Upon approval of the Governor, the duration of the emergency regulation shall be extended for a period of no more than six months. Such approval shall be in the sole discretion of the Governor and shall not be subject to judicial review. Agencies shall notify the Registrar of Regulations of the new expiration date of the emergency regulation as soon as practicable.

E. Emergency regulations shall be published as soon as practicable in the Register.

F. The Regulations of the Marine Resources Commission shall be excluded from the provisions of this section. (1975, c. 503, § 9-6.14:9; 1977, cc. 450, 459; 1981, c. 387; 1982, c. 425; 1983, c. 295; 1984, c. 5; 1985, c. 602, § 9-6.14:4.1; 1986, c. 615; 1987, cc. 375, 652; 1988, cc. 364, 424, 498, 723, 765, 820; 1989, cc. 54, 71, 299, 478; 1990, cc. 721, 968; 1991, cc. 80, 294, 344; 1992, cc. 200, 409, 488, 592, 793, 829; 1993, cc. 537, 669, 898; 1994, cc. 237, 577, 649, 740, 743, 801, 938; 1995, cc. 103, 499, 516; 1996, cc. 51, 152, 158, 189, 205, 279, 320, 345, 573, 590, 598, 638, 705, 735, 818, 1012; 1997, cc. 87, 88, 109, 212, 390, 439, 567, 624, 785, 806, 845, 850, 861, 868; 1998, cc. 39, 619, 784; 1999, cc. 412, 421, 433, 603; 2000, cc. 382, 400, 924, 1011; 2001, c. 844; 2007, cc. 873, 916.)

Editor's note. — Acts 2006, Sp. Sess. I, c. 3, as amended by Acts 2007, c. 847, effective for the biennium ending June 30, 2008, in Item 302 M, provides: "M.1. The Department of Medical Assistance Services shall have the authority to seek federal approval of changes to its MEDALLION waiver and its Medallion II waiver.

"2. In order to conform the state regulations to the federally approved changes and to implement the provisions of this act, the Department shall promulgate emergency regulations to become effective within 280 days or less from the enactment of this act. The Department shall implement these necessary regulatory changes to be consistent with federal approval of the waiver changes."

The 2007 amendments. — The 2007 amendments by cc. 873 and 916 are identical, and redesignated former subsection A as A through C; added the language beginning "may be adopted" to the end of subsection A; substituted "Agencies may also adopt emergency regulations in situations in" for "For the purposes of this subsection, 'emergency situation' means a situation (i) involving an imminent threat to public health or safety or (ii) in" in subsection B; substituted "All emergency" for "The" in subsection C; and inserted subsection D and redesignated the remaining subsections accordingly.

§ 2.2-4012. Purpose; adoption; effective date; filing; duties of Registrar of Regulations. — A.

The purpose of the regulatory procedures shall be to provide a regulatory plan that is predictable, based on measurable and anticipated outcomes, and is inclined toward conflict resolution.

B. Subject to the provisions of §§ 2.2-4013 and 2.2-4014, all regulations, including those that agencies, pursuant to § 2.2-4002, 2.2-4006, or 2.2-4011, may elect to dispense with the public procedures provided by §§ 2.2-4007.01 and 2.2-4009, may be formally and finally adopted by the signed order of the agency so stating. No regulation except an emergency regulation or a noncontroversial regulation promulgated pursuant to § 2.2-4012.1 shall be effective until the expiration of the applicable period as provided in § 2.2-4015. In the case of an emergency regulation filed in accordance with § 2.2-4011, the regulation shall become effective upon its adoption and filing with the Registrar of Regulations, unless a later date is specified. The originals of all regulations shall remain in the custody of the agency as public records subject to judicial notice by all courts and agencies. They, or facsimiles thereof, shall be made available for public inspection or copying. Full and true copies shall also be additionally filed, registered, published, or otherwise made publicly available as required by other laws.

C. Prior to the publication for hearing of a proposed regulation, copies of the regulation and copies of the summary and statement as to the basis, purpose, substance, issues, and the economic impact estimate of the regulation submitted by the Department of Planning and Budget and the agency's response thereto as required by § 2.2-4007.04 shall be transmitted to the Registrar of Regulations, who shall retain these documents.

D. All regulations adopted pursuant to this chapter shall contain a citation to the section of the Code of Virginia that authorizes or requires the regulations and, where the regulations are required to conform to federal law or regulation in order to be valid, a citation to the specific federal law or regulation to which conformity is required.

E. Immediately upon the adoption by any agency of any regulation in final form, a copy of (i) the regulation, (ii) a then current summary and statement as to the basis, purpose, substance, issues, and the economic impact estimate of the regulation submitted by the Department of Planning and Budget, and (iii) the agency's summary description of the nature of the oral and written data, views, or arguments presented during the public proceedings and the agency's comments thereon shall be transmitted to the Registrar of Regulations, who shall retain these documents as permanent records and make them available for public inspection. A draft of the agency's summary description of public comment shall be sent by the agency to all public commenters on the proposed regulation at least five days before final adoption of the regulation. (1975, c. 503, § 9-6.14:9; 1977, cc. 450, 459; 1981, c. 387; 1982, c.

425; 1983, c. 295; 1984, c. 5; 1989, c. 71; 1992, c. 829; 1993, c. 898; 1994, c. 938; 2001, c. 844; 2003, c. 224; 2007, cc. 873, 916.)

The 2007 amendments. — The 2007 amendments by cc. 873 and 916 are identical, and substituted "2.2-4007.01" for "2.2-4007" in subsection B; and substituted "2.2-4007.04" for "2.2-4007" in subsection C.

§ 2.2-4012.1. Fast-track rulemaking process.
— Notwithstanding any other provision, rules that are expected to be noncontroversial may be promulgated or repealed in accordance with the process set out in this section. Upon the concurrence of the Governor, and after written notice to the applicable standing committees of the Senate of Virginia and the House of Delegates, and to the Joint Commission on Administrative Rules, the agency may submit a fast-track regulation without having previously published a Notice of Intended Regulatory Action. The fast-track regulation shall be published in the Virginia Register of Regulations and posted on the Virginia Regulatory Town Hall, along with an agency statement setting out the reasons for using the fast-track rulemaking process. Such regulations shall be subject to the requirements set out in §§ 2.2-4007.03, 2.2-4007.04, and 2.2-4007.05, except that the time for receiving public comment need not exceed 30 days after (i) publication of the regulation in the Virginia Register of Regulations and (ii) a public comment forum opens on the Virginia Regulatory Town Hall. The time for preparation of the economic impact analysis shall not exceed 30 days. If an objection to the use of the fast-track process is received within the public comment period from 10 or more persons, any member of the applicable standing committee of either house of the General Assembly or of the Joint Commission on Administrative Rules, the agency shall (i) file notice of the objection with the Registrar of Regulations for publication in the Virginia Register, and (ii) proceed with the normal promulgation process set out in this article with the initial publication of the fast-track regulation serving as the Notice of Intended Regulatory Action. Otherwise, the regulation will become effective or shall be repealed as appropriate, 15 days after the close of the comment period, unless the regulation or repeal is withdrawn or a later effective date is specified by the agency. (2003, c. 224; 2007, cc. 873, 916.)

The 2007 amendments. — The 2007 amendments by cc. 873 and 916 are nearly identical, and inserted "or repealed," the language beginning "be published in" and ending "Such regulations shall," "or shall be repealed as appropriate," and "or repeal," and substituted the language beginning "§§ 2.2-4007.03" and ending "not exceed 30 days" for "subsections F, H, and I of § 2.2-4007 and shall be published in the Virginia Register of Regulations along with an agency statement setting out the reasons for using the fast-track rulemaking process."

§ 2.2-4013. Executive review of proposed and final regulations; changes with substan-
tial impact. — A. The Governor shall adopt and publish procedures by executive order for review of all proposed regulations governed by this chapter by June 30 of the year in which the Governor takes office. The procedures shall include (i) review by the Attorney General to ensure statutory authority for the proposed regulations; and (ii) examination by the Governor to determine if the proposed regulations are (a) necessary to protect the public health, safety and welfare and (b) clearly written and easily understandable. The procedures may also include review of the proposed regulation by the appropriate Cabinet Secretary.

The Governor shall transmit his comments, if any, on a proposed regulation to the Registrar and the agency no later than fifteen days following the completion of the public comment period provided for in § 2.2-4007.01. The Governor may recommend amendments or modifications to any regulation that would bring that regulation into conformity with statutory authority or state or federal laws, regulations or judicial decisions.

Not less than fifteen days following the completion of the public comment period provided for in § 2.2-4007.01, the agency may (i) adopt the proposed regulation if the Governor has no objection to the regulation; (ii) modify and adopt the proposed regulation after considering and incorporating the Governor's objections or suggestions, if any; or (iii) adopt the regulation without changes despite the Governor's recommendations for change.

B. Upon final adoption of the regulation, the agency shall forward a copy of the regulation to the Registrar of Regulations for publication as soon as practicable in the Register. All changes to the proposed regulation shall be highlighted in the final regulation, and substantial changes to the proposed regulation shall be explained in the final regulation.

C. If the Governor finds that one or more changes with substantial impact have been made to the proposed regulation, he may require the agency to provide an additional thirty days to solicit additional public comment on the changes by transmitting notice of the additional public comment period to the agency and to the Registrar within the thirty-day adoption period described in subsection D, and publishing the notice in the Register. The additional public comment period required by the Governor shall begin upon publication of the notice in the Register.

D. A thirty-day final adoption period for regulations shall commence upon the publication of the final regulation in the Register. The Governor may review the final regulation during this thirty-day final adoption period and if he objects to any portion or all of a regulation, the Governor may file a formal objection to the regulation, suspend the effective date of the regulation in accordance with subsection B of § 2.2-4014, or both.

If the Governor files a formal objection to the regulation, he shall forward his objections to the

Registrar and agency prior to the conclusion of the thirty-day final adoption period. The Governor shall be deemed to have acquiesced to a promulgated regulation if he fails to object to it or if he fails to suspend the effective date of the regulation in accordance with subsection B of § 2.2-4014 during the thirty-day final adoption period. The Governor's objection, or the suspension of the regulation, or both if applicable, shall be published in the Register.

A regulation shall become effective as provided in § 2.2-4015.

E. This section shall not apply to the issuance by the State Air Pollution Control Board of variances to its regulations. (1984, c. 5, § 9-6.14:9.1; 1993, cc. 551, 772, 898; 1995, cc. 25, 736; 2001, c. 844; 2007, cc. 873, 916.)

The 2007 amendments. — The 2007 amendments by cc. 873 and 916 are identical, and substituted "2.2-4007.01" for "2.2-4007" in the second and third paragraphs of subsection A.

§ 2.2-4014. Legislative review of proposed and final regulations.

— A. After publication of the Register pursuant to § 2.2-4031, the standing committee of each house of the General Assembly to which matters relating to the content of the regulation are most properly referable or the Joint Commission on Administrative Rules may meet and, during the promulgation or final adoption process, file with the Registrar and the promulgating agency an objection to a proposed or final adopted regulation. The Registrar shall publish any such objection received by him as soon as practicable in the Register. Within 21 days after the receipt by the promulgating agency of a legislative objection, that agency shall file a response with the Registrar, the objecting legislative committee or the Joint Commission on Administrative Rules, and the Governor. If a legislative objection is filed within the final adoption period, subdivision A 1 of § 2.2-4015 shall govern.

B. In addition or as an alternative to the provisions of subsection A, the standing committee of both houses of the General Assembly to which matters relating to the content are most properly referable or the Joint Commission on Administrative Rules may suspend the effective date of any portion or all of a final regulation with the Governor's concurrence. The Governor and (i) the applicable standing committee of each house or (ii) the Joint Commission on Administrative Rules may direct, through a statement signed by a majority of their respective members and by the Governor, that the effective date of a portion or all of the final regulation is suspended and shall not take effect until the end of the next regular legislative session. This statement shall be transmitted to the promulgating agency and the Registrar within the 30-day adoption period, and shall be published in the Register.

If a bill is passed at the next regular legislative session to nullify a portion but not all of the regulation, then the promulgating agency (i) may promulgate the regulation under the provision of subdivision A 4 a of § 2.2-4006, if it makes no changes to the regulation other than those required by statutory law or (ii) shall follow the provisions of §§ 2.2-4007.01 through 2.2-4007.06, if it wishes to also make discretionary changes to the regulation. If a bill to nullify all or a portion of the suspended regulation, or to modify the statutory authority for the regulation, is not passed at the next regular legislative session, then the suspended regulation shall become effective at the conclusion of the session, unless the suspended regulation is withdrawn by the agency.

C. A regulation shall become effective as provided in § 2.2-4015.

D. This section shall not apply to the issuance by the State Air Pollution Control Board of variances to its regulations. (1984, c. 5, § 9-6.14:9.2; 1993, cc. 551, 772; 2001, c. 844; 2002, c. 677; 2003, c. 212; 2004, c. 777; 2007, cc. 873, 916.)

Editor's note. — Acts 2007, c. 732, cl. 2, provides: "That the Board of Game and Inland Fisheries shall submit the proposed and final regulations authorized under the provisions of this act to the Senate Committee on Agriculture, Conservation and Natural Resources and the House Committee on Agriculture, Chesapeake and Natural Resources at the same time such regulations are submitted to the Virginia Register, so that the Committees may exercise their oversight responsibilities pursuant to § 2.2-4014 of the Code of Virginia."

The 2007 amendments. — The 2007 amendments by cc. 873 and 916 are identical, and substituted "§§ 2.2-4007.01 through 2.2-4007.06" for "§ 2.2-4007" in the second paragraph of subsection B.

§ 2.2-4015. Effective date of regulation; exception.

— A. A regulation adopted in accordance with this chapter and the Virginia Register Act (§ 2.2-4100 et seq.) shall become effective at the conclusion of the thirty-day final adoption period provided for in subsection D of § 2.2-4013, or any other later date specified by the agency, unless:

1. A legislative objection has been filed in accordance with § 2.2-4014, in which event the regulation, unless withdrawn by the agency, shall become effective on a date specified by the agency that shall be after the expiration of the applicable twenty-one-day extension period provided in § 2.2-4014;

2. The Governor has exercised his authority in accordance with § 2.2-4013 to require the agency to provide for additional public comment, in which event the regulation, unless withdrawn by the agency, shall become effective on a date specified by the agency that shall be after the period for which the Governor has provided for additional public comment;

3. The Governor and (i) the appropriate standing committees of each house of the General Assembly or (ii) the Joint Commission on Administrative Rules have exercised their authority in accordance with subsection B of § 2.2-4014 to suspend the effective date of a regulation until the end of the next regular legislative session; or

4. The agency has suspended the regulatory process in accordance with § 2.2-4007.06, or for any reason it deems necessary or appropriate, in which event the regulation, unless withdrawn by the agency, shall become effective in accordance with subsection B.

B. Whenever the regulatory process has been suspended for any reason, any action by the agency that either amends the regulation or does not amend the regulation but specifies a new effective date shall be considered a readoption of the regulation for the purposes of appeal. If the regulation is suspended under § 2.2-4007.06, such readoption shall take place after the thirty-day public comment period required by that subsection. Suspension of the regulatory process by the agency may occur simultaneously with the filing of final regulations as provided in subsection B of § 2.2-4013.

When a regulation has been suspended, the agency must set the effective date no earlier than fifteen days from publication of the readoption action and any changes made to the regulation. During that fifteen-day period, if the agency receives requests from at least twenty-five persons for the opportunity to comment on new substantial changes, it shall again suspend the regulation pursuant to § 2.2-4007.06.

C. This section shall not apply to the issuance by the State Air Pollution Control Board of variances to its regulations. (1984, c. 5, § 9-6.14:9.3; 1993, cc. 551, 772, 898; 1995, c. 25; 2001, c. 844; 2002, cc. 391, 677; 2004, c. 777; 2007, cc. 873, 916.)

The 2007 amendments. — The 2007 amendments by cc. 873 and 916 are identical, and substituted "§ 2.2-4007.06" for "subsection K of § 2.2-4007" in subdivision A 4 and twice throughout subsection B.

ARTICLE 3.

Case Decisions.

§ 2.2-4019. Informal fact finding proceedings.

CASE NOTES

No right to cross-examination in informal hearings. — That a real estate appraiser was not able to cross examine witnesses at her license revocation hearing did not deprive her of due process. Section 2.2-4020, providing for cross-examination of witnesses, was inapplicable, because she had an informal hearing under § 2.2-4019, which did not entitle her to cross-examine witnesses or force them to testify under oath. Haley v. Commonwealth, — Va. App. —, — S.E.2d —, 2006 Va. App. LEXIS 441 (Oct. 3, 2006).

Any error in consideration of challenged evidence was harmless. — Any consideration of evidence challenged by two landfill operators admitted at an informal fact finding conference was harmless as the presiding officer did not refer to the challenged evidence, but referenced certain evidence of the operators; even if the Director of the Virginia Department of Environmental Quality considered the challenged materials, the Director's conclusions were based on some information that was provided by the operators that part of the Columbia aquifer remained at the site. Elbow Farm, Inc. v. Paylor, — Va. App. —, — S.E.2d —, 2007 Va. App. LEXIS 48 (Feb. 13, 2007).

§ 2.2-4020. Formal hearings; litigated issues.

CASE NOTES

Informal hearings. — That a real estate appraiser was not able to cross examine witnesses at her license revocation hearing did not deprive her of due process. This section, providing for cross-examination of witnesses, was inapplicable, because she had an informal hearing under § 2.2-4019, and under § 2.2-4019, she was not entitled to cross-examine witnesses or force them to testify under oath. Haley v. Commonwealth, — Va. App. —, — S.E.2d —, 2006 Va. App. LEXIS 441 (Oct. 3, 2006).

ARTICLE 5.

Court Review.

§ 2.2-4027. Issues on review. — The burden shall be upon the party complaining of agency action to designate and demonstrate an error of law subject to review by the court. Such issues of law include: (i) accordance with constitutional right, power, privilege, or immunity, (ii) compliance with statutory authority, jurisdiction limitations, or right as provided in the basic laws as to subject matter, the stated objectives for which regulations may be made, and the factual showing respecting violations or entitlement in connection with case decisions, (iii) observance of required procedure where any failure therein is not mere harmless error, and (iv) the substantiality of the evidentiary support for findings of fact. The determination of such fact issue shall be made upon the whole evidentiary record provided by the agency if its proceeding was required to be conducted as provided in § 2.2-4009 or 2.2-4020 or, as to subjects exempted from those sections, pursuant to constitutional requirement or statutory provisions for opportunity for an agency record of and decision upon the evidence therein.

In addition to any other judicial review provided by law, a small business, as defined in subsection A of § 2.2-4007.1, that is adversely affected or aggrieved by final agency action shall be entitled to judicial review of compliance with the requirements of subdivision A 2 of § 2.2-4007.04 and § 2.2-4007.1 within one year following the date of final agency action.

When the decision on review is to be made on the agency record, the duty of the court with respect to issues of fact shall be limited to ascertaining whether there was substantial evidence in the agency record upon which the agency as the trier of the facts could reasonably find them to be as it did.

Where there is no agency record so required and made, any necessary facts in controversy shall be determined by the court upon the basis of the agency file, minutes, and records of its proceedings under § 2.2-4007.01 or 2.2-4019 as augmented, if need be, by the agency pursuant to order of the court or supplemented by any allowable and necessary proofs adduced in court except that the function of the court shall be to determine only whether the result reached by the agency could reasonably be said, on all such proofs, to be within the scope of the legal authority of the agency.

Whether the fact issues are reviewed on the agency record or one made in the review action, the court shall take due account of the presumption of official regularity, the experience and specialized competence of the agency, and the purposes of the basic law under which the agency has acted. (1975, c. 503, § 9-6.14:17; 1989, c. 601; 2001, c. 844; 2005, cc. 619, 682; 2007, cc. 873, 916.)

The 2007 amendments. — The 2007 amendments by cc. 873 and 916 are identical, and substituted "subdivision A 2 of § 2.2-4007.04" for "subdivision H 2 of § 2.2-4007" in the second paragraph; and substituted "2.2-4007.01" for "2.2-4007" in the fourth paragraph.

CASE NOTES

I. IN GENERAL.

Any error in consideration of challenged evidence was harmless. — Any consideration of evidence challenged by two landfill operators admitted at an informal fact finding conference was harmless as the presiding officer did not refer to the challenged evidence, but referenced certain evidence of the operators; even if the Director of the Virginia Department of Environmental Quality considered the challenged materials, the Director's conclusions were based on some information that was provided by the operators that part of the Columbia aquifer remained at the site. Elbow Farm, Inc. v. Paylor, — Va. App. —, — S.E.2d —, 2007 Va. App. LEXIS 48 (Feb. 13, 2007).

§ 2.2-4029. Court judgments.

CASE NOTES

Applied in Rice v. Va. Dep't of Soc. Servs., — Va. App. —, — S.E.2d —, 2007 Va. App. LEXIS 123 (Mar. 27, 2007).

§ 2.2-4030. Recovery of costs and attorneys' fees from agency.

CASE NOTES

Applicability.
Claimant who applied for but was denied retirement benefits based on the retiree's Commonwealth employment could not recover attorney fees, as such an award was available only to a prevailing party, which she was not. Shropshire v. Va. Ret. Sys., 48 Va. App. 436, 632 S.E.2d 601, 2006 Va. App. LEXIS 336 (2006).
Denial upheld.
Two landfill operators did not substantially prevail on the merits of their appeals of the decisions of the Director of the Virginia Department of Environmental Quality denying their requests for variances from ground water monitoring requirements and requiring ground water monitoring at a closed portion of a landfill, and the Director's decisions were substantially justified; the trial court did not err by refusing to award the operators attorneys' fees and costs. Elbow Farm, Inc. v. Paylor, — Va. App. —, — S.E.2d —, 2007 Va. App. LEXIS 48 (Feb. 13, 2007).

ARTICLE 6.

Virginia Register of Regulations.

§ 2.2-4031. Publication of Virginia Register of Regulations; exceptions; notice of public hearings of proposed regulations. — A. The Registrar shall publish every two weeks a Virginia Register of Regulations that shall include (i) proposed and final regulations; (ii) emergency regulations; (iii) executive orders; (iv) notices of all public hearings on regulations; (v) petitions for rulemaking made in accordance with § 2.2-4007; and (vi) tax bulletins. The entire proposed regulation shall be published in the Register; however, if an existing regulation has been previously published in the Virginia Administrative Code, then only those sections of regulations to be amended need to be published in the Register. If the length of the regulation falls within the guidelines established by the Registrar for the publication of a summary in lieu of the full text of the regulation, then, after consultation with the promulgating agency, the Registrar may publish only the summary of the regulation. In this event, the full text of the regulation shall be available for public inspection at the office of the Registrar and the promulgating agency.

If a proposed regulation is adopted as published or, in the sole discretion of the Registrar of Regulations, the only changes that have been made are those that can be clearly and concisely explained, the adopted regulation need not be published at length. Instead, the Register shall contain a notation that the proposed regulation has been adopted as published as a proposed regulation without change or stating the changes made. The proposed regulation shall be clearly identified with a citation to the issue and page numbers where published.

A copy of all reporting forms the promulgating agency anticipates will be incorporated into or be used in administering the regulation shall be published with the proposed and final regulation in the Register.

B. Each regulation shall be prefaced with a summary explaining that regulation in plain and clear language. Summaries shall be prepared by the promulgating agency and approved by the Registrar prior to their publication in the Register. The notice required by § 2.2-4007.01 shall include (i) a statement of the date, time and place of the hearing at which the regulation is to be considered; (ii) a brief statement as to the regulation under consideration; (iii) reference to the legal authority of the agency to act; and (iv) the name, address and telephone number of an individual to contact for further information about that regulation. Agencies shall present their proposed regulations in a standardized format developed by the Virginia Code Commission in accordance with subdivision 1 of § 2.2-4104 of the Virginia Register Act (§ 2.2-4100 et seq.). Notwithstanding the exemptions allowed under § 2.2-4002, 2.2-4006 or 2.2-4011, the proposed and final regulations of all agencies shall be published in the Register. However, proposed regulations of the Marine Resources Commission and regulations exempted by subject from the provisions of this chapter by subsection B of § 2.2-4002 shall be exempt from this section.

C. The Virginia Register of Regulations shall be published by posting the Register on the Virginia Code Commission's website. The Virginia Code Commission may arrange for the printing of the Virginia Register as provided in § 30-146. (1984, c. 5, § 9-6.14:22; 1985, cc. 67, 602; 1986, c. 615; 1988, c. 364; 1989, c. 71; 1992, c. 216; 2001, c. 844; 2002, c. 241; 2003, c. 212; 2007, cc. 300, 873, 916.)

The 2007 amendments. — The 2007 amendment by c. 300 deleted "meetings and public" preceding "hearings" and substituted "on regulations" for "of state agencies, legislative committees and study subcommittes" in subsection A; deleted former subsection C regarding requirements for publication of notice of meetings, and redesignated former subsection D as present subsection C.

The 2007 amendments by cc. 873 and 916 are identical, and deleted "subsection A of" preceding "§ 2.2-4007" in the first paragraph of subsection A; substituted "2.2-4007.01" for "2.2-4007" in subsection B; and made minor stylistic changes.

CHAPTER 43.

VIRGINIA PUBLIC PROCUREMENT ACT.

Article 2.

Contract Formation and Administration.

Sec.
2.2-4310. Discrimination prohibited; participation of small, women-, minority- and service disabled veteran-owned business.
2.2-4317. Prequalification generally; prequalification for construction.
2.2-4327. Preference for community reinvestment activities in contracts for investment of funds.

Article 3.

Exemptions and Limitations.

2.2-4343. Exemption from operation of chapter for certain transactions.

ARTICLE 1.

General Provisions.

§ 2.2-4300. Short title; purpose; declaration of intent.

Editor's note. — Acts 2006, Sp. Sess. I, c. 3, as amended by Acts 2007, c. 847, effective for the biennium ending June 30, 2008, in Item 233 F, provides: "Except as provided otherwise in this paragraph, the provisions of the Virginia Public Procurement Act (§ 2.2-4300 et seq., Code of Virginia) shall not apply to the expenditure of funds from the Virginia 400th Anniversary Fund.

However, the provisions of this paragraph shall not be effective until such time as the Board of Trustees of the Jamestown-Yorktown Foundation has adopted guidelines generally applicable to the procurement of goods and services by the Jamestown-Yorktown Foundation and Jamestown 2007 through the expenditure of funds from the Virginia 400th Anniversary Fund. The guidelines shall implement a system of competitive negotiation for professional services; shall prohibit discrimination because of race, religion, color, sex or national origin of the bidder or offeror in the solicitation or award of contracts; may take into account in all cases the dollar amount of the intended procurement, the term of the anticipated contract, and the likely extent of competition; may implement a prequalification procedure for contractors or products; may include provisions for cooperative procurement arrangements; shall incorporate the prompt payment principles of §§ 2.2-4350 and 2.2-4354, Code of Virginia; and may implement provisions of law. The following sections of the Virginia Public Procurement Act shall continue to apply to procurement by the Jamestown-Yorktown Foundation and Jamestown 2007 with funds from the Virginia 400th Anniversary Fund: §§ 2.2-4311, 2.2-4315, 2.2-4330, 2.2-4333 through 2.2-4338, 2.2-4340 through 2.2-4342, and 2.2-4367 through 2.2-4377, Code of Virginia."

Acts 2006, Sp. Sess. I, c. 3, effective for the biennium ending June 30, 2008, in Item 461 E, provides: "E. The Governor is hereby authorized to transfer funds from agency appropriations to the accounts of participating state employees in such amounts as may be necessary to match the contributions of the qualified participating employees, consistent with the requirements of the Code of Virginia governing the deferred compensation cash match program. Such transfers shall be made consistent with the following:

"1. The maximum cash match provided to eligible employees shall not be less than $20.00 per pay period, or $40.00 per month. The Governor may direct the agencies of the Commonwealth to utilize funds contained within their existing appropriations to meet these requirements.

"2. The Governor may direct agencies supported in whole or in part with nongeneral funds to utilize existing agency appropriations to meet these requirements. Such nongeneral revenues and balances are hereby appropriated for this purpose, subject to the provisions of § 4-2.01 b of this act. The use of such nongeneral funds shall be consistent with any existing conditions and restrictions otherwise placed upon such nongeneral funds.

"3. Employees who are otherwise eligible but whose 403(b) provider does not participate in the cash match program by establishing a 401(a) account are ineligible to receive a cash match.

"4. The procurement of services related to the implementation of this program shall be governed by standards set forth in § 51.1-124.30 C, Code of Virginia, and shall not be subject to the provisions of Chapter 7 (§ 11-35 et seq.), Title 11, Code of Virginia."

Law Review.

For article reviewing case law and changes in legislation affecting Virginia construction law, see 40 U. Rich. L. Rev. 143 (2005).

CIRCUIT COURT OPINIONS

Appeal before announcement of award not allowed. — Virginia Public Procurement Act, § 2.2-4300 et seq., did not permit an appeal before the public body's announcement of its decision; a contractor's protest, submitted in response to information that it would not be awarded a contract, was not capable of being appealed as it was filed before announcement of the award. John T. Moore & Assocs., P.C. v. Va. Commonwealth Univ., 69 Va. Cir. 200, 2005 Va. Cir. LEXIS 356 (Richmond 2005).

§ 2.2-4301. Definitions.

Editor's note. — Acts 2006, Sp. Sess. I, c. 3, as amended by Acts 2007, c. 847, effective for the biennium ending June 30, 2008, in § 4-5.06 f., provides: "Institutions that have executed memoranda of understanding with the Secretary of Administration for nongeneral fund capital outlay decentralization programs are hereby granted a waiver from the provisions of § 2.2-4301, Competitive Negotiation, subdivision 3a, Code of Virginia, regarding the not to exceed amount of $100,000 for a single project, the not to exceed sum of $500,000 for all projects performed, and the option to renew for two additional one-year terms."

ARTICLE 2.

Contract Formation and Administration.

§ 2.2-4310. Discrimination prohibited; participation of small, women-, minority- and service disabled veteran-owned business. — A. In the solicitation or awarding of contracts, no public body shall discriminate against a bidder or offeror because of race, religion, color, sex, national origin, age, disability, status as a service disabled veteran, or any other basis prohibited by state law relating to discrimination in employment. Whenever solicitations are made, each public body shall include businesses selected from a list made available by the Department of Minority Business Enterprise.

B. All public bodies shall establish programs consistent with this chapter to facilitate the participation of small businesses and businesses owned by women, minorities, and service disabled veterans in procurement transactions. The programs established shall be in writing and shall comply with the provisions of any enhancement or remedial measures authorized by the Governor pursuant to subsection C or, where applicable, by the chief executive of a local governing body pursuant to § 15.2-965.1, and shall include specific plans to achieve any goals established therein. State agencies shall submit annual progress reports on small, women- and minority-owned business procurement and on service disabled veteran-owned business procurement to the Department of Minority Business Enterprise in a form specified by the Department of Minority Business Enterprise. The Department of Minority Business Enterprise shall make information on service disabled veteran-owned procurement available to the Department of Veterans Services upon request.

C. Whenever there exists (i) a rational basis for small business enhancement or (ii) a persuasive analysis that documents a statistically significant disparity between the availability and utilization of women- and minority-owned businesses, the Governor is authorized and encouraged to require state agencies to implement appropriate enhancement or remedial measures consistent with prevailing law.

D. In the solicitation or awarding of contracts, no state agency, department or institution shall discriminate against a bidder or offeror because the bidder or offeror employs ex-offenders unless the state agency, department or institution has made a written determination that employing ex-offenders on the specific contract is not in its best interest.

E. As used in this section:

"Minority individual" means an individual who is a citizen of the United States or a non-citizen who is in full compliance with United States immigration law and who satisfies one or more of the following definitions:

1. *"African American"* means a person having origins in any of the original peoples of Africa and who is regarded as such by the community of which this person claims to be a part.

2. *"Asian American"* means a person having origins in any of the original peoples of the Far East, Southeast Asia, the Indian subcontinent, or the Pacific Islands, including but not limited to Japan, China, Vietnam, Samoa, Laos, Cambodia, Taiwan, Northern Mariana, the Philippines, a U.S. territory of the Pacific, India, Pakistan, Bangladesh, or Sri Lanka and who is regarded as such by the community of which this person claims to be a part.

3. *"Hispanic American"* means a person having origins in any of the Spanish-speaking peoples of Mexico, South or Central America, or the Caribbean Islands or other Spanish or Portuguese cultures and who is regarded as such by the community of which this person claims to be a part.

4. *"Native American"* means a person having origins in any of the original peoples of North America and who is regarded as such by the community of which this person claims to be a part or who is recognized by a tribal organization.

"Minority-owned business" means a business concern that is at least 51% owned by one or more minority individuals or in the case of a corporation, partnership, or limited liability company or other entity, at least 51% of the equity ownership interest in the corporation, partnership, or limited liability company or other entity is owned by one or more minority individuals and both the management and daily business operations are controlled by one or more minority individuals.

"Service disabled veteran" means a veteran who (i) served on active duty in the United States military ground, naval, or air service, (ii) was discharged or released under conditions other than dishonorable, and (iii) has a service-connected disability rating fixed by the United States Veterans Administration of (a) 50% or greater or (b) 10% or greater if the service-connected disability is combat related.

"Service disabled veteran business" means a business concern that is at least 51% owned by one or more service disabled veterans or, in the case of a corporation, partnership, or limited liability company or other entity, at least 51% of the equity ownership interest in the corporation, partnership, or limited liability company or other entity is owned by one or more individuals who are service disabled veterans and both the management and daily business operations are controlled by one or more individuals who are service disabled veterans.

"Small business" means an independently owned and operated business which, together with affiliates, has 250 or fewer employees, or average annual gross receipts of $10 million or less averaged over the previous three years.

"State agency" means any authority, board, department, instrumentality, institution, agency, or other unit of state government. "State agency" shall not include any county, city, or town.

"Women-owned business" means a business concern that is at least 51% owned by one or more women who are citizens of the United States or non-citizens who are in full compliance with United States immigration law, or in the case of a corporation, partnership, or limited liability company or other entity, at least 51% of the equity ownership interest is owned by one or more women who are citizens of the United States or non-citizens who are in full compliance with United States immigration law, and both the management and daily business operations are controlled by one or more women who are citizens of the United States or non-citizens who are in full compliance with United States immigration law. (1982, c. 647, §§ 11-44, 11-48; 1984, c. 279; 2000, c. 628; 2001, c. 844; 2003, c. 226; 2004, cc. 865, 891; 2006, cc. 831, 921; 2007, c. 787.)

The 2007 amendments. — The 2007 amendment by c. 787, inserted "status as a service disabled veteran" in subsection A; in subsection B, inserted "and service disabled veterans" and "and on service disabled veteran-owned business procurement" and made related changes; and in subsection E, added definitions of "Service disabled veteran" and "Service disabled veteran business."

§ 2.2-4317. Prequalification generally; prequalification for construction. — A. Prospective contractors may be prequalified for particular types of supplies, services, insurance or construction, and consideration of bids or proposals limited to prequalified contractors. Any prequalification procedure shall be established in writing and sufficiently in advance of its implementation to allow potential contractors a fair opportunity to complete the process.

B. Any prequalification of prospective contractors for construction by a public body shall be pursuant to a prequalification process for construction projects adopted by the public body. The process shall be consistent with the provisions of this section.

The application form used in such process shall set forth the criteria upon which the qualifications of prospective contractors will be evaluated. The application form shall request of prospective contractors only such information as is appropriate for an objective evaluation of all prospective contractors pursuant to such criteria. The form shall allow the prospective contractor seeking prequalification to request, by checking the appropriate box, that all information voluntarily submitted by the contractor pursuant to this subsection shall be considered a trade secret or proprietary information subject to the provisions of subsection D of § 2.2-4342.

In all instances in which the public body requires prequalification of potential contractors for construction projects, advance notice shall be given of the deadline for the submission of prequalification applications. The deadline for submission shall be sufficiently in advance of the date set for the submission of bids for such construction so as to allow the procedures set forth in this subsection to be accomplished.

At least thirty days prior to the date established for submission of bids or proposals under the procurement of the contract for which the prequalification applies, the public body shall advise in writing each contractor who submitted an application whether that contractor has been prequalified. In the event that a contractor is denied prequalification, the written notification to the contractor shall state the reasons for the denial of prequalification and the factual basis of such reasons.

A decision by a public body denying prequalification under the provisions of this subsection shall be final and conclusive unless the contractor appeals the decision as provided in § 2.2-4357.

C. A public body may deny prequalification to any contractor only if the public body finds one of the following:

1. The contractor does not have sufficient financial ability to perform the contract that would result from such procurement. If a bond is required to ensure performance of a contract, evidence that the contractor can acquire a surety bond from a corporation included on the United States Treasury list of acceptable surety corporations in the amount and type required by the public body shall be sufficient to establish the financial ability of the contractor to perform the contract resulting from such procurement;

2. The contractor does not have appropriate experience to perform the construction project in question;

3. The contractor or any officer, director or owner thereof has had judgments entered against him within the past ten years for the breach of contracts for governmental or nongovernmental construction, including, but not limited to, design-build or construction management;

4. The contractor has been in substantial noncompliance with the terms and conditions of prior construction contracts with a public body without good cause. If the public body has not contracted with a contractor in any prior construction contracts, the public body may deny prequalification if the contractor has been in substantial noncompliance with the terms and conditions of comparable construction contracts with another public body without good cause. A public body may not utilize this provision to deny prequalification unless the facts underlying such substantial noncompliance were documented in writing in the prior construction project file and such information relating thereto given to the contractor at that time, with the opportunity to respond;

5. The contractor or any officer, director, owner, project manager, procurement manager or chief financial official thereof has been convicted within the past ten years of a crime related to governmental or nongovernmental construction or contracting, in-

cluding, but not limited to, a violation of (i) Article 6 (§ 2.2-4367 et seq.) of this chapter, (ii) the Virginia Governmental Frauds Act (§ 18.2-498.1 et seq.), (iii) Chapter 4.2 (§ 59.1-68.6 et seq.) of Title 59.1, or (iv) any substantially similar law of the United States or another state;

6. The contractor or any officer, director or owner thereof is currently debarred pursuant to an established debarment procedure from bidding or contracting by any public body, agency of another state or agency of the federal government; and

7. The contractor failed to provide to the public body in a timely manner any information requested by the public body relevant to subdivisions 1 through 6 of this subsection.

D. If a public body has a prequalification ordinance that provides for minority participation in municipal construction contracts, that public body may also deny prequalification based on minority participation criteria. However, nothing herein shall authorize the adoption or enforcement of minority participation criteria except to the extent that such criteria, and the adoption and enforcement thereof, are in accordance with the Constitution and laws of the United States and the Commonwealth.

E. The provisions of subsections B, C, and D shall not apply to prequalification for contracts let under § 33.1-12. (1982, c. 647, § 11-46; 1994, c. 918; 1995, c. 527; 2001, c. 844; 2007, c. 154.)

The 2007 amendments. — The 2007 amendment by c. 154 deleted "by the Commonwealth Transportation Board" following "contracts let" in subsection E.

§ 2.2-4327. Preference for community reinvestment activities in contracts for investment of funds.
— Notwithstanding any other provision of law, any county, town, or city that is authorized to and has established affordable housing programs may provide by resolution that in determining the award of any contract for time deposits or investment of its funds, the treasurer or director of finance of such county, town, or city may consider, in addition to the typical criteria, the investment activities of qualifying institutions that enhance the supply of, or accessibility to, affordable housing within the jurisdiction, including the accessibility of such housing to employees of the county, town, or city or employees of the local school board. No more than 50 percent of the funds of the county, town, or city, calculated on the basis of the average daily balance of the general fund during the previous fiscal year, may be deposited or invested by considering such investment activities as a factor in the award of a contract. A qualifying institution shall meet the provisions of the Virginia Security for Public Deposits Act (§ 2.2-4400 et seq.) and all local terms and conditions for security, liquidity and rate of return.

For the purposes of this section, affordable housing means the same as that term is defined in § 15.2-2201. (1993, c. 937, § 11-47.3; 1995, c. 206; 1997, c. 176; 1999, c. 708; 2001, c. 844; 2007, c. 681.)

The 2007 amendments. — The 2007 amendment by c. 681 inserted "town" three times throughout; deleted "pursuant to (i) § 15.2-2304 or § 15.2-2305 or (ii) a local ordinance adopted prior to December 31, 1988" preceding "may provide"; added the language beginning "including the accessibility" to the end of the first sentence; added the final paragraph; and made minor stylistic changes.

§ 2.2-4335. Public construction contract provisions barring damages for unreasonable delays declared void.

Law Review. — For article reviewing case law and changes in legislation affecting Virginia construction law, see 40 U. Rich. L. Rev. 143 (2005).

§ 2.2-4341. Actions on payment bonds; waiver of right to sue.

Law Review. — For article reviewing case law and changes in legislation affecting Virginia construction law, see 40 U. Rich. L. Rev. 143 (2005).

CIRCUIT COURT OPINIONS

Subcontractor for subcontractor could recover on general contractor's payment bond. — Sheet metal company, hired by a subcontractor, fell within the criteria for a claimant, and thus, the sheet metal company could recover against the general contractor's payment bond. Even if the surety was correct that the language of payment bond was more general than Virginia law required, there was no conflict with Virginia Public Procurement Act, § 2.2-4300 et seq., and the broader provisions of the bond took precedence. Stromberg Sheet Metal Works, Inc. v. United States Fid. & Guar. Co., 71 Va. Cir. 122, 2006 Va. Cir. LEXIS 102 (Fairfax County 2006).

ARTICLE 3.

Exemptions and Limitations.

§ 2.2-4343. Exemption from operation of chapter for certain transactions.
— A. The provisions of this chapter shall not apply to:

1. The Virginia Port Authority in the exercise of any of its powers in accordance with Chapter 10 (§ 62.1-128 et seq.) of Title 62.1, provided the Authority implements, by policy or regulation adopted by the Board of Commissioners and approved by the Department of General Services, procedures to ensure fairness and competitiveness in the procurement of goods and services and in the administration of its capital outlay program. This exemption shall be applicable only so long as such policies and procedures meeting the requirements remain in effect.

2. The Virginia Retirement System for selection of services related to the management, purchase or sale of authorized investments, actuarial services, and disability determination services. Selection of these services shall be governed by the standard set forth in § 51.1-124.30.

3. The State Treasurer in the selection of investment management services related to the external management of funds shall be governed by the

standard set forth in § 2.2-4514, and shall be subject to competitive guidelines and policies that are set by the Commonwealth Treasury Board and approved by the Department of General Services.

4. The Department of Social Services or local departments of social services for the acquisition of motor vehicles for sale or transfer to Temporary Assistance to Needy Families (TANF) recipients.

5. The University of Virginia in the selection of services related to the management and investment of its endowment funds, endowment income, gifts, all other nongeneral fund reserves and balances, or local funds of or held by the University pursuant to § 23-76.1. However, selection of these services shall be governed by the Uniform Management of Institutional Funds Act (§ 55-268.1 et seq.) as required by § 23-76.1.

6. The Board of the Virginia College Savings Plan for the selection of services related to the operation and administration of the Plan, including, but not limited to, contracts or agreements for the management, purchase, or sale of authorized investments or actuarial, record keeping, or consulting services. However, such selection shall be governed by the standard set forth in § 23-38.80.

7. Public institutions of higher education for the purchase of items for resale at retail bookstores and similar retail outlets operated by such institutions. However, such purchase procedures shall provide for competition where practicable.

8. The purchase of goods and services by agencies of the legislative branch that may be specifically exempted therefrom by the Chairman of the Committee on Rules of either the House of Delegates or the Senate. Nor shall the contract review provisions of § 2.2-2011 apply to such procurements. The exemption shall be in writing and kept on file with the agency's disbursement records.

9. Any town with a population of less than 3,500, except as stipulated in the provisions of §§ 2.2-4305, 2.2-4308, 2.2-4311, 2.2-4315, 2.2-4330, 2.2-4333 through 2.2-4338, 2.2-4343.1, and 2.2-4367 through 2.2-4377.

10. Any county, city or town whose governing body has adopted, by ordinance or resolution, alternative policies and procedures which are (i) based on competitive principles and (ii) generally applicable to procurement of goods and services by such governing body and its agencies, except as stipulated in subdivision 12.

This exemption shall be applicable only so long as such policies and procedures, or other policies and procedures meeting the requirements of § 2.2-4300, remain in effect in such county, city or town. Such policies and standards may provide for incentive contracting that offers a contractor whose bid is accepted the opportunity to share in any cost savings realized by the locality when project costs are reduced by such contractor, without affecting project quality, during construction of the project. The fee, if any, charged by the project engineer or architect for

determining such cost savings shall be paid as a separate cost and shall not be calculated as part of any cost savings.

11. Any school division whose school board has adopted, by policy or regulation, alternative policies and procedures that are (i) based on competitive principles and (ii) generally applicable to procurement of goods and services by the school board, except as stipulated in subdivision 12.

This exemption shall be applicable only so long as such policies and procedures, or other policies or procedures meeting the requirements of § 2.2-4300, remain in effect in such school division. This provision shall not exempt any school division from any centralized purchasing ordinance duly adopted by a local governing body.

12. Notwithstanding the exemptions set forth in subdivisions 9 through 11, the provisions of subsections C and D of § 2.2-4303, and §§ 2.2-4305, 2.2-4308, 2.2-4311, 2.2-4315, 2.2-4317, 2.2-4330, 2.2-4333 through 2.2-4338, 2.2-4343.1, and 2.2-4367 through 2.2-4377 shall apply to all counties, cities and school divisions, and to all towns having a population greater than 3,500 in the Commonwealth.

The method for procurement of professional services set forth in subdivision 3 a of § 2.2-4301 in the definition of competitive negotiation shall also apply to all counties, cities and school divisions, and to all towns having a population greater than 3,500, where the cost of the professional service is expected to exceed $30,000 in the aggregate or for the sum of all phases of a contract or project. A school board that makes purchases through its public school foundation or purchases educational technology through its educational technology foundation, either as may be established pursuant to § 22.1-212.2:2 shall be exempt from the provisions of this chapter, except, relative to such purchases, the school board shall comply with the provisions of §§ 2.2-4311 and 2.2-4367 through 2.2-4377.

13. A public body that is also a utility operator may purchase services through or participate in contracts awarded by one or more utility operators that are not public bodies for utility marking services as required by the Underground Utility Damage Prevention Act (§ 56-265.14 et seq.). A purchase of services under this subdivision may deviate from the procurement procedures set forth in this chapter upon a determination made in advance by the public body and set forth in writing that competitive sealed bidding is either not practicable or not fiscally advantageous to the public, and the contract is awarded based on competitive principles.

14. Procurement of any construction or planning and design services for construction by a Virginia nonprofit corporation or organization not otherwise specifically exempted when (i) the planning, design or construction is funded by state appropriations of $10,000 or less or (ii) the Virginia nonprofit corporation or organization is obligated to conform to

procurement procedures that are established by federal statutes or regulations, whether those federal procedures are in conformance with the provisions of this chapter.

15. Purchases, exchanges, gifts or sales by the Citizens' Advisory Council on Furnishing and Interpreting the Executive Mansion.

16. The Eastern Virginia Medical School in the selection of services related to the management and investment of its endowment and other institutional funds. The selection of these services shall, however, be governed by the Uniform Management of Institutional Funds Act (§ 55-268.1 et seq.).

17. The Department of Corrections in the selection of pre-release and post-incarceration services.

18. The Board of the Chippokes Plantation Farm Foundation in entering into agreements with persons for the construction, operation, and maintenance of projects consistent with the Chippokes Plantation State Park Master Plan approved by the Director of the Department of Conservation and Recreation pursuant to the requirements of § 10.1-200.1 and designed to further an appreciation for rural living and the contributions of the agricultural, forestry, and natural resource based industries of the Commonwealth, provided such projects are supported solely by private or nonstate funding.

19. The University of Virginia Medical Center to the extent provided by subdivision B 3 of § 23-77.4.

20. The purchase of goods and services by a local governing body or any authority, board, department, instrumentality, institution, agency or other unit of state government when such purchases are made under a remedial plan established by the Governor pursuant to subsection C of § 2.2-4310 or by a chief administrative officer of a county, city or town pursuant to § 15.2-965.1.

21. The contract by community services boards or behavioral health authorities with an administrator or management body pursuant to a joint agreement authorized by § 37.2-512 or 37.2-615.

B. Where a procurement transaction involves the expenditure of federal assistance or contract funds, the receipt of which is conditioned upon compliance with mandatory requirements in federal laws or regulations not in conformance with the provisions of this chapter, a public body may comply with such federal requirements, notwithstanding the provisions of this chapter, only upon the written determination of the Governor, in the case of state agencies, or the governing body, in the case of political subdivisions, that acceptance of the grant or contract funds under the applicable conditions is in the public interest. Such determination shall state the specific provision of this chapter in conflict with the conditions of the grant or contract. (1982, c. 647, §§ 11-35, 11-39, 11-40; 1983, c. 593; 1984, cc. 159, 330, 764, § 11-40.2; 1985, c. 74; 1986, cc. 149, 212, 559; 1987, c. 583; 1991, c. 645; 1994, cc. 661, 918; 1995, c. 18; 1996, cc. 261, 280, 683, 1019; 1997, cc.

85, 488, 785, 861, 863; 1998, cc. 121, 132; 1999, cc. 230, 248, 735, 910, § 11-40.4; 2000, cc. 29, 382, 400, 642, 644, 666, 703; 2001, cc. 392, 409, 736, 753, 774, 844; 2002, cc. 87, 478, 491, 582, 595; 2003, cc. 226, 1008; 2004, cc. 145, 865, 891; 2006, c. 656; 2007, cc. 434, 697.)

Editor's note. — Acts 2007, c. 434, cl. 2, provides: "That the provisions of this act shall not be construed or interpreted to permit or allow the University of Virginia to invest revenues from tuition and educational fees that are used or required for the day-to-day operations of the University in other than cash accounts and fixed income securities."

The 2007 amendments. — The 2007 amendment by c. 434 in subdivision A 5, deleted "or" following "endowment income," and inserted "all other nongeneral fund reserves and balances, or local funds of or held by the University."

The 2007 amendment by c. 697, in subsection A 2, deleted "including but not limited to" preceding "actuarial services," and added "and disability determination services" to the end of the first sentence.

ARTICLE 4.

Prompt Payment.

§ 2.2-4354. Payment clauses to be included in contracts.

CASE NOTES

Applied in In re Jones Constr. & Renovation, Inc., 337 B.R. 579, 2006 Bankr. LEXIS 852 (Bankr. E.D. Va. 2006).

ARTICLE 5.

Remedies.

§ 2.2-4360. Protest of award or decision to award.

CIRCUIT COURT OPINIONS

Appeal before announcement of award not allowed. — Virginia Public Procurement Act, § 2.2-4300 et seq., did not permit an appeal before the public body's announcement of its decision; a contractor's protest, submitted in response to information that it would not be awarded a contract, was not capable of being appealed as it was filed before announcement of the award. John T. Moore & Assocs., P.C. v. Va. Commonwealth Univ., 69 Va. Cir. 200, 2005 Va. Cir. LEXIS 356 (Richmond 2005).

§ 2.2-4363. Contractual disputes.

CIRCUIT COURT OPINIONS

Suit barred for failure to notify. — Contractor's breach of contract claim was barred against a municipal water authority with regard to a water treatment plant construction project as the contractor breached the contract by failing to give notice of the conflicts in the contract documents and drawings prior to proceeding with the work and failed to give timely notice of its claim as required by the contract and by this section. Modern Cont'l South v. Fairfax County Water Auth., 70 Va. Cir. 172, 2006 Va. Cir. LEXIS 39 (Fairfax County 2006).

§ 2.2-4364. Legal actions.

CIRCUIT COURT OPINIONS

Appeal before announcement of award not allowed. — Virginia Public Procurement Act, § 2.2-4300 et seq., did not permit an appeal before the public body's announcement of its decision; a contractor's protest, submitted in response to information that it would not be awarded a contract, was not capable of being appealed as it was filed before announcement of the award. John T. Moore & Assocs., P.C. v. Va. Commonwealth Univ., 69 Va. Cir. 200, 2005 Va. Cir. LEXIS 356 (Richmond 2005).

Failure to comply with invitational bid. — Because a bidder failed to submit a bid that complied with all of the requirements of a city's invitation to bid, it could not be considered a "bidder" for purposes of subsection C of § 2.2-4364, and therefore, lacked standing to bring a breach of contract action against the city; therefore, the city was entitled to summary judgment. Corr. Prods. Co. v. City of Alexandria, — Va. Cir. —, 2006 Va. Cir. LEXIS 278 (Alexandria Nov. 3, 2006).

ARTICLE 6.

Ethics in Public Contracting.

§ 2.2-4369. Proscribed participation by public employees in procurement transactions.

OPINIONS OF THE ATTORNEY GENERAL

Members of health regulatory boards. — It is not a violation of the State and Local Government Conflict of Interests Act or the Virginia Public Procurement Act for a member of a health regulatory board to vote to authorize the board to contract with or join an organization in the business of adminstering licensure examinations, where the Department of Health Professions reimburses the board member for per diem and expenses as allowable under state law and travel regulations. See opinion of Attorney General to Mr. Robert A. Nebiker, Director, Department of Health Professions, 05-029 (6/21/05).

It would be a violation of the State and Local Government Conflict of Interests Act or the Virginia Public Procurement Act for a board member to vote to approve a contract or to join an organization where, at the time of the vote, there is an existing arrangement concerning prospective employment of such board member after departure from the board or the board member accepts the payment of monies in excess of allowable per diem payments and travel reimbursement allowances. See opinion of Attorney General to Mr. Robert A. Nebiker, Director, Department of Health Professions, 05-029 (6/21/05).

Title 8.01.

Civil Remedies and Procedure.

CHAPTER 3.

ACTIONS.

Article 17.

Declaratory Judgments.

Sec.
8.01-187. Condemnation jurors to determine compensation for property taken or damaged.

Article 18.1.

Tort Claims Against the Commonwealth of Virginia.

Sec.
8.01-195.3. Commonwealth, transportation district or locality liable for damages in certain cases.
8.01-195.6. Notice of claim.

ARTICLE 17.

Declaratory Judgments.

§ 8.01-187. Condemnation jurors to determine compensation for property taken or damaged. — Whenever it is determined in a declaratory judgment proceeding that a person's property has been taken or damaged within the meaning of Article I, Section 11 of the Constitution of Virginia and compensation has not been paid or any action taken to determine the compensation within sixty days following the entry of such judgment order or decree, the court which entered the order or decree may, upon motion of such person after reasonable notice to the adverse party, enter a further order appointing condemnation jurors to determine the compensation. The appointment of condemnation jurors and all proceedings thereafter shall be governed by the procedure prescribed for the condemning authority. (Code 1950, § 8-581.1; 1968, c. 782; 1971, Ex. Sess., c. 1; 1977, c. 617; 2007, cc. 450, 720.)

The 2007 amendments. — The 2007 amendments by cc. 450 and 720 are identical, and substituted "Condemnation jurors" for "Commissioners" in the section catchline; and substituted "condemnation jurors" for "commissioners" in the first and last sentences.

ARTICLE 18.

Recovery of Claims Against the Commonwealth of Virginia.

§ 8.01-192. How claims to be prosecuted.

CIRCUIT COURT OPINIONS

Basic statutory requirements for filing pecuniary claim against Commonwealth met. — University's plea in bar was overruled as the developers complied with the basic statutory requirements for filing a pecuniary claim against the Commonwealth of Virginia; while a demand failed to make a demand for damages, an affiant averred that the developers discussed their damages claims with the university's president, who disallowed the claims. The developers' motion to amend their complaint to add the Virginia Comptroller as a necessary party was granted. Geographic Network Affiliates-International, Inc. v. Enter. for Empowerment Found., 69 Va. Cir. 428, 2006 Va. Cir. LEXIS 94 (Norfolk 2006).

§ 8.01-193. Defense and hearing.

CIRCUIT COURT OPINIONS

Motion to add comptroller as party granted. — University's plea in bar was overruled as the developers complied with the basic statutory requirements for filing a pecuniary claim against the

Commonwealth of Virginia; while a demand failed to make a demand for damages, an affiant averred that the developers discussed their damages claims with the university's president, who disallowed the claims. The developers' motion to amend their complaint to add the Virginia Comptroller as a necessary party was granted. Geographic Network Affiliates-International, Inc. v. Enter. for Empowerment Found., 69 Va. Cir. 428, 2006 Va. Cir. LEXIS 94 (Norfolk 2006).

ARTICLE 18.1.

Tort Claims Against the Commonwealth of Virginia.

§ 8.01-195.3. Commonwealth, transportation district or locality liable for damages in certain cases.

— Subject to the provisions of this article, the Commonwealth shall be liable for claims for money only accruing on or after July 1, 1982, and any transportation district shall be liable for claims for money only accruing on or after July 1, 1986, on account of damage to or loss of property or personal injury or death caused by the negligent or wrongful act or omission of any employee while acting within the scope of his employment under circumstances where the Commonwealth or transportation district, if a private person, would be liable to the claimant for such damage, loss, injury or death. However, except to the extent that a transportation district contracts to do so pursuant to § 15.2-4518, neither the Commonwealth nor any transportation district shall be liable for interest prior to judgment or for punitive damages. The amount recoverable by any claimant shall not exceed (i) $25,000 for causes of action accruing prior to July 1, 1988, $75,000 for causes of action accruing on or after July 1, 1988, or $100,000 for causes of action accruing on or after July 1, 1993, or (ii) the maximum limits of any liability policy maintained to insure against such negligence or other tort, if such policy is in force at the time of the act or omission complained of, whichever is greater, exclusive of interest and costs.

Notwithstanding any provision hereof, the individual immunity of judges, the Attorney General, attorneys for the Commonwealth, and other public officers, their agents and employees from tort claims for damages is hereby preserved to the extent and degree that such persons presently are immunized. Any recovery based on the following claims are hereby excluded from the provisions of this article:

1. Any claim against the Commonwealth based upon an act or omission which occurred prior to July 1, 1982.

1a. Any claim against a transportation district based upon an act or omission which occurred prior to July 1, 1986.

2. Any claim based upon an act or omission of the General Assembly or district commission of any transportation district, or any member or staff thereof acting in his official capacity, or to the legislative function of any agency subject to the provisions of this article.

3. Any claim based upon an act or omission of any court of the Commonwealth, or any member thereof acting in his official capacity, or to the judicial functions of any agency subject to the provisions of this article.

4. Any claim based upon an act or omission of an officer, agent or employee of any agency of government in the execution of a lawful order of any court.

5. Any claim arising in connection with the assessment or collection of taxes.

6. Any claim arising out of the institution or prosecution of any judicial or administrative proceeding, even if without probable cause.

7. Any claim by an inmate of a state correctional facility, as defined in § 53.1-1, unless the claimant verifies under oath, by affidavit, that he has exhausted his remedies under the adult institutional inmate grievance procedures promulgated by the Department of Corrections. The time for filing the notice of tort claim shall be tolled during the pendency of the grievance procedure.

Nothing contained herein shall operate to reduce or limit the extent to which the Commonwealth or any transportation district, agency or employee was deemed liable for negligence as of July 1, 1982, nor shall any provision of this article be applicable to any county, city or town in the Commonwealth or be so construed as to remove or in any way diminish the sovereign immunity of any county, city or town in the Commonwealth. (1981, c. 449; 1982, c. 397; 1986, c. 584; 1988, c. 884; 1989, c. 446; 1993, c. 481; 1998, cc. 203, 820; 2007, c. 250.)

The 2007 amendments. — The 2007 amendment by c. 250, deleted former subdivision 8, which read: "Any claim arising from the failure of a computer, software program, database, network, information system, firmware or any other device, whether operated by or on behalf of the Commonwealth of Virginia or one of its agencies, to interpret, produce, calculate, generate, or account for a date which is compatible with the 'Year 2000' date change."

CASE NOTES

Relationship with inmate statute. — To apply the limitations period of the inmate statute, § 8.01-243.2, to an inmate's negligence action against the Commonwealth of Virginia would have impliedly repealed the tolling provisions in subdivision 7 of § 8.01-195.3 of the Virginia Tort Claims Act, §§ 8.01-195.1 to 8.01-195.9; instead of such a disfavored result, the provisions could be harmonized, because the inmate statute applies to all classes of litigation pertaining to conditions of confinement, while the Act applies only to tort actions against the Commonwealth. Ogunde v. Commonwealth, 271 Va. 639, 628 S.E.2d 370, 2006 Va. LEXIS 45 (2006).

CIRCUIT COURT OPINIONS

Punitive damages prohibited. — Administrator of the deceased's estate could not recover punitive damages pursuant to § 8.01-195.3. Ahari v. Fairfax County, 71 Va. Cir. 268, 2006 Va. Cir. LEXIS 141 (Fairfax County 2006).

§ 8.01-195.6. Notice of claim.

— A. Every claim cognizable against the Commonwealth or a transportation district shall be forever barred unless the claimant or his agent, attorney or representative has filed a written statement of the nature of the claim, which includes the time and place at which the injury is alleged to have occurred and the agency or agencies alleged to be liable, within one year after such cause of action accrued. However, if the claimant was under a disability at the time the cause of action accrued, the tolling provisions of § 8.01-229 shall apply.

B. If the claim is against the Commonwealth, the statement shall be filed with the Director of the Division of Risk Management or the Attorney General. If the claim is against a transportation district the statement shall be filed with the chairman of the commission of the transportation district.

C. The notice is deemed filed when it is received in the office of the official to whom the notice is directed. The notice may be delivered by hand, by any form of United States mail service (including regular, certified, registered or overnight mail), or by commercial delivery service.

D. In any action contesting the filing of the notice of claim, the burden of proof shall be on the claimant to establish receipt of the notice in conformity with this section. A signed United States mail return receipt indicating the date of delivery, or any other form of signed and dated acknowledgment of delivery given by authorized personnel in the office of the official with whom the statement is filed, shall be prima facie evidence of filing of the notice under this section.

E. Claims against the Commonwealth involving medical malpractice shall be subject to the provisions of this article and to the provisions of Chapter 21.1 (§ 8.01-581.1 et seq.) of this title. However, the recovery in such a claim involving medical malpractice shall not exceed the limits imposed by § 8.01-195.3. (1981, c. 449; 1984, cc. 638, 698; 1986, c. 584; 1991, c. 23; 1992, c. 796; 2002, c. 207; 2007, c. 368.)

The 2007 amendments. — The 2007 amendment by c. 368, rewrote the section.

CASE NOTES

Applied in Ogunde v. Commonwealth, 271 Va. 639, 628 S.E.2d 370, 2006 Va. LEXIS 45 (2006).

CIRCUIT COURT OPINIONS

Notice not adequate. — Commonwealth's plea in bar was granted because the administrator had not adequately complied with the notice requirements of § 8.01-195.6 when the administrator's first notice was not mailed by certified mail and did not include the agency or agencies that the administrator alleged were liable. The second notice was again deficient for failing to name the agency allegedly liable, and no additional notices of claim were mailed in a timely manner. Ahari v. Fairfax County, 71 Va. Cir. 268, 2006 Va. Cir. LEXIS 141 (Fairfax County 2006).

§ 8.01-195.7. Statute of limitations.

CASE NOTES

Applicability to inmate's tort action. — Inmate's negligence action against the Commonwealth of Virginia was not time-barred by the inmate statute, § 8.01-243.2; instead, § 8.01-195.7, the statute of limitations of the Virginia Tort Claims Act, §§ 8.01-195.1 to 8.01-195.9, controlled the action even if it related to conditions of confinement because it was a tort claim against the Commonwealth. Ogunde v. Commonwealth, 271 Va. 639, 628 S.E.2d 370, 2006 Va. LEXIS 45 (2006).

Title 10.1.
Conservation.

SUBTITLE II.
ACTIVITIES ADMINISTERED BY OTHER ENTITIES.

CHAPTER 11.1.
DEPARTMENT OF ENVIRONMENTAL QUALITY.

Article 1.
General Provisions.

Sec.
10.1-1186.01. Reimbursements to localities for upgrades to treatment works.
10.1-1186.5.   [Expired.]

Article 2.
Environmental Impact Reports of State Agencies.

10.1-1188.   State agencies to submit environmental impact reports on major projects.

ARTICLE 1.
General Provisions.

§ 10.1-1186.01. Reimbursements to localities for upgrades to treatment works. — A. The General Assembly shall fund grants to finance the reasonable costs of design and installation of nutrient removal technology at the publicly owned treatment works designated as significant dischargers contained in subsection E, or as eligible nonsignificant dischargers as defined in § 10.1-2117. Notwithstanding § 10.1-2128, at such time as grant disbursements pursuant to this section reach 200 percent of the appropriations provided for in Chapter 951 of the Acts of Assembly of 2005 and Chapter 10 of the Acts of Assembly of 2006, Special Session I, the House Committee on Agriculture, Chesapeake and Natural Resources, the House Committee on

Appropriations, the Senate Committee on Agriculture, Conservation and Natural Resources, and the Senate Committee on Finance shall review the future funding needs to meet the purposes of the Water Quality Improvement Act and the appropriate funding mechanism for such needs.

B. The disbursement of grants for the design and installation of nutrient removal technology at those publicly owned treatment works included in subsection E and eligible nonsignificant dischargers shall be made as follows: (i) the first phase of a grant shall be disbursed upon written certification that 25% of the local share of the cost of nutrient removal technology for the project has been expended; (ii) the second phase upon written certification that 50% of the local share of the cost of nutrient removal technology for the project has been expended; (iii) the third phase upon written certification that 75% of the local share of the cost of the nutrient removal technology for the project has been expended; and (iv) the final phase upon written certification that 100% of the local share of the cost of the construction, expansion, or upgrade of nutrient removal technology for the project has been expended. The distribution of the grants shall be effected by one of the following methods:

1. In payments to be paid by the State Treasurer out of funds appropriated to the Water Quality Improvement Fund pursuant to § 10.1-2131;

2. Over a specified time through a contractual agreement entered into by the Treasury Board and approved by the Governor, on behalf of the Commonwealth, and the locality or public service authority undertaking the design and installation of nutrient removal technology, such payments to be paid by the State Treasurer out of funds appropriated to the Treasury Board; or

3. In payments to be paid by the State Treasurer upon request of the Director of Environmental Quality out of proceeds from bonds issued by the Virginia Public Building Authority, in consultation with the Department of Environmental Quality, pursuant to §§ 2.2-2261, 2.2-2263, and 2.2-2264, including the Commonwealth's share of the interest costs expended by the locality or regional authority for financing such project during the period from 50% completion of construction to final completion of construction.

C. The General Assembly shall have the sole authority to determine whether disbursement will be made pursuant to subdivision B 1, B 2, or B 3, or a combination thereof; provided that a disbursement shall only be made pursuant to subdivision B 3 upon a certification by the Department of Environmental Quality that project grant reimbursements for the fiscal year will exceed the available funds in the Water Quality Improvement Fund.

D. Exclusive of any deposits made pursuant to § 10.1-2128, the grants awarded pursuant to this section shall include such appropriations as provided for in Chapter 951 of the Acts of Assembly of 2005; and Chapter 10 of the Acts of Assembly of 2006, Special Session I.

E. The disbursement of grants to finance the costs of design and installation of nutrient removal technology at the following 89 publicly owned treatment works and other eligible nonsignificant dischargers shall be provided pursuant to the distribution methodology included in § 10.1-2131. However, in no case shall any publicly owned treatment works receive a grant of less than 35% of the costs of the design and installation of nutrient removal technology.

FACILITY NAME	OWNER
Shenandoah - Potomac River Basin	
ACSA-Fishersville STP	Augusta County Service Authority
Luray STP	Town of Luray
ACSA-Middle River Regional STP	Augusta County Service Authority
HRRSA-North River WWTF	Harrisonburg-Rockingham Regional Sewer Authority
ACSA-Stuarts Draft STP	Augusta County Service Authority
Waynesboro STP	City of Waynesboro
ACSA-Weyers Cave STP	Augusta County Service Authority
Berryville STP	Town of Berryville
Front Royal STP	Town of Front Royal
Mount Jackson STP	Town of Mount Jackson
New Market STP	Town of New Market
Shenandoah Co.-North Fork Regional WWTP	Shenandoah County
Stoney Creek Sanitary District STP	Stoney Creek Sanitary District
Strasburg STP	Town of Strasburg
Woodstock STP	Town of Woodstock
FWSA-Opequon Water Reclamation Facility	Frederick-Winchester Service Authority

FWSA-Parkins Mill WWTF	Frederick-Winchester Service Authority
Purcellville-Basham Simms WWTF	Town of Purcellville
LCSA-Broad Run WRF	Loudoun County Service Authority
Leesburg WPCF	Town of Leesburg
Round Hill WWTP	Town of Round Hill
PWCSA-H.L. Mooney WWTF	Prince William County Service Authority
Upper Occoquan Sewage Authority WWTP	Upper Occoquan Sewage Authority
FCW&SA-Vint Hill WWTF	Fauquier County Water and Sewer Authority
Alexandria Sanitation Authority WWTP	Alexandria Sanitation Authority
Arlington Co. WPCF	Arlington County
Fairfax Co. — Noman-Cole Pollution Control Facility	Fairfax County
Stafford Co.-Aquia WWTP	Stafford County
Colonial Beach STP	Town of Colonial Beach
Dahlgren Sanitary District WWTP	King George County Service Authority
Fairview Beach STP	King George County Service Authority
Purkins Corner WWTP	King George County Service Authority
District of Columbia - Blue Plains STP (Virginia portion)	Loudoun County Service Authority and Fairfax County contract for capacity
Rappahannock River Basin Culpeper WWTP	Town of Culpeper
Marshall WWTP	Town of Marshall
Mountain Run WWTP	Culpeper County
Orange STP	Town of Orange
Rapidan STP	Rapidan Service Authority
FCW&SA-Remington WWTP	Fauquier County Water and Sewer Authority
Warrenton STP	Town of Warrenton
Wilderness Shores WWTP	Rapidan Service Authority
Spotsylvania Co.-FMC WWTF	Spotsylvania County
Fredericksburg WWTF	City of Fredericksburg
Stafford Co.-Little Falls Run WWTF	Stafford County
Spotsylvania Co.-Massaponax WWTF	Spotsylvania County
Montross-Westmoreland WWTP	Westmoreland County
Oakland Park STP	King George County Service Authority
Tappahannock WWTP	Town of Tappahannock
Urbanna WWTP	Hampton Roads Sanitation District
Warsaw STP	Town of Warsaw
Reedville Sanitary District WWTP	Reedville Sanitary District
Kilmarnock WWTP	Town of Kilmarnock
York River Basin Caroline Co. Regional STP	Caroline County
Gordonsville STP	Rapidan Service Authority
Ashland WWTP	Hanover County
Doswell WWTP	Hanover County

HRSD-York River STP	Hampton Roads Sanitation District
Parham Landing WWTP	New Kent County
Totopotomoy WWTP	Hanover County
HRSD-West Point STP	Hampton Roads Sanitation District
HRSD-Mathews Courthouse STP	Hampton Roads Sanitation District
James River Basin	
Buena Vista STP	City of Buena Vista
Clifton Forge STP	Town of Clifton Forge
Covington STP	City of Covington
Lexington-Rockbridge Regional WQCF	Maury Service Authority
Alleghany Co.-Low Moor STP	Alleghany County
Alleghany Co.-Lower Jackson River WWTP	Alleghany County
Amherst-Rutledge Creek WWTP	Town of Amherst
Lynchburg STP	City of Lynchburg
RWSA-Moores Creek Regional STP	Rivanna Water and Sewer Authority
Crewe WWTP	Town of Crewe
Farmville WWTP	Town of Farmville
Chesterfield Co.-Falling Creek WWTP	Chesterfield County
Henrico Co. WWTP	Henrico County
Hopewell Regional WWTF	City of Hopewell
Chesterfield Co.-Proctors Creek WWTP	Chesterfield County
Richmond WWTP	City of Richmond
South Central Wastewater Authority WWTF	South Central Wastewater Authority
Chickahominy WWTP	New Kent County
HRSD-Boat Harbor STP	Hampton Roads Sanitation District
HRSD-James River STP	Hampton Roads Sanitation District
HRSD-Williamsburg STP	Hampton Roads Sanitation District
HRSD-Nansemond STP	Hampton Roads Sanitation District
HRSD-Army Base STP	Hampton Roads Sanitation District
HRSD-Virginia Initiative Plant STP	Hampton Roads Sanitation District
HRSD-Chesapeake/Elizabeth STP	Hampton Roads Sanitation District
Eastern Shore Basin	
Cape Charles WWTP	Town of Cape Charles
Onancock WWTP	Town of Onancock
Tangier Island WWTP	Town of Tangier

F. To the extent that any publicly owned treatment works receives less than the grant specified pursuant to § 10.1-2131, any year-end revenue surplus or unappropriated balances deposited in the Water Quality Improvement Fund, as required by § 10.1-2128, shall be prioritized in order to augment the funding of those projects for which grants have been prorated. Any additional reimbursements to these prorated projects shall not exceed the total reimbursement amount due pursuant to the formula established in subsection E of § 10.1-2131.

G. Notwithstanding the provisions of subsection B of § 10.1-2131, the Director of the Department of Environmental Quality shall not be required to enter into a grant agreement with a facility designated as a significant discharger or eligible nonsignificant discharger if the Director determines that the use of nutrient credits in accordance with the Chesapeake Bay Watershed Nutrient Credit Exchange Program (§ 62.1-44.19:12 et seq.) would be significantly more cost-effective than the installation of nutrient controls for the facility in question. (2007, cc. 851, 900.)

Editor's note. — Acts 2007, cc. 851 and 900, cl. 2 provides: "That the Department of Environmental Quality shall identify and evaluate options to ensure the efficient use of any grants authorized by the Water Quality Improvement Act (§ 10.1-2117 et seq. of the Code of Virginia). Any grant issued after October 1, 2007, shall include policies and guidelines governing the use of such grants that include the enforcement of appropriate cost control measures for the use of the grants. The Department shall work with representatives from local governments and the conservation community to evaluate the optimal use of existing and potential cost control measures, including but not limited to (i) evaluation of eligible and appropriate costs, (ii) applicability of the Virginia Public Procurement Act (§ 2.2-4300 et seq. of the Code of Virginia), (iii) voluntary nutrient credit trading, (iv) basing grant amounts on facility optimization using full life-cycle cost evaluation, (v) the ability to limit or exclude reimbursements based upon a comparison of costs to upgrade or build versus the purchase of credits, and (vi) the ability to prioritize grant agreements based upon the river-basin optimization plans. Such policies and procedures shall be developed no later than October 1, 2007."

Acts 2007, cc 851 and 900, cl. 3 provides: "That based upon a determination by the General Assembly pursuant to subsection C of § 10.1-1186.01 of the Code of Virginia to distribute the grants for the design and installation of nutrient removal technology at publicly owned treatment works designated as significant dischargers or as eligible nonsignificant dischargers as defined in § 10.1-2117 of the Code of Virginia through the use of bonds as provided for in subdivision B 3 of § 10.1-1186.01, the Virginia Public Building Authority is authorized to fund certain Water Quality Improvement Grants through the issuance of bonds as follows:

"§ 1. Pursuant to §§ 2.2-2261, 2.2-2263, and 2.2-2264 of the Code of Virginia, the Virginia Public Building Authority is hereby authorized to finance certain Virginia Water Quality Improvement Grants pursuant to Article 4 (§ 10.1-2128 et seq.) of Chapter 21.1 of Title 10.1 of the Code of Virginia, through the issuance of bonds, without limitation and together with other available funds. Such grants shall be used exclusively to fund a portion of some or all of the acquisition, design, construction, installation, equipping, improvement, or renovation of nutrient removal technology for significant dischargers contained in § 2 of this enactment and eligible nonsignificant dischargers as defined in § 10.1-2117 of the Code of Virginia.

"§ 2. The Virginia Public Building Authority is authorized to take any and all necessary, proper, or convenient steps and to exercise any and all powers granted to it by law to carry out the undertaking and financing contemplated by the provisions of this enactment, including the power to finance grants to fund a portion of the costs of any or all of the projects set forth in this act by the issuance of revenue bonds from time to time in an aggregate principal amount not to exceed $250 million, plus amounts needed to fund issuance costs, reserve funds, original issue discount, and other financing expenses.

"§ 3. The net proceeds of Virginia Public Building Authority bonds shall finance Virginia Water Quality Improvement Grants to fund or reimburse approved capital costs for each such project as and to the extent determined by the Department of Environmental Quality pursuant to the provisions of this enactment and of Article 4 (§ 10.1-2128 et seq.) of Chapter 21.1 of Title 10.1 of the Code of Virginia, including but not limited to the qualifications of projects for Virginia Water Quality Improvement Grants as set forth in §§ 10.1-2129, 10.1-2130, and 10.1-2131 and in written guidelines developed by the Secretary of Natural Resources in accordance with § 10.1-2129. Bond proceeds may not be used to pay debt service on

obligations of regional or local governments or authorities. A separate account shall be maintained for the grants under this enactment and for bonds issued to finance such grants. Upon certification to the Authority by the Department of Environmental Quality that a project qualifies for a grant under the provisions of this act and the provisions of Article 4 (§ 10.1-2128 et seq.) of Chapter 21.1 of Title 10.1 of the Code of Virginia and of the proposed amount and purpose of such grant, the Authority shall cause the disbursement of bond proceeds to fund such grant, but only to the extent of available funds therefore.

"§ 4. The proceeds of such bonds are hereby appropriated for disbursement from the state treasury pursuant to Article X, Section 7 of the Constitution of Virginia, and § 2.2-1819 of the Code of Virginia. Grants funded with proceeds of the bonds will be deposited in a separate account in the Virginia Water Quality Improvement Fund, pursuant to § 10.1-2128 of the Code of Virginia, which authorizes such Fund to consist of such other sums as may be made available to it from any other source, public or private. The general conditions and general provisions of a general appropriation act enacted by the General Assembly, in effect from time to time, and all of the terms and conditions contained therein shall apply to the capital projects listed in this act.

"§ 5. No bonds authorized pursuant to this enactment shall be issued prior to July 1, 2008."

Acts 2007, cc. 851 and 900, cl. 4, contains a severability clause.

Acts 2007, cc. 851 and 900, cl. 5 provides: "That all bonds issued heretofore by the Virginia Public Building Authority to provide funds to pay for all or any portion of the cost of one or more projects or portion thereof are hereby validated, ratified, approved, and confirmed."

§ 10.1-1186.5: Expired.

Editor's note. — Acts 2003, c. 738, cl. 2, provides: "That the provisions of this act shall be effective until submission of the final report." The final report was submitted November 15, 2005. See House Document 103 (2005).

ARTICLE 2.

Environmental Impact Reports of State Agencies.

§ 10.1-1188. State agencies to submit environmental impact reports on major projects. —
A. All state agencies, boards, authorities and commissions or any branch of the state government shall prepare and submit an environmental impact report to the Department on each major state project.

"Major state project" means the acquisition of an interest in land for any state facility construction, or the construction of any facility or expansion of an existing facility which is hereafter undertaken by any state agency, board, commission, authority or any branch of state government, including state-supported institutions of higher learning, which costs $100,000 or more. For the purposes of this chapter, authority shall not include any industrial development authority created pursuant to the provisions of Chapter 49 (§ 15.2-4900 et seq.) of Title 15.2 or Chapter 643, as amended, of the 1964 Acts of Assembly. Nor shall authority include any housing development or redevelopment authority established pursuant to state law. For the purposes of this chapter, branch of state government shall apply to any county, city or town of the Commonwealth only in connection with highway construction, reconstruction, or improvement projects affecting highways or roads undertaken by the county, city, or town.

Such environmental impact report shall include, but not be limited to, the following:

1. The environmental impact of the major state project, including the impact on wildlife habitat;

2. Any adverse environmental effects which cannot be avoided if the major state project is undertaken;

3. Measures proposed to minimize the impact of the major state project;

4. Any alternatives to the proposed construction; and

5. Any irreversible environmental changes which would be involved in the major state project.

For the purposes of subdivision 4 of this subsection, the report shall contain all alternatives considered and the reasons why the alternatives were rejected. If a report does not set forth alternatives, it shall state why alternatives were not considered.

B. For purposes of this chapter, this subsection shall only apply to the review of highway and road construction projects or any part thereof. The Secretaries of Transportation and Natural Resources shall jointly establish procedures for review and comment by state natural and historic resource agencies of highway and road construction projects. Such procedures shall provide for review and comment on appropriate projects and categories of projects to address the environmental impact of the project, any adverse environmental effects which cannot be avoided if the project is undertaken, the measures proposed to minimize the impact of the project, any alternatives to the proposed construction, and any irreversible environmental changes which would be involved in the project. (1973, c. 384, § 10-17.108; 1974, c. 270, § 10.1-1208; 1977, c. 667; 1988, c. 891; 1991, c. 289; 1992, c. 887; 1997, c. 268; 2007, c. 896.)

Editor's note. — Acts 2006, Sp. Sess. I, c. 3, as amended by Acts 2007, c. 847, effective for the biennium ending June 30, 2008, in § 4-4.01 i. 2., provides: "i. Initiation Generally:

"2. The requirements of § 10.1-1190, Code of Virginia, shall be met prior to the release of funds for a major state project, provided, however, that the Governor is authorized to release from any appropriation for a major state project made pursuant to this act such sum or sums as may be necessary to pay for the preparation of the environmental impact report required by § 10.1-1188, Code of Virginia."

Acts 2007, c. 896, cl. 23 contains a severability clause.

The 2007 amendments. — The 2007 amendment by c. 896 substituted "apply to" for "not include" and inserted "only in connection with highway construction, reconstruction, or improvement projects affecting highways or roads undertaken by the county, city, or town" in the last sentence in the definition of "Major state project"; and substituted "only" for "not" in the first sentence of subsection B.

§ 10.1-1190. Approval of Governor required for construction of facility.

Editor's note. — Acts 2006, Sp. Sess. I, c. 3, as amended by Acts 2007, c. 847, effective for the biennium ending June 30, 2008, in

§ 4-4.01 i. 2., provides: "i. Initiation Generally:

"2. The requirements of § 10.1-1190, Code of Virginia, shall be met prior to the release of funds for a major state project, provided, however, that the Governor is authorized to release from any appropriation for a major state project made pursuant to this act such sum or sums as may be necessary to pay for the preparation of the environmental impact report required by § 10.1-1188, Code of Virginia."

SUBTITLE III.

ACTIVITIES ADMINISTERED BY THE DEPARTMENT OF HISTORIC RESOURCES.

CHAPTER 22.

Historic Resources.

Article 1.

Department of Historic Resources.

§ 10.1-2202.1. Historic Resources Fund established; administration; purpose.

Editor's note. — Acts 2006, Sp. Sess. I, c. 3, as amended by Acts 2007, c. 847, effective for the biennium ending June 30, 2008, in Item 370 F, provides: "The Department of Historic Resources is authorized to accept a devise of certain real property under the will of Elizabeth Rust Williams known as Clermont Farm located on Route 7 east of the town of Berryville in Clarke County. If, after due consideration of options, the department determines that the property should be sold or leased to a different public or private entity, and notwithstanding the provisions of § 2.2-1156, Code of Virginia, the department is further authorized to sell or lease such property, provided such sale or lease is not in conflict with the terms of the will. The proceeds of any such sale or lease shall be deposited to the Historic Resources Fund established under § 10.1-2202.1, Code of Virginia."

Title 11.

Contracts.

CHAPTER 1.

General Provisions.

Sec.
11-4.5. Certain indemnification provisions in motor carrier transportation contracts declared void.

§ 11-4.5. Certain indemnification provisions in motor carrier transportation contracts declared void. — A. As used in this section:

"Motor carrier transportation contract" means a contract, agreement, or understanding covering:

1. The transportation of property for compensation or hire by the motor carrier;

2. The entrance on property by the motor carrier for the purpose of loading, unloading, or transporting property for compensation or for hire; or

3. A service incidental to activity described in subdivision 1 or 2 including, but not limited to, storage of property.

For the purposes of this section, the term "motor carrier transportation contract" shall not include the Uniform Intermodal Interchange and Facilities Access Agreement administered by the Intermodal Association of North America, as that agreement may be amended by the Intermodal Interchange Executive Committee, or other agreements providing for the interchange, use, or possession of intermodal chassis, containers, or other intermodal equipment.

B. A provision, clause, covenant, or agreement contained in, collateral to, or affecting a motor carrier transportation contract that purports to indemnify, or hold harmless, or has the effect of indemnifying, or holding harmless, either party from or against any liability for loss or damage resulting from the negligence or intentional acts or omissions of other party, or any agents, employees, servants, or independent contractors who are directly responsible to the other party, is against the public policy and is void and unenforceable.

C. Nothing contained in this section affects a provision, clause, covenant, or agreement where the motor carrier indemnifies or holds harmless the other party against liability for damages to the extent that the damages were caused by and resulting from the negligence of the motor carrier, its agents, employees, servants, or independent contractors who, in whole or in part are directly responsible to the motor carrier. (2006, cc. 237, 423.)

Title 15.2.

Counties, Cities and Towns.

SUBTITLE II.

POWERS OF LOCAL GOVERNMENT.

CHAPTER 9.

GENERAL POWERS OF LOCAL GOVERNMENTS.

Article 5.

Additional Powers.

Sec.
15.2-968.1. Use of photo-monitoring systems to enforce traffic light signals.

ARTICLE 5.

Additional Powers.

§ 15.2-968.1. Use of photo-monitoring systems to enforce traffic light signals. — A. The governing body of any county, city, or town may provide by ordinance for the establishment of a traffic signal enforcement program imposing monetary liability on the operator of a motor vehicle for failure to comply with traffic light signals in such locality in accordance with the provisions of this section. Each such locality may install and operate traffic light signal photo-monitoring systems at no more than one intersection for every 10,000 residents within each county, city, or town at any one time, provided, however, that within planning District 8, each study locality may install and operate traffic light signal photo-monitoring systems at no more than 10 intersections, or at no more than one intersection for every 10,000 residents within each county, city, or town, whichever is greater, at any one time.

B. The operator of a vehicle shall be liable for a monetary penalty imposed pursuant to this section if such vehicle is found, as evidenced by information obtained from a traffic light signal violation monitoring system, to have failed to comply with a traffic light signal within such locality.

C. Proof of a violation of this section shall be evidenced by information obtained from a traffic light signal violation monitoring system authorized pursuant to this section. A certificate, sworn to or affirmed by a law-enforcement officer employed by a locality authorized to impose penalties pursuant to this section, or a facsimile thereof, based upon inspection of photographs, microphotographs, videotape, or other recorded images produced by a traffic light signal violation monitoring system, shall be prima facie evidence of the facts contained therein. Any photographs, microphotographs, videotape, or other recorded images evidencing such a violation shall be available for inspection in any proceeding to adjudicate the liability for such violation pursuant to an ordinance adopted pursuant to this section.

D. In the prosecution for a violation of any local ordinance adopted as provided in this section, prima facie evidence that the vehicle described in the summons issued pursuant to this section was operated in violation of such ordinance, together with proof that the defendant was at the time of such violation the owner, lessee, or renter of the vehicle, shall constitute in evidence a rebuttable presumption that such owner, lessee, or renter of the vehicle was the person who committed the violation. Such presumption shall be rebutted if the owner, lessee, or renter of the vehicle (i) files an affidavit by regular mail with the clerk of the general district court that he was not the operator of the vehicle at the time of the alleged violation or (ii) testifies in open court under oath that he was not the operator of the vehicle at the time of the alleged violation. Such presumption shall also be rebutted if a certified copy of a police report, showing that the vehicle had been reported to the police as stolen prior to the time of the alleged violation of this section, is presented, prior to the return date established on the summons issued pursuant to this section, to the court adjudicating the alleged violation.

E. For purposes of this section, "owner" means the registered owner of such vehicle on record with the Department of Motor Vehicles. For purposes of this section, "traffic light signal violation monitoring system" means a vehicle sensor installed to work in conjunction with a traffic light that automatically produces two or more photographs, two or more microphotographs, video, or other recorded images of each vehicle at the time it is used or operated in violation of § 46.2-833, 46.2-835, or 46.2-836. For each such vehicle, at least one recorded image shall be of the vehicle before it has illegally entered the intersection, and at least one recorded image shall be of the same vehicle after it has illegally entered that intersection.

F. Imposition of a penalty pursuant to this section shall not be deemed a conviction as an operator and shall not be made part of the operating record of the person upon whom such liability is imposed, nor shall it be used for insurance purposes in the provision of motor vehicle insurance coverage. No monetary penalty imposed under this section shall exceed $50, nor shall it include court costs.

G. A summons for a violation of this section may be executed pursuant to § 19.2-76.2. Notwithstanding the provisions of § 19.2-76, a summons for a violation of this section may be executed by mailing by first class mail a copy thereof to the owner, lessee, or renter of the vehicle. In the case of a vehicle owner, the copy shall be mailed to the address contained in the records of the Department of Motor Vehicles; in the case of a vehicle lessee or renter, the copy shall be mailed to the address contained in the records of the lessor or renter. Every such mailing shall include, in addition to the summons, a notice of (i) the summoned person's ability to rebut the presumption that he was the operator of the vehicle at the time of the alleged violation through the filing of an affidavit as provided in subsection D and (ii) instructions for filing such affidavit, including the address to which the affidavit is to be sent. If the summoned person fails to appear on the date of return set out in the summons mailed pursuant to this section, the summons shall be executed in the manner set out in § 19.2-76.3. No proceedings for contempt or arrest of a person summoned by mailing shall be instituted for failure to appear on the return date of the summons. Any summons executed for a violation of this section shall provide to the person summoned at least 60 business days from the mailing of the summons to inspect information collected by a traffic light signal violation monitoring system in connection with the violation.

H. Information collected by a traffic light signal violation monitoring system installed and operated pursuant to subsection A shall be limited exclusively to that information that is necessary for the enforcement of traffic light violations. On behalf of a locality, a private entity may not obtain records regarding the registered owners of vehicles that fail to comply with traffic light signals. Notwithstanding any other provision of law, all photographs, microphotographs, electronic images, or other personal information collected by a traffic light signal violation monitoring system shall be used exclusively for enforcing traffic light violations and shall not (i) be open to the public; (ii) be sold or used for sales, solicitation, or marketing purposes; (iii) be disclosed to any other entity except as may be necessary for the enforcement of a traffic light violation or to a vehicle owner or operator as part of a challenge to the violation; or (iv) be used in a court in a pending action or proceeding unless the action or proceeding relates to a violation of § 46.2-833, 46.2-835, or 46.2-836 or requested upon order from a court of competent jurisdiction. Information collected under this section pertaining to a specific violation shall be purged and not retained later than 60 days after the collection of any civil penalties. If a locality does not execute a summons for a violation of this section within 10 business days, all information collected pertaining to that suspected violation shall be purged within two business days. Any locality operating a traffic light signal violation monitoring system shall annually certify compliance with this section and make all records pertaining to such system available for inspection and audit by the Commonwealth Transportation Commissioner or the Commissioner of the Department of Motor Vehicles or his designee. Any person who discloses personal information in violation of the provisions of this subsection shall be subject to a civil penalty of $1,000.

I. A private entity may enter into an agreement with a locality to be compensated for providing the traffic light signal violation monitoring system or equipment, and all related support services, to include consulting, operations and administration. However, only a law-enforcement officer employed by a locality may swear to or affirm the certificate required by subsection C. No locality shall enter into an agreement for compensation based on the number of violations or monetary penalties imposed.

J. When selecting potential intersections for a traffic light signal violation monitoring system, a locality shall consider factors such as (i) the accident rate for the intersection, (ii) the rate of red light violations occurring at the intersection (number of violations per number of vehicles), (iii) the difficulty experienced by law-enforcement officers in patrol cars or on foot in apprehending violators, and (iv) the ability of law-enforcement officers to apprehend violators safely within a reasonable distance from the violation. Localities may consider the risk to pedestrians as a factor, if applicable. A locality shall submit a list of intersections to the Virginia Department of Transportation for final approval.

K. Before the implementation of a traffic light signal violation monitoring system at an intersection, the locality shall complete an engineering safety analysis that addresses signal timing and other location-specific safety features. The length of the yellow phase shall be established based on the recommended methodology of the Institute of Transportation Engineers. All traffic light signal violation monitoring systems shall provide a minimum 0.5-second grace period between the time the signal turns red and the time the first violation is recorded. If recommended by the engineering safety analysis, the locality shall make reasonable location-specific safety improvements, including signs and pavement markings.

L. Any locality that uses a traffic light signal violation monitoring system shall evaluate the system on a monthly basis to ensure all cameras and traffic signals are functioning properly. Evaluation results shall be made available to the public.

M. Any locality that uses a traffic light signal violation monitoring system to enforce traffic light signals shall place conspicuous signs within 500 feet of the intersection approach at which a traffic light signal violation monitoring system is used. There shall be a rebuttable presumption that such signs were in place at the time of the commission of the traffic light signal violation.

N. Prior to or coincident with the implementation or expansion of a traffic light signal violation monitoring system, a locality shall conduct a public awareness program, advising the public that the locality is implementing or expanding a traffic light signal violation monitoring system. (2007, cc. 836, 903.)

CHAPTER 12.

GENERAL POWERS AND PROCEDURES OF COUNTIES.

Article 1.

Miscellaneous Powers.

Sec.
15.2-1209.1. Counties may regulate carrying of loaded firearms on public highways.

ARTICLE 1.

Miscellaneous Powers.

§ 15.2-1209.1. Counties may regulate carrying of loaded firearms on public highways. — The governing body of any county is hereby empowered to adopt ordinances making it unlawful for any person to carry or have in his possession, for the purpose of hunting, while on any part of a public highway within such county a loaded firearm when such person is not authorized to hunt on the private property on both sides of the highway along which he is standing or walking; and to provide a penalty for violation of such ordinance not to exceed a fine of $100. The provisions of this section shall not apply to persons carrying loaded firearms in moving vehicles or for purposes other than hunting, or to persons acting at the time in defense of persons or property. (Code 1950, § 18.1-272; 1975, cc. 14, 15, § 18.2-287; 2004, c. 462; 2007, c. 203.)

The 2007 amendments. — The 2007 amendment by c. 203 inserted "for the purpose of hunting" in the first sentence and "or for purposes other than hunting" in the second sentence.

CHAPTER 18.

BUILDINGS, MONUMENTS AND LANDS GENERALLY.

Article 1.

Purchase, Sale, etc., of Real Property.

Sec.
15.2-1800. Purchase, sale, use, etc., of real property.

ARTICLE 1.

Purchase, Sale, etc., of Real Property.

§ 15.2-1800. Purchase, sale, use, etc., of real property. — A. A locality may acquire by purchase, gift, devise, bequest, exchange, lease as lessee, or otherwise, title to, or any interests in, any real property, whether improved or unimproved, within its jurisdiction, for any public use. Acquisition of any interest in real property by condemnation is governed by Chapter 19 (§ 15.2-1901 et seq.). The acquisition of a leasehold or other interest in a telecommunications tower, owned by a nongovernmental source, for the operation of a locality's wireless radio communications systems shall be governed by this chapter.

B. Subject to any applicable requirements of Article VII, Section 9 of the Constitution, any locality may sell, at public or private sale, exchange, lease as lessor, mortgage, pledge, subordinate interest in or otherwise dispose of its real property, which includes the superjacent airspace (except airspace provided for in § 15.2-2030) which may be subdivided and conveyed separate from the subjacent land surface, provided that no such real property, whether improved or unimproved, shall be disposed of until the governing body has held a public hearing concerning such disposal. However, the holding of a public hearing shall not apply to (i) the leasing of real property to another public body, political subdivision or authority of the Commonwealth or (ii) conveyance of site development easements across public property, including, but not limited to, easements for ingress, egress, utilities, cable, telecommunications, storm water management, and other similar conveyances, that are consistent with the local capital improvement program, involving improvement of property owned by the locality. The provisions of this section shall not apply to the vacation of public interests in real property under the provisions of Articles 6 (§ 15.2-2240 et seq.) and 7 (§ 15.2-2280 et seq.) of Chapter 22 of this title.

C. A city or town may also acquire real property for a public use outside its boundaries; a county may acquire real property for a public use outside its boundaries when expressly authorized by law.

D. A locality may construct, insure, and equip buildings, structures and other improvements on real property owned or leased by it.

E. A locality may operate, maintain, and regulate the use of its real property or may contract with other persons to do so.

Notwithstanding any contrary provision of law, general or special, no locality providing access and opportunity to use its real property, whether improved or unimproved, may deny equal access or a fair opportunity to use such real property to, or otherwise discriminate against, the Boy Scouts of America or the Girl Scouts of the USA. Nothing in this paragraph shall be construed to require any locality to sponsor the Boy Scouts of America or the Girl Scouts of the USA, or to exempt any such groups from local policies governing access to and use of a locality's real property. The provisions of this paragraph applicable to a locality shall also apply equally to any local governmental entity, including a department, agency, or authority.

F. This section shall not be construed to deprive the resident judge or judges of the right to control the use of the courthouse.

G. *"Public use"* as used in this section shall have the same meaning as in § 1-219.1. (Code 1950, § 15-692; 1962, c. 623, § 15.1-262; 1968, c. 418; 1974, c. 282; 1977, c. 269; 1979, c. 431; 1980, cc. 212, 559; 1984, c. 241; 1986, cc. 477, 573; 1990, c. 813; 1997, c. 587; 1998, c. 696; 2005, c. 822; 2006, c. 57; 2007, cc. 882, 901, 926.)

Editor's note. — Acts 2007, cc. 882, 901 and 926, cl. 3, provides: "That, until July 1, 2010, the provisions of this act shall not affect the ability of a redevelopment and housing authority organized pursuant to Title 36 of the Code of Virginia to acquire property pursuant to any redevelopment or conservation plan adopted prior to January 1, 2007. However, the provisions of this act shall be applicable to all redevelopment and conservation plans adopted after January 1, 2007."

Acts 2007, cc. 882, 901 and 926, cl. 4, provides: "Nothing contained in this act shall prohibit the Norfolk Redevelopment and Housing Authority or the City of Norfolk to acquire property through the use of eminent domain for the location of a recreational facility open to the public to be owned or operated by a not-for-profit entity, provided such acquisitions are instituted prior to July 1, 2010."

The 2007 amendments. — The 2007 amendments by cc. 882, 901 and 926 are identical, and substituted "15.2-1901" for "15.2-1900" in the next-to-last sentence of subsection A; and substituted "1-237.1" [now § 1-219.1] for "15.2-1900" in subsection G.

CHAPTER 19.

CONDEMNATION.

§ 15.2-1904. Possession of property prior to condemnation; authority to utilize expedited acquisition procedure conferred.

CIRCUIT COURT OPINIONS

Taking was for public use. — Landowners' plea in bar was denied as: (1) the purpose of a taking was to facilitate proper storm water runoff into the City's storm sewer system, (2) the public use predominated any private benefit, regardless of any incidental benefit to a developer, (3) the City Council's decree was not without reasonable foundation, (4) the storm sewer box culvert would be held by the City, the terms and manner of enjoyment of the sewer were within the City's control, and it would benefit the public, and (5) the fact that the underlying motivation for the relocation of the storm sewer box culvert was the implementation and development of the Eisenhower East Small Area Plan did not diminish the public use of the taking. City of Alexandria v. Hoffman Family, LLC, 70 Va. Cir. 22, 2005 Va. Cir. LEXIS 309 (Alexandria 2005), aff'd, — Va. —, 634 S.E.2d 722 (2006).

CHAPTER 20.

STREETS AND ALLEYS.

Article 1.

Construction of Roads, Streets and Alleys Generally.

Sec.
15.2-2000. State highway systems excepted; town streets.
15.2-2001. Streets, sidewalks and public rights-of-way generally.

Article 2.

Vacation, etc., of Public Rights-of-Way.

15.2-2007.1. Appointment of viewers in certain cities.

ARTICLE 1.

Construction of Roads, Streets and Alleys Generally.

§ 15.2-2000. State highway systems excepted; town streets. — A. Nothing contained in this chapter, except as otherwise provided, shall apply to any highway, road, street or other public right-of-way which constitutes a part of any system of state highways; however, any highway for which a locality receives highway maintenance funds pursuant to § 33.1-23.5:1 or 33.1-41.1 shall not, for purposes of this section, be deemed to be a part of any system of state highways.

B. Public rights-of-way subject to local control under this chapter which lie within the boundaries of incorporated towns which receive highway maintenance funds pursuant to § 33.1-41.1 shall be subject to the jurisdiction of the town council of such town and not the board of supervisors of the county in which such town is located.

C. The term *"public right-of-way"* as used in this chapter means any area over which the public has a general privilege to travel. It includes, but is not limited to, ways, areas between deeded right-of-way boundary lines, and easements of all descriptions that are available for general travel by the public. (Code 1950, § 15-77.59:1; 1958, c. 328; 1962, c. 623, § 15.1-896; 1994, c. 177; 1997, c. 587; 2005, c. 839.)

The 2005 amendments. — The 2005 amendment by c. 839, effective October 1, 2005, in subsection A, deleted "as defined in § 1-13.40" preceding "however, any highways" and made a minor stylistic change.

§ 15.2-2001. Streets, sidewalks and public rights-of-way generally.

— Every locality may lay out, open, extend, widen, narrow, establish or change the grade of, close, construct, pave, curb, gutter, plant and maintain shade trees on, improve, maintain, repair, clean and light: streets, limited access highways, express highways, roads, alleys, bridges, viaducts, subways and underpasses. Localities may make, improve and repair sidewalks upon all public rights-of-way and may convert sidewalks to bicycle paths. A locality's power and authority over its public rights-of-way and other public places shall be the same, regardless of whether the public right-of-way or place has been expressly or impliedly dedicated to public use, has been conveyed to the locality by deed, or has been acquired by any other means.

Furthermore, any locality may establish highway user fees for highways that are not part of any system of state highways when such highway's traffic-carrying capacity is increased by construction or improvement. (Code 1950, § 15-77.53; 1958, c. 328; 1962, c. 623, § 15.1-889; 1974, c. 407; 1997, c. 587; 2006, c. 924.)

The 2006 amendments. — The 2006 amendment by c. 924 added the second paragraph.

Law Review. — For note, "Virginia Subdivision Law: An Unreasonable Burden on the Unwary," see 34 Wash. & Lee L. Rev. 1223 (1977).

ARTICLE 2.

Vacation, etc., of Public Rights-of-Way.

§ 15.2-2007.1. Appointment of viewers in certain cities.

— Notwithstanding the provisions of § 15.2-2006, the City of Virginia Beach may by ordinance appoint three to five viewers for terms of one year to view each and every street or alley proposed to be altered or vacated during the term. The notice requirements of § 15.2-2204 shall be complied with for each hearing regarding discontinuance of the street or alley proposed to be altered or vacated. The applicant for closure of streets or alleys in such cities that have appointed viewers pursuant to this section shall not be required to advertise, and the governing body shall not be required to hold a separate hearing, for appointment of viewers for each specific street or alley proposed to be altered or vacated. The applicant and the governing body of such city shall comply with all other provisions of § 15.2-2006. (1997, c. 742, § 15.1-364.2; 2007, c. 813.)

Editor's note. — Acts 2007, c. 813, cl. 2, provides: "That the provisions of this act shall not affect the powers of any locality with respect to any ordinance, resolution or bylaw validly adopted and not repealed or rescinded prior to July 1, 2007."

The 2007 amendments. — The 2007 amendment by c. 813 substituted "the City of Virginia Beach" for "any city with a population greater than 350,000" near the beginning of the first sentence.

CHAPTER 22.

PLANNING, SUBDIVISION OF LAND AND ZONING.

Article 1.

General Provisions.

Sec.
15.2-2202.   Duties of state agencies; electric utilities.
15.2-2204.   Advertisement of plans, ordinances, etc.; joint public hearings; written notice of certain amendments.

Article 2.

Local Planning Commissions.

15.2-2220.   Duplicate planning commission authorized for certain local governments.
15.2-2222.1.   Coordination of state and local transportation planning.

Article 3.

The Comprehensive Plan.

15.2-2223.   Comprehensive plan to be prepared and adopted; scope and purpose.
15.2-2223.1.   Comprehensive plan to include urban development areas; new urbanism.
15.2-2224.   Surveys and studies to be made in preparation of plan; implementation of plan.
15.2-2232.   Legal status of plan.

Article 6.

Land Subdivision and Development.

15.2-2241.1.   Bonding requirements for the acceptance of dedication for public use of certain facilities.
15.2-2242.   Optional provisions of a subdivision ordinance.
15.2-2244.1.   Additional method for subdivision of a lot for conveyance to a family member.
15.2-2259.   Local planning commission to act on proposed plat.
15.2-2260.   Localities may provide for submission of preliminary subdivision plats; how long valid.
15.2-2263.   Expedited land development review procedure.
15.2-2266.   Validation of certain plats recorded before January 1, 1975.
15.2-2269.   Plans and specifications for utility fixtures and systems to be submitted for approval.

Article 7.

Zoning.

15.2-2283.1.   Prohibition of sexual offender treatment office in residentially zoned subdivision.

Sec.
15.2-2286. Permitted provisions in zoning ordinances; amendments; applicant to pay delinquent taxes; penalties.
15.2-2288.3. Licensed farm wineries; local regulation of certain activities.
15.2-2291. Group homes of eight or fewer single-family residence.
15.2-2298. Same; additional conditions as a part of rezoning or zoning map amendment in certain high-growth localities.
15.2-2303.1. Development agreements in certain counties.
15.2-2303.2. Proffered cash payments and expenditures.
15.2-2305. Affordable dwelling unit ordinances.
15.2-2308. Boards of zoning appeals to be created; membership, organization, etc.
15.2-2314. Certiorari to review decision of board.

Article 7.1.

Transfer of Development Rights.

15.2-2316.1. Definitions.
15.2-2316.2. Localities may provide for transfer of development rights.

Article 8.

Road Impact Fees.

15.2-2317. Applicability of article.
15.2-2318. Definitions.
15.2-2319. Authority to assess and impose impact fees.
15.2-2320. Impact fee service areas to be established.
15.2-2321. Adoption of road improvements program.
15.2-2322. Adoption of impact fee and schedule.
15.2-2323. When impact fees assessed and imposed.
15.2-2324. Credits against impact fee.
15.2-2325. Updating plan and amending impact fee.
15.2-2326. Use of proceeds.
15.2-2327. Refund of impact fees.

Article 9.

Impact Fees.

15.2-2328. Applicability of article.
15.2-2329. Imposition of impact fees.

ARTICLE 1.

General Provisions.

§ 15.2-2200. Declaration of legislative intent.

CIRCUIT COURT OPINIONS

State health commissioner's issuance of certificate of need does not deprive county of ability to make land use decisions. — That the Virginia State Heath Commissioner issued a hospital owner a certificate of public need to build an acute care hospital did not prevent a county board of supervisors from denying the owner's application to build it in a specific location. The board could exercise its authority to make land use decisions without undermining the Commissioner's authority to evaluate health needs and to authorize the construction of health care facilities where needed. N. Va. Cmty. Hosp., L.L.C. v. Loudoun County Bd. of Supervisors, 70 Va. Cir. 283, 2006 Va. Cir. LEXIS 168 (Loudoun County 2006).

§ 15.2-2202. Duties of state agencies; electric utilities. — A. The Department of Environmental Quality shall distribute a copy of the environmental impact report submitted to the Department for every major state project pursuant to regulations promulgated under § 10.1-1191 to the chief administrative officer of every locality in which each project is proposed to be located. The purpose of the distribution is to enable the locality to evaluate the proposed project for environmental impact, consistency with the locality's comprehensive plan, local ordinances adopted pursuant to this chapter, and other applicable law and to provide the locality with an opportunity to comment. The Department shall distribute the reports to localities, solicit their comments, and consider their responses in substantially the same manner as the Department solicits and receives comments from state agencies.

B. In addition to the information supplied under subsection A, every department, board, bureau, commission, or other agency of the Commonwealth which is responsible for the construction, operation, or maintenance of public facilities within any locality shall, upon the request of the local planning commission having authority to prepare a comprehensive plan, furnish reasonable information requested by the local planning commission relative to the master plans of the state agency which may affect the locality's comprehensive plan. Each state agency shall collaborate and cooperate with the local planning commission, when requested, in the preparation of the comprehensive plan to the end that the local comprehensive plan will coordinate the interests and responsibilities of all concerned.

C. Every state agency responsible for the construction, operation or maintenance of public facilities within the Commonwealth shall notify the chief administrative officer of every locality in which the agency intends to undertake a capital project involving new construction costing at least $100,000. The notice shall be given during the planning phase of the project and prior to preparation of construction and site plans and shall inform localities that preliminary construction and site plans will be available for distribution, upon the request of the locality. Agencies shall not be required to give such notice prior to acquisition of property. The purpose of the notice and distribution is to enable the locality to evaluate the project for consistency with local ordinances other than building codes and to provide the locality with an opportunity to submit comments to the agency during the planning phase of a project. Upon receipt of a request from a locality, the state agency shall transmit a copy of the plans to the locality for comment.

D. Every electric utility that is responsible for the construction, operation, and maintenance of electric transmission lines of 150 kilovolts or more shall furnish reasonable information requested by the local planning commission having authority to prepare a comprehensive plan within the utility's certificated service area relative to any electric transmission line of 150 kilovolts or more that may affect the locality's comprehensive plan. If the locality seeks to include the designation of corridors or routes for electric transmission lines of 150 kilovolts or more in its comprehensive plan, the local planning commission shall give the electric utility a reasonable opportunity for consultation about such corridors or routes. The electric utility shall notify the chief administrative officer of every locality in which the electric utility plans to undertake construction of any electric transmission line of 150 kilovolts or more, prior to the filing of any application for approval of such construction with the State Corporation Commission, of its intention to file any such application and shall give the locality a reasonable opportunity for consultation about such line.

E. Nothing in this section shall be construed to require any state agency or electric utility to duplicate any submission required to be made by the agency or the electric utility to a locality under any other provision of law.

F. Nothing herein shall be deemed to abridge the authority of any state agency or the State Corporation Commission regarding the facilities now or hereafter coming under its jurisdiction.

G. The provisions of this section shall not apply to highway, transit or other projects, as provided in § 10.1-1188 B.

H. The provisions of this section shall not apply to the entering of any option by any state agency or electric utility for any projects listed in subsection C or D. (1993, c. 786, § 15.1-428.1; 1997, c. 587; 2001, c. 281; 2007, c. 761.)

The 2007 amendments. — The 2007 amendment by c. 761 inserted subsection D and redesignated the remaining subsections accordingly; inserted "or electric utility" twice in subsection E and in subsection H; inserted "or the State Corporation Commission" in subsection F; and added "or D" to the end of subsection H.

§ 15.2-2204. Advertisement of plans, ordinances, etc.; joint public hearings; written notice of certain amendments. — A. Plans or ordinances, or amendments thereof, recommended or adopted under the powers conferred by this chapter need not be advertised in full, but may be advertised by reference. Every such advertisement shall contain a descriptive summary of the proposed action and a reference to the place or places within the locality where copies of the proposed plans, ordinances or amendments may be examined.

The local planning commission shall not recommend nor the governing body adopt any plan, ordinance or amendment thereof until notice of intention to do so has been published once a week for two successive weeks in some newspaper published or having general circulation in the locality; however, the notice for both the local planning commission and the governing body may be published concurrently. The notice shall specify the time and place of hearing at which persons affected may appear and present their views, not less than five days nor more than 21 days after the second advertisement appears in such newspaper. The local planning commission and governing body may hold a joint public hearing after public notice as set forth hereinabove.

If a joint hearing is held, then public notice as set forth above need be given only by the governing body. The term "two successive weeks" as used in this paragraph shall mean that such notice shall be published at least twice in such newspaper with not less than six days elapsing between the first and second publication. After enactment of any plan, ordinance or amendment, further publication thereof shall not be required.

B. When a proposed amendment of the zoning ordinance involves a change in the zoning map classification of 25 or fewer parcels of land, then, in addition to the advertising as above required, written notice shall be given by the local planning commission, or its representative, at least five days before the hearing to the owner or owners, their agent or the occupant, of each parcel involved; to the owners, their agent or the occupant, of all abutting property and property immediately across the street or road from the property affected, including those parcels which lie in other localities of the Commonwealth; and, if any portion of the affected property is within a planned unit development, then to such incorporated property owner's associations within the planned unit development that have members owning property located within 2,000 feet of the affected property as may be required by the commission or its agent. Notice sent by registered or certified mail to the last known address of such owner as shown on the current real estate tax assessment books or current real estate tax assessment records shall be deemed adequate compliance with this requirement. If the hearing is continued, notice shall be remailed. Costs of any notice required under this chapter shall be taxed to the applicant.

When a proposed amendment of the zoning ordinance involves a change in the zoning map classification of more than 25 parcels of land, or a change to the applicable zoning ordinance text regulations that decreases the allowed dwelling unit density of any parcel of land, then, in addition to the advertising as above required, written notice shall be given by the local planning commission, or its representative, at least five days before the hearing to the owner, owners, or their agent of each parcel of land involved, provided, however, that written notice of such changes to zoning ordinance text regulations shall not have to be mailed to the owner, owners, or their agent of lots shown on a subdivision plat approved and recorded pursuant to the provisions of Article 6 (§ 15.2-2240 et seq.) of this chapter where such lots are less than 11,500 square feet. One notice sent by first class mail to the last known address of such owner as shown on the current real estate tax assessment books or current real estate tax assessment records shall be deemed adequate compliance with this requirement, provided that a representative of the local commission shall make affidavit that such mailings have been made and file such affidavit with the papers in the case. Nothing in this subsection shall be construed as to invalidate any subsequently adopted amendment or ordinance because of the inadvertent failure by the representative of the local commission to give written notice to the owner, owners or their agent of any parcel involved.

The governing body may provide that, in the case of a condominium or a cooperative, the written notice may be mailed to the unit owners' association or proprietary lessees' association, respectively, in lieu of each individual unit owner.

Whenever the notices required hereby are sent by an agency, department or division of the local governing body, or their representative, such notices may be sent by first class mail; however, a representative of such agency, department or division shall make affidavit that such mailings have been made and file such affidavit with the papers in the case.

A party's actual notice of, or active participation in, the proceedings for which the written notice provided by this section is required shall waive the right of that party to challenge the validity of the proceeding due to failure of the party to receive the written notice required by this section.

C. When a proposed comprehensive plan or amendment thereto; a proposed change in zoning map classification; or an application for special exception for a change in use or to increase by greater than 50 percent of the bulk or height of an existing or proposed building, but not including renewals of previously approved special exceptions, involves any parcel of land located within one-half mile of a boundary of an adjoining locality of the Commonwealth, then, in addition to the advertising and written notification as above required, written notice shall also be given by the local commission, or its representative, at least 10 days before the hearing to the chief administrative officer, or his designee, of such adjoining locality.

D. When (i) a proposed comprehensive plan or amendment thereto, (ii) a proposed change in zoning map classification, or (iii) an application for special exception for a change in use involves any parcel of land located within 3,000 feet of a boundary of a military base, military installation, military airport, excluding armories operated by the Virginia National Guard, or licensed public-use airport then, in addition to the advertising and written notification as above required, written notice shall also be given by the local commission, or its representative, at least 10 days before the hearing to the commander of the military base, military installation, military airport, or owner of such public-use airport, and the notice shall advise the military commander or owner of such public-use airport of the opportunity to submit comments or recommendations.

E. The adoption or amendment prior to July 1, 1996, of any plan or ordinance under the authority of prior acts shall not be declared invalid by reason of a failure to advertise or give notice as may be required by such act or by this chapter, provided a public hearing was conducted by the governing body prior to such adoption or amendment. Every action

contesting a decision of a locality based on a failure to advertise or give notice as may be required by this chapter shall be filed within 30 days of such decision with the circuit court having jurisdiction of the land affected by the decision. However, any litigation pending prior to July 1, 1996, shall not be affected by the 1996 amendment to this section.

F. Notwithstanding any contrary provision of law, general or special, the City of Richmond may cause such notice to be published in any newspaper of general circulation in the city.

G. When a proposed comprehensive plan or amendment of an existing plan designates or alters previously designated corridors or routes for electric transmission lines of 150 kilovolts or more, written notice shall also be given by the local planning commission, or its representative, at least 10 days before the hearing to each electric utility with a certificated service territory that includes all or any part of such designated electric transmission corridors or routes. (Code 1950, § 15-961.4; 1962, c. 407, § 15.1-431; 1964, c. 632; 1968, cc. 354, 714; 1973, cc. 117, 334; 1974, cc. 100, 570; 1975, c. 641; 1976, c. 642; 1977, c. 65; 1982, c. 291; 1990, c. 61; 1992, cc. 353, 757; 1993, cc. 128, 734; 1994, c. 774; 1995, c. 178; 1996, cc. 613, 667; 1997, c. 587; 2001, c. 406; 2002, c. 634; 2004, cc. 539, 799; 2005, c. 514; 2007, cc. 761, 813.)

Editor's note. — Acts 2007, c. 813, cl. 2, provides: "That the provisions of this act shall not affect the powers of any locality with respect to any ordinance, resolution or bylaw validly adopted and not repealed or rescinded prior to July 1, 2007."

The 2007 amendments. — The 2007 amendment by c. 761 added subsection G.

The 2007 amendment by c. 813 substituted "the City of Richmond" for "any city with a population between 200,000 and 210,000 which is required by this title or by its charter to publish a notice" in subsection F.

§ 15.2-2209. Civil penalties for violations of zoning ordinance.

Law Review.
For annual survey article, "Real Estate Law," see 41 U. Rich. L. Rev. 257 (2006).

ARTICLE 2.

Local Planning Commissions.

§ 15.2-2220. Duplicate planning commission authorized for certain local governments. —
The Cities of Chesapeake and Hampton may by ordinance establish a duplicate planning commission solely for the purpose of considering matters arising from the provisions of the Chesapeake Bay Preservation Act (§ 10.1-2100 et seq.). Sections 15.2-2210 through 15.2-2222 shall apply to the commission, mutatis mutandis.

The procedure, timing requirements and appeal to the circuit court set forth in §§ 15.2-2258 through

15.2-2261 shall apply to the considerations of this commission, mutatis mutandis.

To distinguish the planning commission authorized by this section from planning commissions required by § 15.2-2210, the commission established hereunder shall have the words "Chesapeake Bay Preservation" in its title.

The governing body of a city that establishes a commission pursuant to this section, in its sole discretion by ordinance, may abolish the duplicate planning commission. (1993, c. 738, § 15.1-502.1; 1997, c. 587; 2007, c. 813.)

Editor's note. — Acts 2007, c. 813, cl. 2, provides: "That the provisions of this act shall not affect the powers of any locality with respect to any ordinance, resolution or bylaw validly adopted and not repealed or rescinded prior to July 1, 2007."

The 2007 amendments. — The 2007 amendment by c. 813 substituted "The Cities of Chesapeake and Hampton" for "Any city with a population between 140,000 and 160,000 which is subject to the provisions of the Chesapeake Bay Presevation Act (§ 10.1-2100 et seq.)" in the first paragraph.

§ 15.2-2222.1. Coordination of state and local transportation planning.

— A. Prior to adoption of any comprehensive plan pursuant to § 15.2-2223, any part of a comprehensive plan pursuant to § 15.2-2228, or any amendment to any comprehensive plan as described in § 15.2-2229, the locality shall submit such plan or amendment to the Department of Transportation for review and comment if the plan or amendment will substantially affect transportation on state controlled highways as defined by regulations promulgated by the Department. The Department's comments on the proposed plan or amendment shall relate to plans and capacities for construction of transportation facilities affected by the proposal. Within 30 days of receipt of such proposed plan or amendment, the Department may request, and the locality shall agree to, a meeting between the Department and the local planning commission or other agent to discuss the plan or amendment, which discussions shall continue as long as the participants may deem them useful. The Department shall make written comments within 90 days after receipt of the plan or amendment, or by such later deadline as may be agreed to by the parties in the discussions.

B. Upon submission to, or initiation by, a locality of a proposed rezoning under § 15.2-2286, 15.2-2297, 15.2-2298, or 15.2-2303, the locality shall submit the proposal to the Department of Transportation within 10 business days of receipt thereof if the proposal will substantially affect transportation on state-controlled highways. Such application shall include a traffic impact statement if required by local ordinance or pursuant to regulations promulgated by the Department. Within 45 days of its receipt of such traffic impact statement, the Department shall either (i) provide written comment on the proposed rezoning to the locality, or (ii) schedule a meeting, to be held within 60 days of its receipt of the proposal, with the local planning commission or other agent and the rezoning applicant to discuss potential modifications to the proposal to address any concerns or deficiencies. The Department's comments on the proposed rezoning shall be based upon the comprehensive plan, regulations and guidelines of the Department, engineering and design considerations, any adopted regional or statewide plans and short and long term traffic impacts on and off site. The Department shall complete its initial review of the rezoning proposal within 45 days, and its final review within 120 days, after it receives the rezoning proposal from the locality.

C. When a locality receives a subdivision plat pursuant to § 15.2-2258 or 15.2-2260, or a site plan or plan of development pursuant to subdivision A 8 of § 15.2-2286, the locality shall submit such plat or plan to the Department of Transportation in accordance with § 15.2-2260 within 10 business days if the plat or plan substantially affects transportation on state-controlled highways as defined by regulations promulgated by the Department. Such plat or plan shall include supplemental traffic analysis if required by local ordinance or resolution or pursuant to regulations promulgated by the Department. Within 30 days of its receipt of such plat or plan, the Department shall either (i) provide written comment on the plat or plan, or (ii) schedule a meeting, to be held within 60 days of the Department's receipt of the plat or plan, with members of the local planning commission or other agent of the locality to discuss potential modifications to the plat or plan to address any concerns or deficiencies. The Department's comments on the plat or plan shall be based upon the comprehensive plan, regulations or guidelines of the Department, engineering and design considerations, any adopted statewide or regional plans and short and long term traffic impacts on and off site. The Department shall complete its final review within 90 days after it receives such plat or plan from the locality. The submission of the application to the Department shall toll all times for local review set out in this chapter until the locality has received the Department's final comments.

D. If a locality has not received written comments within the timeframes specified in subsections B or C, the locality may assume that the Department has no comments.

E. The review requirements set forth in this section shall be supplemental to, and shall not affect, any requirement for review by the Department of Transportation or the locality under any other provision of law. Nothing in this section shall be deemed to prohibit any additional consultations concerning land development or transportation facilities that may occur between the Department and localities as a result of existing or future administrative practice or procedure, or by mutual agreement.

F. The Department shall impose fees and charges for the review of applications, plans and plats pursuant to paragraphs A, B, and C, and such fees and charges shall not exceed $1,000 for each review.

G. Until July 1, 2008, the Department shall not be subject to the requirements of the Administrative Process Act (§ 2.2-4000 et seq.) in promulgating regulations pursuant to this section, and the Commonwealth Transportation Commissioner may phase the implementation of regulations promulgated pursuant to this section as he may deem appropriate. (2006, cc. 527, 563; 2007, c. 792.)

Editor's note. — Acts 2006, Sp. Sess. I, c. 3, as amended by Acts 2007, c. 847, effective for the biennium ending June 30, 2008, in Item 442 B, provides: "The Commissioner shall be responsible for implementing the provisions of Chapter 527 (2006 Session) concerning the development of traffic impact analyses. If resources are needed in addition to the appropriations included in this act, the Commissioner shall develop and submit a budget request for the 2007 Session to the Secretary of Transportation and the Chairmen of the Senate Finance and House Appropriations Committees. The Director, Department of Planning and Budget, is authorized to increase the appropriation as needed and as supported by the anticipated collection of associated fees."

Acts 2007, c. 792, cl. 2, provides: "That the provisions of this act regarding the ability of the Commonwealth Transportation Commissioner to phase the implementation of regulations are declarative of existing law."

The 2007 amendments. — The 2007 amendment by c. 792 inserted subsection D and redesignated the remaining subsections accordingly; in subsection F, deleted "the actual cost to the Department, or" preceding, and "whichever is less" after, "$1,000"; and added subsection G.

ARTICLE 3.

The Comprehensive Plan.

§ 15.2-2223. Comprehensive plan to be prepared and adopted; scope and purpose. — The local planning commission shall prepare and recommend a comprehensive plan for the physical development of the territory within its jurisdiction and every governing body shall adopt a comprehensive plan for the territory under its jurisdiction.

In the preparation of a comprehensive plan, the commission shall make careful and comprehensive surveys and studies of the existing conditions and trends of growth, and of the probable future requirements of its territory and inhabitants. The comprehensive plan shall be made with the purpose of guiding and accomplishing a coordinated, adjusted and harmonious development of the territory which will, in accordance with present and probable future needs and resources, best promote the health, safety, morals, order, convenience, prosperity and general welfare of the inhabitants, including the elderly and persons with disabilities.

The comprehensive plan shall be general in nature, in that it shall designate the general or approximate location, character, and extent of each feature, including any road improvement and any transportation improvement, shown on the plan and shall indicate where existing lands or facilities are proposed to be extended, widened, removed, relocated, vacated, narrowed, abandoned, or changed in use as the case may be.

As part of the comprehensive plan, each locality shall develop a transportation plan that designates a system of transportation infrastructure needs and recommendations that may include the designation of new and expanded transportation facilities and that support the planned development of the territory covered by the plan and shall include, as appropriate, but not be limited to, roadways, bicycle accommodations, pedestrian accommodations, railways, bridges, waterways, airports, ports, and public transportation facilities. The plan should recognize and differentiate among a hierarchy of roads such as expressways, arterials, and collectors. The Virginia Department of Transportation shall, upon request, provide localities with technical assistance in preparing such transportation plan.

The plan, with the accompanying maps, plats, charts, and descriptive matter, shall show the locality's long-range recommendations for the general development of the territory covered by the plan. It may include, but need not be limited to:

1. The designation of areas for various types of public and private development and use, such as different kinds of residential, including age-restricted, housing; business; industrial; agricultural; mineral resources; conservation; active and passive recreation; public service; flood plain and drainage; and other areas;

2. The designation of a system of community service facilities such as parks, sports playing fields, forests, schools, playgrounds, public buildings and institutions, hospitals, nursing homes, assisted living facilities, community centers, waterworks, sewage disposal or waste disposal areas, and the like;

3. The designation of historical areas and areas for urban renewal or other treatment;

4. The designation of areas for the implementation of reasonable ground water protection measures;

5. A capital improvements program, a subdivision ordinance, a zoning ordinance and zoning district maps, mineral resource district maps and agricultural and forestal district maps, where applicable;

6. The location of existing or proposed recycling centers;

7. The location of military bases, military installations, and military airports and their adjacent safety areas; and

8. The designation of corridors or routes for electric transmission lines of 150 kilovolts or more.

The plan shall include: the designation of areas and implementation of measures for the construction, rehabilitation and maintenance of affordable housing, which is sufficient to meet the current and future needs of residents of all levels of income in the locality while considering the current and future needs of the planning district within which the locality is situated.

The plan shall include: a map that shall show road improvements and transportation improvements, including the cost estimates of such road and transportation improvements as available from the Virginia Department of Transportation, taking into account the current and future needs of residents in the locality while considering the current and future needs of the planning district within which the locality is situated. (1975, c. 641, § 15.1-446.1; 1976, c. 650; 1977, c. 228; 1988, c. 268; 1989, c. 532; 1990, c. 19; 1993, cc. 116, 758; 1996, cc. 585, 600; 1997, c. 587; 2003, c. 811; 2004, cc. 691, 799; 2005, cc. 466, 699; 2006, cc. 527, 563, 564; 2007, c. 761.)

The 2007 amendments. — The 2007 amendment by c. 761 added subdivision 8 and made related changes.

CIRCUIT COURT OPINIONS

Standing to challenge decision. — County water authority's plea in bar was granted because the water authority presented some evidence of reasonableness and, therefore, its action in defining normal service extension of a water main was not ultra vires. Property owners therefore lacked standing to challenge the water authority's implementation of subsection C of § 15.2-2232. Kernan v. Fairfax County Water Auth., 70 Va. Cir. 212, 2006 Va. Cir. LEXIS 34 (Fairfax County 2006).

§ 15.2-2223.1. Comprehensive plan to include urban development areas; new urbanism. —

A. Every county, city, or town that has adopted zoning pursuant to Article 7 (§ 15.2-2280 et seq.) of Chapter 22 of Title 15.2 and that (i) has a population of at least 20,000 and population growth of at least 5% or (ii) has population growth of 15% or more, shall, and any county, city or town may, amend its comprehensive plan to incorporate one or more urban development areas. For purposes of this section, population growth shall be the difference in population from the next-to-latest to the latest decennial census year, based on population reported by the United States Bureau of the Census. For purposes of this section, an urban development area is an area designated by a locality that is appropriate for higher density development due to proximity to transportation facilities, the availability of a public or community water and sewer system, or proximity to a city, town, or other developed area. The comprehensive plan shall provide for commercial and residential densities within urban development areas that are appropriate for reasonably compact development at a density of at least four residential units per gross acre and a minimum floor area ratio of 0.4 per gross acre for commercial development. The comprehensive plan shall designate one or more urban development areas sufficient to meet projected residential and commercial growth in the locality for an ensuing period of at least 10 but not more than 20 years, which may include phasing of development within the urban development areas. Future growth shall be based on official estimates and projections of the Weldon Cooper Center for Public Service of the University of Virginia or other official government sources. The boundaries and size of each urban development area shall be reexamined

and, if necessary, revised every five years in conjunction with the update of the comprehensive plan and in accordance with the most recent available population growth estimates and projections. Such districts may be areas designated for redevelopment or infill development.

B. The comprehensive plan shall further incorporate principles of new urbanism and traditional neighborhood development, which may include but need not be limited to (i) pedestrian-friendly road design, (ii) interconnection of new local streets with existing local streets and roads, (iii) connectivity of road and pedestrian networks, (iv) preservation of natural areas, (v) satisfaction of requirements for stormwater management, (vi) mixed-use neighborhoods, including mixed housing types, (vii) reduction of front and side yard building setbacks, and (viii) reduction of subdivision street widths and turning radii at subdivision street intersections.

C. The comprehensive plan shall describe any financial and other incentives for development in the urban development areas.

D. No county, city, or town that has amended its comprehensive plan in accordance with this section shall limit or prohibit development pursuant to existing zoning or shall refuse to consider any application for rezoning based solely on the fact that the property is located outside the urban development area.

E. Any county, city, or town that would be required to amend its plan pursuant to this section that determines that its plan accommodates growth in a manner consistent with this section, upon adoption of a resolution certifying such compliance, shall not be required to further amend its plan.

F. Any county that amends its comprehensive plan pursuant to this section may designate one or more urban development areas in any incorporated town within such county, if the governing body of the town has also amended its comprehensive plan to designate the same areas as urban development areas with at least the same density designated by the county.

G. To the extent possible, state and local transportation, housing, and economic development funding shall be directed to the urban development area. (2007, c. 896.)

Editor's note. — Acts 2007, c. 896, cl. 10, provides: "That counties shall have until July 1, 2011, to amend their comprehensive plans in accordance with the provisions of § 15.2-2223.1 of the Code of Virginia pursuant to this act."

Acts 2007, c. 896, cl. 23 contains a severability clause.

§ 15.2-2224. Surveys and studies to be made in preparation of plan; implementation of plan. —

A. In the preparation of a comprehensive plan, the local planning commission shall survey and study such matters as the following:

1. Use of land, preservation of agricultural and forestal land, production of food and fiber, characteristics and conditions of existing development, trends

of growth or changes, natural resources, historic areas, ground water, surface water, geologic factors, population factors, employment, environmental and economic factors, existing public facilities, drainage, flood control and flood damage prevention measures, the transmission of electricity, road improvements, and any estimated cost thereof, transportation facilities, transportation improvements, and any cost thereof, the need for affordable housing in both the locality and planning district within which it is situated, and any other matters relating to the subject matter and general purposes of the comprehensive plan.

However, if a locality chooses not to survey and study historic areas, then the locality shall include historic areas in the comprehensive plan, if such areas are identified and surveyed by the Department of Historic Resources. Furthermore, if a locality chooses not to survey and study mineral resources, then the locality shall include mineral resources in the comprehensive plan, if such areas are identified and surveyed by the Department of Mines, Minerals and Energy. The requirement to study the production of food and fiber shall apply only to those plans adopted on or after January 1, 1981.

2. Probable future economic and population growth of the territory and requirements therefor.

B. The comprehensive plan shall recommend methods of implementation and shall include a current map of the area covered by the comprehensive plan. Unless otherwise required by this chapter, the methods of implementation may include but need not be limited to:

1. An official map;
2. A capital improvements program;
3. A subdivision ordinance;
4. A zoning ordinance and zoning district maps;
5. A mineral resource map; and
6. A recreation and sports resource map. (Code 1950, § 15-964.1; 1962, c. 407, § 15.1-447; 1975, c. 641; 1977, c. 228; 1980, c. 322; 1981, c. 418; 1988, c. 438; 1990, c. 97; 1991, c. 280; 1993, cc. 758, 770; 1996, cc. 585, 600; 1997, c. 587; 2006, c. 564; 2007, c. 761.)

The 2007 amendments. — The 2007 amendment by c. 761 inserted "the transmission of electricity" in the first paragraph of subdivision A 1.

§ 15.2-2232. Legal status of plan. — A. Whenever a local planning commission recommends a comprehensive plan or part thereof for the locality and such plan has been approved and adopted by the governing body, it shall control the general or approximate location, character and extent of each feature shown on the plan. Thereafter, unless a feature is already shown on the adopted master plan or part thereof or is deemed so under subsection D, no street or connection to an existing street, park or other public area, public building or public struc-

ture, public utility facility or public service corporation facility other than a railroad facility or an underground natural gas or underground electric distribution facility of a public utility as defined in subdivision (b) of § 56-265.1 within its certificated service territory, whether publicly or privately owned, shall be constructed, established or authorized, unless and until the general location or approximate location, character, and extent thereof has been submitted to and approved by the commission as being substantially in accord with the adopted comprehensive plan or part thereof. In connection with any such determination, the commission may, and at the direction of the governing body shall, hold a public hearing, after notice as required by § 15.2-2204.

B. The commission shall communicate its findings to the governing body, indicating its approval or disapproval with written reasons therefor. The governing body may overrule the action of the commission by a vote of a majority of its membership. Failure of the commission to act within sixty days of a submission, unless the time is extended by the governing body, shall be deemed approval. The owner or owners or their agents may appeal the decision of the commission to the governing body within ten days after the decision of the commission. The appeal shall be by written petition to the governing body setting forth the reasons for the appeal. The appeal shall be heard and determined within sixty days from its filing. A majority vote of the governing body shall overrule the commission.

C. Widening, narrowing, extension, enlargement, vacation or change of use of streets or public areas shall likewise be submitted for approval, but paving, repair, reconstruction, improvement, drainage or similar work and normal service extensions of public utilities or public service corporations shall not require approval unless such work involves a change in location or extent of a street or public area.

D. Any public area, facility or use as set forth in subsection A which is identified within, but not the entire subject of, a submission under either § 15.2-2258 for subdivision or provision 8 of § 15.2-2286 for development or both may be deemed a feature already shown on the adopted master plan, and, therefore, excepted from the requirement for submittal to and approval by the commission or the governing body; provided, that the governing body has by ordinance or resolution defined standards governing the construction, establishment or authorization of such public area, facility or use or has approved it through acceptance of a proffer made pursuant to § 15.2-2303.

E. Approval and funding of a public telecommunications facility by the Virginia Public Broadcasting Board pursuant to Article 12 (§ 2.2-2426 et seq.) of Chapter 24 of Title 2.2 shall be deemed to satisfy the requirements of this section and local zoning ordinances with respect to such facility with the exception of television and radio towers and structures not necessary to house electronic apparatus. The exemption provided for in this subsection shall not apply to facilities existing or approved by the Virginia Public Telecommunications Board prior to July 1, 1990. The Virginia Public Broadcasting Board shall notify the governing body of the locality in advance of any meeting where approval of any such facility shall be acted upon.

F. On any application for a telecommunications facility, the commission's decision shall comply with the requirements of the Federal Telecommunications Act of 1996. Failure of the commission to act on any such application for a telecommunications facility under subsection A submitted on or after July 1, 1998, within ninety days of such submission shall be deemed approval of the application by the commission unless the governing body has authorized an extension of time for consideration or the applicant has agreed to an extension of time. The governing body may extend the time required for action by the local commission by no more than sixty additional days. If the commission has not acted on the application by the end of the extension, or by the end of such longer period as may be agreed to by the applicant, the application is deemed approved by the commission. (Code 1950, §§ 15-909, 15-923, 15-964.10; 1958, c. 389; 1960, c. 567; 1962, c. 407, § 15.1-456; 1964, c. 528; 1966, c. 596; 1968, c. 290; 1975, c. 641; 1976, c. 291; 1978, c. 584; 1982, c. 39; 1987, c. 312; 1989, c. 532; 1990, c. 633; 1997, cc. 587, 858; 1998, c. 683; 2007, c. 801.)

The 2007 amendments. — The 2007 amendment by c. 801 inserted "or an underground natural gas or underground electric distribution facility of a public utility as defined in subdivision (b) of § 56-265.1 within its certificated service territory" in the second sentence in subsection A; and substituted "such work involves" for "involving" in subsection C.

CIRCUIT COURT OPINIONS

Standing to challenge decision. — County water authority's plea in bar was granted because the water authority presented some evidence of reasonableness and, therefore, its action in defining normal service extension of a water main was not ultra vires. Property owners therefore lacked standing to challenge the water authority's implementation of § 15.2-2232. Kernan v. Fairfax County Water Auth., 70 Va. Cir. 212, 2006 Va. Cir. LEXIS 34 (Fairfax County 2006).

ARTICLE 6.

Land Subdivision and Development.

§ 15.2-2241. Mandatory provisions of a subdivision ordinance.

Law Review.
For article reviewing recent developments and changes in legislation, case law, and Virginia Supreme Court Rules affecting civil litigation, "Civil Practice and Procedure," see 40 U. Rich. L. Rev. 95 (2005).

§ 15.2-2241.1. Bonding requirements for the acceptance of dedication for public use of cer-

tain facilities. — Notwithstanding the provisions of § 15.2-2241, provided the developer and the governing body have agreed on the delineation of sections within a proposed development, the developer shall not be required to furnish to the governing body a certified check, cash escrow, bond or letter of credit in the amount of the estimated cost of construction of facilities to be dedicated for public use within each section of the development until such time as construction plans are submitted for the section in which such facilities are to be located. (2007, c. 420.)

§ 15.2-2242. Optional provisions of a subdivision ordinance. — A subdivision ordinance may include:

1. Provisions for variations in or exceptions to the general regulations of the subdivision ordinance in cases of unusual situations or when strict adherence to the general regulations would result in substantial injustice or hardship.

2. A requirement (i) for the furnishing of a preliminary opinion from the applicable health official regarding the suitability of a subdivision for installation of subsurface sewage disposal systems where such method of sewage disposal is to be utilized in the development of a subdivision and (ii) that all buildings constructed on lots resulting from subdivision of a larger tract that abuts or adjoins a public water or sewer system or main shall be connected to that public water or sewer system or main subject to the provisions of § 15.2-2121.

3. A requirement that, in the event streets in a subdivision will not be constructed to meet the standards necessary for inclusion in the secondary system of state highways or for state street maintenance moneys paid to municipalities, the subdivision plat and all approved deeds of subdivision, or similar instruments, must contain a statement advising that the streets in the subdivision do not meet state standards and will not be maintained by the Department of Transportation or the localities enacting the ordinances. Grantors of any subdivision lots to which such statement applies must include the statement on each deed of conveyance thereof. However, localities in their ordinances may establish minimum standards for construction of streets that will not be built to state standards.

For streets constructed or to be constructed, as provided for in this subsection, a subdivision ordinance may require that the same procedure be followed as that set forth in provision 5 of § 15.2-2241. Further, the subdivision ordinance may provide that the developer's financial commitment shall continue until such time as the local government releases such financial commitment in accordance with provision 11 of § 15.2-2241.

4. Reasonable provision for the voluntary funding of off-site road improvements and reimbursements of advances by the governing body. If a subdivider or developer makes an advance of payments for or

construction of reasonable and necessary road improvements located outside the property limits of the land owned or controlled by him, the need for which is substantially generated and reasonably required by the construction or improvement of his subdivision or development, and such advance is accepted, the governing body may agree to reimburse the subdivider or developer from such funds as the governing body may make available for such purpose from time to time for the cost of such advance together with interest, which shall be excludable from gross income for federal income tax purposes, at a rate equal to the rate of interest on bonds most recently issued by the governing body on the following terms and conditions:

a. The governing body shall determine or confirm that the road improvements were substantially generated and reasonably required by the construction or improvement of the subdivision or development and shall determine or confirm the cost thereof, on the basis of a study or studies conducted by qualified traffic engineers and approved and accepted by the subdivider or developer.

b. The governing body shall prepare, or cause to be prepared, a report accepted and approved by the subdivider or developer, indicating the governmental services required to be furnished to the subdivision or development and an estimate of the annual cost thereof for the period during which the reimbursement is to be made to the subdivider or developer.

c. The governing body may make annual reimbursements to the subdivider or developer from funds made available for such purpose from time to time, including but not limited to real estate taxes assessed and collected against the land and improvements on the property included in the subdivision or development in amounts equal to the amount by which such real estate taxes exceed the annual cost of providing reasonable and necessary governmental services to such subdivision or development.

5. In Arlington County, Fairfax County, Loudoun County, and Prince William County, in any town located within such counties, in Bedford County, Pittsylvania County, Spotsylvania County, and Stafford County, or in the Cities of Alexandria, Fairfax, Falls Church, Hampton, Manassas, and Manassas Park, provisions for payment by a subdivider or developer of land of a pro rata share of the cost of reasonable and necessary road improvements, located outside the property limits of the land owned or controlled by him but serving an area having related traffic needs to which his subdivision or development will contribute, to reimburse an initial subdivider or developer who has advanced such costs or constructed such road improvements. Such ordinance may apply to road improvements constructed after July 1, 1988, in Fairfax County; in Arlington County, Loudoun County, and Prince William County, in any town located within such counties, in Bedford County, Pittsylvania County,

Spotsylvania County, and Stafford County, or in the Cities of Alexandria, Fairfax, Falls Church, Hampton, Manassas, and Manassas Park, such ordinance may only apply to road improvements constructed after the effective date of such ordinance.

Such provisions shall provide for the adoption of a pro rata reimbursement plan which shall include reasonable standards to identify the area having related traffic needs, to determine the total estimated or actual cost of road improvements required to adequately serve the area when fully developed in accordance with the comprehensive plan or as required by proffered conditions, and to determine the proportionate share of such costs to be reimbursed by each subsequent subdivider or developer within the area, with interest (i) at the legal rate or (ii) at an inflation rate prescribed by a generally accepted index of road construction costs, whichever is less.

For any subdivision ordinance adopted pursuant to provision 5 of this section after February 1, 1993, no such payment shall be assessed or imposed upon a subsequent developer or subdivider if (i) prior to the adoption of a pro rata reimbursement plan the subsequent subdivider or developer has proffered conditions pursuant to § 15.2-2303 for offsite road improvements and such proffered conditions have been accepted by the locality, (ii) the locality has assessed or imposed an impact fee on the subsequent development or subdivision pursuant to Article 8 (§ 15.2-2317 et seq.) of Chapter 22, or (iii) the subsequent subdivider or developer has received final site plan, subdivision plan, or plan of development approval from the locality prior to the adoption of a pro rata reimbursement plan for the area having related traffic needs.

The amount of the costs to be reimbursed by a subsequent developer or subdivider shall be determined before or at the time the site plan or subdivision is approved. The ordinance shall specify that such costs are to be collected at the time of the issuance of a temporary or final certificate of occupancy or functional use and occupancy within the development, whichever shall come first. The ordinance also may provide that the required reimbursement may be paid (i) in lump sum, (ii) by agreement of the parties on installment at a reasonable rate of interest or rate of inflation, whichever is less, for a fixed number of years, or (iii) on such terms as otherwise agreed to by the initial and subsequent subdividers and developers.

Such ordinance provisions may provide that no certificate of occupancy shall be issued to a subsequent developer or subdivider until (i) the initial developer certifies to the locality that the subsequent developer has made the required reimbursement directly to him as provided above or (ii) the subsequent developer has deposited the reimbursement amount with the locality for transfer forthwith to the initial developer.

6. Provisions for establishing and maintaining access to solar energy to encourage the use of solar

heating and cooling devices in new subdivisions. The provisions shall be applicable to a new subdivision only when so requested by the subdivider.

7. Provisions, in any town with a population between 14,500 and 15,000, granting authority to the governing body, in its discretion, to use funds escrowed pursuant to provision 5 of § 15.2-2241 for improvements similar to but other than those for which the funds were escrowed, if the governing body (i) obtains the written consent of the owner or developer who submitted the escrowed funds; (ii) finds that the facilities for which funds are escrowed are not immediately required; (iii) releases the owner or developer from liability for the construction or for the future cost of constructing those improvements for which the funds were escrowed; and (iv) accepts liability for future construction of these improvements. If such town fails to locate such owner or developer after making a reasonable attempt to do so, the town may proceed as if such consent had been granted. In addition, the escrowed funds to be used for such other improvement may only come from an escrow that does not exceed a principal amount of $30,000 plus any accrued interest and shall have been escrowed for at least five years.

8. Provisions for clustering of single-family dwellings and preservation of open space developments, which provisions shall comply with the requirements and procedures set forth in § 15.2-2286.1.

9. Provisions requiring that where a lot being subdivided or developed fronts on an existing street, and adjacent property on either side has an existing sidewalk, a locality may require the dedication of land for, and construction of, a sidewalk on the property being subdivided or developed, to connect to the existing sidewalk. Nothing in this paragraph shall alter in any way any authority of localities or the Department of Transportation to require sidewalks on any newly constructed street or highway.

10. Provisions for requiring and considering Phase I environmental site assessments based on the anticipated use of the property proposed for the subdivision or development that meet generally accepted national standards for such assessments, such as those developed by the American Society for Testing and Materials, and Phase II environmental site assessments, that also meet accepted national standards, such as, but not limited to, those developed by the American Society for Testing and Materials, if the locality deems such to be reasonably necessary, based on findings in the Phase I assessment, and in accordance with regulations of the United States Environmental Protection Agency and the American Society for Testing and Materials. A reasonable fee may be charged for the review of such environmental assessments. Such fees shall not exceed an amount commensurate with the services rendered, taking into consideration the time, skill, and administrative expense involved in such review.

11. Provisions for requiring disclosure and remediation of contamination and other adverse environmental conditions of the property prior to approval of subdivision and development plans. (Code 1950, §§ 15-781, 15-967.1; 1950, p. 183; 1962, c. 407, § 15.1-466; 1970, c. 436; 1973, cc. 169, 480; 1975, c. 641; 1976, c. 270; 1978, cc. 429, 439, 440; 1979, cc. 183, 188, 395; 1980, cc. 379, 381; 1981, c. 348; 1983, cc. 167, 609; 1984, c. 111; 1985, cc. 422, 455; 1986, c. 54; 1987, c. 717; 1988, cc. 279, 735; 1989, cc. 332, 393, 403, 495; 1990, cc. 170, 176, 287, 708, 973; 1991, cc. 30, 47, 288, 538; 1992, c. 380; 1993, cc. 836, 846, 864; 1994, c. 421; 1995, cc. 386, 388, 389, 452, 457, 474; 1996, cc. 77, 325, 452, 456; 1997, c. 587; 2000, cc. 652, 711; 2002, c. 703; 2005, c. 567; 2006, cc. 421, 514, 533, 903; 2007, c. 813.)

Editor's note. — Acts 2007, c. 813, cl. 2, provides: "That the provisions of this act shall not affect the powers of any locality with respect to any ordinance, resolution or bylaw validly adopted and not repealed or rescinded prior to July 1, 2007."

The 2007 amendments. — The 2007 amendment by c. 813, in subdivision 5, substituted "Arlington County, Fairfax County, Loudoun County, and Prince William County, in any town located within such counties, in Bedford County, Pittsylvania County, Spotsylvania County, and Stafford County, or in the Cities of Alexandria, Fairfax, Falls Church, Hampton, Manassas, and Manassas Park" for "a county having the urban county executive form of government, in any city located within or adjacent thereto, or any county adjacent thereto or a town located within such county, in any county with a population between 57,000 and 57,450, or in any county with a population between 60,000 and 63,000, and in any city with a population between 140,000 and 160,000" in the first sentence and "Fairfax County; in Arlington County, Loudoun County, and Prince William County, in any town located within such counties, in Bedford County, Pittsylvania County, Spotsylvania County, and Stafford County, or in the Cities of Alexandria, Fairfax, Falls Church, Hampton, Manassas, and Manassas Park" for "a county having the urban county executive form of government; in a city located within or adjacent to a county having the urban county executive form of government, or in a county adjacent to a county having the urban county executive form of government or town located within such county and in any county with a population between 57,000 and 57,450, or in any county with a population between 60,000 and 63,000" in the second sentence.

CIRCUIT COURT OPINIONS

Subdivision ordinances facially valid. — Subdivision ordinances adopted by a city pursuant to § 15.2-2242 were facially valid. They provided significant standards, policies, and procedures that made their general delegation of authority to a planning commission's agent valid, and as they were the same or stricter than § 15.2-2242, they were to be harmonized with it. Logan v. City Council for Roanoke, — Va. Cir. —, 2006 Va. Cir. LEXIS 205 (Roanoke Oct. 12, 2006).

§ 15.2-2244. Provisions for subdivision of a lot for conveyance to a family member.

Law Review. — For article reviewing recent developments and changes in legislation, case law, and Virginia Supreme Court Rules affecting civil litigation, "Civil Practice and Procedure," see 40 U. Rich. L. Rev. 95 (2005).

§ 15.2-2244.1. Additional method for subdivision of a lot for conveyance to a family

member. — In addition to § 15.2-2244, a locality may include in its subdivision ordinance provisions permitting a single division of a lot or parcel for the purpose of sale or gift to a member of the immediate family, as defined in § 15.2-2244, of the property owner, if (i) the property has been owned for at least 15 consecutive years by the current owner or member of the immediate family and (ii) the property owner agrees to place a restrictive covenant on the subdivided property that would prohibit the transfer of the property to a nonmember of the immediate family for a period of 15 years. Notwithstanding the provisions of clause (ii), a locality may reduce or provide exceptions to the period of years prescribed in such clause when changed circumstances so require. Upon such modification of a restrictive covenant, a locality shall execute a writing reflecting such modification, which writing shall be recorded in accordance with § 17.1-227. The locality may require that the subdivided lot is no more than one acre and otherwise meets any other express requirement contained in the Code of Virginia or imposed by the local governing body. (2006, c. 456; 2007, c. 856.)

The 2007 amendments. — The 2007 amendment by c. 856 inserted the second and third sentences.

Law Review. — For annual survey article, "Real Estate Law," see 41 U. Rich. L. Rev. 257 (2006).

§ 15.2-2245. Provisions for periodic partial and final release of certain performance guarantees.

Cross references. — As to optional provisions of subdivision ordinance providing alternatives to subsection 5 of § 15.2-2241, see § 15.2-851.1.

§ 15.2-2255. Administration and enforcement of regulations.

Law Review. — For article reviewing recent developments and changes in legislation, case law, and Virginia Supreme Court Rules affecting civil litigation, "Civil Practice and Procedure," see 40 U. Rich. L. Rev. 95 (2005). For annual survey article, "Real Estate Law," see 41 U. Rich. L. Rev. 257 (2006).

§ 15.2-2259. Local planning commission to act on proposed plat. — A. The local planning commission or other agent shall act on any proposed plat within 60 days after it has been officially submitted for approval by either approving or disapproving the plat in writing, and giving with the latter specific reasons therefor. The Commission or agent shall thoroughly review the plat and shall make a good faith effort to identify all deficiencies, if any, with the initial submission. However, if approval of a feature or features of the plat by a state agency or public authority authorized by state law is necessary, the commission or agent shall forward the plat to the appropriate state agency or agencies for review within 10 business days of receipt of such

plat. The state agency shall respond in accord with the requirements set forth in § 15.2-2222.1, which shall extend the time for action by the local planning commission or other agent, as set forth in subsection B. Specific reasons for disapproval shall be contained either in a separate document or on the plat itself. The reasons for disapproval shall identify deficiencies in the plat that cause the disapproval by reference to specific duly adopted ordinances, regulations, or policies and shall identify modifications or corrections as will permit approval of the plat. The local planning commission or other agent shall act on any proposed plat that it has previously disapproved within 45 days after the plat has been modified, corrected and resubmitted for approval.

B. Any state agency or public authority authorized by state law making a review of a plat forwarded to it under this article, including, without limitation, the Virginia Department of Transportation and authorities authorized by Chapter 51 (§ 15.2-5100 et seq.), shall complete its review within 45 days of receipt of the plat upon first submission and within 45 days for any proposed plat that has previously been disapproved, provided, however, that the time periods set forth in § 15.2-2222.1 shall apply to plats triggering the applicability of said section. The Virginia Department of Transportation and authorities authorized by Chapter 51 (§ 15.2-5100 et seq.) shall allow use of public rights-of-way dedicated for public street purposes for placement of utilities by permit when practical and shall not unreasonably deny plat approval. If a state agency or public authority authorized by state law does not approve the plat, it shall comply with the requirements, and be subject to the restrictions, set forth in subsection A, with the exception of the time period therein specified. Upon receipt of the approvals from all state agencies and other agencies, the local agent shall act upon a plat within 35 days.

C. If the commission or other agent fails to approve or disapprove the plat within 60 days after it has been officially submitted for approval, or within 45 days after it has been officially resubmitted after a previous disapproval or within 35 days of receipt of any agency response pursuant to subsection B, the subdivider, after 10-days' written notice to the commission, or agent, may petition the circuit court for the locality in which the land involved, or the major part thereof, is located, to decide whether the plat should or should not be approved. The court shall give the petition priority on the civil docket, hear the matter expeditiously in accordance with the procedures prescribed in Article 2 (§ 8.01-644 et seq.) of Chapter 25 of Title 8.01 and make and enter an order with respect thereto as it deems proper, which may include directing approval of the plat.

D. If a commission or other agent disapproves a plat and the subdivider contends that the disapproval was not properly based on the ordinance applicable thereto, or was arbitrary or capricious, he may appeal to the circuit court having jurisdiction of such land and the court shall hear and determine the case as soon as may be, provided that his appeal is filed with the circuit court within 60 days of the written disapproval by the commission or other agent. (Code 1950, §§ 15-789, 15-967.10; 1952, c. 333; 1962, c. 407, § 15.1-475; 1964, c. 498; 1975, c. 641; 1977, c. 10; 1978, c. 283; 1979, c. 111; 1980, c. 73; 1986, c. 483; 1989, cc. 471, 495; 1990, c. 171; 1992, c. 843; 1993, c. 846; 1996, c. 353; 1997, c. 587; 2003, c. 716; 2007, c. 202.)

The 2007 amendments. — The 2007 amendment by c. 202 inserted the third and fourth sentences of subsection A, added present subsection B, redesignated former subsections B and C as present subsections C and D, and in subsection C, inserted "or within 35 days of receipt of any agency response pursuant to subsection B" in the first sentence.

§ 15.2-2260. Localities may provide for submission of preliminary subdivision plats; how long valid.

— A. Nothing in this article shall be deemed to prohibit the local governing body from providing in its ordinance for the submission of preliminary subdivision plats for tentative approval. The local planning commission, or an agent designated by the commission or by the governing body to review preliminary subdivision plats shall complete action on the preliminary plats within 60 days of submission. However, if approval of a feature or features of the preliminary plat by a state agency or public authority authorized by state law is necessary, the commission or agent shall forward the preliminary plat to the appropriate state agency or agencies for review within 10 business days of receipt of such preliminary plat.

B. Any state agency or public authority authorized by state law making a review of a preliminary plat forwarded to it under this section, including, without limitation, the Virginia Department of Transportation and authorities authorized by Chapter 51 (§ 15.2-5100 et seq.), shall complete its review within 45 days of receipt of the preliminary plat upon first submission and within 45 days for any proposed plat that has previously been disapproved, provided, however, that the time period set forth in § 15.2-2222.1 shall apply to plats triggering the applicability of said section. The Virginia Department of Transportation and authorities authorized by Chapter 51 (§ 15.2-5100 et seq.) shall allow use of public rights-of-way for public street purposes for placement of utilities by permit when practical and shall not unreasonably deny plat approval. If a state agency or public authority authorized by state law does not approve the plat, it shall comply with the requirements, and be subject to the restrictions, set forth in § 15.2-2259 A with the exception of the time period therein specified. Upon receipt of the approvals from all state agencies, the local agent shall act upon a preliminary plat within 35 days.

C. If a commission has the responsibility of review of preliminary plats and conducts a public hearing, it shall act on the plat within forty-five days after receiving approval from all state agencies. If the local agent or commission does not approve the preliminary plat, the local agent or commission shall set forth in writing the reasons for such denial and shall state what corrections or modifications will permit approval by such agent or commission. However, no commission or agent shall be required to approve a preliminary subdivision plat in less than sixty days from the date of its original submission to the commission or agent, and all actions on preliminary subdivision plats shall be completed by the agent or commission and, if necessary, state agencies, within a total of ninety days of submission to the local agent or commission.

D. If the commission or other agent fails to approve or disapprove the preliminary plat within ninety days after it has been officially submitted for approval, the subdivider after ten days' written notice to the commission, or agent, may petition the circuit court for the locality in which the land involved, or the major part thereof, is located to enter an order with respect thereto as it deems proper, which may include directing approval of the plat.

E. If a commission or other agent disapproves a preliminary plat and the subdivider contends that the disapproval was not properly based on the ordinance applicable thereto, or was arbitrary or capricious, he may appeal to the circuit court having jurisdiction of such land and the court shall hear and determine the case as soon as may be, provided that his appeal is filed with the circuit court within sixty days of the written disapproval by the commission or other agent.

F. Once a preliminary subdivision plat is approved, it shall be valid for a period of five years, provided the subdivider (i) submits a final subdivision plat for all or a portion of the property within one year of such approval or such longer period as may be prescribed by local ordinance, and (ii) thereafter diligently pursues approval of the final subdivision plat. "Diligent pursuit of approval" means that the subdivider has incurred extensive obligations or substantial expenses relating to the submitted final subdivision plat or modifications thereto. However, no sooner than three years following such preliminary subdivision plat approval, and upon ninety days' written notice by certified mail to the subdivider, the commission or other agent may revoke such approval upon a specific finding of facts that the subdivider has not diligently pursued approval of the final subdivision plat. (Code 1950, §§ 15-789, 15-967.10; 1952, c. 333; 1962, c. 407, § 15.1-475; 1964, c. 498; 1975, c. 641; 1977, c. 10; 1978, c. 283; 1979, c. 111; 1980, c. 73; 1986, c. 483; 1989, cc. 471, 495; 1990, c. 171; 1992, c. 843; 1993, c. 846; 1996, c. 353; 1997, c. 587; 2002, c. 530; 2006, c. 461; 2007, c. 202.)

The 2007 amendments. — The 2007 amendment by c. 202 inserted "or public authority authorized by state law" in the second sentence of subsection A; and in subsection B, rewrote the first sentence, inserted "and authorities authorized by Chapter 51 (§ 15.2-5100 et seq.)" and "for public street purposes" in the second sentence, inserted "or public authority authorized by state law" in the third sentence; and made minor stylistic changes.

§ 15.2-2263. Expedited land development review procedure.

— A. The Counties of Hanover, Loudoun, Montgomery, Prince William, and Roanoke may establish, by ordinance, a separate processing procedure for the review of preliminary and final subdivision and site plans and other development plans certified by licensed professional engineers, architects, certified landscape architects and land surveyors who are also licensed pursuant to § 54.1-408 and recommended for submission by persons who have received special training in the county's land development ordinances and regulations. The purpose of the separate review procedure is to provide a procedure to expedite the county's review of certain qualified land development plans. If a separate procedure is established, the county shall establish within the adopted ordinance the criteria for qualification of persons and whose work is eligible to use the separate procedure as well as a procedure for determining if the qualifications are met by persons applying to use the separate procedure. Persons who satisfy the criteria of subsection B below shall qualify as plans examiners. Plans reviewed and recommended for submission by plans examiners and certified by the appropriately licensed professional engineer, architect, certified landscape architect or land surveyor shall qualify for the separate processing procedure.

B. The qualifications of those persons who may participate in this program shall include, but not be limited to, the following:

1. A bachelor of science degree in engineering, architecture, landscape architecture or related science or equivalent experience or a land surveyor certified pursuant to § 54.1-408.

2. Successful completion of an educational program specified by the county.

3. A minimum of two years of land development engineering design experience acceptable to the county.

4. Attendance at continuing educational courses specified by the county.

5. Consistent preparation and submission of plans which meet all applicable ordinances and regulations.

C. If an expedited review procedure is adopted by the board of supervisors pursuant to the authority granted by this section, the board of supervisors shall establish an advisory plans examiner board which shall make recommendations to the board of supervisors on the general operation of the program, on the general qualifications of those who may participate in the expedited processing procedure, on initial and continuing educational programs needed to qualify and maintain qualification for such a program and on the general administration and operation of the program. In addition, the plans examiner board shall submit recommendations to the board of supervisors as to those persons who meet the established qualifications for participation in the program, and the plans examiner board shall submit recommendations as to whether those persons who have previously qualified to participate in the program should be disqualified, suspended or otherwise disciplined. The plans examiner board shall consist of six members who shall be appointed by the board of supervisors for staggered four-year terms. Initial terms may be less than four years so as to provide for staggered terms. The plans examiner board shall consist of three persons in private practice as licensed professional engineers or land surveyors certified pursuant to § 54.1-408, at least one of whom shall be a certified land surveyor; one person employed by the county government; one person employed by the Virginia Department of Transportation who shall serve as a nonvoting advisory member; and one citizen member. All members of the board who serve as licensed engineers or as certified surveyors must maintain their professional license or certification as a condition of holding office and shall have at least two years of experience in land development procedures of the county. The citizen member of the board shall meet the qualifications provided in § 54.1-107 and, notwithstanding the proscription of clause (i) of § 54.1-107, shall have training as an engineer or surveyor and may be currently licensed, certified or practicing his profession.

D. The expedited land development program shall include an educational program conducted under the auspices of a state institution of higher education. The instructors in the educational program shall consist of persons in the private and public sectors who are qualified to prepare land development plans. The educational program shall include the comprehensive and detailed study of county ordinances and regulations relating to plans and how they are applied.

E. The separate processing system may include a review of selected or random aspects of plans rather than a detailed review of all aspects; however, it shall also include a periodic detailed review of plans prepared by persons who qualify for the system.

F. In no event shall this section relieve persons who prepare and submit plans of the responsibilities and obligations which they would otherwise have with regard to the preparation of plans, nor shall it relieve the county of its obligation to review other plans in the time periods and manner prescribed by law. (1991, c. 444, § 15.1-501.1; 1997, c. 587; 2007, c. 813.)

Editor's note. — Acts 2007, c. 813, cl. 2, provides: "That the provisions of this act shall not affect the powers of any locality with respect to any ordinance, resolution or bylaw validly adopted and not repealed or rescinded prior to July 1, 2007."

The 2007 amendments. — The 2007 amendment by c. 813 substituted "The Counties of Hanover, Loudoun, Montgomery,

Prince William, and Roanoke" for "Any county having a population between 80,000 and 90,000 or between 212,000 and 216,000" in subsection A.

§ 15.2-2266. Validation of certain plats recorded before January 1, 1975. — Any subdivision plat recorded prior to January 1, 1975, if otherwise valid, is hereby validated and declared effective even though the technical requirements for recordation existing at the time such plat was recorded were not complied with. (1968, c. 279, § 15.1-478.1; 1997, c. 587; 2007, c. 279.)

The 2007 amendments. — The 2007 amendment by c. 279 substituted "1975" for "1953."

§ 15.2-2269. Plans and specifications for utility fixtures and systems to be submitted for approval. — A. If the owners of any such subdivision desire to construct in, on, under, or adjacent to any streets or alleys located in such subdivision any gas, water, sewer or electric light or power works, pipes, wires, fixtures or systems, they shall present plans or specifications therefor to the governing body of the locality in which the subdivision is located or its authorized agent, for approval. If the subdivision is located beyond the corporate limits of a municipality but within the limits set forth in § 15.2-2248, such plans and specifications shall be presented for approval to the governing body of such municipality, or its authorized agent, if the county has not adopted a subdivision ordinance. The governing body, or agent, shall have 45 days in which to approve or disapprove the same. In event of the failure of any governing body, or its agent, to act within such period, such plans and specifications may be submitted, after ten days' notice to the locality, to the circuit court for such locality for its approval or disapproval, and its approval thereof shall, for all purposes of this article be treated and considered as approval by the locality or its authorized agent.

B. Any state agency or public authority authorized by state law making a review of any plat forwarded to it under this article, including, without limitation, the Virginia Department of Transportation and authorities authorized by Chapter 51 (§ 15.2-5100 et seq.), shall complete its review within 45 days of receipt of the plans, provided, however, that the time periods set forth in § 15.2-2222.1 shall apply to plats triggering the applicability of said section. The Virginia Department of Transportation and authorities authorized by Chapter 51 (§ 15.2-5100 et seq.) shall allow use of public rights-of-way dedicated for public street purposes for placement of utilities by permit when practical and shall not unreasonably deny plan approval. If a state agency or public authority by state law does not approve the plan, it shall comply with the requirements, and be subject to the restrictions, set forth in subsection A of § 15.2-2259, with respect to the exception of the time period therein

specified. Upon receipt of the approvals from all state agencies, the local agent shall act upon a preliminary plat within 35 days. (Code 1950, § 15-967.15; 1962, c. 407, § 15.1-480; 1997, c. 587; 2007, c. 202.)

The 2007 amendments. — The 2007 amendment by c. 202 inserted the subsection A designation and substituted "construct in, on, under, or adjacent to any streets" for "construct in, on or under any streets" in the first sentence; added subsection B and made a minor stylistic change.

ARTICLE 7.

Zoning.

§ 15.2-2280. Zoning ordinances generally.

CIRCUIT COURT OPINIONS

Ordinances within county authority. — *Dillon* rule did not apply to the ordinances and regulations that the county imposed in order to preserve a village that was designated as a county historic district, because the county did not exceed the power granted to it to zone, regulate, restrict, permit, prohibit, and determine land uses, building limitations, lot area restrictions, and excavation of natural resources, pursuant to § 15.2-2280. Madison v. Loudoun County Bd. of Supervisors, 69 Va. Cir. 469, 2006 Va. Cir. LEXIS 89 (Loudoun County 2006).

OPINIONS OF THE ATTORNEY GENERAL

Site ordinances. — Adoption of a zoning ordinance is the only method permitted by the General Assembly authorizing a locality to generally control the location of undesirable industries or businesses within a locality, and Wythe County is not authorized to pass a site ordinance restricting or requiring specific requirements of potentially undesirable industries or businesses before locating within Wythe County. See opinion of Attorney General to Mr. Scott S. Farthing, Attorney for Wythe County, 05-011 (3/31/05).

§ 15.2-2283.1. Prohibition of sexual offender treatment office in residentially zoned subdivision. — Notwithstanding any other provision of law, no individual shall knowingly provide sex offender treatment services to a convicted sex offender in an office or similar facility located in a residentially zoned subdivision. (2007, c. 878.)

The number of this section was assigned by the Virginia Code Commission, the 2007 act having provided no number.

§ 15.2-2285. Preparation and adoption of zoning ordinance and map and amendments thereto; appeal.

Law Review.
For article reviewing recent developments and changes in legislation, case law, and Virginia Supreme Court Rules affecting civil litigation, "Civil Practice and Procedure," see 40 U. Rich. L. Rev. 95 (2005).

CASE NOTES

Validity of decision. — Since a majority of council members did not vote on the retailer's applications for rezoning and special use permits, the town council's vote, by less than a majority of council members, meant that a quorum had not voted on the applications, and, thus, the three council members vote to approve the applications was invalid; too, it did not matter that some of the missing council members had absented themselves pursuant to the State and Local Government Conflict of Interests Act (COIA), § 2.2-3100 et seq., since COIA did not apply the laws involving "Meetings of Governing Bodies" since those laws had nothing to do with conflicts of interests. Jakabcin v. Town of Front Royal, 271 Va. 660, 628 S.E.2d 319, 2006 Va. LEXIS 49 (2006).

CIRCUIT COURT OPINIONS

Issues properly raised on appeal of conditional use permit. — Allegations that a board's actions in issuing a conditional use permit, inter alia, were ultra vires, unreasonable and not fairly debatable, were tantamount to granting a variance, amounted to spot zoning, and addressing the predictability of the ordinance were properly raised in an appeal pursuant to § 15.2-2285. Bennett v. Bd. of Supervisors, — Va. Cir. —, 2006 Va. Cir. LEXIS 188 (Nelson County May 25, 2006).

Suit against the county not warranted. — Complainants had not stated grounds for declaratory relief against the county for the regulations it took to preserve a village as an historic district because the regulations did not exceed the authority conferred upon the county pursuant to § 15.2-2306. Additionally the complainants did not object to the proposed regulations as required under § 15.2-2285. Madison v. Loudoun County Bd. of Supervisors, 69 Va. Cir. 469, 2006 Va. Cir. LEXIS 89 (Loudoun County 2006).

§ 15.2-2286. Permitted provisions in zoning ordinances; amendments; applicant to pay delinquent taxes; penalties.

— A. A zoning ordinance may include, among other things, reasonable regulations and provisions as to any or all of the following matters:

1. For variances or special exceptions, as defined in § 15.2-2201, to the general regulations in any district.

2. For the temporary application of the ordinance to any property coming into the territorial jurisdiction of the governing body by annexation or otherwise, subsequent to the adoption of the zoning ordinance, and pending the orderly amendment of the ordinance.

3. For the granting of special exceptions under suitable regulations and safeguards; notwithstanding any other provisions of this article, the governing body of any locality may reserve unto itself the right to issue such special exceptions. Conditions imposed in connection with residential special use permits, wherein the applicant proposes affordable housing, shall be consistent with the objective of providing affordable housing. When imposing conditions on residential projects specifying materials and methods of construction or specific design features, the approving body shall consider the impact of the conditions upon the affordability of housing.

The governing body or the board of zoning appeals of the City of Norfolk may impose a condition upon any special exception relating to retail alcoholic beverage control licensees which provides that such special exception will automatically expire upon a change of ownership of the property, a change in possession, a change in the operation or management of a facility or upon the passage of a specific period of time.

The governing body of the City of Richmond may impose a condition upon any special use permit issued after July 1, 2000, relating to retail alcoholic beverage licensees which provides that such special use permit shall be subject to an automatic review by the governing body upon a change in possession, a change in the owner of the business, or a transfer of majority control of the business entity. Upon review by the governing body, it may either amend or revoke the special use permit after notice and a public hearing as required by § 15.2-2206.

4. For the administration and enforcement of the ordinance including the appointment or designation of a zoning administrator who may also hold another office in the locality. The zoning administrator shall have all necessary authority on behalf of the governing body to administer and enforce the zoning ordinance. His authority shall include (i) ordering in writing the remedying of any condition found in violation of the ordinance; (ii) insuring compliance with the ordinance, bringing legal action, including injunction, abatement, or other appropriate action or proceeding subject to appeal pursuant to § 15.2-2311; and (iii) in specific cases, making findings of fact and, with concurrence of the attorney for the governing body, conclusions of law regarding determinations of rights accruing under § 15.2-2307.

Whenever the zoning administrator of a locality within Planning District 8 has reasonable cause to believe that any person has engaged in or is engaging in any violation of a zoning ordinance that limits occupancy in a residential dwelling unit, which is subject to a civil penalty that may be imposed in accordance with the provisions of § 15.2-2209, and the zoning administrator, after a good faith effort to obtain the data or information necessary to determine whether a violation has occurred, has been unable to obtain such information, he may request that the attorney for the locality petition the judge of the general district court for his jurisdiction for a subpoena duces tecum against any such person refusing to produce such data or information. The judge of the court, upon good cause shown, may cause the subpoena to be issued. Any person failing to comply with such subpoena shall be subject to punishment for contempt by the court issuing the subpoena. Any person so subpoenaed may apply to the judge who issued the subpoena to quash it.

Notwithstanding the provisions of § 15.2-2311, a zoning ordinance may prescribe an appeal period of less than 30 days, but not less than 10 days, for a notice of violation involving temporary or seasonal commercial uses, parking of commercial trucks in residential zoning districts, or similar short-term, recurring violations.

Where provided by ordinance, the zoning administrator may be authorized to grant a modification from any provision contained in the zoning ordinance with respect to physical requirements on a lot or parcel of land, including but not limited to size, height, location or features of or related to any building, structure, or improvements, if the administrator finds in writing that: (i) the strict application of the ordinance would produce undue hardship; (ii) such hardship is not shared generally by other properties in the same zoning district and the same vicinity; and (iii) the authorization of the modification will not be of substantial detriment to adjacent property and the character of the zoning district will not be changed by the granting of the modification. Prior to the granting of a modification, the zoning administrator shall give, or require the applicant to give, all adjoining property owners written notice of the request for modification, and an opportunity to respond to the request within 21 days of the date of the notice. The zoning administrator shall make a decision on the application for modification and issue a written decision with a copy provided to the applicant and any adjoining landowner who responded in writing to the notice sent pursuant to this paragraph. The decision of the zoning administrator shall constitute a decision within the purview of § 15.2-2311, and may be appealed to the board of zoning appeals as provided by that section. Decisions of the board of zoning appeals may be appealed to the circuit court as provided by § 15.2-2314.

The zoning administrator shall respond within 90 days of a request for a decision or determination on zoning matters within the scope of his authority unless the requester has agreed to a longer period.

5. For the imposition of penalties upon conviction of any violation of the zoning ordinance. Any such violation shall be a misdemeanor punishable by a fine of not less than $10 nor more than $1,000. If the violation is uncorrected at the time of the conviction, the court shall order the violator to abate or remedy the violation in compliance with the zoning ordinance, within a time period established by the court. Failure to remove or abate a zoning violation within the specified time period shall constitute a separate misdemeanor offense punishable by a fine of not less than $10 nor more than $1,000, and any such failure during any succeeding 10-day period shall constitute a separate misdemeanor offense for each 10-day period punishable by a fine of not less than $100 nor more than $1,500.

However, any conviction resulting from a violation of provisions regulating the number of unrelated persons in single-family residential dwellings shall be punishable by a fine of up to $2,000. Failure to abate the violation within the specified time period shall be punishable by a fine of up to $2,000, and any such failure during any succeeding 10-day period shall constitute a separate misdemeanor offense for each 10-day period punishable by a fine of up to $2,500. A conviction resulting from a violation of provisions regulating the number of unrelated persons in single-family residential dwellings shall not be punishable by a jail term.

6. For the collection of fees to cover the cost of making inspections, issuing permits, advertising of notices and other expenses incident to the administration of a zoning ordinance or to the filing or processing of any appeal or amendment thereto.

7. For the amendment of the regulations or district maps from time to time, or for their repeal. Whenever the public necessity, convenience, general welfare, or good zoning practice requires, the governing body may by ordinance amend, supplement, or change the regulations, district boundaries, or classifications of property. Any such amendment may be initiated (i) by resolution of the governing body; (ii) by motion of the local planning commission; or (iii) by petition of the owner, contract purchaser with the owner's written consent, or the owner's agent therefor, of the property which is the subject of the proposed zoning map amendment, addressed to the governing body or the local planning commission, who shall forward such petition to the governing body; however, the ordinance may provide for the consideration of proposed amendments only at specified intervals of time, and may further provide that substantially the same petition will not be reconsidered within a specific period, not exceeding one year. Any such resolution or motion by such governing body or commission proposing the rezoning shall state the above public purposes therefor.

In any county having adopted such zoning ordinance, all motions, resolutions or petitions for amendment to the zoning ordinance, and/or map shall be acted upon and a decision made within such reasonable time as may be necessary which shall not exceed 12 months unless the applicant requests or consents to action beyond such period or unless the applicant withdraws his motion, resolution or petition for amendment to the zoning ordinance or map, or both. In the event of and upon such withdrawal, processing of the motion, resolution or petition shall cease without further action as otherwise would be required by this subdivision.

8. For the submission and approval of a plan of development prior to the issuance of building permits to assure compliance with regulations contained in such zoning ordinance.

9. For areas and districts designated for mixed use developments or planned unit developments as defined in § 15.2-2201.

10. For the administration of incentive zoning as defined in § 15.2-2201.

11. For provisions allowing the locality to enter into a voluntary agreement with a landowner that would result in the downzoning of the landowner's undeveloped or underdeveloped property in exchange for a tax credit equal to the amount of excess real estate taxes that the landowner has paid due to the higher zoning classification. The locality may establish reasonable guidelines for determining the amount of excess real estate tax collected and the method and duration for applying the tax credit. For

purposes of this section, "downzoning" means a zoning action by a locality that results in a reduction in a formerly permitted land use intensity or density.

12. Provisions for requiring and considering Phase I environmental site assessments based on the anticipated use of the property proposed for the subdivision or development that meet generally accepted national standards for such assessments, such as those developed by the American Society for Testing and Materials, and Phase II environmental site assessments, that also meet accepted national standards, such as, but not limited to, those developed by the American Society for Testing and Materials, if the locality deems such to be reasonably necessary, based on findings in the Phase I assessment, and in accordance with regulations of the United States Environmental Protection Agency and the American Society for Testing and Materials. A reasonable fee may be charged for the review of such environmental assessments. Such fees shall not exceed an amount commensurate with the services rendered, taking into consideration the time, skill, and administrative expense involved in such review.

13. Provisions for requiring disclosure and remediation of contamination and other adverse environmental conditions of the property prior to approval of subdivision and development plans.

14. For the enforcement of provisions of the zoning ordinance that regulate the number of persons permitted to occupy a single-family residential dwelling unit, provided such enforcement is in compliance with applicable local, state and federal fair housing laws.

B. Prior to the initiation of an application for a special exception, special use permit, variance, rezoning or other land disturbing permit, including building permits and erosion and sediment control permits, or prior to the issuance of final approval, the authorizing body may require the applicant to produce satisfactory evidence that any delinquent real estate taxes owed to the locality which have been properly assessed against the subject property have been paid. (Code 1950, § 15-968.5; 1962, c. 407, § 15.1-491; 1964, c. 564; 1966, c. 455; 1968, cc. 543, 595; 1973, c. 286; 1974, c. 547; 1975, cc. 99, 575, 579, 582, 641; 1976, cc. 71, 409, 470, 683; 1977, c. 177; 1978, c. 543; 1979, c. 182; 1982, c. 44; 1983, c. 392; 1984, c. 238; 1987, c. 8; 1988, cc. 481, 856; 1989, cc. 359, 384; 1990, cc. 672, 868; 1992, c. 380; 1993, c. 672; 1994, c. 802; 1995, cc. 351, 475, 584, 603; 1996, c. 451; 1997, cc. 529, 543, 587; 1998, c. 385; 1999, c. 792; 2000, cc. 764, 817; 2001, c. 240; 2002, cc. 547, 703; 2005, cc. 625, 677; 2006, cc. 304, 514, 533, 903; 2007, cc. 821, 937.)

The 2007 amendments. — The 2007 amendment by c. 821 inserted the present second paragraph in subdivision A 4.

The 2007 amendment by c. 937 added the last paragraph in subdivision A 5 and added subdivision A 13.

The section was set out in the form above at the direction of the Virginia Code Commission.

CIRCUIT COURT OPINIONS

Amendment to zoning ordinance properly enacted. — City's planning commission is not required to make available the actual text of an amendment to the zoning ordinance at the time the motion to initiate the amendment was adopted. Subdivision A 7 of § 15.2-2286 only requires that an amendment be initiated by motion or resolution; the initiation of a text amendment is merely a preliminary step to the adoption of an amendment. Ace Temps., Inc. v. City Council of Alexandria, 70 Va. Cir. 61, 2006 Va. Cir. LEXIS 72 (Alexandria 2006).

City council did not exceed its authority. — Once a city council denied a property owner's request to extend an amortization period, the owner could have been required to cease operations immediately. In allowing the owner an additional 30 days to cease its operations, the council was not, as the owner alleged, improperly exercising zoning enforcement powers granted to the zoning administrator under §§ 15.2-2286 and 15.2-2299, but was merely exercising its inherent authority under § 15.2-1102 to promote the general welfare of the city's inhabitants. Ace Temps., Inc. v. City Council of Alexandria, 70 Va. Cir. 61, 2006 Va. Cir. LEXIS 72 (Alexandria 2006).

§ 15.2-2288.3. Licensed farm wineries; local regulation of certain activities. — A. It is the policy of the Commonwealth to preserve the economic vitality of the Virginia wine industry while maintaining appropriate land use authority to protect the health, safety, and welfare of the citizens of the Commonwealth, and to permit the reasonable expectation of uses in specific zoning categories. Local restriction upon such activities and events of farm wineries licensed in accordance with Title 4.1 to market and sell their products shall be reasonable and shall take into account the economic impact on the farm winery of such restriction and whether such activities and events are usual and customary for farm wineries throughout the Commonwealth. Usual and customary activities and events at farm wineries shall be permitted without local regulation unless there is a substantial impact on the health, safety, or welfare of the public. No local ordinance regulating noise, other than outdoor amplified music, arising from activities and events at farm wineries shall be more restrictive than that in the general noise ordinance. In authorizing outdoor amplified music at a farm winery, the locality shall consider the effect on adjacent property owners and nearby residents.

B, C. [Expired.]

D. No locality may treat private personal gatherings held by the owner of a licensed farm winery who resides at the farm winery or on property adjacent thereto that is owned or controlled by such owner at which gatherings wine is not sold or marketed and for which no consideration is received by the farm winery or its agents differently from private personal gatherings by other citizens.

E. No locality shall regulate any of the following activities of a farm winery licensed in accordance with subdivision 5 of § 4.1-207:

1. The production and harvesting of fruit and other agricultural products and the manufacturing of wine;

2. The on-premises sale, tasting, or consumption of wine during regular business hours within the normal course of business of the licensed farm winery;

3. The direct sale and shipment of wine by common carrier to consumers in accordance with Title 4.1 and regulations of the Alcoholic Beverage Control Board;

4. The sale and shipment of wine to the Alcoholic Beverage Control Board, licensed wholesalers, and out-of-state purchasers in accordance with Title 4.1, regulations of the Alcoholic Beverage Control Board, and federal law;

5. The storage, warehousing, and wholesaling of wine in accordance with Title 4.1, regulations of the Alcoholic Beverage Control Board, and federal law; or

6. The sale of wine-related items that are incidental to the sale of wine. (2006, c. 794; 2007, cc. 611, 657.)

The 2007 amendments. — The 2007 amendments by cc. 611 and 657 rewrote the section.

Subsections B and C as added by the 2007 acts were redesignated as subsections D and E at the direction of the Virginia Code Commission.

Law Review. — For article, "Wine Tasting Activities in Virginia: Is America's First Wine Producing State Destined to Wither on the Vine Due to Overregulation?," see 23 T.M. Cooley L. Rev. 221 (2006).

§ 15.2-2291. Group homes of eight or fewer single-family residence. — A. Zoning ordinances for all purposes shall consider a residential facility in which no more than eight mentally ill, mentally retarded, or developmentally disabled persons reside, with one or more resident counselors or other staff persons, as residential occupancy by a single family. For the purposes of this subsection, mental illness and developmental disability shall not include current illegal use of or addiction to a controlled substance as defined in § 54.1-3401. No conditions more restrictive than those imposed on residences occupied by persons related by blood, marriage, or adoption shall be imposed on such facility. For purposes of this subsection, "residential facility" means any group home or other residential facility for which the Department of Mental Health, Mental Retardation and Substance Abuse Services is the licensing authority pursuant to this Code.

B. Zoning ordinances in the Counties of Arlington, Henry, and York for all purposes shall consider a residential facility in which no more than eight aged, infirm or disabled persons reside, with one or more resident counselors or other staff persons, as residential occupancy by a single family. No conditions more restrictive than those imposed on residences occupied by persons related by blood, marriage, or adoption shall be imposed on such facility. For purposes of this subsection, "residential facility"

means any group home or residential facility in which aged, infirm or disabled persons reside with one or more resident counselors or other staff persons and for which the Department of Social Services is the licensing authority pursuant to this Code.

C. Zoning ordinances in the Cities of Lynchburg and Suffolk for all purposes shall consider a residential facility in which no more than four aged, infirm or disabled persons reside, with one or more resident counselors or other staff persons, as residential occupancy by a single family. No conditions more restrictive than those imposed on residences occupied by persons related by blood, marriage or adoption shall be imposed on such facility. For purposes of this subsection, "residential facility" means any group home or residential facility in which aged, infirm or disabled persons reside with one or more resident counselors or other staff persons and for which the Department of Social Services is the licensing authority pursuant to this Code. (1990, c. 814, § 15.1-486.3; 1993, c. 373; 1997, c. 587; 1998, c. 585; 2007, c. 813.)

Editor's note. — Acts 2007, c. 813, cl. 2, provides: "That the provisions of this act shall not affect the powers of any locality with respect to any ordinance, resolution or bylaw validly adopted and not repealed or rescinded prior to July 1, 2007."

The 2007 amendments. — The 2007 amendment by c. 813 substituted "the Counties of Arlington, Henry, and York" for "counties having adopted the county manager plan of government and any county with a population between 55,800 and 57,000" in subsection B; and substituted "the Cities of Lynchburg and Suffolk" for "any city with a population between 60,000 and 70,000" in subsection C.

§ 15.2-2298. Same; additional conditions as a part of rezoning or zoning map amendment in certain high-growth localities. — A. Except for those localities to which § 15.2-2303 is applicable, this section shall apply to (i) any locality which has had population growth of 5% or more from the next-to-latest to latest decennial census year, based on population reported by the United States Bureau of the Census; (ii) any city adjoining such city or county; (iii) any towns located within such county; and (iv) any county contiguous with at least three such counties, and any town located in that county. However, any such locality may by ordinance choose to utilize the conditional zoning authority granted under § 15.2-2303 rather than this section.

In any such locality, notwithstanding any contrary provisions of § 15.2-2297, a zoning ordinance may include and provide for the voluntary proffering in writing, by the owner, of reasonable conditions, prior to a public hearing before the governing body, in addition to the regulations provided for the zoning district or zone by the ordinance, as a part of a rezoning or amendment to a zoning map, provided that (i) the rezoning itself gives rise to the need for the conditions; (ii) the conditions have a reasonable relation to the rezoning; and (iii) all conditions are in conformity with the comprehensive plan as defined in § 15.2-2223.

Reasonable conditions may include the payment of cash for any off-site road improvement or any off-site transportation improvement that is adopted as an amendment to the required comprehensive plan and incorporated into the capital improvements program, provided that nothing herein shall prevent a locality from accepting proffered conditions which are not normally included in a capital improvement program. For purposes of this section, "road improvement" includes construction of new roads or improvement or expansion of existing roads as required by applicable construction standards of the Virginia Department of Transportation to meet increased demand attributable to new development. For purposes of this section, "transportation improvement" means any real or personal property acquired, constructed, improved, or used for constructing, improving, or operating any (i) public mass transit system or (ii) highway, or portion or interchange thereof, including parking facilities located within a district created pursuant to this title. Such improvements shall include, without limitation, public mass transit systems, public highways, and all buildings, structures, approaches, and facilities thereof and appurtenances thereto, rights-of-way, bridges, tunnels, stations, terminals, and all related equipment and fixtures.

Reasonable conditions shall not include, however, conditions that impose upon the applicant the requirement to create a property owners' association under Chapter 26 (§ 55-508 et seq.) of Title 55 which includes an express further condition that members of a property association pay an assessment for the maintenance of public facilities owned in fee by a public entity, including open space, parks, schools, fire departments, and other public facilities not otherwise provided for in § 15.2-2241; however, such facilities shall not include sidewalks, special street signs or markers, or special street lighting in public rights-of-way not maintained by the Department of Transportation. The governing body may also accept amended proffers once the public hearing has begun if the amended proffers do not materially affect the overall proposal. Once proffered and accepted as part of an amendment to the zoning ordinance, the conditions shall continue in effect until a subsequent amendment changes the zoning on the property covered by the conditions; however, the conditions shall continue if the subsequent amendment is part of a comprehensive implementation of a new or substantially revised zoning ordinance.

No proffer shall be accepted by a locality unless it has adopted a capital improvement program pursuant to § 15.2-2239 or local charter. In the event proffered conditions include the dedication of real property or payment of cash, the property shall not transfer and the payment of cash shall not be made until the facilities for which the property is dedicated or cash is tendered are included in the capital improvement program, provided that nothing herein shall prevent a locality from accepting proffered conditions which are not normally included in a capital improvement program. If proffered conditions include the dedication of real property or the payment of cash, the proffered conditions shall provide for the disposition of the property or cash payment in the event the property or cash payment is not used for the purpose for which proffered.

B. In the event proffered conditions include a requirement for the dedication of real property of substantial value, or substantial cash payments for or construction of substantial public improvements, the need for which is not generated solely by the rezoning itself, then no amendment to the zoning map for the property subject to such conditions, nor the conditions themselves, nor any amendments to the text of the zoning ordinance with respect to the zoning district applicable thereto initiated by the governing body, which eliminate, or materially restrict, reduce, or modify the uses, the floor area ratio, or the density of use permitted in the zoning district applicable to the property, shall be effective with respect to the property unless there has been mistake, fraud, or a change in circumstances substantially affecting the public health, safety, or welfare.

C. Any landowner who has prior to July 1, 1990, proffered the dedication of real property of substantial value, or substantial cash payments for or construction of substantial public improvements, the need for which is not generated solely by the rezoning itself, but who has not substantially implemented such proffers prior to July 1, 1990, shall advise the local governing body by certified mail prior to July 1, 1991, that he intends to proceed with the implementation of such proffers. The notice shall identify the property to be developed, the zoning district, and the proffers applicable thereto. Thereafter, any landowner giving such notice shall have until July 1, 1995, substantially to implement the proffers, or such later time as the governing body may allow. Thereafter, the landowner in good faith shall diligently pursue the completion of the development of the property. Any landowner who complies with the requirements of this subsection shall be entitled to the protection against action initiated by the governing body affecting use, floor area ratio, and density set out in subsection B above, unless there has been mistake, fraud, or a change in circumstances substantially affecting the public health, safety, or welfare, but any landowner failing to comply with the requirements of this subsection shall acquire no rights pursuant to this section.

D. The provisions of subsections B and C of this section shall be effective prospectively only, and not retroactively, and shall not apply to any zoning ordinance text amendments which may have been enacted prior to March 10, 1990. Nothing contained herein shall be construed to affect any litigation pending prior to July 1, 1990, or any such litigation nonsuited and thereafter refiled.

Nothing in this section shall be construed to affect or impair the authority of a governing body to:

1. Accept proffered conditions which include provisions for timing or phasing of dedications, payments, or improvements; or

2. Accept or impose valid conditions pursuant to provision 3 of § 15.2-2286 or other provision of law. (1989, c. 697, § 15.1-492.2:1; 1990, c. 868; 1991, c. 233; 1997, c. 587; 2001, c. 703; 2006, cc. 450, 882; 2007, c. 324.)

The 2007 amendments. — The 2007 amendment by c. 324 added the second sentence in subsection A.

§ 15.2-2299. Same; enforcement and guarantees.

CIRCUIT COURT OPINIONS

City council did not exceed its authority. — Once a city council denied a property owner's request to extend an amortization period, the owner could have been required to cease operations immediately. In allowing the owner an additional 30 days to cease its operations, the council was not, as the owner alleged, improperly exercising zoning enforcement powers granted to the zoning administrator under §§ 15.2-2286 and 15.2-2299, but was merely exercising its inherent authority under § 15.2-1102 to promote the general welfare of the city's inhabitants. Ace Temps., Inc. v. City Council of Alexandria, 70 Va. Cir. 61, 2006 Va. Cir. LEXIS 72 (Alexandria 2006).

§ 15.2-2303.1. Development agreements in certain counties. —

A. In order to promote the public health, safety and welfare and to encourage economic development consistent with careful planning, New Kent County may include in its zoning ordinance provisions for the governing body to enter into binding development agreements with any persons owning legal or equitable interests in real property in the county if the property to be developed contains at least one thousand acres.

B. Any such agreements shall be for the purpose of stimulating and facilitating economic growth in the county; shall not be inconsistent with the comprehensive plan at the time of the agreement's adoption, except as may have been authorized by existing zoning ordinances; and shall not authorize any use or condition inconsistent with the zoning ordinance or other ordinances in effect at the time the agreement is made, except as may be authorized by a variance, special exception or similar authorization. The agreement shall be authorized by ordinance, shall be for a term not to exceed fifteen years, and may be renewed by mutual agreement of the parties for successive terms of not more than ten years each. It may provide, among other things, for uses; the density or intensity of uses; the maximum height, size, setback and/or location of buildings; the number of parking spaces required; the location of streets and other public improvements; the measures required to control stormwater; the phasing or

timing of construction or development; or any other land use matters. It may authorize the property owner to transfer to the county land, public improvements, money or anything of value to further the purposes of the agreement or other public purposes set forth in the county's comprehensive plan, but not as a condition to obtaining any permitted use or zoning. The development agreement shall not run with the land except to the extent provided therein, and the agreement may be amended or canceled in whole or in part by the mutual consent of the parties thereto or their successors in interest and assigns.

C. If, pursuant to the agreement, a property owner who is a party thereto and is not in breach thereof, (i) dedicates or is required to dedicate real property to the county, the Commonwealth or any other political subdivision or to the federal government or any agency thereof, (ii) makes or is required to make cash payments to the county, the Commonwealth or any other political subdivision or to the federal government or any agency thereof, or (iii) makes or is required to make public improvements for the county, the Commonwealth or any other political subdivision or for the federal government or any agency thereof, such dedication, payment or construction therefor shall vest the property owner's rights under the agreement. If a property owner's rights have vested, neither any amendment to the zoning map for the subject property nor any amendment to the text of the zoning ordinance with respect to the zoning district applicable to the property which eliminates or restricts, reduces, or modifies the use; the density or intensity of uses; the maximum height, size, setback or location of buildings; the number of parking spaces required; the location of streets and other public improvements; the measures required to control stormwater; the phasing or timing of construction or development; or any other land use or other matters provided for in such agreement shall be effective with respect to such property during the term of the agreement unless there has been a mistake, fraud or change in circumstances substantially affecting the public health, safety or welfare.

D. Nothing in this section shall be construed to preclude, limit or alter the vesting of rights in accordance with existing law; authorize the impairment of such rights; or invalidate any similar agreements entered into pursuant to existing law. (1997, c. 738, § 15.1-491.001; 2007, c. 813.)

Editor's note. — Acts 2007, c. 813, cl. 2, provides: "That the provisions of this act shall not affect the powers of any locality with respect to any ordinance, resolution or bylaw validly adopted and not repealed or rescinded prior to July 1, 2007."

The 2007 amendments. — The 2007 amendment by c. 813 substituted "New Kent County" for "any county with a population between 10,300 and 11,000 according to the 1990 United States Census through which an interstate highway passes" in subsection A.

§ 15.2-2303.2. Proffered cash payments and expenditures. —

A. The governing body of any

locality accepting cash payments voluntarily proffered on or after July 1, 2005, pursuant to § 15.2-2298, 15.2-2303 or 15.2-2303.1 shall, within seven years of receiving full payment of all cash proffered pursuant to an approved rezoning application, begin, or cause to begin (i) construction, (ii) site work, (iii) engineering, (iv) right-of-way acquisition, (v) surveying, or (vi) utility relocation on the improvements for which the cash payments were proffered. A locality that does not comply with the above requirement, or does not begin alternative improvements as provided for in subsection C, shall forward the amount of the proffered cash payments to the Commonwealth Transportation Board no later than December 31 following the fiscal year in which such forfeiture occurred for direct allocation to the secondary system construction program or the urban system construction program for the locality in which the proffered cash payments were collected. The funds to which any locality may be entitled under the provisions of Title 33.1 for construction, improvement, or maintenance of primary, secondary, or urban roads shall not be diminished by reason of any funds remitted pursuant to this subsection by such locality, regardless of whether such contributions are matched by state or federal funds.

B. The governing body of any locality eligible to accept any proffered cash payments pursuant to § 15.2-2298, 15.2-2303 or 15.2-2303.1 shall, for each fiscal year beginning with the fiscal year 2007, (i) include in its capital improvement program created pursuant to § 15.2-2239, or as an appendix thereto, the amount of all proffered cash payments received during the most recent fiscal year for which a report has been filed pursuant to subsection D, and (ii) include in its annual capital budget the amount of proffered cash payments projected to be used for expenditures or appropriated for capital improvements in the ensuing year.

C. Regardless of the date of rezoning approval, unless prohibited by the proffer agreement accepted by the governing body of a locality pursuant to § 15.2-2298, 15.2-2303, or 15.2-2303.1, a locality may utilize any cash payments proffered for any road improvement or any transportation improvement that is incorporated into the capital improvements program as its matching contribution under § 33.1-23.05. For purposes of this section, "road improvement" includes construction of new roads or improvement or expansion of existing roads as required by applicable construction standards of the Virginia Department of Transportation to meet increased demand attributable to new development. For purposes of this section, "transportation improvement" means any real or personal property acquired, constructed, improved, or used for constructing, improving, or operating any (i) public mass transit system or (ii) highway, or portion or interchange thereof, including parking facilities located within a district created pursuant to this title. Such improvements shall include, without limitation, public mass transit systems, public highways, and all buildings, structures, approaches, and facilities thereof and appurtenances thereto, rights-of-way, bridges, tunnels, stations, terminals, and all related equipment and fixtures.

Regardless of the date of rezoning approval, unless prohibited by the proffer agreement accepted by the governing body of a locality pursuant to § 15.2-2298, 15.2-2303, or 15.2-2303.1, a locality may utilize any cash payments proffered for capital improvements for alternative improvements of the same category within the locality in the vicinity of the improvements for which the cash payments were originally made. Prior to utilization of such cash payments for the alternative improvements, the governing body of the locality shall give at least 30 days' written notice of the proposed alternative improvements to the entity who paid such cash payment mailed to the last known address of such entity, or if proffer payment records no longer exist, then to the original zoning applicant, and conduct a public hearing on such proposal advertised as provided in subsection F of § 15.2-1427. The governing body of the locality prior to the use of such cash payments for alternative improvements shall, following such public hearing, find: (i) the improvements for which the cash payments were proffered cannot occur in a timely manner; (ii) the alternative improvements are within the vicinity of the proposed improvements for which the cash payments were proffered; and (iii) the alternative improvements are in the public interest. Notwithstanding the provisions of the Virginia Public Procurement Act, the governing body may negotiate and award a contract without competition to an entity that is constructing road improvements pursuant to a proffered zoning condition or special exception condition in order to expand the scope of the road improvements by utilizing cash proffers of others or other available locally generated funds. The local governing body shall adopt a resolution stating the basis for awarding the construction contract to extend the scope of the road improvements. All road improvements to be included in the state primary or secondary system of highways must conform to the adopted standards of the Virginia Department of Transportation.

D. The governing body of any locality with a population in excess of 3,500 persons accepting a cash payment voluntarily proffered pursuant to § 15.2-2298, 15.2-2303 or 15.2-2303.1 shall within three months of the close of each fiscal year, beginning in fiscal year 2002 and for each fiscal year thereafter, report to the Commission on Local Government the following information for the preceding fiscal year:

1. The aggregate dollar amount of proffered cash payments collected by the locality;

2. The estimated aggregate dollar amount of proffered cash payments that have been pledged to the locality and which pledges are not conditioned on any event other than time; and

3. The total dollar amount of proffered cash payments expended by the locality, and the aggregate dollar amount expended in each of the following categories:

Schools	$____
Road and other Transportation Improvements	$____
Fire and Rescue/Public Safety	$____
Libraries	$____
Parks, Recreation, and Open Space	$____
Water and Sewer Service Extension	$____
Community Centers	$____
Stormwater Management	$____
Special Needs Housing	$____
Affordable Housing	$____
Miscellaneous	$____
Total dollar amount expended	$____

E. The governing body of any locality with a population in excess of 3,500 persons eligible to accept any proffered cash payments pursuant to § 15.2-2298, 15.2-2303 or 15.2-2303.1 but that did not accept any proffered cash payments during the preceding fiscal year shall within three months of the close of each fiscal year, beginning in 2001 and for each fiscal year thereafter, so notify the Commission on Local Government.

F. The Commission on Local Government shall by November 30, 2001, and by November 30 of each fiscal year thereafter, prepare and make available to the public and the chairmen of the Senate Local Government Committee and the House Counties, Cities and Towns Committee an annual report containing the information made available to it pursuant to subsections D and E. (2001, c. 282; 2003, c. 522; 2005, c. 855; 2006, cc. 583, 872, 882; 2007, c. 321.)

The 2007 amendments. — The 2007 amendment by c. 321, effective March 13, 2007, inserted "or special exception condition" following "proffered zoning condition" in clause (iii) in the second paragraph of subsection C.

§ **15.2-2305. Affordable dwelling unit ordinances.** — A. In furtherance of the purpose of providing affordable shelter for all residents of the Commonwealth, the governing body of any locality, other than localities to which § 15.2-2304 applies, may by amendment to the zoning ordinances of such locality provide for an affordable housing dwelling unit program. Such program shall address housing needs, promote a full range of housing choices, and encourage the construction and continued existence of housing affordable to low and moderate income citizens, determined in accordance with the locality's definition of affordable housing, by providing for increases in density to the applicant in exchange for the applicant providing such affordable housing. Any local ordinance providing optional increases in density for provision of low and moderate income housing adopted before December 31, 1988, shall continue in full force and effect. Any local ordinance may authorize the governing body to (i) establish qualifying jurisdiction-wide affordable dwelling unit sales prices based on local market conditions, (ii) establish jurisdiction-wide affordable dwelling unit qualifying income guidelines, and (iii) offer incentives other than density increases, such as reductions or waiver of permit, development, and infrastructure fees, as the governing body deems appropriate to encourage the provision of affordable housing. Counties to which § 15.2-2304 applies shall be governed by the provisions of § 15.2-2304 for purposes of the adoption of an affordable dwelling unit ordinance.

B. Any zoning ordinance establishing an affordable housing dwelling unit program may include, among other things, reasonable regulations and provisions as to any or all of the following:

1. A definition of affordable housing and affordable dwelling units.

2. For application of the requirements of an affordable housing dwelling unit program to any site, as defined by the locality, or a portion thereof at one location which is the subject of an application for rezoning or special exception or, at the discretion of the local governing body, site plan or subdivision plat which yields, as submitted by the applicant, at an equivalent density greater than one unit per acre and which is located within an approved sewer area.

3. For an increase of up to 30 percent in the developable density of each site subject to the ordinance and for a provision requiring up to 17 percent of the total units approved, including the optional density increase, to be affordable dwelling units, as defined in the ordinance. In the event a 30 percent increase is not achieved, the percentage of affordable dwelling units required shall maintain the same ratio of 30 percent to 17 percent.

4. For increases by up to 30 percent of the density or of the lower and upper end of the density range set forth in the comprehensive plan of such locality applicable to rezoning and special exception applications that request approval of single family detached dwelling units or single family attached dwelling units, when such applications are approved after the effective date of a local affordable housing zoning ordinance amendment.

5. For a requirement that not less than 17 percent of the total number of dwelling units approved pursuant to a zoning ordinance amendment enacted pursuant to subdivision B 4 of this section shall be affordable dwelling units, as defined by the local zoning ordinance unless reduced by the 30 to 17 percent ratio pursuant to subdivision B 3 of this section.

6. For establishment of a local housing fund as part of its affordable housing dwelling unit program to assist in achieving the affordable housing goals of the locality pursuant to this section. The local housing fund may be a dedicated fund within the other funds of the locality, but any funds received pursuant to this section shall be used for achieving the affordable housing goals of the locality.

7. For reasonable regulations requiring the affordable dwelling units to be built and offered for sale or rental concurrently with the construction and certificate of occupancy of a reasonable proportion of the market rate units.

8. For standards of compliance with the provisions of an affordable housing dwelling unit program and for the authority of the local governing body or its designee to enforce compliance with such standards and impose reasonable penalties for noncompliance, provided that a local zoning ordinance provide for an appeal process for any party aggrieved by a decision of the local governing body.

C. For any building which is four stories or above and has an elevator, the applicant may request, and the locality shall consider, the unique ancillary costs associated with living in such a building in determining whether such housing will be affordable under the definition established by the locality in its ordinance adopted pursuant to this section. However, for localities under this section in Planning District Eight, nothing in this section shall apply to any elevator structure four stories or above.

D. Any ordinance adopted hereunder shall provide that the local governing body shall have no more than 280 days in which to process site or subdivision plans proposing the development or construction of affordable housing or affordable dwelling units under such ordinance. The calculation of such period of review shall include only the time that plans are in review by the local governing body and shall not include such time as may be required for revision or modification in order to comply with lawful requirements set forth in applicable ordinances and regulations.

E. A locality establishing an affordable housing dwelling unit program in any ordinance shall establish in its general ordinances, adopted in accordance with the requirements of § 15.2-1427 B, reasonable regulations and provisions as to any or all of the following:

1. For administration and regulation by a local housing authority or by the local governing body or its designee of the sale and rental of affordable units.

2. For a local housing authority or local governing body or its designee to have an exclusive right to purchase up to one-third of the for-sale affordable housing dwelling units within a development within ninety days of a dwelling unit being completed and ready for purchase, provided that the remaining two-thirds of such units be offered for sale exclusively for a ninety-day period to persons who meet the income criteria established by the local housing authority or local governing body or the latter's designee.

3. For a local housing authority or local governing body or its designee to have an exclusive right to lease up to a specified percentage of the rental affordable dwelling units within a development within a controlled period determined by the hous-

ing authority or local governing body or its designee, provided that the remaining for-rental affordable dwelling units within a development be offered to persons who meet the income criteria established by the local housing authority or local governing body or its designee.

4. For the establishment of jurisdiction-wide affordable dwelling unit sales prices by the local housing authority or local governing body or the latter's designee, initially and adjusted semiannually, based on a determination of all ordinary, necessary and reasonable costs required to construct the affordable dwelling unit prototype dwellings by private industry after considering written comment by the public, local housing authority or advisory body to the local governing body, and other information such as the area's current general market and economic conditions, provided that sales prices not include the cost of land, on-site sales commissions and marketing expenses, but may include, among other costs, builder-paid permanent mortgage placement costs and buy-down fees and closing costs except prepaid expenses required at settlement.

5. For the establishment of jurisdiction-wide affordable dwelling unit rental prices by a local housing authority or local governing body or its designee, initially and adjusted semiannually, based on a determination of all ordinary, necessary and reasonable costs required to construct and market the required number of affordable dwelling rental units by private industry in the area, after considering written comment by the public, local housing authority, or advisory body to the local governing body, and other information such as the area's current general market and economic conditions.

6. For a requirement that the prices for resales and rerentals be controlled by the local housing authority or local governing body or designee for a period of fifty years after the initial sale or rental transaction for each affordable dwelling unit, provided that the ordinance further provide for reasonable rules and regulations to implement a price control provision.

7. For establishment of an affordable dwelling unit advisory board which shall, among other things, advise the jurisdiction on sales and rental prices of affordable dwelling units; advise the housing authority or local governing body or its designees on requests for modifications of the requirements of an affordable dwelling unit program; adopt regulations concerning its recommendations of sales and rental prices of affordable dwelling units; and adopt procedures concerning requests for modifications of an affordable housing dwelling unit program. Members of the board, to be ten in number and to be appointed by the governing body, shall be qualified as follows: two members shall be either civil engineers or architects, each of whom shall be registered or certified with the relevant agency of the Commonwealth, or planners, all of whom shall have extensive experience in practice in the locality; one mem-

ber shall be a real estate salesperson or broker, licensed in accordance with Chapter 21 (§ 54.1-2100 et seq.) of Title 54.1; one member shall be a representative of a lending institution which finances residential development in the locality; four members shall consist of a representative from a local housing authority or local governing body or its designee, a residential builder with extensive experience in producing single-family detached and attached dwelling units, a residential builder with extensive experience in producing multiple-family dwelling units, and a representative from either the public works or planning department of the locality; one member may be a representative of a nonprofit housing organization which provides services in the locality; and one citizen of the locality. At least four members of the advisory board shall be employed in the locality.

F. A locality establishing an affordable housing dwelling unit program in any ordinance shall establish in its general ordinances, adopted in accordance with the requirements of subsection B of § 15.2-1427, reasonable regulations and provisions as to the following:

The sales and rental price for affordable dwelling units within a development shall be established such that the owner/applicant shall not suffer economic loss as a result of providing the required affordable dwelling units. "Economic loss" for sales units means that result when the owner or applicant of a development fails to recoup the cost of construction and certain allowances as may be determined by the designee of the governing body for the affordable dwelling units, exclusive of the cost of land acquisition and cost voluntarily incurred but not authorized by the ordinance, upon the sale of an affordable dwelling unit. (1990, c. 834, § 15.1-491.9; 1991, c. 599; 1992, c. 244; 1993, c. 437; 1994, cc. 88, 679; 1996, cc. 233, 426; 1997, cc. 587, 607; 2007, cc. 695, 713.)

The 2007 amendments. — The 2007 amendments by cc. 695 and 713 are identical, and rewrote subsections A through C; substituted "any ordinance" for "its zoning ordinance" in the introductory language of subsection E; and added the introductory language of subsection F and made related changes.

§ 15.2-2306. Preservation of historical sites and architectural areas.

CIRCUIT COURT OPINIONS

Relief against county not warranted. — Complainants had not stated grounds for declaratory relief against the county for the regulations it took to preserve a village as an historic district because the regulations did not exceed the authority conferred upon the county pursuant to § 15.2-2306. Additionally the complainants did not object to the proposed regulations as required under § 15.2-2285. Madison v. Loudoun County Bd. of Supervisors, 69 Va. Cir. 469, 2006 Va. Cir. LEXIS 89 (Loudoun County 2006).

§ 15.2-2307. Vested rights not impaired; nonconforming uses.

Law Review.
For annual survey article, "Real Estate Law," see 41 U. Rich. L. Rev. 257 (2006).

OPINIONS OF THE ATTORNEY GENERAL

Effect of amendment to zoning ordinance on specific use. —A landowner who has secured rezoning of properties for a specific use before the effective date of a subsequent amendment to the zoning ordinance, and who has pursued the project committing and expending significant resources, has obtained a vested right with respect to such use. See opinion of Attorney General to Delegate Bradley P. Marrs, 04-093 (3/25/05).

§ 15.2-2308. Boards of zoning appeals to be created; membership, organization, etc. —

A. Every locality that has enacted or enacts a zoning ordinance pursuant to this chapter or prior enabling laws, shall establish a board of zoning appeals that shall consist of either five or seven residents of the locality, appointed by the circuit court for the locality. Boards of zoning appeals for a locality within the fifteenth or nineteenth judicial circuit may be appointed by the chief judge or his designated judge or judges in their respective circuit, upon concurrence of such locality. Their terms of office shall be for five years each except that original appointments shall be made for such terms that the term of one member shall expire each year. The secretary of the board shall notify the court at least thirty days in advance of the expiration of any term of office, and shall also notify the court promptly if any vacancy occurs. Appointments to fill vacancies shall be only for the unexpired portion of the term. Members may be reappointed to succeed themselves. Members of the board shall hold no other public office in the locality except that one may be a member of the local planning commission. A member whose term expires shall continue to serve until his successor is appointed and qualifies. The circuit court for the City of Chesapeake and the Circuit Court for the City of Hampton shall appoint at least one but not more than three alternates to the board of zoning appeals. At the request of the local governing body, the circuit court for any other locality may appoint not more than three alternates to the board of zoning appeals. The qualifications, terms and compensation of alternate members shall be the same as those of regular members. A regular member when he knows he will be absent from or will have to abstain from any application at a meeting shall notify the chairman twenty-four hours prior to the meeting of such fact. The chairman shall select an alternate to serve in the absent or abstaining member's place and the records of the board shall so note. Such alternate member may vote on any application in which a regular member abstains.

B. Localities may, by ordinances enacted in each jurisdiction, create a joint board of zoning appeals that shall consist of two members appointed from among the residents of each participating jurisdiction by the circuit court for each county or city, plus one member from the area at large to be appointed by the circuit court or jointly by such courts if more than one, having jurisdiction in the area. The term of office of each member shall be five years except that of the two members first appointed from each jurisdiction, the term of one shall be for two years and of the other, four years. Vacancies shall be filled for the unexpired terms. In other respects, joint boards of zoning appeals shall be governed by all other provisions of this article.

C. With the exception of its secretary and the alternates, the board shall elect from its own membership its officers who shall serve annual terms as such and may succeed themselves. The board may elect as its secretary either one of its members or a qualified individual who is not a member of the board, excluding the alternate members. A secretary who is not a member of the board shall not be entitled to vote on matters before the board. For the conduct of any hearing and the taking of any action, a quorum shall be not less than a majority of all the members of the board. The board may make, alter and rescind rules and forms for its procedures, consistent with ordinances of the locality and general laws of the Commonwealth. The board shall keep a full public record of its proceedings and shall submit a report of its activities to the governing body or bodies at least once each year.

D. Within the limits of funds appropriated by the governing body, the board may employ or contract for secretaries, clerks, legal counsel, consultants, and other technical and clerical services. Members of the board may receive such compensation as may be authorized by the respective governing bodies. Any board member or alternate may be removed for malfeasance, misfeasance or nonfeasance in office, or for other just cause, by the court that appointed him, after a hearing held after at least fifteen days' notice.

E. Notwithstanding any contrary provisions of this section, in the City of Virginia Beach, members of the board shall be appointed by the governing body. The governing body of such city shall also appoint at least one but not more than three alternates to the board. (Code 1950, §§ 15-825, 15-850, 15-968.8; 1950, pp. 176, 489; 1952, c. 688; 1962, c. 407, § 15.1-494; 1975, c. 641; 1976, c. 642; 1977, c. 172; 1982, c. 3; 1989, c. 27; 1992, c. 47; 1997, cc. 570, 587; 1998, cc. 346, 520, 528; 1999, c. 838; 2002, cc. 205, 545; 2007, c. 813.)

Editor's note. — Acts 2007, c. 813, cl. 2, provides: "That the provisions of this act shall not affect the powers of any locality with respect to any ordinance, resolution or bylaw validly adopted and not repealed or rescinded prior to July 1, 2007."

The 2007 amendments. — The 2007 amendment by c. 813 substituted "the City of Chesapeake and the Circuit Court for the

City of Hampton" for "a city having a population of more than 140,000 but less than 170,000" in subsection A; and substituted "the City of Virginia Beach" for "any city with a population greater than 390,000" in subsection E.

Law Review. — For article reviewing recent developments and changes in legislation, case law, and Virginia Supreme Court Rules affecting civil litigation, "Civil Practice and Procedure," see 40 U. Rich. L. Rev. 95 (2005).

§ 15.2-2309. Powers and duties of boards of zoning appeals.

Law Review.
For annual survey article, "Real Estate Law," see 41 U. Rich. L. Rev. 257 (2006).

CASE NOTES

Exceptional shallowness of lots does not justify variance. — Variances to permit residential construction on five lots of an owner's land that were rendered unbuildable by overlapping setbacks imposed under the Chesapeake Bay Preservation Act (Act), § 10.1-2100 et seq., were properly denied; the exceptional shallowness of the lots did not require a variance because the owner did not show that the lots existed when the Act was passed, and the denial did not interfere with all reasonable beneficial uses of the land since a single residence could have been built on the entire parcel. Cherrystone Inlet, LLC v. Bd. of Zoning Appeals, 271 Va. 670, 628 S.E.2d 324, 2006 Va. LEXIS 35 (2006).

CIRCUIT COURT OPINIONS

Board taking on litigant's role. — Court denied a board of zoning appeals' motion to have the court reconsider its grant of a county's motion for a voluntary nonsuit. In making the motion, the board was asking the court to sustain the board's position on a totally procedural issue that had nothing to do with the board's responsibility under § 15.2-2309 to assure uniform enforcement of the county zoning ordinance; the board was taking on the role of a litigant, which was contrary to its duties under § 15.2-2309 and to the proper role of a tribunal in the American system of justice. Bd. of Supervisors v. Bd. of Zoning Appeals, — Va. Cir. —, 2006 Va. Cir. LEXIS 262 (Fairfax County Dec. 12, 2006).

§ 15.2-2314. Certiorari to review decision of board. — Any person or persons jointly or severally aggrieved by any decision of the board of zoning appeals, or any aggrieved taxpayer or any officer, department, board or bureau of the locality, may file with the clerk of the circuit court for the county or city a petition specifying the grounds on which aggrieved within 30 days after the final decision of the board.

Upon the presentation of such petition, the court shall allow a writ of certiorari to review the decision of the board of zoning appeals and shall prescribe therein the time within which a return thereto must be made and served upon the relator's attorney, which shall not be less than 10 days and may be extended by the court. The allowance of the writ shall not stay proceedings upon the decision appealed from, but the court may, on application, on notice to the board and on due cause shown, grant a restraining order.

The board of zoning appeals shall not be required to return the original papers acted upon by it but it shall be sufficient to return certified or sworn copies thereof or of the portions thereof as may be called for by the writ. The return shall concisely set forth such other facts as may be pertinent and material to show the grounds of the decision appealed from and shall be verified.

If, upon the hearing, it shall appear to the court that testimony is necessary for the proper disposition of the matter, it may take evidence or appoint a commissioner to take evidence as it may direct and report the evidence to the court with his findings of fact and conclusions of law, which shall constitute a part of the proceedings upon which the determination of the court shall be made. The court may reverse or affirm, wholly or partly, or may modify the decision brought up for review.

In the case of an appeal from the board of zoning appeals to the circuit court of an order, requirement, decision or determination of a zoning administrator or other administrative officer in the administration or enforcement of any ordinance or provision of state law, or any modification of zoning requirements pursuant to § 15.2-2286, the findings and conclusions of the board of zoning appeals on questions of fact shall be presumed to be correct. The appealing party may rebut that presumption by proving by a preponderance of the evidence, including the record before the board of zoning appeals, that the board of zoning appeals erred in its decision. Any party may introduce evidence in the proceedings in the court. The court shall hear any arguments on questions of law de novo.

In the case of an appeal by a person of any decision of the board of zoning appeals that denied or granted an application for a variance, or application for a special exception, the decision of the board of zoning appeals shall be presumed to be correct. The petitioner may rebut that presumption by showing to the satisfaction of the court that the board of zoning appeals applied erroneous principles of law, or where the discretion of the board of zoning appeals is involved, the decision of the board of zoning appeals was plainly wrong and in violation of the purpose and intent of the zoning ordinance.

Costs shall not be allowed against the board, unless it shall appear to the court that it acted in bad faith or with malice in making the decision appealed from. In the event the decision of the board is affirmed and the court finds that the appeal was frivolous, the court may order the person or persons who requested the issuance of the writ of certiorari to pay the costs incurred in making the return of the record pursuant to the writ of certiorari. If the petition is withdrawn subsequent to the filing of the return, the board may request that the court hear the matter on the question of whether the appeal was frivolous. (Code 1950, §§ 15-834 through 15-839, 15-850, 15-958.11; 1950, p. 176; 1962, c. 407, § 15.1-497; 1975, c. 641; 1988, c. 856; 1994, c. 705; 1996, c. 450; 1997, c. 587; 2001, c. 422; 2003, c. 568; 2005, cc. 625, 677; 2006, c. 446.)

Editor's note. — At the direction of the Virginia Code Commission, "relator's attorney" has been substituted for "realtor's attorney" in the second paragraph.

Law Review.

For article reviewing recent developments and changes in legislation, case law, and Virginia Supreme Court Rules affecting civil litigation, "Civil Practice and Procedure," see 40 U. Rich. L. Rev. 95 (2005). For annual survey article, "Real Estate Law," see 41 U. Rich. L. Rev. 257 (2006).

CASE NOTES

Weight of board's decision.

Upon a review of a circuit court's decision, which upheld the findings of both the zoning administrator and the zoning board of appeals, two properties, separated by a 50-foot-wide public street were not "adjacent," and hence, did not constitute one zoning lot under the plain language of Norfolk, Va., Zoning Ordinance § 2-3; hence, a church that owned the property at issue failed to rebut the presumption of correctness of the zoning board's decision. Trustees of the Christ & St. Luke's Episcopal Church v. Bd. of Zoning Appeals of Norfolk, — Va. —, 641 S.E.2d 104, 2007 Va. LEXIS 29 (2007).

Applied in Cherrystone Inlet, LLC v. Bd. of Zoning Appeals, 271 Va. 670, 628 S.E.2d 324, 2006 Va. LEXIS 35 (2006).

CIRCUIT COURT OPINIONS

Tolling of 30-day limitations period. — There is no conflict between §§ 15.2-2314 and 8.01-229, as § 15.2-2314 articulates the limitations period for the initial filing of a claim arising from an adverse decision by a board of zoning appeals, whereas § 8.01-299 creates and defines the contours of a tolling of the limitations period upon the exercise of a voluntary nonsuit. Bd. of Supervisors v. Bd. of Zoning Appeals, 71 Va. Cir. 170, 2006 Va. Cir. LEXIS 103 (Fairfax County 2006).

Appeals' board determination upheld.

Board of zoning appeals' finding that a business was a "day labor agency" and thus was required to obtain a special use permit was not based on erroneous legal principles and was supported by evidence concerning the nature of the business's operations, the nature and length of work performed by its workers, as well as police reports and citizen complaints. Ace Temps., Inc. v. City Council of Alexandria, 70 Va. Cir. 61, 2006 Va. Cir. LEXIS 72 (Alexandria 2006).

ARTICLE 7.1.

Transfer of Development Rights.

§ 15.2-2316.1. Definitions. — As used in this article, the term:

"*Development rights*" means the permitted uses and density of development that are allowed on the sending property under any zoning ordinance of a locality on a date prescribed by the ordinance.

"*Receiving area*" means an area identified by an ordinance and designated by the comprehensive plan as an area authorized to receive development rights transferred from a sending area.

"*Receiving property*" means a lot or parcel within which development rights are increased pursuant to a transfer of development rights. Receiving property shall be appropriate and suitable for development and shall be sufficient to accommodate the transferable development rights of the sending property.

"*Sending area*" means an area identified by an ordinance and designated by the comprehensive plan as an area from which development rights are authorized to be transferred to a receiving area.

"*Sending property*" means a lot or parcel that a locality deems necessary to limit future development in accordance with the ordinance adopted in subsection C of § 15.2-2316.2 or a receiving property that has received development rights from a sending property.

"*Transfer of development rights*" means the process by which development rights from a sending property are affixed to one or more receiving properties. (2006, c. 573; 2007, cc. 363, 410.)

The 2007 amendments. — The 2007 amendments by cc. 363 and 410 are identical, and in the definition of "Development rights" substituted "are" for "would be" and "on a date prescribed by the ordinance" for "in effect on the date an application is submitted pursuant to this article" and deleted "local" preceding "zoning ordinance"; and inserted "or a receiving property that has received development rights from a sending property" in the definition of "Sending propery."

§ 15.2-2316.2. Localities may provide for transfer of development rights. — A. Pursuant to the provisions of this article, the governing body of any locality by ordinance may, in order to conserve and promote the public health, safety, and general welfare, establish procedures, methods, and standards for the transfer of development rights within its jurisdiction. Any locality adopting or amending any such transfer of development rights ordinance shall give notice and hold a public hearing in accordance with § 15.2-2204 prior to approval by the governing body.

B. Any proposed transfer of development rights shall only be initiated upon application by the property owners of both the sending and receiving properties. A locality may not require property owners to transfer development rights as a condition of the development of any property.

C. Prior to any transfer of development rights, a locality shall adopt an ordinance based on findings of public benefit. Such ordinance shall provide for:

1. The issuance and recordation of the instruments necessary to sever development rights from the sending property and to affix development rights to the receiving property. These instruments shall be executed by the affected property owners and lienholders. The instruments shall identify the development rights being transferred, identification of the sending property and the receiving property;

2. The preservation of the character of the sending property and assurance that the prohibitions against the use and development of the sending property shall bind the landowner and every successor in interest to the landowner;

3. The severance of transferable development rights from the sending property and the transfer of development rights to a receiving property;

4. The purchase, sale, exchange, or other conveyance of transferable development rights prior to the rights being affixed to a receiving property;

5. A system for monitoring the severance, ownership, assignment, and transfer of transferable development rights;

6. A map or other description of areas designated as sending and receiving areas for the transfer of development rights between properties;

7. The identification of parcels, if any, within a receiving area that are inappropriate as receiving properties;

8. The ordinance shall include permitted uses and the maximum increases in density in the receiving area;

9. The minimum acreage of a sending property and the minimum reduction in density of the sending property that may be conveyed in a transfer of development rights;

10. An assessment of the infrastructure in the receiving area that identifies the ability of the area to accept increases in density and its plans to provide necessary utility services within any designated receiving area;

11. The review of an application by the planning commission or its agent to determine whether the application complies with the provisions of the ordinance. The application shall be deemed approved upon the determination of compliance with the ordinance and upon recordation of the instrument transferring the development rights in the land records of the office of the circuit court clerk for the locality; and

12. Such other provisions as the locality deems necessary to aid in the implementation of the provisions of this article.

D. The ordinance may provide for the allowance for residential density to be converted to an increase in the square feet of a commercial, industrial or other use on the receiving property.

E. Development rights made transferable pursuant to this article shall be interests in real property and shall be considered as such for purposes of conveyance and taxation. Once an application has been approved and a deed of transferable development rights created pursuant to this article has been sold, conveyed, or otherwise transferred by the owner of the sending property, the transfer of development rights shall vest in the grantee and may be transferred to a successor in interest. Any transfer of the development rights to a different property in a receiving area shall be subject to review pursuant to the provisions of the ordinance adopted pursuant to provision 11 of subsection C.

F. For the purposes of ad valorem real property taxation, the value of a transferable development right shall be deemed appurtenant to the sending property until the transferable development right is recorded as a distinct interest in real property with the appropriate tax assessor or the transferable development right is used at a receiving property and becomes appurtenant thereto.

G. Approved transfers of development rights shall become effective upon the recording of the conveyance and the filing of a certified copy of such recording with the local governing body of the locality.

H. Localities shall incorporate the map identified in provision 6 of subsection C into the comprehensive plan.

I. No amendment to the zoning map, nor any amendments to the text of the zoning ordinance with respect to the zoning district applicable thereto initiated by the governing body, which eliminate, or materially restrict, reduce, or modify the uses, or the density of use permitted in the zoning district applicable to any property to which development rights have been transferred, shall be effective with respect to such property unless there has been mistake, fraud, or a change in circumstances substantially affecting the public health, safety, or welfare.

J. A county adopting an ordinance pursuant to this article may designate eligible receiving areas in any incorporated town within such county, if the governing body of the town has also amended its zoning ordinance to designate the same areas as eligible to receive density being transferred from sending areas in the county.

K. Any county and an adjacent city may enter voluntarily into an agreement to permit the county to designate eligible receiving areas in the city if the governing body of the city has also amended its zoning ordinance to designate the same areas as eligible to receive density being transferred from sending areas in the county. The city council shall designate areas it deems suitable as receiving areas and shall designate the maximum increases in density in each such receiving area. However, if any such agreement contains any provision addressing any issue provided for in Chapter 32 (§ 15.2-3200 et seq.), 33 (§ 15.2-3300 et seq.), 36 (§ 15.2-3600 et seq.), 38 (§ 15.2-3800 et seq.), 39 (§ 15.2-3900 et seq.), or 41 (§ 15.2-4100 et seq.), the agreement shall be subject to the review and implementation process established by Chapter 34 (§ 15.2-3400 et seq.).

1. The terms and conditions of the density transfer agreement as provided in this subsection shall be determined by the affected localities and shall be approved by the governing body of each locality participating in the agreement, provided the governing body of each such locality first holds a public hearing, which shall be advertised once a week for two successive weeks in a newspaper of general circulation in the locality.

2. The governing bodies shall petition a circuit court having jurisdiction in one or more of the localities for an order affirming the proposed agreement. The circuit court shall be limited in its decision to either affirming or denying the agreement and shall have no authority, without the express approval of each local governing body, to amend or change the terms or conditions of the agreement, but shall have the authority to validate the agreement and give it full force and effect. The circuit court

shall affirm the agreement unless the court finds either that the agreement is contrary to the best interests of the Commonwealth or that it is not in the best interests of each of the parties thereto.

3. The agreement shall not become binding on the localities until affirmed by the court under this subsection. Once approved by the circuit court, the agreement shall also bind future local governing bodies of the localities. (2006, c. 573; 2007, cc. 363, 410.)

The 2007 amendments. — The 2007 amendments by cc. 363 and 410 are identical, and substituted "instruments" for "instrument" in the third sentence in subdivision C 1; and added subsection K.

ARTICLE 8.

Road Impact Fees.

§ 15.2-2317. Applicability of article. — This article shall apply to any locality that has adopted zoning pursuant to Article 7 (§ 15.2-2280 et seq.) of Chapter 22 of Title 15.2 and that (i) has a population of at least 20,000 and has a population growth rate of at least 5% or (ii) has population growth of 15% or more. For the purposes of this section, population growth shall be the difference in population from the next-to-latest to the latest decennial census year, based on population reported by the United States Bureau of the Census. (1989, c. 485, § 15.1-498.1; 1997, c. 587; 2000, c. 495; 2006, c. 832; 2007, c. 896.)

Editor's note. — Acts 2007, c. 896, cl. 23 contains a severability clause.

The 2007 amendments. — The 2007 amendment by c. 896 deleted clauses (i) through (vii) listing certain localities and inserted the language beginning "any locality that has adopted" and ending "reported by the United States Bureau of the Census."

§ 15.2-2318. Definitions. — As used in this article, unless the context requires a different meaning:

"*Cost*" includes, in addition to all labor, materials, machinery and equipment for construction, (i) acquisition of land, rights-of-way, property rights, easements and interests, including the costs of moving or relocating utilities, (ii) demolition or removal of any structure on land so acquired, including acquisition of land to which such structure may be moved, (iii) survey, engineering, and architectural expenses, (iv) legal, administrative, and other related expenses, and (v) interest charges and other financing costs if impact fees are used for the payment of principal and interest on bonds, notes or other obligations issued by the locality to finance the road improvement.

"*Impact fee*" means a charge or assessment imposed against new development in order to generate revenue to fund or recover the costs of reasonable road improvements benefiting the new development. Impact fees may not be assessed and imposed for road repair, operation and maintenance, nor to meet demand which existed prior to the new development.

"Impact fee service area" means an area designated within the comprehensive plan of a locality having clearly defined boundaries and clearly related traffic needs and within which development is to be subject to the assessment of impact fees.

"Road improvement" includes construction of new roads or improvement or expansion of existing roads and related appurtenances as required by applicable standards of the Virginia Department of Transportation, or the applicable standards of a locality with road maintenance responsibilities, to meet increased demand attributable to new development. Road improvements do not include on-site construction of roads which a developer may be required to provide pursuant to §§ 15.2-2241 through 15.2-2245. (1989, c. 485, § 15.1-498.2; 1992, c. 465; 1997, c. 587; 2007, c. 896.)

Editor's note. — Acts 2007, c. 896, cl. 23 contains a severability clause.

The 2007 amendments. — The 2007 amendment by c. 896 substituted "benefiting" for "necessitated by and attributable to" and deleted "expand existing roads to" preceding "meet demand" in the definition for "Impact fee"; substituted "an area designated within the comprehensive plan of a locality" for "land designated by ordinance within a locality" in the definition for "Impact fee service area"; inserted "and related appurtenances" following "existing roads," deleted "construction" following "applicable" and inserted "or the applicable standards of a locality with road maintenance responsibilities" in the definition for "Road improvement."

§ 15.2-2319. Authority to assess and impose impact fees.

— Any applicable locality may, by ordinance pursuant to the procedures and requirements of this article, assess and impose impact fees on new development to pay all or a part of the cost of reasonable road improvements that benefit the new development.

Prior to the adoption of the ordinance, a locality shall establish an impact fee advisory committee. The committee shall be composed of not less than five nor more than ten members appointed by the governing body of the locality and at least forty percent of the membership shall be representatives from the development, building or real estate industries. The planning commission or other existing committee that meets the membership requirements may serve as the impact fee advisory committee. The committee shall serve in an advisory capacity to assist and advise the governing body of the locality with regard to the ordinance. No action of the committee shall be considered a necessary prerequisite for any action taken by the locality in regard to the adoption of an ordinance. (1989, c. 485, § 15.1-498.2; 1992, c. 465; 1997, c. 587; 2007, c. 896.)

Editor's note. — Acts 2007, c. 896, cl. 23 contains a severability clause.

The 2007 amendments. — The 2007 amendment by c. 896 substituted "that benefit" for "attibutable in substantial part to" in the first paragraph.

§ 15.2-2320. Impact fee service areas to be established.

— The locality shall delineate one or more impact fee service areas within its comprehensive plan. Impact fees collected from new development within an impact fee service area shall be expended for road improvements benefiting that impact fee service area. An impact fee service area may encompass more than one road improvement project. A locality may exclude urban development areas designated pursuant to § 15.2-2223.1 from impact fee service areas. (1989, c. 485, § 15.1-498.3; 1992, c. 465; 1997, c. 587; 2007, c. 896.)

Editor's note. — Acts 2007, c. 896, cl. 23 contains a severability clause.

The 2007 amendments. — The 2007 amendment by c. 896 substituted "comprehensive plan" for "jurisdiction" in the first sentence and "benefiting" for "within" in the second sentence and inserted the fourth sentence.

§ 15.2-2321. Adoption of road improvements program.

— Prior to adopting a system of impact fees, the locality shall conduct an assessment of road improvement needs benefiting an impact fee service area and shall adopt a road improvements plan for the area showing the new roads proposed to be constructed and the existing roads to be improved or expanded and the schedule for undertaking such construction, improvement or expansion. The road improvements plan shall be adopted as an amendment to the required comprehensive plan and shall be incorporated into the capital improvements program or, in the case of the counties where applicable, the six-year plan for secondary road construction pursuant to § 33.1-70.01.

The locality shall adopt the road improvements plan after holding a duly advertised public hearing. The public hearing notice shall identify the impact fee service area or areas to be designated, and shall include a summary of the needs assessment and the assumptions upon which the assessment is based, the proposed amount of the impact fee, and information as to how a copy of the complete study may be examined. A copy of the complete study shall be available for public inspection and copying at reasonable times prior to the public hearing.

The locality at a minimum shall include the following items in assessing road improvement needs and preparing a road improvements plan:

1. An analysis of the existing capacity, current usage and existing commitments to future usage of existing roads, as indicated by (i) current and projected service levels, (ii) current valid building permits outstanding, and (iii) approved and pending site plans and subdivision plats. If the current usage and commitments exceed the existing capacity of the roads, the locality also shall determine the costs of improving the roads to meet the demand. The analysis shall include any off-site road improvements or cash payments for road improvements accepted by the locality and shall include a plan to fund the

current usages and commitments that exceed the existing capacity of the roads.

2. The projected need for and costs of construction of new roads or improvement or expansion of existing roads attributable in whole or in part to projected new development. Road improvement needs shall be projected for the impact fee service area when fully developed in accord with the comprehensive plan and, if full development is projected to occur more than 20 years in the future, at the end of a 20-year period. The assumptions with regard to land uses, densities, intensities, and population upon which road improvement projections are based shall be presented.

3. The total number of new service units projected for the impact fee service area when fully developed and, if full development is projected to occur more than 20 years in the future, at the end of a 20-year period. A "service unit" is a standardized measure of traffic use or generation. The locality shall develop a table or method for attributing service units to various types of development and land use, including but not limited to residential, commercial and industrial uses. The table shall be based upon the ITE manual (published by the Institute of Transportation Engineers) or locally conducted trip generation studies, and consistent with the traffic analysis standards adopted pursuant to § 15.2-2222.1. (1989, c. 485, § 15.1-498.4; 1992, c. 465; 1997, c. 587; 2007, c. 896.)

Editor's note. — Acts 2007, c. 896, cl. 23 contains a severability clause.

The 2007 amendments. — The 2007 amendment by c. 896 substituted "benefiting" for "within" following "improvement needs" and deleted "and in the locality" following "service area" in the first sentence of the first paragraph; in subdivision 1, inserted "current and projected service levels" as clause (i), deleted former clause (ii) and designated former clause (i) as present clause (ii), inserted "and pending" following "approved" in clause (iii) in the first sentence and inserted "include any off-site road improvements or cash payments for road improvements accepted by the locality and shall" in the second sentence; substituted "20 years" for "ten years" and "20-year" for "ten-year" in subdivisions 2 and 3; and in subdivision 3 inserted "and consistent with the traffic analysis standards adopted pursuant to § 15.2-2222.1."

§ 15.2-2322. Adoption of impact fee and schedule.

— After adoption of a road improvement program, the locality may adopt an ordinance establishing a system of impact fees to fund or recapture all or any part of the cost of providing reasonable road improvements benefiting new development. The ordinance shall set forth the schedule of impact fees. (1989, c. 485, § 15.1-498.5; 1997, c. 587; 2007, c. 896.)

Editor's note. — Acts 2007, c. 896, cl. 23 contains a severability clause.

The 2007 amendments. — The 2007 amendment by c. 896 substituted "benefiting" for "required by."

§ 15.2-2323. When impact fees assessed and imposed.

— The amount of impact fees to be imposed on a specific development or subdivision shall be determined before or at the time the site plan or subdivision is approved. The ordinance shall specify that the fee is to be collected at the time of the issuance of a building permit. The ordinance shall provide that fees (i) may be paid in lump sum or (ii) be paid on installment at a reasonable rate of interest for a fixed number of years. The locality by ordinance may provide for negotiated agreements with the owner of the property as to the time and method of paying the impact fees.

The maximum impact fee to be imposed shall be determined (i) by dividing projected road improvement costs in the impact fee service area when fully developed by the number of projected service units when fully developed, or (ii) for a reasonable period of time, but not less than ten years, by dividing the projected costs necessitated by development in the next ten years by the service units projected to be created in the next ten years.

The ordinance shall provide for appeals from administrative determinations, regarding the impact fees to be imposed, to the governing body or such other body as designated in the ordinance. The ordinance may provide for the resolution of disputes over an impact fee by arbitration or otherwise. (1989, c. 485, § 15.1-498.6; 1992, c. 465; 1997, c. 587; 2007, c. 896.)

Editor's note. — Acts 2007, c. 896, cl. 23 contains a severability clause.

The 2007 amendments. — The 2007 amendment by c. 896 substituted "building permit" for "certificate of occupancy" in the first paragraph; inserted "impact fee" preceding "service area" in the second paragraph and deleted the former fourth paragraph banning fees where developer has proffered conditions for offsite road improvements.

§ 15.2-2324. Credits against impact fee.

— The value of any dedication, contribution or construction from the developer for off-site road or other transportation improvements benefiting the impact fee service area shall be treated as a credit against the impact fees imposed on the developer's project. The locality shall treat as a credit any off-site transportation dedication, contribution, or construction, whether it is a condition of a rezoning or otherwise committed to the locality. The locality may by ordinance provide for credits for approved on-site transportation improvements in excess of those required by the development.

The locality also shall calculate and credit against impact fees the extent to which (i) other developments have already contributed to the cost of existing roads which will benefit the development, (ii) new development will contribute to the cost of existing roads, and (iii) new development will contribute to the cost of road improvements in the future other than through impact fees, including any special taxing districts, special assessments, or community development authorities. (1989, c. 485, § 15.1-498.7; 1992, c. 465; 1997, c. 587; 2007, c. 896.)

Editor's note. — Acts 2007, c. 896, cl. 23 contains a severability clause.

The 2007 amendments. — The 2007 amendment by c. 896 inserted "or other transportation" following "off-site road," substituted "benefiting" for "within" following "improvements" and added the present second sentence in the first paragraph; inserted "other" and substituted "benefit" for "serve" in clause (i) and inserted "including any special taxing districts, special assessments, or community development authorities" at the end of the clause (iii) of the second paragraph.

§ 15.2-2325. Updating plan and amending impact fee.

— The locality shall update the needs assessment and the assumptions and projections at least once every two years. The road improvement plan shall be updated at least every two years to reflect current assumptions and projections. The impact fee schedule may be amended to reflect any substantial changes in such assumptions and projections. Any impact fees not yet paid shall be assessed at the updated rate. (1989, c. 485, § 15.1-498.8; 1997, c. 587; 2007, c. 896.)

Editor's note. — Acts 2007, c. 896, cl. 23 contains a severability clause.

The 2007 amendments. — The 2007 amendment by c. 896 inserted the fourth sentence.

§ 15.2-2326. Use of proceeds.

— A separate road improvement account shall be established for the impact fee service area and all funds collected through impact fees shall be deposited in the interest-bearing account. Interest earned on deposits shall become funds of the account. The expenditure of funds from the account shall be only for road improvements benefiting the impact fee service area as set out in the road improvement plan for the impact fee service area. (1989, c. 485, § 15.1-498.9; 1992, c. 465; 1997, c. 587; 2007, c. 896.)

Editor's note. — Acts 2007, c. 896, cl. 23 contains a severability clause.

The 2007 amendments. — The 2007 amendment by c. 896 substituted "benefiting" for "within" in the third sentence.

§ 15.2-2327. Refund of impact fees.

— The locality shall refund any impact fee or portion thereof for which construction of a project is not completed within a reasonable period of time, not to exceed fifteen years. In the event that impact fees are not committed to road improvements benefiting the impact fee service area within seven years from the date of collection, the locality may commit any such impact fees to the secondary or urban system construction program of that locality for road improvements that benefit the impact fee service area.

Upon completion of a project, the locality shall recalculate the impact fee based on the actual cost of the improvement. It shall refund the difference if the impact fee paid exceeds actual cost by more than fifteen percent. Refunds shall be made to the record owner of the property at the time the refund is made. (1989, c. 485, § 15.1-498.10; 1992, c. 465; 1997, c. 587; 2007, c. 896.)

Editor's note. — Acts 2007, c. 896, cl. 23 contains a severability clause.

The 2007 amendments. — The 2007 amendment by c. 896 inserted the second sentence in the first paragraph.

ARTICLE 9.

Impact Fees.

§ 15.2-2328. Applicability of article.

— The provisions of this article shall apply in their entirety to any locality that has established an urban transportation service district in accordance with § 15.2-2403.1. However, the authority granted by this article may be exercised only in areas outside of urban transportation service districts and on parcels that are currently zoned agricultural and are being subdivided for by-right residential development. The authority granted by this article shall expire on December 31, 2008, for any locality that has not established an urban transportation service district and adopted an impact fee ordinance pursuant to this article by such date. (2007, c. 896.)

Editor's note. — Acts 2007, c. 896, cl. 23 contains a severability clause.

§ 15.2-2329. Imposition of impact fees.

— A. Any locality that includes within its comprehensive plan a calculation of the capital costs of public facilities necessary to serve residential uses may impose and collect impact fees in amounts consistent with the methodologies used in its comprehensive plan to defray the capital costs of public facilities related to the residential development.

B. Impact fees imposed and collected pursuant to this section shall only be used for public facilities that are impacted by residential development.

C. A locality imposing impact fees as provided in this section shall allow credit against the impact fees for cash proffers collected for the purpose of defraying the capital costs of public facilities related to the residential development. A locality imposing impact fees as provided in this section shall also include within its comprehensive plan a methodology for calculating credit for the value of proffered land donations to accommodate public facilities, and for the construction cost of any public facilities or public improvements the construction of which is required by proffer.

D. A locality imposing impact fees under this section may require that such impact fees be paid prior to and as a condition of the issuance of any necessary building permits for residential uses.

E. For the purposes of this section, *"public facilities"* shall be deemed to include: (i) roads, streets, and bridges, including rights-of-way, traffic signals, landscaping, and any local components of federal or state highways; (ii) stormwater collection, retention, detention, treatment, and disposal facilities, flood control facilities, and bank and shore protection and enhancement improvements; (iii) parks, open space, and recreation areas and related facilities; (iv) public safety facilities, including police, fire, emergency medical, and rescue facilities; (v) primary and secondary schools and related facilities; and (vi) libraries and related facilities; however, the definition "public facilities" for counties within the Richmond MSA shall be deemed to include: roads, streets, and bridges, including rights-of-way, traffic signals, landscaping, and any local components of federal or state highways. (2007, c. 896.)

SUBTITLE IV.
OTHER GOVERNMENTAL ENTITIES.

CHAPTER 48.2.

NORTHERN VIRGINIA TRANSPORTATION AUTHORITY.

Sec.
15.2-4838.1. Use of certain revenues by the Authority.
15.2-4839. Authority to issue bonds.
15.2-4840. Other duties and responsibilities of Authority.

§ 15.2-4830. Authority created.

Editor's note. — Acts 2007, c. 896, cl. 4, provides: "That prior to December 1 each year beginning 2008, the Washington Metropolitan Transit Authority shall submit to the Auditor of Public Accounts its annual audit report and financially audited statements for the most recent fiscal year."

Acts 2007, c. 896, cl. 5, provides: "That the Hampton Roads Transportation Authority established under § 33.1-391.7 of the Code of Virginia shall develop as part of a long-range plan quantifiable measures and achievable goals for the area embraced by the Authority relating to, but not limited to, congestion reduction and safety, transit and high-occupancy vehicle (HOV) usage, job-to-housing ratios, job and housing access to transit and pedestrian facilities, air quality, and per-capita vehicle miles traveled. In addition, the Northern Virginia Transportation Authority established under § 15.2-4830 of the Code of Virginia shall also develop as part of a long-range plan quantifiable measures and achievable goals for the area embraced by the Authority relating to, but not limited to, congestion reduction and safety, transit and high-occupancy vehicle (HOV) usage, job-to-housing ratios, job and housing access to transit and pedestrian facilities, air quality, and per-capita vehicle miles traveled. Such goals shall be subject to the approval of the Commonwealth Transportation Board on a biennial basis."

Acts 2007, c. 896, cl. 13, provides: "That the Northern Virginia Transportation Authority established under § 15.2-4830 of the Code of Virginia shall provide written notice to the Clerks of the House of Delegates and the Senate of any affirmative vote of the Authority to assess or impose any fee or tax authorized under this act for imposition or assessment by the Authority. The Authority shall provide such notice as soon as practicable. Upon receiving such written notice, the Clerks shall provide a copy of the same to the Governor. Furthermore, the Authority, the cities and counties embraced by the Authority, the Commissioner of the Department of Taxation, the Commissioner of the Department of Motor Vehicles, and other appropriate entities shall develop guidelines, policies, and procedures for the efficient and effective collection and administration of the fees and taxes authorized by this act for use by the Authority. The guidelines, policies, and procedures shall be made public at least 60 days prior to their implementation. The development of these guidelines, policies, and procedures shall be exempt from the Administrative Process Act (§ 2.2-4000 et seq. of the Code of Virginia). The Secretary of Finance may authorize an anticipation loan for purposes of meeting the requirements of this enactment."

Acts 2007, c. 896, cl. 16, provides: "That, as provided under § 58.1-3221.3, the tax authorized thereunder may only be imposed by a city or county embraced by the Northern Virginia Transportation Authority established under § 15.2-4830, or a city or county embraced by the Hampton Roads Transportation Authority established under § 33.1-391.7."

Acts 2007, c. 896, cl. 18, provides: "That the tax authorized pursuant to § 58.1-540 of the Code of Virginia shall not be imposed by a city or county embraced by the Northern Virginia Transportation Authority if the Authority is imposing any of the fees or taxes authorized under law for imposition or assessment by the Authority."

Acts 2007, c. 896, cl. 20, provides: "That the Northern Virginia Transportation Authority and the counties and cities embraced by the Authority shall work cooperatively with the towns located within such counties for purposes of implementation of the provisions of this act."

§ 15.2-4838.1. Use of certain revenues by the Authority. — A. All moneys received by the Authority and the proceeds of bonds issued pursuant to § 15.2-4839 shall be used by the Authority solely for transportation purposes benefiting those counties and cities that are embraced by the Authority.

B. Forty percent of the revenues shall be distributed on a pro rata basis, with each locality's share being the total of such fees and taxes assessed or imposed by the Authority and received by the Authority that are generated or attributable to the locality divided by the total of such fees and taxes assessed or imposed by the Authority and received by the Authority. Of the revenues distributed pursuant to this subsection (i) in the Cities of Falls Church and Alexandria and the County of Arlington the first 50% shall be used solely for urban or secondary road construction and improvements and for public transportation purposes, and (ii) in the remaining localities, the first 50% shall be used solely for urban or secondary road construction and improvements. The remainder, as determined solely by the applicable locality, shall be used either for additional urban or secondary road construction; for other transportation capital improvements which have been approved by the most recent long range transportation plan adopted by the Authority; or for public transportation purposes. Solely for purposes of calculating the 40% of revenues to be distributed pursuant to this subsection, the revenue generated pursuant to § 58.1-3221.3 and Article 8 (§ 15.2-2317 et seq.) of Chapter 22 of this title by the counties and cities embraced by the Authority shall be considered revenue of the Authority. None of the revenue distributed by this subsection may be used to repay debt issued before July 1, 2007. Each locality shall provide annually to the Northern Virginia Transportation Authority sufficient documentation as required by the Authority showing that the funds distributed under this subsection were used as required by this subsection.

C. The remaining 60% of the revenues from such sources shall be used by the Authority solely for transportation projects and purposes that benefit the counties and cities embraced by the Authority.

1. The revenues under this subsection shall be used first to pay any debt service owing on any bonds issued pursuant to § 15.2-4839, and then as follows:

a. The next $50 million each fiscal year shall be distributed to the Washington Metropolitan Area Transit Authority (WMATA) and shall be used for capital improvements benefiting the area embraced by the Authority for WMATA's transit service (Metro). The Authority shall first make use of that portion of such annual distribution as may be necessary under the requirements of federal law for the payment of federal funds to WMATA, but only if the matching federal funds are exclusive of and in addition to the amount of other federal funds appropriated for such purposes and are in an amount not less than the amount of such funds appropriated in the federal fiscal year ending September 30, 2007;

For each year after 2018 any portion of the amount distributed pursuant to this subsection may be used for mass transit improvements in Prince William County;

b. The next $25 million each fiscal year shall be distributed to the Virginia Railway Express for operating and capital improvements, including but not limited to track lease payments, construction of parking, dedicated rail on the Fredericksburg line, rolling stock, expanded service in Prince William County, and service as may be needed as a result of the Base Realignment and Closure Commission's action regarding Fort Belvoir.

2. All transportation projects undertaken by the Northern Virginia Transportation Authority shall be completed by private contractors accompanied by performance measurement standards, and all contracts shall contain a provision granting the Authority the option to terminate the contract if contractors do not meet such standards. Notwithstanding the foregoing, any locality may provide engineering services or right-of-way acquisition for any project with its own forces. The Authority shall avail itself of the strategies permitted under the Public-Private Transportation Act (§ 56-556 et seq.) whenever feasible and advantageous. The Authority is independent of any state or local entity, including the Virginia Department of Transportation (VDOT) and the Commonwealth Transportation Board (CTB), but the Authority, VDOT and CTB shall consult with one another to avoid duplication of efforts and, at the option of the Authority, may combine efforts to complete specific projects. Notwithstanding the foregoing, at the request of the Authority, VDOT may provide the Authority with engineering services or right-of-way acquisition for the project with its own forces. When determining what projects to construct under this subsection, the Authority shall base its decisions on the combination that (i) equitably distributes the funds throughout the localities, and (ii) constructs projects that move the most people or commercial traffic in the most cost-effective manner,

and on such other factors as approved by the Authority.

3. All revenues deposited to the credit of the Authority shall be used for projects benefiting the localities embraced by the Authority, with each locality's total long-term benefits being approximately equal to the total of the fees and taxes received by the Authority that are generated by or attributable to the locality divided by the total of such fees and taxes received by the Authority.

D. For road construction and improvements pursuant to subsection B, the Department of Transportation may, on a reimbursement basis, provide the locality with planning, engineering, right-of-way, and construction services for projects funded in whole by the revenues provided to the locality by the Authority. (2007, c. 896.)

Editor's note. — Acts 2007, c. 896, cl. 4, provides: "That prior to December 1 each year beginning 2008, the Washington Metropolitan Transit Authority shall submit to the Auditor of Public Accounts its annual audit report and financially audited statements for the most recent fiscal year."

Acts 2007, c. 896, cl. 12, provides: "That in conjunction with the construction of rail mass transit in the right of way of the Dulles Access/Toll Road Connector (DATRC), sound walls shall be constructed along residential properties from the beginning of the DATRC to Dulles International Airport if required by the issued Record of Decisions pursuant to the National Environmental Policy Act (42 U.S.C. § 4321 et seq., as may be amended)."

Acts 2007, c. 896, cl. 20, provides: "That the Northern Virginia Transportation Authority and the counties and cities embraced by the Authority shall work cooperatively with the towns located within such counties for purposes of implementation of the provisions of this act."

Acts 2007, c. 896, cl. 23 contains a severability clause.

§ 15.2-4839. Authority to issue bonds. — The Authority may issue bonds and other evidences of debt as may be authorized by this section or other law. The provisions of Article 5 (§ 15.2-4519 et seq.) of Chapter 45 of this title shall apply, mutatis mutandis, to the issuance of such bonds or other debt. The Authority may issue bonds or other debt in such amounts as it deems appropriate. The bonds may be supported by any funds available except that funds from tolls collected pursuant to subdivision 7 of § 15.2-4840 shall be used only as provided in that subdivision. (2002, c. 846; 2007, c. 896.)

Editor's note. — Acts 2007, c. 896, cl. 4, provides: "That prior to December 1 each year beginning 2008, the Washington Metropolitan Transit Authority shall submit to the Auditor of Public Accounts its annual audit report and financially audited statements for the most recent fiscal year."

Acts 2007, c. 896, cl. 20, provides: "That the Northern Virginia Transportation Authority and the counties and cities embraced by the Authority shall work cooperatively with the towns located within such counties for purposes of implementation of the provisions of this act."

Acts 2007, c. 896, cl. 23 contains a severability clause.

The 2007 amendments. — The 2007 amendment by c. 896 inserted "this section or other" preceding "law" in the first sentence and added the third and fourth sentences.

§ 15.2-4840. Other duties and responsibilities of Authority. — In addition to other powers

herein granted, the Authority shall have the following duties and responsibilities:

1. General oversight of regional programs involving mass transit or congestion mitigation, including, but not necessarily limited to, carpooling, vanpooling, and ridesharing;

2. Long-range regional planning, both financially constrained and unconstrained;

3. Recommending to state, regional, and federal agencies regional transportation priorities, including public-private transportation projects, and funding allocations;

4. Developing, in coordination with affected counties and cities, regional priorities and policies to improve air quality;

5. Allocating to priority regional transportation projects any funds made available to the Authority and, at the discretion of the Authority, directly overseeing such projects;

6. Recommending to the Commonwealth Transportation Board priority regional transportation projects for receipt of federal and state funds;

7. Imposing, collecting, and setting the amount of tolls for use of facilities in the area embraced by the Authority, when the facility is either newly constructed or reconstructed solely with revenues of the Authority or solely with revenues under the control of the Authority in such a way as to increase the facility's traffic capacity, with the amount of any tolls variable by time of day, day of the week, vehicle size or type, number of axles, or other factors as the Authority may deem proper, and with all such tolls to be used for programs and projects that are reasonably related to or benefit the users of the applicable facility, including, but not limited to, for the debt service and other costs of bonds whose proceeds are used for such construction or reconstruction;

8. General oversight of regional transportation issues of a multijurisdictional nature, including but not limited to intelligent transportation systems, signalization, and preparation for and response to emergencies;

9. Serving as an advocate for the transportation needs of Northern Virginia before the state and federal governments;

10. Applying to and negotiating with the government of the United States, the Commonwealth of Virginia, or any agency, instrumentality, or political subdivision thereof, for grants and any other funds available to carry out the purposes of this chapter and receiving, holding, accepting, and administering from any source gifts, bequests, grants, aid, or contributions of money, property, labor, or other things of value to be held, used and applied to carry out the purposes of this chapter subject, however, to any conditions upon which gifts, bequests, grants, aid, or contributions are made. Unless otherwise restricted by the terms of the gift, bequest, or grant, the Authority may sell, exchange, or otherwise dispose of such money, securities, or other property given or bequeathed to it in furtherance of its purposes;

11. Acting as a "responsible public entity" for the purpose of the acquisition, construction, improvement, maintenance and/or operation of a "qualifying transportation facility" under the Public-Private Transportation Act of 1995 (§ 56-556 et seq.); and

12. To decide and vote to impose certain fees and taxes authorized under law for imposition or assessment by the Authority, provided that any such fee or tax assessed or imposed is assessed or imposed in all counties and cities embraced by the Authority. The revenues from such certain fees and taxes shall be kept in a separate account and shall be used only for the purposes provided in this chapter. (2002, c. 846; 2007, c. 896.)

Editor's note. — Acts 2007, c. 896, cl. 8, provides: "That the Virginia Department of Transportation shall, on or before January 1, 2008, submit a written report to the General Assembly on its plans to create opportunities to enhance mobility and free-flowing traffic on Department-controlled toll facilities by embracing technological advances."

Acts 2007, c. 896, cl. 20, provides: "That the Northern Virginia Transportation Authority and the counties and cities embraced by the Authority shall work cooperatively with the towns located within such counties for purposes of implementation of the provisions of this act."

Acts 2007, c. 896, cl. 23 contains a severability clause.

The 2007 amendments. — The 2007 amendment by c. 896 substituted "Imposing, collecting, and setting the amount of" for "Recommending to the Commonwealth Transportation Board use and/or changes in use of" preceding "tolls for," inserted "use of" preceding "facilities" and the language beginning "when the facility is either" and ending "for such construction or reconstruction" in subdivision 7; deleted "or" preceding "instrumentality" and "or political subdivision" following "instrumentality"; added subdivision 12 and made a related change.

Title 17.1.

Courts of Record.

CHAPTER 2.

CLERKS, CLERKS' OFFICES AND RECORDS.

Article 7.

Fees.

Sec.
17.1-275. Fees collected by clerks of circuit courts; generally.

Article 8.

Secure Remote Access.

17.1-292. Applicability; definitions.
17.1-293. Posting and availability of certain information on the Internet; prohibitions.

ARTICLE 7.

Fees.

§ 17.1-275. Fees collected by clerks of circuit courts; generally. — A. A clerk of a circuit court shall, for services performed by virtue of his office, charge the following fees:

1. [Repealed.]

2. For recording and indexing in the proper book any writing and all matters therewith, or for recording and indexing anything not otherwise provided for, $16 for an instrument or document consisting of 10 or fewer pages or sheets; $30 for an instrument or document consisting of 11 to 30 pages or sheets; and $50 for an instrument or document consisting of 31 or more pages or sheets. Whenever any writing to be recorded includes plat or map sheets no larger than eight and one-half inches by 14 inches, such plat or map sheets shall be counted as ordinary pages for the purpose of computing the recording fee due pursuant to this section. A fee of $15 per page or sheet shall be charged with respect to plat or map sheets larger than eight and one-half inches by 14 inches. Only a single fee as authorized by this subdivision shall be charged for recording a certificate of satisfaction that releases the original deed of trust and any corrected or revised deeds of trust. One dollar and fifty cents of the fee collected for recording and indexing shall be designated for use in preserving the permanent records of the circuit courts. The sum collected for this purpose shall be administered by The Library of Virginia in cooperation with the circuit court clerks.

3. For appointing and qualifying any personal representative, committee, trustee, guardian, or other fiduciary, in addition to any fees for recording allowed by this section, $20 for estates not exceeding $50,000, $25 for estates not exceeding $100,000 and $30 for estates exceeding $100,000. No fee shall be charged for estates of $5,000 or less.

4. For entering and granting and for issuing any license, other than a marriage license or a hunting and fishing license, and administering an oath when necessary, $10.

5. For issuing a marriage license, attaching certificate, administering or receiving all necessary oaths or affidavits, indexing and recording, $10.

6. For making out any bond, other than those under § 17.1-267 or subdivision A 4, administering all necessary oaths and writing proper affidavits, $3.

7. For all services rendered by the clerk in any garnishment or attachment proceeding, the clerk's fee shall be $15 in cases not exceeding $500 and $25 in all other cases.

8. For making out a copy of any paper, record, or electronic record to go out of the office, which is not otherwise specifically provided for herein, a fee of $0.50 for each page or, if an electronic record, each image. From such fees, the clerk shall reimburse the locality the costs of making out the copies and pay the remaining fees directly to the Commonwealth. The funds to recoup the cost of making out the copies shall be deposited with the county or city treasurer or Director of Finance, and the governing body shall budget and appropriate such funds to be used to support the cost of copies pursuant to this subdivi-

sion. For purposes of this section, the costs of making out the copies shall include lease and maintenance agreements for the equipment used to make out the copies, but shall not include salaries or related benefits. The costs of copies shall otherwise be determined in accordance with § 2.2-3704. However, there shall be no charge to the recipient of a final order or decree to send an attested copy to such party.

9. For annexing the seal of the court to any paper, writing the certificate of the clerk accompanying it, the clerk shall charge $2 and for attaching the certificate of the judge, if the clerk is requested to do so, the clerk shall charge an additional $0.50.

10. In any case in which a person is convicted of a violation of any provision of Article 1 (§ 18.2-247 et seq.) of Chapter 7 of Title 18.2 or is subject to a disposition under § 18.2-251, the clerk shall assess a fee of $150 for each felony conviction and each felony disposition under § 18.2-251 which shall be taxed as costs to the defendant and shall be paid into the Drug Offender Assessment and Treatment Fund.

11. In any case in which a person is convicted of a violation of any provision of Article 1 (§ 18.2-247 et seq.) of Chapter 7 of Title 18.2 or is subject to a disposition under § 18.2-251, the clerk shall assess a fee for each misdemeanor conviction and each misdemeanor disposition under § 18.2-251, which shall be taxed as costs to the defendant and shall be paid into the Drug Offender Assessment and Treatment Fund as provided in § 17.1-275.8.

12. Upon the defendant's being required to successfully complete traffic school or a driver improvement clinic in lieu of a finding of guilty, the court shall charge the defendant fees and costs as if he had been convicted.

13. In all civil actions that include one or more claims for the award of monetary damages the clerk's fee chargeable to the plaintiff shall be $60 in cases seeking recovery not exceeding $50,000, $10 of which shall be apportioned to the Courts Technology Fund established under § 17.1-132; $110 in cases seeking recovery not exceeding $100,000, $10 of which shall be apportioned to the Courts Technology Fund established under § 17.1-132; and $160 in cases seeking recovery exceeding $100,000, $10 of which shall be apportioned to the Courts Technology Fund established under § 17.1-132. A fee of $25 shall be paid by the plaintiff at the time of instituting a condemnation case, in lieu of any other fees. There shall be no fee charged for the filing of a cross-claim or setoff in any pending action. However, the fees prescribed by this subdivision shall be charged upon the filing of a counterclaim or a claim impleading a third-party defendant. The fees prescribed above shall be collected upon the filing of papers for the commencement of civil actions. This subdivision shall not be applicable to cases filed in the Supreme Court of Virginia.

13a. For the filing of any petition seeking court approval of a settlement where no action has yet been filed, the clerk's fee, chargeable to the petitioner, shall be $50, to be paid by the petitioner at the time of filing the petition.

14. In addition to the fees chargeable for civil actions, for the costs of proceedings for judgments by confession under §§ 8.01-432 through 8.01-440, the clerk shall tax as costs (i) the cost of registered or certified mail; (ii) the statutory writ tax, in the amount required by law to be paid on a suit for the amount of the confessed judgment; (iii) for the sheriff for serving each copy of the order entering judgment, $12; and (iv) for docketing the judgment and issuing executions thereon, the same fees as prescribed in subdivision A 17.

15. For qualifying notaries public, including the making out of the bond and any copies thereof, administering the necessary oaths, and entering the order, $10.

16. For each habeas corpus proceeding, the clerk shall receive $10 for all services required thereunder. This subdivision shall not be applicable to such suits filed in the Supreme Court of Virginia.

17. For docketing and indexing a judgment from any other court of this Commonwealth, for docketing and indexing a judgment in the new name of a judgment debtor pursuant to the provisions of § 8.01-451, but not when incident to a divorce, for noting and filing the assignment of a judgment pursuant to § 8.01-452, a fee of $5; and for issuing an abstract of any recorded judgment, when proper to do so, a fee of $5; and for filing, docketing, indexing and mailing notice of a foreign judgment, a fee of $20.

18. For all services rendered by the clerk in any court proceeding for which no specific fee is provided by law, the clerk shall charge $10, to be paid by the party filing said papers at the time of filing; however, this subdivision shall not be applicable in a divorce cause prior to and including the entry of a decree of divorce from the bond of matrimony.

19, 20. [Repealed.]

21. For making the endorsements on a forthcoming bond and recording the matters relating to such bond pursuant to the provisions of § 8.01-529, $1.

22. For all services rendered by the clerk in any proceeding pursuant to § 57-8 or 57-15, $10.

23. For preparation and issuance of a subpoena duces tecum, $5.

24. For all services rendered by the clerk in matters under § 8.01-217 relating to change of name, $20; however, this subdivision shall not be applicable in cases where the change of name is incident to a divorce.

25. For providing court records or documents on microfilm, per frame, $0.50.

26. In all divorce and separate maintenance proceedings, and all civil actions that do not include one or more claims for the award of monetary damages, the clerk's fee chargeable to the plaintiff shall be $60, $10 of which shall be apportioned to the Courts Technology Fund established under § 17.1-132 to be

paid by the plaintiff at the time of instituting the suit, which shall include the furnishing of a duly certified copy of the final decree. The fees prescribed by this subdivision shall be charged upon the filing of a counterclaim or a claim impleading a third-party defendant. However, no fee shall be charged for the filing of a cross-claim or setoff in any pending suit. In divorce cases, when there is a merger of a divorce of separation a mensa et thoro into a decree of divorce a vinculo, the above mentioned fee shall include the furnishing of a duly certified copy of both such decrees.

27. For the acceptance of credit cards in lieu of money to collect and secure all fees, including filing fees, fines, restitution, forfeiture, penalties and costs, the clerk shall collect a service charge of four percent of the amount paid.

28. For the return of any check unpaid by the financial institution on which it was drawn or notice is received from the credit card issuer that payment will not be made for any reason, the clerk shall collect, if allowed by the court, a fee of $20 or 10 percent of the amount to be paid, whichever is greater, in accordance with § 19.2-353.3.

29. For all services rendered, except in cases in which costs are assessed pursuant to § 17.1-275.1, 17.1-275.2, 17.1-275.3, or 17.1-275.4, in an adoption proceeding, a fee of $20, in addition to the fee imposed under § 63.2-1246, to be paid by the petitioner or petitioners. For each petition for adoption filed pursuant to § 63.2-1201, except those filed pursuant to subdivisions 5 and 6 of § 63.2-1210, an additional $50 filing fee as required under § 63.2-1201 shall be deposited in the Putative Father Registry Fund pursuant to § 63.2-1249.

30. For issuing a duplicate license for one lost or destroyed as provided in § 29.1-334, a fee in the same amount as the fee for the original license.

31. For the filing of any petition as provided in §§ 33.1-124, 33.1-125 and 33.1-129, a fee of $5 to be paid by the petitioner; and for the recordation of a certificate or copy thereof, as provided for in § 33.1-122, as well as for any order of the court relating thereto, the clerk shall charge the same fee as for recording a deed as provided for in this section, to be paid by the party upon whose request such certificate is recorded or order is entered.

32. For making up, certifying and transmitting original record pursuant to the Rules of the Supreme Court, including all papers necessary to be copied and other services rendered, except in cases in which costs are assessed pursuant to § 17.1-275.1, 17.1-275.2, 17.1-275.3, 17.1-275.4, 17.1-275.7, 17.1-275.8, or 17.1-275.9, a fee of $20.

33. [Repealed.]

34. For filings, etc., under the Uniform Federal Lien Registration Act (§ 55-142.1 et seq.), the fees shall be as prescribed in that Act.

35. For filing the appointment of a resident agent for a nonresident property owner in accordance with § 55-218.1, a fee of $10.

36. [Repealed.]

37. For recordation of certificate and registration of names of nonresident owners in accordance with § 59.1-74, a fee of $10.

38. For maintaining the information required under the Overhead High Voltage Line Safety Act (§ 59.1-406 et seq.), the fee as prescribed in § 59.1-411.

39. For lodging, indexing and preserving a will in accordance with § 64.1-56, a fee of $2.

40. For filing a financing statement in accordance with § 8.9A-505, the fee shall be as prescribed under § 8.9A-525.

41. For filing a termination statement in accordance with § 8.9A-513, the fee shall be as prescribed under § 8.9A-525.

42. For filing assignment of security interest in accordance with § 8.9A-514, the fee shall be as prescribed under § 8.9A-525.

43. For filing a petition as provided in §§ 37.2-1001 and 37.2-1013, the fee shall be $10.

44. For issuing any execution, and recording the return thereof, a fee of $1.50.

45. For the preparation and issuance of a summons for interrogation by an execution creditor, a fee of $5. If there is no outstanding execution, and one is requested herewith, the clerk shall be allowed an additional fee of $1.50, in accordance with subdivision A 44.

B. In accordance with § 17.1-281, the clerk shall collect fees under subdivisions A 7, A 13, A 16, A 18 if applicable, A 20, A 22, A 24, A 26, A 29 and A 31 to be designated for courthouse construction, renovation or maintenance.

C. In accordance with § 17.1-278, the clerk shall collect fees under subdivisions A 7, A 13, A 16, A 18 if applicable, A 20, A 22, A 24, A 26, A 29 and A 31 to be designated for services provided for the poor, without charge, by a nonprofit legal aid program.

D. In accordance with § 42.1-70, the clerk shall collect fees under subdivisions A 7, A 13, A 16, A 18 if applicable, A 20, A 22, A 24, A 26, A 29 and A 31 to be designated for public law libraries.

E. The provisions of this section shall control the fees charged by clerks of circuit courts for the services above described. (Code 1950, § 14-123, p. 614; 1952, c. 146; 1954, c. 138; 1956, c. 217; 1964, c. 386, § 14.1-112; 1966, c. 217; 1970, c. 522; 1971, Ex. Sess., c. 95; 1972, cc. 626, 627, 647; 1973, c. 159; 1974, cc. 370, 523; 1975, c. 226; 1976, c. 344; 1977, cc. 449, 463; 1978, c. 502; 1980, c. 145; 1983, c. 103; 1984, cc. 225, 356; 1985, cc. 94, 201; 1986, c. 538; 1988, cc. 49, 52; 1989, c. 595; 1990, cc. 88, 738, 971; 1992, c. 784; 1993, cc. 95, 299, 386; 1994, cc. 64, 432, 498, 842; 1995, cc. 51, 371, 440, 463, 525, § 14.1-111.1; 1996, cc. 344, 976; 1997, cc. 215, 921; 1998, cc. 783, 840, 872; 1999, cc. 9, 1003; 2000, cc. 826, 830; 2001, cc. 481, 496, 501, 836; 2002, cc. 831, 832; 2004, c. 1004; 2005, cc. 373, 681; 2006, cc. 318, 623, 718, 825; 2007, cc. 548, 626, 646.)

The 2007 amendments. — The 2007 amendments by cc. 548 and 626 are identical, and in subdivision A 8, in the first sentence,

inserted "record" following "paper," "electronic" preceding "record," "herein" preceding "a fee" and "or, if an electronic record, each image" at the end; and substituted "$0.50" for "$0.10" at the end of subdivision A 25.

The 2007 amendment by c. 646 repealed former subdivision A 33, which read: "For issuance of hunting and trapping permits in accordance with § 10.1-1154, $0.25."

Law Review.

For annual survey commentary, "The Merger of Common-Law and Equity Pleading in Virginia," see 41 U. Rich. L. Rev. 77 (2006).

ARTICLE 8.

Secure Remote Access.

§ 17.1-292. Applicability; definitions. — A. The provisions of § 17.1-293 of this article shall apply to clerks of the courts of record as defined in § 1-212 and courts not of record as defined in § 16.1-69.5.

B. As used in this article:

"Internet" means the international computer network of interoperable packet-switched data networks.

"Land records" means any writing authorized by law to be recorded on paper or in electronic format that the clerk records affecting title to real property, including but not limited to instruments, orders, or any other writings recorded under this title, Article 5 (§ 8.01-446 et seq.) of Chapter 17 of Title 8.01, Title 8.9A and Chapter 6 (§ 55-106 et seq.) of Title 55. (2007, cc. 548, 626.)

§ 17.1-293. Posting and availability of certain information on the Internet; prohibitions. — A. Notwithstanding Chapter 37 (§ 2.2-3700 et seq.) of Title 2.2 or subsection B of this section, it shall be unlawful for any court clerk to disclose the social security number or other identification numbers appearing on driver's licenses or information on credit cards, debit cards, bank accounts, or other electronic billing and payment systems that was supplied to a court clerk for the purpose of paying fees, fines, taxes, or other charges collected by such court clerk. The prohibition shall not apply where disclosure of such information is required (i) to conduct or complete the transaction for which such information was submitted or (ii) by other law or court order.

B. Beginning January 1, 2004, no court clerk shall post on the Internet any document that contains the following information: (i) an actual signature, (ii) a social security number, (iii) a date of birth identified with a particular person, (iv) the maiden name of a person's parent so as to be identified with a particular person, (v) any financial account number or numbers, or (vi) the name and age of any minor child.

C. Each such clerk shall post notice that includes a list of the documents routinely posted on its website.

D. Nothing in this section shall be construed to prohibit access to any original document as provided by law.

E. This section shall not apply to the following:

1. Providing access to any document among the land records via secure remote access pursuant to § 17.1-294;

2. Postings related to legitimate law-enforcement purposes;

3. Postings of historical, genealogical, interpretive, or educational documents and information about historic persons and events;

4. Postings of instruments and records filed or recorded prior to 1907; and

5. Providing secure remote access to any person and his counsel to documents filed in matters to which such person is a party.

F. Nothing in this section shall prohibit the Supreme Court or any other court from providing online access to a case management system that may include abstracts of case filings and proceedings in the courts of the Commonwealth.

G. The court clerk shall be immune from suit arising from any acts or omissions relating to providing remote access on the Internet pursuant to this section unless the clerk was grossly negligent or engaged in willful misconduct.

This subsection shall not be construed to limit, withdraw, or overturn any defense or immunity already existing in statutory or common law, or to affect any cause of action accruing prior to July 1, 2005. (2007, cc. 548, 626.)

Title 18.2.

Crimes and Offenses Generally.

CHAPTER 7.

CRIMES INVOLVING HEALTH AND SAFETY.

Article 8.

Miscellaneous Dangerous Conduct.

Sec.
18.2-323.02. Prohibition against concealment of dead body; penalty.

ARTICLE 8.

Miscellaneous Dangerous Conduct.

§ 18.2-323.02. Prohibition against concealment of dead body; penalty. — Any person who transports, secretes, conceals or alters a dead body, as defined in § 32.1-249, with malicious intent and to prevent detection of an unlawful act or to prevent the detection of the death or the manner or cause of death is guilty of a Class 6 felony. (2007, c. 436.)

Cross references. — As to punishment for Class 6 felony, see § 18.2-10.

Editor's note. — Acts 2007, c. 436, cl. 2, provides: "That the provisions of this act may result in a net increase in periods of imprisonment or commitment. Pursuant to § 30-19.1:4, the estimated amount of the necessary appropriation cannot be determined for periods of imprisonment in state adult correctional facilities and is $0 for periods of commitment to the custody of the Department of Juvenile Justice."

§ 18.2-323.1. Drinking while operating a motor vehicle; possession of open container while operating a motor vehicle and presumption; penalty.

CASE NOTES

Relationship with offense of driving under the influence. — Where the presence of an open container of alcohol and defendant's appearance gave rise to a rebuttable presumption that defendant consumed alcohol while driving, the fact that an officer did not perceive defendant to be drunk or driving under the influence did not negate the presumption because a driver did not have to be intoxicated to the extent necessary to support a conviction under § 18.2-266 in order to be found guilty of drinking while operating a motor vehicle in violation of § 18.2-323.1. United States v. Washington, 439 F. Supp. 2d 589, 2006 U.S. Dist. LEXIS 52064 (E.D. Va. 2006).

Open container and defendant's appearance justified vehicle search. — Officer who observed a partially empty bottle of alcohol inside defendant's vehicle during a traffic stop did not violate the Fourth Amendment by retrieving the bottle because the presence of the open container of alcohol combined with the officer's observation that defendant's eyes were watery and bloodshot and that defendant's hands were shaking gave rise to a rebuttable presumption that defendant consumed alcohol while driving. United States v. Washington, 439 F. Supp. 2d 589, 2006 U.S. Dist. LEXIS 52064 (E.D. Va. 2006).

Title 19.2.

Criminal Procedure.

CHAPTER 23.

CENTRAL CRIMINAL RECORDS EXCHANGE.

Sec.
19.2-389. Dissemination of criminal history record information.

§ 19.2-389. Dissemination of criminal history record information. — A. Criminal history record information shall be disseminated, whether directly or through an intermediary, only to:

1. Authorized officers or employees of criminal justice agencies, as defined by § 9.1-101, for purposes of the administration of criminal justice and the screening of an employment application or review of employment by a criminal justice agency with respect to its own employees or applicants, and dissemination to the Virginia Parole Board, pursuant to this subdivision, of such information on all state-responsible inmates for the purpose of making parole determinations pursuant to subdivisions 1, 2,

3, and 5 of § 53.1-136 shall include collective dissemination by electronic means every 30 days;

2. Such other individuals and agencies that require criminal history record information to implement a state or federal statute or executive order of the President of the United States or Governor that expressly refers to criminal conduct and contains requirements or exclusions expressly based upon such conduct, except that information concerning the arrest of an individual may not be disseminated to a noncriminal justice agency or individual if an interval of one year has elapsed from the date of the arrest and no disposition of the charge has been recorded and no active prosecution of the charge is pending;

3. Individuals and agencies pursuant to a specific agreement with a criminal justice agency to provide services required for the administration of criminal justice pursuant to that agreement which shall specifically authorize access to data, limit the use of data to purposes for which given, and ensure the security and confidentiality of the data;

4. Individuals and agencies for the express purpose of research, evaluative, or statistical activities pursuant to an agreement with a criminal justice agency that shall specifically authorize access to data, limit the use of data to research, evaluative, or statistical purposes, and ensure the confidentiality and security of the data;

5. Agencies of state or federal government that are authorized by state or federal statute or executive order of the President of the United States or Governor to conduct investigations determining employment suitability or eligibility for security clearances allowing access to classified information;

6. Individuals and agencies where authorized by court order or court rule;

7. Agencies of any political subdivision of the Commonwealth for the conduct of investigations of applicants for public employment, permit, or license whenever, in the interest of public welfare or safety, it is necessary to determine under a duly enacted ordinance if the past criminal conduct of a person with a conviction record would be compatible with the nature of the employment, permit, or license under consideration;

8. Public or private agencies when authorized or required by federal or state law or interstate compact to investigate (i) applicants for foster or adoptive parenthood or (ii) any individual, and the adult members of that individual's household, with whom the agency is considering placing a child or from whom the agency is considering removing a child due to abuse or neglect, on an emergency, temporary, or permanent basis pursuant to §§ 63.2-901.1 and 63.2-1505, subject to the restriction that the data shall not be further disseminated to any party other than a federal or state authority or court as may be required to comply with an express requirement of law;

9. To the extent permitted by federal law or regulation, public service companies as defined in § 56-1, for the conduct of investigations of applicants for employment when such employment involves personal contact with the public or when past criminal conduct of an applicant would be incompatible with the nature of the employment under consideration;

10. The appropriate authority for purposes of granting citizenship and for purposes of international travel, including but not limited to, issuing visas and passports;

11. A person requesting a copy of his own criminal history record information as defined in § 9.1-101 at his cost, except that criminal history record information shall be supplied at no charge to a person who has applied to be a volunteer with (i) a Virginia affiliate of Big Brothers/Big Sisters of America; (ii) a volunteer fire company or volunteer rescue squad; (iii) the Volunteer Emergency Families for Children; (iv) any affiliate of Prevent Child Abuse, Virginia; (v) any Virginia affiliate of Compeer; or (vi) any board member or any individual who has been offered membership on the board of a Crime Stoppers, Crime Solvers or Crime Line program as defined in § 15.2-1713.1;

12. Administrators and board presidents of and applicants for licensure or registration as a child welfare agency as defined in § 63.2-100 for dissemination to the Commissioner of Social Services' representative pursuant to § 63.2-1702 for the conduct of investigations with respect to employees of and volunteers at such facilities, caretakers, and other adults living in family day-care homes or homes approved by family day-care systems, and foster and adoptive parent applicants of private child-placing agencies, pursuant to §§ 63.2-1719 through 63.2-1721, subject to the restriction that the data shall not be further disseminated by the facility or agency to any party other than the data subject, the Commissioner of Social Services' representative or a federal or state authority or court as may be required to comply with an express requirement of law for such further dissemination;

13. The school boards of the Commonwealth for the purpose of screening individuals who are offered or who accept public school employment and those current school board employees for whom a report of arrest has been made pursuant to § 19.2-83.1;

14. The State Lottery Department for the conduct of investigations as set forth in the State Lottery Law (§ 58.1-4000 et seq.), and the Department of Charitable Gaming for the conduct of investigations as set forth in Article 1.1:1 (§ 18.2-340.15 et seq.) of Chapter 8 of Title 18.2;

15. Licensed nursing homes, hospitals and home care organizations for the conduct of investigations of applicants for compensated employment in licensed nursing homes pursuant to § 32.1-126.01, hospital pharmacies pursuant to § 32.1-126.02, and home care organizations pursuant to § 32.1-162.9:1, subject to the limitations set out in subsection E;

16. Licensed homes for adults, licensed district homes for adults, and licensed adult day-care cen-

ters for the conduct of investigations of applicants for compensated employment in licensed homes for adults pursuant to § 63.2-1720, in licensed district homes for adults pursuant to § 63.1-189.1, and in licensed adult day-care centers pursuant to § 63.2-1720, subject to the limitations set out in subsection F;

17. The Alcoholic Beverage Control Board for the conduct of investigations as set forth in § 4.1-103.1;

18. The State Board of Elections and authorized officers and employees thereof in the course of conducting necessary investigations with respect to registered voters, limited to any record of felony convictions;

19. The Commissioner of the Department of Mental Health, Mental Retardation and Substance Abuse Services for those individuals who are committed to the custody of the Commissioner pursuant to §§ 19.2-169.2, 19.2-169.6, 19.2-176, 19.2-177.1, 19.2-182.2, 19.2-182.3, 19.2-182.8, and 19.2-182.9 for the purpose of placement, evaluation, and treatment planning;

20. Any alcohol safety action program certified by the Commission on the Virginia Alcohol Safety Action Program for (i) assessments of habitual offenders under § 46.2-360, (ii) interventions with first offenders under § 18.2-251, or (iii) services to offenders under § 18.2-51.4, 18.2-266, or 18.2-266.1;

21. Residential facilities for juveniles regulated or operated by the Department of Social Services, the Department of Education, or the Department of Mental Health, Mental Retardation and Substance Abuse Services for the purpose of determining applicants' fitness for employment or for providing volunteer or contractual services;

22. The Department of Mental Health, Mental Retardation and Substance Abuse Services and facilities operated by the Department for the purpose of determining an individual's fitness for employment pursuant to departmental instructions;

23. Pursuant to § 22.1-296.3, the governing boards or administrators of private or religious elementary or secondary schools which are accredited by a statewide accrediting organization recognized, prior to January 1, 1996, by the State Board of Education or a private organization coordinating such records information on behalf of such governing boards or administrators pursuant to a written agreement with the Department of State Police;

24. Public and nonprofit private colleges and universities for the purpose of screening individuals who are offered or accept employment;

25. Executive directors of community services boards or the personnel director serving the community services board for the purpose of determining an individual's fitness for employment pursuant to §§ 37.2-506 and 37.2-607;

26. Executive directors of behavioral health authorities as defined in § 37.2-600 for the purpose of determining an individual's fitness for employment pursuant to §§ 37.2-506 and 37.2-607;

27. The Commissioner of the Department of Social Services for the purpose of locating persons who owe child support or who are alleged in a pending paternity proceeding to be a putative father, provided that only the name, address, demographics and social security number of the data subject shall be released;

28. Authorized officers or directors of agencies licensed pursuant to Article 2 (§ 37.2-403 et seq.) of Chapter 4 of Title 37.2 by the Department of Mental Health, Mental Retardation and Substance Abuse Services for the purpose of determining if any applicant who accepts employment in any direct consumer care position has been convicted of a crime that affects their fitness to have responsibility for the safety and well-being of persons with mental illness, mental retardation and substance abuse pursuant to §§ 37.2-416, 37.2-506, and 37.2-607;

29. The Commissioner of the Department of Motor Vehicles, for the purpose of evaluating applicants for a motor carrier certificate or license subject to the provisions of Chapters 20 (§ 46.2-2000 et seq.) and 21 (§ 46.2-2100 et seq.) of Title 46.2;

30. The chairmen of the Committees for Courts of Justice of the Senate or the House of Delegates for the purpose of determining if any person being considered for election to any judgeship has been convicted of a crime;

31. Heads of state agencies in which positions have been identified as sensitive for the purpose of determining an individual's fitness for employment in positions designated as sensitive under Department of Human Resource Management policies developed pursuant to § 2.2-1201.1. Dissemination of criminal history record information to the agencies shall be limited to those positions generally described as directly responsible for the health, safety and welfare of the general populace or protection of critical infrastructures;

32. The Office of the Attorney General, for all criminal justice activities otherwise permitted under subdivision A 1 and for purposes of performing duties required by the Civil Commitment of Sexually Violent Predators Act (§ 37.2-900 et seq.);

33. Shipyards, to the extent permitted by federal law or regulation, engaged in the design, construction, overhaul, or repair of nuclear vessels for the United States Navy, including their subsidiary companies, for the conduct of investigations of applications for employment or for access to facilities, by contractors, leased laborers, and other visitors;

34. Any employer of individuals whose employment requires that they enter the homes of others, for the purpose of screening individuals who apply for, are offered, or have accepted such employment;

35. Public agencies when and as required by federal or state law to investigate (i) applicants as providers of adult foster care and home-based services or (ii) any individual with whom the agency is considering placing an adult on an emergency, temporary, or permanent basis pursuant to

§ 63.2-1601.1, subject to the restriction that the data shall not be further disseminated by the agency to any party other than a federal or state authority or court as may be required to comply with an express requirement of law for such further dissemination, subject to limitations set out in subsection G;

36. The Department of Medical Assistance Services, or its designee, for the purpose of screening individuals who, through contracts, subcontracts, or direct employment, volunteer, apply for, are offered, or have accepted a position related to the provision of transportation services to enrollees in the Medicaid Program or the Family Access to Medical Insurance Security (FAMIS) Program, or any other program administered by the Department of Medical Assistance Services; and

37. Other entities as otherwise provided by law.

Upon an ex parte motion of a defendant in a felony case and upon the showing that the records requested may be relevant to such case, the court shall enter an order requiring the Central Criminal Records Exchange to furnish the defendant, as soon as practicable, copies of any records of persons designated in the order on whom a report has been made under the provisions of this chapter.

Notwithstanding any other provision of this chapter to the contrary, upon a written request sworn to before an officer authorized to take acknowledgments, the Central Criminal Records Exchange, or the criminal justice agency in cases of offenses not required to be reported to the Exchange, shall furnish a copy of conviction data covering the person named in the request to the person making the request; however, such person on whom the data is being obtained shall consent in writing, under oath, to the making of such request. A person receiving a copy of his own conviction data may utilize or further disseminate that data as he deems appropriate. In the event no conviction data is maintained on the data subject, the person making the request shall be furnished at his cost a certification to that effect.

B. Use of criminal history record information disseminated to noncriminal justice agencies under this section shall be limited to the purposes for which it was given and may not be disseminated further.

C. No criminal justice agency or person shall confirm the existence or nonexistence of criminal history record information for employment or licensing inquiries except as provided by law.

D. Criminal justice agencies shall establish procedures to query the Central Criminal Records Exchange prior to dissemination of any criminal history record information on offenses required to be reported to the Central Criminal Records Exchange to ensure that the most up-to-date disposition data is being used. Inquiries of the Exchange shall be made prior to any dissemination except in those cases where time is of the essence and the normal response time of the Exchange would exceed the necessary time period. A criminal justice agency to whom a request has been made for the dissemination of criminal history record information that is required to be reported to the Central Criminal Records Exchange may direct the inquirer to the Central Criminal Records Exchange for such dissemination. Dissemination of information regarding offenses not required to be reported to the Exchange shall be made by the criminal justice agency maintaining the record as required by § 15.2-1722.

E. Criminal history information provided to licensed nursing homes, hospitals and to home care organizations pursuant to subdivision 15 of subsection A shall be limited to the convictions on file with the Exchange for any offense specified in §§ 32.1-126.01, 32.1-126.02 and 32.1-162.9:1.

F. Criminal history information provided to licensed assisted living facilities, licensed district homes for adults, and licensed adult day-care centers pursuant to subdivision 16 of subsection A shall be limited to the convictions on file with the Exchange for any offense specified in § 63.1-189.1 or 63.2-1720.

G. Criminal history information provided to public agencies pursuant to subdivision 35 of subsection A shall be limited to the convictions on file with the Exchange for any offense specified in § 63.2-1719.

H. Upon receipt of a written request from an employer or prospective employer, the Central Criminal Records Exchange, or the criminal justice agency in cases of offenses not required to be reported to the Exchange, shall furnish at the employer's cost a copy of conviction data covering the person named in the request to the employer or prospective employer making the request; provided that the person on whom the data is being obtained has consented in writing to the making of such request and has presented a photo-identification to the employer or prospective employer. In the event no conviction data is maintained on the person named in the request, the requesting employer or prospective employer shall be furnished at his cost a certification to that effect. The criminal history record search shall be conducted on forms provided by the Exchange. (Code 1950, § 19.1-19.2; 1966, c. 669; 1968, c. 537; 1970, c. 118; 1975, c. 495; 1976, c. 771; 1977, c. 626; 1978, c. 350; 1979, c. 480; 1981, c. 207; 1985, c. 360; 1987, cc. 130, 131; 1988, c. 851; 1989, c. 544; 1990, c. 766; 1991, c. 342; 1992, cc. 422, 641, 718, 746, 791, 844; 1993, cc. 48, 313, 348; 1994, cc. 34, 670, 700, 830; 1995, cc. 409, 645, 731, 781, 809; 1996, cc. 428, 432, 747, 881, 927, 944; 1997, cc. 169, 177, 606, 691, 721, 743, 796, 895; 1998, cc. 113, 405, 445, 882; 1999, cc. 383, 685; 2001, cc. 552, 582; 2002, cc. 370, 587, 606; 2003, c. 731; 2005, cc. 149, 914, 928; 2006, cc. 257, 277, 644; 2007, cc. 12, 361, 495, 572.)

The 2007 amendments. — The 2007 amendment by c. 12 deleted "and" at the end of subdivision A 34; added subdivision A 35 [now A 36]; and redesignated the remaining subsection accordingly.

The 2007 amendment by c. 361 added subsection G [now H] and made minor stylistic changes.

The 2007 amendment by c. 495, in subdivision A 8, substituted "authorized or" for "and as," inserted "and the adult members of that individual's household," "or from whom the agency is considering removing a child due to abuse or neglect" and "and 63.2-1505" and deleted "by the agency" following "disseminated" and "for such further dissemination" from the end.

The 2007 amendment by c. 572, in subsection A, added subdivision A 35 and redesignated former subdivision A 35 as present subdivision A 36 [now A 37]; and added subsection G.

Title 22.1.

Education.

CHAPTER 9.

SCHOOL PROPERTY.

Article 1.

General Provisions.

Sec.
22.1-129. Surplus property; sale, exchange or lease of real and personal property.

ARTICLE 1.

General Provisions.

§ 22.1-129. Surplus property; sale, exchange or lease of real and personal property. — A. Whenever a school board determines that it has no use for some of its real property, the school board may sell such property and may retain all or a portion of the proceeds of such sale upon approval of the local governing body and after the school board has held a public hearing on such sale and retention of proceeds, or may convey the title to such real property to the county or city or town comprising the school division or, if the school division is composed of more than one county or city, to the county or city in which the property is located. To convey the title, the school board shall adopt a resolution that such real property is surplus and shall record such resolution along with the deed to the property with the clerk of the circuit court for the county or city where such property is located. Upon the recording of the resolution and the deed, the title shall vest in the appropriate county, city or town.

If a school board sells surplus real property, a capital improvement fund shall be established by such school board and the proceeds of such sale retained by the school board shall accrue to such capital improvement fund. The capital improvement fund shall only be used for new school construction, school renovation, and major school maintenance projects.

B. A school board shall have the power to exchange real and personal property, to lease real and personal property either as lessor or lessee, to grant easements on real property, to convey real property in trust to secure loans, to convey real property to adjust the boundaries of the property and to sell personal property in such manner and upon such terms as it deems proper. As lessee of real property, a school board shall have the power to expend funds for capital repairs and improvements on such property, if the lease is for a term equal to or longer than the useful life of such repairs or improvements.

C. Notwithstanding the provisions of subsections A and B, a school board shall have the power to sell career and technical education projects and associated land pursuant to § 22.1-234.

Notwithstanding the provisions of subsections A and B, a school board of the City of Virginia Beach shall have the power to sell property to the Virginia Department of Transportation or the Commonwealth Transportation Commissioner when the Commissioner has determined that (i) such conveyance is necessary and (ii) when eminent domain has been authorized for the construction, reconstruction, alteration, maintenance, and repair of the public highways of the Commonwealth, and for all other purposes incidental thereto, including, but not limited to, the relocation of public utilities as may be required.

D. School boards may donate obsolete educational technology hardware and software that is being replaced pursuant to subdivision B 4 of § 22.1-199.1. Any such donations shall be offered to other school divisions, to students, as provided in Board of Education guidelines, and to preschool programs in the Commonwealth. (Code 1950, § 22-161; 1968, c. 261; 1973, c. 220; 1980, c. 559; 1989, c. 102; 1991, c. 298; 1995, c. 513; 1997, c. 686; 2000, c. 93; 2001, c. 483; 2005, c. 446; 2007, c. 813.)

Editor's note. — Acts 2007, c. 813, cl. 2, provides: "That the provisions of this act shall not affect the powers of any locality with respect to any ordinance, resolution or bylaw validly adopted and not repealed or rescinded prior to July 1, 2007."

The 2007 amendments. — The 2007 amendment by c. 813 substituted "the City of Virginia Beach" for "a school division comprised of a city having a population of 350,000 or more adjacent to the Atlantic Ocean" in the second paragraph in subsection C.

Title 25.1.

Eminent Domain.

CHAPTER 1.

GENERAL PROVISIONS.

Sec.
25.1-108. Offer of repurchase to former owner.

§ 25.1-100. Definitions.

Law Review.

For annual survey article, "Real Estate Law," see 41 U. Rich. L. Rev. 257 (2006).

§ 25.1-108. Offer of repurchase to former owner.

— A. If a condemnor has acquired a fee simple interest in property by exercise of its power of eminent domain and subsequently declares that the property is surplus, the condemnor shall offer, within 30 days following such determination, to sell such property to the former owner or his heirs or other successors or assigns of record. Upon completion of the stated public use or where the stated public use has been abandoned, the condemnor shall provide written notice, pursuant to subsection B, of such completion or abandonment to the former property owner or his heirs or other successors or assigns of record. Upon completion of the stated public use or where the stated public use has been abandoned, the former property owner or his heirs or other successors or assigns of record may make a written demand that the condemnor declare any excess property as surplus. The right to the offer of repurchase cannot be waived and any contractual provision or agreement waiving such right is void and unenforceable. The offer to sell shall be made by the condemnor at the price paid by the condemnor to the former owner plus interest at the annual rate of six percent; provided that the condemnor may increase the price by the fair market value of the condemnor's improvements, determined at the time the offer to sell is made. In no case shall the price established by the condemnor exceed the fair market value of the property at the time the offer to sell is made. If no written response is received by the condemnor from the former owner within 90 days after the offer to sell has been made, the former owner shall be deemed to have waived his right to the offer of repurchase.

B. Notice of the offer to repurchase shall be sent by certified mail to (i) the last known address of the former owner and (ii) the address of the last owner of record as it appears in the tax records of the local treasurer.

C. This section shall not apply to property acquired by the Commonwealth Transportation Commissioner pursuant to Title 33.1. (2005, c. 2; 2006, c. 246; 2007, cc. 882, 901, 926.)

Editor's note. — Acts 2007, cc. 882, 901, and 926, cl. 3, provides: "That, until July 1, 2010, the provisions of this act shall not affect the ability of a redevelopment and housing authority organized pursuant to Title 36 of the Code of Virginia to acquire property pursuant to any redevelopment or conservation plan adopted prior to January 1, 2007. However, the provisions of this act shall be applicable to all redevelopment and conservation plans adopted after January 1, 2007."

Acts 2007, cc. 882, 901, and 926, cl. 4, provides: "Nothing contained in this act shall prohibit the Norfolk Redevelopment and Housing Authority or the City of Norfolk to acquire property through the use of eminent domain for the location of a recreational facility open to the public to be owned or operated by a not-for-profit

entity, provided such acquisitions are instituted prior to July 1, 2010."

The 2007 amendments. — The 2007 amendments by cc. 882, 901 and 926 are identical, and, in subsection A, in the first paragraph, deleted "within 15 years of being vested with the title to such property" following "property is surplus" and inserted the second and third sentences and deleted the second paragraph, banning requirements for a condemnor to offer to sell property the condemnor has acquired through eminent domain to a former owner 15 years after vestment with the title to the property.

Law Review. — For annual survey article, "Real Estate Law," see 41 U. Rich. L. Rev. 257 (2006).

CHAPTER 2.

CONDEMNATION PROCEDURES.

Article 5.

Determination of Just Compensation by Jurors.

Sec.
25.1-229.   Selection of jurors.

Article 7.

Judgment and Post-Judgment Procedure.

25.1-245.   Costs.

ARTICLE 1.

General Provisions.

§ 25.1-203. Authority of certain condemnors to inspect property; reimbursement for damages; notice prior to entry.

Law Review.

For article reviewing recent developments and changes in legislation, case law, and Virginia Supreme Court Rules affecting civil litigation, "Civil Practice and Procedure," see 40 U. Rich. L. Rev. 95 (2005).

§ 25.1-204. Effort to purchase required; prerequisite to effort to purchase or filing certificate.

CIRCUIT COURT OPINIONS

Bona fide offer made. — Motion by the Commonwealth Transportation Commissioner to amend a certificate of condemnation to properly identify the correct parcel was granted pursuant to § 33.1-125, as the Commissioner had made a bona fide offer to purchase the property under § 25.1-204, and defendants knew which parcel the Commissioner was interested in, and thus defendants were not prejudiced by the clerical error. Commonwealth Transp. Comm'r v. Holly Tree Props., Inc., 71 Va. Cir. 353, 2006 Va. Cir. LEXIS 136 (Fairfax County 2006).

ARTICLE 2.

Condemnation Proceedings.

§ 25.1-205.1. Mandatory dispute resolution orientation session.

Law Review. — For annual survey article, "Real Estate Law," see 41 U. Rich. L. Rev. 257 (2006).

§ 25.1-219. Pretrial settlement conference; determination of preliminary issues; fixing date of trial on issue of just compensation.

CASE NOTES

Matters for jury determination. — In a condemnation proceeding where landowners filed a plea in bar arguing that the condemnation was not for a public use, the trial court properly denied the landowners a jury trial on this issue. In §§ 25.1-219 and 25.1-220, the legislature reserved for decision by the court those issues that did not involve the question of just compensation or the determination of ownership or other interests in the property sought to be condemned. Hoffman Family, LLC v. City of Alexandria, 272 Va. 274, 634 S.E.2d 722, 2006 Va. LEXIS 89 (2006).

§ 25.1-220. Who determines issue of just compensation.

Law Review.
For annual survey article, "Real Estate Law," see 41 U. Rich. L. Rev. 257 (2006).

CASE NOTES

Matters for jury determination. — In a condemnation proceeding where landowners filed a plea in bar arguing that the condemnation was not for a public use, the trial court properly denied the landowners a jury trial on this issue. In §§ 25.1-219 and 25.1-220, the legislature reserved for decision by the court those issues that did not involve the question of just compensation or the determination of ownership or other interests in the property sought to be condemned. Hoffman Family, LLC v. City of Alexandria, 272 Va. 274, 634 S.E.2d 722, 2006 Va. LEXIS 89 (2006).

ARTICLE 5.

Determination of Just Compensation by Jurors.

§ 25.1-229. Selection of jurors. — A. Except as otherwise provided in this section, the provisions of Chapter 11 (§ 8.01-336 et seq.) of Title 8.01 shall apply to the selection of condemnation juries mutatis mutandis. While preserving the random selection process set forth in § 8.01-345, the jury commissioner shall determine the freeholder status of individuals randomly selected by reference to tax rolls or other reliable data the judge of the circuit court deems appropriate.

B. All of the acting jurors and all of the names drawn for alternate jurors shall be freeholders of property within the jurisdiction. On the day set for trial, jurors who appear shall be called to be sworn on their voir dire until a disinterested and impartial panel is obtained. A juror may be stricken for cause. From the impartial panel the judge shall randomly select 13 jurors. From the panel of 13 jurors each party shall have four preemptory strikes. The court may appoint alternate jurors. Five persons from a panel of not fewer than 13 jurors shall constitute a jury in a condemnation case. If fewer than seven jurors remain before the court prior to the exercise of peremptory strikes, the trial may proceed and be heard by less than five jurors provided the parties agree. However, no trial shall proceed with fewer than three jurors.

C. The conclusion of the jurors need not be unanimous, and a majority of the jurors may act in the name of the jury.

D. In condemnation proceedings instituted by the Commonwealth Transportation Commissioner, a person owning structures or improvements for which an outdoor advertising permit has been issued by the Commonwealth Transportation Commissioner pursuant to § 33.1-360 shall be deemed to be an "owner" for purposes of this section. (Code 1919, §§ 4366, 4367; 1928, p. 334; 1948, p. 168; Code 1950, §§ 25-12, 25-16; 1962, c. 426, § 25-46.20; 1968, c. 535; 1973, c. 510; 1974, c. 625; 1975, c. 551; 1991, c. 520; 1993, c. 906; 1997, c. 58; 2000, c. 1029; 2003, c. 940; 2006, c. 586; 2007, cc. 450, 720.)

The 2007 amendments. — The 2007 amendments by cc. 450 and 720 are identical, and rewrote the section.

ARTICLE 7.

Judgment and Post-Judgment Procedure.

§ 25.1-245. Costs. — A. Except as otherwise provided in this chapter, all costs of the proceeding in the trial court that are fixed by statute shall be taxed against the petitioner.

B. The court may in its discretion tax as a cost a fee, not to exceed $1,000, for a survey for the landowner.

C. If an owner whose property is taken by condemnation under this title or under Title 33.1 is awarded at trial, as compensation for the taking of or damage to his real property, an amount that is 30 percent or more greater than the amount of the petitioner's final written offer made not later than 60 days after receipt by the petitioner of a complete copy of the owner's written self contained or summary appraisal report, as referenced in the Uniform Standards of Professional Appraisal Practice, provided it is the same type of report furnished to the landowner that complies with the requirements of the Uniform Standards of Professional Appraisal Practice in effect as of the date of such report on which the owner intends to rely to support the amount of just compensation to which he claims to be entitled, the court may order the petitioner to pay to the owner those (i) reasonable costs, other than attorney fees, and (ii) reasonable fees and travel costs, including reasonable appraisal and engineering fees, for no more than three experts testifying at trial, that the owner incurs. The requirements of this subsection shall not apply to those condemnation actions:

1. Involving easements valued at less than $10,000.

2. In which the petitioner filed, prior to July 1, 2005: (i) a petition in condemnation pursuant to

Chapter 2 (§ 25.1-205 et seq.) of this title; or (ii) a certificate of take or deposit pursuant to Title 33.1, or Chapter 3 (§ 25.1-300 et seq.) of this title.

3. In which the owner does not provide the report described herein.

D. All costs on appeal shall be assessed and assessable in the manner provided by law and the Rules of Court as in other civil cases. (1962, c. 426, § 25-46.32; 1970, c. 345; 2000, c. 1029; 2003, c. 940; 2005, c. 878; 2007, c. 895.)

The 2007 amendments. — The 2007 amendment by c. 895, in subsection C, deleted "the respondent has filed responsive pleadings," inserted "receipt by the petitioner ... claims to be entitled," deleted "as authorized pursuant to § 25.1-419" in clause (i) and inserted "including reasonable appraisal and engineering fees" in clause (ii) and added subdivision C 3.

Law Review.

For article reviewing recent developments and changes in legislation, case law, and Virginia Supreme Court Rules affecting civil litigation, "Civil Practice and Procedure," see 40 U. Rich. L. Rev. 95 (2005).

CHAPTER 4.

RELOCATION ASSISTANCE AND REAL PROPERTY ACQUISITION POLICIES.

Article 3.

Real Property Acquisition Policies.

Sec.
25.1-417.1. (Expires July 1, 2009) Partial reimbursement of costs of an owner obtaining a written appraisal report if no agreement as to the price of property needed for public purposes is reached with the Department of Transportation in certain circumstances and subject to certain conditions.

ARTICLE 3.

Real Property Acquisition Policies.

§ 25.1-417.1. (Expires July 1, 2009) Partial reimbursement of costs of an owner obtaining a written appraisal report if no agreement as to the price of property needed for public purposes is reached with the Department of Transportation in certain circumstances and subject to certain conditions. — A. Notwithstanding any other provision of Title 25.1 to the contrary, whenever the Department of Transportation and the owner do not reach an agreement for the acquisition of private property and the Department of Transportation lawfully files a Certificate of Deposit/Certificate of Take, if authorized to do so, or files a Petition in Condemnation, the owner shall be entitled to partial payment according

to the provisions set out herein for the cost of preparation of one written self contained or summary appraisal report, as referenced in the Uniform Standards of Professional Appraisal Practice, provided it is the same type of report furnished to the landowner that complies with the requirements of the Uniform Standards of Professional Appraisal Practice at that time whenever (i) the offer by the Department of Transportation exceeds $250,000 or (ii) the owner contends, in a responsive pleading filed by the owner, or other written form, that just compensation for the land and interests described in said Certificate or Petition in Condemnation exceeds $250,000. However, the owner shall only be entitled to payment if the owner provides to the Department of Transportation a complete and accurate copy of such written appraisal report, which appraisal is equal to or greater than $250,000, which must relate to the type of acquisition sought by the Department of Transportation, at least 60 days prior to trial. Moreover, the court, in its discretion, may reimburse the landowner for appraisals that are less than $250,000 provided the appraisal otherwise meets the requirements of this section.

B. The amount of payment shall depend on the type of appraisal provided and shall not exceed $10,000. The amount of payment shall be based upon a schedule developed by the Department of Transportation, taking into consideration factors it deems appropriate including, but not limited to the type of acquisition—whole or partial; the complexity of the appraisal (residential, commercial, industrial, agricultural or other); the location of the property within the Commonwealth; the zoning of the property, or its reasonably probable and imminent potential for rezoning.

C. Payment shall be provided within 90 days of the receipt of such written appraisal report by the Department of Transportation according to the Schedule of Payment. Any disputes about the amount of payment shall be resolved by the court.

D. The amount of payment or fact of payment shall not be admissible in any subsequent trial on valuation of the property acquired. (2007, c. 895.)

Editor's note. — Acts 2007, c. 895, cl. 2, provides: "That the provisions of § 25.1-417.1 shall only apply to all acquisitions made by the Department of Transportation by Certificate of Deposit/Certificate of Take or Petition in Condemnation filed after July 1, 2007."

Acts 2007, c. 895, cl. 3, provides: "That the Department of Transportation shall promulgate the Schedule of Reimbursement described in § 25.1-417.1 by October 1, 2007 to become effective that day."

Acts 2007, c. 895, cl. 4, provides: "That the Department of Transportation shall not be subject to the requirements of the Administrative Process Act (§ 2.2-4000 et seq.) as may be necessary to carry out the provisions of the third enactment of this act, but that public participation must be utilized by the Department of Transportation to receive comments and suggestions before the Department of Transportation adopts the Schedule."

Acts 2007, c. 895, cl. 5, provides: "That the provisions of § 25.1-417.1 shall expire on July 1, 2009."

Title 28.2.

Fisheries and Habitat of the Tidal Waters.

SUBTITLE III.

HABITAT.

CHAPTER 13.

WETLANDS.

ARTICLE 1.

General Provisions.

§ 28.2-1300. Definitions.

Law Review.
For article, "New Orleans, the Chesapeake, and the Future of Environmental Assessment Overcoming the Natural Resources Law of unintended Consequences," see 40 U. Rich. L. Rev. 981 (2006).

Title 33.1.

Highways, Bridges and Ferries.

CHAPTER 1.

COMMONWEALTH TRANSPORTATION BOARD AND HIGHWAYS GENERALLY.

Article 1.

Commonwealth Transportation Board.

Sec.
33.1-3. Secretary to be Chairman; Commonwealth Transportation Commissioner.
33.1-12. General powers and duties of Board, etc.; definitions.
33.1-13. (Effective until July 1, 2008) General powers of Commissioner.
33.1-13. (Effective July 1, 2008) General powers of Commissioner.
33.1-13.01. Annual report on outsourcing, privatization and downsizing, maximizing revenue generation, and increasing the role of the private sector.
33.1-13.02. Biennial report on maintaining and operating existing transportation infrastructure.
33.1-19.1. Environmental permits for highway projects; timely review.

Article 1.1.

Allocation of Highway Funds.

33.1-23.02. Definition of the terms "maintenance" and "asset management."
33.1-23.03. Board to develop and update Statewide Transportation Plan.

Sec.
33.1-23.03:002. Goals for addressing transportation needs of populations with limited mobility.
33.1-23.03:8. Priority Transportation Fund established.
33.1-23.03:10. Tolls for use of Interstate Highway System components.
33.1-23.1. Allocation of funds among highway systems.
33.1-23.2. Allocation of construction funds for primary system and interstate match.
33.1-23.4. Allocation of construction funds within secondary system.
33.1-23.4:01. Allocation of proceeds of Commonwealth of Virginia Transportation Capital Projects Revenue Bonds.

Article 2.

The State Highway System.

33.1-41.1. Payments to cities and certain towns for maintenance of certain highways.
33.1-44. Matching highway funds; funding of urban system construction projects, generally.
33.1-46.2. (For expiration date — see Editor's note) Designation of high-occupancy vehicle lanes; use of such lanes; penalties.
33.1-46.2. (For effective date — see Editor's note) Designation of high-occupancy vehicle lanes; use of such lanes; penalties.

Article 6.

Secondary System of State Highways.

33.1-70.3. Requirements for taking new streets into state secondary highway system.
33.1-84.1. Resumption of responsibility for secondary highways by counties.

Article 7.

Eminent Domain and Damages.

33.1-94. Right to enter on land to ascertain its suitability for highway and other transportation purposes; damage resulting from such entry.

Article 15.

Miscellaneous Provisions.

33.1-198. (Effective July 1, 2008) Connections over shoulders of highways for intersecting commercial establishment entrances.
33.1-198.1. (Effective July 1, 2008) Comprehensive highway access management standards.
33.1-199. (Effective July 1, 2008) Replacing entrances destroyed by Commissioner.
33.1-223.2:12. Tolls may vary to encourage travel during off-peak hours.
33.1-223.2:17. Commonwealth Transportation Board may transfer interest in and control over certain highways, highway rights-of-way, and landings.

ARTICLE 1.

Commonwealth Transportation Board.

§ 33.1-3. Secretary to be Chairman; Commonwealth Transportation Commissioner. —
The Chairman of the Commonwealth Transportation Board shall be the Secretary of Transportation. The Commonwealth Transportation Commissioner, hereinafter in this title sometimes called "the Commissioner," shall be the chief executive officer of the Department of Transportation. The Commissioner may, at the time of his appointment, be a

nonresident of Virginia, shall be an experienced administrator, able to direct and guide the Department in the establishment and achievement of the Commonwealth's long-range highway and other transportation objectives and shall be appointed at large.

The Commissioner shall devote his entire time and attention to his duties as chief executive officer of the Department and shall receive such compensation as shall be fixed by the Commonwealth Transportation Board, subject to the approval of the Governor. He shall also be reimbursed for his actual travel expenses while engaged in the discharge of his duties.

In the event of a vacancy due to the death, temporary disability, retirement, resignation or removal of the Commissioner, the Governor may appoint and thereafter remove at his pleasure an "Acting Commonwealth Transportation Commissioner" until such time as the vacancy may be filled as provided in § 33.1-1. Such "Acting Commonwealth Transportation Commissioner" shall have all powers and perform all duties of the Commissioner as provided by law, and shall receive such compensation as may be fixed by the Governor. In the event of the temporary disability, for any reason, of the Commissioner, full effect shall be given to the provisions of § 2.2-605. (Code 1950, § 33-3; 1960, c. 271; 1963, Ex. Sess., c. 3; 1964, c. 265; 1970, c. 322; 1974, c. 462; 1990, cc. 1, 317; 1995, cc. 195, 223; 2007, c. 896.)

Editor's note. — Acts 2007, c. 896, cl. 7, provides: "That the Virginia Department of Transportation, with the advice and consent of the Commonwealth Transportation Board, shall, on or before January 1, 2009, submit to the Governor and the General Assembly a plan to reassign the various highways, bridges, and other facilities comprising the state primary, secondary, and urban highways systems so that the assignment of components to such systems is based, to the maximum degree practicable, on the components' functional classification. Such plan shall include an analysis of the costs, benefits, and programmatic and other implications of such reassignment."

Acts 2007, c. 896, cl. 8, provides: "That the Virginia Department of Transportation shall, on or before January 1, 2008, submit a written report to the General Assembly on its plans to create opportunities to enhance mobility and free-flowing traffic on Department-controlled toll facilities by embracing technological advances."

Acts 2007, c. 896, cl. 23 contains a severability clause.

The 2007 amendments. — The 2007 amendment by c. 896 rewrote the first sentence as the first two paragraphs, inserting the first sentence of the second paragraph; substituted "The Commissioner" for "The Commonwealth Transportation Commissioner, hereinafter in this title sometimes called 'the commissioner;'" and "Commonwealth Transportation Board" for "Governor" and "Governor" for "Board, unless such salary be fixed by the General Assembly in the appropriation act" in the third paragraph.

§ 33.1-12. General powers and duties of Board, etc.; definitions. — The Commonwealth Transportation Board shall be vested with the following powers and shall have the following duties:

(1) Location of routes. To locate and establish the routes to be followed by the roads comprising sys-

tems of state highways between the points designated in the establishment of such systems.

(2) Construction and maintenance contracts and activities related to passenger and freight rail and public transportation.

(a) To let all contracts to be administered by the Virginia Department of Transportation or the Department of Rail and Public Transportation for the construction, maintenance, and improvement of the roads comprising systems of state highways and for all activities related to passenger and freight rail and public transportation in excess of $2 million. The Commonwealth Transportation Commissioner shall have authority to let all Virginia Department of Transportation-administered contracts for highway construction, maintenance, and improvements up to $2 million in value. The Director of the Department of Rail and Public Transportation shall have the authority to let contracts for passenger and freight rail and public transportation improvements up to $2 million in value. The Commonwealth Transportation Commissioner is authorized to enter into agreements with localities, authorities, and transportation districts to administer projects and to allow those localities, authorities, and transportation districts to let contracts for highway construction, maintenance, and improvements within their jurisdictions. The Director of the Department of Rail and Public Transportation is authorized to enter into agreements with localities, authorities, and transportation districts to administer projects and to allow those localities, authorities, and transportation districts to let contracts for passenger and freight rail and public transportation activities within their jurisdictions. The Commonwealth Transportation Commissioner and the Director of the Department of Rail and Public Transportation shall report on their respective transportation contracting activities at least quarterly to the Board.

(b) The Commonwealth Transportation Board may award contracts for the construction of transportation projects on a design-build basis. These contracts may be awarded after a written determination is made by the Commonwealth Transportation Commissioner or the Director of the Department of Rail and Public Transportation, pursuant to objective criteria previously adopted by the Board regarding the use of design-build, that delivery of the projects must be expedited and that it is not in the public interest to comply with the design and construction contracting procedures normally followed. Such objective criteria will include requirements for prequalification of contractors and competitive bidding processes. These contracts shall be of such size and scope to encourage maximum competition and participation by agency prequalified and otherwise qualified contractors. Such determination shall be retained for public inspection in the official records of the Department of Transportation or the Department of Rail and Public Transportation, as the case may be, and shall include a description of the nature and scope of the project and the reasons for the Commissioner's or Director's determination that awarding a design-build contract will best serve the public interest. The provisions of this section shall supersede contrary provisions of subsection D of § 2.2-4303 and § 2.2-4306.

(c) For transportation construction projects valued in excess of $100 million, the Commonwealth Transportation Board shall require that a financial plan be prepared. This plan shall include, but not be limited to, the following: (i) a complete cost estimate for all major project elements; (ii) an implementation plan with the project schedule and cost-to-complete information presented for each year; (iii) identified revenues by funding source available each year to meet project costs; (iv) a detailed cash-flow analysis for each year of the proposed project; and (v) efforts to be made to ensure maximum involvement of private enterprise and private capital.

(3) Traffic regulations. To make rules and regulations, from time to time, not in conflict with the laws of the Commonwealth, for the protection of and covering traffic on and the use of systems of state highways and to add to, amend or repeal the same.

(4) Naming highways, bridges, and interchanges. To give suitable names to state highways, bridges, and interchanges and change the names of any highways, bridges, or interchanges forming a part of the systems of state highways, except such highways, bridges, or interchanges as have been or may hereafter be named by the General Assembly; provided that the name of living persons shall not be used for such purposes. The Department of Transportation shall place and maintain appropriate signs indicating the names of highways, bridges, and interchanges named by the Board or by the General Assembly. The costs of producing, placing, and maintaining these signs shall be paid by the counties, cities, and towns in which they are located. No name shall be given to any state highway, bridge or interchange by the Commonwealth Transportation Board unless and until the Commonwealth Transportation Board shall have received from the local governing body of the locality within which a portion of the facility to be named is located a resolution of that governing body requesting such naming.

(5) Compliance with federal acts. To comply fully with the provisions of the present or future federal aid acts. The Board may enter into all contracts or agreements with the United States government and may do all other things necessary to carry out fully the cooperation contemplated and provided for by present or future acts of Congress in the area of transportation.

(6) Information and statistics. To gather and tabulate information and statistics relating to transportation and disseminate the same throughout the Commonwealth. In addition, the Commissioner shall provide a report to the Governor, the General Assembly, the Commonwealth Transportation Board, and the public concerning the current status of all highway construction projects in the Commonwealth. This report shall be posted at least four times each fiscal year, but may be updated more often as circumstances allow. The report shall contain, at a minimum, the following information for every project in the Six-Year Improvement Program: (i) project description; (ii) total cost estimate; (iii) funds expended to date; (iv) project timeline and completion date; (v) statement of whether project is ahead of, on, or behind schedule; (vi) the name of the prime contractor; (vii) total expenditures of federal transportation funds in each county and city; (viii) total expenditures of state transportation funds in each county and city; (ix) statewide totals for federal, state, and local funds expended for highways; (x) statewide totals for federal, state, and local funds expended for transit; (xi) total funds expended on intercity passenger and freight rail line and trains; and (xii) total funds expended in each federal and state programmatic category. Use of one or more Internet websites may be used to satisfy this requirement. Project specific information posted on the Internet shall be updated daily as information is available.

(7) Policies and operation of Departments. To review and approve policies and transportation objectives of the Department of Transportation and the Department of Rail and Public Transportation, to assist in establishing such policies and objectives, to oversee the execution thereof, and to report thereon to the Commonwealth Transportation Commissioner and the Director of the Department of Rail and Public Transportation, respectively.

(8) Cooperation with other agencies and local governments.

(a) To cooperate with the federal government, the American Association of State Highway and Transportation Officials and any other organization in the numbering, signing and marking of highways, in the taking of measures for the promotion of highway safety, in research activities, in the preparation of standard specifications, in the testing of highway materials and otherwise with respect to transportation projects.

(b) To offer technical assistance and coordinate state resources to work with local governments, upon their request, in developing sound transportation components for their local comprehensive plans.

(9) Transportation.

(a) To monitor and, where necessary, approve actions taken by the Department of Rail and Public Transportation pursuant to Chapter 10.1 (§ 33.1-391.1 et seq.) of this title in order to ensure the efficient and economical development of public transportation, the enhancement of rail transportation, and the coordination of such rail and public transportation plans with highway programs.

(b) To coordinate the planning for financing of transportation needs, including needs for highways, railways, seaports, airports, and public transportation and to set aside funds as provided in § 33.1-23.03:1. To allocate funds for these needs pursuant to §§ 33.1-23.1 and 58.1-638, the Board shall adopt a Six-Year Improvement Program of anticipated projects and programs by July 1 of each year. This program shall be based on the most recent official Transportation Trust Fund revenue forecast and shall be consistent with a debt management policy adopted by the Board in consultation with the Debt Capacity Advisory Committee and the Department of the Treasury.

(c) To recommend to the General Assembly for their consideration at the next session of the General Assembly, objective criteria to be used by the Board in selecting those transportation projects to be advanced from the feasibility to the construction stage. If such criteria are enacted into law, such objectives shall apply to the interstate, primary, and urban systems of highways.

(d) To enter into contracts with local districts, commissions, agencies, or other entities created for transportation purposes.

(e) To promote increasing private investment in Virginia's transportation infrastructure, including but not limited to acquisition of causeways, bridges, tunnels, highways, and other transportation facilities.

(10) Contracts with other states. To enter into all contracts with other states necessary for the proper coordination of the location, construction, maintenance, improvement, and operation of transportation systems, including the systems of state highways with the highways of such other states and, where necessary, to seek the approval of such contracts by the Congress of the United States.

(11) Use of funds. To administer, distribute, and allocate funds in the Transportation Trust Fund as provided by law. The Commonwealth Transportation Board shall ensure that the total funds allocated to any highway construction project are equal to total expenditures within 12 months following completion of the project. However, this requirement shall not apply to debt service apportionments pursuant to § 33.1-23.3 or 33.1-23.4.

(12) Financial and investment advisors. With the advice of the Secretary of Finance and the State Treasurer, to engage a financial advisor and investment advisor who may be anyone within or without the government of the Commonwealth, to assist in planning and making decisions concerning the investment of funds and the use of bonds for transportation purposes. The work of these advisors shall be coordinated with the Secretary of Finance and the State Treasurer.

(13) The powers of the Virginia Aviation Board set out in Chapter 1 (§ 5.1-1 et seq.) of Title 5.1 and the Virginia Port Authority set out in Chapter 10 (§ 62.1-128 et seq.) of Title 62.1 are in no way diminished by the provisions of this title.

(14) To enter into payment agreements with the Treasury Board related to payments on bonds issued by the Commonwealth Transportation Board.

(15) Outdoor theaters. By regulation:

(a) To prevent the erection of moving picture screens of outdoor theaters in such a manner as to be ordinarily visible from any highway;

(b) To require that a sufficient space is left between any highway and the entrance to any outdoor theater to prevent congestion on the highway; and

(c) To require that outdoor theater entrances and exits are adequately lighted and marked.

The term *"public transportation"* or *"mass transit"* as used in this title means passenger transportation by rubber-tired, rail, or other surface conveyance which provides shared ride services open to the general public on a regular and continuing basis. The term does not include school buses; charter or sight-seeing service; vehicular ferry service that serves as a link in the highway network; or human service agency or other client-restricted transportation.

(16) Establishment of highway user fees for the systems of state highways. When the traffic-carrying capacity of any system of state highways or a portion thereof is increased by construction or improvement, the Commonwealth Transportation Board may enter into agreements with localities, authorities, and transportation districts to establish highway user fees for such system of state highways or portion thereof that the localities, authorities, and transportation districts maintain. (Code 1950, § 33-12; 1956, c. 92; 1964, c. 265; 1970, c. 322; 1974, c. 462; 1977, c. 150; 1978, c. 650; 1986, Sp. Sess., c. 13; 1988, cc. 844, 903; 1989, c. 727; 1992, c. 167; 1995, c. 94; 2001, c. 349; 2003, cc. 281, 533, 560; 2004, c. 110; 2005, cc. 839, 919; 2006, cc. 197, 417, 833, 924; 2006, Sp. Sess. I, c. 8; 2007, c. 337.)

The 2006 amendments. — The 2006 amendment by Sp. Sess. I, c. 8, effective January 1, 2007, in subdivision (2)(c), added clause (v) and made minor stylistic changes; and added subdivision (9)(e).

The 2007 amendments. — The 2007 amendment by c. 337 added clauses (vii) through (xii) to subdivision (6).

§ 33.1-13. (Effective until July 1, 2008) General powers of Commissioner. — Except such powers as are conferred by law upon the Commonwealth Transportation Board, the Commonwealth Transportation Commissioner shall have the power to do all acts necessary or convenient for constructing, improving and maintaining the roads embraced in the systems of state highways and to further the interests of the Commonwealth in the areas of public transportation, railways, seaports, and airports. And as executive head of the Transportation Department, the Commissioner is specifically charged with the duty of executing all orders and decisions of the Board and he may, subject to the provisions of this chapter, require that all appointees and employees perform their duties under this chapter.

In addition, the Commissioner, in order to maximize efficiency, shall take such steps as may be appropriate to outsource or privatize any of the

Department's functions that might reasonably be provided by the private sector. (Code 1950, § 33-13; 1970, c. 322; 1974, c. 462; 1978, c. 652; 1986, Sp. Sess., c. 13; 2007, c. 896.)

Section set out twice. — The section above is effective until July 1, 2008. For the version of this section effective July 1, 2008, see the following section, also numbered 33.1-13.

Editor's note. — Acts 2007, c. 896, cl. 23 contains a severability clause.

The 2007 amendments. — The 2007 amendment by c. 896 added the second paragraph.

§ 33.1-13. (Effective July 1, 2008) General powers of Commissioner. — Except such powers as are conferred by law upon the Commonwealth Transportation Board, the Commonwealth Transportation Commissioner shall have the power to do all acts necessary or convenient for constructing, improving, maintaining, and preserving the efficient operation of the roads embraced in the systems of state highways and to further the interests of the Commonwealth in the areas of public transportation, railways, seaports, and airports. And as executive head of the Transportation Department, the Commissioner is specifically charged with the duty of executing all orders and decisions of the Board and he may, subject to the provisions of this chapter, require that all appointees and employees perform their duties under this chapter.

In addition, the Commissioner, in order to maximize efficiency, shall take such steps as may be appropriate to outsource or privatize any of the Department's functions that might reasonably be provided by the private sector. (Code 1950, § 33-13; 1970, c. 322; 1974, c. 462; 1978, c. 652; 1986, Sp. Sess., c. 13; 2007, cc. 863, 896, 928.)

Section set out twice. — The section above is effective July 1, 2008. For this section as in effect until July 1, 2008, see the preceding section, also numbered 33.1-13.

Editor's note. — Acts 2007, cc. 863 and 928, in cl. 2 provide: "That the Commissioner shall solicit and consider public comment in the development of standards required by this act and publish such standards no later than December 31, 2007. Such standards shall become effective on July 1, 2008."

Acts 2007, cc. 863 and 928, in cl. 3 provide: "That the provisions of the first enactment of this act shall become effective July 1, 2008."

Acts 2007, cc. 863 and 928, cl. 4, are nearly identical, and provide: "That, until July 1, 2008, the Commissioner shall not be subject to the requirements of the Administrative Process Act (§ 2.2-4000 et seq.) as may be necessary to carry out the provisions of this act."

The 2007 amendments. — The 2007 amendments by cc. 863 and 928, effective July 1, 2008, are identical, and substituted "maintaining, and preserving the efficient operation of" for "and maintaining."

The 2007 amendment by c. 896 added the second paragraph.

§ 33.1-13.01. Annual report on outsourcing, privatization and downsizing, maximizing revenue generation, and increasing the role of the private sector. — The Commonwealth Transportation Commissioner shall annually report in writing to the General Assembly, no later than November 30 of each year, on all actions and initiatives of the Virginia Department of Transportation in the preceding fiscal year that involved outsourcing, privatization, and downsizing. Further, the Commissioner shall provide, in writing to the General Assembly, detailed and specific plans for outsourcing, privatization, and downsizing in the current fiscal year, including, but not limited to, appropriate asset management and intelligent transportation system functions and services. Such report shall include a description of efforts that have been made, are under way, or are to be undertaken for maximizing the generation of revenue from existing assets of the Department of Transportation, including but not limited to real estate, and increasing the role of the private sector and public-private partnerships in the leasing of real estate and other assets in the development of highway projects. (2006, cc. 420, 544; 2006, Sp. Sess. I, c. 7.)

The 2006 amendments. — The 2006 amendment by Sp. Sess. I, c. 7, effective January 1, 2007, added "maximizing revenue generation, and increasing the role of the private sector" to the section heading, and added the last sentence.

§ 33.1-13.02. Biennial report on maintaining and operating existing transportation infrastructure. — No later than September 15 of each odd-numbered year, the Virginia Department of Transportation shall submit to the Governor, the Joint Legislative Audit and Review Commission, and the Commonwealth Transportation Board a report on the condition of and needs for maintaining and operating the existing transportation infrastructure in the Commonwealth for all asset management and maintenance, based on an asset management methodology. Such methodology shall, in accordance with generally accepted engineering principles and business practices, identify and prioritize maintenance and operations needs, including those for pavement, technology, bridges and other structures, pipes and draining, and congestion management and reduction. Reports shall include (i) the performance standards to be used to determine those needs, (ii) an estimate, for the upcoming two fiscal years, of the budget required to meet them, (iii) employment level goals for the next two years, and (iv) the percentage of asset management under private contract. (2007, cc. 335, 355.)

§ 33.1-19.1. Environmental permits for highway projects; timely review. — Notwithstanding any other provision of state law or regulation, any state agency, board, or commission that issues a permit required for a highway construction project pursuant to Title 10.1, 28.2, 29.1, or 62.1 of the Code of Virginia shall, within 15 days of receipt of an individual permit application, review the application for completeness and either accept the application or request additional specific information from the Department of Transportation. Unless a shorter period is provided by law, regulation, or agreement, the state agency, board, or commission shall within 120 days of receipt of a complete application issue the permit, issue the permit with conditions, deny the permit, or decide whether a public meeting or hearing is required by law. If a public meeting or hearing is held, it shall be held within 45 days of the decision to conduct such a proceeding and a final decision as to the permit shall be made within 90 days of completion of the public meeting or hearing. For coverage under general permits issued pursuant to Title 10.1, 28.2, 29.1, or 62.1, the state agency, board, or commission that issues such permits shall, within 10 business days of receipt of an application from the Department of Transportation for a road or highway construction project, review the application for completeness and either accept the application or request additional specific information from the Department of Transportation. Coverage under the general permit shall be approved, approved with conditions, or denied within 30 business days of receipt of a complete application. (2005, c. 781; 2007, c. 896.)

Editor's note. — Acts 2007, c. 896, cl. 23 contains a severability clause.

The 2007 amendments. — The 2007 amendment by c. 896 deleted "or general" preceding "permit" in the first sentence and added the fourth sentence.

ARTICLE 1.1.

Allocation of Highway Funds.

§ 33.1-23.02. Definition of the terms "maintenance" and "asset management." — A. For the purpose of this title, unless otherwise explicitly provided, the term *"maintenance"* shall include ordinary maintenance, maintenance replacement operations that include but are not limited to traffic signal synchronization, incident management, other intelligent transportation system functions, and any other categories of maintenance which may be designated by the Commissioner.

B. 1. For the purposes of this title, unless otherwise explicitly provided, the term *"asset management"* shall mean a systematic process of operating and maintaining the state system of highways by combining engineering practices and analysis with sound business practices and economic theory to achieve cost-effective outcomes.

2. The Department shall develop asset management practices in the operation and maintenance of the state system of highways.

3. The Commissioner shall advise the Board, on or before June 30 of even-numbered years, of performance targets and outcomes that are expected to be achieved, based upon the funding identified for maintenance, over the biennium beginning July 1 of that year. In addition, not later than September 30 of even-numbered years, the Commissioner shall advise the Board on the Department's accomplishments relative to the expected outcomes and budget expenditures for the biennium ending June 30 of that year and also advise the Board as to the methodology used to determine maintenance needs and the justification as to the maintenance funding by source. (1985, c. 42; 2002, cc. 302, 570; 2006, Sp. Sess. I, c. 9.)

The 2006 amendments. — The 2006 amendment by Sp. Sess. I, c. 9, effective January 1, 2007, inserted "operations that include but are not limited to traffic signal synchronization, incident management, other intelligent transportation system functions" in subsection A and added "and also advise the Board as to the methodology used to determine maintenance needs and the justification as to the maintenance funding by source" at the end of subdivision B 3.

§ 33.1-23.03. Board to develop and update Statewide Transportation Plan. — The Commonwealth Transportation Board shall conduct a comprehensive review of statewide transportation needs in a Statewide Transportation Plan setting forth an inventory of all construction needs for all systems, and based upon this inventory, establishing goals, objectives, and priorities covering a twenty-year planning horizon, in accordance with federal transportation planning requirements. This plan shall embrace all modes of transportation and include technological initiatives. This Statewide Transportation Plan shall be updated as needed, but no less than once every five years. The plan shall promote economic development and all transportation modes, intermodal connectivity, environmental quality, accessibility for people and freight, and transportation safety. The plan shall include quantifiable measures and achievable goals relating to, but not limited to, congestion reduction and safety, transit and high-occupancy vehicle facility use, job-to-housing ratios, job and housing access to transit and pedestrian facilities, air quality, and per capita vehicle miles traveled. The Board shall consider such goals in evaluating and selecting transportation improvement projects. The plan shall incorporate the approved long-range plans' measures and goals developed by the Northern Virginia Transportation Authority and the Hampton Roads Transportation Authority. Each such plan shall be summarized in a public document and made available to the general public upon presentation to the Governor and General Assembly.

It is the intent of the General Assembly that this plan assess transportation needs and assign priorities to projects on a statewide basis, avoiding the production of a plan which is an aggregation of local, district, regional, or modal plans. (1985, c. 320; 2001, cc. 764, 772; 2002, c. 639; 2007, c. 896.)

Editor's note. — Acts 2007, c. 896, cl. 23 contains a severability clause.

The 2007 amendments. — The 2007 amendment by c. 896 substituted "shall promote economic development and all transportation modes" for "will provide consideration of projects and policies and policies affecting all transportation modes and promote economic development" in the third sentence and added the fourth through sixth sentences in the first paragraph.

§ 33.1-23.03:002. Goals for addressing transportation needs of populations with limited mobility. — The Commonwealth Transportation Board, in cooperation with other local, regional, or statewide agencies and entities vested with transportation planning responsibilities, shall establish specific mobility goals for addressing the transportation needs of populations with limited mobility, including, but not necessarily limited to, the elderly, persons with disabilities that limit their mobility, persons not served by any form of mass transit, and those who, for whatever reasons, cannot afford motor vehicles or cannot be licensed to drive them. Such goals, once established, shall be considered in the development and implementation of the Statewide Transportation Plan required by § 33.1-23.03. (2006, cc. 395, 508.)

Editor's note. The section above was enacted as § 33.1-23.03:0001 by Acts 2006, cc. 395 and 508. It was recodified as this section at the direction of the Virginia Code Commission.

§ 33.1-23.03:2. Commonwealth Port Fund, Commonwealth Airport Fund and Commonwealth Mass Transit Fund.

Editor's note. — Acts 2006, Sp. Sess. I, c. 3, as amended by Acts 2007, c. 847, effective for the biennium ending June 30, 2008, in Item 431 B, provides: "The Virginia Aviation Board and the Department of Aviation may obligate funds in excess of the current biennium appropriation for aviation financial assistance programs supported by the Commonwealth Transportation Fund provided 1) sufficient cash is available to cover projected costs in each year and 2) sufficient revenues are projected to meet all cash obligations for new obligations as well as all other commitments and appropriations approved by the General Assembly in the biennial budget."

§ 33.1-23.03:8. Priority Transportation Fund established. — A. There is hereby created in the state treasury a special nonreverting fund to be known as the Priority Transportation Fund, hereafter referred to as "the Fund." The Fund shall be established on the books of the Comptroller. Interest earned on moneys in the Fund shall remain in the Fund and be credited to it. All funds as may be designated in the appropriation act for deposit to the Fund shall be paid into the state treasury and credited to the Fund. Such funds shall include:

1. A portion of the moneys actually collected, including penalty and interest, attributable to any increase in revenues from the taxes imposed under Chapter 22 (§ 58.1-2200 et seq.) of Title 58.1, with such increase being calculated as the difference between such tax revenues collected in the manner prescribed under Chapter 22 less such tax revenues that would have been collected using the prescribed manner in effect immediately before the effective date of Chapter 22, computed without regard to increases in the rates of taxes under Chapter 22 pursuant to enactments of the 2007 Session of the General Assembly. The portion to be deposited to the Fund shall be the moneys actually collected from such increase in revenues and allocated for highway

and mass transit improvement projects as set forth in § 33.1-23.03:2, but not including any amounts that are allocated to the Commonwealth Port Fund and the Commonwealth Airport Fund under such section. There shall also be deposited into the Fund all additional federal revenues attributable to Chapter 22 (§ 58.1-2200 et seq.) of Title 58.1;

2. Beginning with the fiscal year ending June 30, 2000, and for fiscal years thereafter, all revenues that exceed the official forecast, pursuant to § 2.2-1503, for (i) the Highway Maintenance and Operating Fund and (ii) the allocation to highway and mass transit improvement projects as set forth in § 33.1-23.03:2, but not including any amounts that are allocated to the Commonwealth Port Fund and the Commonwealth Airport Fund under such section;

3. All revenues deposited into the Fund pursuant to § 58.1-2531; and

4. Any other such funds as may be transferred, allocated, or appropriated.

All moneys in the Fund shall first be used for debt service payments on bonds or obligations for which the Fund is expressly required for making debt service payments, to the extent needed. The Fund shall be considered a part of the Transportation Trust Fund. Any moneys remaining in the Fund, including interest thereon, at the end of each fiscal year shall not revert to the general fund but shall remain in the Fund. Moneys in the Fund shall be used solely for the purposes enumerated in subsection B of this section. Expenditures and disbursements from the Fund shall be made by the State Treasurer on warrants issued by the Comptroller.

B. The Commonwealth Transportation Board shall use the Fund to facilitate the financing of priority transportation projects throughout the Commonwealth. The Board may use the Fund either (i) by expending amounts therein on such projects directly, (ii) by payment to any authority, locality, commission or other entity for the purpose of paying the costs thereof, or (iii) by using such amounts to support, secure, or leverage financing for such projects. No expenditures from or other use of amounts in the Fund shall be considered in allocating highway maintenance and construction funds under § 33.1-23.1 or apportioning Transportation Trust Fund funds under § 58.1-638, but shall be in addition thereto. The Board shall use the Fund to facilitate the financing of priority transportation projects as designated by the General Assembly; provided, however, that, at the discretion of the Commonwealth Transportation Board, funds allocated to projects within a transportation district may be allocated among projects within the same transportation district as needed to meet construction cash-flow needs.

C. Notwithstanding any other provision of this section, beginning July 1, 2007, no bonds, obligations, or other evidences of debt (the bonds) that expressly require as a source for debt service payments or for the repayment of such bonds the revenues of the Fund, shall be issued or entered into unless at the time of the issuance the revenues then in the Fund or reasonably anticipated to be deposited into the Fund pursuant to the law then in effect are by themselves sufficient to make 100% of the contractually required debt service payments on all such bonds, including any interest related thereto and the retirement of such bonds. (2000, cc. 1019, 1044; 2007, c. 896.)

Editor's note. — For the Commonwealth Transportation Capital Projects Bond Act of 2007, see Acts 2007, c. 896, cl. 2.

Acts 2007, c. 896, cl. 7, provides: "That the Virginia Department of Transportation, with the advice and consent of the Commonwealth Transportation Board, shall, on or before January 1, 2009, submit to the Governor and the General Assembly a plan to reassign the various highways, bridges, and other facilities comprising the state primary, secondary, and urban highways systems so that the assignment of components to such systems is based, to the maximum degree practicable, on the components' functional classification. Such plan shall include an analysis of the costs, benefits, and programmatic and other implications of such reassignment."

Acts 2007, c. 896, cl. 23 contains a severability clause.

The 2007 amendments. — The 2007 amendment by c. 896 inserted "immediately" and "computed without regard to increases in the rates of taxes under Chapter 22 pursuant to enactments of the 2007 Session of the General Assembly" in the first sentence of subdivision A 1; added subdivision A 3 and redesignated former subdivision A 3 as present subdivision A 4 and in that subdivision inserted the first sentence; and added subsection C.

§ 33.1-23.03:9. Concession Payments Account.

Editor's note. — Acts 2007, c. 477, cl. 2, which enacted § 33.1-23.03:10, provides: "That the provisions of this act shall not apply to Chapter 22 of Title 56 or any payment received by the Commonwealth Transportation Board pursuant to § 33.1-23.03:9 of the Code of Virginia."

§ 33.1-23.03:10. Tolls for use of Interstate Highway System components. — A. Notwithstanding any contrary provision of this title and in accordance with all applicable federal and state statutes and requirements, the Commonwealth Transportation Board may impose and collect tolls from all classes of vehicles in amounts established by the Board for the use of any component of the Interstate Highway System within the Commonwealth. Such funds so collected shall be deposited into the Transportation Trust Fund established pursuant to § 33.1-23.03:1, subject to allocation by the Board as provided in this section.

B. The toll facilities authorized by this section shall be subject to the provisions of federal law for the purpose of tolling motor vehicles to finance interstate construction and reconstruction, promote efficiency in the use of highways, reduce traffic congestion, improve air quality and for such other purposes as may be permitted by federal law.

C. In order to mitigate traffic congestion in the vicinity of the toll facilities, no toll facility shall be operated without high-speed automated toll collection technology designed to allow motorists to travel

through the toll facilities without stopping to make payments. Nothing in this subsection shall be construed to prohibit a toll facility from retaining means of non-automated toll collection in some lanes of the facility. The Board shall also consider traffic congestion and mitigation thereof and the impact on local traffic movement as factors in determining the location of the toll facilities authorized pursuant to this section.

D. The revenues collected from each toll facility established pursuant to this section shall be deposited into segregated subaccounts in the Transportation Trust Fund and may be allocated by the Commonwealth Transportation Board as the Board deems appropriate to:

1. Pay or finance all or part of the costs of programs or projects, including without limitation the costs of planning, operation, maintenance and improvements incurred in connection with the toll facility provided that such allocations shall be limited to programs and projects that are reasonably related to or benefit the users of the toll facility. The priorities of metropolitan planning organizations, planning district commissions, local governments, and transportation corridors shall be considered by the Board in making project allocations from such revenues deposited into the Transportation Trust Fund.

2. Repay funds from the Toll Facilities Revolving Account or the Transportation Partnership Opportunity Fund.

3. Pay the Board's reasonable costs and expenses incurred in the administration and management of the Toll Facility. (2007, c. 477.)

Editor's note. — Acts 2007, c. 477, cl. 2, which enacted § 33.1-23.03:10, provides: "That the provisions of this act shall not apply to Chapter 22 of Title 56 or any payment received by the Commonwealth Transportation Board pursuant to § 33.1-23.03:9 of the Code of Virginia."

§ 33.1-23.05. Revenue-sharing funds for systems in certain counties, cities, and towns.

Editor's note. — Acts 2006, Sp. Sess. I, c. 3, as amended by Acts 2007, c. 847, effective for the biennium ending June 30, 2008, in Item 443 A, provides: "Notwithstanding the amounts specified in § 33.1-75.1 C and D of the Code of Virginia, $15,000,000 the first year and $15,000,000 the second year from the Commonwealth Transportation Fund shall be allocated to localities for secondary road revenue sharing."

§ 33.1-23.1. Allocation of funds among highway systems. — A. The Commonwealth Transportation Board shall allocate each year from all funds made available for highway purposes such amount as it deems reasonable and necessary for the maintenance of roads within the interstate system of highways, the primary system of state highways, the secondary system of state highways and for city and town street maintenance payments made pursuant to § 33.1-41.1 and payments made to counties which have withdrawn or elect to withdraw from the

secondary system of state highways pursuant to § 33.1-23.5:1.

B. After funds are set aside for administrative and general expenses and pursuant to other provisions in this title which provide for the disposition of funds prior to allocation for highway purposes, and after allocation is made pursuant to subsection A of this section, the Commonwealth Transportation Board may allocate each year up to 10% of the funds remaining for highway purposes for the undertaking and financing of rail projects that, in the Board's determination, will result in mitigation of highway congestion. After the forgoing allocations have been made, the Board shall allocate the remaining funds available for highway purposes, exclusive of federal funds for the interstate system, among the several highway systems for construction first pursuant to §§ 33.1-23.1:1 and 33.1-23.1:2 and then as follows:

1. Forty percent of the remaining funds exclusive of federal-aid matching funds for the interstate system shall be allocated to the primary system of state highways, including the arterial network, and in addition, an amount shall be allocated to the primary system as interstate matching funds as provided in subsection B of § 33.1-23.2.

2. Thirty percent of the remaining funds exclusive of federal-aid matching funds for the interstate system shall be allocated to urban highways for state aid pursuant to § 33.1-44.

3. Thirty percent of the remaining funds exclusive of federal-aid matching funds for the interstate system shall be allocated to the secondary system of state highways.

C. In addition, the Commonwealth Transportation Board, from funds appropriated for such purpose in the general appropriation act, shall allocate additional funds to the Cities of Newport News, Norfolk, and Portsmouth and the County of Warren in such manner and apportion such funds among such localities as the Board may determine, unless otherwise provided in the general appropriation act. The localities shall use such funds to address highway maintenance and repair needs created by or associated with port operations in those localities.

D. Notwithstanding the foregoing provisions of this section, the General Assembly may, through the general appropriations act, permit the Governor to increase the amounts to be allocated to highway maintenance, highway construction, either or both. (1977, c. 578; 1979, c. 84; 1985, c. 42; 1986, c. 572; 2006, c. 937; 2007, c. 305.)

Editor's note. — Acts 2006, Sp. Sess. I, c. 3, as amended by Acts 2007, c. 847, effective for the biennium ending June 30, 2008, in Item 427 C 2, provides: "Federal funds included in the highway funds distributed pursuant to § 33.1-23.1 B, Code of Virginia, will be distributed to the greatest extent possible to the primary system of state highways and then to the other highway systems taking into consideration the federal eligibility requirements in order to maximize the benefit of the federal funds to the Commonwealth. Such distribution will not change the total amount of funds available to be provided pursuant to § 33.1-23.1."

Acts 2006, Sp. Sess. I, c. 3, as amended by Acts 2007, c. 847,

effective for the biennium ending June 30, 2008, in Item 443 B, provides: "Notwithstanding § 33.1-23.1 of the Code of Virginia, the net proceeds from the lease or sale of surplus and residue property purchased under this program shall be applied to the system and locality where the residue property is located. This funding shall be provided as an adjustment to the allocations distributed to the systems and localities according to § 33.1-23.1 of the Code of Virginia."

The 2007 amendments. — The 2007 amendment by c. 305 rewrote subsection C and redesignated former subsection C as present subsection D.

§ 33.1-23.2. Allocation of construction funds for primary system and interstate match. — A. The Commonwealth Transportation Board shall allocate such funds as are available under § 33.1-23.1 B 1 to the primary system of state highways, including the arterial network, for construction and shall apportion such funds among the nine construction districts so that each construction district shall be allocated a share of such funds equal to the proportion that such construction district bears to the Commonwealth as a whole in terms of: vehicle-miles traveled on the primary system, primary road lane mileage and a primary road need factor which adjusts the weights in the allocation formula for the construction district with the largest under-allocation relative to primary needs, with vehicle-miles traveled weighted seventy percent, primary road lane mileage weighted twenty-five percent, and the primary road need factor weighted five percent.

B. Out of each district's total allocation of primary funds pursuant to paragraph 1 of subsection B of § 33.1-23.1, the Board shall allocate all needed interstate federal-aid matching funds, up to a maximum of twenty-five percent of the district's primary allocation. Any additional interstate federal-aid matching funds needed in a district shall be allocated by the Board from the Interstate Federal-Aid Matching Fund established in § 33.1-23.1:2.

C. Notwithstanding subsection A of this section, the Board may provide for exceptionally heavy expenditures for repairs or replacements made necessary by highway damage resulting from accidents, severe weather conditions, acts of God or vandalism.

D. Notwithstanding subsection A, the Board may, from funds available under subdivision B 1 of § 33.1-23.1, provide funding for the construction of highway projects maintained or to be maintained by a municipality, provided such project involves a component of the National Highway System and such funds are derived from allocations to the highway construction district in which such project is located. Any allocation under this subsection shall not diminish funds allocated or allocable to any such municipality under § 33.1-23.3.

E. Such funds allocated to the primary system shall, as far as possible, be allotted prior to the commencement of the fiscal year and public announcement made of such allotment but the Board shall not approve such allotment until after a public hearing at which political subdivisions of the Commonwealth and interested citizens may be heard.

In any case where any allotment of funds is made under this subsection to any county, all or a part of which subsequently is incorporated as or into a city or town, such allocation shall not be impaired thereby and the funds so allocated shall be expended as if such county or any part thereof had never become an incorporated city, but that portion of such city shall not be eligible to receive funds as a city during the same year it receives the funds allocated as a county or as any part of a county. (1977, c. 578; 1984, c. 748; 1985, c. 42; 2007, cc. 146, 178.)

The 2007 amendments. — The 2007 amendments by cc. 146 and 178 are identical, and added present subsection D and redesignated former subsection D as present subsection E.

§ 33.1-23.3. Allocation of construction funds for urban system highways.

Editor's note. — Acts 2006, Sp. Sess. I, c. 3, as amended by Acts 2007, c. 847, effective for the biennium ending June 30, 2008, in Item 446 D, provides: "For any city or town that assumes responsibility for its construction program as outlined in § 33.1-23.3 D, Code of Virginia, the two percent matching highway fund requirement shall be waived for all new projects approved on or after July 1, 2005."

§ 33.1-23.4. Allocation of construction funds within secondary system. — A. Such funds as are allocated to the secondary system of state highways pursuant to paragraph 3 of subsection B of § 33.1-23.1 shall be apportioned among the several counties in the secondary system by the Commonwealth Transportation Board so that each such county shall be allocated a share of such funds equal to the proportion that such county bears to the Commonwealth as a whole in terms of area and population with population being weighted 80 percent, and area being weighted 20 percent. For the purpose of this section, "area" means the total land area of a county reduced by the area of any military reservations and state or national parks or forests within its boundaries and such other similar areas and facilities of five square miles in area or more, as may be determined by the Commonwealth Transportation Board.

For the purposes of this section, the term "*population*" shall mean either population according to the latest United States census or the latest population estimate of the Center for Public Service of the University of Virginia, whichever is more recent.

If so requested in a resolution adopted by the local governing body, funds allocated to any county under this section may be used to support primary highway system construction projects within the county.

Before allocating funds under the foregoing provisions of this section, the Board may provide for exceptionally heavy expenditures for repairs or replacements made necessary by highway damage resulting from accidents, severe weather conditions, acts of God or vandalism.

B. Notwithstanding other provisions of this section, not more than one-third of the annual secondary system highway funds apportioned to a county under this section may be used to reimburse the county for (i) debt service for bonds or (ii) eligible project costs incurred on approved projects included in the county's Secondary Six-Year Plan and the county's capital improvement program. Such funds may also be used by the county for debt service for bonds issued for, or eligible project costs incurred or to be incurred on, approved projects included, at the time such bonds are issued or such costs are incurred or are to be incurred, in the Six-Year Improvement Program of the Commonwealth Transportation Board and the county's capital improvement program. Any such funds so apportioned to and received by such county, or any portion thereof, may be deposited in a special fund that shall be established separate and apart from any other funds, general or special.

When a county presents a resolution requesting that a portion of its annual secondary construction allocation be set aside for reimbursement for, or payment of, debt service under this section for a specific eligible project, the Commonwealth Transportation Board shall, subject to appropriation and allocation, set aside no more than one-third of the anticipated annual allocation of secondary system construction funding to the county for such purpose, provided such funds have not been previously committed for projects contained in the county's Secondary Six-Year Plan.

The setting aside and use of funds under this section for reimbursement for, or payment of, debt service shall be subject to such terms and conditions as may be prescribed by the Commonwealth Transportation Commissioner.

The provisions of this section shall not constitute a debt or obligation of the Commonwealth Transportation Board or the Commonwealth of Virginia.

C. In counties having elected to manage the construction program for the secondary system of state highways within the county, in accordance with § 33.1-84.1, payment of funds from the allocation of secondary construction funds for the county may be made in equal amounts, one in each quarter of the fiscal year, and shall be reduced by the amount of federal-aid construction funds credited to each county, which will be reimbursed as qualifying expenditures occur and by the amount of funds forecast by the Department of Transportation and by the Department of Rail and Public Transportation to be expended for any construction project or projects or county-wide activities on behalf of the county or other financial obligations. Those counties that decide to take over the responsibility for the secondary construction program shall notify the Commonwealth Transportation Board by July 1 for implementation the following year. Implementation shall take place as specified in the agreement referenced in § 33.1-84.1.

D. The chief administrative officer of counties receiving funds under subsection C of this section shall make annual reports of expenditures to the Department of Transportation in such form as the Commonwealth Transportation Board shall prescribe, accounting for all construction expenditures made from quarterly payments. Such reports shall be included in the scope of the annual audit of each county conducted by independent certified public accountants. (1977, c. 578; 1978, c. 145; 1985, c. 42; 2003, c. 887; 2004, c. 791; 2007, c. 153.)

The 2007 amendments. — The 2007 amendment by c. 153 added subsections C and D.

§ 33.1-23.4:01. Allocation of proceeds of Commonwealth of Virginia Transportation Capital Projects Revenue Bonds.

— The Commonwealth Transportation Board shall allocate, use, and distribute the proceeds of any bonds it is authorized to issue on or after July 1, 2007, pursuant to subdivision 4f of § 33.1-269, as follows:

1. A minimum of 20% of the bond proceeds shall be used for transit capital consistent with subdivision A 4 g of § 58.1-638.

2. A minimum of 4.3% of the bond proceeds shall be used for rail capital consistent with the provisions of §§ 33.1-221.1:1.1 and 33.1-221.1:1.2.

3. The remaining amount of bond proceeds shall be used for paying the costs incurred or to be incurred for construction of transportation projects with such bond proceeds used or allocated as follows: (a) first, to match federal highway funds projected to be made available and allocated to highway and public transportation capital projects by the Commonwealth Transportation Board, for purposes of allowing additional state construction funds to be allocated to the primary, urban, and secondary systems of highways pursuant to subdivisions B 1, B 2, and B 3 of § 33.1-23.1; (b) next, to provide any required funding to fulfill the Commonwealth's allocation of equivalent revenue sharing matching funds pursuant to § 33.1-23.05; and (c) third, to pay or fund the costs of statewide or regional projects throughout the Commonwealth. Costs incurred or to be incurred for construction or funding of these transportation projects shall include, but are not limited to, environmental and engineering studies, rights-of-way acquisition, improvements to all modes of transportation, acquisition, construction and related improvements, and any financing costs or other financing expenses relating to such bonds. Such costs may include the payment of interest on such bonds for a period during construction and not exceeding one year after completion of construction of the relevant project.

4. The total amount of bonds authorized shall be used for purposes of applying the percentages in subdivisions 1 through 3. (2007, c. 896.)

Editor's note. — For the Commonwealth Transportation Capital Projects Bond Act of 2007, see Acts 2007, c. 896, cl. 2.

Acts 2007, c. 896, cl. 7, provides: "That the Virginia Department of Transportation, with the advice and consent of the Common-

wealth Transportation Board, shall, on or before January 1, 2009, submit to the Governor and the General Assembly a plan to reassign the various highways, bridges, and other facilities comprising the state primary, secondary, and urban highways systems so that the assignment of components to such systems is based, to the maximum degree practicable, on the components' functional classification. Such plan shall include an analysis of the costs, benefits, and programmatic and other implications of such reassignment."

Acts 2007, c. 896, cl. 8, provides: "That the Virginia Department of Transportation shall, on or before January 1, 2008, submit a written report to the General Assembly on its plans to create opportunities to enhance mobility and free-flowing traffic on Department-controlled toll facilities by embracing technological advances."

Acts 2007, c. 896, cl. 23 contains a severability clause.

§ 33.1-23.5:1. Funds for counties which have withdrawn or elect to withdraw from the secondary system of state highways.

Editor's note. — Acts 2006, Sp. Sess. I, c. 3, as amended by Acts 2007, c. 847, effective for the biennium ending June 30, 2008, in Item 446 A, provides: "Notwithstanding §§ 33.1-23.5:1 and 33.1-41.1, Code of Virginia, the Department of Transportation shall adjust for inflation the payments made as part of Financial Assistance to Localities distributions and report such inflation adjustment to the Commonwealth Transportation Board."

ARTICLE 2.

The State Highway System.

§ 33.1-41.1. Payments to cities and certain towns for maintenance of certain highways.

— The Commonwealth Transportation Commissioner, subject to the approval of the Commonwealth Transportation Board, shall make payments for maintenance, construction, or reconstruction of highways, as hereinafter provided, to all cities and towns eligible for allocation of construction funds for urban highways under § 33.1-23.3. Such payments, however, shall only be made if those highways functionally classified as principal and minor arterial roads are maintained to a standard satisfactory to the Department of Transportation. Whenever any city or town qualifies under this section for allocation of funds, such qualification shall continue to apply to such city or town regardless of any subsequent change in population and shall cease to apply only when so specifically provided by an act of the General Assembly. All allocations made prior to July 1, 2001, to cities and towns meeting the criteria of the foregoing provisions of this section are hereby confirmed.

No payments shall be made by the Commissioner to any such city or town unless the portion of the highway for which such payment is made either (a) has (i) an unrestricted right-of-way at least 50 feet wide and (ii) a hard-surface width of at least 30 feet; or (b) has (i) an unrestricted right-of-way at least 80 feet wide, (ii) a hard-surface width of at least 24 feet, and (iii) approved engineering plans for the ultimate construction of an additional hard-surface width of at least 24 feet within the same right-of-way; or (c)

(i) is a cul-de-sac, (ii) has an unrestricted right-of-way at least 40 feet wide, and (iii) has a turnaround that meets applicable standards set by the Department of Transportation; or (d) either (i) has been paved and has constituted part of the primary or secondary system of state highways prior to annexation or incorporation or (ii) has constituted part of the secondary system of state highways prior to annexation or incorporation and is paved to a minimum width of 16 feet subsequent to such annexation or incorporation and with the further exception of streets or portions thereof which have previously been maintained under the provisions of § 33.1-79 or § 33.1-82; or (e) was eligible for and receiving such payments under the laws of the Commonwealth in effect on June 30, 1985; or (f) is a street established prior to July 1, 1950, which has an unrestricted right-of-way width of not less than 30 feet and a hard-surface width of not less than 16 feet; or (g) is a street functionally classified as a local street and constructed on or after January 1, 1996, which at the time of approval by the city or town met the criteria for pavement width and right-of-way of the then-current edition of the subdivision street requirements manual for secondary roads of the Department of Transportation (24 VAC 30-90-10 et seq.); (h) is a street previously eligible to receive street payments that is located in the City of Norfolk and the City of Richmond and is closed to public travel, pursuant to legislation enacted by the governing body of the city in which it is located, for public safety reasons, within the boundaries of a publicly funded housing development owned and operated by the local housing authority; or (i) is a local street, otherwise eligible, containing one or more physical protuberances placed within the right-of-way for the purpose of controlling the speed of traffic.

However, the Commissioner may waive the requirements as to hard-surface pavement or right-of-way width for highways where the width modification is at the request of the local governing body and is to protect the quality of the affected local government's drinking water supply or, for highways constructed on or after July 1, 1994, to accommodate some other special circumstance where such action would not compromise the health, safety, or welfare of the public. The modification is subject to such conditions as the Commissioner may prescribe.

For the purpose of calculating allocations and making payments under this section, the Department shall divide affected highways into two categories, which shall be distinct from but based on functional classifications established by the Federal Highway Administration: (i) principal and minor arterial roads and (ii) collector roads and local streets. Payments to affected localities shall be based on the number of moving-lane-miles of highways or portions thereof available to peak-hour traffic in each category of highways in that locality. For the fiscal year 1986, payment to each city and town shall be an amount equal to $7,787 per moving-lane-mile for principal and minor arterials and $4,572 per moving-lane-mile for collector roads and local streets.

The Department of Transportation shall establish a statewide maintenance index of the unit costs for labor, equipment, and materials used on roads and bridges in the fiscal year 1986, and use changes in that index to calculate and put into effect annual changes in the base per-lane-mile rate payable under this section.

The fund allocated by the Board shall be paid in equal sums in each quarter of the fiscal year, and no payment shall be made without the approval of the Board.

The chief administrative officer of the city or town receiving this fund shall make annual categorical reports of expenditures to the Board, in such form as the Board shall prescribe, accounting for all expenditures, certifying that none of the money received has been expended for other than maintenance, construction or reconstruction of the streets, and reporting on their performance as specified in subdivision B 3 of § 33.1-23.02. Such reports shall be included in the scope of the annual audit of each municipality conducted by independent certified public accountants. (1985, c. 42; 1991, c. 353; 1992, c. 267; 1994, c. 459; 1996, cc. 149, 821; 1997, c. 49; 1998, c. 441; 2000, c. 97; 2002, c. 673; 2004, c. 118; 2007, c. 813.)

Editor's note. — Acts 2006, Sp. Sess. I, c. 3, as amended by Acts 2007, c. 847, effective for the biennium ending June 30, 2008, in Item 446 A, provides: "Notwithstanding §§ 33.1-23.5:1 and 33.1-41.1, Code of Virginia, the Department of Transportation shall adjust for inflation the payments made as part of Financial Assistance to Localities distributions and report such inflation adjustment to the Commonwealth Transportation Board."

Acts 2007, c. 813, cl. 2, provides: "That the provisions of this act shall not affect the powers of any locality with respect to any ordinance, resolution or bylaw validly adopted and not repealed or rescinded prior to July 1, 2007."

The 2007 amendments. — The 2007 amendment by c. 813 substituted "the City of Norfolk and the City of Richmond" for "a city having a population of at least 200,000 but no more than 250,000" in the second paragraph.

§ 33.1-44. Matching highway funds; funding of urban system construction projects, generally. — In any case in which an act of Congress requires that federal-aid highway funds made available for the construction or improvement of federal or state highways be matched, the Commonwealth Transportation Board shall contribute such matching funds. However, in the case of municipalities of 3,500 or more population eligible for an allocation of construction funds for urban highways under § 33.1-23.3 and the Town of Wise, the Town of Lebanon, and the Town of Altavista, the Board may contribute toward the cost of construction of any federal-aid highway or street project ninety-eight percent of the necessary funds, including the federal portion, if the municipality contributes the other two percent, and provided further, that within such municipalities the Board may contribute all the required funds on highways in the interstate system.

In the case of municipalities of 3,500 or more population eligible for an allocation of construction funds for urban highways under § 33.1-23.3 and the Town of Wise, the Town of Lebanon, and the Town of Altavista, the Commonwealth Transportation Board may contribute toward the costs of construction or improvement of any highway or street project for which no federal-aid highway funds are made available ninety-eight percent of the necessary funds if the municipality contributes the other two percent.

For purposes of matching highway funds, such contributions shall continue to apply to such municipality regardless of any subsequent change in population and shall cease to apply only when so specifically provided by an act of the General Assembly. All actions taken prior to July 1, 2001, by municipalities meeting the criteria of the foregoing provisions of this section are hereby confirmed.

In the case of municipalities of less than 3,500 in population that on June 30, 1985, maintained certain streets under § 33.1-80 as then in effect, the Commonwealth Transportation Board shall contribute toward the costs of construction or improvement of any highway or street project 100 percent of the necessary funds. The contribution authorized by this paragraph shall be in addition to any other contribution, and projects established in reference to municipalities of less than 3,500 in population shall not in any way be interpreted to change any other formula or manner for the distribution of funds to such municipalities for construction, improvement or maintenance of highways or streets. The Board may accept from a municipality, for right-of-way purposes, contributions of real estate to be credited, at fair market value, against the matching obligation of such municipality under the provisions of this section.

The term "construction or improvement" means the supervising, inspecting, actual building, and all expenses incidental to the construction or reconstruction of a highway, including locating, surveying, design and mapping, costs of rights-of-way, signs, signals and markings, elimination of hazards of railroad grade crossings and expenses incidental to the relocation of any utility or its facilities owned by a municipality or by a public utility district or public utility authority.

If any municipality requesting such Commonwealth Transportation Board contribution subsequently decides to cancel such construction or improvement after the Board has initiated the project at the request of the municipality, such municipality shall reimburse the Board the net amount of all funds expended by the Board for planning, engineering, right-of-way acquisition, demolition, relocation and construction between the date of initiation by the municipality and the date of cancellation. The Board shall have the authority to waive all or any portions of such reimbursement at its discretion.

For purposes of this section, on any construction or improvement project in the Cities of Chesapeake, Hampton, Newport News, or Richmond and funded in accordance with subdivision 2 of subsection B of § 33.1-23.1, the additional cost for placing aboveground utilities below ground may be paid from funds allocated for that project. The maximum cost due to this action shall not exceed five million dollars. Nothing contained herein shall relieve utility owners of their responsibilities and costs associated with the relocation of their facilities when required to accommodate a construction or improvement project. (Code 1950, § 33-35.5; 1958, c. 584; 1964, c. 256; 1970, cc. 322, 403; 1977, c. 578; 1979, c. 84; 1980, c. 128; 1981, c. 370; 1987, c. 545; 1989, c. 303; 1991, c. 353; 2000, c. 762; 2002, c. 673; 2007, c. 813.)

Editor's note. — Acts 2007, c. 813, cl. 2, provides: "That the provisions of this act shall not affect the powers of any locality with respect to any ordinance, resolution or bylaw validly adopted and not repealed or rescinded prior to July 1, 2007."

The 2007 amendments. — The 2007 amendment by c. 813 substituted "the Cities of Chesapeake, Hampton, Newport News, or Richmond" for "any city having either a population of at least 130,000 but less than 150,000 or a population of at least 170,000 but less than 200,000" in the last paragraph.

§ 33.1-46.2. (For expiration date — see Editor's note) Designation of high-occupancy vehicle lanes; use of such lanes; penalties. — A. In order to facilitate the rapid and orderly movement of traffic to and from urban areas during peak traffic periods, the Commonwealth Transportation Board may designate one or more lanes of any highway in the interstate, primary, or secondary highway systems as high-occupancy vehicle lanes, hereinafter referred to in this section as HOV lanes. When lanes have been so designated and have been appropriately marked with such signs or other markers as the Board may prescribe, they shall be reserved during periods designated by the Board for the exclusive use of buses and high-occupancy vehicles. Any local governing body may also, with respect to highways under its exclusive jurisdiction, designate HOV lanes and impose and enforce restrictions on the use of such HOV lanes. Any highway for which the local jurisdiction receives highway maintenance funds pursuant to § 33.1-41.1 shall be deemed to be within the exclusive jurisdiction of the local governing body for the purposes of this section. HOV lanes shall be reserved for high-occupancy vehicles of a specified number of occupants as determined by the Board or, for HOV lanes designated by a local governing body, by that local governing body. Notwithstanding the foregoing provisions of this section, no designation of any lane or lanes of any highway as HOV lanes shall apply to the use of any such lanes by:

1. Emergency vehicles such as fire-fighting vehicles, ambulances, and rescue squad vehicles,

2. Law-enforcement vehicles,

3. Motorcycles,

4. a. Transit and commuter buses designed to transport 16 or more passengers, including the driver,

b. Commuter buses and motor coaches operating under irregular route passenger certificates issued under § 46.2-2010 and any vehicle operating under a certificate of Public Convenience and Necessity or as a common carrier of passengers under § 46.2-2075 or 46.2-2080,

5. Vehicles of public utility companies operating in response to an emergency call,

6. Until July 1, 2008, vehicles bearing clean special fuel vehicle license plates issued pursuant to § 46.2-749.3, or

7. Taxicabs having two or more occupants, including the driver.

In the Hampton Roads Planning District, HOV restrictions may be temporarily lifted and HOV lanes opened to use by all vehicles when restricting use of HOV lanes becomes impossible or undesirable and the temporary lifting of HOV limitations is indicated by signs along or above the affected portion of highway.

The Commissioner of VDOT shall implement a program of the HOV facilities in the Hampton Roads Planning District beginning not later than May 1, 2000. This program shall include the temporary lifting of HOV restrictions and the opening of HOV lanes to all traffic when an incident resulting from nonrecurring causes within the general lanes occurs such that a lane of traffic is blocked or is expected to be blocked for 10 minutes or longer. The HOV restrictions for the facility will be reinstated when the general lane is no longer blocked and is available for use.

The Commissioner shall maintain necessary records to evaluate the effects of such openings on the operation of the general lanes and the HOV lanes. He shall report on the effects of this program. This program will terminate if the Federal Highway Administration requires repayment of any federal highway construction funds because of the program's impact on the HOV facilities in Hampton Roads.

B. In designating any lane or lanes of any highway as HOV lanes, the Board, or local governing body as the case may be, shall specify the hour or hours of each day of the week during which the lanes shall be so reserved, and the hour or hours shall be plainly posted at whatever intervals along the lanes the Board or local governing body deems appropriate. Any person driving a motor vehicle in a designated HOV lane in violation of this section shall be guilty of a traffic infraction which shall not be a moving violation and on conviction shall be fined $100. However, violations committed within the boundaries of Planning District Eight shall be punishable as follows:

For a first offense, by a fine of $125;

For a second offense within a period of five years from a first offense, by a fine of $250;

For a third offense within a period of five years from a first offense, by a fine of $500; and

For a fourth or subsequent offense within a period of five years from a first offense, by a fine of $1,000.

Upon a conviction under this section, the court shall furnish to the Commissioner of the Department of Motor Vehicles in accordance with § 46.2-383 an abstract of the record of such conviction which shall become a part of the person's driving record. Notwithstanding the provisions of § 46.2-492, no driver demerit points shall be assessed for any violation of this section; except that persons convicted of second, third, fourth, or subsequent violations within five years of a first offense committed in Planning District Eight shall be assessed three demerit points for each such violation.

C. In the prosecution of an offense, committed in the presence of a law-enforcement officer, of failure to obey a road sign restricting a highway, or portion thereof, to the use of high-occupancy vehicles, proof that the vehicle described in the HOV violation summons was operated in violation of this section, together with proof that the defendant was at the time of such violation the registered owner of the vehicle, shall constitute in evidence a rebuttable presumption that such registered owner of the vehicle was the person who committed the violation. Such presumption shall be rebutted if the registered owner of the vehicle testifies in open court under oath that he was not the operator of the vehicle at the time of the violation. A summons for a violation of this section may be executed in accordance with § 19.2-76.2. Such rebuttable presumption shall not arise when the registered owner of the vehicle is a rental or leasing company.

D. Notwithstanding the provisions of § 19.2-76, whenever a summons for a violation of this section is served in any county, city, or town, it may be executed by mailing by first-class mail a copy thereof to the address of the owner of the vehicle as shown on the records of the Department of Motor Vehicles. If the summoned person fails to appear on the date of return set out in the summons mailed pursuant to this section, the summons shall be executed in the manner set out in § 19.2-76.3.

No proceedings for contempt or arrest of a person summoned by mailing shall be instituted for his failure to appear on the return date of the summons.

E. Notwithstanding § 33.1-252, high-occupancy vehicles having three or more occupants (HOV-3) may be permitted to use the Omer L. Hirst-Adelard L. Brault Expressway (Dulles Toll Road) without paying a toll.

F. Notwithstanding the contrary provisions of this section, the following conditions shall be met before the HOV-2 designation of Interstate Route 66 outside the Capital Beltway can be changed to HOV-3 or any more restrictive designation:

1. The Department shall publish a notice of its intent to change the existing designation and also immediately provide similar notice of its intent to all

members of the General Assembly representing districts that touch or are directly impacted by traffic on Interstate Route 66.

2. The Department shall hold public hearings in the corridor to receive comments from the public.

3. The Department shall make a finding of the need for a change in such designation, based on public hearings and its internal data and present this finding to the Commonwealth Transportation Board for approval.

4. The Commonwealth Transportation Board shall make written findings and a decision based upon the following criteria:

a. Is changing the HOV-2 designation to HOV-3 in the public interest?

b. Is there quantitative and qualitative evidence that supports the argument that HOV-3 will facilitate the flow of traffic on Interstate Route 66?

c. Is changing the HOV-2 designation beneficial to comply with the federal Clean Air Act Amendments of 1990?

G. [Repealed.] (1973, c. 197; 1983, c. 339; 1988, c. 637; 1989, cc. 573, 744; 1993, cc. 82, 587; 1994, cc. 212, 426, 439; 1995, c. 55; 1996, cc. 34, 187, 191, 695, 921, 1037; 1997, c. 504; 1998, c. 321; 1999, cc. 914, 960; 2000, c. 322; 2002, cc. 89, 757; 2003, c. 324; 2004, c. 704; 2006, cc. 600, 873, 908; 2007, c. 317.)

Section set out twice. — The section above is effective until provisions of Acts 2003, c. 324, expire upon receipt by the Governor of a written communication from the Administrator of the Federal Highway Administration to the effect that the provisions of this act contravene federal law. For the version of this section effective at that time, see the following section also numbered 33.1-46.2.

The 2007 amendments. — The 2007 amendment by c. 317 substituted "2008" for "2007" in subdivision A 6.

§ 33.1-46.2. (For effective date — see Editor's note) Designation of high-occupancy vehicle lanes; use of such lanes; penalties. — A.

In order to facilitate the rapid and orderly movement of traffic to and from urban areas during peak traffic periods, the Commonwealth Transportation Board may designate one or more lanes of any highway in the interstate, primary, or secondary highway systems as high-occupancy vehicle lanes, hereinafter referred to in this section as HOV lanes. When lanes have been so designated and have been appropriately marked with such signs or other markers as the Board may prescribe, they shall be reserved during periods designated by the Board for the exclusive use of buses and high-occupancy vehicles. Any local governing body may also, with respect to highways under its exclusive jurisdiction, designate HOV lanes and impose and enforce restrictions on the use of such HOV lanes. Any highway for which the local jurisdiction receives highway maintenance funds pursuant to § 33.1-41.1 shall be deemed to be within the exclusive jurisdiction of the local governing body for the purposes of this section. HOV lanes shall be reserved for high-occupancy vehicles of a specified number of occupants as determined by the Board or, for HOV lanes designated by a local governing body, by that local governing body. Notwithstanding the foregoing provisions of this section, no designation of any lane or lanes of any highway as HOV lanes shall apply to the use of any such lanes by:

1. Emergency vehicles such as fire-fighting vehicles, ambulances, and rescue squad vehicles,

2. Law-enforcement vehicles,

3. Motorcycles,

4. a. Transit and commuter buses designed to transport 16 or more passengers, including the driver,

b. Commuter buses and motor coaches operating under irregular route passenger certificates issued under § 46.2-2010 and any vehicle operating under a certificate of Public Convenience and Necessity or as a common carrier of passengers under § 46.2-2075 or 46.2-2080,

5. Vehicles of public utility companies operating in response to an emergency call,

6. Until July 1, 2004, vehicles bearing clean special fuel vehicle license plates issued pursuant to § 46.2-749.3, or

7. Taxicabs having two or more occupants, including the driver.

In the Hampton Roads Planning District, HOV restrictions may be temporarily lifted and HOV lanes opened to use by all vehicles when restricting use of HOV lanes becomes impossible or undesirable and the temporary lifting of HOV limitations is indicated by signs along or above the affected portion of highway.

The Commissioner of VDOT shall implement a program of the HOV facilities in the Hampton Roads Planning District beginning not later than May 1, 2000. This program shall include the temporary lifting of HOV restrictions and the opening of HOV lanes to all traffic when an incident resulting from nonrecurring causes within the general lanes occurs such that a lane of traffic is blocked or is expected to be blocked for 10 minutes or longer. The HOV restrictions for the facility will be reinstated when the general lane is no longer blocked and is available for use.

The Commissioner shall maintain necessary records to evaluate the effects of such openings on the operation of the general lanes and the HOV lanes. He shall report on the effects of this program. This program will terminate if the Federal Highway Administration requires repayment of any federal highway construction funds because of the program's impact on the HOV facilities in Hampton Roads.

B. In designating any lane or lanes of any highway as HOV lanes, the Board, or local governing body as the case may be, shall specify the hour or hours of each day of the week during which the lanes shall be so reserved, and the hour or hours shall be plainly posted at whatever intervals along the lanes the Board or local governing body deems appropriate. Any person driving a motor vehicle in a designated HOV lane in violation of this section shall be guilty of a traffic infraction which shall not be a moving violation and on conviction shall be fined $100. However, violations committed within the boundaries of Planning District Eight shall be punishable as follows:

For a first offense, by a fine of $125;

For a second offense within a period of five years from a first offense, by a fine of $250;

For a third offense within a period of five years from a first offense, by a fine of $500; and

For a fourth or subsequent offense within a period of five years from a first offense, by a fine of $1,000.

Upon a conviction under this section, the court shall furnish to the Commissioner of the Department of Motor Vehicles in accordance with § 46.2-383 an abstract of the record of such conviction which shall become a part of the person's driving record. Notwithstanding the provisions of § 46.2-492, no driver demerit points shall be assessed for any violation of this section; except that persons convicted of second, third, fourth, or subsequent violations within five years of a first offense committed in Planning District Eight shall be assessed three demerit points for each such violation.

C. In the prosecution of an offense, committed in the presence of a law-enforcement officer, of failure to obey a road sign restricting a highway, or portion thereof, to the use of high-occupancy vehicles, proof that the vehicle described in the HOV violation summons was operated in violation of this section, together with proof that the defendant was at the time of such violation the registered owner of the vehicle, shall constitute in evidence a rebuttable presumption that such registered owner of the vehicle was the person who committed the violation. Such presumption shall be rebutted if the registered owner of the vehicle testifies in open court under oath that he was not the operator of the vehicle at the time of the violation. A summons for a violation of this section may be executed in accordance with § 19.2-76.2. Such rebuttable presumption shall not arise when the registered owner of the vehicle is a rental or leasing company.

D. Notwithstanding the provisions of § 19.2-76, whenever a summons for a violation of this section is served in any county, city, or town, it may be executed by mailing by first-class mail a copy thereof to the address of the owner of the vehicle as shown on the records of the Department of Motor Vehicles. If the summoned person fails to appear on the date of return set out in the summons mailed pursuant to this section, the summons shall be executed in the manner set out in § 19.2-76.3.

No proceedings for contempt or arrest of a person summoned by mailing shall be instituted for his failure to appear on the return date of the summons.

E. Notwithstanding § 33.1-252, high-occupancy vehicles having three or more occupants (HOV-3) may be permitted to use the Omer L. Hirst-Adelard

L. Brault Expressway (Dulles Toll Road) without paying a toll.

F. Notwithstanding the contrary provisions of this section, the following conditions shall be met before the HOV-2 designation of Interstate Route 66 outside the Capital Beltway can be changed to HOV-3 or any more restrictive designation:

1. The Department shall publish a notice of its intent to change the existing designation and also immediately provide similar notice of its intent to all members of the General Assembly representing districts that touch or are directly impacted by traffic on Interstate Route 66.

2. The Department shall hold public hearings in the corridor to receive comments from the public.

3. The Department shall make a finding of the need for a change in such designation, based on public hearings and its internal data and present this finding to the Commonwealth Transportation Board for approval.

4. The Commonwealth Transportation Board shall make written findings and a decision based upon the following criteria:

a. Is changing the HOV-2 designation to HOV-3 in the public interest?

b. Is there quantitative and qualitative evidence that supports the argument that HOV-3 will facilitate the flow of traffic on Interstate Route 66?

c. Is changing the HOV-2 designation beneficial to comply with the federal Clean Air Act Amendments of 1990?

G. [Repealed.] (1973, c. 197; 1983, c. 339; 1988, c. 637; 1989, cc. 573, 744; 1993, cc. 82, 587; 1994, cc. 212, 426, 439; 1995, c. 55; 1996, cc. 34, 187, 191, 695, 921, 1037; 1997, c. 504; 1998, c. 321; 1999, cc. 914, 960; 2000, c. 322; 2002, cc. 89, 757; 2004, c. 704; 2006, cc. 600, 873, 908; 2007, c. 317.)

Section set out twice. — The section above is effective upon receipt by the Governor of a written communication from the Administrator of the Federal Highway Administration to the effect that the provisions of Acts 2003, c. 324, contravene federal law. For this section as in effect until that time, see the preceding section also numbered 33.1-46.2.

The 2007 amendments. — The 2007 amendment by c. 317 deleted the section symbol preceding "46.2-2080" at the end of subdivision A 4 b.

ARTICLE 6.

Secondary System of State Highways.

§ 33.1-70.3. Requirements for taking new streets into state secondary highway system. — A. The local governing body of any county that has not withdrawn from the state secondary highway system or any town within which the Virginia Department of Transportation maintains the streets, may, by resolution, request the Commonwealth Transportation Board to take any new street into the secondary system of state highways for maintenance if such street has been developed and constructed in accordance with the Board's secondary street acceptance requirements. Only those streets constructed in compliance with the secondary street acceptance requirements shall be taken into the state secondary highway system for maintenance. The Board shall promulgate regulations establishing such secondary street acceptance requirements. The secondary street acceptance requirements established pursuant to this section shall include such provisions as the Board deems necessary or appropriate to achieve the safe and efficient operation of the Commonwealth's transportation network.

B. In addition to such other provisions deemed necessary or appropriate by the Board, the regulations shall include, but not be limited to (i) requirements to ensure the connectivity of road and pedestrian networks with the existing and future transportation network; (ii) provisions to minimize stormwater runoff and impervious surface area, and (iii) provisions for performance bonding of new secondary streets and associated cost recovery fees.

C. No initial regulation establishing secondary street acceptance requirements pursuant to this section shall apply to subdivision plats and subdivision construction plans that have been submitted and accepted for review by the Virginia Department of Transportation on or before the effective date of such initial regulations. No locality shall be obligated to approve any subdivision plat or subdivision construction plans that are inconsistent with these regulations. (2007, c. 382.)

Editor's note. — Acts 2007, c. 382, cl. 2, provides: "The provisions of the Administrative Process Act (§ 2.2-4000 et seq.) shall not apply to initial regulations promulgated by the Board pursuant to this section, but such exemption shall not apply to subsequent regulations or amendments thereto promulgated by the Board."

Acts 2007, c. 382, cl. 3, provides: "That the Board shall solicit and consider public comment in the development of regulations required by this act."

Acts 2007, c. 382, cl. 4, provides: "Until such time as initial regulations establishing secondary street acceptance requirements are adopted pursuant to this section, the subdivision street requirements and the process and criteria for taking such streets into the state secondary system in effect on January 1, 2007, shall continue to apply."

§ 33.1-84.1. Resumption of responsibility for secondary highways by counties. — Notwithstanding any provisions of § 11 of Chapter 415 of the Acts of Assembly of 1932, the Commonwealth Transportation Commissioner, following receipt of a resolution adopted by the Board of Supervisors of a county requesting such action, may enter into an agreement with any county that desires to resume responsibility over all or any portion of the state secondary system of highways within such county's boundaries for the purposes of planning, constructing, maintaining, and operating such highways. Such agreement shall specify the equipment, facilities, personnel, and funding that will be provided to the county in order to implement such agreement's provisions. (2001, cc. 257, 273, 277.)

Editor's note. — At the direction of the Virginia Code Commission, the section has been set out above to correct the text. In the first sentence, "over all or any portion" has been substituted for "over any portion" and, in the last sentence, "provided to the county in order" has been substituted for "provided in order."

ARTICLE 7.

Eminent Domain and Damages.

§ 33.1-90. Acquisition of real property which may be needed for transportation projects; sale of certain real property.

CASE NOTES

Grantor of property acquires a possibility of reverter. — Under a former version of § 33.1-90, the Virginia General Assembly intended to grant to a property owner a contingent right to reconveyance of property acquired by the Commonwealth of Virginia in anticipation of its need for a public highway project if the property so acquired was not ultimately used for that purpose; accordingly, a corporation that made such a conveyance to the Commonwealth in 1973 was granted an interest in that property in the form of a possibility of reverter. Commonwealth Transp. Comm'r v. Windsor Indus., 272 Va. 64, 630 S.E.2d 514, 2006 Va. LEXIS 69 (2006).

Other statutes of limitation are superseded. — In determining whether a successor corporation's claim for reconveyance of land conveyed to the Commonwealth of Virginia by a predecessor was timely, a trial court improperly relied upon §§ 8.01-248 and 8.01-246(4), and § 8.01-255.1, applicable to actions for re-entry upon land for breach of conditions subsequent, was also inapplicable; these provisions were superseded by the more specific time limitations of § 33.1-90, which has a comprehensive and broad scope that in effect contains its own statute of limitations. Commonwealth Transp. Comm'r v. Windsor Indus., 272 Va. 64, 630 S.E.2d 514, 2006 Va. LEXIS 69 (2006).

Reconveyance of property to grantor's successor was required. — Virginia Commissioner of Transportation was properly ordered to reconvey to a successor corporation at its original purchase price property that was acquired by the Commonwealth of Virginia by advance acquisition from the successor's predecessor in 1973 but that was no longer needed for a transportation purpose; amendments made in § 33.1-90 after the original transfer applied to the predecessor's possibility of reverter, the right to demand reconveyance ripened when the Commonwealth offered the property for public sale in 2004, the successor's president was the proper entity to demand reconveyance, and his demand was timely under § 33.1-90. Commonwealth Transp. Comm'r v. Windsor Indus., 272 Va. 64, 630 S.E.2d 514, 2006 Va. LEXIS 69 (2006).

Statutory amendments apply to grantor's possibility of reverter. — Until a possibility of reverter retained by a corporation that conveyed property to the Commonwealth of Virginia in 1973 under a former version of this section vested into an enforceable right, the contingencies upon which it depended and the procedures for exercising the right accrued remained subject to modification by future amendment, including extending the period of time before the right could accrue and establishing periods of limitation on enforcing the right, so long as such amendments did not fully extinguish the corporation's possibility of reverter; amendments made to former § 33.1-90 in 1983 and 1997, before the corporation's possibility of reverter became an enforceable right, therefore, amended the corporation's possibility of reverter. Commonwealth Transp. Comm'r v. Windsor Indus., 272 Va. 64, 630 S.E.2d 514, 2006 Va. LEXIS 69 (2006).

Procedures for demanding reconveyance remain subject to amendment. — When there has been a breach of a condition subsequent on which a possibility of reverter created by an advance acquisition depends, the fee vested in the Commonwealth of Virginia by the original transfer does not automatically revest in the grantor, who must make a written demand under § 33.1-90 to exercise the right to reconveyance; therefore, until 1999 or later when a successor corporation first demanded reconveyance of such property transferred by a predecessor under the version of 33.1-90 in effect in 1973, the Commonwealth remained vested with title to the property, and the contingencies and procedures for making the demand for reconveyance remained subject to change by amendment of § 33.1-90. Commonwealth Transp. Comm'r v. Windsor Indus., 272 Va. 64, 630 S.E.2d 514, 2006 Va. LEXIS 69 (2006).

Notice provision not dependent on prior timely demand. — Requirement in § 33.1-90 that the Virginia Commissioner of Transportation must give notice of an intended sale of property acquired by advance acquisition that is no longer needed for a transportation project and must make a bona fide effort to locate the transferor's heirs and assigns, and a corresponding requirement that a demand for reconveyance must be made within 30 days thereafter are stated in the disjunctive and, thus, are not dependent upon a prior timely demand having been made by the former owner within 90 days from the expiration of the 20-year designated timeframe. Commonwealth Transp. Comm'r v. Windsor Indus., 272 Va. 64, 630 S.E.2d 514, 2006 Va. LEXIS 69 (2006).

Complaint for declaratory judgment was timely demand for reconveyance. — 1999 inquiry by a successor corporation's president about reconveyance of property conveyed to the Commonwealth of Virginia by a predecessor corporation under a former version of this section was not timely under the 90-day requirement as it was then in effect, and the Virginia Transportation Commissioner was statutorily entitled to refuse it, but when the Commissioner offered the property for public sale in 2004, the alternative procedure then in effect for exercising the right to demand reconveyance became operative; publication of the notice of intent to sell triggered a 30-day time period in which the successor could demand reconveyance, and a declaratory judgment action filed by the successor within that time period constituted substantial compliance with the requirement for a written demand. Commonwealth Transp. Comm'r v. Windsor Indus., 272 Va. 64, 630 S.E.2d 514, 2006 Va. LEXIS 69 (2006).

Successor corporation properly demanded reconveyance of property conveyed by predecessor. — Possibility of reverter acquired by a predecessor corporation when it conveyed property to the Commonwealth of Virginia for road use in 1973 was a corporate asset when the predecessor was later dissolved; as trustee of the assets of the dissolved predecessor, its president, who became the president of a successor corporation, was the proper party to make demand on the Virginia Transportation Commissioner for reconveyance of the property, and the successor's subsequent declaratory judgment action was properly filed in the successor's name pursuant to § 13.1-745. Commonwealth Transp. Comm'r v. Windsor Indus., 272 Va. 64, 630 S.E.2d 514, 2006 Va. LEXIS 69 (2006).

§ 33.1-94. Right to enter on land to ascertain its suitability for highway and other transportation purposes; damage resulting from such entry.

— A. The Commonwealth Transportation Commissioner, through his duly authorized officers, agents, or servants, may enter upon any land in the Commonwealth for the purposes of making examination and survey thereof, including but not limited to photographing, testing, including but not limited to soil borings or testing for contamination, making appraisals, and taking such actions as may be necessary or desirable to determine its suitability for highway and other transportation purposes, or for any other purpose incidental thereto. Such officers, agents, or servants shall exercise care to protect any improvements, growing crops, or timber in making such examination or survey.

B. Notice shall be sent to the owner by certified mail, at the address recorded in the tax records, return receipt requested, or delivered by guaranteed overnight courier or otherwise delivered to the owner in person with proof of delivery not less than 15 days prior to the first date of the proposed entry. Notice of intent to enter shall be deemed made on the earlier of the date of mailing, if mailed, or on the date delivered.

C. The notice shall include the anticipated date or dates such entry is proposed to be made and the purpose of such entry. Any entry authorized by this section shall be for the purposes of making examination and survey thereof, including but not limited to photographing, testing, including but not limited to soil borings or testing for contamination, making appraisals, and taking such other actions as may be necessary or desirable to determine the suitability of such property for highway and transportation purposes and shall not be deemed a trespass.

D. The Commonwealth Transportation Commissioner, through his duly authorized officers, agents, or servants, shall make reimbursement for any actual damages to real or personal property resulting from entry upon the property. In any action filed under this section, the court may award the owner his reasonable attorney fees, court costs, and fees for no more than three expert witnesses testifying at trial if: (i) the court finds that the Commissioner maliciously, willfully, or recklessly damaged the owner's property and (ii) the court awards the owner actual damages in an amount 30 percent or more greater than the Commissioner's final written offer made no later than 30 days after the filing of an answer in circuit court or the return date in general district court. A proceeding under this subsection shall not preclude the owner from pursuing any additional remedies available to the landowner. (Code 1950, § 33-57.2; 1960, c. 491; 1970, c. 322; 2007, c. 755.)

The 2007 amendments. — The 2007 amendment by c. 755 rewrote this section.

§ 33.1-125. Reformation, alteration, revision, amendment or invalidation of certificate.

CIRCUIT COURT OPINIONS

Right of condemnor to amend. — Motion by the Commonwealth Transportation Commissioner to amend a certificate of condemnation to properly identify the parcel sought to be condemned was granted pursuant to 33.1-125, as the Commissioner had made a bona fide offer to purchase the property under § 25.1-204, because clerical errors in the offer did not prejudice defendant, as defendants knew which parcel the Commissioner was interested in, and defendants were familiar with condemnation proceedings. Commonwealth Transp. Comm'r v. Holly Tree Props., Inc., 71 Va. Cir. 353, 2006 Va. Cir. LEXIS 136 (Fairfax County 2006).

ARTICLE 15.

Miscellaneous Provisions.

§ 33.1-198. (Effective July 1, 2008) Connections over shoulders of highways for intersecting commercial establishment entrances.

— The Commonwealth Transportation Commissioner

shall permit, at places where commercial establishment entrances are desired to intersect improved highways, suitable connections from such points of intersection over and across the shoulders and unimproved parts of such highways to the paved or otherwise improved parts thereof that comply with the Commonwealth Transportation Commissioner's access management standards for the location, spacing, and design of entrances, taking into account the operating characteristics and federal functional classification of the highway, so as to provide for the users of such entrances safe and convenient means of ingress and egress with motor vehicles to and from the paved or otherwise improved parts of such highways while minimizing the impact of such ingress and egress on the operation of such highways, provided, however, that any person desiring such an entrance shall:

1. Be required first to obtain a permit therefor from the Commonwealth Transportation Commissioner;

2. Provide the entrance at his expense;

3. If required by the Commonwealth Transportation Commissioner, provide for the joint use of the desired entrance with adjacent property owners or provide evidence of such efforts; and

4. Construct the entrance or have the entrance constructed, including such safety structures as are required by the Commonwealth Transportation Commissioner, pursuant to the Department of Transportation's design standards and "Land Use Permit Manual," the latter of which is filed as part of the Virginia Administrative Code.

All commercial entrances whether or not constructed under this section shall be maintained by the owner of the premises at all times in a manner satisfactory to the Commonwealth Transportation Commissioner.

Any person violating the provisions of this section shall be guilty of a misdemeanor, and, upon conviction, shall be fined not less than $5 nor more than $100 for each offense. Following a conviction and 15 days for correction, each day during which the violation continues shall constitute a separate and distinct offense and be punishable as such. Such person shall be civilly liable to the Commonwealth for actual damage sustained by the Commonwealth by reason of his wrongful act. (Code 1950, § 33-116.1; 1956, c. 91; 1966, c. 378; 1970, c. 322; 2005, c. 645; 2007, cc. 863, 928.)

The section above is effective July 1, 2008. For this section as in effect until July 1, 2008, see the section as set out in the 2006 Edition.

Editor's note. — Acts 2007, cc. 863 and 928, in cl. 2 provide: "That the Commissioner shall solicit and consider public comment in the development of standards required by this act and publish such standards no later than December 31, 2007. Such standards shall become effective on July 1, 2008."

Acts 2007, cc. 863 and 928, in cl. 3 provide: "That the provisions of the first enactment of this act shall become effective July 1, 2008."

Acts 2007, cc. 863 and 928, cl. 4, are nearly identical, and provide:

"That, until July 1, 2008, the Commissioner shall not be subject to the requirements of the Administrative Process Act (§ 2.2-4000 et seq.) as may be necessary to carry out the provisions of this act."

The 2007 amendments. — Acts 2007, cc. 863 and 928, effective July 1, 2008, are identical, and redesignated the former provisions as the introductory paragraph and subdivisions 1, 2 and 4; in the introductory paragraph, inserted "that comply with the ... classification of the highway" and "while minimizing the impact of such ingress and egress on the operation of such highways"; inserted subdivision 3; in subdivision 4, substituted the language beginning "the Department of Transportation's" for "'Minimum Standards of Entrances to State Highways' on file in the central office of the Department of Transportation and in the district and residency offices"; and made minor stylistic changes.

CASE NOTES

Commissioners were properly permitted to hear and consider the evidence that curbing around the southern parcel left no openings from state route to the residue of that parcel, and, in the opinion of the landowners' expert, this restriction of access "is going to bring on major trouble". State Highway & Transp. Comm'r v. Dennison, 231 Va. 239, 343 S.E.2d 324 (1986).

§ 33.1-198.1. (Effective July 1, 2008) Comprehensive highway access management standards. — A. Comprehensive highway access management standards are defined as a coordinated set of state standards and guidelines that allow the Commonwealth and its localities to manage access to the systems of state highways according to their federal functional classification or operational characteristics through the control of and improvements to the location, number, spacing, and design of entrances, median openings, turn lanes, street intersections, traffic signals, and interchanges.

B. The General Assembly declares it to be in the public interest that comprehensive highway access management standards be developed and implemented to enhance the operation and safety of the systems of state highways in order to protect the public health, safety, and general welfare while ensuring that private property is entitled to reasonable access to the systems of state highways. The goals of the comprehensive highway access management standards are:

1. To reduce traffic congestion and impacts to the level of service of highways, leading to reduced fuel consumption and air pollution;

2. To enhance public safety by decreasing traffic crash rates;

3. To support economic development in the Commonwealth by promoting the efficient movement of people and goods;

4. To reduce the need for new highways and road widening by improving the performance of the existing systems of state highways; and

5. To preserve public investment in new highways by maximizing their performance.

C. The Commonwealth Transportation Commissioner shall develop and implement comprehensive highway access management standards for managing access to and preserving and improving the efficient operation of the state systems of highways. The comprehensive highway access management standards shall include but not be limited to standards and guidelines for the location, number, spacing, and design of entrances, median openings, turn lanes, street intersections, traffic signals, and interchanges.

Nothing in such standards shall preempt the authority of a local government to regulate the type or density of land uses abutting the state system of highways. (2007, cc. 863, 928.)

Editor's note. — Acts 2007, cc. 863 and 928, in cl. 2 provide: "That the Commissioner shall solicit and consider public comment in the development of standards required by this act and publish such standards no later than December 31, 2007. Such standards shall become effective on July 1, 2008."

Acts 2007, cc. 863 and 928, in cl. 3 provide: "That the provisions of the first enactment of this act shall become effective July 1, 2008."

Acts 2007, cc. 863 and 928, cl. 4, are nearly identical, and provide: "That, until July 1, 2008, the Commissioner shall not be subject to the requirements of the Administrative Process Act (§ 2.2-4000 et seq.) as may be necessary to carry out the provisions of this act."

§ 33.1-199. (Effective July 1, 2008) Replacing entrances destroyed by Commissioner. — The Commonwealth Transportation Commissioner shall review the existing access to any parcel of land having an entrance destroyed in the repair or construction of the systems of state highways and shall provide access to the systems of state highways in a manner that will serve the parcel of land and ensure efficient and safe highway operation. (Code 1950, § 33-117; 1970, c. 322; 2007, cc. 863, 928.)

The section above is effective July 1, 2008. For this section as in effect until July 1, 2008, see the section as set out in the 2006 Edition.

Editor's note. — Acts 2007, cc. 863 and 928, in cl. 2 provide: "That the Commissioner shall solicit and consider public comment in the development of standards required by this act and publish such standards no later than December 31, 2007. Such standards shall become effective on July 1, 2008."

Acts 2007, cc. 863 and 928, in cl. 3 provide: "That the provisions of the first enactment of this act shall become effective July 1, 2008."

Acts 2007, cc. 863 and 928, cl. 4, are nearly identical, and provide: "That, until July 1, 2008, the Commissioner shall not be subject to the requirements of the Administrative Process Act (§ 2.2-4000 et seq.) as may be necessary to carry out the provisions of this act."

The 2007 amendments. — The 2007 amendments by cc. 863 and 928, effective July 1, 2008, are identical, and rewrote the section which read: "The Commonwealth Transportation Commissioner shall replace any entrance destroyed by him in the repair or construction of his highways and replace any such entrance and leave any such entrance in the same condition as it was prior to such repair or improvement."

CASE NOTES

This section contemplated the extinguishment of easements of abutting landowners upon the conversion of a conventional highway into a limited access highway. State Hwy. & Transp. Comm'r v. Linsly, 223 Va. 437, 290 S.E.2d 834 (1982).

Reduction or limitation of direct access to an abutting landowner's property generally is not compensable. State Hwy. & Transp. Comm'r v. Linsly, 223 Va. 437, 290 S.E.2d 834 (1982).

Test for determination of damages in converting highway. — In condemnation proceedings for acquisition of land and easements in the conversion of a conventional highway into a limited access highway, the same test for the determination of damages must be applied as in other cases where the commissioner exercises the right of eminent domain. The damage figure is the difference between the value of the residue immediately before and immediately after the taking. State Hwy. & Transp. Comm'r v. Linsly, 223 Va. 437, 290 S.E.2d 834 (1982).

Difference in fair market value. — The damage, if any, to the residue, over and above any enhancement, is the difference in fair market value immediately before and immediately after the taking. State Hwy. & Transp. Comm'r v. Linsly, 223 Va. 437, 290 S.E.2d 834 (1982).

It was proper to permit the commissioners, in ascertaining damages, to consider the effect on market value of the substitution of indirect access for the easements that formerly afforded direct access to highway. State Hwy. & Transp. Comm'r v. Linsly, 223 Va. 437, 290 S.E.2d 834 (1982).

Commissioners were properly permitted to hear and consider the evidence that curbing around the southern parcel left no openings from state route to the residue of that parcel, and, in the opinion of the landowners' expert, this restriction of access "is going to bring on major trouble". State Highway & Transp. Comm'r v. Dennison, 231 Va. 239, 343 S.E.2d 324 (1986).

Speculative relocation expenses not compensable. — Evidence, to the effect that it would be required to relocate its entrance because the officials of the city would no longer consider its "sight distance" adequate, was based upon speculation and should not have been admitted. Landowner's witnesses admitted that other entrances had been approved by the city which had lesser "sight distances" than that shown on the 1976 plat. They also admitted that the Commissioner's project, which straightened the curve, had the effect of increasing, rather than decreasing, the "sight distance". No evidence was offered to remove the issue from the realm of speculation. Damages to the residue resulting from a partial taking are those which flow directly from the taking, not those which are merely speculative. State Highway and Transp. Comm'r of Va. v. Lanier Farm, Inc., 233 Va. 506, 357 S.E.2d 531 (1987).

§ 33.1-221.1:8. Transportation Partnership Opportunity Fund.

Editor's note. — Acts 2007, c. 847, effective for the biennium ending June 30, 2008, in Item 449.10 1, provides: "$305,000,000 shall be transferred to the Transportation Partnership Opportunity Fund to advance acquisition and construction of the following projects, pursuant to § 33.1-12 or § 56-556 et seq, Code of Virginia: Capital Beltway HOT lanes, Hillsville Bypass, I-64/I-264 interchange, Rt. 50 widening in Loudoun and Fairfax Counties, an updated Environmental Impact Statement for Route 37 Eastern Bypass in Frederick County, and right-of-way owned by the Norfolk Southern Corporation and located between Newtown Road and the Oceanfront. Notwithstanding the limitations contained in § 33.1-221.1:8 E, Code of Virginia, the Governor shall provide sufficient grants and loans from this amount to advance acquisition and construction of the projects listed above."

§ 33.1-223.2:12. Tolls may vary to encourage travel during off-peak hours. — A. In order to provide an incentive for motorists to travel at off-peak hours, and in accordance with federal requirements, wherever a toll is imposed and collected by the Department or such other entity as may be responsible for imposing or collecting such toll, the amount of such toll may vary according to the time of day, day of the week, traffic volume, vehicle speed, vehicle type, similar variables, or combinations thereof. The amount of such toll and the time of day when such toll shall change shall be as fixed and revised by the Commonwealth Transportation Board or such other entity as may be responsible for fixing or revising the amount of such toll; provided,

however, that any such variation shall be reasonably calculated to minimize the reduction in toll revenue generated by such toll.

B. 1. Beginning July 1, 2008, every agency of the Commonwealth or any political subdivision or instrumentality thereof having control of or day-to-day responsibility for the operation of any toll facility in the Commonwealth shall take all necessary actions to ensure that every newly constructed toll facility under its control is capable of fully automated electronic operation, employing technologies and procedures that permit the collection of tolls from users of the facility, to the extent possible, without impeding the traffic flow of the facility. An entity operating a toll facility that substantially upgrades its equipment or substantially renovates its facility after July 1, 2008, shall comply with the provisions of this subsection. The provisions of this section shall also apply to any nongovernmental or quasigovernmental entity operating a toll facility under a comprehensive agreement entered into, pursuant to the Public-Private Transportation Act of 1995 (§ 56-556 et seq.), on or after January 1, 2008. Nothing in this subsection shall be construed to prohibit a toll facility from retaining means of non-automated toll collection in some lanes of the facility.

2. For toll facilities within the territory embraced by the Northern Virginia Transportation Authority, the provisions of subdivision 1 apply to all toll facilities, regardless of whether or not they are newly constructed or substantially upgraded. (2004, c. 1003; 2007, c. 896.)

Editor's note. — Acts 2007, c. 896, cl. 8, provides: "That the Virginia Department of Transportation shall, on or before January 1, 2008, submit a written report to the General Assembly on its plans to create opportunities to enhance mobility and free-flowing traffic on Department-controlled toll facilities by embracing technological advances."

Acts 2007, c. 896, cl. 23 contains a severability clause.

The 2007 amendments. — The 2007 amendment by c. 896 inserted "and in accordance with federal requirements" following "off-peak hours", "similar variables, or combinations thereof" for "or any or all of these variables" in subsection A and added subsection B.

§ 33.1-223.2:17. Commonwealth Transportation Board may transfer interest in and control over certain highways, highway rights-of-way, and landings. — Notwithstanding any contrary provision of this title, the Commonwealth Transportation Board, upon receipt of a written request from a public access authority established pursuant to Title 15.2 and without first abandoning or discontinuing such highway, highway right-of-way, or landing, may transfer to such authority any and all rights and interests of the Board in such highway, highway right-of-way, and landing as the Board may deem in the public interest. Such transfer may be either with or without compensation from the authority. (2007, c. 304.)

CHAPTER 2.

LOCAL AUTHORITY OVER HIGHWAYS.

Article 1.

Miscellaneous Provisions.

Sec.
33.1-225. Levies.

ARTICLE 1.

Miscellaneous Provisions.

§ 33.1-225. Levies. — The boards of supervisors or other governing bodies of the several counties shall not make any levy of county or district road taxes or contract any further indebtedness for the construction, maintenance or improvement of roads; provided, however, that the boards of supervisors or other governing bodies of the several counties shall continue to make county or district levies, as the case may be, upon all real and personal property subject to local taxation, in such county or magisterial district, and not embraced within the corporate limits of any incorporated town which maintains its own streets and is exempt from county and district road taxes unless the citizens of such towns voted on the question of issuing county or district road bonds, sufficient only to provide for the payment of any bonded or other indebtedness and for the interest contracted thereon that may be outstanding as an obligation of any county or district contracted for road purposes or for the sinking fund for the retirement of any bonded indebtedness established for county or district road purposes; and provided, further, that the boards of supervisors or other governing bodies of counties adjacent to cities of the first class may, for the purpose of supplementing funds available for expenditure by the Commonwealth for the maintenance and improvement of roads in such counties when such supplementary funds are necessary on account of the existence of suburban conditions adjacent to such cities, levy county or district road taxes, as the case may be, the proceeds thereof to be expended at the option of the board of supervisors or other governing body either by or under the supervision of the Commonwealth Transportation Commissioner in the maintenance and improvement, including construction and reconstruction, of roads in such suburban district; and provided, further, that any expenditure heretofore made by the board of supervisors of Giles County from the general funds of the county for the improvement of roads which are not in the secondary system of state highways and which are open to public use is hereby validated.

All balances in the hands of the local authorities for county or district road purposes and any taxes levied for years prior to 1932 for county or district road purposes and not collected shall, when collected, and to the extent necessary, be disbursed in payment of obligations heretofore contracted for county or district road purposes and remaining unpaid and the balance, if any, for general county or district purposes.

For the purpose of this section the term "district" shall mean magisterial, sanitary or other special district created by the governing body of a county for the levy of road taxes. (Code 1950, § 33-138; 1964, c. 376; 1968, c. 368; 1970, c. 322; 2007, c. 813.)

Editor's note. — Acts 2007, c. 813, cl. 2, provides: "That the provisions of this act shall not affect the powers of any locality with respect to any ordinance, resolution or bylaw validly adopted and not repealed or rescinded prior to July 1, 2007."

The 2007 amendments. — The 2007 amendment by c. 813 substituted "Giles County" for "any county having a population of more than 17,200 but less than 17,300" near the end of the first paragraph.

CHAPTER 3.

FERRIES, BRIDGES AND TURNPIKES.

Article 5.

State Revenue Bond Act.

Sec.
33.1-268. Definitions.
33.1-269. General powers of Board.
33.1-277. Credit of Commonwealth not pledged.

ARTICLE 5.

State Revenue Bond Act.

§ 33.1-268. Definitions. — As used in this article, the following words and terms shall have the following meanings:

(1) The word *"Board"* means the Commonwealth Transportation Board, or if the Commonwealth Transportation Board is abolished, any board, commission or officer succeeding to the principal functions thereof or upon whom the powers given by this article to the Board shall be given by law.

(2) The word *"project"* or *"projects"* means any one or more of the following:

(a) York River Bridges, extending from a point within the Town of Yorktown in York County, or within York County across the York River to Gloucester Point or some point in Gloucester County.

(b) Rappahannock River Bridge, extending from Greys Point, or its vicinity, in Middlesex County, across the Rappahannock River to a point in the vicinity of White Stone, in Lancaster County, or at some other feasible point in the general vicinity of the two respective points.

(c), (d) [Reserved.]

(e) James River Bridge, from a point at or near Jamestown, in James City County, across the James River to a point in Surry County.

(f), (g) [Reserved.]

(h) James River, Chuckatuck and Nansemond River Bridges, together with necessary connecting roads, in the Cities of Newport News and Suffolk and the County of Isle of Wight.

(i) [Reserved.]

(j) Hampton Roads Bridge, Tunnel, or Bridge and Tunnel System, extending from a point or points in the Cities of Newport News and Hampton on the northwest shore of Hampton Roads across Hampton Roads to a point or points in the City of Norfolk or Suffolk on the southeast shore of Hampton Roads.

(k) The Norfolk-Virginia Beach Highway, extending from a point in the vicinity of the intersection of Interstate Route 64 and Primary Route 58 at Norfolk to some feasible point between London Bridge and Primary Route 60.

(*l*) The Henrico-James River Bridge, extending from a point on the eastern shore of the James River in Henrico County to a point on the western shore, between Falling Creek and Bells Road interchanges of the Richmond-Petersburg Turnpike; however, the project shall be deemed to include all property, rights, easements and franchises relating to any of the foregoing projects and deemed necessary or convenient for the operation thereof and to include approaches thereto.

(m) The limited access highway between the Patrick Henry Airport area and the Newport News downtown area which generally runs parallel to tracks of the Chesapeake and Ohio Railroad.

(n) Transportation improvements in the Dulles Corridor, with an eastern terminus of the East Falls Church Metrorail station at Interstate Route 66 and a western terminus of Virginia Route 772 in Loudoun County, including without limitation the Dulles Toll Road, the Dulles Access Road, outer roadways adjacent or parallel thereto, mass transit, including rail, bus rapid transit, and capacity enhancing treatments such as High-Occupancy Vehicle lanes, High-Occupancy Toll (HOT) lanes, interchange improvements, commuter parking lots, and other transportation management strategies.

(o), (p) [Repealed.]

(q) Subject to the limitations and approvals of § 33.1-279.1, any other highway for a primary highway transportation improvement district or transportation service district which the Board has agreed to finance under a contract with any such district or any other alternative mechanism for generation of local revenues for specific funding of a project satisfactory to the Commonwealth Transportation Board, the financing for which is to be secured by Transportation Trust Fund revenues under any appropriation made by the General Assembly for that purpose and payable first from revenues received under such contract or other local funding source, second, to the extent required, from funds appropriated and allocated, pursuant to the highway allocation formula as provided by law, to the highway construction district in which the project is located or to the county or counties in which the project is located and third, to the extent required from other legally available revenues of the Trust Fund and from any other available source of funds.

(r) U.S. 58 Corridor Development Program projects as defined in §§ 33.1-221.1:2 and 58.1-815.

(s) The Northern Virginia Transportation District Program as defined in § 33.1-221.1:3.

(t) Any program for highways or mass transit or transportation facilities, endorsed by the local jurisdiction or jurisdictions affected, which agree that certain distributions of state recordation taxes will be dedicated and used for the payment of any bonds or other obligations, including interest thereon, the proceeds of which were used to pay the cost of the program. Any such program shall be referred to as a "Transportation Improvement Program."

(u) Any project designated from time to time by the General Assembly financed in whole or part through the issuance of Commonwealth of Virginia Federal Highway Reimbursement Anticipation Notes.

(v) Any project authorized by the General Assembly financed in whole or in part by funds from the Priority Transportation Fund established pursuant to § 33.1-23.03:8 or from the proceeds of bonds whose debt service is paid in whole or in part by funds from such Fund.

(3) The word *"undertaking"* means all of the projects authorized to be acquired or constructed under this article.

(4) The word *"improvements"* means such repairs, replacements, additions and betterments of and to a project acquired by purchase or by condemnation as are deemed necessary to place it in a safe and efficient condition for the use of the public, if such repairs, replacements, additions and betterments are ordered prior to the sale of any bonds for the acquisition of such project.

(5) The term *"cost of project"* as applied to a project to be acquired by purchase or by condemnation, includes the purchase price or the amount of the award, cost of improvements, financing charges, interest during any period of disuse before completion of improvements, cost of traffic estimates and of engineering and legal expenses, plans, specifications and surveys, estimates of cost and of revenues, other expenses necessary or incident to determining the feasibility or practicability of the enterprises, administrative expenses and such other expenses as may be necessary or incident to the financing herein authorized and the acquisition of the project and the placing of the project in operation.

(6) The term *"cost of project"* as applied to a project to be constructed, embraces the cost of construction, the cost of all lands, properties, rights, easements and franchises acquired which are deemed necessary for such construction, the cost of acquiring by purchase or condemnation any ferry which is deemed by the Board to be competitive with any bridge to be constructed, the cost of all machinery and equipment, financing charges, interest prior to and during construction and for one year after completion of construction, cost of traffic estimates and of engineering data, engineering and legal expenses, cost of plans, specifications and surveys, estimates of cost and of revenues, other expenses necessary or incident to determining the feasibility or practicability of the enterprise, administrative expense and such other expenses as may be necessary or incident to the financing herein authorized, the construction of the project, the placing of the project in operation and the condemnation of property necessary for such construction and operation.

(7) The word *"owner"* includes all individuals, incorporated companies, copartnerships, societies or associations having any title or interest in any property rights, easements or franchises authorized to be acquired by this article.

(8) [Repealed.]

(9) The words *"revenue"* and *"revenues"* include tolls and any other moneys received or pledged by the Board pursuant to this article, including, without limitation, legally available Transportation Trust Fund revenues and any federal highway reimbursements and any other federal highway assistance received from time to time by the Commonwealth.

(10) The terms *"toll project"* and *"toll projects"* mean projects financed in whole or in part through the issuance of revenue bonds which are secured by toll revenues generated by such project or projects. (Code 1950, § 33-228; 1950, p. 145; 1954, c. 578; 1956, c. 158; 1962, c. 273; 1964, c. 558; 1970, c. 322; 1972, c. 2; 1974, cc. 52, 297; 1982, c. 261; 1986, Sp. Sess., c. 13; 1988, cc. 844, 903; 1989, Sp. Sess., cc. 9, 11; 1990, c. 710; 1991, cc. 666, 713; 1993, cc. 391, 793; 1994, cc. 520, 589; 1995, c. 354; 2000, cc. 1019, 1044; 2004, c. 807; 2007, c. 896.)

Editor's note. — Acts 2007, c. 896, cl. 23 contains a severability clause.

The 2007 amendments. — The 2007 amendment by c. 896 inserted subdivision 2 (v).

§ 33.1-269. General powers of Board. — The Commonwealth Transportation Board may, subject to the provisions of this article:

1. Acquire by purchase or by condemnation, construct, improve, operate and maintain any one or more of the projects mentioned and included in the undertaking defined in this article;

2. Issue revenue bonds of the Commonwealth, to be known and designated as "Commonwealth of Virginia Toll Revenue Bonds," payable from earnings and from any other available sources of funds, to pay the cost of such projects;

3. Subject to the limitations and approvals of § 33.1-279.1, issue revenue bonds of the Commonwealth to be known and designated as "Common-

wealth of Virginia Transportation Contract Revenue Bonds," secured by Transportation Trust Fund revenues under a payment agreement between the Board and the Treasury Board, subject to their appropriation by the General Assembly and payable first from revenues received pursuant to contracts with a primary highway transportation improvement district or transportation service district or other local revenue sources for which specific funding of any such bonds may be authorized by law; second, to the extent required, from funds appropriated and allocated, pursuant to the highway allocation formula as provided by law, to the highway construction district in which the project or projects to be financed are located or to the county or counties in which the project or projects to be financed are located; and third, to the extent required, from other legally available revenues of the Trust Fund and from any other available source of funds;

4. Issue revenue bonds of the Commonwealth to be known and designated as "Commonwealth of Virginia Transportation Revenue Bonds," secured (i) by revenues received from the U.S. Route 58 Corridor Development Fund, subject to their appropriation by the General Assembly, (ii) to the extent required, from revenues legally available from the Transportation Trust Fund and (iii) to the extent required, from any other legally available funds which have been appropriated by the General Assembly;

4a. Issue revenue bonds of the Commonwealth to be known and designated as "Commonwealth of Virginia Transportation Revenue Bonds," secured, subject to their appropriation by the General Assembly, first from (i) revenues received from the Northern Virginia Transportation District Fund, (ii) to the extent required, funds appropriated and allocated, pursuant to the highway allocation formula as provided by law, to the highway construction district in which the project or projects to be financed are located or to the city or county in which the project or projects to be financed are located, (iii) to the extent required, legally available revenues of the Transportation Trust Fund, and (iv) such other funds which may be appropriated by the General Assembly;

4b. Issue revenue bonds of the Commonwealth to be known and designated as "Commonwealth of Virginia Transportation Program Revenue Bonds" secured, subject to their appropriation by the General Assembly, first from (i) any revenues received from any Set-aside Fund established by the General Assembly pursuant to § 58.1-816.1, (ii) to the extent required, revenues received pursuant to any contract with a local jurisdiction or any alternative mechanism for generation of local revenues for specific funding of a project satisfactory to the Commonwealth Transportation Board, (iii) to the extent required, funds appropriated and allocated, pursuant to the highway allocation formula as provided by law, to the highway construction district in which

the project or projects to be financed are located or to the city or county in which the project or projects to be financed are located, (iv) to the extent required, legally available revenues of the Transportation Trust Fund, and (v) such other funds which may be appropriated by the General Assembly. No bonds for any project or projects shall be issued under the authority of this subsection unless such project or projects are specifically included in a bill or resolution passed by the General Assembly;

4c. Issue revenue bonds of the Commonwealth to be known and designated as "Commonwealth of Virginia Transportation Program Revenue Bonds" secured, subject to their appropriation by the General Assembly, first from (i) any revenues received from the Commonwealth Transit Capital Fund established by the General Assembly pursuant to subdivision A 4 g of § 58.1-638, (ii) to the extent required, legally available revenues of the Transportation Trust Fund, and (iii) such other funds which may be appropriated by the General Assembly. No bonds for any project or projects shall be issued under the authority of this subsection unless such project or projects are specifically included in a bill or resolution passed by the General Assembly;

4d. Issue revenue bonds of the Commonwealth from time to time to be known and designated as "Commonwealth of Virginia Federal Highway Reimbursement Anticipation Notes" secured, subject to their appropriation by the General Assembly, (i) first from any federal highway reimbursements and any other federal highway assistance received from time to time by the Commonwealth, (ii) then, at the discretion of the Board, to the extent required, from legally available revenues of the Transportation Trust Fund, and (iii) then from such other funds, if any, which are designated by the General Assembly for such purpose;

4e. Issue revenue bonds of the Commonwealth from time to time to be known and designated as "Commonwealth of Virginia Credit Assistance Revenue Bonds," secured, subject to their appropriation by the General Assembly, solely from revenues with respect to or generated by the project or projects being financed thereby and any tolls or other revenues pledged by the Board as security therefor and in accordance with the applicable federal credit assistance authorized with respect to such project or projects by the United States Department of Transportation;

4f. Issue revenue bonds of the Commonwealth to be known and designated as "Commonwealth of Virginia Transportation Capital Projects Revenue Bonds," secured, subject to their appropriation by the General Assembly, (i) from the revenues deposited into the Priority Transportation Fund established pursuant to § 33.1-23.03:8; (ii) to the extent required, from revenues legally available from the Transportation Trust Fund; and (iii) to the extent required, from any other legally available funds;

5. Fix and collect tolls and other charges for the use of such projects or to refinance the cost of such projects;

6. Construct grade separations at intersections of any projects with public highways, streets or other public ways or places and change and adjust the lines and grades thereof so as to accommodate the same to the design of such grade separations, the cost of such grade separations and any damage incurred in changing and adjusting the lines and grades of such highways, streets, ways and places to be ascertained and paid by the Board as a part of the cost of the project;

7. Vacate or change the location of any portion of any public highway, street or other public way or place and reconstruct the same at such new location as the Board deems most favorable for the project and of substantially the same type and in as good condition as the original highway, streets, way or place, the cost of such reconstruction and any damage incurred in vacating or changing the location thereof to be ascertained and paid by the Board as a part of the cost of the project. Any public highway, street or other public way or place vacated or relocated by the Board shall be vacated or relocated in the manner provided by law for the vacation or relocation of public roads and any damages awarded on account thereof may be paid by the Board as a part of the cost of the project;

8. Make reasonable regulations for the installation, construction, maintenance, repair, renewal and relocation of pipes, mains, sewers, conduits, cables, wires, towers, poles and other equipment and appliances herein called "public utility facilities," of the Commonwealth and of any municipality, county, or other political subdivision, public utility or public service corporation owning or operating the same in, on, along, over or under the project. Whenever the Board determines that it is necessary that any such public utility facilities should be relocated or removed, the Commonwealth or such municipality, county, political subdivision, public utility or public service corporation shall relocate or remove the same in accordance with the order of the Board. The cost and expense of such relocation or removal, including the cost of installing such public utility facilities in a new location or locations, and the cost of any lands or any rights or interests in lands, and any other rights acquired to accomplish such relocation or removal shall be ascertained by the Board.

On any toll project, the Board shall pay the cost and expense of relocation or removal as a part of the cost of the project for those public utility facilities owned or operated by the Commonwealth or such municipality, county, political subdivision, public utility or public service corporation. On all other projects, under this article, the Board shall pay the cost and expense of relocation or removal as a part of the cost of the project for those public utility facilities owned or operated by the Commonwealth or such municipality, county, or political subdivision. The Commonwealth or such municipality, county, political subdivision, public utility or public service corporation may maintain and operate such public utility facilities with the necessary appurtenances, in the new location or locations, for as long a period and upon the same terms and conditions as it had the right to maintain and operate such public utility facilities in their former location or locations;

9. Acquire by the exercise of the power of eminent domain any lands, property, rights, rights-of-way, franchises, easements and other property, including public lands, parks, playgrounds, reservations, highways or parkways, or parts thereof or rights therein, of any municipality, county or other political subdivision, deemed necessary or convenient for the construction or the efficient operation of the project or necessary in the restoration, replacement or relocation of public or private property damaged or destroyed.

The cost of such projects shall be paid solely from the proceeds of Commonwealth of Virginia Toll or Transportation Contract Revenue Bonds or a combination thereof or from such proceeds and from any grant or contribution which may be made thereto pursuant to the provisions of this article;

10. Notwithstanding any provision of this article to the contrary, the Board shall be authorized to exercise the powers conferred herein, in addition to its general powers to acquire rights-of-way and to construct, operate and maintain state highways, with respect to any project which the General Assembly has authorized or may hereafter authorize to be financed in whole or in part through the issuance of bonds of the Commonwealth pursuant to the provisions of Section 9 (c) of Article X of the Constitution of Virginia; and

11. Enter into any agreements or take such other actions as the Board shall determine in connection with applying for or obtaining any federal credit assistance, including without limitation loan guarantees and lines of credit, pursuant to authorization from the United States Department of Transportation with respect to any project included in the Commonwealth's long-range transportation plan and the approved State Transportation Improvement Program. (Code 1950, § 33-229; 1954, c. 319; 1970, c. 322; 1982, c. 403; 1986, Sp. Sess., c. 13; 1988, cc. 844, 903; 1989, Sp. Sess., cc. 9, 11; 1990, c. 710; 1991, cc. 666, 713; 1993, cc. 391, 793; 1994, cc. 233, 520, 589, 662; 1995, c. 354; 1996, cc. 23, 143; 1999, c. 898; 2000, cc. 1019, 1044; 2004, c. 807; 2007, c. 896.)

Editor's note. — Acts 2007, c. 896, cl. 23 contains a severability clause.

The 2007 amendments. — The 2007 amendment by c. 896 inserted subdivision 4f.

§ 33.1-277. Credit of Commonwealth not pledged. — A. Commonwealth of Virginia Toll Revenue Bonds issued under the provisions of this article shall not be deemed to constitute a debt of the Commonwealth of Virginia or a pledge of the faith and credit of the Commonwealth, but such bonds shall be payable solely from the funds herein provided therefor from tolls and revenues, from bond proceeds or earnings thereon and from any other available sources of funds. All such bonds shall state on their face that the Commonwealth of Virginia is not obligated to pay the same or the interest thereon except from the special fund provided therefor from tolls and revenues under this article, from bond proceeds or earnings thereon and from any other available sources of funds and that the faith and credit of the Commonwealth are not pledged to the payment of the principal or interest of such bonds. The issuance of such revenue bonds under the provisions of this article shall not directly or indirectly or contingently obligate the Commonwealth to levy or to pledge any form of taxation whatever therefor or to make any appropriation for their payment, other than appropriate available funds derived as revenues from tolls and charges under this article or derived from bond proceeds or earnings thereon and from any other available sources of funds.

B. Commonwealth of Virginia Transportation Contract Revenue Bonds issued under the provisions of this article shall not be deemed to constitute a debt of the Commonwealth of Virginia or a pledge of the faith and credit of the Commonwealth, but such bonds shall be payable solely from the funds herein provided therefor (i) from revenues received pursuant to contracts with a primary highway transportation district or transportation service district or any other alternative mechanism for generation of local revenues for specific funding of a project satisfactory to the Commonwealth Transportation Board, (ii) to the extent required, from funds appropriated and allocated, pursuant to the highway allocation formula as provided by law, to the highway construction district in which the project or projects to be financed are located or to the county or counties in which such project or projects are located, (iii) from bond proceeds or earnings thereon, (iv) to the extent required, from other legally available revenues of the Trust Fund, and (v) from any other available source of funds. All such bonds shall state on their face that the Commonwealth of Virginia is not obligated to pay the same or the interest thereon except from revenues in clauses (i) and (iii) hereof and that the faith and credit of the Commonwealth are not pledged to the payment of the principal and interest of such bonds. The issuance of such revenue bonds under the provisions of this article shall not directly or indirectly or contingently obligate the Commonwealth to levy or to pledge any form of taxation whatever or to make any appropriation for their payment, other than to appropriate available funds derived as revenues under this article from the sources set forth in clauses (i) and (iii) hereof. Nothing in this article shall be construed to obligate the General Assembly to make any appropriation of the funds set forth in clause (ii) or (iv) hereof for payment of such bonds.

C. Commonwealth of Virginia Transportation Revenue Bonds issued under the provisions of this article shall not be deemed to constitute a debt of the Commonwealth of Virginia or a pledge of the full faith and credit of the Commonwealth, but such bonds shall be payable solely from the funds herein provided therefor (i) from revenues received from the U.S. Route 58 Corridor Development Fund, subject to their appropriation by the General Assembly, (ii) to the extent required, from revenues legally available from the Transportation Trust Fund and (iii) to the extent required, from any other legally available funds which shall have been appropriated by the General Assembly.

D. Commonwealth of Virginia Transportation Revenue Bonds issued under this article for Category 1 projects as provided in subdivision (2) (s) of § 33.1-268 shall not be deemed to constitute a debt of the Commonwealth of Virginia or a pledge of the faith and credit of the Commonwealth. Such bonds shall be payable solely, subject to their appropriation by the General Assembly, first from (i) revenues received from the Northern Virginia Transportation District Fund, (ii) to the extent required, funds appropriated and allocated, pursuant to the highway allocation formula as provided by law, to the highway construction district in which the project or projects to be financed are located or to the city or county in which the project or projects to be financed are located, (iii) to the extent required, legally available revenues of the Transportation Trust Fund, and (iv) such other funds which may be appropriated by the General Assembly.

E. Commonwealth of Virginia Transportation Program Revenue Bonds issued under this article for projects defined in subdivision (2) (t) of § 33.1-268 shall not be deemed to constitute a debt of the Commonwealth or a pledge of the faith and credit of the Commonwealth. Such bonds shall be payable solely, subject to their appropriation by the General Assembly, first from (i) any revenues received from any Set-aside Fund established by the General Assembly pursuant to § 58.1-816.1, (ii) to the extent required, revenues received pursuant to any contract with a local jurisdiction or any alternative mechanism for generation of local revenues for specific funding of a project satisfactory to the Commonwealth Transportation Board, (iii) to the extent required, funds appropriated and allocated, pursuant to the highway allocation formula as provided by law, to the highway construction district in which the project or projects to be financed are located or to the city or county in which the project or projects to be financed are located, (iv) to the extent required, legally available revenues from the Transportation Trust Fund, and (v) such other funds which may be appropriated by the General Assembly.

F. Commonwealth of Virginia Federal Highway Reimbursement Anticipation Notes issued under this article shall not be deemed to constitute a debt of the Commonwealth of Virginia or a pledge of the full faith and credit of the Commonwealth, but such obligations shall be payable solely, subject to appropriation by the General Assembly, (i) first from any federal highway reimbursements and any other federal highway assistance received from time to time by the Commonwealth, (ii) then, at the discretion of the Board, to the extent required, from legally available revenues of the Transportation Trust Fund, and (iii) then, from such other funds, if any, which are designated by the General Assembly for such purpose.

G. Commonwealth of Virginia Transportation Credit Assistance Revenue Bonds issued under the provisions of this article shall not be deemed to constitute a debt of the Commonwealth of Virginia or a pledge of the full faith and credit of the Commonwealth, but such obligations shall be payable solely, subject to appropriation by the General Assembly, from revenues with respect to or generated by the project or projects being financed thereby and any tolls or other revenues pledged by the Board as security therefor and in accordance with the applicable federal credit assistance authorized with respect to such project or projects by the United States Department of Transportation.

H. Commonwealth of Virginia Transportation Capital Projects Revenue Bonds issued under the provisions of this article for projects as provided in subdivision 2 v of § 33.1-268 shall not be deemed to constitute a debt of the Commonwealth of Virginia or a pledge of the full faith and credit of the Commonwealth, but such bonds shall be payable solely, subject to their appropriation by the General Assembly, (i) from the revenues deposited into the Priority Transportation Fund established pursuant to § 33.1-23.03:8; (ii) to the extent required, from revenues legally available from the Transportation Trust Fund; and (iii) to the extent required, from any other legally available funds. (Code 1950, § 33-237; 1970, c. 322; 1982, c. 403; 1986, Sp. Sess., c. 13; 1988, cc. 844, 903; 1989, Sp. Sess., cc. 9, 11; 1990, c. 710; 1991, cc. 666, 713; 1993, cc. 391, 793; 1994, cc. 233, 520, 589, 662; 1995, c. 354; 2000, cc. 1019, 1044; 2004, c. 807; 2007, c. 896.)

Editor's note. — Acts 2007, c. 896, cl. 23 contains a severability clause.

The 2007 amendments. — The 2007 amendment by c. 896 inserted subsection H.

CHAPTER 7.

OUTDOOR ADVERTISING IN SIGHT OF PUBLIC HIGHWAYS.

ARTICLE 1.

General Regulations.

§ 33.1-370. Special provisions pertaining to interstate, national highway system, and federal-aid primary highways.

CASE NOTES

Applied in Trustees of the Christ & St. Luke's Episcopal Church

v. Bd. of Zoning Appeals of Norfolk, — Va. —, 641 S.E.2d 104, 2007 Va. LEXIS 29 (2007).

CHAPTER 9.

ADJUSTMENT OF CLAIMS RESULTING FROM CONTRACTS EXECUTED AFTER JUNE 30, 1976, FOR CONSTRUCTION OF STATE HIGHWAYS.

Sec.
33.1-386. Submission of claims; initial investigation and notice of decision; appearance before Commissioner; further investigation and notice of decision; settlement.

§ 33.1-386. Submission of claims; initial investigation and notice of decision; appearance before Commissioner; further investigation and notice of decision; settlement. — A. Upon the completion of any contract for the construction of any state highway project awarded by the Commonwealth Transportation Board or by the Commonwealth Transportation Commissioner to any contractor, if the contractor fails to receive such settlement as he claims to be entitled to under the contract for himself or for his subcontractors or for persons furnishing materials for the contract for costs and expenses caused by the acts or omissions of the Department of Transportation, he may, within sixty days after the final estimate date, deliver to the Department of Transportation, through proper administrative channels as determined by the Department, a written claim for such amount to which he deems himself, his subcontractors, or his material persons entitled under the contract. The final estimate date shall be set forth in a letter from the Department to the contractor sent by certified mail. The claim shall set forth the facts upon which the claim is based, provided that written notice of the contractor's intention to file such claim shall have been given to the Department at the time of the occurrence or beginning of the work upon which the claim and subsequent action is based. Within ninety days from receipt of such claim, the Department shall make an investigation and notify the claimant in writing by certified mail of its decision. The claimant and the Department may, however, mutually extend such ninety-day period for another thirty days.

B. If dissatisfied with the decision, the claimant shall, within thirty days from receipt of the Department's decision, notify the Commonwealth Transportation Commissioner, in writing, that he desires to appear before him, either in person or through counsel, and present any additional facts and arguments in support of his claim as previously filed.

C. The Commissioner shall schedule such appearance to be held within thirty days of receiving the claimant's written request. The claimant and the Commissioner may, however, mutually agree to schedule such appearance to be held after thirty days but before sixty days from the receipt of the claimant's written request.

D. Within forty-five days from the date of the appearance before him, the Commissioner shall make an investigation of the claim and notify the contractor in writing of his decision. The claimant and the Commissioner may, however, mutually agree to extend such forty-five-day period for another thirty days. If the Commissioner deems that all or any portion of a claim is valid, he shall have the authority to negotiate a settlement with the contractor, but any such settlement shall be subject to the provisions of § 2.2-514.

E. Failure of the Department or the Commissioner to render a decision within the time period specified in subsections A and D, or within such other period as has been mutually agreed upon as provided in this section, shall be deemed a denial of the claim. Any mutual agreements for time extension permitted herein shall in no way extend the limitations set out in § 33.1-192.1.

If the Commissioner determines that a claim has been denied as the result of an administrative oversight, then the Department reserves the right to reconsider the claim. (1976, c. 230; 1982, c. 320; 1991, c. 691; 1994, c. 67; 2001, c. 175; 2007, c. 162.)

The 2007 amendments. — The 2007 amendment by c. 162, in subsection A, inserted "or by the Commonwealth Transportation Commissioner" and substituted "within sixty days after the final estimate date, deliver to" for "within sixty days from the time of notification of the Department's final estimate, submit to" in the first sentence, inserted the second sentence, and substituted "writing by certified mail" for "writing by registered mail" in the fourth sentence.

CHAPTER 10.1.

DEPARTMENT OF RAIL AND PUBLIC TRANSPORTATION.

Sec.
33.1-391.5. Responsibilities of Department.

§ 33.1-391.5. Responsibilities of Department. — The Department shall have the following responsibilities:

1. Determine present and future needs for, and economic feasibility of providing, public transportation, transportation demand management, and ridesharing facilities and services and the retention, improvement, and addition of passenger and freight rail transportation in the Commonwealth;

2. Formulate and implement plans and programs for the establishment, improvement, development and coordination of public transportation, transportation demand management, and ridesharing facilities and services, and the retention and improvement of passenger and freight rail transportation services and corridors in the Commonwealth, and coordinate transportation demand management and innovative technological transportation initiatives with the Department of Transportation;

3. Coordinate with the Department of Transportation in the conduct of research, policy analysis, and planning for the rail and public transportation modes as may be appropriate to ensure the provision of effective, safe, and efficient public transportation and passenger and freight rail services in the Commonwealth;

4. Develop uniform financial and operating data on and criteria for evaluating all public transportation activities in the Commonwealth, develop specific methodologies for the collection of such data by public transit operators, regularly and systematically verify such data by means of financial audits and periodic field reviews of operating data collection methodologies, and develop such other information as may be required to evaluate the performance and improve the economy or efficiency of public transit or passenger and freight rail operations, transportation demand management programs, and ridesharing in the Commonwealth;

5. Compile and maintain an up-to-date inventory of all abandoned railroad corridors in the Commonwealth abandoned after January 1, 1970;

6. Provide training and other technical support services to transportation operators and ridesharing coordinators as may be appropriate to improve public transportation, ridesharing, and passenger and freight rail services;

7. Maintain liaison with state, local, district and federal agencies or other entities, private and public, having responsibilities for passenger and freight rail, transportation demand management, ridesharing, and public transportation programs;

8. Receive, administer and allocate all planning, operating, capital, and any other grant programs from the Federal Transit Administration, the Federal Railroad Administration, the Federal Highway Administration, and other agencies of the United States government for public transportation, passenger and freight rail transportation, transportation demand management, and ridesharing purposes with approval of the Board and to comply with all conditions attendant thereto;

9. Administer all state grants for public transportation, rail transportation, ridesharing, and transportation demand management purposes with approval of the Board;

10. Promote the use of public transportation, transportation demand management, ridesharing, and passenger and freight rail services to improve the mobility of Virginia's citizens and the transportation of goods;

11. Represent the Commonwealth on local, regional, and national agencies, industry associations, committees, task forces, and other entities, public and private, having responsibility for passenger and freight rail, transportation demand management, ridesharing, and public transportation;

12. Represent the Commonwealth's interests in passenger and freight rail, transportation demand management, ridesharing, and public transportation and coordinate with the Department of Transportation in the planning, location, design, construction, implementation, monitoring, evaluation, purchase, and rehabilitation of facilities and services that affect or are used by passenger and freight rail, transportation demand management, ridesharing, or public transportation;

13. Coordinate with the State Corporation Commission on all matters dealing with rail safety inspections and rail regulations which fall within its purview;

14. Prepare and review state legislation and Commonwealth recommendations on federal legislation and regulations as directed by the Secretary of Transportation; and

15. Promote public transportation, ridesharing, and passenger and freight rail safety. (1992, c. 167; 2002, c. 355; 2007, c. 435.)

The 2007 amendments. — The 2007 amendment by c. 435 added subdivision 5; and redesignated former subdivisions 5 through 14 as subdivisions 6 through 15.

CHAPTER 10.2.

HAMPTON ROADS TRANSPORTATION AUTHORITY.

Sec.
33.1-391.6. Short title.
33.1-391.7. Authority created.
33.1-391.8. Powers of the Authority.
33.1-391.9. Composition of Authority; chairman and vice-chairman; quorum.
33.1-391.10. Additional powers of the Authority.
33.1-391.11. Authority a responsible public entity under Public-Private Transportation Act of 1995.
33.1-391.12. Addition of the Chesapeake Bay Bridge-Tunnel to facilities controlled by Authority; expansion of Authority membership; applicability of local transportation fees to Accomack and Northampton Counties.
33.1-391.13. Issuance of bonds by the Chesapeake Bay Bridge and Tunnel Commission.
33.1-391.14. Continuing responsibilities of the Commonwealth Transportation Board and the Virginia Department of Transportation.
33.1-391.15. Use of revenues by the Authority.

§ **33.1-391.6. Short title.** — This chapter shall be known and may be cited as the Hampton Roads Transportation Authority Act. (2007, c. 896.)

Editor's note. — Acts 2007, c. 896, cl. 5, provides: "That the Hampton Roads Transportation Authority established under § 33.1-391.7 of the Code of Virginia shall develop as part of a long-range plan quantifiable measures and achievable goals for the area embraced by the Authority relating to, but not limited to, congestion reduction and safety, transit and high-occupancy vehicle (HOV) usage, job-to-housing ratios, job and housing access to transit and pedestrian facilities, air quality, and per-capita vehicle miles traveled. In addition, the Northern Virginia Transportation Authority established under § 15.2-4830 of the Code of Virginia shall also develop as part of a long-range plan quantifiable measures and achievable goals for the area embraced by the Authority relating to, but not limited to, congestion reduction and safety, transit and high-occupancy vehicle (HOV) usage, job-to-housing ratios, job and housing access to transit and pedestrian facilities, air quality, and per-capita vehicle miles traveled. Such goals shall be subject to the approval of the Commonwealth Transportation Board on a biennial basis."

Acts 2007, c. 896, cl. 6, provides: "That the fees and taxes authorized by this Act for imposition or assessment by the Hampton Roads Transportation Authority shall only be imposed or assessed by the Authority if (i) at least seven of the twelve governing bodies of the counties and cities embraced by the Authority (but excluding the governing body of the County of Accomack and the governing body of the County of Northampton) that include at least 51% of the population of the counties and cities embraced by the Authority (but excluding the populations of the Counties of Accomack and Northampton) pass a duly adopted resolution stating its approval of such power of the Authority no later than December 31, 2007, and then (ii) at least seven of the twelve voting members of the Authority (but excluding voting members representing the Counties of Accomack and Northampton), that include at least 51% of the population of the counties and cities embraced by the Authority vote in the affirmative to impose or assess all of the fees and taxes authorized under this Act for imposition and assessment by the Authority in all of the counties and cities embraced by the Authority. For purposes of this enactment, "population" means the population as determined by the most recently preceding United States decennial census or the most recent population estimates of the Weldon Cooper Center for Public Service of the University of Virginia, whichever is most recent."

Acts 2007, c. 896, cl. 14, provides: "That the Hampton Roads Transportation Authority, the cities and counties embraced by the Authority, the Commissioner of the Department of Taxation, the Commissioner of the Department of Motor Vehicles, and other appropriate entities shall develop guidelines, policies, and procedures for the efficient and effective collection and administration of the fees and taxes authorized for use by the Authority. The guidelines, policies, and procedures shall be made public at least 60 days prior to their implementation. The development of the guidelines, policies, and procedures shall be exempt from the Administrative Process Act (§ 2.2-4000 et seq. of the Code of Virginia). The Secretary of Finance may authorize an anticipation loan for purposes of meeting the requirements of this enactment."

Acts 2007, c. 896, cl. 15, provides: "That the staff of the Hampton Roads Planning District Commission and the Virginia Department of Transportation shall work cooperatively to assist the proper formation and effective organization of the Hampton Roads Transportation Authority. Until such time as the Authority is fully established and functioning, the staff of the Hampton Roads Planning District Commission shall serve as its staff, and the Hampton Roads Planning District Commission shall provide the Authority with office space and administrative support. The Authority shall reimburse the Hampton Roads Planning District Commission for the cost of such staff, office space, and administrative support as appropriate."

Acts 2007, c. 896, cl. 19, provides: "That the tax authorized pursuant to § 58.1-540 of the Code of Virginia shall not be imposed by a city or county embraced by the Hampton Roads Transportation Authority if the Authority is imposing any of the fees or taxes authorized under law for imposition or assessment by the Authority."

Acts 2007, c. 896, cl. 21, provides: "That the revenue generated by this act shall be used solely for transportation purposes."

Acts 2007, c. 896, cl. 23 contains a severability clause.

§ **33.1-391.7. Authority created.** — The Hampton Roads Transportation Authority, hereinafter in this chapter known as "the Authority" is hereby created as a body politic and as a political subdivision of the Commonwealth. The Authority shall embrace the Counties of Isle of Wight, James City, and York and the Cities of Chesapeake, Hampton, Newport News, Norfolk, Poquoson, Portsmouth, Suffolk, Virginia Beach, and Williamsburg. The membership of the Authority shall be as provided in §§ 33.1-391.9 and 33.1-391.12. In addition, the Counties of Accomack and Northampton shall also be embraced by the Authority at such time that the Chesapeake Bay Bridge-Tunnel facilities become subject to the control of the Authority as provided under § 33.1-391.12. (2007, c. 896.)

Editor's note. — Acts 2007, c. 896, cl. 16, provides: "That, as provided under § 58.1-3221.2, the tax authorized thereunder may only be imposed by a city or county embraced by the Northern Virginia Transportation Authority established under § 15.2-4830, or a city or county embraced by the Hampton Roads Transportation Authority established under § 33.1-391.7."

§ 33.1-391.8. Powers of the Authority.

— Notwithstanding any contrary provision of this title and in accordance with all applicable federal statutes and requirements, the Authority shall control and operate and may impose and collect tolls in amounts established by the Authority for the use of any new or improved highway, bridge, tunnel, or transportation facility to increase capacity on such facility (including new construction relating to, or improvements to, the bridges, tunnels, roadways, and related facilities known collectively as the Chesapeake Bay Bridge-Tunnel as described in § 33.1-391.12, pursuant to the conditions set forth in such section) constructed by the Authority or solely with revenues of the Authority or revenues under the control of the Authority. The amount of any such toll may be varied from facility to facility, by lane, by congestion levels, by day of the week, time of day, type of vehicle, number of axles, or any similar combination thereof, and a reduced rate may be established for commuters as defined by the Authority. For purposes of this section, the Midtown and Downtown tunnels located within the Cities of Norfolk and Portsmouth shall be considered a single transportation facility and both facilities may be tolled if improvements are made to either tunnel. Any tolls imposed by the Authority shall be collected by an electronic toll system that, to the extent possible, shall not impede the traffic flow of the facility or prohibit a toll facility from retaining means of nonautomated toll collection in some lanes of the facility. For all facilities tolled by the Authority, there shall be signs erected prior to the point of toll collection that clearly state how the majority of the toll revenue is being spent by the Authority to benefit the users of the facility. (2007, c. 896.)

§ 33.1-391.9. Composition of Authority; chairman and vice-chairman; quorum.

— The Authority shall consist of the following members: (i) the chief elected officer of the governing body (or in the discretion of the chief elected officer, his designee, who shall be a current elected officer of such governing body) of each of the Counties of Isle of Wight, James City, and York and the Cities of Chesapeake, Hampton, Newport News, Norfolk, Poquoson, Portsmouth, Suffolk, Virginia Beach, and Williamsburg, who shall serve with voting privileges; (ii) a member of the Commonwealth Transportation Board who resides in a county or city embraced by the Authority appointed by the Governor who shall serve ex officio without a vote; (iii) the Director of the Virginia Department of Rail and Public Transportation, or his designee, who shall serve ex officio without a vote; (iv) the Commonwealth Transportation Commissioner, or his designee, who shall serve ex officio without a vote; (v) two members of the Virginia House of Delegates each of whom shall reside in a city or county whose governing body has a voting member on the Authority, neither of whom shall reside in the same city or county, appointed by the Speaker of the House of Delegates, who shall serve ex officio without a vote; and (vi) one member of the Senate of Virginia who shall reside in a city or county whose governing body has a voting member on the Authority, appointed by the Senate Committee on Rules who shall serve ex officio without a vote. Legislative members shall serve terms coincident with their terms of office. Vacancies shall be filled by appointment for the unexpired term by the same process as used to make the original appointment.

The Authority shall appoint a chairman and vice-chairman from among its voting membership.

A majority of the voting members of the Authority shall constitute a quorum for the transaction of business.

Decisions of the Authority shall require a quorum and shall be in accordance with voting procedures established by the Authority. Decisions of the Authority shall require the affirmative vote of a majority of the voting members of the Authority present and voting and such members present and voting in the affirmative shall be representatives of counties and cities that collectively include at least 51% of the population embraced by the Authority at the time of the vote. The population of counties and cities embraced by the Authority shall be the population as determined by the most recently preceding decennial census, except that after July 1 of the fifth year following such census, the population of each county and city shall be adjusted, based on final population estimates made by the Weldon Cooper Center for Public Service of the University of Virginia.

Members of the Authority shall be reimbursed for their actual and necessary expenses incurred in the performance of their duties and, in addition, shall be paid a per diem equal to the amount paid members of the Commonwealth Transportation Board for each day or portion thereof during which they are engaged in the official business of the Authority.

The Auditor of Public Accounts, or his legally authorized representatives, shall annually audit the financial accounts of the Authority, and the cost of such audit shall be borne by the Authority. (2007, c. 896.)

§ 33.1-391.10. Additional powers of the Authority. — The Authority shall have the following powers together with all powers incidental thereto or necessary for the performance of those hereinafter stated:

1. To sue and be sued and to prosecute and defend, at law or in equity, in any court having jurisdiction of the subject matter and of the parties;

2. To adopt and use a corporate seal and to alter the same at its pleasure;

3. To procure insurance, participate in insurance plans, and provide self-insurance; however, the purchase of insurance, participation in an insurance plan, or the creation of a self-insurance plan by the Authority shall not be deemed a waiver or relinquishment of any sovereign immunity to which the Authority or its officers, directors, employees, or agents are otherwise entitled;

4. To establish bylaws and make all rules and regulations, not inconsistent with the provisions of this chapter, deemed expedient for the management of the Authority's affairs;

5. To apply for and accept money, materials, contributions, grants, or other financial assistance from the United States and agencies or instrumentalities thereof, the Commonwealth, and any political subdivision, agency, or instrumentality of the Commonwealth, and from any legitimate private source;

6. To acquire real and personal property or any interest therein by purchase, lease, gift, or otherwise for purposes consistent with this chapter; and to hold, encumber, sell, or otherwise dispose of such land or interest for purposes consistent with this chapter;

7. To acquire by purchase, lease, contract, or otherwise, highways, bridges, tunnels, railroads, rolling stock, and transit and rail facilities and other transportation-related facilities; and to construct the same by purchase, lease, contract, or otherwise;

8. In consultation with the Commonwealth Transportation Board and with each city or county in which the facility or any part thereof is or is to be located, to repair, expand, enlarge, construct, reconstruct, or renovate any or all of the transportation facilities referred to in this section, and to acquire any real or personal property needed for any such purpose;

9. To enter into agreements or leases with public or private entities for the operation and maintenance of bridges, tunnels, transit and rail facilities, and highways;

10. To make and execute contracts, deeds, mortgages, leases, and all other instruments and agreements necessary or convenient for the performance of its duties and the exercise of its powers and functions under this chapter;

11. To the extent funds are made or become available to the Authority to do so, to employ employees, agents, advisors, and consultants, including without limitation, attorneys, financial advisers, engineers, and other technical advisers and, the provisions of any other law to the contrary notwithstanding, to determine their duties and compensation;

12. The authority shall comply with the provisions governing localities contained in § 15.2-2108.23;

13. To decide and vote to impose all of the fees and taxes authorized under law for use by the Authority. Furthermore, no such fee or tax shall apply to Accomack or Northampton County until such time that the Chesapeake Bay Bridge-Tunnel facilities become subject to the control of the Authority as provided under § 33.1-391.12; and

14. To the extent not inconsistent with the other provisions of this chapter, and without limiting or restricting the powers otherwise given the Authority, to exercise all of the powers given to transportation district commissions by §§ 15.2-4518 and 15.2-4519. The Authority shall only undertake those transportation projects that are included in the federally mandated 2030 Regional Transportation Plan approved by the Metropolitan Planning Organization, or any successive plan, and that are located in, or which provide a benefit to, the counties and cities that are members of the Authority, subject to the limitations related to those projects contained in this section.

The Authority shall phase construction of the transportation projects that are included in the federally mandated 2030 Regional Transportation Plan, or any successive plan. Except as specifically provided herein, projects listed in the second phase shall not be undertaken until the Authority has considered and acted upon a financing plan for the maintenance, operation, and construction for the projects listed in the first phase that meet the requirements of this section.

First Phase Projects:

Route 460 Upgrade; I-64 Widening on the Peninsula; I-64 Widening on the Southside; Downtown Tunnel/Midtown Tunnel/MLK Extension; Southeastern Parkway/Dominion Blvd/Route 17; I-664 Widening in Newport News; I-664 Widening on the Southside; I-664 Monitor Merrimac Memorial Bridge Tunnel Widening.

Second Phase Projects:

I-564 from I-64 to the Intermodal Connector; I-564 Connector to the Monitor Merrimac Memorial Bridge Tunnel; Craney Island Connector. (2007, c. 896.)

§ 33.1-391.11. Authority a responsible public entity under Public-Private Transportation Act of 1995. — The Authority is a responsible public entity as defined in the Public-Private Transportation Act of 1995 (§ 56-556 et seq.) (the PPTA).

It is the intent of the General Assembly that the Authority shall encourage private sector participation in the aforementioned projects. Any cost savings realized under the PPTA relating to the construction of first phase projects may be applied to advancing the future construction of second phase projects.

Further, nothing herein shall prohibit the Authority from receiving and acting on PPTA proposals on projects in either phase. (2007, c. 896.)

§ 33.1-391.12. Addition of the Chesapeake Bay Bridge-Tunnel to facilities controlled by Authority; expansion of Authority membership; applicability of local transportation fees to Accomack and Northampton Counties. — The bridges, tunnels, roadways, and related facilities known collectively as the Chesapeake Bay Bridge-Tunnel, which provide a vehicular connection across the mouth of the Chesapeake Bay between the City of Virginia Beach and Northampton County, shall become subject to the control of the Authority subject to the provisions of § 33.1-391.8, at such time as all of the bonds and other evidences of debt now or hereafter issued by or on behalf of the Chesapeake Bay Bridge and Tunnel Commission shall have been satisfied or paid in full. Until such bonds and other evidences of debt have been satisfied or paid in full, control of and responsibility for the operation and maintenance of the Chesapeake Bay Bridge-Tunnel facilities shall remain with the Chesapeake Bay Bridge and Tunnel Commission.

In discharging its responsibilities for the operation and maintenance of the Chesapeake Bay Bridge-Tunnel facilities, the Authority shall have, in addition to the powers it is given by this chapter, all of the powers and authority given to the Chesapeake Bay Bridge and Tunnel Commission by Chapter 693 of the Acts of Assembly of 1954 and by Chapter 714 of the Acts of the Assembly of 1956, as amended and incorporated by reference as § 33.1-253.

At such time as the Chesapeake Bay Bridge-Tunnel facilities become subject to the control of the Authority as contemplated by this section, the Authority shall be enlarged by two members, who shall serve with voting privileges, one of whom shall be the chief elected officer of the governing body of the County of Accomack (or in the discretion of the chief elected officer, his designee, who shall be a current elected officer of such governing body), and one of whom shall be the chief elected officer of the governing body of the County of Northampton (or in the discretion of the chief elected officer, his designee, who shall be a current elected officer of such governing body). (2007, c. 896.)

§ 33.1-391.13. Issuance of bonds by the Chesapeake Bay Bridge and Tunnel Commission. — On a prospective basis, prior to issuing any bonds for the purposes of financing the construction of new or additional tunnels, the Chesapeake Bay Bridge and Tunnel Commission shall affirm that no bond, or payment of any temporary or interim financing shall have a maturity date that extends beyond the maturity date of any existing bond or note until such time as the Authority is consulted about such issuance. (2007, c. 896.)

§ 33.1-391.14. Continuing responsibilities of the Commonwealth Transportation Board and the Virginia Department of Transportation. — Except as otherwise explicitly provided in this chapter, until such time as the Authority and the Virginia Department of Transportation, or the Authority and the Commonwealth Transportation Board, agree otherwise in writing, the Commonwealth Transportation Board shall allocate funding to and the Department of Transportation shall perform or cause to be performed all maintenance and operation of the bridges, tunnels, and roadways pursuant to § 33.1-391.10, and shall perform such other required services and activities with respect to such bridges, tunnels, and roadways as were being performed on January 1, 2008. (2007, c. 896.)

§ 33.1-391.15. Use of revenues by the Authority. — Notwithstanding any other provision of this chapter, all moneys received by the Authority shall be used by the Authority solely for the benefit of those counties and cities that are embraced by the Authority, and such moneys shall be used by the Authority in a manner that is consistent with the purposes stated in this chapter. (2007, c. 896.)

Title 34.

Homestead and Other Exemptions.

CHAPTER 4.

WAGES EXEMPT.

Sec.
34-34. Certain retirement benefits exempt.

§ 34-29. Maximum portion of disposable earnings subject to garnishment.

Law Review.
For article reviewing recent developments and changes in legislation, case law, and Virginia Supreme Court Rules affecting civil litigation, "Civil Practice and Procedure," see 40 U. Rich. L. Rev. 95 (2005).

§ 34-34. Certain retirement benefits exempt. — A. For the purposes of this section:

"*Alternate payee*" shall have the same meaning as provided under § 206 of the Employee Retirement Income Security Act of 1974 (ERISA). In the case of a retirement plan that is not subject to ERISA, the term "*alternate payee*" means an individual who has an interest in a retirement plan pursuant to a judgment, decree, or order, including approval of a property settlement agreement, that would be described in § 206 (d) (3) (B) of ERISA if the retirement plan were subject to ERISA.

"Annual benefit" means an amount payable as an annuity for the lifetime of the individual who claims the exemption provided under this section, assuming that annuity payments will commence upon the individual's attainment of age sixty-five or, if the individual attained age sixty-five on or before the exemption provided under this section is claimed, the individual's age on the date that the exemption is claimed.

"Retirement plan" means a plan, account, or arrangement that is intended to satisfy the requirements of United States Internal Revenue Code §§ 401, 403 (a), 403 (b), 408, 408 A, 409 (as in effect prior to repeal by United States P.L. 98-369), or § 457. Whether a plan, account, or arrangement is intended to satisfy the requirements of one of the foregoing provisions shall be determined based on all of the relevant facts and circumstances including, but not limited to, the issuance of a favorable determination letter by the United States Internal Revenue Service, reports or returns filed with United States or state agencies, and communications from the plan sponsor to participants.

B. Except as otherwise provided in this section, the interest of an individual under a retirement plan shall be exempt from creditor process to the same extent permitted under federal bankruptcy law for such a plan. The exemption provided by this section shall be available whether such individual has an interest in the retirement plan as a participant, beneficiary, contingent annuitant, alternate payee, or otherwise.

C. The exemption provided under subsection B shall not apply to claims made against an individual by the alternate payee of such individual or to claims made against such individual by the Commonwealth in administrative actions pursuant to Chapter 19 (§ 63.2-1900 et seq.) of Title 63.2 or any court process to enforce a child or child and spousal support obligation.

D. If two individuals who are married or were married are entitled to claim the exemption provided under subsection B of an interest under the same retirement plan or plans and such individuals are jointly subject to creditor process as to the same debt or obligation and the debt or obligation arose during the marriage, then the exemption provided under subsection B as to such debts or obligations shall not exceed, in the aggregate, the exemption permitted under federal bankruptcy law for such a plan. The exemption permitted under federal bankruptcy law shall be allocated among such persons in the same proportion as their respective interests in the retirement plan or plans.

E. The exemption provided under this section must be claimed within the time limits prescribed by § 34-17. (1990, c. 425; 1992, c. 716; 1996, c. 330; 1999, cc. 766, 796; 2005, c. 284; 2007, c. 302.)

The 2007 amendments. — The 2007 amendment by c. 302 rewrote the section.

Title 46.2.
Motor Vehicles.

SUBTITLE I.
GENERAL PROVISIONS; DEPARTMENT OF MOTOR VEHICLES.

CHAPTER 1.
GENERAL PROVISIONS.

Sec.
46.2-100. Definitions.

§ 46.2-100. Definitions. — The following words and phrases when used in this title shall, for the purpose of this title, have the meanings respectively ascribed to them in this section except in those instances where the context clearly indicates a different meaning:

"All-terrain vehicle" means a three-wheeled or four-wheeled motor vehicle powered by a gasoline or diesel engine and generally characterized by large, low-pressure tires, a seat designed to be straddled by the operator, and handlebars for steering that is intended for off-road use by an individual rider on various types of unpaved terrain. The term does not include four-wheeled vehicles, commonly known as "go-carts," that have low centers of gravity and are typically used in racing on relatively level surfaces, nor does the term include any "utility vehicle" as defined in this section or any "farm utility vehicle" as defined in this section.

"Antique motor vehicle" means every motor vehicle, as defined in this section, which was actually manufactured or designated by the manufacturer as a model manufactured in a calendar year not less than 25 years prior to January 1 of each calendar year and is owned solely as a collector's item.

"Antique trailer" means every trailer or semi-trailer, as defined in this section, that was actually manufactured or designated by the manufacturer as a model manufactured in a calendar year not less than 25 years prior to January 1 of each calendar year and is owned solely as a collector's item.

"Automobile or watercraft transporters" means any tractor truck, lowboy, vehicle, or combination, including vehicles or combinations that transport motor vehicles or watercraft on their power unit, designed and used exclusively for the transportation of motor vehicles or watercraft.

"Bicycle" means a device propelled solely by human power, upon which a person may ride either on or astride a regular seat attached thereto, having two or more wheels in tandem, including children's bicycles, except a toy vehicle intended for use by

young children. For purposes of Chapter 8 (§ 46.2-800 et seq.) of this title, a bicycle shall be a vehicle while operated on the highway.

"*Bicycle lane*" means that portion of a roadway designated by signs and/or pavement markings for the preferential use of bicycles, electric power-assisted bicycles, and mopeds.

"*Business district*" means the territory contiguous to a highway where 75 percent or more of the property contiguous to a highway, on either side of the highway, for a distance of 300 feet or more along the highway, is occupied by land and buildings actually in use for business purposes.

"*Camping trailer*" means every vehicle that has collapsible sides and contains sleeping quarters but may or may not contain bathing and cooking facilities and is designed to be drawn by a motor vehicle.

"*Cancel*" or "*cancellation*" means that the document or privilege cancelled has been annulled or terminated because of some error, defect, or ineligibility, but the cancellation is without prejudice and reapplication may be made at any time after cancellation.

"*Chauffeur*" means every person employed for the principal purpose of driving a motor vehicle and every person who drives a motor vehicle while in use as a public or common carrier of persons or property.

"*Commission*" means the State Corporation Commission.

"*Commissioner*" means the Commissioner of the Department of Motor Vehicles of the Commonwealth.

"*Crosswalk*" means that part of a roadway at an intersection included within the connections of the lateral lines of the sidewalks on opposite sides of the highway measured from the curbs or, in the absence of curbs, from the edges of the traversable roadway; or any portion of a roadway at an intersection or elsewhere distinctly indicated for pedestrian crossing by lines or other markings on the surface.

"*Decal*" means a device to be attached to a license plate that validates the license plate for a predetermined registration period.

"*Department*" means the Department of Motor Vehicles of the Commonwealth.

"*Disabled parking license plate*" means a license plate that displays the international symbol of access in the same size as the numbers and letters on the plate and in a color that contrasts with the background.

"*Disabled veteran*" means a veteran who (i) has either lost, or lost the use of, a leg, arm, or hand; (ii) is blind; or (iii) is permanently and totally disabled as certified by the U.S. Veterans Administration. A veteran shall be considered blind if he has a permanent impairment of both eyes to the following extent: (i) central visual acuity of 20/200 or less in the better eye, with corrective lenses, or central visual acuity of more than 20/200, if there is a field defect in which the peripheral field has contracted to such an extent that the widest diameter of visual field subtends an angular distance no greater than 20 degrees in the better eye.

"*Driver's license*" means any license, including a commercial driver's license as defined in the Virginia Commercial Driver's License Act (§ 46.2-341.1 et seq.), issued under the laws of the Commonwealth authorizing the operation of a motor vehicle.

"*Electric personal assistive mobility device*" means a self-balancing two-nontandem-wheeled device that is designed to transport only one person and powered by an electric propulsion system that limits the device's maximum speed to 15 miles per hour or less. For purposes of Chapter 8 of this title, an electric personal assistive mobility device shall be a vehicle when operated on a highway.

"*Electric power-assisted bicycle*" means a vehicle that travels on not more than three wheels in contact with the ground and is equipped with (i) pedals that allow propulsion by human power and (ii) an electric motor with an input of no more than 1,000 watts that reduces the pedal effort required of the rider. For the purposes of Chapter 8 of this title, an electric power-assisted bicycle shall be a vehicle when operated on a highway.

"*Essential parts*" means all integral parts and body parts, the removal, alteration, or substitution of which will tend to conceal the identity of a vehicle.

"*Farm tractor*" means every motor vehicle designed and used as a farm, agricultural, or horticultural implement for drawing plows, mowing machines, and other farm, agricultural, or horticultural machinery and implements including self-propelled mowers designed and used for mowing lawns.

"*Farm utility vehicle*" means a vehicle that is designed for off-road use and is used as a farm, agricultural, or horticultural service vehicle, generally having a gasoline or diesel engine, four or more wheels, bench seating for the operator and a passenger, a steering wheel for control, and a cargo bed. "Farm utility vehicle" does not include pickup or panel trucks, golf carts, low-speed vehicles, riding lawn mowers, or all-terrain vehicles.

"*Federal safety requirements*" means applicable provisions of 49 U.S.C. § 30101 et seq. and all administrative regulations and policies adopted pursuant thereto.

"*Financial responsibility*" means the ability to respond in damages for liability thereafter incurred arising out of the ownership, maintenance, use, or operation of a motor vehicle, in the amounts provided for in § 46.2-472.

"*Foreign market vehicle*" means any motor vehicle originally manufactured outside the United States, which was not manufactured in accordance with 49 U.S.C. § 30101 et seq. and the policies and regulations adopted pursuant to that Act, and for which a Virginia title or registration is sought.

"*Foreign vehicle*" means every motor vehicle, trailer, or semitrailer that is brought into the Commonwealth otherwise than in the ordinary course of business by or through a manufacturer or dealer and that has not been registered in the Commonwealth.

"*Golf cart*" means a self-propelled vehicle that is designed to transport persons playing golf and their equipment on a golf course.

"*Governing body*" means the board of supervisors of a county, council of a city, or council of a town, as context may require.

"*Gross weight*" means the aggregate weight of a vehicle or combination of vehicles and the load thereon.

"*Highway*" means the entire width between the boundary lines of every way or place open to the use of the public for purposes of vehicular travel in the Commonwealth, including the streets and alleys, and, for law-enforcement purposes, (i) the entire width between the boundary lines of all private roads or private streets that have been specifically designated "highways" by an ordinance adopted by the governing body of the county, city, or town in which such private roads or streets are located and (ii) the entire width between the boundary lines of every way or place used for purposes of vehicular travel on any property owned, leased, or controlled by the United States government and located in the Commonwealth.

"*Intersection*" means (i) the area embraced within the prolongation or connection of the lateral curblines or, if none, then the lateral boundary lines of the roadways of two highways that join one another at, or approximately at, right angles, or the area within which vehicles traveling on different highways joining at any other angle may come in conflict; (ii) where a highway includes two roadways 30 feet or more apart, then every crossing of each roadway of such divided highway by an intersecting highway shall be regarded as a separate intersection, in the event such intersecting highway also includes two roadways 30 feet or more apart, then every crossing of two roadways of such highways shall be regarded as a separate intersection; or (iii) for purposes only of authorizing installation of traffic-control devices, every crossing of a highway or street at grade by a pedestrian crosswalk.

"*Law-enforcement officer*" means any officer authorized to direct or regulate traffic or to make arrests for violations of this title or local ordinances authorized by law. For the purposes of access to law-enforcement databases regarding motor vehicle registration and ownership only, this term shall also include city and county commissioners of the revenue and treasurers, together with their duly designated deputies and employees, when such officials are actually engaged in the enforcement of §§ 46.2-752, 46.2-753 and 46.2-754 and local ordinances enacted thereunder.

"*License plate*" means a device containing letters, numerals, or a combination of both, attached to a motor vehicle, trailer, or semitrailer to indicate that the vehicle is properly registered with the Department.

"*Light*" means a device for producing illumination or the illumination produced by the device.

"*Low-speed vehicle*" means any four-wheeled electrically-powered vehicle, except a motor vehicle or low-speed vehicle that is used exclusively for agricultural or horticultural purposes or a golf cart, whose maximum speed is greater than 20 miles per hour but not greater than 25 miles per hour and is manufactured to comply with safety standards contained in Title 49 of the Code of Federal Regulations, § 571.500.

"*Manufactured home*" means a structure subject to federal regulation, transportable in one or more sections, which in the traveling mode is eight body feet or more in width or 40 body feet or more in length, or, when erected on site, is 320 or more square feet, and which is built on a permanent chassis and designed to be used as a dwelling with or without a permanent foundation when connected to the required utilities, and includes the plumbing, heating, air conditioning, and electrical systems contained therein.

"*Moped*" means every vehicle that travels on not more than three wheels in contact with the ground that has (i) a seat that is no less than 24 inches in height, measured from the middle of the seat perpendicular to the ground and (ii) a gasoline, electric, or hybrid motor that displaces less than 50 cubic centimeters. For purposes of Chapter 8 (§ 46.2-800 et seq.) of this title, a moped shall be a vehicle while operated on a highway.

"*Motor-driven cycle*" means every motorcycle that has a gasoline engine that (i) displaces less than 150 cubic centimeters; (ii) has a seat less than 24 inches in height, measured from the middle of the seat perpendicular to the ground; and (iii) has no manufacturer-issued vehicle identification number.

"*Motor home*" means every private motor vehicle with a normal seating capacity of not more than 10 persons, including the driver, designed primarily for use as living quarters for human beings.

"*Motor vehicle*" means every vehicle as defined in this section that is self-propelled or designed for self-propulsion except as otherwise provided in this title. Any structure designed, used, or maintained primarily to be loaded on or affixed to a motor vehicle to provide a mobile dwelling, sleeping place, office, or commercial space shall be considered a part of a motor vehicle. For the purposes of this title, any device herein defined as a bicycle, electric personal assistive mobility device, electric power-assisted bicycle, or moped shall be deemed not to be a motor vehicle.

"*Motorcycle*" means every motor vehicle designed to travel on not more than three wheels in contact with the ground and is capable of traveling at speeds in excess of 35 miles per hour. The term "motorcycle" does not include any "electric personal assistive mobility device," "electric power-assisted bicycle," "farm tractor," "golf cart," "moped," "motorized skateboard or scooter," "utility vehicle" or "wheelchair or wheelchair conveyance" as defined in this section.

"Motorized skateboard or scooter" means every vehicle, regardless of the number of its wheels in contact with the ground, that (i) has no seat, but is designed to be stood upon by the operator, (ii) has no manufacturer-issued vehicle identification number, and (iii) is powered by an electric motor having an input of no more than 1,000 watts or a gasoline engine that displaces less than 36 cubic centimeters. The term "motorized skateboard or scooter" includes vehicles with or without handlebars, but does not include "electric personal assistive mobility devices."

"Nonresident" means every person who is not domiciled in the Commonwealth, except: (i) any foreign corporation that is authorized to do business in the Commonwealth by the State Corporation Commission shall be a resident of the Commonwealth for the purpose of this title; in the case of corporations incorporated in the Commonwealth but doing business outside the Commonwealth, only such principal place of business or branches located within the Commonwealth shall be dealt with as residents of the Commonwealth; (ii) a person who becomes engaged in a gainful occupation in the Commonwealth for a period exceeding 60 days shall be a resident for the purposes of this title except for the purposes of Chapter 3 (§ 46.2-300 et seq.) of this title; (iii) a person, other than a nonresident student as defined in this section, who has actually resided in the Commonwealth for a period of six months, whether employed or not, or who has registered a motor vehicle, listing an address in the Commonwealth in the application for registration shall be deemed a resident for the purposes of this title, except for the purposes of the Virginia Commercial Driver's License Act (§ 46.2-341.1 et seq.).

"Nonresident student" means every nonresident person who is enrolled as a full-time student in an accredited institution of learning in the Commonwealth and who is not gainfully employed.

"Off-road motorcycle" means every motorcycle designed exclusively for off-road use by an individual rider with not more than two wheels in contact with the ground. Except as otherwise provided in this chapter, for the purposes of this chapter off-road motorcycles shall be deemed to be "motorcycles."

"Operation or use for rent or for hire, for the transportation of passengers, or as a property carrier for compensation," and *"business of transporting persons or property"* mean any owner or operator of any motor vehicle, trailer, or semitrailer operating over the highways in the Commonwealth who accepts or receives compensation for the service, directly or indirectly; but these terms do not mean a "truck lessor" as defined in this section and do not include persons or businesses that receive compensation for delivering a product that they themselves sell or produce, where a separate charge is made for delivery of the product or the cost of delivery is included in the sale price of the product, but where the person or business does not derive all or a substantial portion of its income from the transpor-

tation of persons or property except as part of a sales transaction.

"Operator" or *"driver"* means every person who either (i) drives or is in actual physical control of a motor vehicle on a highway or (ii) is exercising control over or steering a vehicle being towed by a motor vehicle.

"Owner" means a person who holds the legal title to a vehicle; however, if a vehicle is the subject of an agreement for its conditional sale or lease with the right of purchase on performance of the conditions stated in the agreement and with an immediate right of possession vested in the conditional vendee or lessee or if a mortgagor of a vehicle is entitled to possession, then the conditional vendee or lessee or mortgagor shall be the owner for the purpose of this title. In all such instances when the rent paid by the lessee includes charges for services of any nature or when the lease does not provide that title shall pass to the lessee on payment of the rent stipulated, the lessor shall be regarded as the owner of the vehicle, and the vehicle shall be subject to such requirements of this title as are applicable to vehicles operated for compensation. A "truck lessor" as defined in this section shall be regarded as the owner, and his vehicles shall be subject to such requirements of this title as are applicable to vehicles of private carriers.

"Passenger car" means every motor vehicle other than a motorcycle designed and used primarily for the transportation of no more than 10 persons including the driver.

"Payment device" means any credit card as defined in 15 U.S.C. § 1602(k) or any "accepted card or other means of access" set forth in 15 U.S.C. § 1693a(1). For the purposes of this title, this definition shall also include a card that enables a person to pay for transactions through the use of value stored on the card itself.

"Pickup or panel truck" means every motor vehicle designed for the transportation of property and having a registered gross weight of 7,500 pounds or less.

"Private road or driveway" means every way in private ownership and used for vehicular travel by the owner and those having express or implied permission from the owner, but not by other persons.

"Reconstructed vehicle" means every vehicle of a type required to be registered under this title materially altered from its original construction by the removal, addition, or substitution of new or used essential parts. Such vehicles, at the discretion of the Department, shall retain their original vehicle identification number, line-make, and model year.

"Replica vehicle" means every vehicle of a type required to be registered under this title not fully constructed by a licensed manufacturer but either constructed or assembled from components. Such components may be from a single vehicle, multiple vehicles, a kit, parts, or fabricated components. The kit may be made up of "major components" as

defined in § 46.2-1600, a full body, or a full chassis, or a combination of these parts. The vehicle shall resemble a vehicle of distinctive name, line-make, model, or type as produced by a licensed manufacturer or manufacturer no longer in business and is not a reconstructed or specially constructed vehicle as herein defined.

"*Residence district*" means the territory contiguous to a highway, not comprising a business district, where 75 percent or more of the property abutting such highway, on either side of the highway, for a distance of 300 feet or more along the highway consists of land improved for dwelling purposes, or is occupied by dwellings, or consists of land or buildings in use for business purposes, or consists of territory zoned residential or territory in residential subdivisions created under Chapter 22 (§ 15.2-2200 et seq.) of Title 15.2.

"*Revoke*" or "*revocation*" means that the document or privilege revoked is not subject to renewal or restoration except through reapplication after the expiration of the period of revocation.

"*Roadway*" means that portion of a highway improved, designed, or ordinarily used for vehicular travel, exclusive of the shoulder. A highway may include two or more roadways if divided by a physical barrier or barriers or an unpaved area.

"*Safety zone*" means the area officially set apart within a roadway for the exclusive use of pedestrians and that is protected or is so marked or indicated by plainly visible signs.

"*School bus*" means any motor vehicle, other than a station wagon, automobile, truck, or commercial bus, which is: (i) designed and used primarily for the transportation of pupils to and from public, private or religious schools, or used for the transportation of the mentally or physically handicapped to and from a sheltered workshop; (ii) painted yellow and bears the words "School Bus" in black letters of a specified size on front and rear; and (iii) is equipped with warning devices prescribed in § 46.2-1090. A yellow school bus may have a white roof provided such vehicle is painted in accordance with regulations promulgated by the Department of Education.

"*Semitrailer*" means every vehicle of the trailer type so designed and used in conjunction with a motor vehicle that some part of its own weight and that of its own load rests on or is carried by another vehicle.

"*Shared-use path*" means a bikeway that is physically separated from motorized vehicular traffic by an open space or barrier and is located either within the highway right-of-way or within a separate right-of-way. Shared-use paths may also be used by pedestrians, skaters, users of wheel chairs or wheel chair conveyances, joggers, and other nonmotorized users.

"*Shoulder*" means that part of a highway between the portion regularly traveled by vehicular traffic and the lateral curbline or ditch.

"*Sidewalk*" means the portion of a street between the curb lines, or the lateral lines of a roadway, and the adjacent property lines, intended for use by pedestrians.

"*Snowmobile*" means a self-propelled vehicle designed to travel on snow or ice, steered by skis or runners, and supported in whole or in part by one or more skis, belts, or cleats.

"*Specially constructed vehicle*" means any vehicle that was not originally constructed under a distinctive name, make, model, or type by a generally recognized manufacturer of vehicles and not a reconstructed vehicle as herein defined.

"*Stinger-steered automobile or watercraft transporter*" means an automobile or watercraft transporter configured as a semitrailer combination wherein the fifth wheel is located on a drop frame behind and below the rearmost axle of the power unit.

"*Superintendent*" means the Superintendent of the Department of State Police of the Commonwealth.

"*Suspend*" or "*suspension*" means that the document or privilege suspended has been temporarily withdrawn, but may be reinstated following the period of suspension unless it has expired prior to the end of the period of suspension.

"*Tow truck*" means a motor vehicle for hire (i) designed to lift, pull, or carry another vehicle by means of a hoist or other mechanical apparatus and (ii) having a manufacturer's gross vehicle weight rating of at least 10,000 pounds. "Tow truck" also includes vehicles designed with a ramp on wheels and a hydraulic lift with a capacity to haul or tow another vehicle, commonly referred to as "rollbacks." "Tow truck" does not include any "automobile or watercraft transporter," "stinger-steered automobile or watercraft transporter," or "tractor truck" as those terms are defined in this section.

"*Towing and recovery operator*" means a person engaged in the business of (i) removing disabled vehicles, parts of vehicles, their cargoes, and other objects to facilities for repair or safekeeping and (ii) restoring to the highway or other location where they either can be operated or removed to other locations for repair or safekeeping vehicles that have come to rest in places where they cannot be operated.

"*Toy vehicle*" means any motorized or propellant-driven device that has no manufacturer-issued vehicle identification number, that is designed or used to carry any person or persons, on any number of wheels, bearings, glides, blades, runners, or a cushion of air. The term does not include electric personal assistive mobility devices, electric power-assisted bicycles, mopeds, or motorcycles, nor does it include any nonmotorized or nonpropellant-driven devices such as bicycles, roller skates, or skateboards.

"*Tractor truck*" means every motor vehicle designed and used primarily for drawing other vehicles and not so constructed as to carry a load other than a part of the load and weight of the vehicle attached thereto.

"Traffic infraction" means a violation of law punishable as provided in § 46.2-113, which is neither a felony nor a misdemeanor.

"Traffic lane" or *"lane"* means that portion of a roadway designed or designated to accommodate the forward movement of a single line of vehicles.

"Trailer" means every vehicle without motive power designed for carrying property or passengers wholly on its own structure and for being drawn by a motor vehicle, including manufactured homes.

"Truck" means every motor vehicle designed to transport property on its own structure independent of any other vehicle and having a registered gross weight in excess of 7,500 pounds.

"Truck lessor" means a person who holds the legal title to any motor vehicle, trailer, or semitrailer that is the subject of a bona fide written lease for a term of one year or more to another person, provided that: (i) neither the lessor nor the lessee is a common carrier by motor vehicle or restricted common carrier by motor vehicle or contract carrier by motor vehicle as defined in § 46.2-2000; (ii) the leased motor vehicle, trailer, or semitrailer is used exclusively for the transportation of property of the lessee; (iii) the lessor is not employed in any capacity by the lessee; (iv) the operator of the leased motor vehicle is a bona fide employee of the lessee and is not employed in any capacity by the lessor; and (v) a true copy of the lease, verified by affidavit of the lessor, is filed with the Commissioner.

"Utility vehicle" means a motor vehicle that is (i) designed for off-road use, (ii) powered by an engine of no more than 25 horsepower, and (iii) used for general maintenance, security, agricultural, or horticultural purposes. "Utility vehicle" does not include all-terrain vehicles as defined in this section, riding lawn mowers, or any other vehicle whose definition is included in this section.

"Vehicle" means every device in, on or by which any person or property is or may be transported or drawn on a highway, except devices moved by human power or used exclusively on stationary rails or tracks. For the purposes of Chapter 8 (§ 46.2-800 et seq.) of this title, bicycles, electric personal assistive mobility devices, electric power-assisted bicycles, and mopeds shall be vehicles while operated on a highway.

"Wheel chair or wheel chair conveyance" means a chair or seat equipped with wheels, typically used to provide mobility for persons who, by reason of physical disability, are otherwise unable to move about as pedestrians. The term includes both three-wheeled and four-wheeled devices. So long as it is operated only as provided in § 46.2-677, a self-propelled wheel chair or self-propelled wheel chair conveyance shall not be considered a motor vehicle. (Code 1950, §§ 46-1, 46-169, 46-185, 46-186, 46-343; 1954, c. 59; 1958, cc. 501, 541, §§ 46.1-1, 46.1-161; 1964, c. 618; 1966, c. 643; 1968, cc. 285, 641, 653, 685; 1972, cc. 433, 609; 1974, c. 347; 1975, cc. 382, 426; 1976, c. 372; 1977, cc. 252, 585; 1978, cc. 36, 550, 605; 1979, c. 100; 1980, c. 51; 1981, c. 585; 1983, c. 386; 1984, cc. 404, 780; 1985, c. 447; 1986, cc. 72, 613; 1987, c. 151; 1988, cc. 107, 452, 865; 1989, cc. 645, 705, 727; 1990, cc. 45, 418; 1992, c. 98; 1993, c. 133; 1994, c. 866; 1996, cc. 943, 994; 1997, cc. 9, 186, 486, 783, 904; 1998, c. 888; 1999, cc. 67, 77; 2001, c. 834; 2002, cc. 214, 234, 254; 2003, cc. 29, 46; 2004, cc. 746, 796; 2005, cc. 310, 928; 2006, cc. 529, 538, 540, 874, 891, 896; 2007, cc. 209, 325, 366, 393.)

The 2007 amendments. — The 2007 amendments by cc. 209 and 366 are nearly identical, and added the paragraph defining "Toy vehicle."

The 2007 amendments by cc. 325 and 393 are identical, and added the last sentence to "Reconstructed vehicle"; and inserted the definition of "Replica vehicle."

CASE NOTES

I. General Consideration.
VI. Highway.

I. GENERAL CONSIDERATION.

Applied in McDuffie v. Commonwealth, 49 Va. App. 170, 638 S.E.2d 139, 2006 Va. App. LEXIS 573 (2006).

VI. HIGHWAY.

Military base road was held to be a highway. — Where defendant's vehicle struck a barricade near a military base's gate, defendant's conviction for operating a motor vehicle on a Virginia highway after having been determined an habitual offender was upheld because the road within the base was a highway since members of the public were free to drive on the roads, provided they met the conditions posted on the roadway signs prior to entry. United States v. Scott, — F.3d —, 2006 U.S. App. LEXIS 16899 (4th Cir. July 6, 2006).

Stretch of road between a naval base gate and a drive was open to the public's use for the purposes of vehicular travel and was thus a "highway" under § 46.2-100; thus, defendant's conviction under the Assimilative Crimes Act for driving a motor vehicle on a Virginia highway with a suspended or revoked license was affirmed. United States v. Hill, 473 F.3d 112, 2007 U.S. App. LEXIS 451 (4th Cir. 2007).

United States Marine Corps base road was a highway, because the road was open to the public for purposes of vehicular traffic, there was a town within the base, and the requirement that base visitors produce a valid operator's license, registration, and proof of insurance was a minimal restriction that did not render the base roads inaccessible to public use. United States v. Daniels, 471 F. Supp. 2d 634, 2007 U.S. Dist. LEXIS 5824 (E.D. Va. 2007).

Road leading to the entrance of a federal facility. — Road leading to the entrance to a federal facility, which was open to the use of the public upon inspection of identification, and which was not limited to business invitees of the federal government, was open to the use of the public, and thus, an indictment charging defendant with operating a motor vehicle on a highway while her driving privileges were suspended and of operating a motor vehicle on a highway without a valid operator's license was erroneously dismissed. United States v. Spencer, 422 F. Supp. 2d 589, 2005 U.S. Dist. LEXIS 41423 (E.D. Va. July 26, 2005).

Classification of parking lots.

By defining "highway" to include private parking areas at residential developments containing 100 or more lots or residential dwelling units, a county expanded the scope of the limited authority granted to it by § 46.2-1307, because a "residential dwelling unit" was not necessarily equivalent to a "lot." While an apartment building might be located on a "lot," the living units within that building were not themselves "lots." Eberth v. County of Prince William, 49 Va. App. 105, 637 S.E.2d 338, 2006 Va. App. LEXIS 545 (2006).

CIRCUIT COURT OPINIONS

Residency. — Because defendant, who had an Oregon commercial driver's license, had actually resided in Virginia for a period of six months, the defendant could either drive commercial vehicles only or obtain a Virginia operator license in order to drive noncommercial vehicles in the state. Commonwealth v. Meierotto, 69 Va. Cir. 493, 2006 Va. Cir. LEXIS 84 (Northampton County 2006).

CHAPTER 2.

DEPARTMENT OF MOTOR VEHICLES.

Article 1.

Powers and Duties of Department, Generally.

Sec.
46.2-206.1. (Contingent expiration date — see Editor's note) Imposition of certain additional fees on certain drivers.

ARTICLE 1.

Powers and Duties of Department, Generally.

§ 46.2-206.1. (Contingent expiration date — see Editor's note) Imposition of certain additional fees on certain drivers. — A. The purpose of the civil remedial fees imposed in this section is to generate revenue from drivers whose proven dangerous driving behavior places significant financial burdens upon the Commonwealth. The civil remedial fees established by this section shall be in addition to any other fees, costs, or penalties imposed pursuant to the Code of Virginia.

B. The civil remedial fees established by this section shall be assessed on any resident of Virginia operating a motor vehicle on the highways of Virginia, including persons to whom Virginia driver's licenses, commercial driver's licenses, or learner's permits have been issued pursuant to this title; and persons operating motor vehicles without licenses or whose license has been revoked or suspended.

C. The court shall assess a person with the following fees upon each conviction of the following offenses:

1. Driving while his driver's license was suspended or revoked pursuant to § 18.2-272, 46.2-301, 46.2-302, 46.2-341.21, or 46.2-391 shall be assessed a fee to be paid in three annual payments of $250 each;

2. Reckless driving in violation of Article 7 (§ 46.2-852 et seq.) of Chapter 8 or aggressive driving in violation of § 46.2-868.1 shall be assessed a fee to be paid in three annual payments of $350 each;

3. Driving while intoxicated in violation of § 18.2-266, 18.2-266.1, or 46.2-341.24 shall be assessed a fee to be paid in three annual payments of $750 each;

4. Any other misdemeanor conviction for a driving and/or motor vehicle related violation of Title 18.2 or this title that is not included in one of the preceding three subdivisions shall be assessed a fee to be paid in three annual payments of $300 each; and

5. Any felony conviction for a driving or motor vehicle-related offense under Title 18.2 or this title, shall be assessed a fee to be paid in three annual payments of $1,000 each.

D. For the purposes of subsection C:

1. A finding of guilty in the case of a juvenile and a conviction under a substantially similar valid local ordinance of any locality of the Commonwealth, shall be a conviction.

2. The fees assessed under subsection C shall be implemented in a manner whereby no convictions for offenses committed prior to July 1, 2007, shall be considered.

E. The court shall collect, in full, the first annual payment of the fee imposed under subsection C at the time of conviction and shall order the person assessed a fee to submit the second annual payment to the Department within 14 calendar months of the date of conviction and the third annual payment to the Department within 26 months of the date of conviction. When transmitting conviction information to the Department the court shall also transmit notice that a fee has been imposed under this section and the deadline upon which the second and third annual payments must be submitted to the Department. The court shall order suspension of the driver's license or privilege to drive a motor vehicle in Virginia as provided in § 46.2-395 of any person failing to pay the first annual payment of the fee assessed under subsection C.

F. For all convictions reported to the Department for which fees are established under subsection C, the person assessed the fee shall submit the second annual payment to the Commissioner within 14 calendar months of the date of conviction and the third annual payment within 26 months of the date of conviction. The Commissioner, or his designee, shall establish guidelines, policies, or procedures to notify every person assessed a fee pursuant to subsection C of the second and the third annual payments. If the person fails to make such payment, the Commissioner shall suspend his driver's license or privilege to operate a motor vehicle in Virginia. No license shall be reissued or reinstated until all fees assessed pursuant to this section have been paid and all other reinstatement requirements as provided in this title have been satisfied.

G. In addition to any fees set forth in subsection C, any person whose driver's record with the Department shows a balance of eight or more driver demerit points on July 15 shall be assessed a fee of $100 plus $75 for each demerit point in excess of eight, but not greater than $700, provided that only those demerit points attributable to offenses which occurred on or after July 1, 2007 shall be used to calculate and assess such fees.

H. The Commissioner, or his designee, shall assess the fees set forth in subsection G annually, beginning on July 15, 2007.

I. The Commissioner, or his designee, shall establish guidelines, policies, or procedures to notify every person assessed a fee pursuant to subsection G. If any assessment made under subsection G remains unpaid 60 days following the date on which the notice of assessment was mailed, the Commissioner shall suspend the driver's license or privilege to drive a motor vehicle in Virginia of the person against whom the assessment was imposed. No license shall be reissued or reinstated until all fees assessed pursuant to this section have been paid and all other reinstatement requirements as provided in this title have been satisfied.

J. In the event that a person disputes a conviction on his driver's record based upon identity, if the person presents the Department a certified copy of a petition to a court of competent jurisdiction seeking to vacate an order of such conviction, the Department shall suspend the imposition of the assessment. Such suspension shall be valid for one year from the date of the commencement or until 30 days after an entry of a final order on such petition, whichever occurs first.

K. Funds collected through the imposition of the fees as provided for in this section shall be used to pay the Department's cost in imposing and collecting such assessments as provided in the general appropriation act, and any remainder shall be deposited into the Highway Maintenance and Operating Fund. (2007, c. 896.)

Editor's note. — Acts 2007, c. 896, cl. 3, provides: "That the revenues generated by the provisions of this act shall not be used to calculate or reduce the share of local, federal, and state revenues otherwise available to participating jurisdictions. Further, such revenues and moneys shall not be included in any computation of, or formula for, a locality's ability to pay for public education, upon which appropriations of state revenues to local governments for public education are determined."

Acts 2007, c. 896, cl. 11, provides: "That the fees collected pursuant to § 46.2-206.1 in the fiscal year ending June 30, 2008, shall be deposited and held in a special fund in the state treasury and transferred on August 15, 2008, to the Highway Maintenance and Operating Fund."

Acts 2007, c. 896, cl. 17, provides: "That the Department of Motor Vehicles shall work with the appropriate state agencies to develop guidelines, policies, and procedures for the efficient and effective collection and administration of the fees set forth under § 46.2-206.1 of the Code of Virginia. The guidelines, policies, and procedures shall be made public at least 60 days before their implementation. The development of the guidelines, policies, and procedures shall be exempt from the Administrative Process Act (§ 2.2-4000 et seq. of the Code of Virginia)."

Acts 2007, c. 896, cl. 21, provides: "That the revenue generated by this act shall be used solely for transportation purposes."

Acts 2007, c. 896, cl. 22, provides: "That the provisions of this act which generate additional revenue for the Transportation Trust Fund, established under § 33.1-23.03:1 of the Code of Virginia, or the Highway Maintenance and Operating Fund shall expire on December 31 of any year in which the General Assembly appropriates any of the revenues designated under general law to the Highway Maintenance and Operating Fund or the Transportation Trust Fund for any non-transportation related purpose."

Acts 2007, c. 896, cl. 23 contains a severability clause.

SUBTITLE II.
TITLING, REGISTRATION AND LICENSURE.

CHAPTER 6.
TITLING AND REGISTRATION OF MOTOR VEHICLES.

Article 2.
Titling Vehicles.

Sec.
46.2-625. Specially constructed, reconstructed, replica, or foreign vehicles.
46.2-629. Odometer reading to be reported on certificate of title, application, or power of attorney.

Article 7.
Fees for Registration.

46.2-694. (Contingent expiration date — see Editor's note) Fees for vehicles designed and used for transportation of passengers; weights used for computing fees; burden of proof.
46.2-694.1. (Contingent expiration date — see Editor's note) Fees for trailers and semitrailers not designed and used for transportation of passengers.
46.2-697. (Contingent expiration date — see Editor's note) Fees for vehicles not designed or used for transportation of passengers.
46.2-702.1. (Contingent expiration — see Editor's note) Distribution of certain revenue.

Article 10.
Special License Plates.

46.2-739. Special license plates for certain disabled veterans; fees.

Article 11.
State and Local Motor Vehicle Registration.

46.2-752. Taxes and license fees imposed by counties, cities, and towns; limitations on amounts; disposition of revenues; requiring evidence of payment of personal property taxes and certain fines; prohibiting display of licenses after expiration; failure to display valid local license required by other localities; penalty.

ARTICLE 2.
Titling Vehicles.

§ 46.2-625. Specially constructed, reconstructed, replica, or foreign vehicles. — If a vehicle for which the registration or a certificate of title is applied is a specially constructed, reconstructed, replica, or foreign vehicle, the fact shall be stated in the application and, in the case of any foreign vehicle registered outside the Commonwealth, the owner shall present to the Department the certificate of title and registration card or other evidence of registration as he may have. The Commissioner may require such other evidence of ownership as he may deem advisable and promulgate regulations establishing what additional evidence of ownership, if any, shall be required for titling and registration of specially constructed, reconstructed, replica, or foreign vehicles. All titles and registrations for specially constructed, reconstructed, and replica vehicles shall be branded with the words "specially constructed," "reconstructed," or "replica" as appropriate. (Code 1950, § 46-51; 1958, c. 541, § 46.1-53; 1970, c. 632; 1989, c. 727; 2007, cc. 325, 393.)

The 2007 amendments. — The 2007 amendments by cc. 325 and 393 are identical, and inserted "replica," in the first two sentences and added the last sentence to this section.

§ 46.2-629. Odometer reading to be reported on certificate of title, application, or power of attorney.

— A. Every owner or transferor of any motor vehicle, including a dealer, shall, at the time of transfer of ownership of any motor vehicle by him, record on the certificate of title, if one is currently issued on the vehicle in the Commonwealth, and on any application for certificate of title the reading on the odometer or similar device plus any known additional distance traveled not shown by the odometer or similar device of the motor vehicle at the time of transfer. If, however, a transferor gives his power of attorney to a dealer or other person for the purpose of assigning the transferor's interest in a motor vehicle, the transferor shall conspicuously record on the power of attorney the reading on the odometer or similar device at the time of the assignment.

B. The Department shall not issue to any transferee any new certificate of title to a motor vehicle unless subsection A of this section has been complied with.

C. It shall be unlawful for any person knowingly to record an incorrect odometer or similar device reading plus any known additional distance not shown by the odometer or similar device on any certificate of title or application for a title, or on any power of attorney as described in subsection A of this section.

D. Notwithstanding other provisions of this section, an owner or transferor, including a dealer, of any of the following types of motor vehicles need not disclose the vehicle's odometer reading:

1. Vehicles having gross vehicle weight ratings of more than 16,000 pounds; and

2. Vehicles that were manufactured for a model year at least 10 years earlier than the calendar year in which the sale or transfer occurs and were previously exempt from recording an odometer reading on the certificate of title in another state, provided that the Department shall brand the titles of all such vehicles to indicate this exemption.

E. Violation of this section shall constitute a Class 1 misdemeanor.

F. The provisions of subsections A and B of this section shall not apply to transfers under § 46.2-633.

G. This section shall not apply to transfers or application for certificates of title of all-terrain vehicles or off-road motorcycles as defined in § 46.2-100. (1972, c. 851, § 46.1-89.1; 1978, c. 294; 1986, c. 490; 1989, c. 727; 2004, c. 724; 2006, c. 896; 2007, c. 225.)

The 2007 amendments. — The 2007 amendment by c. 225 rewrote subsection D, to add subdivision D 2.

ARTICLE 6.

Exemptions from Registration.

§ 46.2-665. Vehicles used for agricultural or horticultural purposes.

CIRCUIT COURT OPINIONS

Farm tractor was exempt from registration. — Although an insured's nephew was driving a tractor on a highway when an accident occurred, and vehicles used for agricultural and horticultural purposes that are driven over highways are not exempt from registration under § 46.2-665, the tractor was covered under a homeowner's insurance policy that covered farm vehicles not subject to registration for purposes of a suit arising out of the accident; the tractor only traveled on the highway when moving between tracts of land, and § 46.2-667, which specifically governed farming tractors, provided that tractors that used public highways solely to travel between tracts of land did not have to be registered. Erie Ins. Exch. v. Young, 69 Va. Cir. 34, 2005 Va. Cir. LEXIS 361 (Warren County 2005).

§ 46.2-667. Farm machinery and tractors.

CIRCUIT COURT OPINIONS

Tractor operated between tracts of land was exempt. — Although an insured's nephew was driving a tractor on a highway when an accident occurred, and vehicles used for agricultural and horticultural purposes that are driven over highways are not exempt from registration under § 46.2-665, the tractor was covered under a homeowner's insurance policy that covered farm vehicles not subject to registration for purposes of a suit arising out of the accident; the tractor only traveled on the highway when moving between tracts of land, and § 46.2-667, which specifically governed farming tractors, provided that tractors that used public highways solely to travel between tracts of land did not have to be registered. Erie Ins. Exch. v. Young, 69 Va. Cir. 34, 2005 Va. Cir. LEXIS 361 (Warren County 2005).

ARTICLE 7.

Fees for Registration.

§ 46.2-685. Payment of fees into special fund.

Editor's note. — Acts 2006, Sp. Sess. I, c. 3, as amended by Acts 2007, c. 847, effective for the biennium ending June 30, 2008, in § 3-6.02 A, provides: "Notwithstanding the provisions of Article 7, Chapter 6, Title 46.2, Code of Virginia the Department of Motor Vehicles shall transfer to the general fund $1,725,000 on or before June 30, 2007 the additional medical services revenue which shall be distributed in accordance with Chapter 794, Acts of Assembly of 2002."

§ 46.2-694. (Contingent expiration date — see Editor's note) Fees for vehicles designed and used for transportation of passengers; weights used for computing fees; burden of proof. — A. The annual registration fees for motor vehicles, trailers, and semitrailers designed and used for the transportation of passengers on the highways in the Commonwealth are:

1. Thirty-three dollars for each private passenger car or motor home if the passenger car or motor home weighs 4,000 pounds or less, provided that it is not used for the transportation of passengers for compensation and is not kept or used for rent or for hire, or is not operated under a lease without a chauffeur.

2. Thirty-eight dollars for each passenger car or motor home which weighs more than 4,000 pounds, provided that it is not used for the transportation of passengers for compensation and is not kept or used for rent or for hire, or is not operated under a lease without a chauffeur.

3. Thirty cents per 100 pounds or major fraction thereof for a private motor vehicle other than a motorcycle with a normal seating capacity of more than 10 adults including the driver if the private motor vehicle is not used for the transportation of passengers for compensation and is not kept or used for rent or for hire or is not operated under a lease without a chauffeur. In no case shall the fee be less than $23 if the vehicle weighs 4,000 pounds or less or $28 if the vehicle weighs more than 4,000 pounds.

4. Thirty cents per 100 pounds or major fraction thereof for a school bus. In no case shall the fee be less than $23 if the vehicle weighs 4,000 pounds or less or $28 if the vehicle weighs more than 4,000 pounds.

5. Twenty-three dollars for each trailer or semitrailer designed for use as living quarters for human beings.

6. Thirteen dollars plus $ 0.30 per 100 pounds or major fraction thereof for each motor vehicle, trailer, or semitrailer used as a common carrier of passengers, operating either intrastate or interstate. Interstate common carriers of interstate passengers may elect to be licensed and pay the fees prescribed in subdivision 7 of this subsection on submission to the Commissioner of a declaration of operations and equipment as he may prescribe. An additional $5 shall be charged if the motor vehicle weighs more than 4,000 pounds.

7. Thirteen dollars plus $ 0.70 per 100 pounds or major fraction thereof for each motor vehicle, trailer, or semitrailer used as a common carrier of interstate passengers if election is made to be licensed under this subsection. An additional $5 shall be charged if the motor vehicle weighs more than 4,000 pounds. In lieu of the foregoing fee of $ 0.70 per 100 pounds, a motor carrier of passengers, operating two or more vehicles both within and outside the Commonwealth and registered for insurance purposes with the Surface Transportation Board of the United States Department of Transportation, Federal Highway Administration, may apply to the Commissioner for prorated registration. Upon the filing of such application, in such form as the Commissioner may prescribe, the Commissioner shall apportion the registration fees provided in this subsection so that the total registration fees to be paid for such vehicles of such carrier shall be that proportion of the total fees, if there were no apportionment, that the total number of miles traveled by such vehicles of such carrier within the Commonwealth bears to the total number of miles traveled by such vehicles within and outside the Commonwealth. Such total mileage in each instance is the estimated total mileage to be traveled by such vehicles during the license year for which such fees are paid, subject to the adjustment in accordance with an audit to be made by representatives of the Commissioner at the end of such license year, the expense of such audit to be borne by the carrier being audited. Each vehicle passing into or through Virginia shall be registered and licensed in Virginia and the annual registration fee to be paid for each such vehicle shall not be less than $33. For the purpose of determining such apportioned registration fees, only those motor vehicles, trailers, or semitrailers operated both within and outside the Commonwealth shall be subject to inclusion in determining the apportionment provided for herein.

8. Thirteen dollars plus $ 0.80 per 100 pounds or major fraction thereof for each motor vehicle, trailer or semitrailer kept or used for rent or for hire or operated under a lease without a chauffeur for the transportation of passengers. An additional fee of $5 shall be charged if the vehicle weighs more than 4,000 pounds. This subsection does not apply to vehicles used as common carriers.

9. Twenty-three dollars for a taxicab or other vehicle which is kept for rent or hire operated with a chauffeur for the transportation of passengers, and which operates or should operate under permits issued by the Department as required by law. An additional fee of $5 shall be charged if the vehicle weighs more than 4,000 pounds. This subsection does not apply to vehicles used as common carriers.

10. Eighteen dollars for a motorcycle, with or without a sidecar. To this fee shall be added a surcharge of $3 which shall be distributed as provided in § 46.2-1191.

11. Twenty-three dollars for a bus used exclusively for transportation to and from church school, for the purpose of religious instruction, or church, for the purpose of divine worship. If the empty weight of the vehicle exceeds 4,000 pounds, the fee shall be $28.

12. Thirteen dollars plus $ 0.70 per 100 pounds or major fraction thereof for other passenger-carrying vehicles.

13. An additional fee of $4 per year shall be charged and collected at the time of registration of each pickup or panel truck and each motor vehicle under subdivisions 1 through 12 of this subsection.

All funds collected pursuant to this subdivision shall be paid into the state treasury and shall be set aside as a special fund to be used only for emergency medical service purposes. The moneys in the special fund shall be distributed as follows:

a. Two percent shall be distributed to the State Department of Health to provide funding to the Virginia Association of Volunteer Rescue Squads to be used solely for the purpose of conducting volunteer recruitment, retention and training activities;

b. Thirty percent shall be distributed to the State Department of Health to support (i) emergency medical services training programs (excluding advanced life support classes); (ii) advanced life support training; (iii) recruitment and retention programs (all funds for such support shall be used to recruit and retain volunteer emergency medical services personnel only, including public awareness campaigns, technical assistance programs, and similar activities); (iv) emergency medical services system development, initiatives, and priorities based on needs identified by the State Emergency Medical Services Advisory Board; (v) local, regional, and statewide performance contracts for emergency medical services to meet the objectives stipulated in § 32.1-111.3; (vi) technology and radio communication enhancements; and (vii) improved emergency preparedness and response. Any funds set aside for distribution under this provision and remaining undistributed at the end of any fiscal year shall revert to the Rescue Squad Assistance Fund;

c. Thirty-two percent shall be distributed to the Rescue Squad Assistance Fund;

d. Ten percent shall be available to the State Department of Health's Office of Emergency Medical Services for use in emergency medical services; and

e. Twenty-six percent shall be returned by the Comptroller to the locality wherein such vehicle is registered, to provide funding for training of volunteer or salaried emergency medical service personnel of licensed, nonprofit emergency medical services agencies and for the purchase of necessary equipment and supplies for use in such locality for licensed, nonprofit emergency medical and rescue services.

The Comptroller shall clearly designate on the warrant, check, or other means of transmitting these funds that such moneys are only to be used for purposes set forth in this subdivision. Such funds shall be in addition to any local appropriations and local governing bodies shall not use these funds to supplant local funds. Each local governing body shall report annually to the Board of Health on the use of the funds returned to it pursuant to this section. In any case in which the local governing body grants the funds to a regional emergency medical services council to be distributed to the licensed, nonprofit emergency medical and rescue services, the local governing body shall remain responsible for the proper use of the funds. If, at the end of any fiscal year, a report on the use of the funds

returned to the locality pursuant to this section for that year has not been received from a local governing body, any funds due to that local governing body for the next fiscal year shall be retained until such time as the report has been submitted to the Board.

B. All motor vehicles, trailers, and semitrailers registered as provided in subsection B of § 46.2-646 shall pay a registration fee equal to one-twelfth of all fees required by subsection A of this section or § 46.2-697 for such motor vehicle, trailer, or semitrailer, computed to the nearest cent, multiplied by the number of months in the registration period for such motor vehicles, trailers, and semitrailers.

C. The manufacturer's shipping weight or scale weight shall be used for computing all fees required by this section to be based upon the weight of the vehicle.

D. The applicant for registration bears the burden of proof that the vehicle for which registration is sought is entitled by weight, design, and use to be registered at the fee tendered by the applicant to the Commissioner or to his authorized agent. (Code 1950, §§ 46-154 through 46-156, 46-158.1, 46-159, 46-163.1, 46-166.1; 1950, p. 621; 1952, cc. 224, 418; 1956, cc. 132, 597, 705; 1958, c. 541, § 46.1-149; 1960, c. 243; 1964, c. 218; 1972, c. 609; 1974, c. 170; 1978, c. 708; 1980, c. 25; 1982, c. 671; 1983, c. 566; 1984, cc. 476, 545; 1985, c. 333; 1986, Sp. Sess., c. 11; 1988, cc. 701, 704; 1989, c. 727; 1990, c. 508; 1991, c. 472; 1994, c. 279; 1997, c. 283; 2002, c. 794; 2004, c. 194; 2005, c. 928; 2007, c. 896.)

The section above is effective until December 31 of any year revenues designated for the Highway Maintenance and Operating Fund or the Transportation Trust Fund are appropriated for any non-transportation related purposes. For this section effective until that time, see the section as set out in the 2006 Edition.

Editor's note. — Acts 2006, Sp. Sess. I, c. 3, as amended by Acts 2007, c. 847, effective for the biennium ending June 30, 2008, in Item 286 B, provides: "Distributions made under § 46.2-694 A 13 b (iii), Code of Virginia, shall be made only to nonprofit emergency medical services organizations."

Acts 2007, c. 896, cl. 3, provides: "That the revenues generated by the provisions of this act shall not be used to calculate or reduce the share of local, federal, and state revenues otherwise available to participating jurisdictions. Further, such revenues and moneys shall not be included in any computation of, or formula for, a locality's ability to pay for public education, upon which appropriations of state revenues to local governments for public education are determined."

Acts 2007, c. 896, cl. 21, provides: "That the revenue generated by this act shall be used solely for transportation purposes."

Acts 2007, c. 896, cl. 22, provides: "That the provisions of this act which generate additional revenue for the Transportation Trust Fund, established under § 33.1-23.03:1 of the Code of Virginia, or the Highway Maintenance and Operating Fund shall expire on December 31 of any year in which the General Assembly appropriates any of the revenues designated under general law to the Highway Maintenance and Operating Fund or the Transportation Trust Fund for any non-transportation related purpose."

Acts 2007, c. 896, cl. 23 contains a severability clause.

The 2007 amendments. — The 2007 amendment by c. 896 substituted "Thirty-three dollars" for "Twenty-three dollars" at the beginning of subdivision A 1 and "Thirty-eight dollars" for "Twenty-eight dollars" at the beginning of subdivision A 2. For contingent expiration, see Editor's note.

§ 46.2-694.1. (Contingent expiration date — see Editor's note) Fees for trailers and semi-

trailers not designed and used for transportation of passengers. — Unless otherwise specified in this title, the registration fees for trailers and semitrailers not designed and used for the transportation of passengers on the highways in the Commonwealth shall be as follows:

Registered Gross Weight	1-Year Fee	2-Year Fee	Permanent Fee
0-1,500 lbs	$18.00	$36.00	$70.00
1,501-4,000 lbs	$28.50	$57.00	$75.00
4,001 lbs & above	$40.00	$80.00	$100.00

From the foregoing registration fees, the following amounts, regardless of weight category, shall be paid by the Department into the state treasury and set aside for the payment of the administrative costs of the safety inspection program provided for in Article 21 (§ 46.2-1157 et seq.) of Chapter 10 of this title: (i) from each one-year registration fee, one dollar and fifty cents; (ii) from each two-year registration fee, three dollars; and (iii) from each permanent registration fee, four dollars. (1997, c. 283; 2007, c. 896.)

The section above is effective until December 31 of any year revenues designated for the Highway Maintenance and Operating Fund or the Transportation Trust Fund are appropriated for any non-transportation related purposes. For this section effective until that time, see the section as set out in the 2006 Edition.

Editor's note. — Acts 2007, c. 896, cl. 3, provides: "That the revenues generated by the provisions of this act shall not be used to calculate or reduce the share of local, federal, and state revenues otherwise available to participating jurisdictions. Further, such revenues and moneys shall not be included in any computation of, or formula for, a locality's ability to pay for public education, upon which appropriations of state revenues to local governments for public education are determined."

Acts 2007, c. 896, cl. 21, provides: "That the revenue generated by this act shall be used solely for transportation purposes."

Acts 2007, c. 896, cl. 22, provides: "That the provisions of this act which generate additional revenue for the Transportation Trust Fund, established under § 33.1-23.03:1 of the Code of Virginia, or the Highway Maintenance and Operating Fund shall expire on December 31 of any year in which the General Assembly appropriates any of the revenues designated under general law to the Highway Maintenance and Operating Fund or the Transportation Trust Fund for any non-transportation related purpose."

Acts 2007, c. 896, cl. 23 contains a severability clause.

The 2007 amendments. — The 2007 amendment by c. 896 changed all of the fees in the table following the first paragraph.

§ 46.2-697. (Contingent expiration date — see Editor's note) Fees for vehicles not designed or used for transportation of passengers.

— A. Except as otherwise provided in this section, the fee for registration of all motor vehicles not designed and used for the transportation of passengers shall be $23 plus an amount determined by the gross weight of the vehicle or combination of vehicles of which it is a part, when loaded to the maximum capacity for which it is registered and licensed, according to the schedule of fees set forth in this section. For each 1,000 pounds of gross weight, or major fraction thereof, for which any such vehicle is registered, there shall be paid to the Commissioner the fee indicated in the following schedule immediately opposite the weight group and under the classification established by the provisions of subsection B of § 46.2-711 into which such vehicle, or any combination of vehicles of which it is a part, falls when loaded to the maximum capacity for which it is registered and licensed. The fee for a pickup or panel truck shall be $33 if its gross weight is 4,000 pounds or less, and $38 if its gross weight is 4,001 pounds through 6,500 pounds. The fee shall be $39 for any motor vehicle with a gross weight of 6,501 pounds through 10,000 pounds.

Fee Per Thousand Pounds of Gross Weight

Gross Weight Groups (pounds)	Private Carriers	For Rent or For Hire Carriers
10,001 — 11,000	$3.17	$4.75
11,001 — 12,000	3.42	4.90
12,001 — 13,000	3.66	5.15
13,001 — 14,000	3.90	5.40
14,001 — 15,000	4.15	5.65
15,001 — 16,000	4.39	5.90
16,001 — 17,000	4.88	6.15
17,001 — 18,000	5.37	6.40
18,001 — 19,000	5.86	7.50
19,001 — 20,000	6.34	7.70
20,001 — 21,000	6.83	7.90
21,001 — 22,000	7.32	8.10
22,001 — 23,000	7.81	8.30
23,001 — 24,000	8.30	8.50
24,001 — 25,000	8.42	8.70
25,001 — 26,000	8.48	8.90
26,001 — 27,000	10.07	10.35
27,001 — 28,000	10.13	10.55
28,001 — 29,000	10.18	10.75
29,001 — 40,000	10.31	10.95
40,001 — 45,000	10.43	11.15
45,001 — 50,000	10.68	11.25
50,001 — 55,000	11.29	13.25
55,001 — 76,000	13.73	15.25
76,001 — 80,000	16.17	16.25

For all such motor vehicles exceeding a gross weight of 6,500 pounds, an additional fee of five dollars shall be imposed.

B. In lieu of registering any motor vehicle referred to in this section for an entire licensing year, the owner may elect to register the vehicle only for one or more quarters of a licensing year, and in such case, the fee shall be twenty-five percent of the annual fee plus five dollars for each quarter that the vehicle is registered.

C. When an owner elects to register and license a motor vehicle under subsection B of this section, the provisions of §§ 46.2-646 and 46.2-688 shall not apply.

D. Notwithstanding any other provision of law, no vehicle designed, equipped, and used to tow disabled or inoperable motor vehicles shall be required to register in accordance with any gross weight other than the gross weight of the towing vehicle itself, exclusive of any vehicle being towed.

E. All registrations and licenses issued for less than a full year shall expire on the date shown on the license and registration. (Code 1950, § 46-162; 1956, c. 477; 1958, c. 541, § 46.1-154; 1962, c. 86; 1964, c. 218; 1964, Ex. Sess., c. 22; 1973, c. 517; 1974, c. 150; 1979, c. 244; 1982, c. 671; 1984, c. 144; 1986 Sp. Sess., c. 11; 1989, c. 727; 1997, c. 283; 2007, c. 896.)

The section above is effective December 31 of any year revenues designated for the Highway Maintenance and Operating Fund or the Transportation Trust Fund are appropriated for any non-transportation related purposes. For this section as in effect until that time, see the section as set out in the 2006 Edition.

Editor's note. — Acts 2007, c. 896, cl. 3, provides: "That the revenues generated by the provisions of this act shall not be used to calculate or reduce the share of local, federal, and state revenues otherwise available to participating jurisdictions. Further, such revenues and moneys shall not be included in any computation of, or formula for, a locality's ability to pay for public education, upon which appropriations of state revenues to local governments for public education are determined."

Acts 2007, c. 896, cl. 21, provides: "That the revenue generated by this act shall be used solely for transportation purposes."

Acts 2007, c. 896, cl. 22, provides: "That the provisions of this act which generate additional revenue for the Transportation Trust Fund, established under § 33.1-23.03:1 of the Code of Virginia, or the Highway Maintenance and Operating Fund shall expire on December 31 of any year in which the General Assembly appropriates any of the revenues designated under general law to the Highway Maintenance and Operating Fund or the Transportation Trust Fund for any non-transportation related purpose."

Acts 2007, c. 896, cl. 23 contains a severability clause.

The 2007 amendments. — The 2007 amendment by c. 896 substituted "$23" for "thirteen dollars," "$33" for "twenty-three dollars," "$38" for "twenty-nine dollars" and "$39" for "twenty-nine dollars" in subsection A and increased all of the fee amounts under table heading "Private Carriers" following the first paragraph of subsection A.

§ 46.2-702.1. (Contingent expiration — see Editor's note) Distribution of certain revenue.
— A. Except as provided in subsection B, the net additional revenues generated by increases in the registration fees under §§ 46.2-694, 46.2-694.1, and 46.2-697 pursuant to enactments of the 2007 Session of the General Assembly, shall be deposited into the Highway Maintenance and Operating Fund.

B. In the case of vehicles registered under the International Registration Plan, an amount that is approximately equal to the net additional revenues generated by increases in the registration fees under §§ 46.2-694, 46.2-694.1, and 46.2-697 that are in regard to such vehicles pursuant to enactments of the 2007 Session of the General Assembly shall be deposited into the Highway and Maintenance Operating Fund.

C. For purposes of this title, *"net additional revenues"* shall mean the additional revenues provided pursuant to enactments of the 2007 Session of the General Assembly minus any refunds or remittances required to be paid. (2007, c. 896.)

Editor's note. — Acts 2007, c. 896, cl. 3, provides: "That the revenues generated by the provisions of this act shall not be used to calculate or reduce the share of local, federal, and state revenues otherwise available to participating jurisdictions. Further, such revenues and moneys shall not be included in any computation of, or formula for, a locality's ability to pay for public education, upon

which appropriations of state revenues to local governments for public education are determined."

Acts 2007, c. 896, cl. 21, provides: "That the revenue generated by this act shall be used solely for transportation purposes."

Acts 2007, c. 896, cl. 22, provides: "That the provisions of this act which generate additional revenue for the Transportation Trust Fund, established under § 33.1-23.03:1 of the Code of Virginia, or the Highway Maintenance and Operating Fund shall expire on December 31 of any year in which the General Assembly appropriates any of the revenues designated under general law to the Highway Maintenance and Operating Fund or the Transportation Trust Fund for any non-transportation related purpose."

Acts 2007, c. 896, cl. 23 contains a severability clause.

ARTICLE 10.
Special License Plates.

§ 46.2-739. Special license plates for certain disabled veterans; fees.
— A. On receipt of an application, the Commissioner shall issue special license plates to applicants who are disabled veterans as defined in § 46.2-100 or unremarried surviving spouses of such disabled veterans. These license plates shall be special permanent red, white, and blue license plates bearing the letters "DV." The application shall be accompanied by a certification from the U.S. Veterans Administration that the veteran has been so designated and that his disability is service-connected. License plates issued under this subsection shall not permit the vehicles upon which they are displayed to use parking spaces reserved for persons with disabilities that limit or impair their ability to walk.

B. On receipt of an application, the Commissioner shall issue special DV disabled parking license plates displaying the international symbol of access in the same size as the numbers and letters on the plate and in a color that contrasts to the background to veterans who are also persons with disabilities that limit or impair their ability to walk as defined in § 46.2-100. The Commissioner shall require that such application be accompanied by a certification signed by a licensed physician, licensed podiatrist, licensed chiropractor, licensed nurse practitioner, or licensed physician assistant to that effect. Special DV disabled parking license plates issued under this subsection shall authorize the vehicles upon which they are displayed to use parking spaces reserved for persons with disabilities that limit or impair their ability to walk.

No annual registration fee, as prescribed in § 46.2-694, and no annual fee, as set forth in subdivision 3 of subsection B of § 46.2-725, shall be required for any one motor vehicle owned and used personally by any veteran, provided such vehicle displays license plates issued under this section.

The provisions of subdivisions 1 and 2 of subsection B of § 46.2-725 shall not apply to license plates issued under this section. (1972, c. 80, § 46.1-149.1; 1976, c. 410; 1977, c. 167; 1989, c. 727; 1994, c. 866; 1995, c. 747; 1997, cc. 774, 816; 2007, c. 715.)

The 2007 amendments. — The 2007 amendment by c. 715, in subsection B, in the second sentence, substituted "signed by" for "from" and inserted "licensed podiatrist, licensed chiropractor, licensed nurse practitioner, or licensed physician assistant" following "licensed physician."

ARTICLE 11.

State and Local Motor Vehicle Registration.

§ 46.2-752. Taxes and license fees imposed by counties, cities, and towns; limitations on amounts; disposition of revenues; requiring evidence of payment of personal property taxes and certain fines; prohibiting display of licenses after expiration; failure to display valid local license required by other localities; penalty. — A. Except as provided in § 46.2-755, counties, cities, and towns may levy and assess taxes and charge license fees on motor vehicles, trailers, and semitrailers. However, none of these taxes and license fees shall be assessed or charged by any county on vehicles owned by residents of any town located in the county when such town constitutes a separate school district if the vehicles are already subject to town license fees and taxes, nor shall a town charge a license fee to any new resident of the town, previously a resident of a county within which all or part of the town is situated, who has previously paid a license fee for the same tax year to such county. The amount of the license fee or tax imposed by any county, city, or town on any motor vehicle, trailer, or semitrailer shall not be greater than the annual or one-year fee imposed by the Commonwealth on the motor vehicle, trailer, or semitrailer. The license fees and taxes shall be imposed in such manner, on such basis, for such periods, and subject to proration for fractional periods of years, as the proper local authorities may determine. Local licenses may be issued free of charge for any or all of the following:

1. Vehicles powered by clean special fuels as defined in § 46.2-749.3, including dual-fuel and bi-fuel vehicles,

2. Vehicles owned by volunteer rescue squads,

3. Vehicles owned by volunteer fire departments,

4. Vehicles owned or leased by active members or active auxiliary members of volunteer rescue squads,

5. Vehicles owned or leased by active members or active auxiliary members of volunteer fire departments,

6. Vehicles owned or leased by auxiliary police officers,

7. Vehicles owned or leased by volunteer police chaplains,

8. Vehicles owned by surviving spouses of persons qualified to receive special license plates under § 46.2-739,

9. Vehicles owned or leased by auxiliary deputy sheriffs or volunteer deputy sheriffs,

10. Vehicles owned by persons qualified to receive special license plates under § 46.2-739,

11. Vehicles owned by any of the following who served at least 10 years in the locality: former members of volunteer rescue squads, former members of volunteer fire departments, former auxiliary police officers, former volunteer police chaplains, and former volunteer special police officers appointed under § 15.2-1737. In the case of active members of volunteer rescue squads and volunteer fire departments, applications for such licenses shall be accompanied by written evidence, in a form acceptable to the locality, of their active membership, and no member shall be issued more than one such license free of charge,

12. All vehicles having a situs for the imposition of licensing fees under this section in the locality;

13. Vehicles owned or leased by deputy sheriffs; however, no deputy sheriff shall be issued more than one such license free of charge,

14. Vehicles owned or leased by police officers; however, no police officer shall be issued more than one such license free of charge,

15. Vehicles owned or leased by officers of the State Police; however, no officer of the State Police shall be issued more than one such license free of charge,

16. Vehicles owned or leased by salaried firefighters; however, no salaried firefighter shall be issued more than one such license free of charge; or

17. Vehicles owned or leased by salaried emergency medical technicians; however no salaried emergency medical technician shall be issued more than one such license free of charge.

The governing body of any county, city, or town issuing licenses under this section may by ordinance provide for a 50 percent reduction in the fee charged for the issuance of any such license issued for any vehicle owned or leased by any person who is 65 years old or older. No such discount, however, shall be available for more than one vehicle owned or leased by the same person.

The governing body of any county, city, or town issuing licenses free of charge under this subsection may by ordinance provide for (i) the limitation, restriction, or denial of such free issuance to an otherwise qualified applicant, including without limitation the denial of free issuance to a taxpayer who has failed to timely pay personal property taxes due with respect to the vehicle and (ii) the grounds for such limitation, restriction, or denial.

The situs for the imposition of licensing fees under this section shall in all cases, except as hereinafter provided, be the county, city, or town in which the motor vehicle, trailer, or semitrailer is normally garaged, stored, or parked. If it cannot be determined where the personal property is normally garaged, stored, or parked, the situs shall be the domicile of its owner. In the event the owner of the motor vehicle is a full-time student attending an institution of higher education, the situs shall be the domicile of such student, provided the student has presented sufficient evidence that he has paid a personal property tax on the motor vehicle in his domicile.

B. The revenue derived from all county, city, or town taxes and license fees imposed on motor vehicles, trailers, or semitrailers shall be applied to general county, city, or town purposes.

C. A county, city, or town may require that no motor vehicle, trailer, or semitrailer shall be locally licensed until the applicant has produced satisfactory evidence that all personal property taxes on the motor vehicle, trailer, or semitrailer to be licensed have been paid and satisfactory evidence that any delinquent motor vehicle, trailer, or semitrailer personal property taxes owing have been paid which have been properly assessed or are assessable against the applicant by the county, city, or town. A county, city, or town may also provide that no motor vehicle license shall be issued unless the tangible personal property taxes properly assessed or assessable by that locality on any tangible personal property used or usable as a dwelling titled by the Department of Motor Vehicles and owned by the taxpayer have been paid. Any county and any town within any such county may by agreement require that all personal property taxes assessed by either the county or the town on any vehicle be paid before licensure of such vehicle by either the county or the town.

C1. The Counties of Dinwiddie, Lee, and Wise may, by ordinance or resolution adopted after public notice and hearing and, with the consent of the treasurer, require that no license may be issued under this section unless the applicant has produced satisfactory evidence that all fees, including delinquent fees, payable to such county or local solid waste authority, for the disposal of solid waste pursuant to the Virginia Water and Waste Authorities Act (§ 15.2-5100 et seq.), or pursuant to § 15.2-2159, have been paid in full. For purposes of this subsection, all fees, including delinquent fees, payable to a county for waste disposal services described herein, shall be paid to the treasurer of such county; however, in Wise County, the fee shall be paid to the county or its agent.

D. The Counties of Arlington, Fairfax, Loudoun, and Prince William and towns within them and any city may require that no motor vehicle, trailer, or semitrailer shall be licensed by that jurisdiction unless all fines owed to the jurisdiction by the owner of the vehicle, trailer, or semitrailer for violation of the jurisdiction's ordinances governing parking of vehicles have been paid. The provisions of this subsection shall not apply to vehicles owned by firms or companies in the business of renting motor vehicles.

E. If in any county imposing license fees and taxes under this section, a town therein imposes like fees and taxes on vehicles of owners resident in the town, the owner of any vehicle subject to the fees or taxes shall be entitled, on the owner's displaying evidence that he has paid the fees or taxes, to receive a credit on the fees or taxes imposed by the county to the extent of the fees or taxes he has paid to the town. Nothing in this section shall deprive any town now imposing these licenses and taxes from increasing them or deprive any town not now imposing them from hereafter doing so, but subject to the limitations provided in subsection D of this section. The governing body of any county and the governing body of any town in that county wherein each imposes the license tax herein provided may provide mutual agreements so that not more than one license plate or decal in addition to the state plate shall be required.

F. Notwithstanding the provisions of subsection E of this section, in a consolidated county wherein a tier-city exists, the tier-city may, in accordance with the provisions of the agreement or plan of consolidation, impose license fees and taxes under this section in addition to those fees and taxes imposed by the county, provided that the combined county and tier-city rates do not exceed the maximum provided in subsection A of this section. No credit shall be allowed on the fees or taxes imposed by the county for fees or taxes paid to the tier-city, except as may be provided by the consolidation agreement or plan. The governing body of any county and the governing body of any tier-city in such county wherein each imposes the license tax herein may provide by mutual agreement that no more than one license plate or decal in addition to the state license plate shall be required.

G. Any county, city, or town may by ordinance provide that it shall be unlawful for any owner or operator of a motor vehicle, trailer, or semitrailer (i) to fail to obtain and, if any required by such ordinance, to display the local license required by any ordinance of the county, city or town in which the vehicle is registered, or (ii) to display upon a motor vehicle, trailer, or semitrailer any such local license, required by ordinance to be displayed, after its expiration date. The ordinance may provide that a violation shall constitute a misdemeanor the penalty for which shall not exceed that of a Class 4 misdemeanor and may, in the case of a motor vehicle registered to a resident of the locality where such vehicle is registered, authorize the issuance by local law-enforcement officers of citations, summonses, parking tickets, or uniform traffic summonses for violations. Any such ordinance may also provide that a violation of the ordinance by the registered owner of the vehicle may not be discharged by payment of a fine except upon presentation of satisfactory evidence that the required license has been obtained. Nothing in this section shall be construed to require a county, city, or town to issue a decal or any other tangible evidence of a local license to be displayed on the licensed vehicle if the county's, city's, or town's ordinance does not require display of a decal or other evidence of payment. No ordinance adopted pursuant to this section shall require the display of any local license, decal, or sticker on any vehicle owned by a public service company, as defined in § 56-76, having a fleet of at least 2,500 vehicles garaged in the Commonwealth.

H. Except as provided by subsections E and F, no vehicle shall be subject to taxation under the provisions of this section in more than one jurisdiction. Furthermore, no person who has purchased a local vehicle license, decal, or sticker for a vehicle in one county, city, or town and then moves to and garages his vehicle in another county, city, or town shall be required to purchase another local license, decal, or sticker from the county, city, or town to which he has moved and wherein his vehicle is now garaged until the expiration date of the local license, decal, or sticker issued by the county, city, or town from which he moved.

I. Purchasers of new or used motor vehicles shall be allowed at least a 10-day grace period, beginning with the date of purchase, during which to pay license fees charged by local governments under authority of this section.

J. Beginning October 1, 1992, the treasurer or director of finance of any county, city, or town may enter into an agreement with the Commissioner whereby the Commissioner will refuse to issue or renew any vehicle registration of any applicant therefor who owes to such county, city or town any local vehicle license fees or delinquent tangible personal property tax or parking citations issued only to residents of such county, city, or town. Before being issued any vehicle registration or renewal of such license or registration by the Commissioner, the applicant shall first satisfy all such local vehicle license fees and delinquent taxes or parking citations and present evidence satisfactory to the Commissioner that all such local vehicle license fees and delinquent taxes or parking citations have been paid in full. The Commissioner shall charge a reasonable fee to cover the costs of such enforcement action, and the treasurer or director of finance may add the cost of this fee to the delinquent tax bill or the amount of the parking citation. The treasurer or director of finance of any county, city, or town seeking to collect delinquent taxes or parking citations through the withholding of registration or renewal thereof by the Commissioner as provided for in this subsection shall notify the Commissioner in the manner provided for in his agreement with the Commissioner and supply to the Commissioner information necessary to identify the debtor whose registration or renewal is to be denied. Any agreement entered into pursuant to the provisions of this subsection shall provide the debtor notice of the intent to deny renewal of registration at least 30 days prior to the expiration date of a current vehicle registration. For the purposes of this subsection, notice by first-class mail to the registrant's address as maintained in the records of the Department of Motor Vehicles shall be deemed sufficient. In the case of parking violations, the Commissioner shall only refuse to issue or renew the vehicle registration of any applicant therefor

pursuant to this subsection for the vehicle that incurred the parking violations. The provisions of this subsection shall not apply to vehicles owned by firms or companies in the business of renting motor vehicles.

K. The governing bodies of any two or more counties, cities, or towns may enter into compacts for the regional enforcement of local motor vehicle license requirements. The governing body of each participating jurisdiction may by ordinance require the owner or operator of any motor vehicle, trailer, or semitrailer to display on his vehicle a valid local license issued by another county, city, or town that is a party to the regional compact, provided that the owner or operator is required by the jurisdiction of situs, as provided in § 58.1-3511, to obtain and display such license. The ordinance may also provide that no motor vehicle, trailer, or semitrailer shall be locally licensed until the applicant has produced satisfactory evidence that (i) all personal property taxes on the motor vehicle, trailer, or semitrailer to be licensed have been paid to all participating jurisdictions and (ii) any delinquent motor vehicle, trailer, or semitrailer personal property taxes that have been properly assessed or are assessable by any participating jurisdiction against the applicant have been paid. Any city and any county having the urban county executive form of government, the counties adjacent to such county and towns within them may require that no motor vehicle, trailer, or semitrailer shall be licensed by that jurisdiction or any other jurisdiction in the compact unless all fines owed to any participating jurisdiction by the owner of the vehicle for violation of any participating jurisdiction's ordinances governing parking of vehicles have been paid. The ordinance may further provide that a violation shall constitute a misdemeanor the penalty for which shall not exceed that of a Class 4 misdemeanor. Any such ordinance may also provide that a violation of the ordinance by the owner of the vehicle may not be discharged by payment of a fine except upon presentation of satisfactory evidence that the required license has been obtained. The provisions of this subsection shall not apply to vehicles owned by firms or companies in the business of renting motor vehicles.

L. In addition to the taxes and license fees permitted in subsection A, counties, cities, and towns may charge a license fee of no more than $1 per motor vehicle, trailer, and semitrailer. Except for the provisions of subsection B, such fee shall be subject to all other provisions of this section. All funds collected pursuant to this subsection shall be paid pursuant to § 51.1-1204 to the Volunteer Firefighters' and Rescue Squad Workers' Service Award Fund to the accounts of all members of the Fund who are volunteers for fire departments or rescue squads within the jurisdiction of the particular county, city, or town. (Code 1950, § 46-64; 1950, p. 240; 1952, c. 169; 1954, cc. 491, 594; 1956, cc. 66,

549, 570; 1958, c. 541, § 46.1-65; 1959, Ex. Sess., cc. 22, 55; 1962, c. 574; 1964, c. 218; 1972, c. 200; 1974, c. 621; 1975, c. 105; 1977, c. 166; 1979, c. 185; 1980, c. 105; 1982, c. 85; 1984, cc. 308, 630, 695; 1986, c. 123; 1987, cc. 208, 243; 1989, cc. 321, 706, 727; 1990, cc. 181, 187, 188, 455; 1991, c. 622; 1992, cc. 226, 355, 794, 806; 1993, cc. 50, 63, 175, 565; 1994, cc. 528, 962; 1995, cc. 91, 412, 449, 460, 479, 659; 1996, cc. 89, 562; 1997, cc. 246, 499, 905, 911; 1998, c. 649; 1999, c. 236; 2000, c. 303; 2001, cc. 338, 471, 605, 606; 2002, cc. 206, 553; 2003, c. 326; 2004, cc. 689, 723; 2005, c. 317; 2006, c. 148; 2007, cc. 213, 230, 813, 865.)

Editor's note. — Acts 2007, c. 813, cl. 2, provides: "That the provisions of this act shall not affect the powers of any locality with respect to any ordinance, resolution or bylaw validly adopted and not repealed or rescinded prior to July 1, 2007."

The 2007 amendments. — The 2007 amendment by c. 213 added the last sentence in subsections G and H.

The 2007 amendment by c. 230 substituted "shall not be greater than the annual or one-year fee imposed" for "shall not be greater than the amount of the license tax imposed" in the third sentence of subsection A.

The 2007 amendment by c. 813, in subsection C1, substituted "The Counties of Dinwiddie, Lee, and Wise" for "Any county having a population of at least 24,000, but no more than 24,600, or having a population of at least 39,550, but no more than 41,550" in the first sentence and "Wise County" for "any county with a population between 39,550 and 41,550" in the second sentence.

The 2007 amendment by c. 865, deleted "or" at the end of subdivision A 11; substituted a comma for a period at the end of subdivision A 12; and added subdivisions A 13 through A 17.

CASE NOTES

Lack of decal did not provide cause for traffic stop. — Because a vehicle that was registered in Fredericksburg, Virginia, did not required a Fairfax County registration decal under § 46.2-752, the lack of such a decal on defendant's vehicle did not provide sufficient cause under the Fourth Amendment to stop the vehicle. United States v. Washington, 439 F. Supp. 2d 589, 2006 U.S. Dist. LEXIS 52064 (E.D. Va. 2006).

OPINIONS OF THE ATTORNEY GENERAL

Collection of unpaid decal fee. — A locality eliminating the physical decal may carry forward an unpaid decal fee and collect it from the locality's residents in subsequent years, and such collection is subject to a limitation of five years from the tax year for which the assessment is made. See opinion of Attorney General to Ms. Barbara O. Carraway, Treasurer for the City of Chesapeake, 05-003 (4/26/05).

SUBTITLE III.
OPERATION.

CHAPTER 8.
REGULATION OF TRAFFIC.

Article 1.
General and Miscellaneous.

Sec.
46.2-804. Special regulations applicable on highways laned for traffic.

Sec.
46.2-805. Lane direction control signals.
46.2-808. Commonwealth Transportation Board may prohibit certain uses of controlled access highways; penalty.
46.2-819.1. Installation and use of photo-monitoring system or automatic vehicle identification system in conjunction with certain toll facilities; penalty.
46.2-819.3. Use of toll facility without payment of toll; enforcement; penalty.
46.2-819.4. Smoking in proximity to gas pumps; penalty.

Article 8.
Speed.

46.2-870. Maximum speed limits generally.
46.2-871. Maximum speed limit for school buses.
46.2-873. Maximum speed limits at school crossings; penalty.
46.2-874.1. Exceptions to maximum speed limits in residence districts; penalty.

Article 10.
Stopping on Highways.

46.2-891. Exemption for highway construction and maintenance vehicles.

Article 12.
Bicycles.

46.2-905. Riding bicycles, electric personal assistive mobility devices, electric power-assisted bicycles, motor-driven cycles, and mopeds on roadways and bicycle paths.
46.2-908.1. Electric personal assistive mobility devices, electrically powered toy vehicle, and electric power-assisted bicycles.

Article 13.
Motorcycles and Mopeds and All-Terrain Vehicles.

46.2-915. Stickers required on mopeds.

Article 16.
Pedestrians.

46.2-932. Playing on highways; use of toy vehicle on highways, persons riding bicycles, electric personal assistive mobility devices, electric power-assisted bicycles, mopeds, etc., not to attach to vehicles; exception.

ARTICLE 1.

General and Miscellaneous.

Michie's Jurisprudence. — For related discussion, see 2B M.J. Automobiles, §§ 20, 27, 28, 66, 123; 3A M.J. Bicycles, § 1.

§ 46.2-804. Special regulations applicable on highways laned for traffic. — Whenever any roadway has been divided into clearly marked lanes for traffic, drivers of vehicles shall obey the following:

1. Any vehicle proceeding at less than the normal speed of traffic at the time and place and under the conditions existing, shall be driven in the lane nearest the right edge or right curb of the highway when such lane is available for travel except when overtaking and passing another vehicle or in preparation for a left turn or where right lanes are reserved for slow-moving traffic as permitted in this section;

2. A vehicle shall be driven as nearly as is practicable entirely within a single lane and shall not be moved from that lane until the driver has ascertained that such movement can be made safely;

3. Except as otherwise provided in subdivision 5 of this section, on a highway which is divided into three lanes, no vehicle shall be driven in the center lane except when overtaking and passing another vehicle or in preparation for a left turn or unless such center lane is at the time allocated exclusively to traffic moving in the direction the vehicle is proceeding and is signed or marked to give notice of such allocation. Traffic-control devices may be erected directing specified traffic to use a designated lane or designating those lanes to be used by traffic moving in a particular direction regardless of the center of the roadway and drivers of vehicles shall obey the directions of every such device;

4. The Commonwealth Transportation Board, or local authorities in their respective jurisdictions, may designate right lanes for slow-moving vehicles and the Virginia Department of Transportation shall post signs requiring trucks and combination vehicles to keep to the right on Interstate Highway System components with no more than two travel lanes in each direction where terrain is likely to slow the speed of such vehicles climbing hills and inclines to a speed that is less than the posted speed limit;

5. Wherever a highway is marked with double traffic lines consisting of a solid line immediately adjacent to a broken line, no vehicle shall be driven to the left of such line if the solid line is on the right of the broken line, but it shall be lawful to make a left turn for the purpose of entering or leaving a public, private, or commercial road or entrance. Where the middle lane of a highway is marked on both sides with a solid line immediately adjacent to a broken line, such middle lane shall be considered a left-turn or holding lane and it shall be lawful to drive to the left of such line if the solid line is on the right of the broken line for the purpose of turning left into any road or entrance, provided that the vehicle may not travel in such lane further than 150 feet;

6. Wherever a highway is marked with double traffic lines consisting of two immediately adjacent solid lines, no vehicle shall be driven to the left of such lines, except when turning left. (Code 1950, § 46-222; 1952, c. 671; 1958, c. 541, § 46.1-206; 1962, c. 87; 1979, c. 25; 1985, c. 481; 1989, c. 727; 2007, c. 501.)

Cross references. — As to additional penalties for aggressive driving, see § 46.2-868.1.

The 2007 amendments. — The 2007 amendment by c. 501 added the language beginning "and the Virginia Department of Transportation" at the end of subdivision 4.

CASE NOTES

Editor's note. — Many of the cases below were decided under former Title 46.1 or prior law.

The caption of this section shows that it was intended to apply to city streets as well as open highways. Ragsdale v. Jones, 202 Va. 278, 117 S.E.2d 114 (1960).

Section does not relate to duty of driver to pedestrian. — This section and former §§ 46.1-211 and 46.1-289 (see now §§ 46.2-842 and 46.2-1082) deal with the duties of an operator of a motor vehicle turning from one lane to another where the movement of another vehicle is involved, and with the requirement of equipping a motor vehicle with a rear view mirror. They do not relate to the duty of the operator of a motor vehicle to a pedestrian. Thus an instruction in the words of these statutes was inappropriate under the evidence in an action for the death of a pedestrian who was struck by a motor vehicle. Russell v. Hammond, 200 Va. 600, 106 S.E.2d 626 (1959).

Former subdivision (b) (see now subdivision 2) applies to movement of vehicle from one lane to another on same road. Wallingford v. Karnes, 194 Va. 648, 74 S.E.2d 161 (1953), holding that subdivision was not applicable to the facts established in case growing out of collision at intersection.

Former subdivision (b) (see now subdivision 2) is also applicable to movements within an intersection as well as to those upon city streets and open highways. Ragsdale v. Jones, 202 Va. 278, 117 S.E.2d 114 (1959).

The manifest purpose of former subdivision (e) (see now subdivision 5) of this section was to prevent cars driving on the left side of the road for purposes of passing where there was not sufficient vision ahead to allow the passing to be made in safety in view of the fact that the car being passed was in motion. Burcham v. J.P. Stevens & Co., 209 F.2d 35 (4th Cir. 1954).

If passing movement is commenced across broken line, it must be completed before reaching solid traffic line to the right of a broken line under this section. Neighbors v. Moore, 216 Va. 514, 219 S.E.2d 692 (1975).

The fact that defendant/driver commenced to pass when a single broken line marked the lanes gave him no license to continue north in that lane after he reached the solid line. That traffic control marking required the defendant to return to the northbound lane before he reached the solid line. Neighbors v. Moore, 216 Va. 514, 219 S.E.2d 692 (1975).

Turning left across solid lines. — It was not unlawful for motorist to cross yellow line of oncoming turn lane for purpose of turning left onto entrance ramp to Interstate highway. Commonwealth v. Reynolds, No. 2626-98-1 (Ct. of Appeals May 28, 1999).

Burden of explanation. — This section forbids driving to the left of two adjacent solid lines marking double traffic lanes on a highway. Therefore, one whose car is to the left of such lines has a burden of explanation. Bizzaro v. Payne, 169 F.2d 851 (4th Cir. 1948); Interstate Veneer Co. v. Edwards, 191 Va. 107, 60 S.E.2d 4 (1950).

Instructions. — In a civil case, it was correct for the trial court to refuse an instruction stating defendant's duty to drive in the lane nearest the right-hand edge where the evidence did not show that the failure to drive in the correct lane was a proximate cause of the accident. Baker v. Richardson, 201 Va. 834, 114 S.E.2d 599 (1960).

An instruction was objected to because it was stated therein that where a highway is divided into three lanes an automobile should not be driven in the center lane except where overtaking and passing another vehicle, but should be driven in the lane nearest the right-hand edge of the highway. The court said that this part of the instruction simply stated the statutory rule where the highway is divided into three lanes. Chick Transit Corp. v. Edenton, 170 Va. 361, 196 S.E. 648 (1938).

An instruction based on this section defining the duty of a driver not to move from one lane to another on a laned highway until he has exercised ordinary care to ascertain that the move can be made with safety was properly given. Nicholaou v. Harrington, 217 Va. 618, 231 S.E.2d 318 (1977).

CIRCUIT COURT OPINIONS

Where facts did not support a valid stop. — Suppression was granted where the facts and circumstances did not support a stop of the vehicle in which defendant was a passenger; moreover, the officer who stopped the vehicle failed to issue a citation for the alleged infraction. Commonwealth v. Lincoln, 60 Va. Cir. 369, 2002 Va. Cir. LEXIS 406 (Louisa County 2002).

§ 46.2-805. Lane direction control signals. —

When lane direction control signals are placed over the individual lanes of a highway, vehicular traffic may travel in any lane over which a green signal is shown, but shall not enter or travel in any lane over which a red signal is shown and shall vacate as soon as possible any lane over which an amber signal is shown. (1974, c. 347, § 46.1-206.1; 1989, c. 727.)

§ 46.2-808. Commonwealth Transportation Board may prohibit certain uses of controlled access highways; penalty. — A. The Common-

wealth Transportation Board may, when necessary to promote safety, prohibit the use of controlled access highways or any part thereof by any or all of the following:

1. Pedestrians,
2. Persons riding bicycles, electric power-assisted bicycles, electric personal assistive mobility devices, or mopeds,
3. Animal-drawn vehicles,
4. Self-propelled machinery or equipment, and
5. Animals led, ridden or driven on the hoof.

B. The termini of any section of controlled access highways, use of which is restricted under the provisions of this section, shall be clearly indicated by a conspicuous marker.

C. This section shall not apply to any vehicle or equipment owned or controlled by the Virginia Department of Transportation, while actually engaged in the construction, reconstruction, or maintenance of highways or to any vehicle or equipment for which a permit has been obtained for operation on such highway.

Any person violating a restriction or prohibition imposed pursuant to this section shall be guilty of a traffic infraction. (1964, c. 239, § 46.1-171.1; 1966, c. 365; 1981, c. 585; 1983, c. 262; 1989, c. 727; 1991, c. 55; 2004, cc. 947, 973; 2006, cc. 529, 538; 2007, cc. 209, 366.)

The 2007 amendments. — The 2007 amendments by cc. 209 and 366 are identical, and deleted "motorized skateboards or scooters" following "electric power-assitsted bicycles" in subdivision A 2.

§ 46.2-819.1. Installation and use of photo-monitoring system or automatic vehicle identification system in conjunction with certain toll facilities; penalty. — A. The operator of any

toll facility or the locality within which such toll facility is located may install and operate or cause to be installed and operated a photo-monitoring system or automatic vehicle identification system, or both, at locations where tolls are collected for the use of such toll facility. The operator of a toll facility shall send an invoice or bill for unpaid tolls to the registered owner of a vehicle as part of an electronic or manual toll collection process, prior to seeking remedies under this section.

B. Information collected by a photo-monitoring system or automatic vehicle identification system installed and operated pursuant to subsection A shall be limited exclusively to that information that is necessary for the collection of unpaid tolls. Notwithstanding any other provision of law, all photographs, microphotographs, electronic images, or other data collected by a photo-monitoring system or automatic vehicle identification system shall be used exclusively for the collection of unpaid tolls and shall not (i) be open to the public; (ii) be sold and/or used for sales, solicitation, or marketing purposes; (iii) be disclosed to any other entity except as may be necessary for the collection of unpaid tolls or to a vehicle owner or operator as part of a challenge to the imposition of a toll; and (iv) be used in a court in a pending action or proceeding unless the action or proceeding relates to a violation of this section or upon order from a court of competent jurisdiction. Information collected under this section shall be purged and not retained later than 30 days after the collection and reconciliation of any unpaid tolls, administrative fees, and/or civil penalties. Any entity operating a photo-monitoring system or automatic vehicle identification system shall annually certify compliance with this section and make all records pertaining to such system available for inspection and audit by the Commonwealth Transportation Commissioner or the Commissioner of the Department of Motor Vehicles or their designee. Any violation of this subsection shall constitute a Class 1 misdemeanor. In addition to any fines or other penalties provided for by law, any money or other thing of value obtained as a result of a violation of this section shall be forfeited to the Commonwealth.

The toll facility operator may impose and collect an administrative fee in addition to the unpaid toll so as to recover the expenses of collecting the unpaid toll, which administrative fee shall be reasonably related to the actual cost of collecting the unpaid toll and not exceed $100 per violation. Such fee shall not be levied upon the operator of the vehicle until the second unpaid toll has been documented. The operator of the vehicle shall pay the unpaid tolls and any administrative fee detailed in an invoice or bill issued by a toll facility operator. If paid within 30 days of notification, the administrative fee shall not exceed $25.

C. If the matter proceeds to court, the registered owner or operator of a vehicle shall be liable for a civil penalty as follows: for a first offense, $50; for a second offense within one year from the first offense, $100; for a third offense within two years from the second offense, $250; and for a fourth and any subsequent offense within three years from the second offense, $500 plus, in each case, the unpaid toll, all accrued administrative fees imposed by the toll facility operator, and applicable court costs if the vehicle is found, as evidenced by information obtained from a photo-monitoring system or automatic vehicle identification system as provided in this section, to have used such a toll facility without payment of the required toll.

D. Any action under this section shall be brought in the General District Court of the city or county in which the toll facility is located.

E. Proof of a violation of this section shall be evidenced by information obtained from a photo-monitoring system or automatic vehicle identification system as provided in this section. A certificate, sworn to or affirmed by a technician employed or authorized by the operator of a toll facility or by the locality wherein the toll facility is located, or a facsimile of such a certificate, based on inspection of photographs, microphotographs, videotapes, or other recorded images produced by a photo-monitoring system, or of electronic data collected by an automatic vehicle identification system, shall be prima facie evidence of the facts contained therein. Any photographs, microphotographs, videotape, or other recorded images or electronic data evidencing such a violation shall be available for inspection in any proceeding to adjudicate the liability for such violation under this section. A record of communication by an automatic vehicle identification device with the automatic vehicle identification system at the time of a violation of this section shall be prima facie evidence that the automatic vehicle identification device was located in the vehicle registered to use such device in the records of the Virginia Department of Transportation.

F. It shall be prima facie evidence that the vehicle described in the summons issued pursuant to subsection K of this section was operated in violation of this section.

Upon a finding by a court of competent jurisdiction that the vehicle described in the summons issued pursuant to subsection K of this section was in violation of this section, the court shall impose a civil penalty upon the registered owner or operator of such vehicle in accordance with the amounts specified in subsection C of this section, together with applicable court costs, the operator's administrative fee and the toll due. Penalties assessed as the result of action initiated by the Virginia Department of Transportation shall be remanded by the clerk of the court which adjudicated the action to the Virginia Department of Transportation's Toll Facilities Revolving Fund. Penalties assessed as the result of action initiated by an operator of a toll facility other than the Virginia Department of Transportation shall be remanded by the clerk of the court which adjudicated the action to the treasurer or director of finance of the county or city in which the violation occurred for payment to the toll facility operator.

The registered owner of such vehicle shall be given reasonable notice by way of a summons as provided in subsection K of this section that his vehicle had been used in violation of this section and such owner shall be given notice of the time and place of the hearing as well as the civil penalty and costs for such offense.

Upon the filing of an affidavit with the court at least 14 days prior to the hearing date by the registered owner of the vehicle stating that he was not the driver of the vehicle on the date of the violation and providing the legal name and address of the operator of the vehicle at the time of the violation, a summons will also be issued to the alleged operator of the vehicle at the time of the offense.

In any action against a vehicle operator, an affidavit made by the registered owner providing the name and address of the vehicle operator at the time of the violation shall constitute prima facie evidence that the person named in the affidavit was operating the vehicle at all the relevant times relating to the matter named in the affidavit.

If the registered owner of the vehicle produces a certified copy of a police report showing that the vehicle had been reported to the police as stolen prior to the time of the alleged offense and remained stolen at the time of the alleged offense, then the court shall dismiss the summons issued to the registered owner of the vehicle.

G. Upon a finding by a court that a person has three or more unpaid tolls and such person fails to pay the required penalties, fees, and unpaid tolls, the court shall notify the Commissioner of the Department of Motor Vehicles, who shall refuse to issue or renew any vehicle registration certificate of any applicant or the license plate issued for the vehicle driven in the commission of the offense until the court has notified the Commissioner that such penalties, fees, and unpaid tolls have been paid. If it is proven that the vehicle owner was not the operator at the time of the offense and upon a finding by a court that the person identified in an affidavit pursuant to subsection F as the operator violated this section and such person fails to pay the required penalties, fees, and unpaid tolls, the court shall notify the Commissioner, who shall refuse to issue or renew any vehicle registration certificate of any applicant or the license plate issued for any vehicle owned or co-owned by such person until the court has notified the Commissioner that such penalties, fees, and unpaid tolls have been paid. Such funds representing payment of unpaid tolls and all administrative fees of the toll facility operator shall be transferred from the court to the Virginia Department of Transportation's Toll Facilities Revolving Fund or, in the case of an action initiated by an operator of a toll facility other than the Virginia Department of Transportation, to the treasurer or director of finance of the county or city in which the violation occurred for payment to the toll facility operator. The Commissioner shall collect a $40 administrative fee from the registered owner or operator of the vehicle to defray the cost of processing and removing an order to deny registration or registration renewal.

H. For purposes of this section, *"operator of a toll facility other than the Virginia Department of Transportation"* means any agency, political subdivision, authority, or other entity that operates a toll facility; *"owner"* means the registered owner of a vehicle on record with the Department of Motor Vehicles. For purposes of this section, "owner" does not mean a vehicle rental or vehicle leasing company; *"photo-monitoring system"* means a vehicle sensor installed to work in conjunction with a toll collection device that automatically produces one or more photographs, one or more microphotographs, a videotape, or other recorded images of each vehicle at the time it is used or operated in violation of this section; *"automatic vehicle identification system"* means an electronic vehicle identification system installed to work in conjunction with a toll collection device that automatically produces an electronic record of each vehicle equipped with an automatic vehicle identification device that uses a toll facility; and *"automatic vehicle identification device"* means an electronic device that communicates by wireless transmission with an automatic vehicle identification system.

I. Any vehicle rental or vehicle leasing company, if named in a summons, shall be released as a party to the action if it provides the operator of the toll facility a copy of the vehicle rental agreement or lease or an affidavit identifying the renter or lessee prior to the date of hearing set forth in the summons. Upon receipt of such rental agreement, lease, or affidavit, a notice shall be mailed to the renter or lessee identified therein. Release of this information shall not be deemed a violation of any provision of the Government Data Collection and Dissemination Practices Act (§ 2.2-3800 et seq.) or the Insurance Information and Privacy Protection Act (§ 38.2-600 et seq.). The toll facility operator shall allow at least 30 days from the date of such mailing before pursuing other remedies under this section. In any action against the vehicle operator, a copy of the vehicle rental agreement, lease, or affidavit identifying the renter or lessee of the vehicle at the time of the violation is prima facie evidence that the person named in the rental agreement, lease, or affidavit was operating the vehicle at all the relevant times relating to the matter named in the summons.

J. Imposition of a civil penalty pursuant to this section shall not be deemed a conviction as an operator and shall not be made part of the driving record of the person upon whom such civil penalty is imposed nor shall it be used for insurance purposes in the provision of motor vehicle insurance coverage. The provisions of § 46.2-395 shall not be applicable to any civil penalty, fee, unpaid toll, fine or cost imposed or ordered paid under this section for a violation of this section.

K. On a form prescribed by the Supreme Court, a summons for a violation of this section may be executed pursuant to § 19.2-76.2. Toll facility personnel or their agents mailing such summons shall be considered conservators of the peace for the sole and limited purpose of mailing such summons. Notwithstanding the provisions of § 19.2-76, a summons for a violation of this section may be executed by mailing by first-class mail a copy thereof to the address of the owner of the vehicle as shown on the records of the Department of Motor Vehicles or, if the registered owner has named and provided a valid address for the operator of the vehicle at the time of the violation in an affidavit executed pursuant to subsection F, such named operator of the vehicle. If the summoned person fails to appear on the date of return set out in the summons mailed pursuant to this section, the summons shall be executed in the manner set out in § 19.2-76.3.

L. The operator of a toll facility may enter into an agreement with the Department of Motor Vehicles, in accordance with the provisions of subdivision 21 of subsection B of § 46.2-208, to obtain vehicle owner information regarding the registered owners of vehicles that fail to pay tolls required for the use of toll facilities and with the Virginia Department of Transportation to obtain any information that is necessary to conduct electronic toll collection. Information provided to the operator of a toll facility shall only be used for the collection of unpaid tolls and the operator of the toll facility shall be subject to the same conditions and penalties regarding release of the information as contained in subsection B.

M. No person shall be subject to both the provisions of this section and to prosecution under § 46.2-819 for actions arising out of the same transaction or occurrence. (1998, c. 802; 2001, cc. 803, 852; 2003, c. 768; 2004, c. 924; 2005, c. 862; 2006, c. 859; 2007, cc. 78, 200.)

The 2007 amendments. — The 2007 amendments by cc. 78 and 200 are identical, and substituted "that operates a toll facility" for "authorized by the Code of Virginia to operate such toll facility" in the first sentence of subsection H; and added the last sentence in subsection J.

§ 46.2-819.3. Use of toll facility without payment of toll; enforcement; penalty. — A. The toll facility operator may impose and collect an administrative fee in addition to the unpaid toll so as to recover the expenses of collecting the unpaid toll, which administrative fee shall be reasonably related to the actual cost of collecting the unpaid toll and not exceed $100 per violation. Such fee shall not be levied upon the operator of the vehicle until the second unpaid toll has been documented. The owner or operator of the vehicle shall pay the unpaid tolls and any administrative fee detailed in an invoice or bill issued by a toll facility operator. If paid within 30 days of notification, the administrative fee shall not exceed $25.

B. If the matter proceeds to court, the owner or operator of the vehicle shall be liable for a civil penalty as follows: for a first offense, $50; for a second offense within one year from the first offense, $100; for a third offense within two years from the second offense, $250; and for a fourth and any subsequent offense within three years from the second offense, $500 plus, in each case, the unpaid toll, all accrued administrative fees imposed by the toll facility operator and applicable court costs if the vehicle operator is found, as evidenced by information obtained from the toll facility operator, to have used such a toll facility without payment of the required toll.

C. A written promise to pay an unpaid toll within a specified period of time executed by the driver of a motor vehicle, accompanied by a certificate sworn to or affirmed by an authorized agent of the toll facility that the unpaid toll was not paid within such specified period, shall be prima facie evidence of the facts contained therein.

D. The operator of a toll facility may send an invoice or bill to the driver of a motor vehicle using a toll facility without payment of the specified toll as part of an electronic or manual toll collection process prior to seeking remedies under this section. Any action under this section shall be brought in the general district court of the city or county in which the toll facility is located.

E. Upon a finding by a court of competent jurisdiction that the driver of a motor vehicle identified in the summons issued pursuant to subsection I was in violation of this section, the court shall impose a civil penalty upon the driver of a motor vehicle in accordance with the amounts specified in subsection B, together with applicable court costs, the operator's administrative fee, and the toll due. Penalties assessed as the result of action initiated by the Virginia Department of Transportation shall be remanded by the clerk of the court which adjudicated the action to the Virginia Department of Transportation's Toll Facilities Revolving Fund. Penalties assessed as the result of action initiated by an operator of a toll facility other than the Virginia Department of Transportation shall be remanded by the clerk of the court which adjudicated the action to the treasurer or director of finance of the county or city in which the violation occurred for payment to the toll facility operator.

F. Upon a finding by a court that a person has three or more unpaid tolls and such person fails to pay the required penalties, fees, and unpaid tolls, the court shall notify the Commissioner of the Department of Motor Vehicles, who shall refuse to issue or renew any vehicle registration certificate of any applicant or the license plate issued for any vehicle owned or co-owned by the offender. The Commissioner shall collect a $40 administrative fee from the owner or operator of the vehicle to defray the cost of processing and removing an order to deny registration or registration renewal.

G. For purposes of this section, *"operator of a toll facility other than the Virginia Department of Transportation"* means any agency, political subdivision, authority, or other entity that operates a toll facility.

H. Imposition of a civil penalty pursuant to this section shall not be deemed a conviction as an operator and shall not be made part of the driving record of the person upon whom such civil penalty is imposed nor shall it be used for insurance purposes in the provision of motor vehicle insurance coverage. The provisions of § 46.2-395 shall not be applicable to any civil penalty, fee, unpaid toll, fine or cost imposed or ordered paid under this section for a violation of this section.

I. A summons for a violation of this section may be executed pursuant to § 19.2-76.2. Toll facility personnel or their agents mailing such summons shall be considered conservators of the peace for the sole and limited purpose of mailing such summons. Notwithstanding the provisions of § 19.2-76, a summons for a violation of this section may be executed by mailing by first-class mail a copy thereof to the address of the driver of a motor vehicle as shown on the records of the Department of Motor Vehicles. If the summoned person fails to appear on the date of return set out in the summons mailed pursuant to this section, the summons shall be executed in the manner set out in § 19.2-76.3.

J. No person shall be subject to both the provisions of this section and to prosecution under § 46.2-819 for actions arising out of the same transaction or occurrence. (2004, c. 924; 2006, c. 859; 2007, cc. 78, 200.)

The 2007 amendments. — The 2007 amendments by cc. 78 and 200 are identical, and substituted "that operates a toll facility" for "authorized by the Code of Virginia to operate such toll facility" at the end of subsection G; and added the last sentence in subsection H.

§ 46.2-819.4. Smoking in proximity to gas pumps; penalty. — Any person who smokes or uses an open flame within 20 feet of a pump used to fuel motor vehicles or a fueling tanker being used to deliver gasoline to a gasoline station is guilty of a Class 3 misdemeanor if smoking or the use of an open flame is prohibited by a sign at the pump. Any person who causes a fire or explosion as a result of a violation of this section is guilty of a Class 1 misdemeanor. (2007, c. 848.)

ARTICLE 8.

Speed.

Michie's Jurisprudence. — For related discussion, see 2B M.J. Automobiles, §§ 11, 15, 17, 27, 99, 126.1.

§ 46.2-870. Maximum speed limits generally. — Except as otherwise provided in this article, the maximum speed limit shall be 55 miles per hour on interstate highways or other limited access highways with divided roadways, nonlimited access highways having four or more lanes, and all state primary highways.

The maximum speed limit on all other highways shall be 55 miles per hour if the vehicle is a passenger motor vehicle, bus, pickup or panel truck, or a motorcycle, but 45 miles per hour on such highways if the vehicle is a truck, tractor truck, or combination of vehicles designed to transport property, or is a motor vehicle being used to tow a vehicle designed for self-propulsion, or a house trailer.

Notwithstanding the foregoing provisions of this section, the maximum speed limit shall be 65 miles per hour where indicated by lawfully placed signs, erected subsequent to a traffic engineering study and analysis of available and appropriate accident and law-enforcement data, on: (i) interstate highways, (ii) multilane, divided, limited access highways, and (iii) high-occupancy vehicle lanes if such lanes are physically separated from regular travel lanes. The maximum speed limit on Interstate Route 85 shall be 70 miles per hour where indicated by lawfully placed signs, erected subsequent to a traffic engineering study and analysis of available and appropriate accident and law-enforcement data. The maximum speed limit shall be 60 miles per hour where indicated by lawfully placed signs, erected subsequent to a traffic engineering study and analysis of available and appropriate accident and law-enforcement data, on U.S. Route 29, U.S. Route 58, U.S. Route 360, U.S. Route 460, and on U.S. Route 17 between the town of Port Royal and Saluda where they are nonlimited access, multilane, divided highways. (Code 1950, § 46-212; 1950, p. 881; 1952, c. 666; 1954, c. 244; 1956, c. 364; 1958, c. 541, §§ 46.1-193, 46.1-401; 1960, c. 153; 1962, c. 307; 1964, cc. 118, 408; 1966, c. 85; 1968, c. 641; 1972, cc. 89, 546, 553, 608; 1974, c. 528; 1975, c. 533; 1977, c. 577; 1978, c. 605; 1980, c. 347; 1986, c. 639; 1988, cc. 662, 897; 1989, cc. 276, 526, 727; 1992, c. 598; 1994, c. 423; 1996, c. 1; 1998, cc. 546, 560; 1999, c. 142; 2001, c. 298; 2002, c. 872; 2003, c. 838; 2004, c. 696; 2005, cc. 266, 267, 268; 2006, c. 213; 2007, cc. 222, 544.)

Editor's note. — Acts 2007, c. 222, cl. 2, provides: "That the provisions of this act shall not be applicable to posted speed limits in effect prior to July 1, 2007."

Acts 2007, c. 544, cl. 2, provides: "That the provisions of this act shall not be applicable to posted speed limits in effect on June 30, 2007."

The 2007 amendments. — The 2007 amendment by c. 222 inserted "and analysis of available and appropriate accident and law-enforcement data" in the third sentence of the third paragraph.

The 2007 amendment by c. 544, in the last paragraph, inserted "and analysis of available and appropriate accident and law-enforcement data" following "traffic engineering study" in the first through last sentences.

§ 46.2-871. Maximum speed limit for school buses.
— The maximum speed limit for school buses shall be 45 miles per hour or the minimum speed allowable, whichever is greater, on any highway where the maximum speed limit is 55 miles per hour or less, and 60 miles per hour on all interstate highways and on other highways where the maximum speed limit is more than 55 miles per hour. (Code 1950, § 46-212; 1950, p. 881; 1952, c. 666; 1954, c. 244; 1956, c. 364; 1958, c. 541, § 46.1-193; 1960, c. 153; 1962, c. 307; 1964, cc. 118, 408; 1966, c.

85; 1968, c. 641; 1972, cc. 89, 546, 553, 608; 1974, c. 528; 1977, c. 577; 1978, c. 605; 1980, c. 347; 1989, c. 727; 1993, c. 278; 1994, c. 676; 1999, c. 166; 2006, c. 416; 2007, c. 98.)

The 2007 amendments. — The 2007 amendment by c. 98 substituted "60 miles per hour on all interstate highways" for "55 miles per hour on all interstate highways."

§ 46.2-873. Maximum speed limits at school crossings; penalty.
— A. The maximum speed limit shall be twenty-five miles per hour between portable signs, tilt-over signs, or fixed blinking signs placed in or along any highway and bearing the word "school" or "school crossing." Any signs erected under this section shall be placed not more than 600 feet from the limits of the school property or crossing in the vicinity of the school. However, "school crossing" signs may be placed in any location if the Department of Transportation or the council of the city or town or the board of supervisors of a county maintaining its own system of secondary roads approves the crossing for such signs. If the portion of the highway to be posted is within the limits of a city or town, such portable signs shall be furnished and delivered by such city or town. If the portion of highway to be posted is outside the limits of a city or town, such portable signs shall be furnished and delivered by the Department of Transportation. The principal or chief administrative officer of each school or a school board designee, preferably not a classroom teacher, shall place such portable signs in the highway at a point not more than 600 feet from the limits of the school property and remove such signs when their presence is no longer required by this section. Such portable signs, tilt-over signs, or fixed blinking signs shall be placed in a position plainly visible to vehicular traffic approaching from either direction, but shall not be placed so as to obstruct the roadway.

B. Such portable signs, tilt-over signs, or blinking signs shall be in a position, or be turned on, for thirty minutes preceding regular school hours, for thirty minutes thereafter, and during such other times as the presence of children on such school property or going to and from school reasonably requires a special warning to motorists. The governing body of any county, city, or town may, however, decrease the period of time preceding and following regular school hours during which such portable signs, tilt-over signs, or blinking signs shall be in position or lit if it determines that no children will be going to or from school during the period of time that it subtracts from the thirty-minute period.

C. The governing body of any city or town may, if the portion of the highway to be posted is within the limits of such city or town, increase or decrease the speed limit provided in this section only after justification for such increase or decrease has been shown by an engineering and traffic investigation, and no such increase or decrease in speed limit shall be effective unless such increased or decreased speed limit is conspicuously posted on the portable signs, tilt-over signs, or fixed blinking signs required by this section.

D. The City of Virginia Beach may establish school zones as provided in this section and mark such zones with flashing warning lights as provided in this section on and along all highways adjacent to Route 58.

E. Any person operating any motor vehicle in excess of a maximum speed limit established specifically for a school crossing zone, when such school crossing zone is (i) indicated by appropriately placed signs displaying the maximum speed limit and (ii) in operation pursuant to subsection B of this section shall be guilty of a traffic infraction punishable by a fine of not more than $250, in addition to other penalties provided by law.

For the purposes of this section, "school crossing zone" means an area located within the vicinity of a school at or near a highway where the presence of children on such school property or going to and from school reasonably requires a special warning to motorists. Such zones are marked and operated in accordance with the requirements of this section with appropriate warning signs or other traffic control devices indicating that a school crossing is in progress.

F. Notwithstanding the foregoing provisions of this section, the maximum speed limit in school zones in residential areas may be decreased to fifteen miles per hour if (i) the school board having jurisdiction over the school nearest to the affected school zone passes a resolution requesting the reduction of the maximum speed limit for such school zone from twenty-five miles per hour to fifteen miles per hour and (ii) the local governing body of the jurisdiction in which such school is located enacts an ordinance establishing the speed-limit reduction requested by the school board. (Code 1950, § 46-212; 1950, p. 881; 1952, c. 666; 1954, c. 244; 1956, c. 364; 1958, c. 541, § 46.1-193; 1960, c. 153; 1962, c. 307; 1964, cc. 118, 408; 1966, c. 85; 1968, c. 641; 1972, cc. 89, 546, 553, 608; 1974, c. 528; 1977, c. 577; 1978, c. 605; 1980, c. 347; 1989, c. 727; 1990, c. 928; 1994, c. 157; 1997, cc. 629, 781; 2007, c. 813.)

Editor's note. — Acts 2007, c. 813, cl. 2, provides: "That the provisions of this act shall not affect the powers of any locality with respect to any ordinance, resolution or bylaw validly adopted and not repealed or rescinded prior to July 1, 2007."

The 2007 amendments. — The 2007 amendment by c. 813 substituted "The City of Virginia Beach" for "Any city having a population of 390,000 or more" in subsection D.

§ 46.2-874.1. Exceptions to maximum speed limits in residence districts; penalty. — A. The governing body of any town with a population between 14,000 and 15,000 may by ordinance (i) prohibit the operation of a motor vehicle at a speed of twenty miles per hour or more in excess of the applicable maximum speed limit in a residence

district and (ii) provide that any person who violates the prohibition shall be subject to a mandatory civil penalty of $100, not subject to suspension.

B. The governing body of the City of Falls Church, or the City of Manassas may by ordinance (i) prohibit the operation of a motor vehicle at a speed of fifteen miles per hour or more in excess of the applicable maximum speed limit in a residence district, as defined in § 46.2-100 of the Code of Virginia, when indicated by appropriately placed signs displaying the maximum speed limit and the penalty for violations, and (ii) provide that any person who violates the prohibition shall be subject to a civil penalty of $100, in addition to other penalty provided by law. (1999, c. 865; 2000, c. 957; 2007, c. 813.)

Editor's note. — Acts 2007, c. 813, cl. 2, provides: "That the provisions of this act shall not affect the powers of any locality with respect to any ordinance, resolution or bylaw validly adopted and not repealed or rescinded prior to July 1, 2007."

The 2007 amendments. — The 2007 amendment by c. 813 substituted "the City of Falls Church, or the City of Manassas" for "any city with a population between 9,000 and 11,000" in subsection B.

ARTICLE 10.

Stopping on Highways.

§ 46.2-891. Exemption for highway construction and maintenance vehicles. — The provisions of this article shall not apply to any vehicle owned or controlled by the Virginia Department of Transportation or counties, cities or towns, while actually engaged in the construction, reconstruction, maintenance, or emergency road clearance of highways. (Code 1950, § 46-256; 1952, c. 671; 1958, c. 541, § 46.1-248; 1962, c. 175; 1972, c. 63; 1974, c. 230; 1977, cc. 284, 326; 1985, c. 93; 1989, c. 727; 2007, cc. 189, 918.)

The 2007 amendments. — The 2007 amendments by cc. 189 and 918 are identical, and substituted "reconstruction, maintenance, or emergency road clearance of highways" for "reconstruction, or maintenance of highways."

ARTICLE 11.

Accidents.

§ 46.2-894. Duty of driver to stop, etc., in event of accident involving injury or death or damage to attended property; penalty.

CASE NOTES

Knowledge necessarily is an essential element of the crime.

Defendant was properly convicted of a violation of this section because the circumstantial evidence, including the observations of two other motorists that he drove in the oncoming lane of traffic when another vehicle was approaching, allowed the trial court, as fact finder, to conclude that he had actual knowledge that an accident with injuries would have occurred, and whether defendant drove in the oncoming lane to pass a slower vehicle or because he "nodded off" was irrelevant, as the dispositive question was whether he knew his action caused an accident in which the other vehicle's occupants would have sustained personal injury. Tooke v. Commonwealth, 47 Va. App. 759, 627 S.E.2d 533, 2006 Va. App. LEXIS 110 (2006).

But the extent of damage or number of people injured or killed does not constitute an element of the offense.

When defendant was convicted of two violations of § 46.2-894, requiring him to stop and render assistance in an accident in which he was involved, because there were two occupants injured in a vehicle he caused to go off the road, this was a miscarriage of justice, because defendant was convicted twice for conduct that was but one criminal offense, so his failure to object did not bar the appellate court, under Va. Sup. Ct. R. 5A:18, from finding that the ends of justice exception to that Rule applied. Tooke v. Commonwealth, 47 Va. App. 759, 627 S.E.2d 533, 2006 Va. App. LEXIS 110 (2006).

"Involved." — Because defendant's conduct, accelerating in an attempt to reach the end of the merge lane first, contributed to the other driver's high speed, defendant was "involved" in the accident and should have reported identifying information to a law enforcement officer. Robinson v. Commonwealth, 48 Va. App. 623, 633 S.E.2d 737, 2006 Va. App. LEXIS 400 (2006).

Evidence sufficient for conviction.

Evidence supported defendant's conviction of leaving the scene of an accident where another driver was killed after he and defendant had been drag racing. Although defendant claimed that he had left the scene to make a telephone call and report the accident, two witnesses had seen him use a telephone at the scene, and the telephone was later found in defendant's car; defendant's path behind and between houses suggested that he was trying to avoid detection; defendant had had an opportunity to give information to an off-duty state trooper before the trooper left the scene; and defendant never attempted to render assistance to anyone. O'Connell v. Commonwealth, 48 Va. App. 719, 634 S.E.2d 379, 2006 Va. App. LEXIS 415 (2006).

ARTICLE 12.

Bicycles.

§ 46.2-905. Riding bicycles, electric personal assistive mobility devices, electric power-assisted bicycles, motor-driven cycles, and mopeds on roadways and bicycle paths. — Any person operating a bicycle, electric personal assistive mobility device, electric power-assisted bicycle, or moped on a roadway at less than the normal speed of traffic at the time and place under conditions then existing shall ride as close as safely practicable to the right curb or edge of the roadway, except under any of the following circumstances:

1. When overtaking and passing another vehicle proceeding in the same direction;

2. When preparing for a left turn at an intersection or into a private road or driveway;

3. When reasonably necessary to avoid conditions including, but not limited to, fixed or moving objects, parked or moving vehicles, pedestrians, animals, surface hazards, or substandard width lanes that make it unsafe to continue along the right curb or edge;

4. When avoiding riding in a lane that must turn or diverge to the right; and

5. When riding upon a one-way road or highway, a person may also ride as near the left-hand curb or edge of such roadway as safely practicable.

For purposes of this section, a "substandard width lane" is a lane too narrow for a bicycle, electric personal assistive mobility device, electric power-assisted bicycle, motorized skateboard or scooter, or moped and another vehicle to pass safely side by side within the lane.

Persons riding bicycles, electric personal assistive mobility devices, or electric power-assisted bicycles on a highway shall not ride more than two abreast. Persons riding two abreast shall not impede the normal and reasonable movement of traffic, shall move into a single file formation as quickly as is practicable when being overtaken from the rear by a faster moving vehicle, and, on a laned roadway, shall ride in a single lane.

Notwithstanding any other provision of law to the contrary, the Department of Conservation and Recreation shall permit the operation of electric personal assistive mobility devices on any bicycle path or trail designated by the Department for such use. (1974, c. 347, § 46.1-229.1; 1980, c. 130; 1981, c. 585; 1989, c. 727; 2001, c. 834; 2002, c. 254; 2003, cc. 29, 46; 2004, cc. 947, 973; 2006, cc. 529, 538; 2007, cc. 209, 366.)

The 2007 amendments. — The 2007 amendments by cc. 209 and 366 are identical, and deleted "motorized skateboard or scooter" following "electric power-assisted bicycle" in the introductory paragraph, and in the next-to-last paragraph, deleted "motorized skateboards or scooters" following "electric personal assistive mobility devices."

§ 46.2-908.1. Electric personal assistive mobility devices, electrically powered toy vehicle, and electric power-assisted bicycles. — All electric personal assistive mobility devices, electrically powered toy vehicles, and electric power-assisted bicycles shall be equipped with spill-proof, sealed, or gelled electrolyte batteries. No person shall at any time or at any location drive an electric personal assistive mobility device, or an electric power-assisted bicycle faster than twenty-five miles per hour. No person less than fourteen years old shall drive any electric personal assistive mobility device, motorized skateboard or scooter, or electric power-assisted bicycle unless under the immediate supervision of a person who is at least eighteen years old.

An electric personal assistive mobility device or motorized skateboard or scooter may be operated on any highway with a maximum speed limit of twenty-five miles per hour or less. An electric personal assistive mobility device shall only operate on any highway authorized by this section if a sidewalk is not provided along such highway or if operation of the electric personal assistive mobility device on such sidewalk is prohibited pursuant to § 46.2-904. Nothing in this section shall prohibit the operation of an electric personal assistive mobility device or motorized skateboard or scooter in the crosswalk of any highway where the use of such crosswalk is authorized for pedestrians, bicycles, or electric power-assisted bicycles. (2001, c. 834; 2002, c. 254; 2006, cc. 529, 538; 2007, cc. 209, 366.)

The 2007 amendments. — The 2007 amendments by cc. 209 and 366 are identical, and, in the first paragraph, substituted "electrically powered toy vehicles" for "motorized skateboards or scooters" and "gelled electrolyte batteries" for "gel batteries" in the first sentence and deleted "a motorized skateboard or scooter" following "assistive mobility device" in the second sentence; and in the second paragraph, deleted "or motorized skateboard or scooter" following "assistive mobility device" twice in the second sentence.

ARTICLE 13.

Motorcycles and Mopeds and All-Terrain Vehicles.

§ 46.2-915. Stickers required on mopeds. — Any dealer who sells any moped at retail shall affix to any such moped, or verify that there is affixed thereto a permanent decal or sticker which states (i) that the operation of mopeds on highways and public vehicular areas by persons under the age of sixteen is prohibited by Virginia law, (ii) the maximum horsepower of the moped, and (iii) the maximum speed at which the moped may be ridden.

Any dealer who sells any such moped which does not have affixed thereto such a permanent decal or sticker or who sells a motorcycle with such a sticker or decal attached thereto indicating that its motor is rated at no more than two brake horsepower producing only ordinary speeds up to a maximum of 35 miles per hour shall be guilty of a Class 1 misdemeanor. (1976, c. 264, § 46.1-172.03; 1981, c. 585; 1987, c. 344; 1989, c. 727; 2007, c. 111.)

The 2007 amendments. — The 2007 amendment by c. 111 substituted "35 miles per hour" for "thirty miles per hour" in the last paragraph.

ARTICLE 16.

Pedestrians.

Michie's Jurisprudence. — For related discussion, see 2B M.J. Automobiles, §§ 28, 29, 30, 32 - 36, 68; 5C M.J. Death by Wrongful Act, § 4; 17 M.J. Street Railroads, § 21.

§ 46.2-932. Playing on highways; use of toy vehicle on highways, persons riding bicycles, electric personal assistive mobility devices, electric power-assisted bicycles, mopeds, etc., not to attach to vehicles; exception. — A. No person shall play on a highway, other than on the sidewalks thereof, within a city or town or on any part of a highway outside the limits of a city or town designated by the Commonwealth Transportation Commissioner exclusively for vehicular travel. No person shall use any toy vehicle on the roadway of any highway that (i) has a speed limit greater than 25 miles per hour, (ii) has more than two travel lanes, or (iii) is located outside a residence district as defined in § 46.2-100. The governing bodies of coun-

ties, cities, and towns may designate areas on highways under their control where play is permitted and may impose reasonable restrictions on play on such highways. Persons using such devices, except bicycles, electric personal assistive mobility devices, electric power-assisted bicycles, mopeds, and motorcycles, shall keep as near as safely practicable to the far right side or edge of the right traffic lane so that they will be proceeding in the same direction as other traffic.

No person riding on any bicycle, electric personal assistive mobility device, electric power-assisted bicycle, moped, roller skates, skateboards or other devices on wheels or runners, shall attach the same or himself to any vehicle on a highway.

B. Notwithstanding the provisions of subsection A of this section, the governing body of Arlington County may by ordinance permit the use of devices on wheels or runners on highways under such county's control, subject to such limitations and conditions as the governing body may deem necessary and reasonable. (Code 1950, § 46-248; 1958, c. 541, § 46.1-235; 1972, c. 817; 1973, c. 288; 1981, c. 585; 1989, c. 727; 2001, cc. 170, 834; 2002, c. 254; 2004, cc. 947, 973; 2006, cc. 529, 538; 2007, cc. 209, 366, 813.)

Editor's note. — Acts 2007, c. 813, cl. 2, provides: "That the provisions of this act shall not affect the powers of any locality with respect to any ordinance, resolution or bylaw validly adopted and not repealed or rescinded prior to July 1, 2007."

The 2007 amendments. — The 2007 amendments by cc. 209 and 366 are identical, and in subsection A, rewrote the second sentence, and deleted "If the highways have only two traffic lanes" at the beginning of the fourth sentence of the first paragraph, substituted "skateboards or other devices" for "skateboards, motorized skateboards or scooters, toys, or other devices" and "highway" for "roadway" in the second paragraph.

The 2007 amendment by c. 813 substituted "Arlington County" for "any county having a population of at least 170,000 but less than 200,000" in subsection B.

CHAPTER 10.

MOTOR VEHICLE AND EQUIPMENT SAFETY.

Article 15.

Maximum Vehicle Widths and Heights.

Sec.
46.2-1110. Height of vehicles; damage to overhead obstruction; penalty.

Article 17.

Maximum Vehicle Weights.

46.2-1130.1. Overweight permits granted to cross bridges and culverts by certain emergency response vehicles responding to an emergency call.
46.2-1135. (Contingent effective date — see Editor's notes) Liquidated damages for violation of weight limits.

Article 18.

Permits for Excessive Size and Weight. 46.2-1142 for vehicles used to haul concrete; fees.

46.2-1143. Overweight permits for coal haulers; trucks hauling gravel, sand, crushed stone, or liquids produced from

Sec.
       gas or oil wells in certain counties; penalties.
46.2-1144.1. Overweight permits for tank wagons.
46.2-1149.3. Payment of fees into special fund.
46.2-1149.5. Overweight permits for underground pipe cleaning,
       hydroexcavating, and water blasting equipment.

ARTICLE 15.

Maximum Vehicle Widths and Heights.

§ 46.2-1110. Height of vehicles; damage to overhead obstruction; penalty. — No loaded or unloaded vehicle shall exceed a height of 13 feet, six inches.

Nothing contained in this section shall require either the public authorities or railroad companies to provide vertical clearances of overhead bridges or structures in excess of 12 feet, six inches, or to make any changes in the vertical clearances of existing overhead bridges or structures crossing highways. The driver or owner of vehicles on highways shall be held financially responsible for any damage to overhead bridges or structures that results from collisions therewith.

The driver or owner of any vehicle colliding with an overhead bridge or structure shall immediately notify, either in person or by telephone, a law-enforcement officer or the public authority or railroad company, owning or maintaining such overhead bridge or structure of the fact of such collision, and his name, address, driver's license number, and the registration number of his vehicle. Failure to give such notice immediately, either in person or by telephone, shall constitute a Class 1 misdemeanor.

On any highway over which there is a bridge or structure having a vertical clearance of less than 14 feet, the Commonwealth Transportation Commissioner shall have at least two signs erected setting forth the height of the bridge or structure. Such signs shall be located at least 1,500 feet ahead of the bridge or structure.

The Virginia Department of Transportation may install and use overheight vehicle optical detection systems to identify vehicles that exceed the overhead clearance of the westbound tunnel of the Hampton Roads Bridge Tunnel on Interstate Route 64. When the optical system sensor located closest to the westbound tunnel entrance is used in identifying such vehicles, the system shall be installed at the specified height as determined by measurement standards that have been certified by the Commissioner of the Virginia Department of Agriculture and Consumer Services, and are traceable to national standards of measurement. Such identification by such system shall, for all purposes of law, be equivalent to having measured the height of the vehicle with a tape measure or other measuring device.

Any person who drives or attempts to drive any vehicle or combination of vehicles into or through any tunnel when the height of such vehicle, any vehicle in a combination of vehicles, or any load on any such vehicle exceeds that permitted for such tunnel, shall be guilty of a misdemeanor and, in addition, shall be assessed three driver demerit points. In addition, the driver of any such vehicle shall be fined $1,000, of which $1,000 shall be a mandatory minimum. For subsequent offenses, the owner of any such vehicle shall be fined $2,500, of which $2,500 shall be a mandatory minimum.

A violation of this section shall be deemed for all purposes a moving violation. (Code 1950, § 46-327; 1950, p. 480; 1958, c. 541, § 46.1-329; 1962, c. 85; 1984, c. 780; 1989, c. 727; 2001, c. 94; 2005, cc. 542, 543; 2006, Sp. Sess. I, c. 6.)

The 2006 amendments. — The 2006 amendment by Sp. Sess. I, c. 6, effective January 1, 2007, in the next-to-last paragraph, deleted "Class 3" preceding "misdemeanor" near the end of the first sentence, and added the second and third sentences; and added the last paragraph.

ARTICLE 17.

Maximum Vehicle Weights.

§ 46.2-1130.1. Overweight permits granted to cross bridges and culverts by certain emergency response vehicles responding to an emergency call. — Notwithstanding the provisions of §§ 46.2-1104 and 46.2-1130, emergency response vehicles, including fire and emergency medical apparatus responding to and returning from an emergency call, may be permitted to exceed the gross weight limit posted on a bridge or culvert, except those maintained by a railroad, provided that a determination has been made by a licensed professional engineer, qualified in the appropriate discipline, that the emergency response vehicle can safely cross that bridge or culvert and that determination has been documented by the issuance of a written permit or letter of authorization by the agency or entity responsible for the maintenance of that bridge or culvert.

The permitting agency or entity shall not be held liable for any damage or injury caused as a result of an emergency response vehicle crossing a bridge or culvert while responding to or returning from an emergency call under the conditions specified in the overweight permit pursuant to this section. (2007, cc. 177, 540.)

§ 46.2-1135. (Contingent expiration date — see Editor's notes) Liquidated damages for violation of weight limits. — A. Any person violating any weight limit as provided in this chapter or in any permit issued pursuant to Article 18 (§ 46.2-1139 et seq.) of this chapter by the Department or its designee or by local authorities pursuant to this chapter shall be assessed liquidated damages. The amount of those damages shall be:

Excess weight over the prescribed or permitted axle weight limits	Assessed amount per pound	Excess weight over the prescribed gross weight limit	Assessed amount per pound
2,000 pounds or less	1¢ per pound	2,000 pounds or less	1¢ per pound
2,001 to 4,000 pounds	3¢ per pound	2,001 to 4,000 pounds	3¢ per pound
4,001 to 8,000 pounds	12¢ per pound	4,001 to 8,000 pounds	7¢ per pound
8,001 to 12,000 pounds	22¢ per pound	8,001 to 12,000 pounds	12¢ per pound
12,001 pounds or more	35¢ per pound	12,001 pounds or more	20¢ per pound

All gross permit violations shall be assessed $.20 per pound over the permitted weight limit.

In addition to all damages assessed herein, for every violation of any weight limit as provided in this chapter or in any permit issued pursuant to Article 18 (§ 46.2-1139 et seq.) of this chapter, there shall be assessed additional liquidated damages of $20.

If a person has no prior violations under the motor vehicle weight laws, and the excess weight does not exceed 1,500 pounds, the general district court may waive the liquidated damages against such person. Except as provided by § 46.2-1138, such assessment shall be entered by the court or by the Department as a judgment for the Commonwealth, the entry of which shall constitute a lien upon the overweight vehicle. Except as provided by § 46.2-1138, such sums shall be paid to the Department or collected by the attorney for the Commonwealth and forwarded to the State Treasurer and allocated to the fund appropriated for the construction and maintenance of state highways.

B. If the gross weight of the vehicle exceeds lawful limits by at least 25 percent but no more than 50 percent, the amount of the liquidated damages shall be two times the amount provided for in the foregoing provisions of this section; if the gross weight of the vehicle exceeds lawful limits by more than 50 percent, the amount of the liquidated damages shall be three times the amount provided for in the foregoing provisions of this section. The provisions of this subsection shall not apply to pickup or panel trucks.

C. The increases in the liquidated damages under subsection A pursuant to enactments of the 2007 Session of the General Assembly shall not be applicable to any motor vehicle hauling forest or farm products from the place where such products are first produced, cut, harvested, or felled to the location where they are first processed. The amount of liquidated damages assessed against such motor vehicles shall be:

Excess weight over the prescribed or permitted axle weight limits	Assessed amount per pound	Excess weight over the prescribed gross weight limit	Assessed amount per pound
4,000 pounds or less	1¢ per pound	4,000 pounds or less	1¢ per pound
4,001 to 8,000 pounds	10¢ per pound	4,001 to 8,000 pounds	5¢ per pound
8,001 to 12,000 pounds	20¢ per pound	8,001 to 12,000 pounds	10¢ per pound
12,001 pounds or more	30¢ per pound	12,001 pounds or more	15¢ per pound

(Code 1950, § 46-338.2; 1956, c. 215; 1958, cc. 541, 612, § 46.1-342; 1968, c. 184; 1974, c. 331; 1977, c. 644; 1981, c. 187; 1986, c. 588; 1987, c. 372; 1989, c. 727; 1994, c. 922; 1997, c. 479; 2001, cc. 411, 433; 2003, c. 314; 2007, c. 896.)

The section above is effective December 31 of any year revenues designated for the Highway Maintenance and Operating Fund or the Transportation Trust Fund are appropriated for any non-transportation related purposes. For this section as in effect until that time, see the section as set out in the 2006 Edition.

Editor's note. — Acts 2007, c. 896, cl. 3, provides: "That the revenues generated by the provisions of this act shall not be used to calculate or reduce the share of local, federal, and state revenues otherwise available to participating jurisdictions. Further, such revenues and moneys shall not be included in any computation of, or formula for, a locality's ability to pay for public education, upon which appropriations of state revenues to local governments for public education are determined."

Acts 2007, c. 896, cl. 21, provides: "That the revenue generated by this act shall be used solely for transportation purposes."

Acts 2007, c. 896, cl. 22, provides: "That the provisions of this act which generate additional revenue for the Transportation Trust Fund, established under § 33.1-23.03:1 of the Code of Virginia, or the Highway Maintenance and Operating Fund shall expire on December 31 of any year in which the General Assembly appropriates any of the revenues designated under general law to the

Highway Maintenance and Operating Fund or the Transportation Trust Fund for any non-transportation related purpose."

Acts 2007, c. 896, cl. 23 contains a severability clause.

The 2007 amendments. — The 2007 amendment by c. 896 rewrote both tables and added the second paragraph following the second table of subsection A; substituted "1,500" for "2,500" in the third paragraph of subsection A; and added subsection C.

ARTICLE 18.

Permits for Excessive Size and Weight.

§ 46.2-1143. Overweight permits for coal haulers; trucks hauling gravel, sand, crushed stone, or liquids produced from gas or oil wells in certain counties; penalties. — A. The Commissioner and local authorities of cities and towns in their respective jurisdictions, upon written application by the owner or operator of vehicles used exclusively for hauling coal from a mine or other place of production to a preparation plant, loading dock, or railroad shall issue, without cost, a permit authorizing those vehicles to operate with gross weights in excess of those established in § 46.2-1126 on the conditions set forth in this section.

B. Vehicles with three axles may have a maximum gross weight, when loaded, of no more than 60,000 pounds, a single axle weight of not more than 24,000 pounds and a tandem axle weight of no more than 45,000 pounds. Vehicles with four axles may have a maximum gross weight, when loaded, of no more than 70,000 pounds, a single axle weight of no more than 24,000 pounds, and a tri-axle weight of no more than 50,000 pounds. Vehicles with five axles having no less than 35 feet of axle space between extreme axles may have a maximum gross weight, when loaded, of no more than 90,000 pounds, a single axle weight of no more than 20,000 pounds, and a tandem axle weight of no more than 40,000 pounds. Vehicles with six axles may have a maximum gross weight, when loaded, of no more than 110,000 pounds, a single axle weight of no more than 24,000 pounds, a tandem axle weight of no more than 44,000 pounds, and a tri-axle weight of no more than 54,500 pounds.

C. No load of any vehicle operating under a permit issued according to this section shall rise above the top of the bed of such vehicle, not including extensions of the bed. Three-axle vehicles shall not carry loads in excess of the maximum bed size in cubic feet for such vehicle which shall be computed by a formula of 60,000 pounds minus the weight of the empty truck divided by the average weight of coal. For the purposes of this section, the average weight of coal shall be 52 pounds per cubic foot. Four-axle vehicles shall not carry loads in excess of the maximum bed size for such vehicle which shall be computed by a formula of 70,000 pounds minus the weight of the truck empty divided by the average weight of coal. Five-axle vehicles shall not carry loads in excess of the maximum bed size for such vehicle, which shall be computed by a formula of 90,000 pounds minus the weight of the truck empty divided by the average weight of coal. Six-axle vehicles shall not carry loads in excess of the maximum bed size for such vehicle, which shall be computed by a formula of 110,000 pounds minus the weight of the truck empty divided by the average weight of coal.

D. For the purposes of this section, the term bed shall mean that part of the vehicle used to haul coal. Bed size shall be measured by its interior dimensions with volume expressed in cubic feet. In order to ensure compliance with this section by visual inspection, if the actual bed size of the vehicle exceeds the maximum as provided above, the owner or operator shall be required to paint a horizontal line two inches wide on the sides of the outside of the bed of the vehicle, clearly visible to indicate the uppermost limit of the maximum bed size applicable to the vehicle as provided in this section. In addition, one hole two inches high and six inches long on each side of the bed shall be cut in the center of the bed and at the top of the painted line. Any vehicle in violation of this section shall subject the vehicle's owner or operator or both to a penalty of $250 for a first offense, $500 for a second offense within a 12-month period, and $1,000 and revocation of the permit for a third offense within a 12-month period from the first offense.

E. If the bed of any vehicle is enlarged beyond the maximum bed size for which its permit was granted, or if the line or holes required are altered so that the vehicle exceeds the bed size for which its permit was granted, the owner, operator, or both shall be subject to a penalty of $1,000 for each offense and revocation of the permit. Upon revocation, a permit shall not be reissued for six months. The penalties provided in this section shall be in lieu of those imposed under § 46.2-1135.

F. For any vehicle with a valid permit issued pursuant to the conditions required by this section, when carrying loads which do not rise above the top of the bed or the line indicating the bed's maximum size, if applicable, it shall be, in the absence of proof to the contrary, prima facie evidence that the load is within the applicable weight limits. If any vehicle is stopped by enforcement officials for carrying a load rising above the top of the bed or the line indicating the bed's maximum size, the operator of the vehicle shall be permitted to shift his load within the bed to determine whether the load can be contained in the bed without rising above its top or above the line.

G. No such permit shall be valid for the operation of any such vehicle for a distance of more than 85 miles from the preparation plant, loading dock, or railroad.

H. Until July 1, 2009, in counties that impose a severance tax on coal and gases as authorized by § 58.1-3712, the weight limits prescribed in subsection B of this section shall also apply to trucks hauling gravel, sand, or crushed stone no more than 50 miles from origin to destination. Nothing contained in this subsection shall authorize any extension of weight limits provided in § 46.2-1127 for operation on interstate highways. Any weight violation hauling sand, gravel, or crushed stone under this subsection shall be subject to the penalties authorized by § 46.2-1135.

I. In counties that impose a severance tax on coal and gases as authorized by § 58.1-3712, the weight limits prescribed in subsection B shall also apply to motor vehicles hauling liquids produced from a gas or oil well and water used for drilling and completion of a gas or oil well no more than 50 miles from origin to destination. Nothing contained in this subsection shall authorize any extension of weight limits provided in § 46.2-1127 for operation on interstate highways. Any weight violation involving hauling liquids produced from a gas or oil well and water used for drilling and completion of a gas or oil well under this subsection shall be subject to the penalties authorized by § 46.2-1135. (1973, c. 62, § 46.1-343.3; 1989, c. 727; 1996, cc. 36, 87; 1999, c. 915; 2001, c. 417; 2002, c. 264; 2003, cc. 314, 315; 2005, c. 556; 2007, c. 523.)

Editor's note. — Acts 2007, c. 523, cl. 2, provides: "That the Department of Transportation, in consultation with the Commonwealth Transportation Board, shall recommend legislation regarding the operation of vehicles pursuant to subsection H of § 46.2-1143 as amended by this act. Such proposed legislation shall be presented to the Governor and Chairmen of the House and Senate Committees on Transportation no later than December 1, 2007."

The 2007 amendments. — The 2007 amendment by c. 523 substituted "July 1, 2009" for "July 1, 2007" in subsection H.

§ 46.2-1144.1. Overweight permits for tank wagons.

— The Commissioner, upon written application and payment of a fee by the owner of tank wagon vehicles as defined in § 58.1-2201, shall issue overweight permits for operation of said vehicles.

The overweight permit fees shall be based on a fee schedule established by the Commonwealth Transportation Commissioner. Such fees shall be dedicated to and deposited into the Highway Maintenance and Operating Fund.

The Commissioner may also assess a separate application fee for applications pursuant to this section that covers the administrative expenses of the Department. Funds from the application fee are to be designated as specified in § 46.2-1149.3.

No permit issued under this section shall authorize a single axle weight of more than 24,000 pounds and a total gross weight in excess of 36,000 pounds. Permits issued under this section shall be valid for one year from the date of issuance. No permit issued under this section shall authorize violation of any weight limitation, promulgated and posted in accordance with § 46.2-1130, applicable to bridges or culverts. This permit shall not be combined with any other overweight permit or extension of weight limits. (2007, c. 738.)

Editor's note. — Acts 2007, c. 738, cl. 2, provides: "That from July 1, 2007, to July 1, 2008, the annual overweight permit fee shall be $800 for each eligible vehicle. The Commonwealth Transportation Commissioner shall establish a fee structure that shall become effective on July 1, 2008, based on the results of a study of overweight vehicles."

Acts 2007, c. 738, cl. 3, provides: "That the fee structure established by the Commonwealth Transportation Commissioner pursuant to § 46.2-1144.1 shall not be subject to the requirements of the Administrative Process Act (§ 2.2-4000 et seq.)."

§ 46.2-1149.3. Payment of fees into special fund.

— Except as provided in § 46.2-1144.1, all fees collected by the Commissioner under §§ 46.2-1139 through 46.2-1149.2 shall be paid into the state treasury and set aside as a special fund to be used to meet the expenses of the Department. (2003, c. 314; 2007, c. 738.)

Editor's note. — Acts 2007, c. 738, cl. 2, provides: "That from July 1, 2007, to July 1, 2008, the annual overweight permit fee shall be $800 for each eligible vehicle. The Commonwealth Transportation Commissioner shall establish a fee structure that shall become effective on July 1, 2008, based on the results of a study of overweight vehicles."

The 2007 amendments. — The 2007 amendment by c. 738 inserted "Except as provided in § 46.2-1144.1" at the beginning.

§ 46.2-1149.5. Overweight permits for underground pipe cleaning, hydroexcavating, and water blasting equipment.

— The Commissioner and local authorities of cities and towns, in their respective jurisdictions, upon written application made by the owner or operator, shall issue an overweight permit for the operation of underground pipe cleaning, hydroexcavating, and water blasting equipment. Any vehicle operating under a permit issued pursuant to this section shall have a gross weight of no more than 64,000 pounds, a single axle weight of no more than 20,000 pounds, and a tandem axle weight of no more than 44,000 pounds. Such permit shall not designate the route to be traversed nor contain restrictions or conditions not applicable to other vehicles in their general use of the highways.

For purposes of this section, *"underground pipe cleaning equipment"* means a self-propelled motor vehicle manufactured for the specific purpose of vacuuming and cleaning underground sanitary and storm pipe. *"Hydroexcavating equipment"* means a self-propelled motor vehicle manufactured for the specific purpose of digging with water and vacuuming of debris. *"Water blasting equipment"* means a self-propelled motor vehicle manufactured for the specific purpose of waterblasting flat concrete surfaces and vacuuming spent water for reuse. (2007, c. 429.)

Editor's note. — Acts 2007, c. 429, cl. 2, provides: "That the Department of Transportation, in consultation with the Commonwealth Transportation Board, shall recommend legislation regarding the operation of vehicles pursuant to the provisions of this act. Such proposed legislation shall be presented to the Governor and Chairmen of the House and Senate Committees on Transportation no later than December 1, 2007."

CHAPTER 12.

ABANDONED, IMMOBILIZED, UNATTENDED AND
TRESPASSING VEHICLES; PARKING.

Article 3.

Trespassing Vehicles, Parking, and Towing.

Sec.
46.2-1216. Removal or immobilization of motor vehicles against
which there are outstanding parking violations; ordinances.
46.2-1219.2. Parking of vehicles in commuter parking lots owned
by the Virginia Department of Transportation.
46.2-1222.2. Local ordinances prohibiting parking of certain vehicles.

ARTICLE 2.

Immobilized and Unattended Vehicles.

Michie's Jurisprudence. — For related discussion, see 1A M.J.
Abandonment, § 1; 2B M.J. Automobiles, § 27.

ARTICLE 3.

Trespassing Vehicles, Parking, and Towing.

Michie's Jurisprudence. — For related discussion, see 1A M.J.
Abandonment, § 1; 2B M.J. Automobiles, §§ 5, 13.

**§ 46.2-1216. Removal or immobilization of
motor vehicles against which there are outstanding parking violations; ordinances.** —
The governing body of any county, city, or town may
provide by ordinance that any motor vehicle parked
on the public highways or public grounds against
which there are three or more unpaid or otherwise
unsettled parking violation notices may be removed
to a place within such county, city, or town or in an
adjacent locality designated by the chief law-enforcement officer for the temporary storage of the
vehicle, or the vehicle may be immobilized in a
manner which will prevent its removal or operation
except by authorized law-enforcement personnel.
The governing body of Fairfax County, and any town
adjacent to such county, Loudoun County, the Cities
of Alexandria, Fairfax, Falls Church, Manassas,
Manassas Park, and Virginia Beach may also provide by ordinance that whenever any motor vehicle
against which there are three or more outstanding
unpaid or otherwise unsettled parking violation
notices is found parked upon private property, including privately owned streets and roads, the vehicle may, by towing or otherwise, be removed or
immobilized in the manner provided above; provided
that no motor vehicle may be removed or immobilized from property which is owned or occupied as a
single family residence. Any such ordinance shall
further provide that no such vehicle parked on
private property may be removed or immobilized
unless written authorization to enforce this section
has been given by the owner of the property or an

association of owners formed pursuant to Chapter
4.1 (§ 55-79.1 et seq.) or Chapter 4.2 (§ 55-79.39 et
seq.) of Title 55 and that the local governing body
has provided written assurance to the owner of the
property that he will be held harmless from all loss,
damage, or expense, including costs and attorney's
fees, that may be incurred as a result of the towing
or otherwise of any motor vehicle pursuant to this
section. The ordinance shall provide that the removal or immobilization of the vehicle shall be by or
under the direction of, an officer or employee of the
police department or sheriff's office.

Any ordinance shall provide that it shall be the
duty of the law-enforcement personnel removing or
immobilizing the motor vehicle or under whose
direction such vehicle is removed or immobilized, to
inform as soon as practicable the owner of the
removed or immobilized vehicle of the nature and
circumstances of the prior unsettled parking violation notices for which the vehicle was removed or
immobilized. In any case involving immobilization of
a vehicle pursuant to this section, there shall be
placed on the vehicle, in a conspicuous manner, a
notice warning that the vehicle has been immobilized and that any attempt to move the vehicle
might damage it.

Any ordinance shall provide that the owner of an
immobilized vehicle, or other person acting on his
behalf, shall be allowed at least twenty-four hours
from the time of immobilization to repossess or
secure the release of the vehicle. Failure to repossess
or secure the release of the vehicle within that time
period may result in the removal of the vehicle to a
storage area for safekeeping under the direction of
law-enforcement personnel.

Any ordinance shall provide that the owner of the
removed or immobilized motor vehicle, or other
person acting on his behalf, shall be permitted to
repossess or to secure the release of the vehicle by
payment of the outstanding parking violation notices for which the vehicle was removed or immobilized and by payment of all costs incidental to the
immobilization, removal, and storage of the vehicle,
and the efforts to locate the owner of the vehicle.
Should the owner fail or refuse to pay such fines and
costs, or should the identity or whereabouts of the
owner be unknown and unascertainable, the ordinance may provide for the sale of the motor vehicle
in accordance with the procedures set forth in
§ 46.2-1213. (1977, c. 666, § 46.1-3.02; 1978, c. 282;
1984, c. 64; 1988, c. 520; 1989, c. 727; 1990, c. 686;
2007, c. 813.)

Editor's note. — Acts 2007, c. 813, cl. 2, provides: "That the
provisions of this act shall not affect the powers of any locality with
respect to any ordinance, resolution or bylaw validly adopted and
not repealed or rescinded prior to July 1, 2007."
The 2007 amendments. — The 2007 amendment by c. 813
substituted "The governing body of Fairfax County, and any town
adjacent to such county, Loudoun County, the Cities of Alexandria,
Fairfax, Falls Church, Manassas, Manassas Park, and Virginia
Beach" for "The governing body of any county having the urban
county executive form of government and any county, city, or town

adjacent to such county except any county having the county manager plan of government and any city having a 1980 census population of more than 262,000 but less than 265,000" in the second sentence in the first paragraph.

§ 46.2-1219.2. Parking of vehicles in commuter parking lots owned by the Virginia Department of Transportation. — A. It shall constitute a traffic infraction for any person to park any vehicle in any commuter parking lot owned by the Virginia Department of Transportation in any manner not in conformance with posted signs and pavement markings.

B. In the prosecution of an offense established under this section, prima facie evidence that the vehicle described in the summons issued pursuant to this section was parked in violation of this section, together with proof that the defendant was at the time of such violation the owner, lessee, or renter of the vehicle, shall constitute in evidence a rebuttable presumption that such owner, lessee, or renter of the vehicle was the person who committed the violation. Such presumption shall be rebutted if the owner, lessee, or renter of the vehicle (i) files an affidavit by regular mail with the clerk of the general district court that he was not the operator of the vehicle at the time of the alleged violation or (ii) testifies in open court under oath that he was not the operator of the vehicle at the time of the alleged violation. Such presumption shall also be rebutted if a certified copy of a police report, showing that the vehicle had been reported to the police as stolen prior to the time of the alleged violation of this section, is presented, prior to the return date established on the summons issued pursuant to this section, to the court adjudicating the alleged violation. A violation of this section may be charged on the uniform traffic summons form.

C. Notwithstanding the provisions of § 19.2-76, whenever a summons for a violation of this section is served in any county, city, or town, it may be executed by mailing by first-class mail a copy thereof to the address of the owner of the vehicle as shown on the records of the Department of Motor Vehicles. If the summoned person fails to appear on the date of return set out in the summons mailed pursuant to this section, the summons shall be executed in the manner set out in § 19.2-76.3.

Enforcement of the provisions of this section may be enforced by any law-enforcement officer as defined in § 9.1-101. (2007, c. 263.)

§ 46.2-1222.2. Local ordinances prohibiting parking of certain vehicles. — The governing body of any county, city, or town may by ordinance limit to no more than two hours the length of time of parking on streets, adjacent to commercial business areas, of vehicles with gross weights in excess of 12,000 pounds or lengths of 30 feet or more, unless such vehicles are actively engaged in loading or unloading operations or waiting to be loaded or

unloaded or are engaged in or preparing to engage in utility or similar service work. (2007, c. 487.)

CHAPTER 13.

Powers of Local Governments.

Sec.
46.2-1304.   Local regulation of trucks and buses.
46.2-1307.   Designation of private roads as highways for law-enforcement purposes.
46.2-1307.1. Designation of private roads as highways for law-enforcement purposes in Warren County.

§ 46.2-1304. Local regulation of trucks and buses. — The governing bodies of counties, cities, and towns may by ordinance, whenever in their judgment conditions so require:

1. Prohibit the use of trucks, except for the purpose of receiving loads or making deliveries on certain designated streets under their jurisdiction;

2. Restrict the use of trucks passing through the city or town to such street or streets under their jurisdiction as may be designated in such ordinance.

The Cities of Poquoson and Williamsburg may restrict the operation of nonscheduled buses, other than school buses, over designated streets under its jurisdiction. (Code 1950, § 46-206; 1958, c. 541, § 46.1-181; 1968, c. 463; 1989, c. 727; 1998, cc. 547, 574; 2007, c. 813.)

Editor's note. — Acts 2007, c. 813, cl. 2, provides: "That the provisions of this act shall not affect the powers of any locality with respect to any ordinance, resolution or bylaw validly adopted and not repealed or rescinded prior to July 1, 2007."

The 2007 amendments. — The 2007 amendment by c. 813 substituted "The Cities of Poquoson and Williamsburg" for "Any city having a population of at least 11,200 but no more than 15,000" in the last paragraph.

§ 46.2-1307. Designation of private roads as highways for law-enforcement purposes. — The governing body of any county, city, or town may adopt ordinances designating the private roads, within any residential development containing 100 or more lots or residential dwelling units, as highways for law-enforcement purposes. Such ordinance may also provide for certification of road signs and speed limits by private licensed professional engineers using criteria developed by the Commonwealth Transportation Commissioner, and, for law-enforcement purposes, such certification shall have the same effect as if certified by the Commonwealth Transportation Commissioner. (1979, c. 100, § 46.1-181.5; 1987, c. 152; 1989, c. 727; 2007, cc. 74, 187, 310.)

The 2007 amendments. — The 2007 amendments by cc. 74 and 310 are identical, and inserted "or residential dwelling units" near the end.

The 2007 amendment by c. 187 added the second sentence.

Ordinance that exceeded scope of county's authority held invalid. — By defining "highway" to include private parking areas at residential developments containing 100 or more lots or residential dwelling units, a county expanded the scope of the limited authority granted to it by § 46.2-1307, because a "residential dwelling unit" was not necessarily equivalent to a "lot." While an apartment building might be located on a "lot," the living units within that building were not themselves "lots." Eberth v. County of Prince William, 49 Va. App. 105, 637 S.E.2d 338, 2006 Va. App. LEXIS 545 (2006).

§ 46.2-1307.1. Designation of private roads as highways for law-enforcement purposes in Warren County. — Notwithstanding the provisions of § 46.2-1307, the governing body of Warren County may adopt ordinances designating the private roads, within any residential development containing 50 or more lots, as highways for law-enforcement purposes. Such ordinance may also provide for certification of road signs and speed limits by private licensed professional engineers using criteria developed by the Commonwealth Transportation Commissioner, and, for law-enforcement purposes, such certification shall have the same effect as if certified by the Commonwealth Transportation Commissioner. (2006, c. 870; 2007, c. 187.)

The 2007 amendments. — The 2007 amendment by c. 187 added the second sentence.

Title 53.1.

Prisons and Other Methods of Correction.

CHAPTER 2.

STATE CORRECTIONAL FACILITIES.

ARTICLE 1.

General Provisions.

§ 53.1-21. Transfer of prisoners into and between state and local correctional facilities.

Nor to remain in a particular prison.
State prisoner's liberty interest in remaining in a particular correctional facility was not protected by the Due Process Clause of the Fourteenth Amendment because the Director of the Virginia Department of Corrections had the authority to transfer inmates into and between correctional facilities. Lamp v. Wallace, — F. Supp. 2d —, 2005 U.S. Dist. LEXIS 43932 (E.D. Va. Mar. 23, 2005).

Title 54.1.

Professions and Occupations.

SUBTITLE II.

PROFESSIONS AND OCCUPATIONS REGULATED BY THE DEPARTMENT OF PROFESSIONAL AND OCCUPATIONAL REGULATION AND BOARDS WITHIN THE DEPARTMENT.

CHAPTER 4.

ARCHITECTS, ENGINEERS, SURVEYORS, LANDSCAPE ARCHITECTS AND INTERIOR DESIGNERS.

Article 1.

Architects, Engineers, Surveyors and Landscape Architects.

Sec.
54.1-402.2. Cease and desist orders for unlicensed activity; civil penalty.

ARTICLE 1.

Architects, Engineers, Surveyors and Landscape Architects.

§ 54.1-402.2. Cease and desist orders for unlicensed activity; civil penalty. — A. Notwithstanding § 54.1-111, the Board may issue an order requiring any person to cease and desist from (i) practicing or offering to practice as an architect, professional engineer, or land surveyor when such person is not licensed or registered by the Board in accordance with this chapter or (ii) holding himself out as a landscape architect or certified landscape architect or certified interior designer when such person is not certified or registered by the Board in accordance with this chapter. The order shall be effective upon its entry and shall become final unless such person files an appeal with the Board in accordance with the Administrative Process Act (§ 2.2-4000 et seq.) within 21 days of the date of entry of the order.

B. If the person fails to cease and desist the unlicensed, uncertified, or unregistered activity after entry of an order in accordance with subsection A, the Board may refer the matter for enforcement pursuant to § 54.1-306.

C. Any person engaging in unlicensed, uncertified, or unregistered activity shall be subject to further proceedings before the Board and the Board may impose a civil penalty not to exceed $2,500. Any penalties collected under this section shall be paid to the Literary Fund after deduction of the administrative costs of the Board in furtherance of this section.

D. Nothing contained in this section shall apply to any person engaged in activity exempted from the provisions of this chapter. (2007, c. 618.)

Title 56.

Public Service Companies.

CHAPTER 1.

GENERAL PROVISIONS.

Article 3.

Occupation of Streets and Roads.

Sec.
56-15.　Permits to place poles, wires, etc., in roads and streets in certain counties; charge therefor.

ARTICLE 3.

Occupation of Streets and Roads.

§ 56-15. Permits to place poles, wires, etc., in roads and streets in certain counties; charge therefor. — The governing body of Albemarle County, Chesterfield County, Henrico County, Prince William County, or York County, may adopt an ordinance requiring any person, firm or corporation to obtain a permit from the county engineer or such other officer as may be designated in such ordinance before placing any pole or subsurface structures under, along or in any county road or street in such county which is not included within the primary or secondary system of state highways, or any lines or wires that cross any such road or street, whether or not such road or street be actually opened, and may provide in such ordinance reasonable charges for the issuance of such a permit and penalties for violations of the terms of such ordinance to be imposed by the court, judge or justice trying the case.

In the event the county engineer or such other officer as may be designated fails or refuses to issue any such permit requested within thirty days after application therefor, or attaches to such permit conditions to which such person, firm or corporation is unwilling to consent, then such person, firm or corporation may proceed to make such crossing pursuant and subject to the provisions of §§ 56-23 to 56-32, as if the application had been made to the

board of supervisors or other governing body of the county. (1942, p. 222; Michie Code 1942, § 3885a; 2007, c. 813.)

Editor's note. — Acts 2007, c. 813, cl. 2, provides: "That the provisions of this act shall not affect the powers of any locality with respect to any ordinance, resolution or bylaw validly adopted and not repealed or rescinded prior to July 1, 2007."

The 2007 amendments. — The 2007 amendment by c. 813 substituted "The governing body of Albemarle County, Chesterfield County, Henrico County, Prince William County, or York County" for "The board of supervisors or other governing body of any county adjoining a city having a population of 175,000 inhabitants or more according to the last preceding United States census, or of any county which has adopted the county executive form of county government" at the beginning of the first paragraph.

CHAPTER 22.

PUBLIC-PRIVATE TRANSPORTATION ACT OF 1995.

Sec.
56-573.1:1.　Posting of conceptual proposals; public comment; public access to procurement records.

§ 56-556. Title.

Editor's note. — Acts 2007, c. 477, cl. 2, which enacted § 33.1-23.03:10, provides: "That the provisions of this act shall not apply to Chapter 22 of Title 56 or any payment received by the Commonwealth Transportation Board pursuant to § 33.1-23.03:9 of the Code of Virginia."

§ 56-573.1:1. Posting of conceptual proposals; public comment; public access to procurement records. — A. Conceptual proposals submitted in accordance with subsection A or B of § 56-560 to a responsible public entity shall be posted by the responsible public entity within 10 working days after acceptance of such proposals as follows:

1. For responsible public entities that are state agencies, departments, and institutions, posting shall be on the Department of General Service's web-based electronic procurement program commonly known as "eVA;" and

2. For responsible public entities that are local public bodies, posting shall be on the responsible public entity's website or by publication, in a newspaper of general circulation in the area in which the contract is to be performed, of a summary of the proposals and the location where copies of the proposals are available for public inspection. Posting may also be on the Department of General Service's web-based electronic procurement program commonly known as "eVA," in the discretion of the local responsible public entity.

In addition to the posting requirements, at least one copy of the proposals shall be made available for public inspection. Nothing in this section shall be construed to prohibit the posting of the conceptual proposals by additional means deemed appropriate by the responsible public entity so as to provide maximum notice to the public of the opportunity to inspect the proposals. Trade secrets, financial records, or other records of the private entity excluded from disclosure under the provisions of subdivision 11 of § 2.2-3705.6 shall not be required to be posted, except as otherwise agreed to by the responsible public entity and the private entity.

B. In addition to the posting requirements of subsection A, for 30 days prior to entering into an interim or comprehensive agreement, a responsible public entity shall provide an opportunity for public comment on the proposals. The public comment period required by this subsection may include a public hearing in the sole discretion of the responsible public entity. After the end of the public comment period, no additional posting shall be required.

C. Once the negotiation phase for the development of an interim or a comprehensive agreement is complete and a decision to award has been made by a responsible public entity, the responsible public entity shall present the major business points of the interim or comprehensive agreement, including the use of any public funds, to its oversight board at a regularly scheduled meeting of the board that is open to the public.

D. Once an interim agreement or a comprehensive agreement has been entered into, a responsible public entity shall make procurement records available for public inspection, in accordance with the Virginia Freedom of Information Act (§ 2.2-3700 et seq.). For the purposes of this subsection, procurement records shall not be interpreted to include (i) trade secrets of the private entity as defined in the Uniform Trade Secrets Act (§ 59.1-336 et seq.) or (ii) financial records, including balance sheets or financial statements of the private entity that are not generally available to the public through regulatory disclosure or otherwise.

E. Cost estimates relating to a proposed procurement transaction prepared by or for a responsible public entity shall not be open to public inspection.

F. Any inspection of procurement transaction records under this section shall be subject to reasonable restrictions to ensure the security and integrity of the records.

G. The provisions of this section shall apply to accepted proposals regardless of whether the process of bargaining will result in an interim or a comprehensive agreement. (2006, c. 936; 2006, Sp. Sess. I, c. 1; 2007, c. 374.)

Editor's note. — Acts 2006, Sp. Sess. I, c. 1, effective July 1, 2006, in cl. 2, provides: "That the provisions of this act shall expire on July 1, 2007."

Acts 2006, Sp. Sess. I, c. 1, effective July 1, 2006, in cl. 3, provides: "That an emergency exists and this act shall become effective July 1, 2006."

The 2007 amendments. — The 2007 amendment by c. 374, in subsection D, deleted the parenthetical "(Effective July 1, 2007)" at the beginning and substituted "in accordance with the Virginia

Freedom Infomation Act (§ 2.2-3700 et seq.)" for "upon request" in the first sentence.

<hr>

Title 58.1.

Taxation.

SUBTITLE I.

TAXES ADMINISTERED BY THE DEPARTMENT OF TAXATION.

<hr>

CHAPTER 8.

STATE RECORDATION TAX.

Sec.
58.1-815.4. (Contingent expiration — see Editor's notes) Distribution of recordation tax for certain transportation-related purposes.

§ 58.1-815.4. (Contingent expiration — see Editor's notes) Distribution of recordation tax for certain transportation-related purposes. — Effective July 1, 2008, of the state recordation taxes imposed pursuant to §§ 58.1-801 and 58.1-803, the revenues collected each fiscal year from $0.03 of the total tax imposed under each section shall be deposited by the Comptroller as follows:

1. The revenues collected from $0.02 of the total tax shall be deposited into the Commonwealth Mass Transit Fund pursuant to subdivision A 4 e of § 58.1-638; and

2. The revenues collected from $0.01 of the total tax shall be deposited into the Highway Maintenance and Operating Fund. (2007, c. 896.)

Editor's note. — Acts 2007, c. 896, cl. 3, provides: "That the revenues generated by the provisions of this act shall not be used to calculate or reduce the share of local, federal, and state revenues otherwise available to participating jurisdictions. Further, such revenues and moneys shall not be included in any computation of, or formula for, a locality's ability to pay for public education, upon which appropriations of state revenues to local governments for public education are determined."

Acts 2007, c. 896, cl. 21, provides: "That the revenue generated by this act shall be used solely for transportation purposes."

Acts 2007, c. 896, cl. 22, provides: "That the provisions of this act which generate additional revenue for the Transportation Trust Fund, established under § 33.1-23.03:1 of the Code of Virginia, or the Highway Maintenance and Operating Fund shall expire on December 31 of any year in which the General Assembly appropriates any of the revenues designated under general law to the Highway Maintenance and Operating Fund or the Transportation Trust Fund for any non-transportation related purpose."

Acts 2007, c. 896, cl. 23 contains a severability clause.

CHAPTER 17.

MISCELLANEOUS TAXES.

Article 4.1.

Motor Vehicle Fuel Sales Tax in Certain Localities.

Sec.
58.1-1724.2. Rules and regulations; bracket system.
58.1-1724.3. Sales tax on fuel in certain localities.
58.1-1724.4. Exclusion from professional license tax.
58.1-1724.5. Refund of motor vehicle fuel sales tax.
58.1-1724.6. Disposition of tax revenues.
58.1-1724.7. Disclosure of information; penalties.

ARTICLE 4.1.

Motor Vehicle Fuel Sales Tax in Certain Localities.

§ 58.1-1724.2. Rules and regulations; bracket system. — The Tax Commissioner shall promulgate rules and regulations for the registration of dealers and the procedures for filing returns for the payment of the tax imposed pursuant to this article. Such regulations shall include provisions for a bracket system, designed so that the tax will appear on the fuel pump as a part of the total cost of a unit of fuel, whether the unit is a gallon or other measure. The bracket system shall state the tax per unit measure in tenths of a cent, and shall be in increments of no more than 2 ½ cents. (2007, c. 896.)

Editor's note. — Acts 2007, c. 896, cl. 23 contains a severability clause.

§ 58.1-1724.3. Sales tax on fuel in certain localities. — A. In addition to all other taxes, fees, and other charges imposed on fuels subject to tax under Chapter 22 (§ 58.1-2200 et seq.) of this title, the Hampton Roads Transportation Authority may impose a sales tax of 2% of the retail price of such fuels sold at retail within any county or city embraced by the Authority. The Commissioner shall transfer the revenues collected to the Hampton Roads Transportation Authority established under § 33.1-391.7. As used in this section *"sold at retail"* means a sale to a consumer or to any person for any purpose other than resale.

B. The tax imposed under this section shall be subject to the provisions of the Virginia Retail Sales and Use Tax Act (§ 58.1-600 et seq.), except that the exemption provided for motor vehicle fuels under § 58.1-609.1, and the bracket system provided in such act, shall not be applicable. (2007, c. 896.)

§ 58.1-1724.4. Exclusion from professional license tax. — The amount of the tax imposed by this article and collected by a dealer in any taxable year shall be excluded from gross receipts for purposes of any tax imposed under Chapter 37 (§ 58.1-3700 et seq.) of this title. (2007, c. 896.)

§ 58.1-1724.5. Refund of motor vehicle fuel sales tax. — Anyone who purchases fuel (i) that is taxed under the provisions of § 58.1-1724.3 and (ii) upon which a refund is granted for motor fuels taxes paid pursuant to the provisions of Chapter 22 (§ 58.1-2200 et seq.), may file a claim for a refund of taxes paid under this article within 30 days after receipt of a refund under the above chapter on forms and under regulations adopted by the Department of Taxation. (2007, c. 896.)

§ 58.1-1724.6. Disposition of tax revenues. — All taxes paid to the Commissioner pursuant to this article, after subtraction of the direct costs of administration by the Department, shall be transferred to the Hampton Roads Transportation Authority on a monthly basis. (2007, c. 896.)

§ 58.1-1724.7. Disclosure of information; penalties. — For purposes of administering the tax levied under this article, the Commissioner, upon written request, is authorized to provide to the finance officer of the Hampton Roads Transportation Authority, such information as may be necessary for the performance of his official duties. Any person to whom information is provided pursuant to this section shall be subject to the prohibitions and penalties prescribed in § 58.1-3. (2007, c. 896.)

SUBTITLE II.

TAXES ADMINISTERED BY OTHER AGENCIES.

CHAPTER 22.

VIRGINIA FUELS TAX ACT.

Article 3.

Motor Fuel Tax; Liability.

Sec.
58.1-2217. Taxes levied; rate.

Article 5.

Provisions Applicable to Alternative Fuels.

58.1-2249. Tax on alternative fuel.

Article 9.

Disposition of Tax Revenues.

58.1-2289. (Contingent expiration date — see Editor's notes)
            Disposition of tax revenue generally.

ARTICLE 3.

Motor Fuel Tax; Liability.

§ 58.1-2217. Taxes levied; rate. — A. There is hereby levied a tax at the rate of seventeen and one-half cents per gallon on gasoline and gasohol.

B. **(Contingent expiration date — see Editor's notes)** There is hereby levied a tax at the rate of seventeen and one-half cents per gallon on diesel fuel.

B. **(Contingent effective date — see Editor's notes)** There is hereby levied a tax at the rate of sixteen cents per gallon on diesel fuel.

C. Blended fuel that contains gasoline shall be taxed at the rate levied on gasoline. Blended fuel that contains diesel fuel shall be taxed at the rate levied on diesel fuel.

D. There is hereby levied a tax at the rate of five cents per gallon on aviation gasoline. Any person, whether or not licensed under this chapter, who uses, acquires for use, sells or delivers for use in highway vehicles any aviation gasoline shall be liable for the tax at the rate of seventeen and one-half cents per gallon, along with any penalties and interest that may accrue.

E. **(Contingent expiration date — see Editor's notes)** There is hereby levied a tax at the rate of five cents per gallon on aviation jet fuel purchased or acquired for use by a user of aviation fuel other than an aviation consumer. There is hereby levied a tax at the rate of five cents per gallon upon the first 100,000 gallons of aviation jet fuel, excluding bonded aviation jet fuel, purchased or acquired for use by any aviation consumer in any fiscal year. There is hereby levied a tax at the rate of one-half cent per gallon on all aviation jet fuel, excluding bonded aviation jet fuel, purchased or acquired for use by an aviation consumer in excess of 100,000 gallons in any fiscal year. Any person, whether or not licensed under this chapter, who uses, acquires for use, sells or delivers for use in highway vehicles any aviation jet fuel taxable under this chapter shall be liable for the tax imposed at the rate of seventeen and one-half cents per gallon, along with any penalties and interest that may accrue.

E. **(Contingent effective date — see Editor's notes)** There is hereby levied a tax at the rate of five cents per gallon on aviation jet fuel purchased or acquired for use by a user of aviation fuel other than an aviation consumer. There is hereby levied a tax at the rate of five cents per gallon upon the first 100,000 gallons of aviation jet fuel, excluding bonded aviation jet fuel, purchased or acquired for use by any aviation consumer in any fiscal year. There is hereby levied a tax at the rate of one-half cent per gallon on all aviation jet fuel, excluding bonded aviation jet fuel, purchased or acquired for use by an aviation consumer in excess of 100,000 gallons in any fiscal year. Any person, whether or not licensed under this chapter, who uses, acquires for use, sells or delivers for use in highway vehicles any aviation jet fuel taxable under this chapter shall be liable for the tax imposed at the rate of sixteen cents per gallon, along with any penalties and interest that may accrue.

F. In accordance with § 62.1-44.34:13, a storage tank fee is imposed on each gallon of gasoline, aviation gasoline, diesel fuel (including dyed diesel fuel), blended fuel, and heating oil sold and delivered or used in the Commonwealth. (2000, cc. 729, 758; 2007, c. 896.)

Subsections B and E set out twice. — The first version of subsections B and E set out above are effective until December 31 of any year revenues designated for the Highway Maintenance and Operating Fund or the Transportation Trust Fund are appropriated for non-transportation related purposes.

Editor's note. — Acts 2007, c. 896, cl. 3, provides: "That the revenues generated by the provisions of this act shall not be used to calculate or reduce the share of local, federal, and state revenues otherwise available to participating jurisdictions. Further, such revenues and moneys shall not be included in any computation of, or formula for, a locality's ability to pay for public education, upon which appropriations of state revenues to local governments for public education are determined."

Acts 2007, c. 896, cl. 21, provides: "That the revenue generated by this act shall be used solely for transportation purposes."

Acts 2007, c. 896, cl. 22, provides: "That the provisions of this act which generate additional revenue for the Transportation Trust Fund, established under § 33.1-23.03:1 of the Code of Virginia, or the Highway Maintenance and Operating Fund shall expire on December 31 of any year in which the General Assembly appropriates any of the revenues designated under general law to the Highway Maintenance and Operating Fund or the Transportation Trust Fund for any non-transportation related purpose."

Acts 2007, c. 896, cl. 23 contains a severability clause.

The 2007 amendments. — The 2007 amendment by c. 896 substituted "seventeen and one-half cents" for "sixteen cents" in subsections B and E. See Acts 2007, c. 896, cl. 22, for contingent expiration.

ARTICLE 5.

Provisions Applicable to Alternative Fuels.

§ 58.1-2249. Tax on alternative fuel. —
A. **(Contingent expiration date — see Editor's notes)** There is hereby levied a tax at the rate of seventeen and one-half cents per gallon on liquid alternative fuel used to operate a highway vehicle by means of a vehicle supply tank that stores fuel only for the purpose of supplying fuel to operate the vehicle. There is hereby levied a tax at a rate equivalent to seventeen and one-half cents per gallon on all other alternative fuel used to operate a highway vehicle. The Commissioner shall determine the equivalent rate applicable to such other alternative fuels.

A. **(Contingent effective date — see Editor's notes)** There is hereby levied a tax at the rate of sixteen cents per gallon on liquid alternative fuel used to operate a highway vehicle by means of a vehicle supply tank that stores fuel only for the purpose of supplying fuel to operate the vehicle. There is hereby levied a tax at a rate equivalent to sixteen cents per gallon on all other alternative fuel used to operate a highway vehicle. The Commissioner shall determine the equivalent rate applicable to such other alternative fuels.

B. In addition to any tax imposed by this article, there is hereby levied an annual license tax of fifty dollars per vehicle on each highway vehicle that is fueled from a private source if the alternative fuels tax levied under this article has not been paid on fuel used in the vehicle. If such a highway vehicle is not in operation by January 1 of any year, the license tax shall be reduced by one-twelfth for each complete month which shall have elapsed since the beginning of such year. (2000, cc. 729, 758; 2007, c. 896.)

Subsection A set out twice. — The first version of subsection A set out above is effective until December 31 of any year revenues designated for the Highway Maintenance and Operating Fund or the Transportation Trust Fund are appropriated for non-transportation related purposes.

Editor's note. — Acts 2007, c. 896, cl. 3, provides: "That the revenues generated by the provisions of this act shall not be used to calculate or reduce the share of local, federal, and state revenues otherwise available to participating jurisdictions. Further, such revenues and moneys shall not be included in any computation of, or formula for, a locality's ability to pay for public education, upon which appropriations of state revenues to local governments for public education are determined."

Acts 2007, c. 896, cl. 21, provides: "That the revenue generated by this act shall be used solely for transportation purposes."

Acts 2007, c. 896, cl. 22, provides: "That the provisions of this act which generate additional revenue for the Transportation Trust Fund, established under § 33.1-23.03:1 of the Code of Virginia, or the Highway Maintenance and Operating Fund shall expire on December 31 of any year in which the General Assembly appropriates any of the revenues designated under general law to the Highway Maintenance and Operating Fund or the Transportation Trust Fund for any non-transportation related purpose."

Acts 2007, c. 896, cl. 23 contains a severability clause.

The 2007 amendments. — The 2007 amendment by c. 896 substituted "seventeen and one-half cents" for "sixteen cents" in two places in subsection A. See Acts 2007, c. 896, cl. 22, for contingent expiration.

ARTICLE 9.

Disposition of Tax Revenues.

§ 58.1-2289. (Contingent expiration date — see Editor's notes) Disposition of tax revenue generally. — A. Unless otherwise provided in this section, all taxes and fees, including civil penalties, collected by the Commissioner pursuant to this chapter, less a reasonable amount to be allocated for refunds, shall be promptly paid into the state treasury and shall constitute special funds within the Commonwealth Transportation Fund. Any balances remaining in these funds at the end of the year shall be available for use in subsequent years for the purposes set forth in this chapter, and any interest income on such funds shall accrue to these funds. Except as provided in § 33.1-23.03:1, no portion of the revenue derived from taxes collected pursuant to §§ 58.1-2217, 58.1-2249 or 58.1-2701, and remaining after authorized refunds for nonhighway use of fuel, shall be used for any purpose other than the construction, reconstruction or maintenance of the roads and projects comprising the State Highway System, the Interstate System and the secondary system of state highways and expenditures directly and necessarily required for such purposes, including the retirement of revenue bonds.

Revenues collected under this chapter may be also used for (i) contributions toward the construction, reconstruction or maintenance of streets in cities and towns of such sums as may be provided by law and (ii) expenditures for the operation and maintenance of the Department of Transportation, the Department of Rail and Public Transportation, the Department of Aviation, the Virginia Port Authority, and the Department of Motor Vehicles as may be provided by law.

The Governor is hereby authorized to transfer out of such fund an amount necessary for the inspection of gasoline and motor grease measuring and distributing equipment, and for the inspection and analysis of gasoline for purity.

B. Except as provided in subsection F, the tax collected on each gallon of aviation fuel sold and delivered or used in this Commonwealth, less refunds, shall be paid into a special fund of the state treasury. Proceeds of this special fund within the Commonwealth Transportation Fund shall be disbursed upon order of the Department of Aviation, on warrants of the Comptroller, to defray the cost of the administration of the laws of this Commonwealth relating to aviation, for the construction, maintenance and improvement of airports and landing fields to which the public now has or which it is proposed shall have access, and for the promotion of aviation in the interest of operators and the public generally.

C. One-half cent of the tax collected on each gallon of fuel on which a refund has been paid for gasoline, gasohol, diesel fuel, blended fuel, or alternative fuel, for fuel consumed in tractors and unlicensed equipment used for agricultural purposes shall be paid into a special fund of the state treasury, known as the Virginia Agricultural Foundation Fund, to be disbursed to make certain refunds and defray the costs of the research and educational phases of the agricultural program, including supplemental salary payments to certain employees at Virginia Polytechnic Institute and State University, the Department of Agriculture and Consumer Services and the Virginia Truck and Ornamentals Research Station, including reasonable expenses of the Virginia Agricultural Council.

D. One and one-half cents of the tax collected on each gallon of fuel used to propel a commercial watercraft upon which a refund has been paid shall be paid to the credit of the Game Protection Fund of the state treasury to be made available to the Board of Game and Inland Fisheries until expended for the purposes provided generally in subsection C of § 29.1-701, including acquisition, construction, improvement and maintenance of public boating access areas on the public waters of this Commonwealth and for other activities and purposes of direct benefit and interest to the boating public and for no other purpose. However, one and one-half cents per gallon on fuel used by commercial fishing, oystering, clamming, and crabbing boats shall be paid to the Department of Transportation to be used for the construction, repair, improvement and maintenance of the public docks of this Commonwealth used by said commercial watercraft. Any expenditures for the acquisition, construction, improvement and maintenance of the public docks shall be made according to a plan developed by the Virginia Marine Resources Commission.

From the tax collected pursuant to the provisions of this chapter from the sales of gasoline used for the propelling of watercraft, after deduction for lawful refunds, there shall be paid into the state treasury for use by the Marine Resources Commission, the Virginia Soil and Water Conservation Board, the State Water Control Board, and the Commonwealth Transportation Board to (i) improve the public docks as specified in this section, (ii) improve commercial and sports fisheries in Virginia's tidal waters, (iii) make environmental improvements including, without limitation, fisheries management and habitat enhancement in the Chesapeake and its tributaries, and (iv) further the purposes set forth in § 33.1-223, a sum as established by the General Assembly.

E. Notwithstanding other provisions of this section, there shall be transferred from moneys collected pursuant to this section to a special fund within the Commonwealth Transportation Fund in the state treasury, to be used to meet the necessary expenses of the Department of Motor Vehicles, an amount equal to one percent of a sum to be calculated as follows: the tax revenues collected pursuant to this chapter, at the tax rates in effect on December 31, 1986, less refunds authorized by this chapter and less taxes collected for aviation fuels.

F. The additional revenues, less any additional refunds authorized, generated by increases in the rates of taxes under this chapter pursuant to enactments of the 2007 Session of the General Assembly shall be collected pursuant to Article 4 of this chapter and deposited into the Highway Maintenance and Operating Fund. (2000, cc. 729, 758; 2007, c. 896.)

The section above is effective until the appropriation of revenues by the General Assembly to the Highway Maintenance and Operating Fund or the Transportation Trust Fund for any non-tranportation related purpose. For this section as in effect upon such approval, see the section as set out in the 2006 Edition.

Editor's note. — Acts 2007, c. 896, cl. 3, provides: "That the revenues generated by the provisions of this act shall not be used to calculate or reduce the share of local, federal, and state revenues otherwise available to participating jurisdictions. Further, such revenues and moneys shall not be included in any computation of, or formula for, a locality's ability to pay for public education, upon which appropriations of state revenues to local governments for public education are determined."

Acts 2007, c. 896, cl. 21, provides: "That the revenue generated by this act shall be used solely for transportation purposes."

Acts 2007, c. 896, cl. 22, provides: "That the provisions of this act which generate additional revenue for the Transportation Trust Fund, established under § 33.1-23.03:1 of the Code of Virginia, or the Highway Maintenance and Operating Fund shall expire on December 31 of any year in which the General Assembly appropriates any of the revenues designated under general law to the Highway Maintenance and Operating Fund or the Transportation Trust Fund for any non-transportation related purpose."

Acts 2007, c. 896, cl. 23 contains a severability clause.

The 2007 amendments. — The 2007 amendment by c. 896

deleted the section symbol preceding "58.1-2701" in subsection A; substituted "Except as provided in subsection F, the tax" for "The tax" at the beginning of subsection B; substituted "a refund has been paid for gasoline, gasohol, diesel fuel, blended fuel, or alternative fuel" for "the refund has been paid at the rate of seventeen cents per gallon, or in the case of diesel fuel, fifteen and one-half cents per gallon" in subsection C and added subsection F. See Acts 2007, c. 896, cl. 22, for contingent expiration.

CHAPTER 24.

VIRGINIA MOTOR VEHICLE SALES AND USE TAX.

Sec.
58.1-2402.1. Local rental car transportation fee.
58.1-2403. Exemptions.
58.1-2425. Disposition of revenues.

§ 58.1-2402.1. Local rental car transportation fee. — A. In addition to all other taxes, fees, and other charges imposed under law, the Hampton Roads Transportation Authority established pursuant to § 33.1-391.7 and the Northern Virginia Transportation Authority established pursuant to § 15.2-4830, may impose a fee of 2% of the gross proceeds on the daily rental of a vehicle in any county or city embraced by the respective Authority wherein the daily rental of the vehicle occurs, regardless of whether such vehicle is required to be licensed in the Commonwealth. The fee shall not be levied upon a rental to a person for re-rental as an established business or part of an established business or incidental or germane to such business.

B. After subtraction of the direct costs of administration by the Department, the Commissioner shall transfer the revenues collected pursuant to this section to the Hampton Roads Transportation Authority and the Northern Virginia Transportation Authority, as appropriate.

C. Any and all fees imposed pursuant to this section shall be collected by the Department of Motor Vehicles. The Commissioner shall maintain records of the fee imposed and collected by locality.

D. The fee imposed pursuant to the authority granted under this section shall be implemented, enforced, and collected in the same manner that rental taxes under this chapter are implemented, enforced, and collected. (2007, c. 896.)

Editor's note. — Acts 2007, c. 896, cl. 23 contains a severability clause.

§ 58.1-2403. Exemptions. — No tax shall be imposed as provided in § 58.1-2402 or 58.1-2402.1 if the vehicle is:

1. Sold to, rented or used by the United States government or any governmental agency thereof;

2. Sold to, rented or used by the Commonwealth of Virginia or any political subdivision thereof;

3. Registered in the name of a volunteer fire department or rescue squad not operated for profit;

4. Registered to any member of the Mattaponi, Pamunkey, or Chickahominy Indian tribes or any other recognized Indian tribe of the Commonwealth living on the tribal reservation;

5. Transferred incidental to repossession under a recorded lien and ownership is transferred to the lienholder;

6. A manufactured home permanently attached to real estate and included in the sale of real estate;

7. A gift to the spouse, son, or daughter of the transferor. With the exception of a gift to a spouse, this exemption shall not apply to any unpaid obligation assumed by the transferee incidental to the transfer;

8. Transferred from an individual or partnership to a corporation or limited liability company or from a corporation or limited liability company to an individual or partnership if the transfer is incidental to the formation, organization or dissolution of a corporation or limited liability company in which the individual or partnership holds the majority interest;

9. Transferred from a wholly owned subsidiary to the parent corporation or from the parent corporation to a wholly owned subsidiary;

10. Being registered for the first time in this Commonwealth and the applicant holds a valid, assignable title or registration issued to him by another state or a branch of the United States Armed Forces and (i) has owned the vehicle for longer than 12 months or (ii) has owned the vehicle for less than 12 months and provides evidence of a sales tax paid to another state. However, when a vehicle has been purchased by the applicant within the last 12 months and the applicant is unable to provide evidence of a sales tax paid to another state, the applicant shall pay the Virginia sales tax based on the fair market value of the vehicle at the time of registration in Virginia;

11. Titled in a Virginia or non-Virginia motor vehicle dealer's name for resale;

12. A motor vehicle having seats for more than seven passengers and sold to an urban or suburban bus line the majority of whose passengers use the buses for traveling a distance of less than 40 miles, one way, on the same day;

13. Purchased in the Commonwealth by a nonresident and a Virginia title is issued for the sole purpose of recording a lien against the vehicle if the vehicle will be registered in a state other than Virginia;

14. A motor vehicle designed for the transportation of 10 or more passengers, purchased by and for the use of a church conducted not for profit;

15. Loaned or leased to a private nonprofit institution of learning, for the sole purpose of use in the instruction of driver's education when such education is a part of such school's curriculum for full-time students;

16. Sold to an insurance company or local government group self-insurance pool, created pursuant to

§ 15.2-2703, for the sole purpose of disposition when such company has paid the registered owner of such vehicle a total loss claim;

17. Owned and used for personal or official purposes by accredited consular or diplomatic officers of foreign governments, their employees or agents, and members of their families, if such persons are nationals of the state by which they are appointed and are not citizens of the United States;

18. A self-contained mobile computerized axial tomography scanner sold to, rented or used by a nonprofit hospital or a cooperative hospital service organization as described in § 501 (e) of the United States Internal Revenue Code;

19. A motor vehicle having seats for more than seven passengers and sold to a restricted common carrier or common carrier of passengers;

20. Beginning July 1, 1989, a self-contained mobile unit designed exclusively for human diagnostic or therapeutic service, sold to, rented to, or used by a nonprofit hospital, or a cooperative hospital service organization as described in § 501 (e) of the United States Internal Revenue Code, or a nonprofit corporation as defined in § 501 (c) (3) of the Internal Revenue Code, established for research in, diagnosis of, or therapy for human ailments;

21. Transferred, as a gift or through a sale to an organization exempt from taxation under § 501 (c) (3) of the Internal Revenue Code, provided the motor vehicle is not titled and tagged for use by such organization;

22. A motor vehicle sold to an organization which is exempt from taxation under § 501 (c) (3) of the Internal Revenue Code and which is organized for the primary purpose of distributing food, clothing, medicines and other necessities of life to, and providing shelter for, needy persons in the United States and throughout the world;

23. A truck, tractor truck, trailer, or semitrailer, as severally defined in § 46.2-100, except trailers and semitrailers not designed or used to carry property and vehicles registered under § 46.2-700, with a gross vehicle weight rating or gross combination weight rating of 26,001 pounds or more, in which case no tax shall be imposed pursuant to subdivisions 1 and 3 of subsection A of § 58.1-2402;

24. Transferred to the trustees of a revocable inter vivos trust, when the individual titleholder of a Virginia titled motor vehicle and the beneficiaries of the trust are the same persons, regardless of whether other beneficiaries of the trust may also be named in the trust instrument, when no consideration has passed between the titleholder and the beneficiaries; and transferred to the original titleholder from the trustees holding title to the motor vehicle;

25. Transferred to trustees of a revocable inter vivos trust, when the owners of the vehicle and the beneficiaries of the trust are the same persons, regardless of whether other beneficiaries may also be named in the trust instrument, or transferred by

trustees of such a trust to beneficiaries of the trust following the death of the grantor, when no consideration has passed between the grantor and the beneficiaries in either case;

26. Sold by a vehicle's lessor to its lessee upon the expiration of the term of the vehicle's lease, if the lessee is a natural person and this natural person has paid the tax levied pursuant to this chapter with respect to the vehicle when he leased it from the lessor, and if the lessee presents an original copy of the lease upon request of the Department of Motor Vehicles or other evidence that the sales tax has been paid to the Commonwealth by the lessee purchasing the vehicle; or

27. Titled in the name of a deceased person and transferred to the spouse or heir, or under the will, of such deceased person. (Code 1950, §§ 58-685.13, 58-685.13:1; 1966, c. 587; 1970, c. 409; 1972, cc. 302, 680; 1973, c. 457; 1974, c. 477; 1976, c. 610; 1977, c. 537; 1978, cc. 758, 766; 1982, c. 541; 1984, c. 675; 1988, c. 372; 1990, cc. 40, 849; 1995, cc. 27, 247, 786; 1997, c. 283; 1998, c. 322; 1999, c. 77; 2000, cc. 576, 602, 1027; 2002, c. 513; 2003, c. 278; 2005, cc. 246, 274; 2006, c. 604; 2007, c. 896.)

Editor's note. — Acts 2007, c. 896, cl. 23 contains a severability clause.

The 2007 amendments. — The 2007 amendment by c. 896 inserted "or 58.1-2402.1" following "§ 58.1-2402" in the introductory paragraph.

Law Review.

For annual survey of Virginia law on taxation, see 40 U. Rich. L. Rev. 291 (2005).

§ 58.1-2425. Disposition of revenues. —

A. Except as provided in § 58.1-2402.1 funds collected hereunder by the Commissioner shall be forthwith paid into the state treasury. Except as otherwise provided in § 58.1-2402.1 and in this section, these funds shall constitute special funds within the Commonwealth Transportation Fund. Any balances remaining in these funds at the end of the year shall be available for use in subsequent years for the purposes set forth in this chapter, and any interest income on such funds shall accrue to these funds. The revenue so derived, after refunds have been deducted, is hereby allocated for the construction, reconstruction and maintenance of highways and the regulation of traffic thereon and for no other purpose. However, (i) all funds collected pursuant to the provisions of this chapter from manufactured homes, as defined in § 46.2-100, shall be distributed to the city, town, or county wherein such manufactured home is to be situated as a dwelling; (ii) all funds collected from the additional tax imposed by subdivision A 4 of § 58.1-2402 on the rental of daily rental vehicles shall be distributed quarterly to the city, town, or county wherein such vehicle was delivered to the rentee; (iii) effective January 1, 1987, an amount equivalent to the net additional revenues generated by enactments of the 1986 Special Session of the Virginia General Assem-

bly which amended §§ 46.2-694, 46.2-697, 58.1-2401, 58.1-2402 and this section shall be distributed to and paid into the Transportation Trust Fund, a special fund within the Commonwealth Transportation Fund, and are hereby appropriated to the Commonwealth Transportation Board for transportation needs; (iv) except as otherwise provided in clause (iii) of this sentence, all moneys collected from the tax on the gross proceeds from the rental in Virginia of any motor vehicle pursuant to subdivision A 3 of § 58.1-2402 at the tax rate in effect on December 31, 1986, shall be paid by the Commissioner into the state treasury and shall be paid into the Rail Enhancement Fund established by § 33.1-221.1:1.1; and (v) all additional revenues resulting from the fee imposed under subdivision A 5 of § 58.1-2402 as enacted by the 2004 Session of the General Assembly shall be used to pay the debt service on the bonds issued by the Virginia Public Building Authority for the Statewide Agencies Radio System (STARS) for the Department of State Police pursuant to the authority granted by the 2004 Session of the General Assembly.

B. As provided in subsection A of § 58.1-638, of the funds becoming part of the Transportation Trust Fund pursuant to clause (iii) of subsection A of this section, an aggregate of 4.2 percent shall be set aside as the Commonwealth Port Fund; an aggregate of 2.4 percent shall be set aside as the Commonwealth Airport Fund; and an aggregate of 14.5 percent in fiscal year 1998-1999 and 14.7 percent in fiscal year 1999-2000 and thereafter shall be set aside as the Commonwealth Mass Transit Fund. (Code 1950, § 58-685.23; 1966, c. 587; 1976, c. 567; 1981, c. 145; 1984, c. 675; 1986, Sp. Sess., c. 11; 1987, c. 696; 1991, c. 323; 1997, cc. 283, 423, 853; 1998, cc. 905, 907; 1999, c. 77; 2004, c. 522; 2005, c. 323; 2007, c. 896.)

Editor's note. — Acts 2007, c. 896, cl. 23 contains a severability clause.

The 2007 amendments. — The 2007 amendment by c. 896, in subsection A, substituted "Except as provided in § 58.1-2402.1 funds" for "All funds" at the beginning of the first sentence and inserted "in § 58.1-2402.1 and" in the second sentence.

SUBTITLE III.
LOCAL TAXES.

CHAPTER 37.
License Taxes.

Sec.
58.1-3713. (Expires December 31, 2012) Local coal and gas road improvement and Virginia Coalfield Economic Development Authority tax.

§ 58.1-3713. (Expires December 31, 2012) Local coal and gas road improvement and Vir-

ginia Coalfield Economic Development Authority tax. — A. In addition to the taxes authorized under § 58.1-3712, any county or city may adopt a license tax on every person engaging in the business of severing coal or gases from the earth. The rate of such tax shall not exceed one percent. The provisions of § 58.1-3712 as they relate to measurement of gross receipts, filing of reports and record keeping shall be applicable to the tax imposed under this section.

The moneys collected for each county or city from the tax imposed under authority of this section shall be paid into a special fund of such county or city to be called the Coal and Gas Road Improvement Fund of such county or city, and shall be spent for such improvements to public roads as the coal and gas road improvement advisory committee and the governing body of such county or city may determine as provided in subsection B of this section. The county may also, in its discretion, elect to improve city or town roads with its funds if consent of the city or town council is obtained. Such funds shall be in addition to those allocated to such counties from state highway funds which allocations shall not be reduced as a result of any revenues received from the tax imposed hereunder. In those localities which comprise the Virginia Coalfield Economic Development Authority, the tax imposed under this section shall be paid as follows: (i) three-fourths of the revenue shall be paid to the Coal and Gas Road Improvement Fund and used for the purposes set forth herein; however, one-fourth of such revenue may be used to fund the construction of new water and/or sewer systems and lines in areas with natural water supplies which are insufficient from the standpoint of quality or quantity, and (ii) one-fourth of the revenue shall be paid to the Virginia Coalfield Economic Development Fund. Furthermore, with regard to the portion paid to the Coal and Gas Road Improvement Fund, a county or city may provide for an additional one-fourth allocation for the construction of new water or sewer systems or lines or the repair or enhancement of existing water or sewer systems or lines in areas with natural water supplies which are insufficient from the standpoint of quality or quantity; however, if this option is initi-

ated by a county or city, it must satisfy the requirements set forth in § 58.1-3713.01. Notwithstanding the foregoing limitations regarding revenues used for water systems and/or sewer systems, such revenues designated for water and water systems and/or sewer systems shall be distributed directly to the local public service authority for such purposes instead of the local governing body.

B. Any county or city imposing the tax authorized in this section shall establish a Coal and Gas Road Improvement Advisory Committee, to be composed of four members: (i) a member of the governing body of such county or city, appointed by the governing body, (ii) a representative of the Department of Transportation, and (iii) two citizens of such county or city connected with the coal and gas industry, appointed for a term of four years, initially commencing July 1, 1989, by the chief judge of the circuit court.

Such committee shall develop on or before July 1 of each year a plan for improvement of roads during the following fiscal year. Such plan shall have the approval of three members of the committee and shall be submitted to the governing body of the county or city for approval. The governing body may approve or disapprove such plan, but may make no changes without the approval of three members of the committee.

C. The provisions of this section shall expire on December 31, 2012. (Code 1950, § 58-266.1:2; 1978, c. 646; 1984, c. 675; 1986, c. 58; 1988, c. 784; 1989, cc. 265, 380; 1991, c. 164; 1993, c. 163; 1996, c. 706; 2004, cc. 871, 893; 2005, c. 645; 2006, cc. 78, 497; 2007, cc. 57, 586.)

Sunset provision. — Acts 1978, c. 646 enacted § 58-266.1:2 and by a second enactment clause provided that it would expire December 31, 1986, and provided a provision relating to taxes assessed prior to the expiration date. That section, along with all other sections in Title 58, was repealed by Acts 1984, c. 675, which also added Title 58.1. Section 58.1-3713, as a part of new Title 58.1, was enacted substantially the same as § 58-266.1:2, but no reference was made to an expiration. Acts 1978, c. 646, cl. 2, as amended by Acts 1985, c. 539, by Acts 1991, c. 393, cl. 1, by Acts 1995, cc. 614 and 635, and by Acts 2002, c. 274, cl. 1, provided for a December 31, 2007, sunset provision, which was subsequently repealed by Acts 2007, cc. 57 and 586, cl. 2. See now subsection C of this section.

The 2007 amendments. — The 2007 amendments by cc. 57 and 586 are identical, and inserted subsection C.

Index to Statutes

This index supplements the index found in the main edition. The Publishers have only included entries when the addition of or changes to material contained in the main edition have rendered the index in the main edition incomplete or obsolete.

A

ADMINISTRATION OF STATE GOVERNMENT.
Administrative process act, §§2.2-4000 to 2.2-4031.

ADMINISTRATIVE PROCESS.
Amendment of regulations.
  Air pollution control board.
    Applicability of provisions.
      Variances, §2.2-4007.07.
  Economic impact analysis, §2.2-4007.04.
  Informational proceedings, §2.2-4007.03.
  Noncompliance, effect, §2.2-4007.03.
  Notice of intended regulatory action, §2.2-4007.01.
  Petitions, §2.2-4007.
  Public hearing, §2.2-4007.01.
  Public participation guidelines, §2.2-4007.02.
  Revisions, §§2.2-4007.03, 2.2-4007.06.
  Submission of proposed regulations, §2.2-4007.05.
Appeals. See within this heading, "Court review."
Hearings.
  Regulations.
    New or amended, §2.2-4007.01.
New regulations.
  Air pollution control board.
    Applicability of provisions.
      Variances, §2.2-4007.07.
  Economic impact analysis, §2.2-4007.04.
  Informational proceedings, §2.2-4007.03.
  Noncompliance, effect, §2.2-4007.03.
  Notice of intended regulatory action, §2.2-4007.01.
  Petitions, §2.2-4007.
  Public hearing, §2.2-4007.01.
  Public participation guidelines, §2.2-4007.02.
  Revisions, §§2.2-4007.03, 2.2-4007.06.
  Submission of proposed regulations, §2.2-4007.05.
Notice.
  Public comment.
    Hearing, §2.2-4007.01.
    Notice of intended regulatory action, §2.2-4007.01.
    Revisions, §§2.2-4007.03, 2.2-4007.06.
  Regulations.
    Notice of intended regulatory action, §2.2-4007.01.
    Petitions, §2.2-4007.
    Revisions, §§2.2-4007.03, 2.2-4007.06.
Public comment.
  Air pollution control board.
    Applicability of provisions.
      Variances, §2.2-4007.07.
  Economic impact analysis, §2.2-4007.04.
  Informational proceedings, §2.2-4007.03.
  Noncompliance, effect, §2.2-4007.03.
  Notice of intended regulatory action, §2.2-4007.01.
  Petitions, §2.2-4007.
  Public participation guidelines, §2.2-4007.02.
  Revisions, §§2.2-4007.03, 2.2-4007.06.
  Submission of proposed regulations, §2.2-4007.05.
Registrar.
  Proposed regulations.
    Notice of intended regulatory action, §2.2-4007.01.
    Petitions, §2.2-4007.
  Submission of proposed regulations, §2.2-4007.05.

ADMINISTRATIVE PROCESS —Cont'd
Regulations.
  Economic impact analysis, §2.2-4007.04.
  Informational proceedings, §2.2-4007.03.
  Noncompliance, effect, §2.2-4007.03.
  Notice of intended regulatory action, §2.2-4007.01.
  Petitions, §2.2-4007.
  Public hearing, §2.2-4007.01.
  Public participation guidelines, §2.2-4007.02.
  Revisions, §§2.2-4007.03, 2.2-4007.06.
  Submission of proposed regulations, §2.2-4007.05.

AGGRESSIVE DRIVING.
Civil remedial fee, §46.2-206.1.

AIR POLLUTION CONTROL BOARD.
Administrative process.
  Proposed regulations.
    Applicability of provisions.
      Variances, §2.2-4007.07.

ALBEMARLE COUNTY.
Poles or subsurface structures.
  Placing under or along road or street.
    Permit from county engineer, authority to adopt ordinance requiring, §56-15.

ALEXANDRIA.
Parking violations.
  Removal or immobilization of vehicles.
    Outstanding parking violations, §46.2-1216.

ALLOCATION OF HIGHWAY FUNDS.
Interstate highway system.
  Tolls for use of interstate highway system components, §33.1-23.03:10.
Secondary system of state highways, §§33.1-23.4, 33.1-23.4:01, 33.1-79, 33.1-82.
Transportation trust fund.
  Interstate highway system.
    Tolls for use of interstate highway system components, §33.1-23.03:10.

APPRAISALS AND APPRAISERS.
Eminent domain.
  Partial payment to owner for purposes of appraisal, §25.1-417.1.

ARCHITECTS.
Unlicensed activities.
  Cease and desist orders, civil penalty, §54.1-402.2.

ARLINGTON COUNTY.
Mentally ill, mentally retarded or developmentally disabled persons.
  Zoning of group homes of eight or fewer single-family residences, §15.2-2291.
Playing on roads, devices on wheels or runners.
  Ordinance permitting use on highways, §46.2-932.

AUTHORITIES.
Administrative process act, §§2.2-4000 to 2.2-4031.
Hampton Roads transportation authority.
  General provisions, §§33.1-391.6 to 33.1-391.15.

B

BICYCLE PATHS.
Converting sidewalks to, §15.2-2001.

181

BICYCLES.
Attaching to vehicle on highway.
Persons riding on, §46.2-932.
Electric power-assisted bicycles.
Controlled access highways.
Prohibited, §46.2-808.
Paths.
Converting sidewalks to, §15.2-2001.

BOARDS.
Administrative process act, §§2.2-4000 to 2.2-4031.

BOND ISSUES.
Northern Virginia transportation authority, §15.2-4839.
Use of certain revenues, §15.2-4838.1.

BONDS, SURETY.
Subdivisions.
Dedication for public use of certain facilities.
Bonding requirement for acceptance of, §15.2-2241.1.

BRIDGES.
Emergency vehicles crossing bridges and culverts.
Overweight permits granted.
Vehicles responding to emergency calls, §46.2-1130.1.

C

CAMP PENDLETON.
Acquisition, conveyance or transfer of property by state agency.
Notice to members of General Assembly, §2.2-1150.

CEASE AND DESIST ORDERS.
Architects, engineers, land surveyors.
Unlicensed activities, §54.1-402.2.

CHESAPEAKE.
Planning commission.
Duplicate commissions in Chesapeake and Hampton, §15.2-2220.

CHESTERFIELD COUNTY.
Poles or subsurface structures.
Placing under or along road or street.
Permit from county engineer, authority to adopt ordinance, §56-15.

CHIEF INFORMATION OFFICER (CIO).
Information technologies agency.
Duties, §2.2-2009.
Powers.
Geographic information system, §2.2-2029.
Security of Commonwealth's databases and data communications, §2.2-2009.

CIGARETTES.
Gas pumps.
Smoking in proximity to, §46.2-819.4.

CITIES.
Photo-monitoring systems to enforce traffic light signals, §15.2-968.1.
Private roads.
Residential developments.
Designation as highways for law enforcement purposes, §46.2-1307.
Residential developments.
Private roads.
Designation as highways for law enforcement purposes, §46.2-1307.
Road impact fees, §§15.2-2317 to 15.2-2329.
Roads, streets and public rights of way.
Powers and authority of localities, §15.2-2001.
Streets.
Powers and authority of localities, §15.2-2001.
Road impact fees, §§15.2-2317 to 15.2-2329.
See ROAD IMPACT FEES.
Viewers to view streets or alleys proposed for vacation or alteration.
Appointment in Virginia Beach, §15.2-2007.1.

CLAIMS AGAINST THE COMMONWEALTH.
Limitation of actions.
Tort claims act, §§8.01-195.6, 8.01-195.7.
Statute of limitations.
Tort claims act, §§8.01-195.6, 8.01-195.7.
Tort claims act.
Statute of limitations, §§8.01-195.6, 8.01-195.7.

COLLEGIAL BODIES.
Administrative process act, §§2.2-4000 to 2.2-4031.

COMMERCIAL DRIVERS' LICENSES.
Driving while disqualified.
Civil remedial fee, §46.2-206.1.
Out-of-service orders.
Driving while out-of-service.
Civil remedial fee, §46.2-206.1.

COMMISSIONS.
Administrative process act, §§2.2-4000 to 2.2-4031.

COMMUTER PARKING LOTS.
Parking not in conformance with signs, §46.2-1219.2.

COMPREHENSIVE HIGHWAY ACCESS MANAGEMENT STANDARDS, §33.1-198.1.

COMPREHENSIVE PLAN.
New urbanism.
Incorporation of principles, §15.2-2223.1.
Traditional neighborhood development.
Incorporation of principles, §15.2-2223.1.
Urban development area.
Inclusion, §15.2-2223.1.

COMPUTER CONFERENCES.
Freedom of information act.
Electronic communication meetings.
Exceptions to prohibition, §2.2-3708.1.

CONTROLLED ACCESS HIGHWAYS.
Unauthorized use, §46.2-808.

CORRECTIONS DEPARTMENT.
Freedom of information act exclusions, §2.2-3705.7.

COUNCILS.
Administrative process act, §§2.2-4000 to 2.2-4031.

COUNTIES.
Firearms.
Highways.
Regulation of loaded firearms on public highways, §15.2-1209.1.
Highway construction funds.
Allocation for secondary system, §§33.1-23.4, 33.1-23.4:01.
Hunting.
Regulation of loaded firearms on public highways, §15.2-1209.1.
Photo-monitoring systems to enforce traffic light signals, §15.2-968.1.
Planning and development.
Road impact fees, §§15.2-2317 to 15.2-2329.
Powers.
Firearms.
Regulation of loaded firearms on public highways, §15.2-1209.1.
Private roads.
Residential developments.
Designation as highways for law enforcement purposes, §46.2-1307.
Residential developments.
Private roads.
Designation as highways for law enforcement purposes, §46.2-1307.
Road impact fees, §§15.2-2317 to 15.2-2329.
Roads and streets.
Powers and authority of localities, §15.2-2001.
Private roads.
Residential developments.
Designation as highway for law enforcement purposes, §46.2-1307.

COUNTIES —Cont'd
Secondary system of state highways.
New streets.
Requirements for taking new streets into system, §33.1-70.3.

COUNTY ROADS.
Private roads.
Residential developments.
Designation as highway for law enforcement purposes, §46.2-1307.

CRIMINAL OFFENSES.
Commuter parking lots owned by VDOT.
Parking not in conformance with signs, §46.2-1219.2.
Dead bodies.
Alteration to prevent detection of death or cause of death, §18.2-323.02.
Concealment, §18.2-323.02.
Gas pumps.
Smoking in proximity to, §46.2-819.4.
Motor vehicle or traffic offenses.
Commuter parking lots owned by VDOT.
Parking not in conformance with signs, §46.2-1219.2.
Smoking in proximity to gas pumps, §46.2-819.4.

CULVERTS.
Emergency vehicles crossing.
Overweight permits granted.
Vehicles responding to emergency calls, §46.2-1130.1.

D

DEAD BODIES.
Alteration to prevent detection of death or cause of death, §18.2-323.02.
Concealment, §18.2-323.02.

DEDICATION FOR PUBLIC USE.
Subdivision ordinance provision.
Bonding requirements for acceptance of dedication, §15.2-2241.1.

DEFINED TERMS.
Electronic communication.
Freedom of information act, §2.2-3701.
Net additional revenues.
Disposition of vehicle registration fees, §46.2-702.1.
Owner.
Traffic light signal violation-monitoring system, §§15.2-968.1, 46.2-833.01.
Public right-of-way, §15.2-2000.
Regional public body.
Freedom of information act, §2.2-3701.
Replica vehicle, §46.2-100.
Toy vehicle, §46.2-100.
Traffic light signal violation-monitoring system.
Traffic infractions, §§15.2-968.1, 46.2-833.01.

DEVELOPMENTAL HOMES.
Zoning of group homes for mentally ill, mentally retarded or developmentally disabled, §15.2-2291.

DINWIDDIE COUNTY.
Local licensing of motor vehicles, trailers or semitrailers.
Evidence of payment of all fees due county or solid waste authority.
Required prior to issuing license, §46.2-752.

DISABILITY OR HANDICAP.
Freedom of information.
Open meetings.
Electronic communication meetings.
Exceptions to prohibition, §2.2-3708.1.

DRIVERS' LICENSES.
Dangerous driving behavior.
Civil remedial fees, §46.2-206.1.
Driving while privilege to drive suspended or revoked.
Civil remedial fee, §46.2-206.1.

DRIVERS' LICENSES —Cont'd
Revocation.
Driving while privilege to drive revoked.
Civil remedial fee, §46.2-206.1.
Suspension.
Civil remedial fee.
Failure to pay assessment, §46.2-206.1.
Driving while privilege to drive suspended.
Civil remedial fee, §46.2-206.1.
Unlicensed driving.
Driving on suspended or revoked license or permit.
Civil remedial fee, §46.2-206.1.

DRIVING WHILE INTOXICATED.
Civil remedial fee, §46.2-206.1.
Fees.
Civil remedial fee, §46.2-206.1.

DRIVING WHILE LICENSE SUSPENDED OR REVOKED.
Civil remedial fee, §46.2-206.1.

DRIVING WITHOUT LICENSE.
Driving on suspended or revoked license or permit.
Civil remedial fee, §46.2-206.1.

E

ELECTRIC PERSONAL ASSISTIVE MOBILITY DEVICES.
Attaching to vehicle on highway, §46.2-932.
Controlled access highways.
Prohibited, §46.2-808.

ELECTRIC POWER-ASSISTED BICYCLES.
Controlled access highways.
Prohibited, §46.2-808.

EMERGENCY VEHICLES.
Crossing bridges and culverts.
Overweight permits granted.
Vehicles responding to emergency calls, §46.2-1130.1.

EMINENT DOMAIN.
Appraisal, partial payment for, §25.1-417.1.
Just compensation.
Partial payment for appraisal report, §25.1-417.1.

ENGINEERS.
Unlicensed activities.
Cease and desist orders, civil penalty, §54.1-402.2.

ENVIRONMENTAL QUALITY DEPARTMENT.
Treatment works.
Reimbursements to localities for upgrades to, §10.1-1186.01.

EVASION OF TRAFFIC CONTROL DEVICES.
Traffic light signal violation-monitoring system, §§15.2-968.1, 46.2-833.01.

F

FAIRFAX, CITY OF.
Parking violations.
Removal or immobilization of vehicles.
Outstanding parking violations, §46.2-1216.

FAIRFAX COUNTY.
Parking violations.
Removal or immobilization of vehicles.
Outstanding parking violations, §46.2-1216.

FALLS CHURCH.
Parking violations.
Removal or immobilization of vehicles.
Outstanding parking violations, §46.2-1216.
Speed limit in residential district, §46.2-874.1.

FEES.
Motor vehicles department.
Civil remedial fees, §46.2-206.1.
Road impact fees, §§15.2-2317 to 15.2-2329.

FELONIES.
Dead bodies.
Alteration to prevent detection of death or cause of death, §18.2-323.02.
Concealment, §18.2-323.02.
Motor vehicles.
Civil remedial fee for felony convictions, §46.2-206.1.

FINES.
Firearms.
Regulation of loaded firearms on county highways, §15.2-1209.1.

FIREARMS.
Counties.
Highways.
Regulation of loaded firearms on county highways, §15.2-1209.1.
Ordinances.
Regulation of loaded firearms on county highways, §15.2-1209.1.

FREEDOM OF INFORMATION ACT.
Electronic communication meetings.
Exceptions to prohibition, §2.2-3708.1.
Open meetings.
Electronic communication meetings.
Exceptions to prohibition, §2.2-3708.1.
General assembly meetings, electronic mode prohibited, §2.2-3707.01.
Minutes, §2.2-3707.

G

GASOLINE PUMPS.
Smoking in proximity, §46.2-819.4.

GASOLINE STATIONS.
Smoking in proximity to gas pumps, §46.2-819.4.

GRANTS.
Waste management.
Upgrades to treatment works, reimbursement to localities for, §10.1-1186.01.

H

HAMPTON ROADS.
Planning commission.
Duplicate commissions in Chesapeake and Hampton, §15.2-2220.

HAMPTON ROADS TRANSPORTATION AUTHORITY,
§§33.1-391.6 to 33.1-391.15.
Audit of financial accounts, §33.1-391.9.
Chesapeake Bay bridge and tunnel commission.
Bond issues.
Issuance of bonds, §33.1-391.13.
Chesapeake Bay bridge-tunnel facilities.
Tunnel under control of authority, §33.1-391.12.
Citation of act, §33.1-391.6.
Corporate powers, §§33.1-391.8, 33.1-391.10.
Creation, §33.1-391.7.
Downtown and midtown tunnels.
Authority to impose separate tolls, §33.1-391.8.
First phase projects, §33.1-391.10.
Local rental car transportation fee.
Authority to impose, §58.1-2402.1.
Local transportation fees.
Applicability to Accomack and Northampton counties, §§33.1-391.10, 33.1-391.12.
Use of revenue, §33.1-391.15.
Meetings.
Quorum, §33.1-391.9.
Membership.
Composition of members, §33.1-391.9.
Expansion of membership, §33.1-391.12.

HAMPTON ROADS TRANSPORTATION AUTHORITY
—Cont'd
Membership —Cont'd
Meeting quorum, §33.1-391.9.
Midtown and downtown tunnels.
Authority to impose separate tolls, §33.1-391.8.
Motor fuel sales tax.
Authority to impose on fuel, §58.1-1724.3.
Disposition of tax revenues, §58.1-1724.6.
Tax commissioner.
Disclosure of information to authority, §58.1-1724.7.
Officers, §33.1-391.9.
Powers and duties, §§33.1-391.8, 33.1-391.10.
Private sector entities.
Participation encouraged, §33.1-391.11.
Second phase projects, §33.1-391.10.
Taxes.
Power to impose fees and taxes, §33.1-391.10.
Use of revenue, §33.1-391.12.
Title of act, §33.1-391.6.
Tolls.
Authority to impose, §33.1-391.8.
Use of revenue, §33.1-391.15.
Transportation board.
Continuing responsibilities, §33.1-391.14.
Transportation department.
Continuing responsibilities, §33.1-391.14.
Travel expenses.
Reimbursement, §33.1-391.9.

HANOVER COUNTY.
Subdivisions.
Expedited land development review procedures, §15.2-2263.

HENRICO COUNTY.
Poles or subsurface structures.
Placing under or along road or street not in state highway system.
Permit from county engineer.
Ordinance requiring, authority to adopt, §56-15.

HENRY COUNTY.
Mentally ill, mentally retarded or developmentally disabled persons.
Zoning of group homes of eight or fewer single-family residences, §15.2-2291.

HIGHWAY MAINTENANCE AND OPERATING FUND.
Vehicle registration fee increases.
Disposition of revenue generated by, §46.2-702.1.

HUNTING.
Highways.
Regulation of loaded firearms on county highways, §15.2-1209.1.

I

IMPACT FEES.
Road impact fees, §§15.2-2317 to 15.2-2329.

INFORMATION TECHNOLOGIES AGENCY.
Chief information officer (CIO).
Duties, §2.2-2009.
Security of government information, §2.2-2009.
Security of government information.
Chief information officer (CIO), §2.2-2009.

INTERSTATE HIGHWAY SYSTEM.
School buses.
Maximum speed limit, §46.2-871.
Tolls for use of interstate highway system components, §33.1-23.03:10.
Trucks and combination vehicles required to keep to right.
Signs requiring under certain circumstances.
DOT to post signs, §46.2-804.

L

LANDINGS.
Transportation board.
Acquisitions, conveyances and transfers of property.
Request to board for transfer to authority, §33.1-223.2:17.

LANE DIRECTION CONTROL SIGNALS, 46.2-805.

LEE COUNTY.
Local licensing of motor vehicles, trailers or semitrailers.
Evidence of payment of all fees due county or solid waste authority.
Required prior to issuing license, §46.2-752.

LICENSE TAXES.
Motor fuel sales taxes.
Exclusion from professional license tax, §58.1-1724.4.

LIMITATION OF ACTIONS.
Claims against the Commonwealth.
Tort claims act, §§8.01-195.6, 8.01-195.7.
State.
Tort claims against the Commonwealth, §§8.01-195.6, 8.01-195.7.
Tort claims act, §§8.01-195.6, 8.01-195.7.

LOCAL GOVERNMENT.
Planning and development.
Road impact fees, §§15.2-2317 to 15.2-2329.
Road impact fees, §§15.2-2317 to 15.2-2329.

LOCALITIES.
Bicycle paths.
Converting sidewalks to, §15.2-2001.
Photo-monitoring systems to enforce traffic light signals, §15.2-968.1.
Planning and development.
Road impact fees, §§15.2-2317 to 15.2-2329.
Powers of local government.
Motor vehicles.
Traffic light signals.
Photo-monitoring systems to enforce, §15.2-968.1.
Traffic light signals.
Photo-monitoring systems to enforce, §15.2-968.1.
Road impact fees, §§15.2-2317 to 15.2-2329.
Sidewalks.
Powers, §15.2-2001.
Waste management.
Reimbursements to localities for upgrades to treatment works, §10.1-1186.01.

LOCAL PLANNING.
Road impact fees, §§15.2-2317 to 15.2-2329.

LOCAL SCHOOL BOARDS.
Department of transportation or Commonwealth transportation commissioner.
Sale of property to by school board in city located in Virginia Beach, §22.1-129.

LOUDOUN COUNTY.
Local licensing of motor vehicles, trailers and semitrailers.
Payment of fines for ordinance and parking violations.
Evidence required before issuing license, §46.2-752.
Parking violations.
Removal or immobilization of vehicles.
Outstanding parking violations, §46.2-1216.
Subdivisions.
Expedited land development review procedures, §15.2-2263.

LYNCHBURG.
Mentally ill, mentally retarded or developmentally disabled persons.
Zoning of group homes of eight or fewer single-family residences, §15.2-2291.

M

MAIL.
Traffic light signal violation-monitoring system.
Service of summons, §§15.2-968.1, 46.2-833.01.

MANASSAS.
Parking violations.
Removal or immobilization of vehicles.
Outstanding parking violations, §46.2-1216.
Speed limit in residence district, §46.2-874.1.

MANASSAS PARK.
Parking violations.
Removal or immobilization of vehicles.
Outstanding parking violations, §46.2-1216.

MEDICAL MALPRACTICE.
Tort claims act.
Statute of limitations, §§8.01-195.6, 8.01-195.7.

MISDEMEANORS.
Gas pumps.
Smoking in proximity to, §46.2-819.4.
Motor vehicles.
Civil remedial fee for misdemeanor convictions, §46.2-206.1.
Smoking in proximity to gas pumps, §46.2-819.4.

MONTGOMERY COUNTY.
Subdivisions.
Expedited land development review procedures, §15.2-2263.

MOPEDS.
Attaching to vehicle on highway, §46.2-932.

MOTOR VEHICLE AND TRAFFIC OFFENSES.
Aggressive driving.
Civil remedial fee, §46.2-206.1.
Civil remedial fee.
Dangerous driving behavior, §46.2-206.1.
Commuter parking lots owned by VDOT.
Parking not in conformance with signs, §46.2-1219.2.
Dangerous driving behavior.
Civil remedial fee, §46.2-206.1.
Driving while license suspended or revoked.
Civil remedial fee, §46.2-206.1.
Photo-monitoring systems to enforce traffic light signals, §§15.2-968.1, 46.2-833.01.

MOTOR VEHICLE REGISTRATION.
Fees.
Additional revenue generated by fee increases.
Disposition, §46.2-702.1.
Highway maintenance and operating fund.
Disposition of additional revenue generated by fee increases, §46.2-702.1.
Foreign vehicles, §46.2-625.
Reconstructed and specially constructed vehicles, §§46.2-625, 46.2-734.
Replica vehicle, §§46.2-602.1, 46.2-625.
Specially constructed vehicles, §§46.2-625, 46.2-734.

MOTOR VEHICLES.
Aggressive driving.
Civil remedial fee, §46.2-206.1.
Civil remedial fees, §46.2-206.1.
Dangerous driving behavior.
Civil remedial fees, §46.2-206.1.
Odometer.
Reporting odometer reading on certificate of title, §46.2-629.
Photo-monitoring systems to enforce traffic lights signals, §15.2-968.1.
Replica vehicle.
Defined, §46.2-100.
Titling and registration, §§46.2-602.1, 46.2-625.
Slow moving traffic vehicles.
Designation of lanes for.
Commonwealth transportation board or local authorities, §46.2-804.
Toy vehicles.
Defined, §46.2-100.
Electrically powered vehicles.
Battery requirements to operate, §46.2-908.1.
Use on highways, restrictions, §46.2-932.

MOTOR VEHICLES DEPARTMENT.
Civil remedial fees, §46.2-206.1.

MOTOR VEHICLES DEPARTMENT —Cont'd
Local rental car transportation fee.
  Maintenance of records of collection by locality, §58.1-2402.1.

MOTOR VEHICLE SIZE AND WEIGHT.
Crossing bridge or culvert.
  Emergency response vehicles responding to emergency calls.
    Overweight permits granted, §46.2-1130.1.
Emergency response vehicles.
  Overweight permits to cross bridges and culverts granted,
    §46.2-1130.1.
Excessive size and weight permits, §§46.2-1139 to
  46.2-1149.5.
  Emergency response vehicles.
    Overweight permits to cross bridges and culverts granted,
      §46.2-1130.1.
  Tank wagons.
    Overweight permits, §46.2-1144.1.
  Underground pipe cleaning, hydroexcavating and water
      blasting equipment.
    Overweight permits, §46.2-1149.5.
Permits for excessive size and weight, §§46.2-1139 to
  46.2-1149.5.
Tank wagons.
  Overweight permits, §46.2-1144.1.
Underground pipe cleaning, hydroexcavating and water
    blasting equipment.
  Overweight permits, §46.2-1149.5.

MOTOR VEHICLE TITLING.
Odometer reading.
  Reporting on certificate of title, §46.2-629.
Reconstructed vehicles, §§46.2-625, 46.2-734.
Replica vehicle, §§46.2-602.1, 46.2-625.
Transfer of vehicle ownership.
  Odometer reading reported on certificate of title, §46.2-629.

MOVING TRAFFIC VIOLATIONS.
Aggressive driving.
  Civil remedial fee, §46.2-206.1.
Civil remedial fee, §46.2-206.1.
Evasion of traffic control devices.
  Signal violation-monitoring system, §§15.2-968.1, 46.2-833.01.
Photo-monitoring systems to enforce traffic light signals,
  §§15.2-968.1, 46.2-833.01.
Traffic lights.
  Signal violation-monitoring system, §§15.2-968.1, 46.2-833.01.

N

NEWPORT NEWS.
Hampton Roads transportation authority.
  General provisions, §§33.1-391.6 to 33.1-391.15.

NORFOLK.
Hampton Roads transportation authority.
  General provisions, §§33.1-391.6 to 33.1-391.15.

NORTHERN VIRGINIA TRANSPORTATION AUTHORITY.
Bond issues.
  Use of certain revenues, §15.2-4838.1.
Local rental car transportation fee.
  Authority to impose, §58.1-2402.1.

NOTICE.
Administrative process act.
  Regulations.
    Notice of intended regulatory action, §2.2-4007.01.
    Petitions, §2.2-4007.
    Revisions, §§2.2-4007.03, 2.2-4007.06.
Eminent domain.
  Right to enter land to ascertain suitability for highway
    purposes, §33.1-94.
Motor vehicle, civil remedial fee.
  Assessment, §46.2-206.1.
Regulations.
  Notice of intended regulatory action, §2.2-4007.01.
  Petitions for new or amended regulations, §2.2-4007.

NOTICE —Cont'd
Regulations —Cont'd
  Revisions, §§2.2-4007.03, 2.2-4007.06.

NUTRIENT REMOVAL TECHNOLOGY.
Design and installation at treatment works.
  Reimbursements to localities for upgrades, §10.1-1186.01.

O

ONLINE CONFERENCES.
Open meetings.
  Freedom of information act.
    Electronic communication meetings.
      Exceptions to prohibition, §2.2-3708.1.

OPEN MEETINGS.
Freedom of information act.
  Electronic communication meetings.
    Exceptions to prohibition, §2.2-3708.1.

ORDINANCES.
Parking.
  Limiting length of time of parking adjacent to commercial
      business areas.
    Vehicles of certain weight and length, §46.2-1222.2.
Road impact fees.
  Generally, §§15.2-2317 to 15.2-2329.
Traffic light signal violation-monitoring system.
  Photo-monitoring systems to enforce, §15.2-968.1.

OVERWEIGHT PERMITS.
Excessive size and weight permits, §§46.2-1139 to
  46.2-1149.5.
  See MOTOR VEHICLE SIZE AND WEIGHT.

P

PARKING.
Commuter parking lots owned by VDOT.
  Traffic infraction, §46.2-1219.2.
Limiting length of time of parking adjacent to commercial
    business areas.
  Vehicles of certain weight and length.
    Authority of local government, §46.2-1222.2.
Ordinances.
  Limiting length of time of parking adjacent to commercial
      business areas.
    Vehicles of certain weight and length, §46.2-1222.2.
Vehicles of certain weight and length.
  Limiting length of time of parking adjacent to commercial
      business areas.
    Authority of local government, §46.2-1222.2.

PARKING LOTS OR OTHER FACILITIES.
Commuter parking lots owned by VDOT.
  Parking not in conformance with signs and pavement
      markings.
    Traffic infraction, §46.2-1219.2.

PERMITS.
Motor vehicle size and weight.
  Excessive size and weight permits, §§46.2-1139 to 46.2-1149.5.

PHOTO-MONITORING SYSTEMS.
Enforcement of traffic light signals.
  Local powers, §15.2-968.1.

PLANNING AND BUDGET DEPARTMENT.
Administrative process act.
  Proposed regulations.
    Economic impact analysis, §2.2-4007.04.

PLANNING AND DEVELOPMENT.
Comprehensive plan.
  New urbanism.
    Incorporation of principles, §15.2-2223.1.
  Traditional neighborhood development.
    Incorporation of principles, §15.2-2223.1.

PLANNING AND DEVELOPMENT —Cont'd
Comprehensive plan —Cont'd
Urban development areas.
  Inclusion, §15.2-2223.1.

PLANNING COMMISSIONS.
Chesapeake.
Duplicate commission in Chesapeake and Hampton,
  §15.2-2220.
Duplicate commission in Chesapeake and Hampton,
  §15.2-2220.
Hampton.
Duplicate commission in Chesapeake and Hampton,
  §15.2-2220.

POLITICAL SUBDIVISIONS.
Planning, subdivision of land and zoning.
Road impact fees, §§15.2-2317 to 15.2-2329.
Road impact fees, §§15.2-2317 to 15.2-2329.

POQUOSON.
Buses.
Restricting nonscheduled buses over designated streets,
  §46.2-1304.

PRESUMPTIONS.
Traffic infractions.
Traffic light signal violation-monitoring system, §§15.2-968.1,
  46.2-833.01.

PRIMA FACIE EVIDENCE.
Commuter parking lots owned by VDOT.
Parking not in conformance with signs and pavement
  markings, §46.2-1219.2.

PRINCE WILLIAM COUNTY.
Local licensing of motor vehicles, trailers and
  semitrailers.
Payment of fines for ordinance and parking violations.
  Evidence required before issuing license, §46.2-752.
Poles or subsurface structures.
Placing under or along road or street not in state highway
  system.
  Permit from county engineer.
    Ordinance requiring, authority to adopt, §56-15.
Subdivisions.
Expedited land development review procedures, §15.2-2263.

PRIVATE ROADS.
Residential developments.
Designation as highways for law enforcement purposes.
  Authority of local government, §46.2-1307.

PUBLICATION.
Administrative process act.
Emergency regulations, §2.2-4011.

PUBLIC FUNDS.
Highway maintenance and operating fund.
Vehicle registration fee increases.
  Disposition of additional revenue generated by, §46.2-702.1.

PUBLIC OFFICERS AND EMPLOYEES.
Administrative process act, §§2.2-4000 to 2.2-4031.

PURCHASES AND SUPPLY DIVISION.
Purchases through division.
Purchases made in accordance with Virginia public
  procurement act, §2.2-1111.

R

RABIES.
Certificate of inoculation.
Freedom of information act exclusions, §2.2-3705.7.

RECKLESS DRIVING.
Civil remedial fee, §46.2-206.1.

RECORDATION TAX, STATE.
Distribution of recordation tax.
Transportation-related purposes, §58.1-815.4.

REGISTRAR.
Administrative process act.
Proposed regulations.
  Notice of intended regulatory action, §2.2-4007.01.
  Petitions, §2.2-4007.
Proposed regulations.
Submission, §2.2-4007.05.

REGULATIONS OF STATE AGENCIES.
Administrative process act.
Generally, §§2.2-4000 to 2.2-4031.

REPLICA VEHICLES.
Defined, §46.2-100.
Titling and registration, §§46.2-602.1, 46.2-625.

REPORTS.
Transportation board.
Biennial report.
  Maintaining and operating existing transportation
    infrastructure, §33.1-13.02.

ROAD IMPACT FEES, §§15.2-2317 to 15.2-2329.
Applicability of provisions.
Urban transportation service districts, §15.2-2328.
Urban transportation service districts.
Applicability of provisions, §15.2-2328.
Imposition of impact fees, §15.2-2329.

ROAD RAGE.
Aggressive driving.
Civil remedial fee, §46.2-206.1.

ROADS, STREETS AND PUBLIC RIGHTS OF WAY.
Acquisitions, conveyances and transfers of property.
Transportation board.
  Request to board for transfer to authority, §33.1-223.2:17.
Alteration and vacation.
Viewers.
  Virginia Beach, §15.2-2007.1.
Bicycle paths.
Converting sidewalks to, §15.2-2001.
Cleaning.
Powers of localities, §15.2-2001.
Dedication for public use.
Subdivision ordinance provision.
  Bonding requirements for acceptance of dedication,
    §15.2-2241.1.
Hampton Roads transportation authority.
General provisions, §§33.1-391.6 to 33.1-391.15.
Maintenance.
Powers of localities, §15.2-2001.
Powers and authority of locality generally, §15.2-2001.
Repairs.
Powers of localities, §15.2-2001.
Road impact fees, §§15.2-2317 to 15.2-2329.
Sidewalks.
Powers of locality generally, §15.2-2001.
State highway systems excepted, §15.2-2000.
Town streets, §15.2-2000.
Transportation board.
Acquisitions, conveyances and transfers of property.
  Request to board for transfer to authority, §33.1-223.2:17.
Viewers.
Alteration and vacation.
  Virginia Beach, §15.2-2007.1.

ROANOKE COUNTY.
Subdivisions.
Expedited land development review procedures, §15.2-2263.

ROLLER SKATING.
Attaching to vehicle on highway, §46.2-932.

RULES AND REGULATIONS.
Administrative process generally, §§2.2-4000 to 2.2-4031.

S

SECONDARY SYSTEM OF STATE HIGHWAYS.
Counties.
New streets.
  Requirements for taking new streets into system, §33.1-70.3.

SEXUAL OFFENDER TREATMENT OFFICE.
Zoning.
Prohibited in residentially zoned subdivision, §15.2-2283.1.

SIDEWALKS.
Converting to bicycle paths, §15.2-2001.
Powers of localities, §15.2-2001.

SKATEBOARDS.
Attaching to vehicle on highway, §46.2-932.

SLOW MOVING TRAFFIC TO KEEP TO RIGHT, §46.2-804.

SLOW MOVING VEHICLES.
Designation of lanes for, §46.2-804.
Slow moving traffic to keep to right, §46.2-804.
Maximum fine for violating Title 46.2, §46.2-113.

SMALL BUSINESSES.
Administrative process.
Appeal of final agency action, right to, §2.2-4027.
Regulatory flexibility provisions, §2.2-4007.1.

SMOKING IN PROXIMITY TO GAS PUMPS, §46.2-819.4.

STATE DEPARTMENTS AND AGENCIES.
Acquisitions, conveyances and transfers of property.
Camp Pendleton or other military property.
Notice to members of General Assembly, §2.2-1150.
Administrative process act, §§2.2-4000 to 2.2-4031.

STATE GOVERNMENT.
Administrative process act, §§2.2-4000 to 2.2-4031.

STATE OFFICERS AND EMPLOYEES.
Administrative process act, §§2.2-4000 to 2.2-4031.

STATUTE OF LIMITATIONS.
Claims against the Commonwealth.
Tort claims against the Commonwealth, §§8.01-195.6, 8.01-195.7.

STREETS.
Road impact fees, §§15.2-2317 to 15.2-2329.

SUBDIVISIONS.
Dedication for public use, ordinance to include provisions.
Bonding requirements for acceptance of dedication, §15.2-2241.1.
Road impact fees, §§15.2-2317 to 15.2-2329.

SUFFOLK.
Mentally ill, mentally retarded or developmentally disabled persons.
Zoning of group homes of eight or fewer single-family residences, §15.2-2291.

SUMMONS AND PROCESS.
Traffic infractions.
Commuter parking lot owned by VDOT.
Parking not in conformance with signs and pavement markings, §46.2-1219.2.
Traffic light signal violation-monitoring system.
How summons served, §§15.2-968.1, 46.2-833.01.

SURVEYORS.
Unlicensed activities.
Cease and desist order, civil penalty, §54.1-402.2.

T

TANK WAGONS.
Overweight permits, §46.2-1144.1.

TAX COMMISSIONER AND DEPARTMENT OF TAXATION.
Local rental car transportation fee.
Maintenance of records of collection by locality, §58.1-2402.1.
Motor fuel sales tax in certain transportation districts.
Bracket system, rule promulgation, §58.1-1724.2.

TAXES.
Motor vehicle fuel sales tax in certain counties, §§58.1-1724.2 to 58.1-1724.7.
Road impact fees, §§15.2-2317 to 15.2-2329.

TAX REFUNDS.
Motor vehicle sales and use tax, §§58.1-1724.5, 58.1-2423.

TELECOMMUNICATIONS.
Open meetings.
Freedom of information act.
Electronic communication meetings.
Exceptions to prohibition, §2.2-3708.1.

TELECONFERENCES.
Open meetings.
Freedom of information act.
Electronic communication meetings.
Exceptions to prohibition, §2.2-3708.1.

THREATS.
Security of government information.
Chief information officer (CIO), duties, §2.2-2009.

TOBACCO.
Gas pumps.
Smoking in proximity to, §46.2-819.4.

TOLL BRIDGES.
Failure to pay toll.
Administrative fee.
Recovery of expenses for collecting unpaid toll, §46.2-819.3.
Civil penalty, §46.2-819.3.

TOLL PROJECTS ON INTERSTATE SYSTEM.
Collection and deposit of tolls.
Transportation trust fund, §33.1-23.03:10.

TOLL ROADS.
Failure to pay toll.
Administrative fee.
Recovery of expenses for collecting unpaid toll, §46.2-819.3.
Civil penalty, §46.2-819.3.
Interstate highway system.
Tolls for use of interstate highway system components, §33.1-23.03:10.

TORT CLAIMS ACT.
Statute of limitations, §§8.01-195.6, 8.01-195.7.

TOWNS.
Private roads.
Residential developments.
Designation as highways for law enforcement purposes, §46.2-1307.
Residential developments.
Private roads.
Designation as highways for law enforcement purposes, §46.2-1307.
Road impact fees, §§15.2-2317 to 15.2-2329.
Streets and alleys, §15.2-2000.

TOY VEHICLES.
Defined, §46.2-100.
Electrically powered toy vehicles.
Spill-proof, sealed or gelled electrolyte batteries.
Required to operate, §46.2-908.1.
Use on highways, restrictions, §46.2-932.

TRAFFIC CONTROL DEVICES.
Lane direction control signals, §46.2-805.
Monitoring system, traffic light violations.
Photo-monitoring, §§15.2-968.1, 46.2-833.01.
Photo-monitoring systems to enforce traffic light signals.
Local powers, §15.2-968.1.

TRAFFIC INFRACTIONS.
Civil remedial fees, §46.2-206.1.
Commuter parking lots owned by VDOT.
Parking not in conformance with signs and pavement markings, §46.2-1219.2.
Dangerous driving behavior.
Civil remedial fees, §46.2-206.1.
Parking.
Commuter parking lots owned by VDOT.
Parking not in conformance with signs and pavement markings, §46.2-1219.2.

TRAFFIC INFRACTIONS —Cont'd
Playing on highways, §46.2-932.
Toy vehicles.
Use on highways, restrictions, §46.2-932.
TRANSPORTATION.
Public-private transportation act.
Conceptual proposal.
Posting, public comment, §56-573.1:1.
Local public entities.
Conceptual proposal.
Posting, public comment, §56-573.1:1.
Procurement records.
Public inspection, making available.
Interim or comprehensive agreement entered into, §56-573.1:1.
Public inspection.
Conceptual proposal.
Making available for, §56-573.1:1.
State agencies, departments and institutions.
Conceptual proposal.
Posting, public comment, §56-573.1:1.
TRANSPORTATION BOARD.
Acquisitions, conveyances and transfers of property.
Highways, rights-of-ways and landings.
Request to board for transfer to authority, §33.1-223.2:17.
Hampton Roads transportation authority.
General provisions, §§33.1-391.6 to 33.1-391.15.
Public access authorities.
Highways, rights-of-ways and landings.
Request to board for transfer to authority, §33.1-223.2:17.
Transfer of interest in and control over highways to, §33.1-223.2:17.
Reports.
Biennial report.
Maintaining and operating existing transportation infrastructure, §33.1-13.02.
School board in Virginia Beach.
Sale of property to transportation commissioner, §22.1-129.
Transfer of interest in and control over highways, §33.1-223.2:17.
TRANSPORTATION DEPARTMENT.
Commuter parking lots.
Parking not in conformance with signs and pavement markings.
Traffic infraction, §46.2-1219.2.
Hampton Roads transportation authority.
General provisions, §§33.1-391.6 to 33.1-391.15.
Intermodal planning and investment, office of, §2.2-229.
Office of intermodal planning and investment of the secretary, §2.2-229.
School board in Virginia Beach.
Sale of property to department, §22.1-129.
Secretary of transportation.
Office of intermodal planning and investment, §2.2-229.
TRANSPORTATION TRUST FUND.
Allocation of highway funds.
Interstate highway system.
Tolls for use of components of system, §33.1-23.03:10.
Interstate highway system.
Tolls for use of components of system, §33.1-23.03:10.

U

UNDERGROUND PIPE CLEANING, HYDROEXCAVATING AND WATER BLASTING EQUIPMENT.
Overweight permits, §46.2-1149.5.

URBAN TRANSPORTATION SERVICE DISTRICTS.
Impact fees, §§15.2-2328, 15.2-2329.

V

VENUE.
Freedom of information act.
Enforcement, §2.2-3713.
VIDEOCONFERENCES.
Open meetings.
Freedom of information act.
Electronic communication meetings.
Exceptions to prohibition, §2.2-3708.1.
VIRGINIA BEACH.
Hampton Roads transportation authority.
General provisions, §§33.1-391.6 to 33.1-391.15.
Parking violations.
Removal or immobilization of vehicles.
Outstanding parking violations, §46.2-1216.
School zones.
Establishing authorized, marking, §46.2-873.
Streets and alleys.
Alteration and vacation.
Viewers, §15.2-2007.1.

W

WASTE MANAGEMENT.
Upgrade to treatment works, reimbursements to localities for, §10.1-1186.01.
WILLIAMSBURG.
Buses.
Restricting nonscheduled buses over designated streets, §46.2-1304.
WISE COUNTY.
Local licensing of motor vehicles, trailers or semitrailers.
Evidence of payment of all fees due county or solid waste authority.
Required prior to issuing license, §46.2-752.

Y

YORK COUNTY.
Mentally ill, mentally retarded or developmentally disabled persons.
Zoning of group homes of eight or fewer single-family residences, §15.2-2291.
Poles or subsurface structures.
Placing under or along road or street not in state highway system.
Permit from county engineer.
Ordinance requiring, authority to adopt, §56-15.

Z

ZONING.
Residential uses.
Sexual offender treatment office.
Prohibited in residentially zoned subdivision, §15.2-2283.1.
Sexual offender treatment office.
Prohibited in residentially zoned subdivision, §15.2-2283.1.

Notes

Notes

Notes

Notes

Notes

Notes

Notes

Notes

Notes

Notes

Notes

Notes

Notes